D0948216

"Dr. Woodhouse's customary rigor with the text, combined with acute observation and wide-ranging Biblical and theological reflection, makes this commentary a must-have for any preacher of the book. The commentary does far more than explain the text, it feeds the soul. I could not recommend it more highly."

William Taylor, Rector, St. Helen Bishopsgate, London; author, *Understanding the Times* and *Partnership*

"John Woodhouse's commentaries on 1 and 2 Samuel are not written to gather dust on the shelf. They are the rare commentaries worthy of being read cover to cover and are destined to be thoroughly underlined and oft quoted. Again and again Woodhouse helps readers see through the shadows of King David into the rule and reign of his greater Son, King Jesus."

Nancy Guthrie, Bible Teacher; author, Seeing Jesus in the Old Testament Bible study series

"Dr. Woodhouse is one of my favorite interpreters of Scripture. He has an uncanny ability to so carefully read a text, that you will see things you never noticed, only then to wonder why you had not seen them before. He does justice to a text in its own historical and literary contexts, while showing how it resonates with the whole story of the Bible. Finally, he is a master of conceiving preaching trajectories from the Old Testament for the edification of the Church. These features, and more, characterize this outstanding volume on 2 Samuel. With its guidance, pastors will read, learn, and preach the message of 2 Samuel with greater depth of insight to the glory of the greater Davidic King."

Constantine R. Campbell, Associate Professor of New Testament, Trinity Evangelical Divinity School; author, *Paul and Union with Christ*

"This book is the ideal commentary for a preacher. It summarizes wide and deep scholarship clearly and concisely, offers perceptive and persuasive judgments on matters of translation and interpretation, and contains thoughtful suggestions for hearing these narratives as a part of Christian Scripture fulfilled in great David's greater Son. It is a marvelous resource."

Christopher Ash, Director of the PT Cornhill Training Course, The Proclamation Trust; author, *The Priority of Preaching*

"Dr. Woodhouse's masterly exposition of 2 Samuel takes us through the life and story of King David in a gripping way, setting David within the whole story of God's salvation, which culminates in the news about Jesus Christ, 'the Son of David' and ultimate King. Woodhouse writes with clarity and warmth that will not only excite preachers of God's Word, but also challenge and encourage others who love the Scriptures. Highly recommended."

Peter T. O'Brien, Retired Vice-Principal and Emeritus Faculty Member, Moore Theological College, Australia

"John Woodhouse's commentaries on 1 and 2 Samuel set a new benchmark for faithful, detailed engagement with the text of Scripture that warms the heart as it informs the mind. John explains each passage, not only in the context of the book but also in the grand sweep of Biblical theology, culminating in the gospel of our Lord Jesus Christ."

Phillip D. Jensen, Dean, St. Andrew's Cathedral, Sydney, Australia

"This is not simply the best and most sufficient commentary on 2 Samuel that explores every sentence in the light of the whole of Scripture, but is also a model of brilliant exposition for any preacher to adopt."

Archie Poulos, Head of the Ministry Department and Director of the Centre for Ministry Development, Moore Theological College, Australia

2 SAMUEL

PREACHING THE WORD
Edited by R. Kent Hughes

2 SAMUEL

YOUR KINGDOM COME

JOHN WOODHOUSE

R. Kent Hughes
Series Editor

■■ **CROSSWAY**

WHEATON, ILLINOIS

2 Samuel

Copyright © 2015 by John Woodhouse

Published by Crossway
　　　　　1300 Crescent Street
　　　　　Wheaton, Illinois 60187

Cover design: Jon McGrath, Simplicated Studio

Cover image: Adam Greene, illustrator

First printing 2015

Printed in the United States of America

Unless otherwise indicated, Scripture quotations are from the ESV® Bible (The Holy Bible, English Standard Version®), copyright © 2001 by Crossway, a publishing ministry of Good News Publishers. Used by permission. All rights reserved.

Scripture quotations marked AT are the author's translation.

Scripture quotations marked HCSB have been taken from *The Holman Christian Standard Bible*®. Copyright © 1999, 2000, 2002, 2003 by Holman Bible Publishers. Used by permission.

Scripture references marked JB are from *The Jerusalem Bible*. Copyright © 1966, 1967, 1968 by Darton, Longman & Todd Ltd. and Doubleday & Co., Inc.

Scripture quotations marked KJV are from the *King James Version* of the Bible.

Scripture quotations marked NASB are from *The New American Standard Bible*®. Copyright © The Lockman Foundation 1960, 1962, 1963, 1968, 1971, 1972, 1973, 1975, 1977, 1995. Used by permission.

Scripture references marked NIV are taken from The Holy Bible, New International Version®, NIV®. Copyright © 1973, 1978, 1984, 2011 by Biblica, Inc.™ Used by permission. All rights reserved worldwide.

Scripture references marked NRSV are from *The New Revised Standard Version*. Copyright © 1989 by the Division of Christian Education of the National Council of the Churches of Christ in the U.S.A. Published by Thomas Nelson, Inc. Used by permission of the National Council of the Churches of Christ in the U.S.A.

Scripture references marked REB are from The Revised English Bible. Copyright ©1989, 2002 by Oxford University Press and Cambridge University Press. Published by Oxford University Press.

Scripture references marked RSV are from *The Revised Standard Version*. Copyright ©1946, 1952, 1971, 1973 by the Division of Christian Education of the National Council of the Churches of Christ in the U.S.A.

Scripture quotations marked RV are from *The Revised Version*.

All emphases in Scripture quotations have been added by the author.

Hardcover ISBN: 978-1-4335-4613-6
ePub ISBN: 978-1-4335-4616-7
PDF ISBN: 978-1-4335-4614-3
Mobipocket ISBN: 978-1-4335-4615-0

Library of Congress Cataloging-in-Publication Data

Woodhouse, John, 1949– author.
　　2 Samuel : your kingdom come / John Woodhouse ;
R. Kent Hughes, General Editor.
　　　　pages cm. — (Preaching the word)
　　Includes bibliographical references and index.
　　ISBN 978-1-4335-4613-6 (hc)
　　1. Bible. Samuel, 1st—Commentaries. I. Hughes, R.
Kent, editor. II. Title. III. Title: Second Samuel.
BS1325.53.W663　　　　2015
222'.4407—dc23　　　　　　　　　　　2014009505

Crossway is a publishing ministry of Good News Publishers.

VP		25	24	23	22	21	20	19	18	17	16	15
15	14	13	12	11	10	9	8	7	6	5	4	3	2	1

For
Elisabeth & Andrew
Luke & Victoria
Anne & Adrian
Susan & Jason
much loved fellow servants of the King

*And your house and your kingdom shall
be made sure forever before me. Your
throne shall be established forever.*

2 SAMUEL 7:16

Contents

A Word to Those Who Preach the Word

There are times when I am preaching that I have especially sensed the pleasure of God. I usually become aware of it through the unnatural silence. The ever-present coughing ceases, and the pews stop creaking, bringing an almost physical quiet to the sanctuary—through which my words sail like arrows. I experience a heightened eloquence, so that the cadence and volume of my voice intensify the truth I am preaching.

There is nothing quite like it—the Holy Spirit filling one's sails, the sense of his pleasure, and the awareness that something is happening among one's hearers. This experience is, of course, not unique, for thousands of preachers have similar experiences, even greater ones.

What has happened when this takes place? How do we account for this sense of his smile? The answer for me has come from the ancient rhetorical categories of *logos*, *ethos*, and *pathos*.

The first reason for his smile is the *logos*—in terms of preaching, God's Word. This means that as we stand before God's people to proclaim his Word, we have done our homework. We have exegeted the passage, mined the significance of its words in their context, and applied sound hermeneutical principles in interpreting the text so that we understand what its words meant to its hearers. And it means that we have labored long until we can express in a sentence what the theme of the text is—so that our outline springs from the text. Then our preparation will be such that as we preach, we will not be preaching our own thoughts about God's Word, but God's actual Word, his *logos*. This is fundamental to pleasing him in preaching.

The second element in knowing God's smile in preaching is *ethos*—what you are as a person. There is a danger endemic to preaching, which is having your hands and heart cauterized by holy things. Phillips Brooks illustrated it by the analogy of a train conductor who comes to believe that he has been to the places he announces because of his long and loud heralding of them. And that is why Brooks insisted that preaching must be "the bringing of truth through personality." Though we can never perfectly embody the truth we preach, we must be subject to it, long for it, and make it as much a part of our ethos as possible. As the Puritan William Ames said, "Next to the Scriptures, nothing makes a sermon more to pierce, than when it comes out of the inward affection of the heart without any affectation." When a preacher's *ethos* backs up his *logos*, there will be the pleasure of God.

Last, there is *pathos*—personal passion and conviction. David Hume, the Scottish philosopher and skeptic, was once challenged as he was seen going to hear George Whitefield preach: "I thought you do not believe in the gospel." Hume replied, "I don't, but he does." Just so! When a preacher believes what he preaches, there will be passion. And this belief and requisite passion will know the smile of God.

The pleasure of God is a matter of *logos* (the Word), *ethos* (what you are), and *pathos* (your passion). As you preach the Word may you experience his smile—the Holy Spirit in your sails!

R. Kent Hughes
Wheaton, Illinois

Introduction

Kingdom Matters

2 SAMUEL AND MATTHEW 6:9, 10

David is one of the most important figures of world history. This assessment, and the reasons for it, will emerge in the course of our study of the account of his reign through the pages of 2 Samuel. In general terms, however, the claim can hardly be doubted. In cultures that have been touched by his story, David has captured the imagination of great artists, sculptors, and writers. From children's storybooks to (perhaps the most famous representation) Michelangelo Buonarroti's *David*, this man is remembered and recognized by people of many backgrounds over 3,000 years after he lived.

A large part of the reason for this is the remarkable account of his life and reign found in the books of 1 and 2 Samuel. The story is captivating. In one of the world's finest pieces of narrative literature, the greatness and the weaknesses of this man's life are portrayed in vivid and gripping detail. This remarkable literary work has made David known to the world and provided the basis for every other representation of him. David's impact on human history, thought, and culture has been, directly or indirectly, through the books of 1 and 2 Samuel.

However, we miss the significance of David almost entirely if we do not take careful note of the fact that his story belongs to the whole Bible story. While David, the man and the king, is as interesting as almost any great figure of human history, this is magnified many times over when we understand that he is a major figure in the history of God's purposes for the whole world. Again this fact, and its importance, will be elaborated as we see the narrative of 2 Samuel unfold.

As a great and significant historical figure, David can be (and has been) viewed from many different angles.[1] Each of these may or may not have a convincing claim to yield true insights into the importance of David. However the perspective from which to properly and fully understand David is that of Christian faith.[2] While this claim might sound puzzling (or even offensive) at first, it follows simply from recognizing that the whole Bible story (in which David's story is set) culminates in the news about Jesus Christ (importantly introduced in the first sentence of the New Testament as "the son of David," Matthew 1:1). Those who believe this message are in a position to understand the importance of David as the Bible presents him, rather than arbitrarily taking his story out of this context. In the pages that follow we will repeatedly consider the importance of David for those who have faith in Jesus Christ.

This does not mean that David should be of interest only to Christian believers. On the contrary. But the biggest reason that David should interest believer and unbeliever alike is that his story illuminates the most important story in the history of the world—the story of Jesus Christ. David's story is an essential part of the story of Jesus Christ. Even a person who does not yet believe that story deserves to understand it.[3]

In the course of listening to the story of David in the book of 2 Samuel we will discover many facets to the way in which this story illuminates the story of Jesus and the life of faith in him. The central idea is the kingdom of God. David's story and Jesus' story are about the kingdom of God. What is the kingdom of God?

The Kingdom and Jesus

Jesus taught his disciples to pray for this kingdom:

> Our Father in heaven,
> hallowed be your name.
> Your kingdom come,
> your will be done,
>   on earth as it is in heaven. (Matthew 6:9, 10)

This is an astonishing prayer. That *God's kingdom* would come means *God's perfect will* being done here on earth as it is in Heaven. The kingdom of God is God's own rule, his reign over all. We are praying for a kingdom of goodness, glory, righteousness, grace, peace, blessing.

Christian believers pray "Your kingdom come" (v. 10) because we believe the promise on which this prayer is based. The promise has come to us from Jesus Christ, who began his public life "proclaiming the gospel of the kingdom" (Matthew 4:23; 9:35). "The gospel of the kingdom"[4] (or in Christian vocabulary simply "the gospel") is the news ("gospel" means "news"[5]) about God's kingdom made known by Jesus. His message was, "The time is fulfilled, and the kingdom of God is at hand; repent and believe in the gospel" (Mark 1:15). He taught about what the kingdom is like (see Matthew 13:24, 31, 33, 44, 45, 47; 18:23; 22:2; 25:1) and about "enter[ing]" the kingdom (Matthew 18:3; 19:23, 24; 21:31; 23:13; cf. 25:34; John 3:5). This kingdom was his constant theme (see Acts 1:3) because it is *his* kingdom (Matthew 16:28; Luke 1:33; 22:29, 30; John 18:36; 2 Timothy 4:1; Hebrews 1:8; 2 Peter 1:11; Revelation 11:15); he is its king (Matthew 21:5; 25:34; Luke 19:38; John 12:15; 18:37; Acts 17:7; Revelation 17:14; 19:16).[6]

The Kingdom in Christian Experience

This kingdom is therefore the theme of the Christian message (see Acts 8:12; 14:22; 19:8; 20:25; 28:23, 31). The kingdom is central to the Christian experience: we have been transferred to, are being called into, and are receiving the kingdom (Colossians 1:13; 1 Thessalonians 2:12; Hebrews 12:28). We are looking forward to this kingdom (2 Timothy 4:1, 18; 2 Peter 1:11) and to the day when Christ "delivers the kingdom to God the Father" (1 Corinthians 15:24).[7]

Furthermore the kingdom defines the Christian mission. Just days before his death Jesus said to his disciples, "And this gospel of the kingdom will be proclaimed throughout the whole world as a testimony to all nations, and then the end will come" (Matthew 24:14). Those engaged in the task of making known the news of the kingdom are "workers for the kingdom" (Colossians 4:11; cf. Revelation 1:9).

Christian believers are therefore kingdom people. We receive the kingdom of God by humbly coming under the royal rule of Jesus Christ. We pray for the coming of God's kingdom (just as we pray "Come, Lord Jesus," Revelation 22:20). We are committed to the task of proclaiming the news of his kingdom to all people everywhere.

This way of speaking, thoroughly Biblical as we have seen it to be, can be difficult for us. It is certainly awkward for our contemporaries who may be seeking to understand the Christian faith. These days most of us have little, if anything, to do with kings and kingdoms. We may be aware that historically these ideas can have terrible associations. Kings have been tyrants. Monarchies have become acceptable in today's world only when transformed into a largely ceremonial and symbolic role, as we see in Britain's "constitutional monarchy." Even then many (in countries like my homeland of Australia) long to be rid of such archaic forms with their associations of privilege, power, and worse. Only a short time ago (in historical terms) the people of the United States of America fought a bitter eight-year-long war to gain independence from a king and declared, in an apparent repudiation of the very idea of kingship, that "All men are created equal."[8]

We, for whom kings and kingdoms are at best strange ideas, may well ask, what is the *kingdom* of God, for which Christians have been praying for 2,000 years, and of which the New Testament says so much?

The Kingdom of God: The Bible's Theme

The Bible's answer to that question is astounding. On the one hand, the kingdom of God is what the history of all things has been about. On the other hand, the kingdom of God is the ultimate solution to all of the world's troubles.

However, this kingdom is not a human achievement. Human activity, political or otherwise, will never establish God's kingdom. Indeed the Bible's promise, and the Christian hope, is that this kingdom will come *despite* the weakness, foolishness, and wickedness of human efforts. The kingdom of God will come as God's gift, not our accomplishment.

When Jesus spoke of the kingdom of God, he was not introducing a new idea. Indeed, his message was that the time for the kingdom was "fulfilled" (Mark 1:15). That is, the long-expected time had come. This expectation was created, in no small measure, by the story of David, the king who had reigned over Israel 1,000 years before the birth of Jesus Christ. Our reading of 2 Samuel will help us understand the expectation that makes sense of Jesus' announcement.

The kingdom of God can be rightly seen as the theme of the whole Bible. The idea is not limited to the actual expression.[9] God's kingdom is both his *rule* as king (in this sense "kingdom" means "king*ship*") and the *realm* that is under his rule. To say that the theme of the Bible is the kingdom of God is to recognize that the Bible is about God's rule and the bringing of all things under his rule.

David's Reign and the Bible's Theme

Before we begin to read the story of David's reign it is important to see that it is, in a significant sense, pivotal in the Old Testament's presentation of the kingdom of God. At the risk of oversimplification, we can say that everything in the Old Testament before David (Genesis to 1 Samuel) is leading up to his reign, and everything after David (1 Kings to Malachi) looks back to David's kingdom and confirms the expectation that this was the beginning of something of monumental importance for the whole world.

In brief, the Bible's story prior to David's reign may be summarized as follows: God created all things by his sovereign will and word (Genesis 1, 2). His kingdom is seen in creation itself.[10] However, humankind repudiated God's good and wise rule, and the goodness of the whole creation was disrupted by this upheaval (Genesis 3—11). And yet, despite humanity's corruption, God promised to yet bring blessing to the world through a nation descended from Abraham (Genesis 12—50; especially 12:1–3), a nation in which his rule would be honored.[11] He redeemed this nation from bondage to another king, Pharaoh of Egypt (Exodus—Leviticus) and brought them into the land he had promised Abraham (Numbers—Joshua). Sadly, this nation repeatedly turned away from God (Judges), ultimately demanding a human king so that they could be like the pagan nations around them rather than the people over whom the Lord God was king (1 Samuel 8:4–8; 12:12, 17, 19). Astonishingly God gave them the king they asked for (1 Samuel 8:22), but he refused to forsake the people he had made his own (1 Samuel 12:22). They could have their king only so long as both king and people followed the Lord (1 Samuel 12:13–15). Saul was that king (1 Samuel 10:1, 24; 11:15). But he failed to fulfill the condition of his kingship (1 Samuel 13:13; 15:10, 17–23; 28:17–19). When God rejected Saul, he promised that he would provide a different king, one of *his* choosing (in this sense "a man after *his* [God's] own heart," 1 Samuel 13:14), and therefore "better" than Saul (1 Samuel 15:28). This king was David. In contrast to Saul, he was not chosen *by the people for themselves* (1 Samuel 8:18; 12:17, 19), but he was a king provided *by God for himself* (1 Samuel 16:1).[12]

As the book of 2 Samuel begins, therefore, we may anticipate that God's king will at last rule over God's people in God's way. In David's reign, in other words, we expect to see the kingdom of God. Up to a point, that is what we will see. However, too soon we will find that even David failed to be the righteous and faithful king we have been led to expect.[13]

After David's death, and after the brief period of glory in the early part of his son Solomon's reign, the kingdom that had been David's disintegrated. The books of 1 and 2 Kings tell the story. Where then, we reasonably ask, is the kingdom of God? What has become of the promises that supported its expectation? The answers to these questions come through the prophets who appear during and after the collapse of the kingdom that had been David's. Their message includes the clear promise that the hopes that had rightly become attached to David will yet be realized. For example:

> Behold, the days are coming, declares the Lord, when I will fulfill the promise I made to the house of Israel and the house of Judah. In those days and at that time I will cause a righteous Branch to spring up for David, and he shall execute justice and righteousness in the land. (Jeremiah 33:14, 15)[14]

We have therefore seen that the story 2 Samuel tells is central to the Bible's message. God is the King. He is at work in the history of the world establishing his kingdom. As we hear of David's remarkable reign, we will see this purpose of God taking shape. We will more clearly understand what Jesus meant when he announced, "The time is fulfilled, and the kingdom of God is at hand; repent and believe in the gospel" (Mark 1:15). More than this, we will know more deeply what it means to pray, "Your kingdom come" (Matthew 6:10).

Part 1

THE KING
IS DEAD

2 Samuel 1

1

A Dead King,
a Victorious King,
and a Time of Waiting

2 SAMUEL 1:1

*After the death of Saul, when David had
returned from striking down the Amalekites,
David remained two days in Ziklag.*

1:1

THE BOOKS WE KNOW AS 1 Samuel and 2 Samuel tell the story of the first two kings of God's Old Testament people, the nation Israel.[1] Saul's reign occupied the last couple of decades of the second millennium BC.[2] The tragic story is told in 1 Samuel. It is a story of monumental failure, ending with Saul's violent death by his own hand (1 Samuel 31). Then David reigned for the first forty years of the first millennium BC.[3] He was to be remembered as Israel's greatest king. The brilliant but complicated story of his extraordinary reign is the subject of 2 Samuel.

The whole story is about leadership—Israel's longing for leadership they could trust, how and why Saul failed them, how and why David did so much better but also failed.

The opening words of 2 Samuel mention three events that, as we will see, turn out to have very great consequences for the whole world:

(1) The death of Saul (v. 1a).

(2) The victory of David (v. 1b).

(3) Two days that changed everything (v. 1c).

The fact that few today are even aware of these events underlines the importance of hearing the message of the book that begins in this way. The story of King David has more to teach us than almost any other human life in the history of the world. There is a reason that Jesus Christ was known as the son of *David*.

The Death of Saul (v. 1a)

"After the death of Saul" (v. 1a) would make a fitting title for the book of 2 Samuel.[4] There is evidence that the two books of 1 and 2 Samuel may once have been considered one.[5] Certainly they tell one continuous story.[6] However, it is clear that the story has two distinct parts, and Part Two is about what happened "after the death of Saul" (v. 1a).[7] The break between 1 Samuel 31 and 2 Samuel 1 is appropriate and significant.[8]

Saul's death (and the manner of his death) was the culmination of his tragic life. It marked the end of what might be described as a failed "experiment" in Israel. Saul had been appointed king by the prophet Samuel, in obedience to God (see 1 Samuel 8:22; 9:16; 10:24; 11:14, 15). However, this had been the Lord's response to the insistent demand of the people for a king because they wanted to be "like all the nations" (1 Samuel 8:20; cf. 1 Samuel 8:5). They wanted the security that the leaders of other nations seemed to provide. They were in effect rejecting God as the one who could deliver them. In response to this faithless demand God did two things.

First, he gave them what they had asked for. Ironically Saul's very name meant, "Asked For."[9] Therefore Saul was "the king whom *you* have chosen, for whom *you* have asked" (1 Samuel 12:13); "*your* king, whom *you* have chosen *for yourselves*" (1 Samuel 8:18).

Second, God set the terms by which Saul would reign. The Lord had no intention of abandoning the people he had made his own (1 Samuel 12:22). He would *not* allow them to become "like all the nations" (see Exodus 19:4–6, 1 Samuel 8:20). They could have the king they "ask[ed] for" (and perhaps they would learn their lesson, see 1 Samuel 8:9–18), but the king would be chosen by God and reign on conditions set by him: he and his people must "fear the Lord and serve him and obey his voice and not rebel against the commandment of the Lord" (1 Samuel 12:14). In other words, God would allow his people to have the king that they asked for, only so long as both king and people lived in obedience to God.

Saul was also therefore, in this sense, "him whom *the Lord* has chosen" (1 Samuel 10:24). He was, in this context, "the LORD's anointed" (see 1 Samuel 2:10; 10:1; 12:3, 5; 15:17; 24:6, 10; 26:9, 11, 16, 23).

And so Saul became the God-appointed king of his people Israel, with all the solemn responsibilities this entailed (see 1 Samuel 10:25; 15:1).

The death of Saul was therefore terrible. Death is always terrible, but this was the death of one who had been the Lord's anointed king. At the same time it was the end of one in whom the people had once placed such high expectations, such hopes.

Saul died because he failed to fulfill the conditions God had placed on his kingship. Saul "did not obey the voice of the LORD" (1 Samuel 28:18; cf. 15:1). 1 Samuel 13 and 15 tell the story. It was a catastrophe (see 1 Samuel 13:11a, 13; 15:11, 19, 22, 23, 26). Only a king who was fully and perfectly obedient to God could reign over the people whose true king was God himself (1 Samuel 8:7; 12:12). Saul's death was God's judgment on his disobedience (1 Samuel 28:16–19).

At the same time Saul's ugly death was dreadful proof of the people's foolishness in desiring a king "like all the nations" (1 Samuel 8:5). In human terms, Saul had once appeared to hold great promise as a leader (1 Samuel 10:23, 24). He had the qualities Israel was looking for in a leader. What hopes had once rested on Saul! The people wanted a king to "go out before us and fight our battles" (1 Samuel 8:20). The Lord himself had said, "He shall save my people from the hands of the Philistines" (1 Samuel 9:16). And in fact he accomplished quite a lot (see 1 Samuel 11:1–11; 14:47, 48). In the end, however, the Philistines defeated Saul and drove him to suicide (1 Samuel 31). He died a failure. It is not difficult to imagine an Israelite in those days lamenting, "We had hoped that he was the one to redeem Israel."

The book of 2 Samuel opens with the implied question, what will happen "after the death of Saul" (v. 1)? If Saul could not secure Israel's life, what hope was there?

The Death of Saul and the Death of Jesus

A thousand years later there was another death that appeared to have similarities to the death of Saul. Like Saul this man had been known as "the Christ" (in Hebrew *mashiakh* [Messiah], meaning "anointed one"). Certainly some who had believed in this man *did* say, when he died, "We had hoped that he was the one to redeem Israel" (Luke 24:21). Jesus' shameful, humiliating death (so like Saul's in this respect; see especially 1 Samuel 31:8–10) dashed the hopes of those who had believed in him, just as the death of Saul had shattered his followers (see 1 Samuel 31:7).

Certainly some saw Jesus' terrible death (like Saul's) as God's judgment on him (see Deuteronomy 21:23), and they were not entirely wrong (see Galatians 3:13). They drew the apparently reasonable conclusion that his death (like Saul's) marked his disqualification from being the Messiah he had claimed to be (see, for example, Mark 15:29–32). In the days immediately following his crucifixion, the death of Jesus raised the same question as the one posed by the death of Saul: What will happen *after the death of Jesus*?

The Victory of David (v. 1b)

Let's return to the question raised by Saul's death, 1,000 years earlier. It will be answered by the whole story that the book of 2 Samuel has to tell. However, in the opening words of the book the answer is signaled. Alongside the death of Saul, the first sentence of 2 Samuel sets a very different event in the life of another man, to whom our attention is now drawn: "David had returned from striking down the Amalekites"[10] (v. 1b).

Anyone who has read 1 Samuel (and every reader of 2 Samuel should have done that first) knows that the earlier book has told the story of Saul and his failure. But alongside that tragic account there has been the beginning of another story, the story of David. David was introduced in 1 Samuel 16, immediately after Saul's calamitous act of disobedience in 1 Samuel 15, and his story could hardly have been more different from that of Saul.

After Saul had decisively failed to be the fully obedient king he was required to be, David had been chosen by God to be king over Israel. However, the Lord's choice of David was different from his choice of Saul. This time it had not been a response to the rebellious demand of the people, but, as Samuel put it, "According to *his own heart* the LORD has sought *for himself* a man."[11] That is, this time God was not giving the people what *they* had asked for, but out of God's own good will ("his own heart" 1 Samuel 13:14)[12] God was choosing a man for his own purpose ("for himself"). This was the essential difference between Saul and David, and the reason that David was a "better" man than Saul to be Israel's king (1 Samuel 15:28). Saul was the kind of king the people wanted so they could be like the nations around them. David was chosen out of a very different purpose—God's own heart.

Although David did not become king immediately, his story from 1 Samuel 16 on displays his superiority to Saul. He was more successful in fighting Israel's enemies (see 1 Samuel 17; then 18:5, 7, 14, 15, 30). This was because "the LORD was with him" (1 Samuel 18:14b) in a way he was evidently not with Saul (see 1 Samuel 16:13, 14). He repeatedly displayed faithfulness and righteousness of character and conduct (1 Samuel 26:23), while Saul was utterly unreliable and downright wicked (1 Samuel 24:17). This, too, must be seen as a consequence of the Lord's favor resting on David (rather than the basis for this fact).[13]

The last five chapters of 1 Samuel interweave the two contrasting stories of Saul and David in a way that suggests that the events described in each narrative were happening at about the same time.[14] As the terrified Saul approached his final confrontation with the Philistines (see 1 Samuel 28:15), and at last took his own life on Mount Gilboa (1 Samuel 31:4), David (for rather complicated reasons, see 1 Samuel 27, 29) was three days journey away, to the south, smashing Amalekites (1 Samuel 30:1, 17–20).

The death of the king and the terrible defeat suffered by Israel at the hands of the Philistines up north was devastating. We are told that the Philistines proclaimed the "good news" of their decisive triumph throughout their land (1 Samuel 31:9). An observer could be excused for failing even to notice what was happening with David, far away to the south. In any case it would have been difficult to think that whatever was happening down there near Ziklag could have any bearing on the dismal future now faced by the vanquished people of Israel.

By setting the death of Saul alongside the victory of David over the Amalekites in 1:1[15] the writer has signaled three things.

First, the death of Saul (monumentally tragic as it was) and the resounding defeat suffered by Israel at that time was *not the end of the story*. At the same time there was a victory. The victory may have been hardly noticed at the time, but it was the hope of Israel's future.

Second, the victorious one was David, the one about whom 1 Samuel has already said so much. Any hope in Saul was now gone. The hope of Israel now rested in David. Not all Israelites yet realized or accepted this, and there were understandable reasons for that. However 2 Samuel opens by drawing our attention from *Saul* and his final failure to *David* and his distant victory over Israel's enemies.

Third, nothing could better represent David's greater credentials for reigning over Israel than the fact that the enemies he had defeated were, of all people, the Amalekites.[16] The Amalekites had played an ominous role in the life of Saul. On the one hand we have been briefly told that during his reign Saul "struck the Amalekites and delivered Israel" (1 Samuel 14:48). However, on the other hand it was precisely Saul's failure to obey a command of God *with regard to the Amalekites* that was central to his failure as king (1 Samuel 15; see especially vv. 2, 3, 5–9, 18, 19, 32, 33). Indeed Saul was told, the night before he died, "Because you did not obey the voice of the LORD and did not carry out his fierce wrath *against Amalek*, therefore the LORD has done this thing to you this day" (1 Samuel 28:18). But at the very time Saul died *because of his failure to deal with the Amalekites*, David had been "*striking down* the Amalekites." The verb is vivid and might remind us of the same Hebrew word used rather often of David's military successes, particularly against the Philistines (1 Samuel 17:26, 35, 36, 46, 49, 50, 57; 18:6, 7, 27; 19:5, 8; 21:9, 11; 23:2, 5; 27:9; 29:5; 30:17). It is the same word that was used of the Philistines' violence against Saul's sons on Mount Gilboa (1 Samuel 31:2). However, it is also the word that was used to describe what Saul *should* have done to the Amalekites (1 Samuel 15:3) and what he incompletely did do (1 Samuel 15:7).

Therefore, if the book of 2 Samuel is going to answer the question, what will happen "after the death of Saul?" (1:1) the first hint is that: (1) the death of Saul was not all that was happening on that dreadful day: there was a victory being won, even if it was unnoticed by most; (2) the victory was being won by David, the one who had been chosen by God to be a better king than Saul; and (3) the victory was in fact reversing Saul's momentous failure.[17]

David's Victory and Jesus' Victory

A thousand years later, when Jesus died a death surprisingly like the death of Saul, the truth was that on that day: (1) a victory was won, even if it was unnoticed by most (Colossians 2:15); (2) the victory was won by the one chosen by God to be king over all, "great David's greater son"[18]; and (3) his victory was in fact reversing humanity's momentous failure (see, for example, Romans 5:19).

The great difference between the questions, what will happen after the death of Saul? and what will happen after the death of Jesus? is that the answer to the latter does not require us to look away from Jesus and his death to another king. In this case it was the one who had died who won the victory, and he did so in the very act of dying.

Two Days That Changed Everything (v. 1c)

The third element in 1:1 is a reference to the period of time after David had won his victory, but before the news of Saul's death had reached him: "David remained two days in Ziklag" (v. 1c).

Ziklag had been the starting and end point for the Amalekite conflict referred to in the previous phrase (see 1 Samuel 30:1, 26). Through a rather strange sequence of events Ziklag had been given to David by the Philistine king Achish (1 Samuel 27:6).[19] We need not rehearse here all that had happened at Ziklag (although the reference is certainly meant as a reminder of the story in 1 Samuel 30). We are simply told that David remained there for two days before the next major event occurred.

These two days would have been days of suspense for David. He knew that far to the north the Philistine forces had massed to fight against Saul and Israel. But he did not yet know the outcome. They were two days in which we (the readers) know that the old king had died, but the one we expect to become the new king did not yet know this. They were two days in which there was in fact "no king in Israel." This was the situation that had prevailed immediately prior to the beginning of the book of 1 Samuel (see Judges 21:25). In these two days Israel returned in this regard to the situation with which the story that had led to Saul's appointment had begun. The difference now was that David was waiting in Ziklag.

As we read the Gospel accounts in the New Testament, it is interesting to notice that after the death of Jesus there were two days in which the future was uncertain—at least to those who were afraid and waiting for they knew not what. It was on the third day that the next major event occurred. The New Testament writers understood that Jesus' resurrection "on the third day" had been anticipated in the Scriptures (1 Corinthians 15:4). It is not unreasonable to suggest that the two days between the death of Saul and the emergence of David "on the third day" (2 Samuel 1:2) was a part of the pattern.[20]

The question for which we have been prepared by the opening sentence of 2 Samuel is, what happened on the third day after the death of Saul? When leadership like Saul's had finally failed, what hope was there? These questions will be answered in the pages that follow.

2

Who Says Crime Doesn't Pay?

2 SAMUEL 1:2–10

TWO CONTRADICTORY VIEWS of life are captured in the sayings "Crime doesn't pay" and "Who says crime doesn't pay?" The first sounds noble, good, and wise. It recognizes the bitter fruit that doing wrong can produce and warns would-be perpetrators to think again. "Crime doesn't pay." The second, however, reflects realistic observation of life—crime often *does* pay. "Who says crime doesn't pay?"

Which do you believe—really? And why?

There is ample evidence to support the second perspective. Few really believe there is nothing to be gained from criminal activity. Otherwise by this time most intelligent criminals would have learned the lesson. However, all over the world, in every nation and people group, every city and village, crime continues to be part of life. Those who engage in unlawful activities believe they will benefit. It is far from obvious that they are wrong.

Of course they are *sometimes* wrong. Some criminals are caught, some crimes fail in their intentions, some wrongdoing has unexpected dire consequences for the perpetrator. But this does not gainsay the fact that we live in a world where crime often *does* pay very handsomely indeed. "Crime doesn't pay" sounds good, but it also sounds more like wishful thinking than persuasive truth.

Those responsible for crime prevention in any community have the unenviable task of persuading would-be criminals that the potential penalty for unlawful behavior and the risk of being caught outweigh the potential benefits. "Crime *probably* will not pay" is a difficult message to convey and is never completely successful.

Perhaps we could defend the view that "crime doesn't pay" by arguing that such benefits as may be attained through crime and misdeeds are superficial and short-lived and do not offset the damage that will be suffered one way or another by the wrongdoer, whether or not their offenses ever come to light. Over time the advantages of ill-gotten gains can be seriously diminished by a troubled conscience, an increasingly flawed character, a tarnished reputation, an inability to earn trust, or ongoing fears of being exposed. However, this is also a difficult argument to sustain effectively. Crime continues the world over because at least some people estimate that the intangible downside is worth it: crime can pay *enough* to make the pain (such as it may be) worthwhile. So it is widely believed.

I suspect that few readers of this book are criminals (in the usual sense of that word). However, what if we include all forms of wrongdoing? Consider some of the wrong things you have done recently—an untruthfulness, a less-than-kind action, a broken promise, some selfish and inconsiderate behavior, some good you could have done but didn't. Many of us will be able to think of more serious wrongs that we have committed. Perhaps no one else knows of the misconduct. Here is my suggestion. In every case you did the wrong thing because you believed that you would derive *some* benefit from doing it. In other words, all of us who do wrong of *any* kind (that is, all of us) actually believe that *doing wrong* (at least sometimes) *does pay*. We believe that we can gain pleasure, prosperity, security, status, power, or some other advantage by doing the wrong thing. Otherwise we would never do it. "Who says crime doesn't pay?"

What do you think it would take to persuade us to think differently? How different would our lives be if we *really did believe* there is nothing to be gained by doing wrong?

Second Samuel begins with a remarkable incident in which someone was convinced that crime would pay. He sought to gain from a lie and a more dramatic act of which we will hear. He was wrong. He made a terrible miscalculation. His experience holds the key to one of life's most important lessons.

We have already been reminded (1:1a) that Saul, Israel's king, had died. This happened on Mount Gilboa, where the Israelites had suffered a terrible defeat at the hands of the Philistines, long-time bitter enemies of Saul and the Israelites. The detailed account of what happened has been provided in 1 Samuel 31.

At the time of Saul's death David was about a three-day journey to the south, in the town of Ziklag (1 Samuel 30:1).[1] Ziklag was the town that had been given to David in the rather complicated circumstances described in 1 Samuel 27 (see v. 6). While Saul's forces had been suffering the Philistine assault to the north in the vicinity of Mount Gilboa, David and his men had been rather busy down south in Ziklag. They had been pursuing and dealing with the Amalekites (1:1b) who had earlier destroyed the town of Ziklag and "taken captive the women and all who were in [Ziklag], both small and great" (1 Samuel 30:2a). David had now returned to Ziklag, having rescued and recovered all that the Amalekites had taken (1 Samuel 30:18), and had been there for two days (1:1c).

To appreciate what happened next we must remember two things about David. First, he was fully aware of the conflict far to the north (see 1 Samuel 28:1, 2; 29:1–11). He had left that scene just before the hostilities had begun. Second, he did not yet know the outcome. Specifically he had not yet heard the news of Saul's death. During the two days he waited in Ziklag he was, no doubt, anxious to know how the hostilities to the north had gone.

The narrative now invites us to join David in Ziklag. We will see:

(1) What happened "on the third day" (v. 2).
(2) The man's story (vv. 3–10).

What Happened "On the Third Day" (v. 2)

And on the third day, behold, a man came from Saul's camp, with his clothes torn and dirt on his head. And when he came to David, he fell to the ground and paid homage. (v. 2)

The arrival of this man that day in Ziklag was surprising, perplexing, and ominous. He is neither named nor identified in any other way (yet). Who was he? Where had he come from? Why had he come to Ziklag? What news did he bring? The answers to these questions were far from obvious to anyone witnessing the scruffy stranger's entrance into the ruined town of Ziklag that day.

The narrator tells us that the man came "from Saul's camp" (v. 2). Literally the text says, "from the camp, from with Saul." Two things are important to note about this piece of information.

First, since it is the narrator who tells us this, we understand that it is true.[2] This is perplexing for us as we read the account. We have heard in 1 Samuel 31 (again from the narrator, and therefore authoritatively) what happened to Saul. The only persons whom we know were with Saul at the end (three of his sons and his armor-bearer) had died on Mount Gilboa along with Saul (see 1 Samuel 31:2, 5). Who, then, was this man who came (literally) "from with Saul"?

Second, the text subtly suggests that "from the camp, from with Saul" is not only information provided to the reader by the narrator, but also *how David saw this man* as he arrived in Ziklag. The word "behold" in verse 2 represents an idiom in Hebrew that, in this context, seems to focus our attention on the described scene *as it would have appeared to David* and those with him in Ziklag that day.[3]

This suggests that as he waited for two days in Ziklag (1:1c) David was on the lookout for news "from the camp, from with Saul." The urgency of the difficulties that had faced him on his return to Ziklag (1 Samuel 30:1) would not have diminished his apprehension about the outcome of the conflict with the Philistines that he had left behind only a few days earlier. The disheveled man who arrived on the third day was immediately (and rightly, the narrator has confirmed) assumed by David to have come with news of "the camp of Israel" (v. 3), and especially of Saul.

However, David could not have known for certain that this was the case. In recent times he had been living a dangerous double life. To all appearances he had become a trusted servant of the Philistine king Achish (1 Samuel 27:12). This, however, was a deceit. David had been driven to the land of the Philistines to escape Saul's murderous plots against him (1 Samuel 27:1), but there he had duped Achish into trusting him, while in fact never ceasing to serve the interests of the people of Israel (see 1 Samuel 27:8–12). Therefore it would have been conceivable that the man who arrived on the third day had come from the *Philistine* camp with news for the supposed trusted servant of Achish about how the battle had gone *for the Philistines*. Indeed it would have been reasonable to assume this because Achish and the Philistines knew that David had returned to Ziklag (1 Samuel 29:4, 10, 11).

However, David appears to have seen the man who arrived in the light of his own real concerns, which were for the Israelites and for Saul. He saw the man as he hoped he was: "from the camp, from with Saul."

The appearance of the man who arrived was ominous. "Clothes torn and dirt on his head" (v. 3) signaled bad news. These were conventional expressions of mourning. On a much earlier occasion a man looking just like this had come from another battle between the Israelites and the Philistines (1 Samuel 4:12[4]). He was the "man of Benjamin" (1 Samuel 4:12) who brought the terrible news to old Eli in Shiloh that the Israelite forces had been crushed, Eli's sons had been killed, and the ark of the covenant had been captured by the enemy. This news had killed Eli (1 Samuel 4:18). The scene in Ziklag many years later is reminiscent of that day in Shiloh.[5] We (who have read 1 Samuel 31) know that a man who came to Ziklag from "with Saul" would be bringing news as devastating as the news brought similarly years before to Shiloh.

We will soon have reason to question the genuineness of this man's expressions of grief.[6] For the moment we see him as David saw him—one who appeared to be bringing bad news from the battlefront.

The scene creates a puzzle that must have perplexed David as much as it should bother us who are hearing the account at this point. Who could this man be, bringing news from the conflict in the north to David here in Ziklag? Those who supported David were there with him in Ziklag (see 1 Samuel 27:3; 29:11; 30:1, 18, 19). Those who had stayed with Saul, loyal to their king, knew that David had earlier fled from the land of Israel. They had heard that he joined the Philistines (1 Samuel 27:4). How could they have known that David was now in Ziklag? Who was this man, and why had he come to Ziklag?

The man's actions when he approached David were extraordinary. "He fell to the ground and paid homage" (v. 2c). While this may not be entirely unambiguous,[7] in this context we (the readers) must see this man (genuinely or otherwise) acknowledging what we know, namely that David is now the king. We might compare the similar act of Abigail, who certainly understood David's future (see 1 Samuel 25:23, 28–30). Indeed there have been many in the story so far who have recognized that David would succeed Saul as Israel's king (see this idea develop through 1 Samuel 18:3, 4, 7, 16, 30; 20:15, 16, 31; 21:11; 23:17; 24:20; 26:25; 28:17). It will be some time before all in Israel acknowledge this fact (5:1–3). However, on that day in Ziklag the man who came to David seemed to understand. This adds to the mystery. Who was he—apparently the first person to bow before the new king?

Again we will shortly have reason to doubt the integrity of the man's bowing before David. Indeed we will come to see him as "nothing but an insincere flatterer."[8] At this stage, however, we see him as David saw him—a surprisingly subservient individual about whom there are many questions.

The Man's Story (vv. 3–10)

The story now unfolds as David proceeded to ask the man a series of these questions, and the man responded.

Question 1: "Where Do You Come From?" (v. 3)

David's first question was to confirm his first impressions: "David said to him, 'Where do you come from?'" (v. 3a). David had no evidence yet to confirm that the man had come from Saul's camp. From David's point of view it was still possible that the man had come from the Philistine lines, or perhaps from somewhere else altogether.

The man's reply did a little more than provide the confirmation David sought. "And he said to him, 'I have escaped from the camp of Israel'" (v. 3b). "From the camp of Israel" (v. 3) would have answered David's question and, as the narrator has informed us in verse 2, done so truly. But what did he mean that he had "escaped"? The obvious meaning is that he had come "from the camp of Israel" (v. 3), having escaped *from the Philistines*. However, by saying, "I have escaped *from the camp of Israel*," the stranger (perhaps unintentionally) made a connection with the man to whom he had come. For a long time now David had repeatedly "escaped" from Saul (see the refrain-like occurrences of the Hebrew verb in the story of David's flight from the threats of Saul—1 Samuel 19:10, 11, 12, 17, 18; 22:1; 23:13; 27:1[9]). The man who had now come to David had, he said, "escaped" from Saul's camp. Was he subtly putting himself on David's side of any breach that there might still be between David and "the camp of Israel"? He, too, was an escapee from the sphere of Saul's influence.[10]

The important and obvious point is that David's first impressions were confirmed. The bedraggled man was indeed from the Israelite camp and therefore could be expected to have news of the conflict.

Question 2: "How Did It Go?" (v. 4)

David's second question was therefore predictable, expressing the concern he must have had since leaving the vicinity of the dreaded engagement some days earlier: "And David said to him, 'How did it go? Tell me'" (v. 4a).

"How did it go?" (more literally, "What was the situation?"[11]) is precisely the question old Eli asked the messenger in that earlier encounter at Shiloh (1 Samuel 4:16), of which we have already been reminded. We are probably right to see a parallel between the devastating news brought on these two occasions. Each signaled the end of an era of leadership in Israel. Eli's period as judge ended that day years earlier (see 1 Samuel 2:31; 4:18). David's echo of the question that had been asked on that day will bring the news of the end of Saul's reign as king.[12]

The mysterious messenger responded with the news he had brought:

"And he answered, 'The people[13] fled from the battle, and also many of the people have fallen and are dead, and Saul and his son Jonathan are also dead'" (v. 4b). As on the earlier occasion at Shiloh (see 1 Samuel 4:16), the messenger's news unfolds one piece of information at a time, moving toward what will be the climactic news for David.[14] First he reported the rout: the people fled. Second, he told of the large death toll: many are dead. Third, he gave the most significant news of all: even Saul is dead. And, fourth, as though he knew something of David's particular concern, he added: Jonathan, Saul's son, is also dead.

All of this we know to be true because the narrator has recounted these things in 1 Samuel 31. Certainly the messenger reduced his report to essentials. For some reason he did not mention the deaths of two other sons of Saul (1 Samuel 31:2). This suggests that his news had been given a particular emphasis. Saul and his heir apparent ("his son," v. 4) were dead. It may also suggest that the messenger knew something of the remarkable and important relationship between David and Jonathan (most recently see 1 Samuel 23:16–18). In any case the fact that the deaths of Abinadab and Malchi-shua were not considered to have the same urgent importance as the facts reported does not undermine the complete truthfulness of the report to this point.

It was, of course, momentous news. For a long time David had known that Saul's day would come. He had said, "As the LORD lives, the LORD will strike him, or his day will come to die, or he will go down into battle and perish" (1 Samuel 26:10). Now all three of these things had come to pass in the one event. David had also known that Saul's death would usher in his own succession to kingship over Israel. Although we have not heard as much from David's lips, it has been said again and again by others, usually in David's hearing. David had only ever disagreed with those who anticipated his reign in the question of how it would come about. Repeatedly he had insisted that he would not be the one to raise his hand against Saul. The news that Saul was indeed dead was the most important news David could hear.

Question 3: The Full Story (vv. 5–10)

David was no fool. Was there something about this man's manner that suggested a lack of integrity? Perhaps there was an incongruity between the expressions of mourning (v. 2) and the way in which he conveyed the news of the Israelite deaths (v. 4). Did he sound as if he thought he was bringing *good* news? That is how David will recall this moment some time later (see 4:10). Whatever the reason, David considered that the man could not be taken simply at his word. So David's third question pressed the young man for more details: "Then David said to the young man who told him, 'How do you know that Saul and his son Jonathan are dead?'" (v. 5).

The narrator focuses our attention on the man's activity in telling David his story. He is described (literally) as "the young man[15] who was telling him."[16] The messenger will be referred to in precisely this way three times (see also vv. 6, 13). The man's telling is the focus of attention. We know that so far his telling has been truthful. But how could David know this? That was David's question, and we will see he was shrewd to have asked it.

The Young Man Was There (v. 6)

"The young man who was telling" David these things responded to David's question with much more detail. His reply begins to answer some of the questions that his arrival in Ziklag raised but also presents us with further perplexities. His response, like his initial report, unfolded step by step. This is how it began:

> And the young man who told him said, "By chance I happened to be on Mount Gilboa, and there was Saul leaning on his spear, and behold, the chariots and the horsemen were close upon him." (v. 6)

The young man was claiming to be an eyewitness to the events he was telling.[17] While he had not yet given David evidence that this claim was true, we (the readers) have good reason to believe him. His report is very close to the truth as we know it from 1 Samuel 31, and it is difficult to know how anyone who had not seen these things could have known the details.

First, Mount Gilboa was indeed the location of Saul's death (1 Samuel 31:1). We may be a little puzzled at how the young man "by chance happened" to be there.[18] "Does one accidentally stumble onto a battle field while the killing is still going on?"[19] Be that as it may, such questions are hardly enough to dismiss the credibility of this witness.

It is certainly believable that he saw "Saul leaning on his spear" (v. 6). We know that Saul was badly wounded (or greatly distressed[20]) by the Philistine archers (1 Samuel 31:3). The plausible image of Saul leaning on his spear is a reminder to us (as it may have been to David) of the role of that spear in Saul's life, especially in his hostilities toward David. Saul and Jonathan were the only Israelites (at one time at least) to have a spear (1 Samuel 13:22). The spear was often in Saul's hand; it was almost his badge of office (1 Samuel 18:10; 19:9; 22:6; 26:7). David had quietly stolen the spear once, without harming Saul, as a bold demonstration of his faithfulness to

Saul (1 Samuel 26:11, 12, 16, 22, 23). Twice Saul had hurled that spear at David himself (1 Samuel 18:11; 19:10) and once at Jonathan because of his friendship with David (1 Samuel 20:33).[21] This detail of the young man's testimony enhances his credibility.

If we were particularly suspicious we may have some questions about the claim that "the chariots and the horsemen[22] were close upon him" (v. 6). We heard only of archers in 1 Samuel 31:3, and there are reasons to think that chariots, while effective in the valley of Jezreel just to the north of Mount Gilboa, would not have been able to negotiate the more rugged terrain of the mountain itself. However, this is to claim to know too much. We do not know exactly where on Mount Gilboa this scene was located, nor the details of the topography. Furthermore archers are known to have operated from chariots. The apparent conflict between the man's testimony and the narrator's account in 1 Samuel 31:3 is no more than the variation we would expect from independent eyewitnesses who each provide different details of a complex scene.[23]

So far neither we (the readers) nor David have any reason to doubt "the young man who was telling" all this. It sounds as though the young man was indeed a witness to the events reported in 1 Samuel 31.

The Young Man Was Called by Saul (v. 7)

At this point, however, his story takes a turn that could only be noticed by those who (unlike David) have already heard what really happened on Mount Gilboa. In 1 Samuel 31 the narrator tells us how the exhausted, and possibly wounded, Saul called on his armor-bearer to finish him off (1 Samuel 31:4a). If we suppose (as seems reasonable) that the young man telling the story now to David was there and witnessed that dreadful conversation, listen to how he now twisted it. He purported that the conversation in question had taken place not with Saul's armor-bearer but with himself—and that it went rather differently.

He continued his tale: "And when he [Saul] looked behind him, he saw me, and called to me. And I answered, 'Here I am'" (v. 7). So he not only witnessed the events on Mount Gilboa (he says). He was close enough to have spoken with Saul himself.

David had no reason to doubt he was telling the truth. But we do. In the context of what really happened as it has been narrated in 1 Samuel 31:4, 5 it is difficult to imagine how the conversation claimed by the young man could possibly have taken place.[24]

The Young Man Was an Amalekite (v. 8)

According to the story the young man was telling David, Saul then asked the question that has been important since the man arrived in Ziklag but is as yet unanswered: "And he said to me, 'Who are you?'" (v. 8a). Who indeed? Who could have been there on Mount Gilboa but not known to Saul? Saul's question suggests that the man was not one of the king's servants.[25] Presumably he was not a Philistine. Who then?

The answer the young man claimed to have given to Saul is astonishing: "I answered him, 'I am an Amalekite'" (v. 8b).

Imagine the shock for David at this reply, and also for Saul (if it had actually been made to him). David had just finished "striking down the Amalekites" (v. 1b). They had destroyed his town of Ziklag and dragged off all the women, children, and possessions. Now (and only now) he and we learn that the mystery man who had arrived in Ziklag was (or claimed to be) an *Amalekite*!

The narrator has carefully kept this piece of information from us all until this point, just as the man himself had kept it from David.[26] Now that it is out, more questions are raised. An Amalekite! Any impression we may have been forming that the man was a credible witness must now be rethought.[27] In Bible history the Amalekites had long been hostile enemies not only of the Israelites but of Israel's God.[28] What was an Amalekite doing on Mount Gilboa, and what was he doing now in Ziklag? Why was he bringing this report to David—the man God had chosen to be *his* (that is, God's) king? What was he doing prostrated before David? An Amalekite!

We have reason to doubt that this man ever, in fact, spoke to Saul. But we cannot miss the impact that the words "I am an Amalekite" (v. 8) *would* have had on Saul had they been spoken as claimed. The previous night Saul had been told the terrible reason that he had lost the kingdom and would die in the battle with the Philistines the next day. It was "because you did not obey the voice of the LORD and did not carry out his fierce wrath against *Amalek*" (1 Samuel 28:18). The Amalekites had been at the center of Saul's downfall. Saul's decisive act of disobedience had been his failure to do what God had told him to do to the Amalekites. The full account is in 1 Samuel 15. What an irony it would have been for Saul, in the last moments of his life, to be face-to-face with an Amalekite![29]

The Amalekite is a profound symbol, on the one hand, of the failure of Saul and, on the other hand, of the promise of David. The Amalekites represented opposition to God's will (see Exodus 17:16).[30] Saul had failed to carry out God's judgment on Amalek (1 Samuel 15) and therefore had proven himself to be unacceptable as king over God's people (see 1 Samuel 15:23, 26, 27; 28:17–19). David had dealt with the Amalekites just as he had dealt with Goliath (1:1b; 1 Samuel 17:50). There is something strangely fitting, therefore, about an Amalekite bringing the news of Saul's death to David.

Let's pause for a moment and see if we can piece together what must really have happened on Mount Gilboa. Why did the young man choose to disclose his surprising identity at *this point* in the story he was telling?

It seems clear (as we have seen) that he really was on Mount Gilboa and that he did witness what happened to Saul, at fairly close quarters. He was close enough to observe the conversation that did take place between Saul and his armor-bearer. He saw, and possibly understood, the armor-bearer's refusal to accede to Saul's request to end his life (1 Samuel 31:4). The armor-bearer had refused because he "feared greatly" (1 Samuel 31:4) the request Saul had made of him. Things might have gone rather differently, however, if Saul had made his request to an Amalekite. For reasons that we will soon see, the man who brought the news of Saul's death to David wanted his story to go rather differently from the actual events. Crucial to his version of what happened was his identity as an Amalekite.

The Amalekites were descended from a grandson of Esau (Genesis 36:12) and were therefore related to the Edomites who were the descendants of Esau (Genesis 36:1–17). On an earlier occasion one notorious Edomite, named Doeg, had been among Saul's servants (1 Samuel 21:7). At that terrible time Doeg had obeyed Saul's command when none of his Israelite servants dared to do so. He slaughtered eighty-five priests and every man, woman, child, and animal in the town of Nob (1 Samuel 22:17–19). David knew about and had been deeply troubled by what Doeg did at Nob (1 Samuel 22:21, 22). According to the story the young man was now telling David years later in Ziklag, "by chance" (v. 6) Saul had a kinsman of Doeg available to do his will on Mount Gilboa.[31] We know that there was an Israelite servant there who did not dare to do so (1 Samuel 31:4).

The Young Man Said He Was Asked to Kill Saul (v. 9)

The young man continued his story: "And he said to me, 'Stand beside me and kill me,[32] for anguish[33] has seized me, and yet my life still lingers'"[34] (v. 9).

We know the young man was lying,[35] but like all the best lies it was close enough to the truth to be believable.[36] Saul had indeed asked to be killed (1 Samuel 31:4). It is possible that if he had known of the presence of a Doeg-like character he *would* have directed his request to him. Like Doeg previously, an Amalekite could be expected to be free from the scruples that kept his armor-bearer (to whom Saul actually addressed his appeal) from doing the deed. The lie was credible.

As we hear the young man's story what really happened is becoming clearer. He almost certainly did witness the events on Mount Gilboa, but the probability is that he did so unobserved by Saul or anyone else. However, his answer to David's question, "How do you know . . . ?" (v. 5), claims more—that he was not only there, but that Saul spoke to him and asked him to finish him off. The young man distorted the truth just enough to claim the status not only of a credible eyewitness but also of a participant in the events he was telling.

The Young Man Said He Was Obedient (v. 10a)

Indeed his claim to have been involved went one astonishing step further: "So I stood beside him and killed him, because I was sure [literally, I knew] that he could not live after he had fallen" (v. 10a).

The young man justified his breathtaking claim with an argument that sounds surprisingly like today's defenses of euthanasia. Saul was about to die anyway. Hastening his death was an act of kindness. We will see that his reasoning was no more valid then than it is today.

The lie was brazen. But remember that David had none of our reasons for recognizing the deception. True, David still had no *proof* that the young man was speaking truthfully. He had answered David's question, "How do you know?" (v. 5) with the claim to have inflicted the fatal blow himself—out of kindness and with Saul's informed consent. The further (unspoken) question (how could David know he was telling the truth?) was about to be answered.

The Young Man Had Proof (v. 10b)

The climax of the young man's story is now reached: "And I took the crown[37] that was on his head and the armlet that was on his arm, and I have brought them here to my lord" (v. 10b).

The young man's story had been breathtaking in its daring and suddenly became utterly convincing to those in Ziklag who were hearing it. With a closing flourish the young man produced Saul's royal insignia, no doubt instantly recognizable by David and those with him. These objects must have appeared as positive proof of the story the young man was telling. How else could they have come into his possession?

The scene is remarkable. The first person to bow before the one who we know will succeed Saul and be king of God's people was an Amalekite who, by bringing these objects to David, symbolically "crowned" the new king of Israel[38] and was the first now to call him "my lord" (v. 10).[39]

Nonetheless as we listen to his story we realize that the man's cunning was astonishing. His possession of Saul's royal emblems certainly demonstrates the substantial truthfulness of his story that we have already recognized. He must indeed have been on Mount Gilboa and close to Saul. However, from what we know of the actual course of the events on Mount Gilboa, we must conclude that the young man witnessed Saul's suicide and the death of his armor-bearer in like manner (1 Samuel 31:4–6), and *then* (before the Philistines came to strip the bodies the next day, 1 Samuel 31:8) this young man stole the crown and the armlet from the fallen body of Saul.[40]

We have no idea when he concocted the story that he was now telling David, but his motives are becoming clear. While some questions remain unanswered, the man's efforts in traveling to Ziklag, prostrating himself before David and now presenting David with the symbols of kingship, show that he knew David as at least a contender to be Saul's successor.[41] He hoped to benefit from the favor of the new king. David's understanding of the man's motives is revealed some time later. David believed that the man expected to receive a reward for bringing to David the "good news" of Saul's death (4:10). David's response to the news (1:11, 12) will demonstrate how wrong he was. Furthermore the man evidently expected to gain additional favor with David if he had been personally involved in Saul's death. He would soon learn what a mistake that was. Finally he thought he could gain these benefits by constructing a lie that completely misrepresented his own role in the events concerned. His ingenious efforts were about to bring the very opposite of their intended effects—for a reason that he had completely overlooked. He had made a terrible miscalculation.

As we (quite rightly) find ourselves disapproving of the lying Amalekite, the searching question is whether we are likewise deluded into thinking that we can win some advantage in life by wrong behavior—a lie, a deception, a broken promise, a betrayal. How easy it is to think that a moral compromise (which we always see as slight) may be advantageous. The Amalekite only distorted the truth a little. He is a striking example of "the deceitfulness of sin" (Hebrews 3:13). His sinful heart (like ours) allowed him to think that crime might pay. The crime he falsely claimed (killing Saul) and the lie with which he claimed it were motivated by twisted thinking that is all too familiar to us. The idea that we live in a world where wrongdoing can benefit us is a terrible miscalculation because it completely overlooks the decisive factor.

In our next chapter we will see that the decisive factor overlooked by the Amalekite was the character of God's king. The young man dared to bow before God's king and thought he could gain some benefit from his lie and his claimed act of violence. He thought that David's ways were like his ways. He had an ultimate lesson to learn.

It was David's righteous character that shattered the idea that the Amalekite might profit from his crimes. David's righteousness was a mere shadow of the righteousness of the one who is now God's King (see Isaiah 9:7; 11:4, 5; 16:5; Acts 3:14; 7:52; 17:31; 22:14; 2 Timothy 4:8; 1 Peter 3:18; 2 Peter 1:1; 1 John 2:1, 29; 3:7).

This little Amalekite was a deluded fool, and so are we whenever we think we can be servants of God's King, the Lord Jesus Christ, and advance our cause with anything other than righteousness. "For we [like the young man who came to Ziklag] must all appear before the judgment seat of Christ, so that each one may receive what is due for what he has done in the body, whether good or evil" (2 Corinthians 5:10). Crime *doesn't* pay. Do you believe that? Really?

3

Crime *Doesn't* Pay

2 SAMUEL 1:11–16

GOD'S RULE OVER HIS CREATION (Jesus called this "the kingdom of God" [Mark 4:26]) is the theme of the whole Bible. The Bible recounts the history of both human rebellion against God's rule (beginning in Genesis 3) and God's gracious commitment to establish his perfect rule. This is the huge story that makes sense of the world as it is and reveals what the world and life ought to be like and ultimately will be like.

The second book of Samuel is an important part of that story. It tells how, 1,000 years before Jesus, David became Israel's king "after the death of Saul" (1:1a). David was the man chosen by God to rule as king over his chosen people, the nation of Israel. David's kingdom was—for a time—the expression in this world of the kingdom of God.

The scene we left at the end of our last chapter had a young Amalekite bowing before David and delivering his embellished account of how Saul had died. For what he expected would be his own benefit he had distorted the truth just enough to make himself the "hero" of his story. He had made himself out to be the one who had mercifully and obediently hastened Saul's death. He was the one, therefore, who had removed David's enemy and opened the way for David to take Saul's crown and kingdom.

It was a lie. We know that because in 1 Samuel 31 the narrator has told us what really happened. However, David had no way of knowing the young man was lying. Indeed the trophies he was carrying must have looked like irrefutable proof of his audacious story.

The Amalekite believed that his lie (and the deed he falsely claimed to have performed) would bring him some reward from David, the man who (because of Saul's death) would soon be king. That expectation was about to be shattered. For a reason that he had fatally misunderstood, he was about to learn that in his situation crime *doesn't* pay.

What was it about the situation that made his scheme a disaster? We will see that the situation in the days of David anticipates the situation in which we find ourselves—Jesus Christ, the son of David, has become king. We will see:

(1) David's grief (vv. 11, 12)
(2) David's judgment (v. 13–16).

David's Grief (vv. 11, 12)

We take up the story in 1:11 with what happened once the young Amalekite's tale had been told. The narrator takes some liberty with the chronology. The precise *sequence* of events is often less important for the writers of the Bible than it normally is for us.[1] The first thing we hear about is the *impact* of the news brought by the young Amalekite.

> Then David took hold of his clothes and tore them, and so did all the men who were with him. And they mourned and wept and fasted until evening for Saul and for Jonathan his son and for the people of the LORD and for the house of Israel, because they had fallen by the sword. (vv. 11, 12)

I do not think this was the response the Amalekite had expected. (Whether or not he actually witnessed it is, as we will see, another matter.) Perhaps some distress at the defeat and suffering of the people generally would be understandable. But how could David not rejoice at the end of his archenemy Saul? Had the roles been reversed, we can be sure that Saul would have been overjoyed at David's demise. I have no doubt that the death of David would have caused no weeping in the camp of Saul! On this day, however, David wept, as did his companions.

Now that we have heard his story, we see the expressions of mourning with which the Amalekite came to Ziklag (v. 2) for the sham that they were. We no longer believe this opportunist liar. We no longer believe his show of grief.

But there was no sham in David's grief that day. His sorrow was as real as that of the people of Jabesh-gilead (1 Samuel 31:13), if differently motivated. David may well have understood that Saul's death was God's doing (1 Samuel 26:10), as indeed it was (1 Samuel 28:19). This did not diminish the tragedy—any more than the coming divine judgment on Jerusalem many years later diminished the sorrow of Jesus over that city's demise (Matthew 23:37).[2] We know that God himself takes no pleasure in the death of anyone, no matter how much that death is deserved (Ezekiel 18:32). In our next chapter we will have the opportunity to reflect more deeply on the significance of David's grief.

For now we notice that the grief of David (and his fellows) is said to be first "for Saul" (v. 12). Careful readers of this history may not be surprised. David never sought Saul's death (see 1 Samuel 19:4; 20:1; 22:14; 24:6, 10, 11, 17–19; 26:9, 11, 18), despite Saul's concerted campaign to eliminate David (see this theme develop through 1 Samuel 18:8, 9, 11, 15, 17, 25, 29; 19:1, 5, 10, 11, 17; 20:1, 30, 31; 22:23; 23:7, 14, 15; 24:1; 26:2; 27:1, 4). When it came, David saw and felt Saul's death for the tragedy it was.

Second, David and those with him wept over the death of Saul's son, Jonathan. Jonathan's death could have been seen as the elimination of a potential rival to the throne. David did not see it that way. There had been a wonderful friendship between David and Jonathan. The death of Jonathan was devastating for David. But it was more than the tragedy of a lost friend. Jonathan, though Saul's heir apparent, had been the first to recognize and gladly acknowledge David as Israel's future king. Years earlier Jonathan had abandoned any claim to the throne in favor of David (see 1 Samuel 18:3, 4), and Jonathan had loved and had been unswervingly faithful to his future king. Both David and Jonathan had hoped and expected that Jonathan would serve at David's side when he became king over Israel (1 Samuel 23:17). It was not to be. So David wept for Jonathan.[3]

Third, the mourning that day in Ziklag was "for the people of the LORD and for the house of Israel" (v. 12). This is a description of the same people in two respects: they were the Lord's people, and they were members of the one "house" or household (figuratively speaking).[4] The suffering of the Lord's people at the hands of their enemies grieved David.[5]

David's Judgment (vv. 13–16)

What we are told next probably happened before the period of mourning described in verses 11, 12.[6] The importance of that response to the news the Amalekite brought has given it priority in the narrative, overriding the chronology.

David had two more questions (following those in verses 3, 4, and 5) for "the young man who told him" his story (v. 13). (Remember that David had no reason to doubt that he was telling the truth.)

Question 4: Identity (v. 13)

The first of these last two questions was to confirm the identity of the messenger: "And David said to the young man who told him, 'Where do you come from?'" (v. 13a). The translation is not precise, for this is not the same as the question David asked at the beginning of this conversation. There David had asked, "Where do you *come* from?" (v. 3a)—inquiring about just where the new arrival had recently been. This time he asked (literally), "Where are *you* from?" (NIV)—inquiring about the man's identity (more like Saul's reported question in verse 8). It was as though David said, "Where did you say you were from again?"[7]

The young man's reply (if it is to be believed) added an important detail: "And he answered, 'I am the son of a sojourner, an Amalekite'" (v. 13b). Only now do we (and David) learn that he was not simply an Amalekite, but the son of "a sojourner." This term is variously translated "stranger" (RV), "foreigner" (HCSB, NIV), "alien" (REB), and "resident alien" (JB, NRSV). It refers to a non-Israelite who lived more or less permanently in Israel.[8] "Resident alien" expresses the idea best. In Israel the resident alien enjoyed certain rights. This, like so much in Israel, was because of the people's historical experience—they had been "resident aliens" in Egypt (see Exodus 22:21; 23:9; Deuteronomy 10:19; 23:7). Resident aliens did not enjoy all the privileges of Israelite citizens, but they were entitled to justice under the Law. They were also subject to its penalties.

This new information about the young man who had come to Ziklag answers a number of the questions we may have had about him. It is possible that, as a resident alien, he was serving in Saul's army.[9] Is that how he "by chance . . . happened to be on Mount Gilboa" (v. 6b)? Being a resident alien in Israel may well explain his knowledge of David and his reputation.

The man's motive in claiming resident alien status was almost certainly to make clear to David that, though an Amalekite, he was not an enemy. He did not belong to *the* Amalekites. His status in the Israelite community was presented with an expectation of David's goodwill. He was not *just* an Amalekite. Or so he would like David to believe.[10]

Question 5: Guilt (v. 14)

The young man's expectation was shattered by David's final question, which neither required nor received a response. "David said to him, 'How is it you were not afraid to put out your hand to destroy the LORD's anointed?'" (v. 14). *How did you dare!*

Here is a theme that has run like a thread through the account in 1 Samuel.[11] The Lord's "anointed" was first mentioned in the last words of Hannah's great prayer at the beginning of that book (1 Samuel 2:10) and again rather enigmatically in the Lord's message about the end of the house of

Eli (1 Samuel 2:35). In due course the Lord told Samuel to "anoint" Saul (1 Samuel 9:16; 15:1), which he did (1 Samuel 10:1). Saul was therefore understood to have been anointed *by the Lord* (1 Samuel 10:1; 15:17) and therefore to be the Lord's "anointed" (1 Samuel 12:3, 5). After Saul was rejected as king (because he disobeyed the Lord), the Lord told Samuel to anoint David (1 Samuel 16:3, 12, 13), who would therefore become "the Lord's anointed" (1 Samuel 16:6). However, despite this development, as long as Saul lived David insisted that he (Saul) was "the Lord's anointed" against whom he (David) consistently refused to do any harm (1 Samuel 24:6, 10; 26:9, 11, 23; cf. 26:16). David's view that no one should dare to act against "the Lord's anointed" (v. 14) was shared by Saul's armor-bearer who was asked by Saul to kill him. He would not do it, "for he feared greatly" (1 Samuel 31:4). How come, David asked the young Amalekite, *you* did not tremble?

"The Lord's anointed" is Bible language for the one chosen and appointed by the Lord to represent the Lord as his king. There are two important ideas here. The first is that only God himself may both appoint and remove his king. Even when Saul had been rejected by God, and David had been chosen and designated as his successor, no one but the Lord had the right to act against the one whom the Lord had anointed. Even David refused to do such a thing. The second idea is that to oppose "the Lord's anointed" is to oppose the Lord (see Psalm 2:2). All this David understood. Saul's armor-bearer got it. The young Amalekite did not.

The Hebrew term for "anointed" is *mashiakh* (which has come into English as "messiah"). The Greek translation is *christos* (which has likewise come into English as "christ"). This is the very title that would eventually be applied to Jesus. Ultimately he has become "the Lord's Christ" (see, for example, Luke 2:26; Acts 3:18; Revelation 11:15; 12:10). David's outrage at the reported action of the young man against Saul may therefore be seen as a shadowy anticipation of the outrage that ought to be felt about the execution of Jesus (see Acts 2:23, 36; 5:30; 10:38, 39; 1 Corinthians 2:8) and all opposition to the Lord's Christ. How do they dare!

As we watch the mockery of Christ and of faith in Christ that has become a public media sport in our day, don't you tremble? There is one who sits enthroned in Heaven. He cares about those who rage against the Lord and his anointed (Psalm 2:4). I would not want to be in their shoes when he speaks to them in his wrath and terrifies them in his fury (Psalm 2:5). Would you? I would not like to be in this young Amalekite's shoes when David turned on him. Would you? How did he dare!

We know that the young man who came to David had not in fact killed Saul. He just claimed that he had. He thought that by claiming such an act he could gain the favor of the new king. He fabricated his lie in order to achieve this. What he did not understand was David's righteousness and faithfulness (see 1 Samuel 26:23). He tragically, terrifyingly, stupidly miscalculated. He did not take into account the character of God's king. His privileged status as a resident alien did not excuse him. It magnified his guilt. He ought to have known better. So should many. How is it that they are not terrified to oppose the Lord's Christ?

The Sentence (v. 15)

The consequences were terrible and swift. "Then David called one of the young men and said, 'Go, execute him.' And he struck him down so that he died" (v. 15).

This Amalekite was "struck . . . down" (v. 15), just as David had struck down the others (v. 1b). David completed the work Saul had failed to do. He executed God's judgment on the Amalekites. Do not be deceived. The Lord's king does not reward evil. With this king crime does not pay.

David may have had this very day in mind when he wrote:

> No one who practices deceit
>   shall dwell in my house;
> no one who utters lies
>   shall continue before my eyes. (Psalm 101:7)

The Verdict (v. 16)

The last element of the episode is again probably slightly out of chronological order, unless we are to imagine David addressing the young man's corpse.[12] It is likely that verse 16 tells us what happened between verses 14 and 15. Putting these words last has dramatic effect. "And David said to him, 'Your blood be on your head, for your own mouth has testified against you, saying, "I have killed the LORD's anointed"'" (v. 16).

The death of Saul is now the first and last thing mentioned in this episode, seen first in simple factual terms (v. 1a) and finally in terms of David's interpretation of the Amalekite's lie (v. 16d).[13]

"Your blood" (v. 16) probably means "the blood you have shed."[14] The dirt that was pretentiously "on his head" when he arrived at Ziklag (v. 2) is replaced by the guilt for what he had claimed to have done.[15]

The Amalekite had imagined that he could profit from his lie in the new kingdom of David. He fancied that he could have David as his king while remaining an Amalekite at heart. He dreamed that he could seek David's kingdom without pursuing his righteousness. He became an example to all who think that wrongdoing can pay when God's king reigns. Those who entertain that thought fail to reckon with the character of God's king. This young man made a terrible miscalculation about David—he disastrously misunderstood the kingdom of God.

As we hear his terrible story I want to ask you to examine your own unacknowledged beliefs about the benefits to be gained by wrongdoing. Jesus Christ, descended from David according to the flesh, has now been declared by God to be his powerful king by his resurrection from the dead (Romans 1:3, 4). Do you see God's King as he really is—"Jesus Christ the *righteous*" (1 John 2:1)? His kingdom is a kingdom of *righteousness* (Matthew 6:33; Romans 14:17). He will judge the whole world in *righteousness* (Acts 17:31; cf. 2 Timothy 4:8). Will you learn from what the young Amalekite learned (too late) about God's king? If you take God's kingdom seriously, you must take *righteousness* seriously. Jesus is King: do not imagine that *any* wrongdoing will ever bring you a benefit worth having. *Jesus* is the Christ! To seek first the kingdom of God will mean to seek his *righteousness* (Matthew 6:33). There is no place in this kingdom "for the cowardly, the faithless, the detestable . . . for murderers, the sexually immoral, sorcerers, idolaters, and all liars" (Revelation 21:8). Whether I *believe* that will be shown in my repudiation of every temptation to find pleasure, satisfaction, fulfillment, achievement, security, or happiness through wrongdoing—of any kind.[16]

This opening episode of 2 Samuel, set in the context of the Bible as a whole, teaches us that whatever gain we may anticipate when we do wrong is short-sighted and deluded. That is because this is God's world. "The fleeting pleasures of sin" (Hebrews 11:25) are just that—fleeting, transitory. It may not *seem* like that, but it *is* like that, because the one who determines the final outcome of all things is the one who made and rules the world—the righteous and holy God.

The ultimate foolishness of believing that crime (or any wrongdoing) does pay can only be seen by those who believe God's Word, who know that Jesus is King. In other words, only those who believe God's Word can really believe that crime *doesn't* pay—and understand why.

Of course, there is more to be said about our King. He forgives those who repent. He restores those who turn to him for help. He has mercy on those who seek his mercy. He heals those who cry out to him. But he does not reward unrighteousness. Learn from the deluded Amalekite.

4

What the Victorious King Said about the Dead King

2 SAMUEL 1:17–27

DEATH IS COMPLICATED. It not only terrifies us, it confuses us. Even when death comes by so-called natural causes after a long and full life, we mourn. Samuel's death had been like that. Though Samuel was an old man (see 1 Samuel 8:1) known to have lived a full and honest life (see 1 Samuel 12:2–5), all Israel mourned for him when he died (1 Samuel 25:1; 28:3). There are times when death comes at the end of a period of pain and suffering, and we speak of it as a relief. But still we weep. Although nothing is more certain than our own death, there are few who know how to come to terms with this reality and are accepting of it.

Death silences us. It is hard to know what to say in the face of death. What do you say to a dying friend or a grieving family?

At the same time death has a way of putting things in perspective. Petty things are seen to be petty. The good qualities of a person are rarely seen as clearly as they are at his or her funeral. Why is this? How are we to respond to the reality of death? What can we say in the face of death?

The Bible has much important light to shine on this difficult subject. Death is profoundly connected with human sin and God's judgment (see Genesis 2:17; 3:3, 4; Romans 5:12; 6:23). It is even more terrible than we feel it to be. However, Jesus Christ by his own sin-bearing, substitutionary death and his resurrection from the dead has drawn the sting of death (1 Corinthians 15:55–57), has delivered us from our slavery to the fear of death

(Hebrews 2:15), and has given us "a living hope" that sees beyond death (1 Peter 1:3). Death is the last enemy of God's kingdom to be destroyed (1 Corinthians 15:26), but it certainly will be destroyed (Revelation 21:4). This enemy will, in the end, have no place in the kingdom of God (see 1 Corinthians 15:24–26). No wonder those who know all this pray earnestly, "Your kingdom come" (Matthew 6:10).

In the meantime death is still complicated. Although God has given us all the answers we *need*, we do not have all the answers we would *like*. We find it hard to know what to say about death.

We return to the third day after the death of King Saul, to the little town of Ziklag, where David was poised to become Israel's king at last. God's own king (see 1 Samuel 16:1) was about to begin his reign. It took a death to make him king. David's reign has been anticipated again and again (trace this theme through 1 Samuel 2:10; 13:14; 15:28; 16:1, 12, 13; 18:4, 8, 12, 30; 20:13–17, 31; 21:11; 23:17; 24:20; 25:28–31; 26:25; 28:17), but it was only when Saul died that it could begin. What did the new king have to say about that death?

We have seen that the young Amalekite who came to Ziklag with the news of Saul's death had expected David to welcome him and his message. David's first act as king (a status yet to be formally recognized; see 2:4; 5:3) was to order the execution of the young man (1:15). That was the "reward" he received for his "news" (see 4:10). He had seriously misjudged the new king. David's second act as king (although the narrator mentions it first, perhaps suggesting it was the more important act) was to lead his companions in mourning for Saul and for Jonathan and for the Israelite people (1:11, 12). Contrary to the expectations of the messenger, the death of Saul and his son Jonathan was not received as good news by David.

In 1:17–27 we hear David's words concerning the deaths of Saul and Jonathan. They constitute what someone has described as "the most beautiful heroic lament of all time."[1] They are called a "lamentation" in verse 17, which may be defined as grief put into words.[2] David's first act as king toward his people was to teach them a psalm that not only expressed their mourning but gave it a surprising shape.[3]

The first book of Samuel began with a narrative about the birth of one who would become a new leader for Israel (1 Samuel 1), followed by a poem (Hannah's prayer, 1 Samuel 2:1–10) that anticipated the major themes of the history that would follow. The second book of Samuel begins with similarities and differences. First there is a narrative about the circumstances in which God brought a new leader to Israel (1:1–16). This time those circumstances involved not a birth but deaths.[4] Then there is a poem (David's lament, 1:17–27) that takes up themes from Hannah's prayer in a surprising way.[5]

Our passage has two unequal sections:

(1) Introducing David's lament (vv. 17, 18)
(2) David's lament (vv. 19–27).

Introducing David's Lament (vv. 17, 18)

David's lamentation is introduced as follows:

> And David lamented with this lamentation over Saul and Jonathan his son, and he said it should be taught to the people of Judah; behold, it is written in the Book of Jashar. (vv. 17, 18)

Here we are told four things about the words that follow. The first is that they were *David's* lamentation: "David lamented" (v. 17). David's grief was not merely private, but it was certainly personal. The lament is an "eloquent testimony to the depth and sincerity of David's grief."[6] Many years later it would be said of the great son of David, "Jesus wept" (John 11:35). On that day David wept (see 1:12).

Second, the focus of his lament was "Saul and Jonathan his son" (v. 17). David grieved, too, for the whole people of Israel who had suffered so greatly (1:12). But the lament focused on Saul and his son Jonathan—the old king and the crown prince.

The relationships between David, Saul, and Jonathan had a complex history. Certainly David's relationships with the king and with his son were very different. Jonathan was consistently devoted to David (1 Samuel 18:1–4; 19:1, 4; 20:4, 9, 35, 41, 42; 23:16–18). Saul, although at first positively disposed to the young man who killed the monster Goliath (1 Samuel 18:5; 19:5) and came into his court with his soothing music (1 Samuel 16:21), soon came to hate David with a bitter and murderous jealousy (1 Samuel 18:8, 9, 11, 12, 15, 17, 21, 25, 29; 19:1, 10, 17, 20; 20:1, 3, 30, 31; 22:7, 8, 13, 17, 23; 23:7, 14, 15, 19–24; 24:2, 14; 26:2, 18, 20; 27:1). Yet David "lamented . . . over Saul and Jonathan his son" (v. 17). That is not to say that his grief over each was the same, but it was (as we will see) connected.[7]

The third thing said here about David's words of lamentation is that he required them to "be taught to the people of Judah" (v. 18).[8] Here is the first act of the new king toward his subjects. "The sweet psalmist of Israel" (23:1)[9] began his reign by teaching the following words to his people. There would be many more similar poems composed by King David, many of which are to be found in the Book of Psalms.

The reference to "the people of *Judah*" (v. 18), the tribe of the Israelite nation to which David belonged (1 Samuel 17:12; see also 1 Samuel 30:26), anticipates the fact that the people of Judah were the first to acknowledge him as king (2:4). There was some time and trouble before the whole nation came to this mind (5:3). We may assume that David's instruction that the lament be taught to the people was made before all Israel had accepted him as king.[10]

The fourth thing said about the poem is that readers of this book should know it well because "behold,[11] it is written in the Book of Jashar" (v. 18). Unfortunately, today's readers of 2 Samuel cannot know the Book of Jashar (or "The Book of the Upright") as well as the ancient audience. The book has long been lost.[12] It was probably a collection of songs or poetry associated with major figures of Israel's history ("The Upright"). David's instruction that his lamentation be taught to the people was apparently obeyed. By the time this account of his life was written, the narrator could point to it in the then well-known Book of The Upright.

David's Lament (vv. 19–27)

Fortunately for us the historian did not simply refer readers to the Book of Jashar. He reproduced the words of David's lamentation here. The beauty and depth of the poem are extraordinary. In the space available here we can hardly do them justice.

The poem defies simple analysis. Here we will listen to it in three parts (vv. 20, 21; vv. 22–24; vv. 25, 26), with an introductory line announcing the tragedy (v. 19) and a concluding line echoing the introduction and looking back on it (v. 27).[13]

The Tragedy Announced (v. 19)
He said:[14]

> "Your glory, O Israel, is slain on your high places!
> How the mighty have fallen!" (vv. 18b, 19)

David's lament begins by addressing the nation ("O Israel," v. 19). What had happened was a tragedy *for Israel*. These words may have been taught first to the people of Judah (v. 18), but from the beginning David was concerned for the whole nation.

The first word in the original is something of an enigma. The ESV "Your glory" (v. 19) does not convey the oddity of the Hebrew word, which can mean either "the ornament" or "the gazelle."[15] The context does not clearly indicate one or the other meaning.[16] Perhaps he is saying that "the ornament" of Israel (in that sense "the glory") lies shattered on the hills where Saul and Jonathan died. However, the use of the harsh term "slain" (v. 19)[17] may suggest the animate sense of the word: "The gazelle, O Israel, is slain on your high places" (v. 19).[18]

The "high places" (v. 19) would later become the sites of Israelite apostasy, of pagan sacrifice (see Leviticus 26:30; Numbers 33:52; 1 Kings 3:2, 3; 12:31, 32; 13:2, 32, 33; 2 Kings 12:3; 14:4; 15:4; Psalm 78:58; Jeremiah 7:31; 19:5; 32:35; Ezekiel 6:3, 6; Hosea 10:8; Amos 7:9). Today what had been slain on the high places is Israel's *ornament* or Israel's *gazelle*. We will return to this enigmatic expression shortly.

The ambiguity dissolves with the cry, "How the mighty have fallen!" (v. 19). This cry will be repeated like a refrain through the poem (vv. 25a, 27a). "The mighty" (v. 19) is now a plural word. While the reference could include all those Israelites who had died in the battle with the Philistines, it will soon be clear that the focus is on Saul and Jonathan.

The horror of the tragedy is *what was* (they were "mighty") and *what now is* (they are "fallen," v. 19). Sense the loss—the greatness that once was is no longer.[19] This is the pain of grief. It is the terrible sense of loss. We weep because of *what was*, but *now is not. The mighty have fallen.* Strangely, death casts a bright light on *what has been lost.* Much of the pain in grief comes from how aware we become of what we have lost.

This reversal (*the mighty* now *fallen*) should remind readers of the prayer prayed by Hannah years earlier (1 Samuel 2:1–10). Hannah made explicit what must be read between the lines of David's lament. It is the Lord who brings down the mighty. "The bows of the mighty are broken," said Hannah (1 Samuel 2:4a). If Saul and Jonathan were "the mighty," then Hannah's words had found a shocking fulfillment.

David's lament now unfolds in three main sections. First we hear a kind of denial in verses 20, 21: "No!" Second, in verses 22–24 we are pointed back to "the mighty" who have fallen and hear eloquent words about what had been lost. Third, David's most intense emotions and the aspect of this tragedy that distressed him most keenly are given voice in verses 25, 26.

Part 1: No! (vv. 20, 21)

In verses 20, 21 we hear David longing for the impossible. On the one hand he longed that certain inescapable consequences of the deaths would not come about (v. 20). On the other hand he wished that the tragedy would be recognized on an impossible scale (v. 21).

No Joy for the Enemy (v. 20)

> Tell[20] it not in Gath,
>> publish it not in the streets of Ashkelon,
> lest the daughters of the Philistines rejoice,
>> lest the daughters of the uncircumcised exult. (v. 20)

The "good news" of Israel's defeat, and particularly of Saul's death, had already been broadcast in macabre form throughout the land of the Philistines (1 Samuel 31:9).[21] David may not have known this yet. In any case he longed for the impossible, namely that the Philistines might not hear of what had happened.[22]

Gath was the Philistine town with which David had had the most experience. It was located in the foothills of the central mountains, toward the eastern edge of the coastal area that was the land of the Philistines.[23] Gath was the home of the first Philistine he ever met, the great Goliath (1 Samuel 17:4). Remarkably David had twice sought refuge from the threats of Saul in Gath (1 Samuel 21:10; 27:2). On the second of these occasions David had won the trust of the Philistine king and to all appearances had become his loyal subject (1 Samuel 27:12). The appearances were false. The finest proof of David's true commitment is this lament, in which he shows himself to be profoundly on the side of Israel. He longed that the inhabitants of Gath might not hear of what had happened. "Tell it not in Gath" (v. 20). This was an ironic sequel to recent days in which David had been keen to keep other secrets from those in Gath (1 Samuel 27:11).[24] Then he had succeeded. But no one would keep *this* news from being told in Gath.

Ashkelon was another of the five leading Philistine cities (1 Samuel 6:17). It was on the Mediterranean coast and therefore on the opposite edge of Philistine territory from Gath. These two towns stood for the whole land of the Philistines. "Publish it not in the streets of Ashkelon" (v. 20).

David was not *literally* telling the people of Israel to refrain from announcing their tragedy in the Philistine cities.[25] That was hardly likely. He was rather expressing a desire that the news might not be told there by anyone. The reason was that he could hardly bear the idea of the exultant joy that the news was bound to bring to Philistine hearers.

Years earlier when by David's own action the Israelites had defeated the Philistines, the women of the Israelite cities sang songs of joy (see 1 Samuel

18:6, 7). The idea of the tables being turned and the Philistine women now exulting was intolerable to David.

One of the unusual features of this lament is the absence of any explicit reference to God. However, David's commitment to the Lord is just beneath the surface. The horror he felt at the idea of the Philistines rejoicing over Israel's demise was so intense because they were "the uncircumcised" (v. 20). Years earlier David had expressed his disdain for Goliath and his threats against "the armies of the living God" by calling him "this uncircumcised Philistine" (1 Samuel 17:26, 36). Earlier still, Jonathan, while expressing his firm faith in the Lord, had called the Philistine enemy "these uncircumcised" (1 Samuel 14:6). The term underlines the identity of the Philistines as *not* the Lord's people. More recently even Saul had been horrified at the prospect of being killed and mistreated by "these uncircumcised" (1 Samuel 31:4). We may detect just beneath the surface of David's words his dismay at the harm to the Lord's reputation when the Philistines sing their songs of joy at the death of the one who had been the Lord's anointed.[26]

In this way David gives words to a second dimension of his grief. Not only is there profound loss (v. 19), but this loss would enable the enemies to delight in their evidently successful hostility to God and his people.

No Joy for the Place (v. 21)

From one impossible wish David turned to another:

> You mountains of Gilboa,
>> let there be no dew or rain upon you,
>> nor fields of offerings![27] (v. 21a)

"Your high places" (v. 19a) are now specified and addressed: "You mountains of Gilboa" (v. 21).[28] The young Amalekite had truthfully informed David of this location (1:6; see 1 Samuel 31:1). David now expressed his wish that the shattering significance of what had happened should be seen in a permanent curse on the place where it happened.[29]

Of course, the only one who can actually do something like what David described is God himself.[30] David did not imagine that his words here would be effective, but he gave voice to a further dimension of the tragedy. It was as though the good order of the world had been disrupted. The place where such a catastrophe occurred should not be unaffected. The good order of things (dew, rain, crops) ought not to continue as though nothing had happened.

Here is a third dimension to David's anguish. The pain of a death is intensified by the fact that the world seems to go on *as though nothing has happened*, though something *terrible* has happened. Some might want to tell us that death is "only natural." In our grief we want to cry out that nothing is more *unnatural*. David put this agony into words.

He reinforced his longing with a stark picture of what had happened on Mount Gilboa:

> For there the shield of the mighty was defiled,
>   the shield of Saul, not anointed with oil. (v. 21b)

The picture is stark. Saul's shield lies in the dirt, splattered, no doubt, with blood. Perhaps there is a hint of many such shields ("the mighty" is plural as in verse 19b), but the focus of attention is on one of them. It is clear from its filthy state that it is not "anointed with oil" (v. 21).

The scene can be taken in directly and literally. Leather shields, studded with metal plates, were oiled before battle in order to both enhance their effectiveness in deflecting weapons and to make it difficult for the enemy to take hold of it in hand-to-hand combat (cf. Isaiah 21:5).[31] The grimy shield lying in the mud would never again receive such careful treatment.

The tragedy was deeper than that, however. The words "not anointed with oil" may be applied to "Saul" as well as to his "shield" (v. 21).[32] Twice in this chapter David has reminded us that Saul had been "the Lord's anointed" (vv. 14, 16). The unoiled shield in the dirt on Gilboa is a graphic symbol of the unanointed Saul now finally rejected by God.[33]

Again if we are attentive I believe that we can hear, just beneath the surface of his words, David's disturbing understanding of the theological dimension of this event. The great tragedy of Saul is *what he might have been* as the Lord's anointed king. Long ago Samuel had told Saul that had he been obedient to the Lord's words, "the LORD would have established your kingdom over Israel forever" (1 Samuel 13:13). The end result of Saul's disobedience is now seen and symbolized in the picture that David's words paint of the defiled shield on the slopes of Gilboa—no longer anointed.

Part 2: What Has Been Lost (vv. 22–24)

In the second part of the lament David looks back for a moment at what Saul and Jonathan had been, what had been lost.

They Were Great Warriors (v. 22)

First there was their greatness as warriors.

From the blood of the slain,
   from the fat of the mighty,
the bow of Jonathan turned not back,
   and the sword of Saul returned not empty. (v. 22)

Here terms that have been used already of Saul and Jonathan ("slain," v. 19a and "mighty," vv. 19b, 21b) are taken up and applied to their foes. There had been many past occasions when the situation David now mourned had been just the opposite. Saul and Jonathan had often advanced against the enemy and triumphed.

The image here is of the soldiers' weapons consuming the "blood" and the "fat" of the enemy.[34] Saul's considerable success as a soldier has not been a major theme of this history, largely because he was so overshadowed in this by David (1 Samuel 18:7). However, beginning with his remarkable defeat of Nahash the Ammonite (1 Samuel 11:1–11), there had been numerous occasions of courageous, skillful, and successful battles under Saul's leadership (see 1 Samuel 14:47, 48; 15:7; also 23:28; 24:1). Jonathan, too, had been a remarkable warrior (notably 1 Samuel 14:1–23). Jonathan's bow (1 Samuel 20:20, 36) and Saul's sword (1 Samuel 17:39; 31:4) have featured in the earlier story.

This is not the whole truth, and it is not a balanced account of Saul's life. But David rightly understood Saul's death as a time to appreciate *what had been lost.*

There is something important here about grief. The pain is our sense of *what we have lost.* When we attempt to put our grief into words (perhaps in a eulogy at a funeral or more informally in our talking with friends and family) it is entirely proper that we speak about *the good that has been lost.* Of course, we should not pretend that the person concerned was something they were not, but neither should we expect in this context a balanced picture of the person and his or her life. Words that express grief *should* speak of *the good that we have lost.* That is why we are grieving. Putting our grief into words in this way helps us to understand our sadness by helping us to see its cause—*the good that has been lost.*

Of course, Saul's death also meant the end of his bitterness, rage, and violent crazy jealousy. But that is beside the point. That is not the reason his death was tragic. David wept because Saul's death also meant the end of what was good. That is what he put into words.

They Were Loved Leaders (v. 23)
Saul and Jonathan, beloved and lovely!
   In life and in death they were not divided;

they were swifter than eagles;
    they were stronger than lions. (v. 23)

If you have read the earlier history recently, you might wonder at David's words. "They were not divided" (v. 23)? In reality there had been *terrible* uproars in the relationship between Saul and his son, to the point where the king twice attempted to take Jonathan's life (see especially 1 Samuel 14:29, 44; 20:33, 34)! However, again all that was beside David's point *here*. Jonathan *had* been astonishingly faithful to his father. Despite Jonathan's devotion to David, despite Saul's murderous hatred of David, Jonathan never betrayed or abandoned his father. To the very end Jonathan stayed with Saul (1 Samuel 31:2). This is the point David wants to be remembered now: "in life and in death they were not divided" (v. 23).

Furthermore, David insists, the king and his son were "beloved and lovely" (v. 23). That may not be a realistic description of Saul toward the end as he deteriorated into dark paranoia. But there was a time when he was hailed by the nation, which recognized that in all Israel there was "none like him" (1 Samuel 10:24). They "rejoiced" in their triumphant king (1 Samuel 11:15). The summary of Saul's reign in 1 Samuel 14:47, 48 indicates that there was much that was positive. Furthermore (although David did not yet know about this, see 2:4b) the final scene in 1 Samuel records an act of devotion toward Saul and his sons by the inhabitants of Jabesh-gilead (1 Samuel 31:11–13). David was not exaggerating when he said of Saul *and* Jonathan that they were "beloved and lovely" (v. 23).

This is what all Israel must understand. The deaths of Saul and Jonathan were a terrible loss to the nation. "The mighty have fallen" (v. 19). In Saul's case, it is true, the fall had begun some time earlier. David, of all people, had reason to point out Saul's grave faults and offenses. But this was not the time for that. David's words focus on *the good that had been lost*—and, he insisted, there was much.

Saul Did You Good (v. 24)

This second part of the lament has one more note to strike in its articulation of what had been lost. In sharp contrast to the rejoicing that was inevitable among the Philistine women (no matter what David might wish, v. 20b):

You daughters of Israel, weep over Saul,
    who clothed you luxuriously in scarlet,
    who put ornaments of gold on your apparel. (v. 24)

Saul's reign, despite all its problems, evidently brought prosperity to at least parts of Israelite society. Again David was insisting that the good should not be forgotten, and if the good was remembered, then there was reason to weep. The good had been lost. Hannah's prayer again found a strange fulfillment here: "The LORD makes poor and makes rich; he brings low and he exalts" (1 Samuel 2:7).

Part 3: David's Anguish (vv. 25, 26)

The third and final part of David's lament takes a surprising turn. Verse 25a could mark the end of the lament:

> How the mighty have fallen
> in the midst of the battle! (v. 25a)

This is a clear echo of the opening two lines in reverse order, so that, from a formal point of view, verses 19 and 25 form a neat frame for the poem with an AB—BA pattern. If this was the end of the lament it would neatly round it off by taking us back to the beginning. The theme has been what had happened in "the battle" on Mount Gilboa, the fall of "the mighty," namely Saul and Jonathan (v. 25).

However, the second half of verse 25 has a surprise that will expand into several more lines from David that shift the emphasis of the whole lament. In a clear echo of the very first line of the poem, David inserts a crucial change. The exact words of verse 19a are repeated, except that the enigmatic first word, "the gazelle," is replaced by a name:[35] "Jonathan lies slain on your high places" (v. 25b).

Without uttering a disparaging word about Saul, David managed to indicate that "the gazelle" or "the ornament" of Israel had not really been Saul. It had been Jonathan.[36] As far as David was concerned (again without undermining what he had already said about Saul) the tragedy on Mount Gilboa focused on Jonathan.[37]

The main body of the lament concludes with an expression of David's own grief at the death of his friend. For the first time in the whole poem David speaks in the first person. He addresses his words to the departed Jonathan:

> I am distressed for you, my brother Jonathan;
> very pleasant have you been to me;
> your love to me was extraordinary,
> surpassing the love of women. (v. 26)

These moving words are undoubtedly intimately personal. But they are more than that. The relationship between David and Jonathan was of public importance. Certainly it was a deep personal friendship. At what was to be one of the last times they saw each other they both wept, "David weeping the most" (1 Samuel 20:41). However, it was more than that. Jonathan was the crown prince, the heir of Saul, and yet he was the first to gladly acknowledge David as Israel's next king—*his* king (see especially 1 Samuel 18:3, 4; 20:13–17; 23:17).

Up to this point, in both the preceding narrative and in David's lament, every time Jonathan has been mentioned reference has been made to his relationship to Saul. Repeatedly Jonathan is called "his [Saul's] son" (1:4, 5, 12, 17). Then in verses 22, 23 of the lament Saul and Jonathan are presented together as a pair. In verse 25b, however, Jonathan is singled out and is mentioned without any reference to Saul. Then in verse 26a he is characterized as "my [David's] brother." It is astonishing that the lament climaxes not with Saul, but with Jonathan; and not with Jonathan as Saul's "son" but as David's "brother" (1:4, 2:26).

Since Saul's daughter Michal was David's wife (1 Samuel 18:27), Jonathan was, of course, David's brother-in-law. However that is beside the point and almost certainly not what David had in mind when he called Jonathan "my brother" (v. 26). This is a reference to the covenant between them (see 1 Samuel 18:3; 20:8, 16; 22:8; 23:18). Although some details are implicit, it is clear enough that Jonathan and David made a covenant that included at least:

- Jonathan's love for David (1 Samuel 18:1, 3; 19:1b; 20:17, 30; see 20:34).[38]
- Jonathan's renunciation of any claim to Saul's throne (1 Samuel 18:4;[39] see 20:31).
- Jonathan's glad acceptance of David's future reign (1 Samuel 20:13; 23:17).
- Jonathan's regarding David's enemies as his enemies (1 Samuel 20:16).
- David's commitment to deal kindly with Jonathan (1 Samuel 20:14, 17) and indeed to have him second in rank to himself (1 Samuel 23:17, 18).
- David's promise to deal kindly with Jonathan's family (1 Samuel 20:15, 42).
- The Lord's support for this relationship (1 Samuel 20:13–16, 23, 42; 23:16).

All of this is caught up in David's reference to Jonathan as "my brother" (v. 26).

If the role of the lament has been to give appropriate words for the people to express their grief, it has also very carefully given a direction to their sorrow. Certainly there is the recognition of the great loss of Saul's actual and potential greatness, but the people were to particularly understand the loss of Jonathan through David's eyes. They are to learn to grieve for Jonathan as David grieved for him. This implies understanding the goodness of Jonathan's love for David.

David celebrated the goodness of this love in what strikes us as extravagant language.[40] In Hebrew two words from verse 23a ("beloved" and "lovely"), which applied to the people's love and admiration for Saul and Jonathan, are strikingly now applied to the relationship between David and Jonathan ("pleasant" and "love"),[41] but now intensified ("*very* pleasant" and "*extraordinary . . . love*," v. 26).

We should note that the words "surpassing the love of women" (v. 26) have been improperly taken by some to suggest that there was a sexual aspect to the relationship between David and Jonathan.[42] I have briefly discussed this issue in my commentary on 1 Samuel.[43] In this very public lament the suggestion that David would even hint at any such thing is ludicrous. Rather he was saying that the extraordinary relationship between himself and Jonathan (as outlined above) was more important than even the most cherished relationship between a man and a woman. The point is not so much the man-to-man friendship they shared[44] as the covenant between them. Jonathan's love for David had everything to do with David's kingship.

Jonathan's love for David—slain now on the mountain—is the climax of the lamentation David taught the people of Israel for a very good reason (to which I will return in a moment).

The Tragedy Summed Up (v. 27)

The lament is concluded. David closes with another echo of the opening lines.

> How the mighty have fallen,
>   and the weapons of war perished! (v. 27)

"The mighty," as in verses 19 and 25, is plural and returns us to the situation that was the occasion for the lament—the deaths of Saul and Jonathan. "The weapons of war" that had "perished" are probably a poetic reference to the dead king and his son (v. 27).[45]

There are at least three dimensions to what we should learn from David's remarkable lament over Saul and Jonathan.

First, there are lessons here about the nature of grief and putting grief into appropriate words. Of course, the situation was unique, and our experiences of mourning will never be identical to what David and his people experienced at that time. However. it is valuable to observe how and why David spoke so positively about Saul. There was so much else that could have been said but was not.[46] The lament put the grief into words and therefore properly focused on what had been lost. This was not the time for a balanced biography. It was a recognition that Saul's death was a tragedy and why. It was because there had been, by God's kindness, good in Saul and his reign. If the people were to understand and experience their grief properly, they needed to see that.

As we grieve it is important for us to understand that it's about *the good that has been lost*. This will mean remembering the good. It is a time to put into words what we have lost and to therefore recognize those things that were God's gift to us. And therefore to learn to *thank* God in our grief. David taught his people to grieve well.

Second, let us appreciate the king God was about to set over his people. With breathtaking care and skill David taught the people to understand that Saul's death, and especially Jonathan's death, prepared the way for the new king.[47] David was the one who had been chosen to replace Saul. Remembering what had been lost in Saul's death was a way of anticipating what David would be for Israel. Remembering Jonathan's relationship to David pointed to an example of how all Israel should now love and rejoice in their new king. "The mighty" had indeed "fallen" (v. 27). An even mightier one was about to take their place. His reign began with words of grace.[48]

Third, as the lament prepared the way for David, it is appropriate for us to reflect on the way in which it also pointed forward to Jesus. In due course David would fall as Saul did. "The mighty have fallen" expresses more than the deaths of Saul and Jonathan (v. 19, 25, 27). All human rulers and leaders eventually fall. As we grieve, let us recognize that the good that has been lost has been provided in a new way. As Jonathan looked forward to the new king with joy and love, let us look forward to King Jesus at whose coming every tear will be wiped away, and death will be no more (Revelation 21:4).

Part 2

THE COMING OF
THE KINGDOM

2 Samuel 2:1—5:3

5

Who Will Have This King?

2 SAMUEL 2:1–11

AS WE HEAR THE BIBLE'S ACCOUNT of the reign of King David, we must not forget its purpose. We could easily enjoy the narrative for the engaging story that it is. Here is a rich mixture of dramatic action, personal conflict, corrupt behavior, and exemplary conduct with complex, intriguing characters and enthralling, page-turning plots. We could, more particularly, focus on the biographical interest of the story. In David we have one of the most interesting characters in world literature—brilliant but also submissive to God; ruthless but also merciful and kind; capable of costly integrity but also (as we will see) of astonishingly self-serving wickedness. We could take an interest in the historical significance of the persons and events here recorded. Here is one of the greatest figures in world history, whose influence is arguably still felt. Each of these interests is valid, but none is adequate.

David became king of the nation of Israel as part of God's unfolding purpose for the world he has made. We now know that this purpose is to bring all things under the Lordship of Jesus Christ (see Matthew 28:18; Acts 2:36; Romans 14:9; 1 Corinthians 15:27; Ephesians 1:10, 21, 22; Philippians 2:9; Colossians 1:19, 20; 2:10; Hebrews 1:2; 1 Peter 3:22; Revelation 11:15). Unlike Saul, who had been given to the people in response to their rebellious demand for a king "like all the nations" (1 Samuel 8:5, 19, 20, 22), David was chosen to be king according to God's own purpose. In that sense he was "a man after [God's] own heart" (1 Samuel 13:14).[1] While Saul was undoubtedly appointed by God (1 Samuel 9:16; 10:24; 15:1), David's place in God's purpose was very different: he was the king God had chosen *for himself* (1 Samuel 16:1).

Any interest in David that falls short of understanding him as God's king is inadequate. David and his reign revealed the kingdom that God will finally establish. The kingdom that Jesus came to announce (Matthew 4:17), inaugurate (Colossians 1:13), and finally establish (1 Corinthians 15:24–28) is the kingdom that David's kingdom was introducing to the world. John Calvin put it well: "The earthly reign [of David] is a token in which we must contemplate the reign of our Lord Jesus Christ and the salvation of his Church to the end of the world."[2]

The second chapter of 2 Samuel brings us to the day when David's reign began. Here we have a wonderful opportunity to "contemplate the reign of our Lord Jesus Christ." We will see:

(1) How the new king began his reign (vv. 1–4a).
(2) How the new king treated his enemies (vv. 4b–7).
(3) How the new king was opposed (vv. 8–11).

How the New King Began His Reign (vv. 1–4a)

The long-awaited moment had arrived. David's years on the run from Saul (1 Samuel 19—31) were over. Remarkably his integrity was intact. Despite extreme provocation he had not acted against Saul or against the people of Israel. He had not sought his own advantage, but had maintained righteousness and faithfulness. He had suffered for this. Now, however, Saul was dead. It was time for God's purpose for David, anticipated when he was a lad (1 Samuel 16:13) and confirmed again and again in his experience and in the eyes of others (see, for example, 1 Samuel 18:12, 14, 28), to advance.

The Ascent of the King (vv. 1–3)

How would that happen? The situation was dire. Just three days journey to the north (from Ziklag, where David was), the Israelite people had suffered a terrible defeat at the hands of the Philistines. That enemy now occupied many of the Israelite cities in the north and northeast areas of the land, on both sides of the Jordan River (1 Samuel 31:7). What role would the Philistines play in the days following their resounding defeat of Saul's army? While it is difficult to imagine that the Philistines simply withdrew from Israel's affairs (and indeed it will later become clear that they did not), our historian did not consider their power to be decisive in the course that events now took. We will hear nothing more from him about the Philistines until some years have passed and David is established as king over all Israel in Jerusalem (5:17).[3] It is clear from their reappearance in the story at that point that they had not gone away. However, the interests of the historian are very particular, and whatever the Philistines were doing was irrelevant as he explains how David became king.

What he wants us to understand about David becoming king is this: *David's ascent was in obedience to the words of the Lord.*[4] Years earlier Samuel had told Saul that as the Lord's anointed king over his people Israel, one thing was required of him above all else: he must "listen to the sound [or voice] of the words of the LORD" (1 Samuel 15:1 AT). Saul's kingship had failed, and he died at the hands of the Philistines precisely because he "did not obey the voice of the LORD" (1 Samuel 28:18).

David's movement to become king began in stark contrast to Saul's disobedience.

> After this David inquired of the LORD, "Shall I go up into any of the cities of Judah?" And the LORD said to him, "Go up." David said, "To which shall I go up?" And he said, "To Hebron." (2 Samuel 2:1)

"After this" (v. 1) suggests that little time elapsed between the events of the previous chapter, namely David's receiving and responding to the news of Saul's death, and what happened next.

David's initiative was to ask God about the next step (ESV, "inquired," v. 1). Here perhaps is a subtle irony. Saul's name was significant in his story. He was the one "asked for" by the people, and "Asked For" was his name.[5] David's movement toward the kingship began with a very different asking. David asked the Lord.

The narrative here (as often in the Bible) does not pause to satisfy our curiosity as to how David made his inquiry of the Lord and how he received an answer. The inquiry and the answer are all that matters here, not the method. From the few places in which more details are given we know that throughout the Old Testament period God spoke "in many ways" (Hebrews 1:1). Specifically we know that David had on previous occasions "inquired of the LORD" (v. 9) by means of the ephod with the help of the priest Abiathar (1 Samuel 23:9–12; 30:7, 8). Unfortunately (for our curiosity), we know very little about what this process was and how it worked. It is commonly assumed that it was a kind of casting lots, but this is not certain.[6] We also know that there were occasions when David received words from the Lord by means of a prophet (see 1 Samuel 22:5) and others when he received the Lord's words, but no indication is given of how it happened (see 1 Samuel 23:2–4). It has been assumed by numerous commentators that on this occasion David made his inquiry by means of Abiathar and the ephod, and that may be so.[7]

David's question introduces the key word translated "go up" that is repeated five times in verses 1–3.[8] The leading idea is David's ascent, not just "to the higher elevation of Judah, as compared with Ziklag,"[9] but to the kingship. The crucial point is that he "went up" in obedience to the Lord.[10]

In this David foreshadowed the one who would, many years later, be "highly exalted" by a path of obedience (see Philippians 2:8, 9). God's king (first David and finally Jesus) did not grasp power out of selfish ambition. The path to their kingship was obedience to God.

David's question supposed that if he were to "go up," it would be to one of "the cities of Judah" (v. 1).[11] Just as Saul the Benjaminite (1 Samuel 9:1, 16, 21; 10:20, 21) had based himself in the town of Gibeah in Benjamin (1 Samuel 10:26; 11:4; 13:2, 15; 14:2, 16; 15:34; 22:6; 26:1), it may have been reasonable to assume that David's future base would be in his home territory of Judah (1 Samuel 17:12). Moreover, it had been in Judah that David had been anointed (in Bethlehem, 1 Samuel 16:4, 13) and had first come to public attention by defeating Goliath (1 Samuel 17:1, 50). The prophet Gad had once directed him to "the land of Judah" (1 Samuel 22:5). Perhaps most important of all, the elders of Judah were his friends. Only recently he had recognized this friendship with gifts to them from his raid on the Amalekites (1 Samuel 30:26). It is possible that the Philistine occupation of much of the north was also a factor in David's thinking.[12] If David was to "go up" (v. 1) into the land of the people of Israel, it is not surprising that he would assume it should be to one of the cities of Judah. The Lord's reply—"Go up" (v. 1)—confirmed that he was right.

As though to emphasize the exactness of David's obedience at this point, the general permission to "Go up" was followed by a request for specific direction: "To where shall I go up?" (AT). The Lord's reply was unambiguous: "To Hebron" (v. 1).

Hebron was an important city located on a mountain ridge in Judah, about nineteen miles south-southeast of Jerusalem.[13] It was the last mentioned in a list of "all the places where David and his men had roamed" (1 Samuel 30:31).

It is difficult to overstate the significance of the Lord's direction to David to go up "to Hebron" (v. 1). Hebron was the city of Abraham. Abraham settled "by the oaks of Mamre, which are at Hebron" and built an altar there to the Lord (Genesis 13:18; 14:13). This was where "the LORD appeared to him" when three men visited him with the message that Sarah would have a son (Genesis 18:1–15). Sarah died at Hebron (Genesis 23:2) and was buried in a cave east of the city (Genesis 23:19). Later Abraham himself (Genesis

25:9, 10) and his son Isaac (Genesis 35:27–29) and Rebekah, Jacob, and Leah (Genesis 49:31; 50:13) were buried there too. Indeed Hebron was the location of the only portion of the promised land to become the possession of Abraham (Genesis 23) and therefore the first part of the land to be given to Abraham and his descendants as promised by the Lord (Genesis 12:1; 15:7, 18–21). Hebron, we might say, is where Israel's life in the land of God's promise began.

The power of these associations must not be overlooked. David's going up "to Hebron" (in accordance with the word of the Lord) links David's story to Abraham. It suggests that David's rise is the continuation of the story that began there with Abraham. In other words, David's move to Hebron connects him with the promises that God had made to Abraham.[14] If we are right to see David's move to Hebron in this light (and subsequent events will confirm that we are), it is an important indication that what God will do through David is of enormous significance. It is connected to God's promise to Abraham to bring blessing to "all the families of the earth" (Genesis 12:3). Indeed David's going up to Hebron anticipates the fact that Jesus will be introduced in the first sentence of the New Testament as "the son of David" *and* "the son of Abraham" (Matthew 1:1). The key to understanding David is the key to understanding Jesus—God's promises to Abraham. God's words "To Hebron" (v. 1) were of momentous significance.

> So David went up there, and his two wives also, Ahinoam of Jezreel and Abigail the widow of Nabal of Carmel. And David brought up his men who were with him, everyone with his household, and they lived in the towns of Hebron. (vv. 2, 3)

David's exactly obedient response[15] to the Lord's word is reminiscent of Abraham's similar response such a long time previously (compare Genesis 12:4: "So Abram went"[16]).

It is clear that this was no temporary visit on David's part. He transferred a company that must have numbered several thousand from his base in Ziklag to Hebron and the surrounding towns. This was the crowd that had gone with David when he fled from Saul to the land of the Philistines. Then there were 600 with their households (1 Samuel 27:2, 3). We cannot know how long David spent in the Philistine territory, but it was not brief (see the account in 1 Samuel 27). During that time it is likely that his company grew, just as it had grown from the 400 men who had joined him earlier in the cave of Adullam (1 Samuel 22:2).

Of this vast contingent the first mentioned are David's two wives. David had taken Ahinoam and Abigail to be his wives during his time on the run from Saul (1 Samuel 25:42, 43).[17] They had been among those who went with David to the land of the Philistines (1 Samuel 27:3). They had been captured by the Amalekites (1 Samuel 30:5) and rescued by David (1 Samuel 30:18). Their hometowns, Jezreel and Carmel respectively, were in the Hebron region.[18] David's wives, going up with him from Ziklag to Hebron, were therefore returning home.[19]

These were David's second and third wives. His first wife, Saul's daughter Michal, had been taken by Saul after David was forced to flee and was given to another man by the name of Palti (1 Samuel 25:44). We will hear more about Michal in due course. The circumstances of David's marriage to Abigail (see 1 Samuel 25) were remembered. She is repeatedly referred to as "the widow[20] of Nabal" (1 Samuel 27:3; 30:5; 2 Samuel 2:2; 3:3), a reminder of her remarkable speech while still Nabal's wife, in which she anticipated what was now about to happen to David (1 Samuel 25:24–31). We know less about Ahinoam, but she would become the mother of David's first son, Amnon (3:2). David would take several more wives over the coming years (3:2–5).

The story told by the books of Samuel began with a man who had two wives (1 Samuel 1:2). Polygamy was not forbidden in the Old Testament, although problems were anticipated (see Deuteronomy 21:15–17) and often recounted (as in 1 Samuel 1). There is no obvious criticism of David implied in the report of his several wives (at this point). However we will find ourselves rethinking this when we come to 3:2–5.

The Acceptance of the King (v. 4a)

The arrival of David and his company in Hebron and the nearby towns would have been a major event. We are only told one thing about the welcome they received.

> And the men of Judah came, and there they anointed David king over the house of Judah. (v. 4a)

As so often in the Biblical record, we are tantalized by the brevity of the account. "The men of Judah" were, no doubt, "the elders of Judah," also described earlier as David's "friends" (1 Samuel 30:26; see also 2 Samuel 19:11). At that time David's "friends" were contrasted with "the enemies of the LORD" (1 Samuel 30:26). It is almost certain that "friends" here has political overtones. At a time when Saul regarded himself and David as mutual enemies (1 Samuel 18:29; 19:17; cf. 24:4; 26:8),[21] the "friends" of David would be those who distanced themselves from Saul's attitude.[22]

These "friends"(1 Samuel 30:26) came to Hebron, but we know nothing of what passed between them and David except that they anointed him as their king. The brevity of the account suggests that the elders of Judah had no hesitation in doing this. Perhaps we are to understand that they had been waiting for this day and were more than ready for it. Although we are told nothing of the thoughts and motivations of the men of Judah, their act was a recognition and affirmation of the anointing that David had received many years earlier in Bethlehem (1 Samuel 16:13).[23] At last the man on whom God had set his heart (1 Samuel 13:14) to be his king (1 Samuel 16:1b) had begun his reign.

It was a small beginning, but a massively significant one. As one writer has put it, "It is a small beginning, but it is the kingdom of God—concrete, visible, earthly. The kingdom of God has for the moment tucked itself away in the hills of Judah. The kingdom of God *is* like a mustard seed."[24] But it was only the beginning.

How the New King Treated His Enemies (vv. 4b–7)

There have been numerous unambiguous indications that David was to be king over the whole kingdom that had been Saul's (1 Samuel 13:14; 15:28; 16:1; 28:17). The tribe of Judah over whom David was now recognized and accepted as king occupied only the southernmost portion of the Israelite territory (although a very substantial portion). The north was occupied by the Philistines (although we do not know the extent of their occupation).

What the Men of Jabesh Had Done (v. 4b)

David's first recorded official act after becoming king in Hebron was prompted by some news. David was informed, "It was the men of Jabesh-gilead who buried Saul" (v. 4b). The details of this incident were given at the very end of 1 Samuel (31:11–13). Jabesh-gilead (or Jabesh[25]) was the town that had been dramatically saved by Saul, at the very beginning of his reign, from the brutal Nahash the Ammonite (1 Samuel 11:1–11). The people of Jabesh-gilead did not forget and many years later risked their own lives to honor Saul's body. They had shown themselves to be Saul's friends.[26]

What response would the new king of Judah make to this news about the friends of the one who had considered himself David's enemy? The situation was far from straightforward. Jabesh-gilead was located some seventy miles north of Hebron and on the eastern side of the Jordan River. It was directly opposite Gilboa and the Jezreel Valley where the Israelites had suffered the recent crushing defeat by the Philistines. The area was now occupied by Philistines. The people of Jabesh were once again under enemy oppression, the very oppression that Saul had been appointed to save them from (1 Samuel 9:16) and that David had gained such a reputation for dealing with (1 Samuel 17:36, 50, 51; 18:6, 27, 30; 19:5, 8; 23:5). Recently David's relationship to the Philistines had been more ambiguous (see 1 Samuel 27:4, 12). For these and perhaps other reasons, those who told David the news about the people of Jabesh-gilead must have wondered what he would do.

The King's Words to the Men of Jabesh (vv. 5–7)

David's response took the form of a surprising message.

> David sent messengers to the men of Jabesh-gilead and said to them, "May you be blessed by the LORD, because you showed this loyalty to Saul your lord and buried him. Now may the LORD show steadfast love and faithfulness to you. And I will do [this][27] good to you because you have done this thing. Now therefore let your hands be strong, and be valiant, for Saul your lord is dead, and the house of Judah has anointed me king over them." (vv. 5–7)

The messengers' assignment was dangerous. On the one hand there were the occupying forces of the Philistines. On the other there was the uncertainty of how the people of Jabesh would receive messengers from Saul's old enemy. The message they brought to Jabesh, however, must have astonished all who heard it. It contained four elements.

What They Had Done (vv. 5c, 6c)

First, David *commended* the people of Jabesh for what they had done. David described their act of burying Saul as "this loyalty" (v. 5c in the ESV rendering). It was more than that. The Hebrew word (*khesed*) is an important Biblical term and a key-word of David's message. It was more than "loyalty" (v. 5). A better translation would be "mercy" or "kindness." In a context like this the word typically refers to "exceptional acts of one human to another, meeting an extreme need outside the normal run of perceived duty, and arising from personal affection or pure goodness."[28] "Loyalty" (v. 5) is not quite it.

David praised the people of Jabesh-gilead for their kindness toward Saul, who had been their "lord" (v. 5). David saw their action in exactly the opposite terms to the deed of the young Amalekite in 2 Samuel 1. The Amalekite may have thought he was showing kindness to both Saul and David in the act he claimed to have committed, but David saw his (alleged) act as treachery. David was persisting in his long-running refusal to accept the role of Saul's enemy. If the people of Jabesh-gilead had shown themselves to be Saul's friends, that did not make them David's enemies. On the contrary.

What The Lord Will Do (vv. 5b, 6a)

Second, David prayed that the Lord would *bless* the people of Jabesh-gilead because of their kindness to Saul. We (the readers) have been prepared for this by David's conduct through the later chapters of 1 Samuel and especially by the report of his responses to the news of Saul's death in 2 Samuel 1. This should not blind us to the fact that David's message was extraordinary. It was the young Amalekite who had (not unreasonably) expected to be rewarded by David for his claimed role in Saul's death. David heard that the men of Jabesh-gilead had treated Saul in exactly the opposite way to the Amalekite. Anyone with the Amalekite's understanding of things (which, I say again, was not unreasonable) could well expect David to be angry with the people of Jabesh. David, however, surprised everyone by being angry with the Amalekite and praying for God's blessing on the people of Jabesh-gilead.

More particularly he prayed that the Lord would show to them *khesed* (v. 6a; ESV, "steadfast love,"), that is, exceptional kindness, just as they had shown such kindness to Saul (the same Hebrew word translated in the ESV as "loyalty" in verse 5c).

David's prayer went further—that the Lord would show "steadfast love [*khesed*] and faithfulness ['*emet*]" (v. 6a). If *khesed* is God's kindness and mercy, his '*emet* (the Hebrew word means "truth") is what we need in order to be able to rely on his mercy. These two words are often found together in the Bible's descriptions of God's ways: he is "abounding in steadfast love and faithfulness" (Exodus 34:6; also Genesis 24:27, 49; 32:10; 2 Samuel 15:20; Psalm 25:10; 40:10, 11; 57:3, 10; 61:7; 85:10; 86:15; 89:14; 108:4; 115:1; 117:2; 138:2). They comprehend "all that we could desire from and ask of God."[29] They speak of his forgiving grace and his trustworthiness, his promises and their sure fulfillment.[30] That God is like this is what makes faith in him possible.

> And where will we find assurance unless we know his faithfulness—that is, that he is constant in his promises—and also that he makes us taste and feel that everything that he promises to us is certain and infallible? For when

someone speaks to us of his mercy, we will only be able to conceive of a confused fantasy unless we have actually known that he, indeed, wants to be our father. Therefore, unless God speaks to testify to us that he chooses us for his children and that he wishes to undertake the responsibility for our salvation, it is certain that we will always be unstable, and tortured with many doubts and worries.[31]

David's message to those who had every reason to regard him as their enemy (and to consider themselves his enemies) was about God's grace. If the people of Jabesh-gilead talked together about this message they might have said, "though we were his enemies, David spoke to us of God's love" (cf. Romans 5:8).

What The King Will Do (v. 6b)

The third element of David's message to the people of Jabesh-gilead was the most astonishing: "And I will do [this] good to you" (v. 6b). In the Hebrew "I" is particularly emphatic: "*I am the one* who will do this good to you."

He was not simply saying that *just as* he prayed God would be good to them, he would *also* be kind.[32] It was more than that. He was asserting that he was the one through whom the Lord would bless them and show his steadfast love and faithfulness to them. "I am the one who will do *this good* to you (namely, the good that I have prayed that the Lord will show to you)."[33]

Who was David to speak like this? On the one hand he was setting himself up as the one who would deal with the people of Jabesh-gilead. What gave him the right to do anything (good or ill) to the people of this northern town? On the other hand (and more remarkably still) he was claiming to be the answer to his own prayer: the Lord would bless these people by David's dealings with them.

In both of these claims David was presenting himself to the people of Jabesh-gilead (at least implicitly) as God's own king and was inviting them to accept his goodness (which he identified with God's goodness) toward them.

What They Should Now Do (v. 7)

The fourth and final element of David's message made his invitation explicit: "let your hands be strong, and be valiant" (v. 7a). Take courage. Be confident and bold.

Courage was needed. Why? Because "Saul your lord is dead" (v. 7b), and those who destroyed him now occupied their territory (1 Samuel 31:7). The future for the people of Jabesh-gilead was bleak (especially if the Philistines discovered their audacious deed for Saul).[34]

On what basis could David call for such courage? On the one hand, the invitation is based ("Now therefore") on his prayer and his promise in verses 5, 6. On the other hand both the prayer and the promise should be taken seriously because "the house of Judah has anointed me king over them" (v. 7c). Again there is an emphasis on "me": "*I am the one* the house of Judah has anointed king over them."[35]

David's message to the people of Jabesh-gilead was wonderfully like the gospel of our Lord Jesus Christ in which the grace of God is offered to his enemies (Romans 5:10) because the one who once held their allegiance is defeated (Hebrews 2:14) and Jesus has begun to reign (Acts 2:36). Of course, the parallel is not exact, but the character of God's king and his message of grace is clear.

How the New King Was Opposed (vv. 8–11)

We are not told how the people of Jabesh responded to the message from David. We will hear of them once more much later in the story of David, but only in terms that recall their brave deed on behalf of Saul (21:12). They were no doubt caught up in the movement that eventually made David king of "all the tribes of Israel" (5:1–4), but if there was any earlier agreement between them and the king in Hebron we are told nothing about it.

Instead we learn that there was another powerful man in the north who did not want David to be his king. He was Abner, a cousin of the late King Saul. Abner had commanded Saul's army (see 1 Samuel 14:50). Abner was the son of Ner, a brother of Saul's father, Kish (1 Samuel 14:50, 51). Abner had been by Saul's side on the day that both of them saw with astonishment the young David slay Goliath (1 Samuel 17:55) and had brought the young hero to Saul after the event (1 Samuel 17:57). At a later time Abner shared a place at Saul's table with David (1 Samuel 20:25). David and Abner knew one another well. Abner's attitude to David was no doubt influenced by his master's bitter and jealous hatred. It would also have been colored by the humiliation he must have suffered from David's superior military performance (1 Samuel 18:30). This would hardly have been ameliorated by David's public rebuke of the commander on the day that David stole Saul's spear and water jar (1 Samuel 26:14, 15).

After the death of Saul, and with the news spreading that the people of Judah had recognized David as their king, Abner took action:

> But Abner the son of Ner, commander of Saul's army, took Ish-bosheth the son of Saul and brought him over to Mahanaim, and he made him king

over Gilead and the Ashurites and Jezreel and Ephraim and Benjamin and all Israel. (vv. 8, 9)

Abner's action is presented in contrast to that of the house of Judah (*"But Abner . . . ,"* v. 8). We will see shortly that what Abner did almost certainly occurred several years after the men of Judah had anointed David. The narrator, however, presents his action immediately after the report of David's gracious message to the people of Jabesh-gilead. It almost appears in the narrative as though Abner's action is in response to David's message. Certainly his action stands in contrast to what we might have hoped was the response of the people of Jabesh. Rather than welcome the "good" (v. 6) that David was offering to Saul's former followers, Abner installed another king, a son of Saul. In this way he rejected David as king.

Abner's action amounted to a refusal to accept that Saul's kingship had come to an end. It should be remembered that Abner had witnessed Saul's acknowledgment of David's future in 1 Samuel 26:25 and almost certainly also the even clearer words of Saul some time earlier: "I know that you shall surely be king, and that the kingdom of Israel shall be established in your hand" (1 Samuel 24:20). However, this was not a development Abner was (yet) willing to accept.[36]

The son of Saul taken by Abner had obviously survived the slaughter of the other three sons of Saul on Mount Gilboa (1 Samuel 31:2, 6). His name here, Ish-bosheth, appears to be a derogatory nickname. His real name was probably Ish-baal (or Eshbaal), Saul's youngest son (see 1 Chronicles 8:33; 9:39).[37] "Baal" was a word in Hebrew that could mean "husband," "lord," "master," or "owner."[38] "Ish-baal" would then mean "man of the lord (or possibly Lord[39])." However, Baal was also the name of a famous pagan Canaanite god or gods (see, for example, Numbers 25:3; Judges 6:25, 31; 1 Kings 16:31; 18:19; 22:53). Therefore, names containing "baal" sometimes had "baal" replaced with the word "bosheth," which means "shame."[40] Ish-baal is called by our historian "Man of Shame."[41]

It is clear from his action here and the ensuing events that Abner was the powerful figure among the northern Israelites. Ish-bosheth (as we will call him, since that is his name in our text) was Abner's puppet.

Abner chose to bring the surviving son of the dead king to Mahanaim. Mahanaim was about fifteen miles south of Jabesh-gilead, by the Jabbok River, a tributary flowing east to west into the Jordan River about halfway between the Dead Sea and Lake Galilee.[42] Mahanaim was therefore central to the region east of the Jordan, known as Gilead. Later David would use Mahanaim as a base after he was forced to flee from Jerusalem during Absalom's revolt (17:24, 27; 19:32; 1 Kings 2:8). Later still Mahanaim would be a significant administrative center in Solomon's kingdom (1 Kings 4:14). All of this suggests that Mahanaim was an obvious choice for Abner's installation of Ish-bosheth, especially when we add the consideration that it located the new power base as far as possible from the Philistine territory to the west.[43]

As always, however, it is important to notice the historical associations that place names in the Bible story carry. While Mahanaim (which means "two camps") may not be as weighty with memories as Hebron, it was named by Jacob when he met angels on his way to his reunion with Esau (Genesis 32:2) and divided the company who were with him into "two camps" (Genesis 32:7, 10). There is some irony in Abner's choice of Mahanaim. He was again dividing the people of Israel into "two camps."[44]

Many years later, after the death of Solomon, there would be a permanent split into two kingdoms named "Israel" and "Judah" (1 Kings 12). The seeds of that division may be traced back to the day that the northern tribes, at Abner's initiative, chose to have a king other than David. The term "Israel" became ambiguous. It could refer to the whole people of the Lord (as in 1:3, 12, 19, 24) or just to the northern tribes (excluding the large southern tribe of Judah, as in 2:10; 3:10; 5:5).[45]

Israel (in the fullest sense) would only be united when they came under their true king (see 5:1–3). After the later division of the kingdom, one of the important blessings of the promised Messiah was that he would make them one nation again (see Isaiah 11:12, 13; Jeremiah 3:18; 50:4, 5; Ezekiel 34:23; 37:22; Hosea 1:11; Zechariah 10:6). God's people would only be united when they came under their true king.

Abner made Ish-bosheth king over an area that is partially designated with a list of territories and then summed up as "all Israel" (v. 9). Gilead (as we have seen) is the land east of the Jordan where Ish-bosheth was based. "The Ashurites" (v. 9) is possibly intended to be a reference to the tribe of Asher, located to the northwest on the Mediterranean coast (but this is not clear[46]). "Jezreel" (v. 9) is almost certainly the northern location of that name, where the recent disastrous conflict with the Philistines had begun (1 Samuel 29:1). "Ephraim" (v. 9) was the Israelite heartland, and "Benjamin" was the tribal territory just to the north of Judah to which Saul and his family belonged. These places do not constitute an exhaustive list, for the writer adds at the end, "and all Israel" (v. 9). Since the scope of the territory outlined in verse 9 is almost certainly the *claim* of Ish-bosheth's kingship rather than a description of his actual control, "all Israel" here probably extends his claim over David's kingdom of Judah.[47]

David did not receive the welcome he really should have received as God's king. We might say, "he came to his own [his own being all Israel], and his own people did not receive him" (cf. John 1:11). They did not want this man to reign over them (cf. Luke 19:14). Under Abner's influence they chose another king (cf. John 19:15).

Our passage concludes with three short notes. First, there are the summary details of Ish-bosheth's reign: "Ish-bosheth, Saul's son, was forty years old when he began to reign over Israel, and he reigned two years" (v. 10a). Ish-bosheth's brief reign reminds us of Saul's "two years over Israel" (1 Samuel 13:1).[48] Abner's bold initiative with Ish-bosheth lasted no longer than Saul's legitimate reign. They were two turbulent years, as we will soon see, but only two years.

There remained some who did not accept the kingship of Ish-bosheth: "But the house of Judah followed David" (v. 10b). This note has been struck at the end of each part of our passage (vv. 4a, 7c, and 10b). The narrator keeps returning to the fact that there were some who did receive him (cf. John 1:12).

A concluding note about David's time in Hebron unveils the chronology of events that, presumably for dramatic effect, the narrator has condensed. "And the time that David was king in Hebron over the house of Judah was seven years and six months" (v. 11). Since, as we will see, the end of David's time in Hebron and the end of Ish-bosheth's reign were probably quite close in time, this means that Abner did not take the step of installing Ish-bosheth in Mahanaim until some five years or so *after* David was anointed in Hebron.[49] David's move to Hebron had been a response to Saul's death ("After this . . . ," v. 1). We can now see that Abner's move, about five years later, was not a response to Saul's death but to David's kingship and possibly to the news of his gracious message to Saul's former subjects.[50]

We are told nothing about the first five years of David's reign from Hebron except the message he sent to Jabesh-gilead.[51] The narrator's interest will now focus on the two years in which there were two claims on the allegiance of the people of Israel. One claim had been graciously and gently expressed in the message from Hebron to the people of Jabesh-gilead. The other had been enacted by Abner's installation of Ish-bosheth in Mahanaim. What happened next brought the two sides into terrible conflict.

These events provide us with an opportunity to contemplate the reign of our Lord Jesus Christ. Our King Jesus has begun to reign, not in Hebron, but in Heaven. He is the King who in *perfect* obedience exercises God's good rule. His kingdom really is God's kingdom. His word (even to his would-be enemies) is a word of grace, extraordinary mercy, and kindness. He is the one who will bring the kindness of God to those who come to him.

At the same time there are many Ish-bosheths—alternative rulers seeking our allegiance. But "No one can serve two masters, for either he will hate the one and love the other, or he will be devoted to the one and despise the other" (Matthew 6:24).

Will you, like the people of Judah so long ago, follow God's King? Or will you be drawn to another—a man of shame?

6

Human Politics and the Kingdom

2 SAMUEL 2:12–32

FROM 2 SAMUEL 2:12 to the end of 2 Samuel 4 we hear a story of human politics. A number of men attempted to have an influence on the coming kingdom of David by their own efforts. Some sought to hasten it. Some sought to defeat it. Some sought to turn the kingdom to their own advantage. But none of them was good enough, wise enough, or powerful enough to accomplish what they intended.

Human politics is often messy. *Politics* can be a dirty word. One dictionary offers the following definition of *politics*: "the use of underhanded and unscrupulous methods in obtaining power or advancement within an organization."[1]

Why should politics have such a bad name? If politics is the process by which policies and actions are formulated and enacted in an organization or a society, it is difficult to see that politics as such is dishonorable. Indeed the Bible's general teaching encourages honor and respect for those who hold what we call political office (see, for example, Matthew 17:25–27; 22:21; John 19:11; Romans 13:1–7; Titus 3:1, 2). This is because God has put the authorities in place for the good of human society. They are (whether they know it or not) responsible to God for the exercise of their authority. We should pray for them, thank God for them (1 Timothy 2:1, 2), and honor them (1 Peter 2:13–17). The widespread cynicism today about politics and politicians is not good. But it is understandable.

The problem is that power in the hands of human beings is never completely wise and good. Just as we individually mess up our lives in various ways and hurt others from time to time, so those who have power in an organization or a society are never entirely pure in their motives, nor wholly wise in their thinking, nor thoroughly good in their actions. This, of course, is putting it mildly. In many cases those with power (and those who seek power) are self-serving in their motives, foolish in their thinking, dishonest in their words, and corrupt in their actions.

But even at its best, political activity falls short of our hopes. The dreams *never* match the reality. It is never really like *West Wing*.[2] We are simply not good enough, wise enough, or strong enough to make human communities work as we believe they should. If you place your hopes in politics, you will be disappointed.

The Bible has the answer as to why this is so. It is that *sinners* are not good enough, wise enough, or strong enough to build a just, peaceful, and prosperous society.

Our only realistic hope is the *kingdom of God*. The Bible's message is that God has promised a King who will be wise and understanding, a just Judge who will rule with righteousness and faithfulness. And he will succeed. He will bring perfect and complete peace, not just to one nation, not even only to the whole human race, but to all of God's creation (see Isaiah 11:1–9). More than that, this King has already come and has begun to reign. The King, Jesus Christ, is calling all people everywhere to come into this kingdom by changing the direction of their lives and trusting *him* (see Mark 1:15).

Human politics, although capable of a measure of wisdom, goodness, and effectiveness (as well as much foolishness, evil, and failure), cannot bring in the kingdom of God. Only God's King can do that. The early pages of 2 Samuel will help us see whether we really believe that.

The situation as we come to 2:12 was this. In *Hebron* David had been acknowledged as God's king some five years earlier. In *Mahanaim* Ish-bosheth had been more recently installed as a rival king by Saul's old army commander, Abner. Having two kings in Israel was untenable. What was to be done?

The events of one day now unfold in three scenes:

(1) The two sides "together" in Gibeon (vv. 12–17).
(2) The two sides in conflict all day (vv. 18–24).
(3) The two sides reach a truce (of sorts) (vv. 25–32).

Neither the king in Hebron (David) nor the king in Mahanaim (Ish-bosheth) were directly involved in the events of this day. In particular it is important to notice that what happened that day was not David's doing. This was an attempt by the followers of each king (led by their strong men, Abner and Joab) to resolve the situation by talk and action. It was politics. It failed. The politicians were not wise enough, good enough, or strong enough to solve the problems facing them. The limitations of human politics were displayed that day.

Scene 1: The Two Sides "Together" in Gibeon (vv. 12–17)

Two Armies Meet "Together" (vv. 12, 13)

The action of the day began with Abner: "Abner the son of Ner, and the servants of Ish-bosheth the son of Saul, went out from Mahanaim to Gibeon" (v. 12).

"Son of Ner" (v. 12) is a reminder of the family connections: Saul and Abner had been cousins (see 1 Samuel 14:50). On this day Abner and "the servants" (v. 12, that is, soldiers) of Saul's son Ish-bosheth, whom Abner had installed as Israel's king, made the journey west from Mahanaim across the Jordan River and south to Gibeon. This was fifty miles or more, depending on the route taken.

Gibeon was close to the northern border of Judah and in the territory of the tribe of Benjamin (Joshua 18:25), the tribe to which Abner and Ish-bosheth belonged. Gibeon was famous because during the conquest of the land under Joshua, its Hivite inhabitants had tricked Joshua into making a covenant of peace with them (Joshua 9). This town and its history will impact the story of David again in due course. There Joab will kill his rival Amasa (20:8–10), and David will have to honor the covenant made in the days of Joshua (21:1–9). At this point, however, Gibeon was about to add a terrible incident to its fame.

For the first time in the Bible we now meet the commander of David's army. His name was Joab:[3] "And Joab the son of Zeruiah and the servants of David went out and met them at the pool of Gibeon" (v. 13a).

Joab had two brothers (Abishai and Asahel). Their mother, Zeruiah, was David's sister (1 Chronicles 2:16[4]). This family connection probably accounts for the repeated identification of the brothers in terms of their mother's name.

These three nephews of David will prove to be intensely loyal to him in different ways but will also cause considerable difficulty for the king. A glimpse of their character was given some time earlier when one of them (Abishai) had said to David, "Now please let me pin [Saul] to the earth with one stroke of the spear, and I will not strike him twice" (1 Samuel 26:8b). We will see too many examples of the eagerness of the sons of Zeruiah for violent solutions.

The symmetry of the text (notice how the wording of verse 13a closely parallels verse 12a) suggests that Joab was to David what Abner was to Ishbosheth, namely the commander of the king's army. Joab will be a major player in the course of David's life (and beyond).

No explanation is given for the movement of Joab and "the servants" (v. 13, again, soldiers) of David from Hebron to Gibeon, about twenty-five miles to the north.[5] The action may have been in response to news of the advance of Abner's men toward Judah. Joab had about half the distance Abner had to travel. This may have given him time to receive intelligence of Abner's advance and take his men to what may have been a predictable meeting point. It is also possible that the meeting at Gibeon had been prearranged. The relatively calm manner of the initial encounter gives some weight to this suggestion.

At Gibeon there was a pool, presumably of some considerable size.[6] Here the two groups "met" (v. 13). The Hebrew adds a word here that suggests a certain "coming together" in this meeting.[7] It was not, at least initially, a confrontation.

"And they sat down, the one on the one side of the pool, and the other on the other side of the pool" (v. 13b). The scene appears placid—the seated soldiers with the still water of the pool between them. But we sense the tension. This is, after all, a "coming together" of fighting men who serve two rival kings.

The two groups seated on opposite sides of the pool are described in terms that suggest a striking symmetry.[8] Our memory of recent events, however, imposes a certain asymmetry. On one side of the pool were the men who had recently (in this narrative) succeeded in striking down the Amalekites (1:1). On the other side were representatives of the army that had (at about the same time) been decisively crushed by the Philistines (1 Samuel 31 and, of course, the news and lament of 2 Samuel 1). On one side were the servants of the man who had gone up to Hebron in obedience to the Lord and was there anointed as king. On the other side were the servants of the man who had been made king by the commander who had lost the battle with the Philistines. On the one side were the men who may well have been thought by those on the other to have been collaborators with the Philistines. On the other side there may well have been those who had rejected the gracious offer of the king in Hebron (2:6). The apparent symmetry of the scene is superficial.

Two Commanders Talk (v. 14)

However, the symmetry is suggestive of the unity that both sides ought to share. The untranslated word "together" in verse 13 may likewise hint at what ought to be. They represented one people (see 1:12). This point will eventually triumph over the others just mentioned (see 5:1). The men on either side of the pool seem to have no thirst for a fight. They were aware (as we shall hear) that they were "brothers" (2:26, 27).[9]

But what was to be done? While there was no indication that David intended to coerce the northern tribes to accept his rule, did the advance of Abner's troops to Gibeon suggest that he had intentions to make Ish-bosheth's claim over "all Israel" (2:9) a reality? David's presence had been perceived as a threat to Saul's kingdom during Saul's lifetime (1 Samuel 13:14; 15:28; 18:8; 20:31; 24:20; 28:17). How much more it must have been after Saul's death!

Could negotiation help? Could the supporters of either king be persuaded to change allegiance? Could both kings agree to renounce any claim to the territory of the other? Could either king be intimidated or persuaded to step down? There were various possibilities for resolving the situation.

Abner again took the initiative. "And Abner said to Joab, 'Let the young men arise and compete before us'" (v. 14a). At first hearing this proposal is perplexing. The word translated "compete" suggests entertainment (Judges 16:25), play (Psalm 104:26), rejoicing (1 Samuel 18:7; 2 Samuel 6:5; 1 Chronicles 15:29; Proverbs 8:30, 31), or even joking (Proverbs 26:19) rather than anything violent. It is possible, then, that Abner was proposing some kind of joust. Given the circumstances mere entertainment seems unlikely, but he may have been proposing some form of competition between teams from each side that might make some contribution to resolving the standoff.[10]

Joab's quick agreement suggests that he saw the idea as harmless enough. "And Joab said, 'Let them arise'" (v. 14b). The two commanders were taking tentative steps in their negotiation, probably hoping to avoid violence.

Two Teams Engage (vv. 15, 16)

If that was the intention, they had miscalculated. This is what happened:

> Then they arose and passed over by number, twelve for Benjamin and Ish-bosheth the son of Saul, and twelve of the servants of David. And each caught his opponent by the head and thrust his sword in his opponent's

side, so they fell down together. Therefore that place was called Helkath-hazzurim, which is at Gibeon. (vv. 15, 16)

The two teams, perhaps each claiming to represent all "twelve" (v. 15) tribes of Israel, moved out without any indication of the horror about to come. Abner's men are described as representing Benjamin (Saul's tribe, in whose territory all this was taking place) and Ish-bosheth. Those on Joab's team were "servants of David" (v. 15). The teams, therefore, in their number and description represented the two kings and their claims.

It was no doubt more messy than the brief symmetrical description in verse 16. Whatever the young men were meant to do, they attacked each other with deadly violence. The outcome was twenty-four dead young men. "They fell down *together*" (v. 16). Here we have the word we noted in verse 13 (where it is untranslated in the ESV). They had "met *together*" at the pool in Gibeon. Now the young men "fell down *together*" (v. 16) there. The possibility of peaceful unity hinted at as they came together earlier was dashed as they destroyed one another.

Abner and Joab had sought a wise solution (or at least a way forward). They were not wise enough. The site of this horror was given a name that would perpetuate its memory. The place became known as Helkath-hazzurim—"the field of stone knives."[11]

The Aftermath (in Summary) (v. 17)

Whatever hope there might have been that day for a peaceful resolution had been destroyed. A terrible battle raged for the remainder of the day. The narrator does not, on this occasion, keep us in suspense. He provides a brief summary of the whole day before recounting one awful sequence of events. The summary is: "And the battle was very fierce that day. And Abner and the men of Israel were beaten before the servants of David" (v. 17).

Abner was the real power on one side of this conflict. For the first time in 2 Samuel "Israel" (v. 17) clearly refers to the northern part of the nation, excluding Judah. "The servants of David" (v. 17) suggests that at this stage the other side was defined by their personal allegiance to David.

Scene 2: The Two Sides in Conflict All Day (vv. 18–24)

The narrator spares us many of the details of that terrible day. He does, however, follow one particular incident in some detail, for this incident will have repercussions for years to come, even beyond David's lifetime. The sequence of events that was set in motion that day will end (if I may spoil a good story by turning to its last page) with the execution of Joab by Solomon on the orders of David (see 1 Kings 2:5, 6, 28–35). That may seem to be a long way off, but this day was where it began.

Meet the Sons of Zeruiah (v. 18)

We have noted that Joab and his two brothers were passionately loyal supporters of David. On the day of the fierce battle referred to in verse 17 the narrator's interest focuses on these three men: "And the three sons of Zeruiah were there, Joab, Abishai, and Asahel" (v. 18a). To begin with, our attention is drawn to the third of the brothers, with a vital piece of information about his athleticism: "Now Asahel was as swift of foot as a wild gazelle" (v. 18b).

Like his brothers, Asahel was a young man of action. In the Hebrew text the description of him is a striking reminder of the first word of David's earlier lament. We noted that the word rendered "Your glory" in the ESV of 1:19 could be translated "The gazelle." By the end of David's poem we saw that "the gazelle" (v. 18) was a reference to the mighty warrior Jonathan. Asahel is likened to (literally) "one of the gazelles which are in the field." At least in his agility he was like Jonathan (see 1 Samuel 14:13).

Asahel's Chase (v. 19)

The fighting that followed the mutual slaughter of the twenty-four young men was no doubt chaotic. There is no suggestion that Abner or Joab were directing events. Asahel chose to use his speed to make his contribution to the conflict. "And Asahel pursued Abner, and as he went, he turned neither to the right hand nor to the left from following Abner" (v. 19). Obsessive and determined, Asahel did not deviate from his mission.

Abner's Warning (vv. 20–23a)

This was not what Abner or Joab had hoped for. As Asahel closed in on Abner, the older soldier thought he recognized the young man. He did not want a fight. The seasoned warrior could easily have dispensed with the younger man. Instead he chose to speak to him. "Then Abner looked behind him and said, 'Is it you, Asahel?'"[12] The younger man responded, "It is I" (v. 20).[13]

Abner had some sage advice for the eager youth. "Abner said to him, 'Turn aside to your right hand or to your left, and seize one of the young men and take his spoil'" (v. 21a). *Here's some good advice, Asahel. Pick on someone more of a match for you than an experienced commander.* However, the young man's obsession blinded him to his own limitations and the capability of the one he pursued. "But Asahel would not turn aside from following him" (v. 21b).

Abner was wise enough to see the consequences of a confrontation with this youth. There was little question about who would win. And killing Joab's brother would hardly help the present situation. So he pleaded with the lad in deadly earnest. "And Abner said again to Asahel, 'Turn aside from following me. Why should I strike you to the ground? How then could I lift up my face to your brother Joab?'" (v. 22). Although events will prove the wisdom of Abner's words, Asahel was in no mood to listen. "But he refused to turn aside" (v. 23a). Great warrior that he was, Abner could not avert this terrible confrontation.

Asahel's End (v. 23b, c)

> Therefore Abner struck him in the stomach with the butt of his spear, so that the spear came out at his back. And he fell there and died where he was. (v. 23b, c)

As Asahel rushed on toward Abner, his own speed brought him down. The veteran soldier played an old trick. He stopped in his tracks, projecting his spear backwards into Asahel's path, so that Asahel drove himself onto the deadly butt of Abner's spear. On that very spot he dropped and died.

The Aftermath (vv. 23d, 24)

Asahel's crumpled, lifeless body transfixed everyone who saw it. "And all who came to the place where Asahel had fallen and died, stood still" (v. 23d).

"All who came" (v. 23) included at least many of "the servants of David" (vv. 13, 17), who we may now understand were also pursuing Abner, some distance behind the swift-footed Asahel. They recognized the dead lad. They knew his family. The possible consequences of this death were terrifying to contemplate. Everyone was stunned. They knew that the conflict had just moved to another level. Shocked at the prospects, they stood motionless.

It is possible that some from the other side were included in "all who came" (v. 23). Just as Abner had recognized the young man and knew his family connections, others among "the servants of Ish-bosheth" (v. 12) may now have come upon the fallen warrior. They too would realize that this was a shocking development. They stood in stunned silence.

There were, however, two who did not allow the horror of Asahel's corpse to immobilize them. "But Joab and Abishai pursued Abner" (v. 24a). The brothers took up Asahel's mission where he had left off.[14] Abner had been right to anticipate that the killing of Asahel would bring him into direct conflict with Joab.

This eventful day was coming to an end. "And as the sun was going down they came to the hill of Ammah, which lies before Giah on the way to the wilderness of Gibeon" (v. 24b). Ammah is probably a hill to the east of Gibeon, and Giah may be a valley on its eastern side.[15] Abner and his men were fleeing toward the Jordan and on their way back to Mahanaim. Joab and Abishai were close behind them on the route eastward.[16]

If the military leaders had earlier lacked the wisdom to resolve the conflict, it is clear that the eager young Asahel had not helped the situation in any way at all. His efforts had just made things worse. With the sun going down on Joab and Abishai on the hill of Ammah, we wonder where this will all end.

Scene 3: The Two Sides Reach a Truce (of Sorts) (vv. 25–32)

Abner's Men (v. 25)

Our attention shifts from the hill of Ammah to another group: "And the people of Benjamin gathered themselves together behind Abner and became one group and took their stand on the top of a [literally, one] hill" (v. 25).

The scene has Abner defensively surrounded by his men on the top of the hill as Joab and Abishai reached the nearby hill of Ammah, presumably just to the west.[17]

Abner's men are called "the people [literally, sons] of Benjamin." This may indicate that Abner had swelled his forces from local people, naturally inclined to support their kinsman Ish-bosheth. The unity that was hinted at when the two groups of soldiers "came together" at the pool of Gibeon (v. 13) had not been realized. The "one group" that formed as night fell consisted only of the sons of Benjamin.

Two Commanders Talk (Again) (vv. 26, 27)

The situation was again tense. If, as the narrator seems to have suggested, Joab and Abishai were on their own, it seems unlikely that they could overcome the company that had now gathered around Abner on the next hill to the east. On the other hand, it is becoming clear that Abner did not want a solution through bloodshed. Perhaps the sons of Benjamin could easily have overwhelmed the two surviving sons of Zeruiah. This, however, was not what Abner sought. He attempted to restart the negotiations that had been so disastrously interrupted by the slaughter in the Field of the Stone Knives.

In the darkness a familiar voice called out from the top of the easternmost hill.

> Then Abner called to Joab, "Shall the sword devour forever? Do you not know that the end will be bitter? How long will it be before you tell your people to turn from the pursuit of their brothers?" (v. 26)

The earlier conversation at the pool of Gibeon had (unintentionally) set a terrible train of events in motion. This conversation must bring them to an end.[18] Abner asked three pointed rhetorical questions. (1) Should this conflict, with its cost in bloodshed, be allowed to go on "forever" (v. 26), Joab? (2) Can't you see, Joab, that if this does go on, "the end will be bitter" (v. 26) for us all? (3) This is a family conflict, Joab, brother against brother. How long will you allow it to go on?

This noble-sounding speech had a problem (as Joab must have heard it). It seemed to lay the blame for the fighting on *Joab*. The Hebrew text at this point has some difficulties but should in my judgment be translated:

> And Joab said, "As God lives, if you had not spoken, the people would have withdrawn this morning, each from following his brother." (v. 27 AT[19])

In other words, "You started this, Abner, with your speech this morning. If you had not spoken, suggesting your 'competition,' then what you are now wanting to stop would never have begun."

This exchange hardly settled matters. Like so many attempts at diplomatic solutions, it amounted to little more than blame shifting. It will turn out to be no more effective than the earlier talk between the commanders.

Joab's Men Stop (v. 28)

However, the immediate outcome was a cessation of hostilities. Joab no doubt recognized that he could not expect to succeed in the present circumstances.

> So[20] Joab blew the trumpet, and all the men stopped and pursued Israel no more, nor did they fight anymore. (v. 28)

Joab's trumpet blast echoed far and wide and conveyed its message to the servants of David, wherever they were now scattered. The day's fighting was over.

Abner's Men Withdraw (v. 29)

This enabled Abner and his men to march through the night and return to Mahanaim.

> And Abner and his men went all that night through the Arabah. They crossed the Jordan, and marching the whole morning [perhaps better, through the whole Bithron[21]], they came to Mahanaim. (v. 29)

The hard overnight march brought Abner's battered troops back across the Jordan valley[22] to where they had begun: Mahanaim—"two camps." There were indeed now two camps, and the chasm between them was deeper than it had been one day earlier.

The Aftermath (vv. 30–32)

The author now takes stock of this day on which two able men had made attempts to resolve the difficult situation of two kings in Israel, but had succeeded only in making matters worse. There is a note about each side.

David's Servants (v. 30)

> Joab returned from the pursuit of Abner. And when he had gathered all the people together, there were missing from David's servants nineteen men besides Asahel. (v. 30)

On David's side, just twenty casualties. If this includes the twelve at the beginning of the day, the ensuing battle had cost just seven more lives plus Asahel.

Abner's Men (v. 31)

"But the servants of David had struck down of Benjamin 360 of Abner's men" (v. 31). For every man on David's side who had fallen, there had been eighteen on Abner's side. This result may have a lot to do with Abner's eagerness for a truce.

The End of the Matter? (v. 32)

Where did all this leave the situation? As the account draws to its close, our attention is drawn again to the death that stands at its center. "And they took up Asahel and buried him in the tomb of his father, which was at Bethlehem" (v. 32a). Bethlehem was approximately midway on the journey back from Gibeon to Hebron. Importantly, of course, it was David's hometown (1 Samuel 16:4; 17:12, 15; 20:6, 28). We are reminded, therefore, of the family connection between Asahel and David. What trouble would yet flow from this unnecessary death?

More importantly, the mention of Bethlehem reminds us of what this day has been all about. Do you remember what happened, years earlier, in Bethlehem? God had designated David as the one he had chosen to be his king (1 Samuel 16). If you wanted to be on the right side of history, you didn't need to know the plans and strategies of Abner and Joab. You needed to know about what had happened at Bethlehem.

As Abner and his men marched eastward through the night, Joab's troops trudged south (via the stop at Bethlehem). They reached Hebron in time to see the sun rise. "And Joab and his men marched all night, and the day broke upon them at Hebron" (v. 32b).

What a day it had been! It would be possible to look back on the day and pass judgment. What was wise? What was foolish? Who was right? Who was wrong? The Bible writer seems to be content to leave such questions alone. The point of it all is rather the hopelessness of the situation. What was needed was not another clever strategy. If this day had taught anything, it was that the best men of action from both sides only made matters worse. They were not wise enough (or perhaps good enough or strong enough) to solve this. What hope was left?

Bethlehem.

God's kingdom would come, but by means that are completely different from the failed strategies of Abner and Joab in the days of David.

Bethlehem would feature again in God's strange ways of establishing his kingdom. A millennium after the events of 2 Samuel 2 a son of David was born in Bethlehem (see Micah 5:2; Matthew 2:1, 5, 6; Luke 2:4; John 7:42). He is the King whom David could only dimly foreshadow. In God's strange ways the death and resurrection of Jesus was God's victory over all evil, and the kingdom of his Christ is now advancing in the world by the weak foolishness of the word of the cross. We *pray* "Your kingdom come" (Matthew 6:10) precisely because *we* are not good enough or wise enough or powerful enough ourselves to make any progress.

Our strategies and plans, our negotiations and proposals are no more able to bring peace and harmony, justice and righteousness than the efforts of Abner and Joab. How pathetic are our efforts to advance God's kingdom!

Do not be surprised that the best human efforts achieve less than we hope for. Often much less. Do not be disillusioned when what we do achieve is weak and fragile. It is (as it has always been) *God's* work to bring in his kingdom. Only when *he* establishes *his kingdom* will we know the peace for which we long. Only when we remember Bethlehem will we pray authentically, "Your kingdom come" (Matthew 6:10).

7

Ambitious Opportunism and the Kingdom

2 SAMUEL 3:1–21

THE GREAT AND DECISIVE question of life is not what we achieve, nor how good we become, and certainly not how much we acquire. It is, who is your king? It will do no good at all to be highly successful, seriously virtuous, and even ridiculously wealthy if you are on the wrong side of history. Likewise, even if you achieve little (or fail in much), have a deeply flawed character, and lose everything, but have the right king, all will be well.

This simple point is difficult for us to grasp because we hate the idea that we are weak and are not masters of our own destinies. We love to pretend that we are in control. The truth is that we are utterly dependent on our King. We need a king who is powerful *for us*, one who is able to save us from our enemies and give us security. If we have such a king, all is well. If we do not, then our lives will ultimately end in failure.

This does not mean that how we live is unimportant. On the contrary. But it does mean that what our King does is *more* important.

The King of whom I speak is Jesus Christ. Those who belong to his kingdom know well that his powerful goodness is decisive. Of course, with Jesus as our King, how we live and what we do with our life matters. But it does not matter as much as having him as our King.

In the days of David, the way was being prepared for the coming of Jesus by the establishment of a kingdom that foreshadowed his kingdom. As a shadow of the kingdom yet to come, David's kingdom was both like and unlike the kingdom that would come with Jesus. It was a shadow but only a shadow, of that kingdom. We learn much about that kingdom as we see the similarities *and* the differences between King David and the Lord Jesus.

In the early chapters of 2 Samuel David's kingdom was not immediately or universally acknowledged. In this respect it was like the kingdom of Jesus. By his death Jesus has defeated his enemies, and by his resurrection he has been declared to be God's King. However, his kingdom is not yet universally acknowledged. Enemies oppose him, and rivals vie for power (see 1 Corinthians 15:25).

The great and decisive question in those days in Israel was, who will be Israel's king? The people of Judah had decided. David was their king, and he began his reign over them in Hebron (2:4). However, up north, across the Jordan in Mahanaim, Abner had decided for the rest of the nation that Saul's son Ish-bosheth would be their king (2:8, 9). We have not yet heard what the people generally thought about this. Abner, not public opinion, was the power behind Ish-bosheth's throne.

The resolution of this situation was not going to be easy. Ish-bosheth claimed (with some apparently reasonable grounds, it should be said) to be the rightful inheritor of Saul's kingdom. David was understood, at least by the people of Judah, to be the man God had chosen to rule the same kingdom. Initial attempts at negotiation (if that is what it was at the pool of Gibeon) had resulted in bloodshed but no solution (2:12–28). Abner and his men were back in Mahanaim. Joab and his company had returned to Hebron (2:29–32). Israel still had two claimants to the throne.

Chapter 3 of 2 Samuel begins with a brief summary of David's time as king in Hebron (vv. 1–5). We then follow the story of how one key player in this drama changed sides (vv. 6–21), with historic consequences. It is a story of ambition, sex, power, and politics. But the big question was, who will be king? The story unfolds as follows:

(1) David's time in Hebron: A summary (vv. 1–5).
(2) Abner and Ish-bosheth: Breakdown (vv. 6–11).
(3) Abner and David: Negotiation (vv. 12–16).
(4) Abner for David: Delivering the kingdom (vv. 17–21).

David's Time in Hebron: A Summary (vv. 1–5)

Before we hear the details of how the standoff between Hebron and Mahanaim was broken, the narrator gives us a glimpse of the whole period during which David was king in Hebron, highlighting the last two years, since Ish-bosheth's installation in Mahanaim.[1]

The Conflict (v. 1)

The latter part of that period was a time of conflict. What had begun on the day by the pool of Gibeon (2:12–32) did not end when the parties withdrew to Mahanaim and Hebron respectively. "There was a long war [literally, The war[2] was long] between the house of Saul and the house of David" (v. 1a).

The repeated expression "house of" (v. 1) is a little unusual but has appeared several times in the narrative so far. On the one hand it suggests a dynasty. As Saul's son and would-be heir, Ish-bosheth represented "the house of Saul" (v. 1) in this sense. But David's reign had just begun; the question of a dynasty was some way off (but note vv. 2–5).[3] Nonetheless, after the death of Israel's first king, if there was to be a lasting kingdom the issue was the establishment of a dynasty. On the other hand "house of" suggests family. The long "war" (v. 1) is properly understood as a family dispute.[4] Indeed it was a struggle between branches of one family ("brothers," as Abner and Joab had said, 2:26, 27). Whether it consisted of actual battles (as on the day that began at the pool of Gibeon) or simply a continuing state of hostility[5] is not said.

David's "house" at this time was "the house of Judah" over whom he was king (2:4, 7, 10, 11). The wider family was "the house of Israel" who were "the people of the LORD" (1:12), over whom Abner had set Ish-bosheth (2:8, 9).[6] However, Ish-bosheth is so unimportant that he is not even mentioned in this summary of David's years in Hebron. We will notice as the narrative unfolds that a number of times the narrator seems quite deliberately to avoid mentioning Ish-bosheth. The alternative kingdoms were that of "David" or that of the late "Saul" (v. 1).

The advantage in this conflict continued as it had begun (2:17, 30b, c, 31): "And David grew stronger and stronger, while the house of Saul became weaker and weaker" (v. 1b, c). There may well have been times when this was far from obvious to those in the thick of the struggle. Today the kingdom of Jesus is growing stronger and stronger, although many cannot see it. The truth is that *God is at work*, sovereign over all human wickedness, foolishness, and weakness, and he is establishing his kingdom and his King. So it was in these early days of David's kingdom.

In what way was David growing stronger? The first answer to that question has to do with David's growing family and potential dynasty. The second answer will involve a turn of events in Mahanaim that decisively weakened the house of Saul.

David's Sons (vv. 2–5)

First the narrator takes a step further back and surveys David's seven and a half years in Hebron from one particular point of view: "And sons were born to David at Hebron" (v. 2a). Six sons were born to David in these years, to six different wives. The "house of David" was in this respect growing "stronger and stronger."

The absence of any explicit comment by the narrator on the multiplication of wives taken by David should not be understood as a neutral stance to this development. While it is true that the Old Testament does not condemn all instances of polygamy, and there is no law forbidding the practice, there is at least what we might describe as a lack of enthusiasm for it (see, for example, the difficult situation in 1 Samuel 1; also Deuteronomy 21:15–17). More than this, however, the book of Deuteronomy clearly states that a king in Israel "shall not acquire many wives for himself" (Deuteronomy 17:17). For anyone who knows God's Law in the book of Deuteronomy, this list of David's sons, with their various mothers, is therefore troubling.

Furthermore, for anyone who knows what lies ahead for David, the list of sons is disturbing. There are names here that we will hear again. They will be the cause of much pain and terrible trouble for David and his family.[7]

"His firstborn was Amnon, of Ahinoam of Jezreel" (v. 2b). Ahinoam was one of the two wives David had brought with him to Hebron (see 2:2). This first son of David will appear again in the story, years later. His shocking and wayward behavior then (the incestuous rape of his half-sister Tamar, 13:1–22) will play a major role in the disastrous and bloody family feud that will all but destroy David's family and his kingdom. Amnon will be murdered by his own half-brother (13:23–33), who will then attempt to overthrow his father as king, meeting his own death in the ensuing conflict (14—18). The story of David's firstborn son will not be a happy one. However, all this lies in the future.

". . . and his second, Chileab, of Abigail the widow of Nabal of Carmel" (v. 3a). Abigail was the other wife David had brought with him to Hebron (see 2:2). This son probably died at a young age because he is never mentioned again,[8] and at a later date David's third (and later again his fourth) son appears to be the oldest surviving.

". . . and the third, Absalom the son of Maacah the daughter of Talmai king of Geshur" (v. 3b). This was the brother of Tamar who avenged his sister's rape by killing Amnon and who attempted to seize David's throne. Again, for those who know the story, the mention of Absalom is a reminder of the tragic side of David's life. At this point, however, the sadness was yet to come.

The marriage of David to Maacah, the daughter of a foreign king, had a political dimension. Geshur was a small kingdom on the east side of the Jordan River, to the north. In other words, it was on the other side of Ish-bosheth's base in Mahanaim. During his time in Hebron David formed a relationship, by this marriage, with a kingdom that was strategically located to bring pressure on "the house of Saul" (v. 1). This marriage was no doubt part of David's growing "stronger and stronger (v. 1)."[9]

". . . and the fourth, Adonijah the son of Haggith" (v. 4a). As David's death drew near, Adonijah would be the oldest surviving son of David and would claim the succession, leading once again to much strife (1 Kings 1:5—2:25). Other than being the mother of Adonijah (1 Kings 1:5, 11; 2:13), we know nothing about Haggith.

". . . and the fifth, Shephatiah the son of Abital; and the sixth, Ithream, of Eglah, David's wife"[10] (vv. 4b, 5a). Of these two sons and their mothers we have no further knowledge.

At first sight this list of David's growing family may support the assertion that he "grew stronger and stronger" (v. 1). In due course, however, we will look back and see that these names were harbingers of trouble to come for David's kingdom. We may reasonably wonder whether this is related to the dissonance between this list and Deuteronomy 17:17. If so, this is the first time the narrator has signaled that there may be a problem with King David.

Since these sons of David were born to different mothers, there is no indication of how their births were spread in time.[11] The impression given, however, is that the births spanned David's years in Hebron: "These were born to David in Hebron" (v. 5b).

Abner and Ish-botheth: Breakdown (vv. 6–11)

The big-picture summary of David's period in Hebron is followed by an account of a particular sequence of events that were a crucial part of David's growing stronger. They started with a critical weakening of the house of Saul, but led to David's becoming the unchallenged king of all Israel.

The action began in Mahanaim. Abner, the strong man who had made Ish-bosheth king, appeared to be having second thoughts.

Abner's Ambition (v. 6)

> While there was war between the house of Saul and the house of David,
> Abner was making himself strong in the house of Saul. (v. 6)

The house of Saul may have been becoming "weaker and weaker" (v. 1), but one man in Mahanaim was becoming stronger. Rather, he was "*making himself* strong" (v. 6). Abner was a man who made things happen. He had made Ish-bosheth king in the first place (2:8, 9). He was the one who initiated events on the terrible day that began with bringing his men to Gibeon and his proposal there to Joab (2:14; then see 2:20–23, 26). Ish-bosheth, however, seems to have been a disappointment.

The failure of leaders' sons to live up to their fathers has been an important feature of the story told by the books of Samuel. Eli's sons were a disaster (1 Samuel 2:12–25). Samuel's were no better (1 Samuel 8:3). Ironically the failure of Samuel's sons was the occasion for the people's demand that led to the appointment of King Saul (1 Samuel 8:5). Although Saul had one exemplary son in Jonathan, that son had died on Mount Gilboa. Ish-bosheth does not appear to have filled his father's shoes well.

Ish-bosheth's Complaint (v. 7)

Was Abner maneuvering himself into a position where he could usurp Saul's son? Ish-bosheth thought so. It had to do with a woman. "Now Saul had a concubine whose name was Rizpah, the daughter of Aiah" (v. 7a).

Like multiple wives, the practice of having concubines receives less attention by the Biblical narrators than we might wish.[12] It is a practice seen in the days of the patriarchs (Genesis 22:24; 36:12). Abraham and Jacob had concubines (Genesis 16:2, 3; 25:6; 35:22; 1 Chronicles 1:32[13]). Manasseh had at least one (1 Chronicles 7:14), as did a certain Caleb (1 Chronicles 2:46, 48). At a later time Gideon had a concubine (Judges 8:31), as did "a certain Levite" (see Judges 19:1—20:7). Saul had at least one (3:7; 21:11), and David had several (2 Samuel 5:13; 15:16; 16:21, 22; 19:5; 20:3; 1 Chronicles 3:9). Solomon took this to extremes: along with his 700 wives, he had 300 concubines (1 Kings 11:3; see Ecclesiastes 2:8; Song of Solomon 6:8, 9). His son Rehoboam did not quite match his father: he had only eighteen wives and sixty concubines (2 Chronicles 11:21)! Concubines and children born to them had a lower status than wives and their children (implied in Exodus 23:12; 1 Chronicles 3:9), although there could be rivalry (Genesis 21:9, 10). The children of a concubine could "belong" to a wife (Genesis 30:3). There seems to be some ambiguity around the rights or status of a concubine (see the dreadful story in Judges 19), although the Law offered some protection (Exodus 21:7–11; Deuteronomy 21:10–14[14]). In a royal family, to have sexual relations with a concubine of the king was understood as an assault on the king's position (as Absalom did, 16:21, 22; see also 1 Kings 2:21–24).

What are we to make of all this? In these practices Israel reflected the wider culture of its time (see Esther 2:14; Daniel 5:2, 3, 23),[15] and moral judgments are difficult.[16] God's purpose from the beginning is for monogamous marriage (Genesis 2:24; Matthew 19:4–6; 1 Timothy 3:2). This was the most common form of marriage in Israel[17] and should be the basis of our understanding of marriage.[18] However, deviations from this ideal occurred, arguably under the influence of the prevailing culture.[19] Some deviations were unambiguously condemned by the Law and other parts of Scripture (such as adultery and homosexual practice). Others, such as polygamy and concubines, receive less direct attention.[20] In these situations God's Law provided some protection for the vulnerable, but the Biblical historians rarely passed explicit moral judgments on these practices.[21]

Returning to 3:7, a concubine of the late King Saul is introduced to us here by name (Rizpah) as is her otherwise unknown father (Aiah). Rizpah will appear much later in the story, where she will play an honorable role in a tragic episode (21:1–14). At this stage in the story, however, she remains in the background of a devastating conversation that took place between Ish-bosheth and Abner.

"And Ish-bosheth[22] said to Abner, 'Why have you gone in to my father's concubine?'" (v. 7b). If (as the course of this conversation will confirm) Abner had sexually taken Rizpah, this would not have been a private matter. It was no less than a bold public challenge to the throne (compare Absalom's later public act in 16:20–22).[23] Ish-bosheth did not ask *whether* Abner had done this. That was apparently not in dispute. He asked *why*. "What do you think you are doing, Abner?"

Abner's response will confirm that the allegation was true and therefore that Abner had his eye on Ish-bosheth's throne. We can reasonably speculate that Abner's disappointment in Saul's son had driven him to do what he thought was necessary if the kingdom was to be kept in the hands of those who were loyal to Saul. Taking Saul's concubine was a first step to taking Saul's throne.

Abner's Anger (vv. 8–10)

However, for the proud Abner to be rebuked by this weakling whom he had come to despise was more than the strong man could bear.

Abner was insulted. "Then Abner was very angry over the words of Ish-bosheth" (v. 8a). That's putting it mildly. Who did Ish-bosheth think he was addressing? Was Abner no more than "a dog's head" (v. 8b)?[24] Moreover, did Ish-bosheth think that Abner was on the side of the enemy ("of Judah," v. 8b)?

"After all I have done for you!" he shouted in effect. Abner was not one to be talked down to, even by the man he had made king. Indeed Abner immediately assumed the position of the superior in this exchange. "To this day I keep showing steadfast love to the house of Saul your father, to his brothers, and to his friends" (v. 8c). He was the one who was constantly showing "steadfast love" (v. 8, Hebrew, *khesed*). This is the word we heard from David in 2:5, 6 (ESV, "loyalty" in v. 5). The men of Jabesh had shown *khesed* to the dead Saul, and the Lord himself would now show *khesed* to them. While the term can be used in a variety of contexts, it is typically the more powerful one who shows *khesed* to the weaker or more needy.[25] How dare Ish-bosheth speak as he had to the man who was constantly showing *khesed* to everyone around him!

Mind you, Abner did not go so far as to say that he had shown *khesed* to Ish-bosheth himself. He was not going to give the man that dignity. Instead he pointed out what he had *not* done to Ish-bosheth: ". . . and have not given you into the hand of David" (v. 8d). That was a kindness that Ish-bosheth did not deserve, and he should have recognized that it put him deeply in Abner's debt.

Instead this ungrateful wretch now had the effrontery to "charge me today with a fault concerning a woman" (v. 8e). "Today" means after all I have done "*to this day*" (v. 8c). Of course, Ish-bosheth's accusation was much more than "a fault concerning a woman" (v. 8), precisely because of who this woman was. Abner had made no attempt to deny the charge.[26] He just expressed outrage that the man before him should make it and trivialized the offense.

The tirade from Abner reached its climax with an oath: "God do so to Abner and more also . . ." (v. 9a). Such strong words from the furious Abner would have been terrifying. If he had paused at this point, anyone listening (and especially Ish-bosheth) would have trembled at what he might be about to say. The oath had the tone of a terrible threat.

Such fears were warranted. At this moment Abner abandoned his allegiance to Saul and committed himself (with that oath) to use his considerable power to the benefit of David and the detriment of the house of Saul. There would be no more "steadfast love to the house of Saul" (v. 8) from Abner.

The surprise is that he expressed this in terms that acknowledged God's promise to David. He called on God to deal with him "if I do not accomplish for David what the LORD has sworn to him" (v. 9b). Abner was quite clear about what the Lord had sworn to David: "to transfer the kingdom from the house of Saul and set up the throne of David over Israel and over Judah, from Dan to Beersheba" (v. 10). These words are astonishing at several levels.

First, where did Abner learn "what the LORD has sworn to" (v. 9) David? He had witnessed David's remarkable career since the day he felled Goliath (1 Samuel 17:55–57). He, like Saul, may well have deduced that "the LORD was with David" (1 Samuel 18:12, 28). Saul had been told by Samuel that his kingdom was to be given to another (1 Samuel 13:14; 15:28), and his fears that this other was David were confirmed (1 Samuel 24:20; 28:17). All of this was likely to have reached a man as powerful and as close to King Saul as Abner. He did not need to have personally received a prophetic word to this effect.[27] The terms of God's promise elaborated in verse 10 go no further than what Saul (and therefore probably Abner) knew by the end: (a) the house of Saul would lose the kingdom; (b) the throne of David would be established; and (c) David's kingdom would cover the whole of Israel's land.[28] It seems likely that this promise was by now public knowledge.

Second, if Abner knew "what the LORD has sworn to" (v. 9) David, why had he given his considerable support to the house of Saul "to this day" (v. 8)? This is relatively simple to answer. Abner, like so many people in every age, had not wanted to believe the word of God that he had heard. He did not want Saul's kingdom to be transferred to David. He had therefore been able to convince himself (against reason) that there was a future for the house of Saul. Such irrationality is a common human response to God's word. Consider how many people have heard that Jesus is Lord, but simply do not want it to be true. But now Abner was resisting God's promise to David no longer.

Third, and perhaps most striking of all, what kind of arrogance led Abner to swear that *he* would be the one who would "accomplish" (v. 9) what the Lord had sworn? Abner continued to see himself as the man who made things happen. He was, remember, "making himself strong in the house of Saul" (v. 6). He considered himself to be the one in control of that which the Lord had promised to transfer from the house of Saul to David. Furthermore his words imply that he will "set up the throne of David" (v. 10). He overestimated his power (as we will see).

Abner's change of allegiance was not exactly admirable. His motivation was a mixture of disillusionment with Ish-bosheth and vindictiveness toward the man who had let him down and now dared to accuse him. Like many characters in this story, however, his words were better than either his motivations or his actions.

Ish-bosheth's Fear (v. 11)

Abner's furious speech terrified Ish-bosheth. "And Ish-bosheth[29] could not answer Abner another word, because he feared him" (v. 11). The strong man (v. 6) had silenced the weak one (v. 1) and weakened him further.

Abner and David: Negotiation (vv. 12–16)

Abner's heated words were no empty threat. Immediately[30] he made contact with David. Abner, remember, was a man who made things happen. He had the sense to realize the danger of going to Hebron himself, so he sent messengers.

Abner's Offer (v. 12)

> And Abner sent messengers to David on his behalf, saying, "To whom does the land belong? Make your covenant with me, and behold, my hand shall be with you to bring over all Israel to you." (v. 12)

"To whom does the land belong?" (v. 12) is tantalizingly ambiguous.[31] Was Abner implying a recognition on his part that the land belonged to David?[32] I do not think so, although the ambiguity may have suited his purpose. Abner was rather making the suggestion (as his following words will make clear) that he was the one who had control of "the land" (v. 12).

Abner followed this question with a proposal that David should make a covenant with Abner. Again the high-handed approach is staggering. It is almost as though he were saying, "It would be in your interests, David, to deal with me." Mind you, Abner maintained a stance of open generosity. He spoke of "*your* covenant" (v. 12); that is, the terms were to be defined by David. The assumption, of course, is that Abner would be looked after in this arrangement.

Abner, for his part, would give David his full support ("my hand," v. 12) and cause the whole nation to come over to David. He did see himself as a man who made things happen! It would be fair to suggest that Abner was "playing God." We could imagine his promise to David being spoken by God himself.[33]

The implication of Abner's offer is that should David be so foolish as to refuse to make his covenant with the commander, then Abner would ensure that the nation did *not* come over to David. He seemed to believe that the kingdom, the throne, was in his hands.

David's Conditional Acceptance (vv. 13, 14)

We have not heard anything from David himself since his gracious message to the people of Jabesh-gilead (also sent by messengers, 2:5–7). The chronological information in 2:10, 11 indicates that the narrative has now reached some time in the last two of David's seven and a half years in Hebron. We have almost no idea of David's activity through most of his time in Hebron.

His response to the apparently arrogant offer of Abner is astonishing. "And he said, 'Good; I will make a covenant with you'" (v. 13a). David sent back the messengers to Abner with this clear and decisive acceptance of his offer.

However, the acceptance was very definitely on David's terms. "I will make a covenant with you" (v. 13) has a marked emphasis on the word "I." This is followed by a firm and non-negotiable condition: "'But one thing I require of you; that is, you shall not see my face unless you first bring Michal, Saul's daughter, when you come to see my face'" (v. 13b).

We have seen that through his years in Hebron David had learned the political value of marriages. The political importance of Michal is noted: she was "Saul's daughter" (v. 13). Michal had loved David at the height of his early popularity (see 1 Samuel 18:16, 20, 28). David, for his part, had slain 200 Philistines to earn the right to marry her (1 Samuel 18:20–29). This had been part of a plot by Saul that had backfired. He had demanded "a hundred foreskins of the Philistines" (1 Samuel 18:25) as a bride-price for Michal, confident that the Philistines would kill David. It was not the last time that Saul underestimated David. David's marriage to Michal brought him into Saul's family as the king's son-in-law. Some time later Michal helped David escape from Saul by warning David and lying to her father (1 Samuel 19:11–17). It seems likely that David had not seen Michal since that day. While he was on the run from Saul, the king had given this daughter of his to another man by the name of Palti (1 Samuel 25:44).

What was David's motivation in insisting that Abner bring Michal back to him? It was probably more than (but not necessarily less than) his personal affection for his first wife. Michal had been wrongly taken from him by Saul, presumably against her will. This was one expression of Saul's persecution of David. The return of Michal would represent an acknowledgment on the part of the house of Saul of David's rights. It would imply that Saul had been wrong, not only in taking Michal from David, but in all his opposition to David. The return of Michal, in other words, would represent a change in the house of Saul's attitude toward David. It would, we might say, be an expression of repentance. Michal's return would be a token of the nation being transferred to David.[34] Furthermore, David's desire to have Michal as his wife was an expression of David's positive attitude toward the house of Saul, already expressed in other ways (see 1:19–27; 2:5, 6).

David's immediate and definite response, sent to Abner, displayed (a) his willingness (eagerness?) to receive all Israel and (b) his determination that this would happen on his terms.

No sooner had the messengers left to take David's reply to Abner than David sent another message.

> Then David sent messengers to Ish-bosheth, Saul's son, saying, "Give me my wife Michal, for whom I paid the bridal price of a hundred foreskins of the Philistines." (v. 14)

David wasn't going to leave Abner in charge of the transfer of the kingdom. Without waiting for a response from Abner, he made his demand directly to Saul's son. Recalling the circumstances of his marriage to Michal (1 Samuel 18:17–27),[35] David demanded that Ish-bosheth (once again with his identity as "Saul's son" emphasized, v. 14) return his wife.

Obedience to David in Mahanaim (vv. 15, 16)

The response in Mahanaim to David's message was astonishing. Both Ish-bosheth and Abner obeyed David.

> And Ish-bosheth sent and took her from her husband Paltiel the son of Laish. But her husband went with her, weeping after her all the way to Bahurim. Then Abner said to him, "Go, return." And he returned. (vv. 15, 16)

Ish-bosheth, weakened even more than before by the loss of Abner's allegiance, lacked the strength to withstand David. He acquiesced. He sent to Gallim (cf. 1 Samuel 25:44) and had Michal taken from her husband. There is much human interest in this small scene. As readers we wish we knew something of Michal's feelings about all of this. Instead we witness the pathetic scene of the distraught Paltiel[36] reduced to tears as he helplessly followed the woman who was being taken from him (as she had once been taken from David). Oh, the cruelty of what Saul had done!

Abner appeared in time to send Paltiel back home. He played his part in ensuring that David's word was obeyed. There is some evidence that Paltiel's town, Gallim, was located north of Jerusalem and therefore not very far from Bahurim.[37] In other words, Paltiel was not able to go very far weeping for

Michal. The village where he was forced to turn back will appear later in this story (16:5; 17:18; 19:16; 23:31), where its location not far from Jerusalem will be significant.

However, while recognizing the pathos of the scene, that is not the most important thing here. What was astonishing was that the leaders in Mahanaim were obeying the king in Hebron, and Michal, the daughter of Saul, was on her way back to David. This was the beginning of something big.

Abner for David: Delivering the Kingdom (vv. 17–21)

We will hear nothing more of Michal until the day when she has a serious falling out with David (6:16–23). The story of Michal is not a happy one. That, however, lies in the future.

Now the scene shifts from Michal, on her way south to Hebron, to Abner and his energetic activity, now on the side of of David and among "the elders of Israel" (v. 17).

Abner's Word to Israel: "Come to David" (vv. 17–19a)

The chronological sequence of events is unclear. On the assumption (which is only an assumption) that on his visit to David in Hebron described in verse 19 Abner was accompanying Michal, Abner's activity described in verse 17 had probably taken place some time earlier. It would have taken weeks, probably months, somewhere between the falling out with Ish-bosheth in verses 7–11 and Michal's journey back to David, the beginning of which we have seen in verse 16. This suggests that the to and fro of messengers between Mahanaim and Hebron took some time.

> And Abner conferred [or *had* conferred] with the elders of Israel, saying, "For some time past you have been seeking David as king over you. Now then bring it about, for the LORD has promised David, saying, 'By the hand of my servant David I will save my people Israel from the hand of the Philistines, and from the hand of all their enemies.'" Abner also spoke [or *had also spoken*] to Benjamin. (vv. 17–19a)

"And the word of Abner had been with the elders of Israel" (v. 17a AT). This makes Abner sound like Samuel (see 1 Samuel 4:1). He was preaching the good news of the kingdom of David. Abner the evangelist!

"The elders of Israel" (v. 17) here refers to the leaders of the Israelite tribes other than Judah, the tribes who had yet to acknowledge David as king. Abner's "word" to them had three points.

First, the elders, like Abner himself now, were not enthusiastic about

Ish-bosheth. They knew in their hearts that David was the king for them. This had been so, said Abner, "for some time past" (literally "both yesterday and the day before yesterday"). Abner may have been pointing back to the time when "all Israel and Judah loved David" (1 Samuel 18:16). He may have had in mind the more recent time as David was growing stronger and the house of Saul was growing weaker (v. 1). Perhaps he was overstating the situation when he said that they had been "seeking" (v. 17) David as king. The powerful negotiator, skilled with words, may have been giving shape to as yet unexpressed desires. In due course they would be expressed (see 5:1–3).

Second, Abner urged the elders to act now. "You know you want David as your king. Make him your king. Do it!"

Third, Abner provided the most powerful endorsement of the desire that he had attributed to them and the action he was proposing. These things were in accordance with the Lord's promise. They were right to want David as their king because he was the one God promised would deliver Israel from the Philistines and who had recently crushed them and indeed "all their enemies" (v. 18).

It is particularly noted that he also brought this message to Saul's own tribe, Benjamin. Located immediately to the north of Judah, the small tribe of Benjamin had the strongest reasons to maintain allegiance to the house of Saul. Abner took his word for David there too.

We have already noted that characters in Biblical narratives often speak more truthfully than they know, and their words are often better than their actions or motivations. This was again the case with Abner. Every indication is that Abner was self-serving. He turned to David only when it suited him to do so, and for his own purposes. However, it is difficult to fault the "gospel" he preached to the elders of Israel. Abner had not (to our knowledge) heard directly the words he attributed to God concerning David. However, he was remarkably accurate. "My servant David" (v. 18) is precisely how the Lord will speak of David in 7:5, 8. It is astonishing that this designation of David as the Lord's "servant" (v. 18), which will become an important title for that great king (see 1 Kings 3:6; 8:24, 25, 26; 11:32; 14:8; 2 Kings 19:34; Psalm 132:10; Isaiah 37:35; Ezekiel 34:23, 24; 37:24; Luke 1:69), is first recorded on the lips of Abner, who had set up a king to rival David! Furthermore, "my [that is, the Lord's] people Israel" (v. 18) is a surprisingly true description of the nation (see 1 Samuel 2:29; 9:16, 17; 2 Samuel 5:2; 7:7, 8, 10, 11) from the man who had tried to defy the will of God by keeping "all Israel" under the house of Saul (2:9). Saul had made the mistake of thinking that Israel was *his* people (1 Samuel 15:30). "I will save my people Israel from the hand of the Philistines" (v. 18) is remarkably close to what God had said to Samuel about Saul (1 Samuel 9:16). Abner's message rightly transferred that promise now to David.

What we do not hear from Abner is any confession of his own failure. "I was wrong to make Ish-bosheth king." "I have acted as though Israel were my people." "I have tried to use my own power to defy God's purpose." These are words we never hear from Abner. He wasn't that kind of guy.

Abner's Word to David (vv. 19b–21d)

Abner's campaign was a success, and he was able to take the news to Hebron (presumably now picking up the story of Abner's travel south with Michal from verse 16, after the brief flashback of verses 17–19a).

> And then[38] Abner went to tell David at Hebron all that Israel and the whole house of Benjamin thought good to do. When Abner came[39] with twenty men to David at Hebron, David made a feast for Abner and the men who were with him. And Abner said to David, "I will arise and go and will gather all Israel to my lord the king, that they may make a covenant with you, and that you may reign over all that your heart desires." (vv. 19b–21d)

The ready response of Israel, and particularly all of Benjamin, to Abner's word suggests that the only reason they had not turned to David earlier was Abner. Once Abner had abandoned both his resistance to David and his rival scheme to keep the house of Saul in power, the people saw how "good" (v. 19) David was.[40]

The greatest surprise in this surprising sequence of events is the welcome Abner received from David. A feast was prepared for him and his delegation. No recriminations. David received Abner not on the basis of his past (which was reprehensible), nor on the basis of his integrity (which even now was dubious). Despite, rather than because of, these things Abner found in David a generous, gracious welcome.

Abner was still the man who (in his own opinion) made things happen. His response to David's welcome was to promise that he would now "accomplish for David what the LORD has sworn to him" (v. 9). He reiterated personally and directly the word he had sent by messengers earlier (v. 12). Abner did still seem to think that David's future depended on him. Although he now called David "my lord the king" (and remarkably Abner is the first character in the narrative to address David as "king,"[41] v. 21), the man of action was taking charge of events (or so he thought): "I will arise . . . go . . .

gather" (v. 21). Little did Abner know that his power to control events would soon come to an end.

". . . all that your heart [or soul] desires" (v. 21) may, on the lips of Abner, carry a tone of political ambition. However, it is an apt description of David's desire to do good to all Israel (2:6).[42]

Peace (v. 21e)

"So David sent Abner away, and he went in peace" (v. 21e). This episode closes with David sending Abner to do what he had said he would do and Abner departing from David "in peace" (v. 21, Hebrew, *shalom*). Between the king and this rebel who had caused so much trouble (see v. 1), there was now "peace" (v. 21).

This is a glimpse of the nature of God's king and his kingdom. Former rebels find peace. The history of Abner's relationship with David could be described as "once . . . alienated and hostile in mind, doing evil deeds" (cf. Colossians 1:21). Most recently he was the power behind the "war" (v. 1) with which this chapter began. He was "now reconciled," and this depended not on any goodness in him, but on the goodness of David (cf. Colossians 1:22). Of course, Abner had much to learn, and if he was going to be a servant of his new king, that would change him. For now the most important change for Abner was the change in who his lord and king was.

Abner's story has not yet run its course. It will shortly take a terrible turn. At this point I want to urge you to see how the kingdom of David was a shadow of the kingdom of Jesus Christ. We "who once were alienated and hostile in mind, doing evil deeds, he has now reconciled in his body of flesh by his death, in order to present [us] holy and blameless and above reproach before him" (Colossians 1:21, 22). Like Israel and the whole house of Benjamin so long ago, do you see the *goodness* of our King?

8

Personal Vengeance and the Kingdom

2 SAMUEL 3:22–39

MAHATMA GANDHI is reported to have said, "I like your Christ, I do not like your Christians. Your Christians are so unlike your Christ."

While it is probable that Gandhi himself had a view of Christ that was at least partly imagined (and surprisingly like Gandhi), his words ring true. We Christians *are* so unlike our Christ. We acknowledge this to our shame. We long and expect to become *more* like Christ, but in this life we know that whenever we are compared to him Gandhi's words will have validity.

To put it simply, Christian people are not as good as Jesus Christ. Therefore it is foolish to dismiss the claims of Christianity because of the faults seen in Christian people. Those investigating Christianity should understand that the Christian message is about Jesus Christ, not about Christians. This is not an excuse for Christian failings. We who have been welcomed by our Savior must strive to live in ways that please and honor him. It is simply the nature of Christianity. Christian believers are sinners who have been forgiven and are being changed but who still have a long way to go.

Those of us who are Christian believers need to be reminded that we are not as good as Jesus Christ. The kingdom of God depends on the goodness of the King, not on the goodness of those who follow him. I am using the word *goodness* in the widest possible sense. The kingdom of God depends on the wisdom, power, righteousness, faithfulness, kindness, gentleness, justice (this list could be greatly expanded) of Jesus Christ, not on those qualities in Christian believers. Of course, our lives must be genuinely transformed by the goodness of our King. But the kingdom of God, the progress of Christianity, indeed the authenticity of Christianity, depends on him, not on us.

Those of us in any form of Christian ministry should take this to heart. We work hard, in whatever sphere of responsibility we have been given, to make Christ known, to show care in the name of Christ, to build his church. But our ways are never quite his ways. Our wisdom always falls short of his wisdom. Our abilities are always less than adequate. Our integrity is always tarnished beside his righteousness. The kingdom of God, the progress of Christianity, indeed the integrity of Christianity depends on him, not on us.

This can be very confusing because the visible form of the kingdom of God advancing in this world is Christian believers. As the gospel of our Lord Jesus Christ is proclaimed, men and women, boys and girls are coming into the kingdom as they receive Jesus Christ as Savior and Lord. For unbelievers it is easier to assess Christianity by looking at the believers whom they meet than by looking at Jesus Christ as he is presented to us in the Bible. This is foolishness. And for believers it is tempting to think that our plans and efforts correspond exactly with the good purposes of our King. This is a recipe for disillusionment.

The principle we are considering (that the kingdom of God depends on the goodness of the King, not on the goodness of his followers) was displayed as David's kingdom was being established. The kingdom of David was a manifestation in history of the kingdom of God and so foreshadowed Jesus Christ's kingdom. In the rather long and tortuous story of how David came to reign over all Israel, we now hear how Joab, David's military commander, took matters into his own hands. Joab made the mistake of thinking that he knew better than his king.

It would be as foolish to evaluate the kingdom of David by looking at Joab as it is to judge the kingdom of Jesus Christ by the imperfections of Christians. Joab was as foolish as Christians today who think that their ways are better than the ways of Jesus for advancing the kingdom.

A glance back at the story so far will help us understand what happened next. After the death of King Saul (1:1) David had been made king in the southern town of Hebron over the tribe of Judah (2:4). A son of Saul had been set up as a rival king to the northeast, in Mahanaim, claiming sovereignty over "all Israel" (2:9). This was Ish-bosheth. His elevation had been the work of Abner, who had been Saul's military commander (2:8, 9). An attempt of sorts to resolve this situation had been made by Abner and his counterpart on David's side, Joab (2:12–32). But this had led to war (2:17), "a long war" (3:1) between the followers of the two kings. On the first day of that conflict Abner had killed Joab's brother, Asahel (2:23). The account makes clear that Abner did all he could to avoid this killing, but Asahel's persistence, in the context of the fierce battle, made it unavoidable.

During the long period of war there was, in Mahanaim, a serious falling out between Ish-bosheth and Abner, the man who had put him in power (3:6–11). As a consequence Abner abandoned his allegiance to Ish-bosheth and went over to David in Hebron, with the promise that he would bring the whole nation with him (3:12–21). Remarkably Abner, who had been more responsible than anyone else for the "long *war* between the house of Saul and the house of David" (3:1) went from the presence of David "in peace" (3:21).

This was remarkable because "peace" had proved so elusive. When the two commanders had made an attempt to resolve the situation, the result had been "war" (3:1). Only when David became involved was the result "peace" (3:21).

However, Abner's departure from Hebron "in peace" was very troubling to one man who had been absent during Abner's brief visit to David. We hear now of:

(1) Joab's revenge (vv. 22–27).
(2) David's goodness (vv. 28–35).
(3) Knowing David (vv. 36–39).

Joab's Revenge (vv. 22–27)

Joab (like Abner, his opposite number from the north) was a man of action who was inclined to take matters into his own hands. No doubt his brief absence from Hebron had contributed to the "peace" (3:21) that had come about between Abner and David. On the day of the battle in which Asahel had been killed by Abner, Joab and his brother Abishai had attempted to avenge their brother's death (2:24). Between Joab and Abner there was anything but "peace" (3:21). For this reason it is possible that David had arranged for Joab to be absent at the time of Abner's visit to Hebron.[1] He was not absent for long.

Joab Hears (vv. 22, 23)

> Just then the servants of David arrived with Joab from a raid, bringing much spoil with them. But Abner was not with David at Hebron, for he had sent him away, and he had gone in peace. When Joab and all the army that was with him came, it was told Joab, "Abner the son of Ner came to the king, and he has let him go, and he has gone in peace." (vv. 22, 23)

Suddenly,[2] just as Abner was out of sight, who should arrive in Hebron with a clamor but Joab and his men. "The servants of David" (v. 22a) refers to the soldiers under Joab's command (as in 2:13, 15, 17, 31). In this time of conflict Joab had been doing what Joab did—fighting. No details are given of this particular engagement. It may have been part of the continuing conflict with the northerners referred to at the beginning of this chapter, or Joab may have been engaging in other exploits (as David had done earlier, 1 Samuel 27:8). Whatever it was, Joab and his men were returning as victors with "much spoil" (v. 22).

The narrator underlines the contrast between this scene and the one it interrupted by reminding us that Abner had left Hebron, having been sent away "in peace" by David (v. 22b; cf. v. 21e).

Someone (we are not told who[3]) informed Joab of this situation (v. 23). Again the circumstance described at the end of verse 21 is repeated.[4] Three times in as many verses we have heard that David had sent Abner and Abner had gone "in peace" (v. 21, 22, 23). Particularly striking is the threefold "in peace." Joab returned with the spoils of war, only to hear that Abner had departed "in peace." This was not good news to Joab's ears.

Apart from the personal bitterness Joab felt toward Abner because of the death of Asahel (2:24, 27), this man of action who always wanted to control events would not have welcomed the news that the king had brokered some kind of "peace" with his enemy, without consulting Joab.

Joab Speaks (vv. 24, 25)

Joab's response to what he had heard was vehement. Like Abner's response to Ish-bosheth earlier (in very different circumstances, 3:8–10), Joab was clearly very angry with his king.

> Then Joab went to the king and said, "What have you done? Behold, Abner came to you. Why is it that you have sent him away, so that he is gone? You know that Abner the son of Ner came to deceive you and to know your going out and your coming in, and to know all that you are doing." (vv. 24, 25)

At this point we are not allowed to lose sight of David's position. As Abner had addressed David as "my lord *the king*" (v. 21) and Joab had just been told that "Abner son of Ner came to *the king*" (v, 23), so now we are told that "Joab went to *the king*" (v. 24a).[5]

"What have you done?" Joab demanded (v. 24b). The question implies that the one addressed has done a terrible wrong, in the opinion of the questioner (cf. Genesis 3:13; 4:10; 20:9; 31:26; Exodus 14:11; Numbers 23:11; Joshua 7:19). These are the words of an accuser to an accused. Joab was accusing the king. Importantly he asked precisely the question Samuel had asked Saul when Saul had disobeyed God's word to him, thus forfeiting the kingship (1 Samuel 13:11). But Joab was not Samuel, David was not Saul, and the action in question was right, not wrong. In this setting Joab's question was presumptuous.

Boldly he presented his accusation with the vivid "Behold . . ." (v. 24). That is, "Just look at what you have done!"

The terrible thing that David had done, in Joab's view, was to allow Abner to get away (alive?). For the fourth time in four verses we hear (now from Joab's lips) that David had sent Abner away and that he had gone. Joab cannot quite bring himself to use the expression "in peace" (v. 21, 22, 23). It was not a peace he was willing to acknowledge. Instead of "in peace" he substitutes an expression in Hebrew that emphasizes that Abner has really, completely *gone*.[6]

With biting sarcasm Joab asserted that David knew what he clearly did not know (v. 25). "Surely you *must* have known that he came to deceive you." What kind of fool would not know that? Of course, Joab was implying (without any attempt at subtlety) that Abner had succeeded in deceiving David. He had come to Hebron, spied out what he wanted to know about David's affairs,[7] and now (thanks to the king's utter stupidity, we can almost hear Joab say) he had completely gone.

Joab saw the gentleness of David toward his old adversary Abner as (at best) naïveté and (at worst) culpable, weak, stupidity. We will shortly see that Joab was driven by forces other than concern for the king's security. There was more to his fury at the king's kindness to Abner than he expressed. What troubled Joab most was that Joab's king had treated Joab's enemy as a friend.

No response to Joab from David is recorded. This was certainly not for the same reason that Ish-bosheth had been unable to answer Abner earlier (3:11). Abner had so intimidated Ish-bosheth that he could defy him to his face. However, Joab had to proceed with his actions behind David's back. He had to do what he had accused Abner of doing: deceive the king.

Joab Acts (vv. 26, 27)

Like Abner a little earlier (see 3:12), this military commander, angry with his king, took action by sending messengers to Abner who was heading back north. "When Joab came out from David's presence, he sent messengers after Abner, and they brought him back from the cistern of Sirah" (v. 26a–c).

Apart from what can be deduced from this text, the location of Sirah and the cistern there is unknown.[8] Presumably, however, ancient readers of this narrative knew the whereabouts of the cistern (or well) some short distance to the north of Hebron. Abner and his delegation of twenty men (3:20) had probably stopped there for refreshment. We do not know what message was used to persuade Abner and his men to return to Hebron. It is probable (in the light of their last conversation, 2:26, 27) that Joab was not mentioned.

It is important to note that (in contrast to Abner's earlier sending of messengers, which was not kept a secret from Ish-bosheth), "David did not know about it" (v. 26d). This tells us something about Joab's relationship to David. Powerful man of action that he was, Joab did not dare to openly defy the king in the way that Abner had defied Ish-bosheth. The fact that Abner was brought back to Hebron *without David's knowledge* will be important for another reason that will soon become clear.[9]

On whatever pretense Abner was enticed to return to Hebron, he was no doubt surprised to be met by Joab, who gave the impression that the two commanders needed to have a quiet chat: "And when Abner returned to Hebron, Joab took him aside into the midst of the gate to speak with him privately" (v. 27a, b).

Joab had assured the king that Abner had come to Hebron to deceive him. Now Joab deceived Abner. There was no intention of a private conference in "the midst of the gate." Instead "there he struck him in the stomach, so that he died" (v. 27c, d). He did to Abner just what Abner had done to his brother some time earlier (see 2:23[10]). In case we miss the symbolism of the identical killings, the narrator explicitly tells us that Joab's motivation was "for the blood of Asahel his brother" (v. 27e).

Joab was not concerned about the security of David's kingdom, as he had implied when he rebuked the king. We now see that he, not Abner, had deceived David. Joab's fury was over his brother's earlier death at Abner's hands. We know, however, that Abner had gone to quite extraordinary lengths to avoid that death and the consequences that were now playing out (see 2:21, 22).

Furthermore Asahel's death had occurred in "battle" (2:17). But Joab murdered Abner after "peace" had been won (3:21). It was an act of unjustifiable vengeance (see 1 Kings 2:5).[11]

David's Goodness (vv. 28–35)

In his own mind Joab believed he was fiercely loyal to David. His ways, however, were not the king's ways. He was able to carry out his deed only by keeping it secret from David. However, the secret could not be kept from the king for long.

David Hears (v. 28a)

The time lapse between verses 27 and 28 could not have been long, but it was significant. David did not learn of Joab's plot or his action until it was too late to do anything about it. "*Afterward*, when David heard of it . . ." (v. 28a).[12] Like Joab's hearing in verse 23, we do not know who told David. It certainly would not have been Joab.

David Speaks (vv. 28b–31b)

When the news reached David's ears, he was distressed. What Joab had done was precisely what David, at very great cost to himself, had refused to do through the years of persecution by Saul (see 1 Samuel 24:6, 10, 11; 26:9, 11). David had learned from the astute Abigail that "the LORD has restrained you from bloodguilt and from saving with your own hand" (1 Samuel 25:26). He knew that the qualities God required of him were "righteousness and . . . faithfulness" (1 Samuel 26:23). Joab's way was not the way of God's king.

Joab was not unlike Peter in the Garden of Gethsemane, who thought his own violent strength could save Jesus (John 18:10). Jesus' response to Peter emphatically rejected his disciple's way: "Put your sword into its sheath; shall I not drink the cup that my Father has given me?" (John 18:11). The cause of Christ cannot be advanced by "disgraceful, underhanded ways" or "cunning" (2 Corinthians 4:2).

Like Jesus and his apostle, David immediately and emphatically distanced himself from what Joab had done. He did this with three dramatic statements.

First, "he said, 'I and my kingdom are forever guiltless before the LORD for the blood of Abner the son of Ner'" (v. 28b). In the Hebrew the emphatic first word is the one translated here "guiltless" (v. 28). The word has legal overtones and means "free of liability for an offense and its consequences."[13] The deed of Joab must not be attributed to David or his kingdom. That is not what this king or his kingdom is like. This innocence of David and his kingdom, David claimed, is absolute: it is "forever" and "before the LORD" (v. 28).

Second, he insisted that the one who did this deed must bear the guilt. In this matter Joab had not acted for the king. David uttered a terrible curse on Joab and his family for what they had done: "'May it fall upon the head of Joab and upon all his father's house, and may the house of Joab never be without one who has a discharge or who is leprous or who holds a spindle or who falls by the sword or who lacks bread!'" (v. 29). The details of this curse matter less than the horror of it.[14] David's words are charged with emotion and are not to be pressed for literal sense. They are reminiscent of the words of judgment on Eli and his house in 1 Samuel 2:31–36,[15] and the meaning is: "May God avenge the murder of Abner upon Joab and his family, by punishing them continually with terrible diseases, violent death, and poverty."[16] Joab had set himself against the will of the king and had therefore placed himself in the position of an enemy of the king.

The narrator now sums up what had happened, adding one new piece of information that explains the extent of David's curse: "So Joab and Abishai his brother killed Abner, because he had put their brother Asahel to death in the battle at Gibeon" (v. 30). Both brothers were involved in Abner's death, as they had been in the earlier pursuit of him (2:24). These brothers were the surviving sons of Zeruiah (2:18). David's words against "all [Joab's] father's house" (v. 29) appropriately included them both. The narrator underlines the fact that we have already observed—the murder was an act of family vengeance for a death that had occurred in battle.

David's third dramatic statement was a command to Joab and others. "Then David said to Joab and to all the people who were with him,[17] 'Tear your clothes and put on sackcloth and mourn before Abner'" (v. 31a, b).

To Joab's undoubted distress and embarrassment David was about to give Abner a state funeral and insisted that Joab don mourning gear (torn clothes and sackcloth; cf. 1:2 and 1 Samuel 4:12) and, with his men and the others present, march ahead of the body of Abner ("before Abner," v. 31) in the funeral procession.[18] This was a public humiliation of Joab. The funeral would acknowledge that Abner was not the king's enemy but his friend. By forcing Joab to join the public mourning for Abner, David was requiring from Joab a public acknowledgment that his deed was not an act of loyalty to his king, but the very opposite.

We assume that Joab and his men complied with the king's command. What went through his mind as he did so is left to our imagination.

David Acts (vv. 31c, 32)

David involved himself fully in the public honoring of Abner and the grief over his death.

David took his place prominently, directly behind the corpse of Abner. "And King David followed the bier" (v. 31c). This is the first time David is referred to as "King David," with the full weight of his official title (see 5:3; 6:12, 16; 7:18; and twelve more uses of the title in 2 Samuel). This public act of the king contrasts with and passes judgment on the secret act of Joab.

"They buried Abner" not in the home of his family, which would have been in the territory of Benjamin, but "at Hebron" (v. 32a). Abner had changed kings, and so he had changed his old allegiances. Burial at Hebron signified his new relationship to the king in Hebron.

As David had led the people in weeping over the death of Saul (1:11, 12), so he did for Abner. "And the king lifted up his voice and wept at the grave of Abner, and all the people wept" (v. 32b, c).

David Speaks Again (vv. 33–35)

The similarity between David's response to Saul's death and his actions now after the death of Saul's commander continued as David composed a lament for Abner (v. 33a; cf. 1:17). This was much shorter than the lament for Saul (1:19–27), but nonetheless put into words (fine words!) the grief David felt at Abner's death, and therefore added to the public demonstration that this death was not the king's doing.

And the king lamented for Abner, saying,

> "Should Abner die as a fool dies?
> Your hands were not bound;
>   your feet were not fettered;
> as one falls before the wicked
>   you have fallen." (vv. 33, 34a–d)

The lament was pointed. The opening rhetorical question (v. 33b) gave a perspective on what had happened. Abner's death had been like the death of "a fool" (v. 33). "Fool" suggests moral and spiritual stupidity. "The *fool* says in his heart, 'There is no God'" (Psalm 14:1). "For the *fool* . . . his heart is busy with iniquity" (Isaiah 32:6). David may have had in mind the death of Nabal. "As a fool dies" (v. 33) could be translated "like the death of Nabal" (1 Samuel 25).[19] Nabal was a fool who abused David and would have lost his life at David's hand if it had not been for the shrewd intervention of his wife Abigail, who was now, of course, David's wife (see 2:2; 3:3, where we were reminded of Nabal).

Joab had treated Abner as "a fool" (v. 33). He had deceived him and used the man's goodwill toward David to entrap him and murder him. More than this, he had treated him as though he was like Nabal, who had made David his enemy. David challenged this assessment of Abner. Abner had changed sides. David had sent him away "in peace" (v. 31). "Did Abner *have* to die the death of a villain?"[20]

David's response to his own question is a poetic description of Abner (addressed to the dead man; cf. 1:26) as free from guilt. He was not a criminal in chains who had met a deserved death (v. 34a, b). Rather he had been wickedly murdered (v. 34c).[21]

Abner was no "fool" (v. 33), but Joab and Abishai had been "wicked."[22] There is no escaping the fact that David here publicly called his general and his brother "wicked" (v. 34). We cannot be sure how widely known was the involvement of Joab and Abishai. Nothing in the text suggests it was kept secret. The impression given is that this royal rebuke of Joab and Abishai would have been understood by all who heard it.

The lament had such an impact on the people that "all the people wept again over him" (v. 34d). Their endorsement of the lament carried the implicit endorsement of its judgment of Joab and Abishai. Joab's ways were not the ways of this king or his kingdom.

Earlier when David and the people had heard the news of the deaths of Saul and Jonathan, they had "fasted until evening" (1:12). David was now doing the same because of Abner's death. "Then all the people came to persuade David to eat bread while it was yet day" (v. 35a). The people were united in their concern for their king. The impression is that they were united with him in his grief. "But David swore, saying, 'God do so to me and more also, if I taste bread or anything else till the sun goes down!'" (v. 35b).

David's oath echoes the almost identical earlier oath of Abner (3:9) about what he intended to do for David. Abner was not able to keep his promise. David, on the other hand, honored the man who had once been his adversary by fulfilling his vow.

Knowing David (vv. 36–39)

Joab may have imagined that in the events of that day he had taken matters into his own hands and had won a victory for his king. But Joab had treated David as a fool, accusing him of being deceived by Abner, and then deceiving him himself. In truth the events of that day presented qualities of the king that contrasted starkly with all that Joab had done. The people could see it.

The Good King (v. 36)

"And all the people took notice of it, and it pleased them, as everything that the king did pleased all the people" (v. 36). The translation is a little weak. Behind the language of "pleasing" are Hebrew words for "good." "It pleased them" (v. 36) is more literally, "it was *good* in their eyes." "Everything that the king did pleased all the people" (v. 36) is literally, "everything that the king did, in the eyes of all the people was *good.*" In the events of this day the people saw the *goodness* of their king.

David's message to the people of Jabesh-gilead had included the promise to "do *good* to you" (2:6). The good David promised to do (as we have seen) was to be the one through whom the Lord would show them steadfast love and faithfulness. The people's response to Abner's message about David had been to see David as "good" (3:19). David's words after the death of Abner confirmed for all the people that he was "good."

The Innocent King (v. 37)

In verse 37 the narrator draws our attention, for the seventh time since verse 31, to "all the people." In verse 31 "all the people" referred to those who were present with David at the time. In verse 32, in the context of the public funeral, the phrase "all the people" referred to the large crowds that witnessed this public event. This is the sense of the phrase in verses 34, 35, and 36. However, the narrator now wants to tell us that the goodness of the king that was seen by those present on that day became known far and wide. "So all the people *and all Israel* understood [literally, knew] that day that it had not been the king's will to put to death Abner the son of Ner" (v. 37).

"All the people and all Israel" (v. 37) could be understood in various ways,[23] but the details matter less than the clear affirmation that throughout the whole nation (not just the crowd at Abner's funeral, nor Judah only, but everywhere) all came to know that what Joab had done that day was not the king's doing (literally, "was not from the king").

This has been a story about what people did and did not "know." Joab claimed that David should have *known* that Abner had come to Hebron to deceive him—to *know* all the king's doings (v. 25). David did not *know* about Joab's deception of Abner (v. 26). But now the whole nation *knew* the innocence of their king.

The Gracious King (v. 38)

The king spoke again, apparently to a smaller circle of "his servants" (v. 38). There was something he wanted to ensure that they *knew*. "And the king said to his servants, 'Do you not *know* that a prince and a great man has fallen this day in Israel?'" (v. 38).

As was the case in the lament (vv. 33, 34), and indeed in the earlier lament over Saul and Jonathan (1:19–27), these unqualified positive words about the man who had died must be understood in their context. David was responding to the death of one who could have been regarded as his enemy by seeing the tragedy of his death. The tragedy of death lies in the good that has been lost. David recognized and gave words to what had been good in Abner. "A prince" (v. 38) over-translates a Hebrew word that has a wide range of uses and generally indicates official leaders, often military, but does not suggest royalty.[24] It is the word translated "commander" in 2:8. In this context "leader" may convey the sense. "A leader, a great one, has fallen in Israel today."

The grace that had accepted Abner (3:13) and sent him "in peace" (3:21) was expressed in David's non-recriminatory words about Abner.

The Gentle King (v. 39)

All this was summed up in a remarkable statement by David about himself, a surprising comparison with Joab and Abishai, and a devastating prayer.

About himself he said, "And I was gentle today, though anointed king" (v. 39a). The word rendered "gentle" is a remarkable term in this context. It often has a negative sense of weakness (as in Genesis 33:13; Deuteronomy 20:8; 2 Chronicles 13:7).[25] As the next sentence makes clear, the point is one of comparison. The toughness of Joab and Abishai was not the character of David.

"*Though* anointed king" (v. 39) is literally (and more properly), "*and* anointed king."[26] Whether David was referring to the anointing that had taken place some years earlier in Hebron (2:7) or what happened much earlier when he was a lad in Bethlehem (1 Samuel 16:13), David had long understood that violence was not the way for him to become king. There was a place for strong, even violent action (1:1, 15, 16), but not "today" (v. 39). Today he had been "gentle" (v. 39). This was not inconsistent with being anointed king. It was the character of this king.

In contrast, "'These men, the sons of Zeruiah, are more severe than I'" (v. 39b). They were "more severe" or "harder" than David. The difference between these two and their king was seen much earlier when Abishai had offered to kill Saul for David. "I will not strike him twice," he had said (1 Samuel 26:8). The harsh, tough characters we have seen in the sons of

Zeruiah were *unlike* their king. They were hard-liners who were harder than their king.

However, David did not at this time take action against Joab and his brother (other than the humiliation of the day). Some (even today) criticize this as weakness.[27] I prefer to think that this was David's gentleness again. On this occasion he left vengeance to the Lord: "The LORD repay the evil-doer according to his wickedness!" (v. 39c). Joab's time would come (see 1 Kings 2:5, 6).

What do we learn from this episode in the story of David's kingdom?

Actions taken in the name of the king in God's kingdom are not always compatible with the character of the king or his kingdom. It would have been understandable for the people to have evaluated David's kingdom on the basis of Joab's actions. But they were wiser. They saw the goodness of the king *despite* the actions of Joab. Joab's passionate and energetic deeds against the one he considered to be the king's enemy only brought David's condemnation. Joab was self-deceived. He was pursuing nothing other than his own wicked agenda, not the will of the king.

So it is with the kingdom of which David's kingdom was a shadow. The goodness of Jesus surpasses the goodness of anyone who does anything in his name. Those who serve this King must take heed that they are not like Joab. They must pray for spiritual wisdom and understanding "so as to walk in a manner *worthy of the Lord, fully pleasing to him*, bearing fruit in every *good* work" (Colossians 1:10). But even then the kingdom depends on the King's goodness, not on ours.

9

Wicked Violence
and the Kingdom

2 SAMUEL 4

AS WE HAVE BEEN FOLLOWING the tangled story of David and the coming of his kingdom, I have been suggesting that the story is a striking display of the ineptitude of various human efforts to establish, secure, or even advance the kingdom of God. There is an important lesson here for people engaged in any form of Christian ministry, particularly those who may be tempted with the spirit of our time that sees "success" as the measure and justification of all things.[1] We are tempted to evaluate Christian ministry and leadership on "success" criteria. Indeed we can hardly imagine how else to think. But it is hopeless. What will happen when we discover the truth—that we are *not* good enough or wise enough or powerful enough to build God's kingdom? Our best efforts produce little observable success.

We have seen that political and military effort (like that of Abner and Joab in 2:12–32), clever grasping of opportunity (like that of Abner in 3:1–21), and strong decisive action (like that of Joab in 3:22–39) were not the keys of the kingdom of David. Repeatedly men had proven to be neither good, wise, nor powerful enough to secure (or to overthrow) David's kingdom. That is because the kingdom of David was God's kingdom. Human effort will never secure or destroy God's kingdom. *God* is at work. Despite human wickedness, folly, and weakness, "David grew stronger and stronger, while the house of Saul became weaker and weaker" (3:1).

We have reached the final stage in the story of the house of Saul growing weaker and weaker while the house of David was growing stronger and stronger.

(1) The "weaker and weaker" house of Saul (vv. 1–4).
(2) Ish-bosheth's end (vv. 5–7).
(3) The "stronger and stronger" house of David (vv. 8–12).

We are about to see how desperate two men became when it at last became clear to them that they were on the wrong side of this struggle. At the beginning of 2 Samuel 4 we are taken from Hebron (where chapter 3 had left us) about sixty miles northeast, across the Jordan River, to Mahanaim, the northern base of the rival king in Israel.[2]

The "Weaker and Weaker" House of Saul (vv. 1–4)

Panic in Mahanaim (v. 1)

Ish-bosheth knew that his commander, Abner, had defected and gone over to Hebron. He also knew that Abner had entered negotiations with David. It is not clear how much he knew of Abner's progress in persuading the northern tribes to join him in going over to David, but there is no reason to think this had been kept secret from him. He was terrified.

The news that now reached Mahanaim shattered what little remained of his courage: "When Ish-bosheth,[3] Saul's son, heard that Abner had died at Hebron, his courage failed" (v. 1a). Literally that last phrase is, "his hands became slack." He lost his grip. While Abner had terrified him (3:11), Ish-bosheth was nothing without the strong man who had "made him king" (2:9). What would become of him without Abner? He knew nothing of the particular circumstances of Abner's death. What did the death of Ish-bosheth's general *in Hebron* signal about the intentions of the king in Hebron toward the north and in particular toward Ish-bosheth? No wonder his hands dropped.

"And all Israel was dismayed" (v. 1b). "Terrified" might be a better rendering.[4] Was all Israel panicked because they saw their king losing his grip or because they, too, heard about Abner's death in Hebron? Probably both. What would now become of the people who had rejected David and given their allegiance to the trembling weakling in Mahanaim? They had recently been persuaded by Abner that their future lay with David (3:17–19, 21). But they did not know that their change of heart had been communicated to David, nor did they know how he had responded to the news. The news that Abner had been killed in Hebron hardly suggested that he had received a warm welcome there. If they had not yet heard about Joab's role and that "it had not been the king's will" (3:37), they (like Ish-bosheth) could only understand the news of Abner's death "at Hebron" (4:1) as terribly threatening.[5]

We are witnessing the last stages of the disintegration of "the house of Saul" (3:1), a weak and quivering king with a terrified people.

Ish-bosheth's Two Men (vv. 2, 3)

On the reasonable assumption that the narrator's theme is now the weakness of Ish-bosheth's hold on power, in the face of Abner's death in Hebron, what follows points to his best hope in this perilous situation. He did have two men who, perhaps, might go some way to filling the void left by Abner's death. We are introduced to these two at some length.

> Now Saul's son[6] had two men who were captains of raiding bands; the name of the one was Baanah, and the name of the other Rechab, sons of Rimmon a man of Benjamin from Beeroth (for Beeroth also is counted part of Benjamin; the Beerothites fled to Gittaim and have been sojourners there to this day). (vv. 2, 3)

"Captains of raiding bands" (v. 2) is not a particularly promising designation.[7] "Raiding bands" (v. 2) is what the Amalekite mob were called in 1 Samuel 30:8, 15, 23 (where the ESV has, simply, "band").[8] Are we to understand that these two men were Ish-bosheth's best hope?

The unusually detailed account of their family, tribe, and hometown background emphasizes the blood ties between Baanah, Rechab, and Ish-bosheth. Rimmon, the father of Baanah and Rechab, is otherwise unknown in the Biblical record. The important thing about him in this context is that he was (literally) "from the sons of Benjamin," as were Kish (Saul's father, 1 Samuel 9:1) and therefore Saul (1 Samuel 9:21; 10:20, 21; 22:7) and Ish-bosheth (2:15).

Beeroth,[9] the hometown of Baanah and Rechab, has a curious history that probably accounts for the details emphasizing its Benjaminite credentials.[10] In the days of Joshua the native (non-Israelite) inhabitants of Beeroth had joined with those of Gibeon and two other nearby towns in a deception that tricked Joshua into making a covenant with them (Joshua 9; see especially v. 17), so that (unlike other inhabitants of the land) they survived Joshua's conquest (Joshua 9:18). If Rimmon and his sons lived in Beeroth, later readers of this account might wonder whether they were really Benjaminites. The narrator explains that "the Beerothites [that is, the original inhabitants] fled to Gittaim"[11] (v. 3a). This may have been when Saul had attempted to annihilate them (as we will learn later in the story, 21:1, 2). This relocation, still known at the time 2 Samuel was written ("to this day," v. 3b), clarifies a possible confusion: Rimmon and his sons, though they lived in Beeroth, did not belong to the earlier inhabitants of the town but to the tribe of Benjamin.

This has been a rather roundabout way of indicating that with the death of Abner the future for the frightened Ish-bosheth depended on the likes of these two fellow Benjaminites, Baanah and Rechab. We will hear more of them very shortly.

Jonathan's Son (v. 4)

Where else might the "house of Saul" (3:1) look, now that Ish-bosheth had lost his grip? Three other sons of Saul had died (1 Samuel 31:2). We might think therefore that the only future for Saul's dynasty would be to skip a generation. It so happens that Saul did have a grandson.[12]

> Jonathan, the son of Saul, had a son who was crippled in his feet. He was five years old when the news about Saul and Jonathan came from Jezreel, and his nurse took him up and fled, and as she fled in her haste, he fell and became lame. And his name was Mephibosheth. (v. 4)

Mephibosheth[13] was a casualty of the same disaster that had befallen Saul and Jonathan, for it was the news of that tragedy that occasioned the accident. We do not know where the child was being cared for while his father, Jonathan, was fighting alongside his grandfather, Saul, on the slopes of Mount Gilboa (1 Samuel 31:1, 2). Presumably it was in or near Saul's town of Gibeah.[14] News of Israel's defeat and the deaths of Saul and Jonathan would have traveled quickly from Jezreel (in the valley below and to the north of Mount Gilboa, where the Israelite army had been based, 1 Samuel 29:1). Although Gibeah was more than fifty miles to the south from the battle, the crushing defeat of the Israelite forces, and especially the death of the king, spelled danger for all Israel and especially for Saul's family (see 1 Samuel 31:7). In the panic of escaping from the too well known location of Saul's family home, the five-year-old Mephibosheth had either fallen or been dropped and suffered the injury that crippled him in both legs.

The accident had occurred about seven years before Abner's death in Hebron.[15] Mephibosheth would now have been about twelve years old and unable to walk or perhaps even stand. We will hear more of Mephibosheth in due course (2 Samuel 9). Here we observe that this surviving member of Saul's family was too young to rule and would be unable to fight even when older. No one would be looking to Mephibosheth to take up Ish-bosheth's lost cause.

Ish-bosheth's End (vv. 5–7)

Our attention is therefore taken back to Baanah and Rechab. What kind of support might the house of Saul receive from these two men? Not a lot, as we are about to see.

An Arrival (v. 5)

> Now the sons of Rimmon the Beerothite, Rechab and Baanah,[16] set out, and about the heat of the day they came to the house of Ish-bosheth as he was taking his noonday rest. (v. 5)

If Beeroth was near Gibeon, it would take the equivalent of an overnight plus a half-day march to reach Mahanaim (cf. 2:29). The purpose of the arrival in Mahanaim of these two kinsmen of Ish-bosheth is not yet clear, just as it was certainly not known to any who witnessed their arrival in the town.

Their business was with Ish-bosheth. But they reached his house at an inconvenient time. He was taking a midday rest. The timing was, however, no accident.

A Killing (v. 6a)

> And they came into the midst of the house as if to get wheat, and they stabbed him in the stomach. (v. 6a)[17]

There was no reason to suspect these two kinsmen of Ish-bosheth. They appeared to be on a mundane mission—to get wheat. Without further explanation we must suppose that wheat supplies were available from somewhere within the building that was Ish-bosheth's house and that Rechab and Baanah had an acceptable reason to be fetching provisions. However, once inside they carried out their real intent and assassinated the sleeping Ish-bosheth.

Despite the rather different circumstances, the narrator describes this killing in terms that remind us of the killing of Asahel (see 2:23) and the subsequent corresponding killing of Abner (see 3:27).[18] These two had, in a sense, stepped into the shoes of the departed Abner. They killed like Abner killed. Indeed the two brother assassins were also like the brothers Joab and Abishai in their killing (3:30). But whereas Abner had reluctantly killed an adversary in battle, these two purposefully assassinated their king, with no apparent reservation. Whereas Joab and Abishai had killed for vengeance, we are left wondering why Rechab and Baanah performed their bloody deed.

A Departure (v. 6b)

The question raised by the assassination (why?) will have to wait for an answer. The account of the killing is concluded with a note about the departure of the assassins. "Then Rechab and Baanah his brother escaped" (v. 6b). Their plan had been carried out without a hitch.[19]

The Killing (Again) (v. 7a)

The assassination of Ish-bosheth is the pivotal event of 2 Samuel 4 and the climactic event of 2 Samuel 2—4. It will change everything. Our first hearing of the killing is shocking. So far we have heard only the bare facts. Indeed we have not yet been told that Ish-bosheth actually died.

As the shock of the violence of the sons of Rimmon sinks in, the narrator takes us through the event one more time, because there is an important detail we need to learn.

> When they came into the house, as he lay on his bed in his bedroom, they struck him and put him to death and beheaded him. (v. 7a)

If the first playing of this scene had left any doubt, we now learn unambiguously that the blow was fatal. Ish-bosheth died. The detail that will now be part of this story until the last verse of the chapter is that they not only killed him, they also beheaded him. Ish-bosheth's head was crucial to the purpose of this premeditated murder.

In this gruesome detail Ish-bosheth's death was like his father's (see 1 Samuel 31:9).

The Departure (Again) (v. 7b)

This crucial detail is now added to the second account of the pair's departure, not just from the house now, but from Mahanaim and the north altogether. "They took his head and went by the way of the Arabah all night" (v. 7b).

With their grisly trophy in hand the two brothers retraced, in the opposite direction, the steps of Abner after his act of killing. Like him they went by way of the Arabah (that is, in this context, the Jordan Valley). Like him they traveled all night (see 2:29). Abner had been returning north *to* Mahanaim from Gibeon. These two were traveling *from* Mahanaim. Where were they going?

The "Stronger and Stronger" House of David (vv. 8–12)

We are kept in suspense no longer: they "brought the head of Ish-bosheth to David at Hebron" (v. 8a). They were not just retracing Abner's steps back to Gibeon. They followed him all the way to Hebron (3:20), where he had died (4:1).

A Message for the King (v. 8)

They had killed like Abner and now, like Abner, they came to David with a message (see 3:12, 21). Their hope not to die like Abner in Hebron (4:1) rested on this message.

> And they said to the king, "Here is the head of Ish-bosheth, the son of Saul, your enemy, who sought your life. The LORD has avenged my lord the king this day on Saul and on his offspring." (v. 8b)

They spoke to David with full recognition of his position as "the king" (v. 8). Like Abner before them, they addressed him as "my lord the king" (cf. 3:21). This put into words what had been expressed in their violent action. The sons of Rimmon had abandoned their allegiance to the house of Saul and intended to transfer it to David.

Their message to the king was displayed in the gruesome trophy they had brought all the way from Mahanaim to Hebron, "the head of Ish-bosheth" (v. 8).[20] It was like the less macabre but equally portentous objects brought to David about seven years previously by the Amalekite, the crown and armlet of Saul (1:10). Like that young man, these two imagined that the trophy in their hands was good news for David.

While the bloody prize they held out before David had obvious significance (Ish-bosheth was dead!), the sons of Rimmon gave their own spin to that message as they put it into words. What they said was true, but it was distorted by what they did not say.

First, they articulated the significant identity of Ish-bosheth: "the son of Saul" (v. 8). Saul's death (1:1) had not brought Saul's kingdom to an end, as the Amalekite youth had thought and symbolically expressed by bringing the king's crown and armlet to David. The death of "the son of Saul" was necessary. Surely the head of Ish-bosheth was therefore good news for David. But they either did not know or did not understand that David had never sought the death of Saul or his sons.

Second, they presented the relationship of Saul to David: "your enemy" (v. 8). Saul was, indeed, "David's enemy" (see 1 Samuel 18:29). This, however, was always only from Saul's side of the relationship (as in 1 Samuel 19:17). In characterizing Saul as "your enemy" (v. 8), Rechab and Baanah were sounding like the men in the cave near Wildgoats' Rocks and like

Abishai at the hill of Hachilah (see 1 Samuel 24:4; 26:8). They either did not know or did not understand that David himself had consistently refused to treat Saul as his enemy (as even Saul had to acknowledge, 1 Samuel 24:19).

Third, they referred to the concrete expression of Saul's enmity that David had experienced for a long time: "who sought your life" (v. 8). The long story of Saul's seeking David's life occupies nine chapters of 1 Samuel (1 Samuel 19—27; see this very expression in 1 Samuel 20:1; 22:23; 23:15; 25:29; cf. 24:11). What these two failed to understand (as had the young Amalekite before them) was that David had never sought Saul's or Ish-bosheth's life.

Fourth, they presented Ish-bosheth's death as the Lord's gift to David: "The LORD has avenged" (v. 8, literally, "The LORD has given vengeance [or recompense]").

Saul's death was certainly God's judgment on him for his disobedience (1 Samuel 28:18, 19). It is a distortion, however, to regard it as a gift to David. David certainly did not see it that way (1:11, 12, 19–27). Nor would he see the death of this son of Saul in those terms. While the Lord may use the wicked acts of men to advance his own good purposes, it is the height of presumption for the perpetrator of the wickedness to present his evil deed as a gift from God (cf. Acts 2:23).

Again we are reminded of David's men earlier who had presumed that the opportunity to kill Saul was God's gift to David (1 Samuel 24:4; 26:8).[21] As on those occasions this king saw things very differently. An opportunity to do evil is never a gift from God (see James 1:13–18).

We have seen that the passage of the sons of Rimmon from Mahanaim to David in Hebron recalls the earlier journey (identical in starting point and destination) by Abner. They were, however, not like Abner who (for all the ambiguities of his motives) knew the promise of God to David and (in his imperfect way) relied on it (see 3:9, 10, 12, and especially 18). Rechab and Baanah were far more like the young Amalekite of 2 Samuel 1.

A Message from the King (vv. 9–11)

"But David answered Rechab and Baanah his brother, the sons of Rimmon the Beerothite . . ." (v. 9a). David's response to the brothers was not what they were expecting. In three devastating affirmations any hope that they had of a welcome from David was crushed.

The God of the King (v. 9b)

First he spoke of the Lord his God: "As the LORD lives, who has redeemed my life out of every adversity . . ." (v. 9b). Saul may have sought David's "life," but the Lord had redeemed his "life."[22] As the Lord had delivered David "from the paw of the lion and from the paw of the bear" (1 Samuel 17:37), from Goliath (1 Samuel 17:46), and from many enemies (1 Samuel 18:14), so he had saved him from Saul (and indeed from many other adversities). Here is the reason that David had never sought Saul's life. He trusted God (see 1 Samuel 24:15; 26:10). He had never thought that he needed to act unrighteously or unfaithfully in order to take hold of the kingship that God would give him. Why? Because he trusted God (see 1 Samuel 26:23, 24). He waited for the Lord to *give* him the kingdom in his own time and way. He refused to *take* it with his own hand (cf. 1 Samuel 25:26, 30, 31).[23]

The "Reward" of the King (v. 10)

Second, David saw the similarity we have already noted between the intentions of the sons of Rimmon and those of the Amalekite years earlier. "[W]hen one told me,[24] 'Behold,[25] Saul is dead,' and thought he was bringing good news, I seized him and killed him at Ziklag, which was the reward I gave him for his news" (v. 10).

By this time David had (almost certainly) learned more accurately about the death of Saul than he had known that day about seven years earlier when the Amalekite had told him his self-serving version of events. Then David had ordered that man's execution on the grounds of his own confession that he had killed Saul (1:16). It seems that David had now learned that Saul had not died at the Amalekite's hands as claimed. He showed no remorse, however, over the execution. He now understood that the lying young man had implicated himself in Saul's death, thinking that this would be good news to David and that he would be rewarded. His reward was his execution. We can only speculate about what might have happened if the Amalekite had brought the news of Saul's death but had not claimed to have killed him. It seems likely that he would not have died since it was the killing of Saul that David cited as the offense that deserved death.

The Judgment of the King (v. 11)

We have not heard the brothers who now came to David explicitly claim to have killed Ish-bosheth, but the awful thing they were carrying was testimony enough. Furthermore what David said next shows that he knew details of the killing that he could only have heard from them. They were, therefore, very much like the Amalekite, except they were telling the truth. So David continued:

How much more, when wicked men have killed a righteous man in his own
house on his bed, shall I not now require his blood at your hand and destroy
you from the earth? (v. 11)

The crime of these two was "more" (v. 11) than that of the Amalekite.
They were "wicked men" (v. 11). Long ago in this story Hannah had prayed,
"[The Lord] will guard the feet of his faithful ones, but *the wicked* shall be
cut off in darkness, for not by might shall a man prevail" (1 Samuel 2:9;
cf. 12:25; 24:13). Much more recently David had called Joab and Abishai
"the wicked" for their murder of Abner (3:34, 39). Rechab and Baanah were
"wicked men" because they had killed "a righteous man" (v. 11). This was
not an absolute statement about Ish-bosheth, but in this context he was innocent of any offense that might be cited to justify his slaughter.

The sons of Rimmon had put themselves in precisely the same place
as the young Amalekite had done earlier, imagining that wickedness could
advantage them in David's kingdom. They were as wrong as he was.

Justice in Hebron (v. 12)

This sorry episode closes with grim justice being carried out in Hebron. "And
David commanded his young men, and they killed them and cut off their
hands and feet and hanged them beside the pool at Hebron" (v. 12a).

The efforts of men to bring in (or destroy) David's kingdom had begun
at another pool, some twenty-five miles to the north, in Gibeon (2:13).
First Abner and Joab had attempted a political/military solution (2:12–32).
Then Abner had tried to sort matters out by himself and perhaps for himself
(3:1–21). Joab had then taken control with his agenda of personal vengeance
(3:22–39). Finally the sons of Rimmon had wickedly killed in order to hasten David's kingdom and advance their own fortunes. The terrible failure
of those efforts was displayed at the pool in Hebron, where the bodies of
the two assassins were hung in a gruesome reminder of what had happened
to the body of Saul (1 Samuel 31:10; see Deuteronomy 21:22, 23). The
schemes of these men failed in their intentions. They were not good enough,
wise enough, or powerful enough to bring in David's kingdom or even to join
David's kingdom. However, their wickedness, foolishness, and weakness did
not destroy this kingdom either. The kingdom was (as it had always been) in
God's hands to give in his own way and in his own time.

The grim justice against the assassins was matched by an act of grace
toward a former rival. "But they took the head of Ish-bosheth and buried it
in the tomb of Abner at Hebron" (v. 12b). Saul's son and Saul's general were

honored by David and buried together in Hebron. But Saul's kingdom had surely now come to its end.

Looking back over the chapter, we note that it was Ish-bosheth's *hands* that signaled his demise in verse 1 (AT). Mephibosheth's crippled *feet* exemplified the failing house of Saul in verse 4. The removal (v. 7), taking (v. 8a), showing (v. 8b), and burying (v. 12) of Ish-bosheth's *head* was the final sign of his fall. It has been a chapter in which body parts have represented the disintegration of the house of Saul.[26]

Wickedness (like that of Rechab and Baanah) is doubly deceptive. On the one hand, the men who did the evil deed imagined that the end justified the means. If the outcome of their actions was David becoming king of Israel, wouldn't the king be pleased with them? On the contrary. God's kingdom is a kingdom of righteousness (see 1 Kings 10:9; Psalm 72:1; 99:4; Proverbs 16:12, 13; 25:5; Isaiah 9:7; 32:1; Jeremiah 22:15; 23:5; Zechariah 9:9; Matthew 5:10, 20; 6:33; 13:43; Romans 14:17). God's king condemns all wickedness.

Christian reader, take heed. Never compromise righteousness, even when you imagine that good will come of some unrighteous action. I doubt that you will be tempted to think that an assassination is called for to advance the gospel. But in our own day it is more common than we like to think for Christians to try to advance God's kingdom by disgraceful and unworthy means. Be sure that you love righteousness more than success.

On the other hand, wickedness is never able to *thwart* God's kingdom. In his infinite wisdom and power God uses even wicked deeds (which he hates and judges) to advance his purposes. The wickedness of Rechab and Baanah (like the wickedness of Judas and those who put Jesus to death) in God's remarkable sovereignty accomplished God's purposes *despite* the evil of the actions (cf. Genesis 50:20; Acts 2:23). Do not fear that the wickedness of men will ever hinder God's kingdom. God's King is good, he is wise, and he is very powerful. It is just that his ways are seldom our ways. Success for him can look like failure to us. "Oh, the depth of the riches and wisdom and knowledge of God! How unsearchable are his judgments and how inscrutable his ways!" (Romans 11:33).

10

Coming to the King

2 SAMUEL 5:1–3

WHY IS IT THAT human beings have never been able to build a society that is all we would like it to be? Why are harmony and happiness so difficult to attain and so fleeting on the occasions we think we have managed to find them? Why do leaders who appear to promise so much *always* let us down? Why do conflict, suffering, injustice, disappointment, anxiety, and fear continue so powerfully in human lives and societies? Why have we never been able to build communities that are completely secure, prosperous, peaceful, and joyful?

The simple but true answer is that we are not good, wise, or strong enough.

We are not good enough. *Human wickedness* undermines every group of people in various ways. The Bible calls it sin, and it is displayed in the many expressions of self-centeredness with which we are all too familiar. Greed, resentment, pride, perversity, untruthfulness, immorality, malice, and much more are present in every human group. Neither education nor regulation has ever been able to make us good enough to live completely happily together.

We are not wise enough. *Human foolishness* means that mistakes are always made. We are not clever enough to solve all our problems. Decisions are made with good intentions that have terrible unintended consequences. Many of our worthy plans for making things better fail simply because the planners were not able to take into account every possibly relevant factor. Despite massive advances in human knowledge we have not become wise enough to organize and manage human communities that are good for all.

We are not strong enough. *Human weakness* prevents even the best and wisest humans from overcoming all obstacles to harmony and happiness among us. There are difficulties that are simply beyond human solutions. It seems highly unlikely that medical science will ever eradicate sickness and disease completely. So-called natural disasters will continue to be almost entirely beyond our control. Accidents cannot always be avoided. Death awaits us all and will always be tragic. For all the wonders of development and progress over the centuries, human beings and human communities face challenges that are beyond human solution. We are not strong enough.

It follows that the Bible's message about the kingdom of God is enormously important. God has promised to do what humans lack the goodness, wisdom, and power to accomplish. Only the kingdom *of God* guarantees the righteousness we humans consistently fail to exhibit, the peace we find so elusive, and the joy that is always transitory (cf. Romans 14:17).

In the Old Testament history of the people of Israel the kingdom of David was the kingdom of God. That is, David was God's king. His was not the full or perfect expression of God's kingdom. That only came into the world with Jesus Christ (Matthew 12:28; Mark 1:15) and will culminate only when he returns (Matthew 13:41; Luke 22:16, 18, 30; 1 Corinthians 15:24; 2 Thessalonians 1:5; 2 Timothy 4:1). Nonetheless the surprising and often perplexing story of David's journey from Bethlehem (where he was anointed to be God's king, 1 Samuel 16:1–13) to Jerusalem (where the Lord will establish him as king over his people, 5:12) teaches us a great deal about the kingdom of God. In particular we see how this kingdom is so very different from the wickedness, foolishness, and weakness of humans.

First it was Goliath and the Philistines, the enemies of God's people, who threatened to destroy them with their impressive might. The apparently small, weak, and insignificant David prevailed, and the Philistines fled (1 Samuel 17). This was the Lord's doing (1 Samuel 17:37, 46). "The bows of the mighty [were] broken. . . . The adversaries of the LORD [were] broken to pieces" (1 Samuel 2:4, 10).

Then there was Saul, the rejected king of Israel whose jealousy toward David drove him mad and led to the long story of Saul's murderous pursuit of David (beginning at 1 Samuel 18:8 and continuing at least until 1 Samuel 27:4). Through those years David maintained his righteousness and faithfulness by refusing to *take* the throne from Saul by violence (see 1 Samuel 26:23). He would wait until the Lord *gave* it to him (see 1 Samuel 26:10). As Saul did everything in his power to destroy him, David suffered. But it could be said of him, as it was later said of Jesus, "When he was reviled, he did not revile in return; when he suffered, he did not threaten, but continued entrusting himself to him who judges justly" (1 Peter 2:23; see especially 1 Samuel 24, 26).

When Saul died and a man came to David claiming to have done him the service of killing his adversary, David neither welcomed the news nor rewarded the man (2 Samuel 1). At the news of the death of Saul (and Jonathan), David wept (1:12).

When the time had come for David to be recognized as king, it was only the southern tribe of Judah who acknowledged him (2:4). David's word from Hebron to the people of the north, and particularly to those most loyal to Saul, was full of grace (2:5–7).

However, the north did not welcome David's kindness. Instead Ishbosheth was made king over them in Mahanaim (2:8, 9).

When Abner and Joab attempted to resolve the situation of the two rival kingdoms, the outcome was bloodshed that accomplished nothing (2:12–32). Neither of the two generals was good, wise, or powerful enough to settle the matter.

When at last Abner (for dubious reasons and with suspicious intentions) decided to abandon Ish-bosheth and go over to David, he found a surprisingly gracious welcome and left David "in peace" (3:1–21).

However, Abner underestimated the hatred of Joab, who thought that he would protect David's kingdom by assassinating Abner (3:22–27). David repudiated Joab's action as wickedness (3:28–39).

The final episode in the long struggle between David and the house of Saul came when two of Ish-bosheth's men assassinated him, thinking they were doing David a service. David saw it very differently (2 Samuel 4).

Those who were caught up in this course of events would have been hard-pressed to see where it would all end. There were moments, to be sure, when it was clear that David's cause seemed strong (see, for example, 1 Samuel 18:14, 30; 2 Samuel 2:17, 30, 31). At other times it was far from clear how David could ever become king (see, for example, 1 Samuel 22:1, 2; 27:1; 2 Samuel 3:39). The historian summed up the last couple of years of this story in these terms: "David grew stronger and stronger, while the house of Saul became weaker and weaker" (3:1b). These words have the benefit of both hindsight and divine inspiration. It is far from clear that everyone involved at the time could see that this is what was happening. That is because human ways often seem to be good, wise, and strong when in reality they are wicked, foolish, and weak.

In fact all human efforts to either destroy or establish David's kingdom had not achieved their end. But the time had come for David to receive the kingdom.

Since David had become king in the southern town of Hebron (Abraham's town, we recall) he had received several significant visitors. Abner, the man who put Ish-bosheth on the throne in Mahanaim, "came . . . to David at Hebron" (3:20), as did Rechab and Baanah, Ish-bosheth's two kinsmen who had removed his head (which they had hopefully brought with them to Hebron, 4:8). These visits were very different. On the one hand David had welcomed Abner's change of allegiance, despite his excessive self-confidence. On the other hand David had passed judgment on Rechab and Baanah for their assassination of Ish-bosheth, despite the advantage this brought to David.

The next time that we hear of someone who "came to David at Hebron" the ambiguities of these earlier occasions have gone. We will note:

(1) How they came (vv. 1, 2).
(2) How they were received (v. 3).

How They Came (vv. 1, 2)

"Then all the tribes of Israel came to David at Hebron" (v. 1a). This was not literally what happened (several million visitors would have strained Hebron's facilities[1]). In verse 3 we will learn that the tribes came to David representatively.[2] It was their elders who came. Nonetheless the wording of verse 1a should be taken seriously. The elders really did represent "all the tribes of Israel" (v. 1).[3]

Why did they come? The short answer is that they had come to their senses. The attempt to set up a king other than David had been foolish from the beginning. Both Abner and the people should have known better.

When people come to God's King today, they recognize that they have come to their senses. Previous attempts to live without Jesus Christ as their Lord have been foolish. They should have known better.

What brought the tribes of Israel to their senses? Some time earlier "the elders of Israel" had heard the good news of the kingdom of David from Abner (3:17, 18).[4] If Abner is to be believed (and at this point we have no reason to doubt him), their response was positive (it was "good in their eyes," literal translation of the phrase in 3:19). Some time later the news of Abner's death in Hebron had alarmed "all Israel" (4:1). However (presumably some time later again), "all Israel" understood that Abner's death was not David's doing (3:37). Now Ish-bosheth's death (2 Samuel 4) had removed any final obstacle to all the tribes of Israel doing what they had wanted to do for a long time (3:17).

Likewise today the means by which people come to their senses is hearing the good news of the kingdom of Jesus Christ. There may be obstacles and excuses in people's lives that stand in the way of coming to Christ. We long that the gospel will be proclaimed and heard in such a way that these hindrances (whatever they may be) will be swept away (cf. 2 Corinthians 10:4, 5).

When they came to David the elders of Israel put into words (on behalf of all the tribes of Israel) three reasons for their coming. They had come to understand and to believe the gospel of the kingdom in its 1000 BC form.

Who We Are: Your Body (v. 1b)

First, they had come to understand something about themselves. "Behold, we are your bone and flesh" (v. 1b). This unusual phrase is at least a vivid representation of what we would call blood relationship.[5] In this sense the common ancestry of all Israelites back to Jacob is what lies behind the statement.[6]

It was a basic requirement for a king over the people of Israel that he must be "one from among your brothers" (Deuteronomy 17:15). The elders of Israel were at least affirming that David fulfilled this requirement. They came to him as a brother, not as a stranger, foreigner, or enemy.

Today those who come to God's King, Jesus Christ, likewise should understand that he has been "made like his brothers in every respect" (Hebrews 2:17) and calls us "brothers" (Hebrews 2:11; cf. John 1:14; Romans 8:3; Galatians 4:4; Philippians 2:7). The incarnation[7] means that what was once true between "all the tribes of Israel" (5:1) and King David is now true between the whole human race and Jesus Christ. We come to him not as a stranger, foreigner, or enemy but as a brother.

However, I am inclined to think that the elders of Israel were saying even more than this to David. The emphasis of their words falls less on *his relationship to them* than on *who they are in relation to him*.[8] "We are your bone and your flesh" is a way of saying, "We are your body." They were acknowledging David as their king. On the one hand it was a remarkable expression of submission to David's rule. The tribes of Israel are claiming to belong to their king and to be responsive to his will as though they were his very body. On the other hand they were expressing profound trust in their king. They looked to him to care for them as a man nourishes his own body.[9] "We are your bone and your flesh—that's who we are!"

This understanding, like so much we see in the kingdom of David, anticipates an even more profound truth in the kingdom of Jesus Christ. Those gathered under the rule of Jesus ("the church"[10]) are "the body of Christ," that is the body of the King (see, for example, 1 Corinthians 12:27; Ephesians 1:23; 4:12; 5:23, 30; Colossians 1:24).

Those who come to God's King today join the assembly that is the King's "body." This is an expression of the submission and trust that believers have toward Christ Jesus. He is the "head" of his "body" and is himself its Savior (Ephesians 5:23, 24). He cares for and nourishes his "body" (Ephesians 5:25–30). We who have come to Jesus Christ belong to him, respond to his will, and look to him for sustenance and protection. We are his body—that's who we are!

Who You Are: Our Savior (v. 2a)

The second reason all the tribes of Israel gave for coming to David in Hebron that day was something they understood and believed about David: "In times past, when Saul was king over us, it was you[11] who led out and brought in Israel" (v. 2a).

Here is a clear echo of the earlier words in which Abner had sought to persuade the elders of Israel to come over to David. The elders' "In times past" (v. 2) is very close to (the Hebrew is almost identical to) Abner's "For some time past" (3:17). Abner had spoken of the longstanding (even if recently suppressed) desire of the elders to have David as their king: "You have been seeking David as king over you" (3:17). The elders now gave expression to that desire by describing its cause. When Saul had been their king, it was David who had been their savior. He was the one who (literally) "caused Israel to go out and come in." "Going out and coming in" "is an expression for leadership in battle"[12] (see Numbers 27:17; 1 Samuel 18:13, 16; 29:6; 2 Samuel 3:25). It was David who had led them out against their enemies and brought them back safe and victorious. The basis for this description of David has been amply laid out in the narrative of 1 Samuel, where David repeatedly saved the people from their enemies, especially the Philistines (see 1 Samuel 17:1–58; 18:5–7, 13b–16, 27, 30; 19:4, 5, 8; 21:11; 23:1–5; 27:8, 9; 29:5; 30:1–31; 2 Samuel 1:1b).

David's role as Israel's savior had been evident for a long time. The tribes of Israel had been foolish not to embrace David as their king much earlier. It is an interesting exercise to read 5:1–3 immediately after 2:1–7. That sequence of events would have been sensible: David goes up to Hebron, is made king by the tribe of Judah, and extends a gracious offer to people in the north, who then come to him in Hebron, recognizing him as the king of all Israel. This sensible sequence was interrupted by the foolish act of Abner making Ish-bosheth king in Mahanaim. It took some time and bloodshed before all Israel came to their senses and at last came to David. They had been foolish to follow another king. This acknowledgment is implicit in their recognition that even when Saul had been king, David had been their savior.

Today those who come to God's King, Jesus Christ, recognize that he is the one who has defeated our enemies. The enemies are variously described in the New Testament. Behind them all stands Satan, the Accuser. In his hands the power of sin and death threatens human lives. The "thrones or dominions or rulers or authorities" (Colossians 1:16) are the spiritual powers by which Satan opposes God's good purposes for his creation and for humanity. The decisive victory over all these enemies was won, paradoxically, by Jesus Christ's death on the cross, where the power of Satan to accuse us was stripped away as the record of our debt was obliterated (see Colossians 2:14, 15[13]). Like the tribes of Israel in Hebron that day, we come to Jesus saying, "You are the one who has defeated our enemies and made us safe."

The connection between the first two reasons given by the elders of Israel (Israel is David's body; David is Israel's savior) is also profoundly deepened in the relationship between Jesus Christ and his people. His headship of this body is seen most clearly in his being "its Savior," giving himself up for her (see Ephesians 5:23, 25).

What God Has Promised: "Shepherd of My People" (v. 2b)

The third thing that the tribes of Israel at last understood as they came to David in Hebron was God's promise concerning him: "And the LORD said to you, 'You shall be shepherd of my people Israel,[14] and you shall be prince over Israel'" (v. 2b).

When the tribes of Israel at last acknowledged God's promise concerning David, it was the climax of a long story. Abner had reminded them of the Lord's promise (see 3:18), but behind Abner's message was the long story that had led to this point.

This is an appropriate place for us to look back and review God's promise concerning David prior to this point in the story. The careful reader should already realize (as the tribes of Israel did) a great deal of what God had promised concerning David. However, it is surprising how little had (at this stage) been explicitly put into words. What do we know (at this point in the story) of God's purpose for David?

A convenient starting point is Samuel's address to the people of Israel at

Gilgal at the time of Saul's appointment as king (1 Samuel 12). At the heart of that speech was the Lord's commitment to his people: "For the LORD will not forsake his people, for his great name's sake, because it has pleased the LORD to make you a people for himself" (1 Samuel 12:22). This commitment can be traced back to the promise first made to Abraham: "I will make of you a great nation, and I will bless you and make your name great, so that you will be a blessing . . . and in you all the families of the earth shall be blessed" (Genesis 12:2, 3).

The appointment of Saul (and the terms of that appointment) must be understood in the context of God's commitment "to make . . . a people for himself" (1 Samuel 12:22) and through them to bring blessing to "all the families of the earth" (Genesis 12:3). The rejection of Saul after his disobedience and the consequent choice of David are only properly seen as God's faithfulness to this same purpose.

As the story is told in the books of Samuel, God's purpose for his king is anticipated as early as Hannah's prayer in 1 Samuel 2. "The LORD will judge the ends of the earth; he will give strength to his king and exalt the horn of his anointed" (1 Samuel 2:10b). It became clear that this expectation must be applied to someone other than Saul when Saul failed to obey the word of the Lord. "The LORD has sought out [for himself[15]] a man after his own heart, and the LORD has commanded him to be prince over his people, because you have not kept what the LORD commanded you" (1 Samuel 13:14).

In the context of the rejection of Saul, God's purpose for David continued to take shape. "The LORD has torn the kingdom of Israel from you [Saul] this day and has given it to a neighbor of yours, who is better than you" (1 Samuel 15:28).

When the Lord sent Samuel to Jesse in Bethlehem, he said, "I have provided for myself a king among his sons" (1 Samuel 16:1). When David at last appeared, the Lord said to Samuel, "Arise, anoint him, for this is he" (1 Samuel 16:12).

From this point onward in the narrative there are recorded surprisingly few words from God about David.[16] There are several examples of David expressing his confidence in God, apparently based on God's promise to him (1 Samuel 17:37, 45–47; 24:12, 15; 25:39; 26:10, 23, 24; cf. 23:16, 18). Many people recognized, from his remarkable military successes, that "the LORD was with him" (1 Samuel 18:12, 14, 28; cf. 19:5). More and more people came to understand that David would be Israel's next king (see 1 Samuel 18:3, 8; 20:13d–17, 31; 21:11; 23:17; 24:20; 25:26, 28–31; 26:25). This was finally confirmed in the word from the departed Samuel to Saul on the night before his death: "The LORD has torn the kingdom out of your hand and given it to your neighbor, David" (1 Samuel 28:17).

When we now hear the elders of Israel come to David in Hebron and speak of the Lord's promise to David, we understand that they were at last acknowledging the truth that had been known in Israel at least since the young David had slain Goliath. No previous recorded word from God was in precisely the terms quoted by the elders of Israel (just as Abner's earlier expression of the promise in 3:18 was new). It is possible, of course, that the elders were quoting an otherwise unrecorded prophetic message. It is more likely that the elders were expressing their understanding of what God had promised from all that had gone before.[17] If so, like Abner earlier, their words are remarkably perceptive. Like many characters in Biblical narratives, they spoke more truly and profoundly than they may have known.

Three terms in 5:2b are particularly striking: "shepherd," "my people," and "prince."

David was to be "*prince* over Israel." The Hebrew term translated "prince" was used for the first time in the Old Testament of Saul (1 Samuel 9:16). It is not a term that itself has royal connotations and is probably better translated with a neutral word like "leader"[18] because at least in some contexts it seems to be deliberately chosen to avoid some associations of the term "king."[19] David was, of course, to be king over Israel, but his kingship would be so different from anything the world had known that sometimes another word is needed (cf. 1 Samuel 13:14; 25:30).

The people whom David would lead were "*my people* Israel" (v. 2). As Samuel had reminded the people long ago, "It has pleased the LORD to make . . . a people for himself" (1 Samuel 12:22). One critical aspect of David's unique kingship was that the people of his kingdom were the Lord's people. You follow this king because you belong to God.

"You shall be *shepherd* of my people Israel" (v. 2). David had been a shepherd in Bethlehem when he was a boy. This is repeatedly noted in the early parts of his story (see 1 Samuel 16:11, 19; 17:15, 20, 28, 34, 40; cf. 2 Samuel 7:8) and was no doubt well-known.[20] David himself had drawn a comparison between his activity as shepherd and his defeat of the Philistine (1 Samuel 17:36, 37). Saving the sheep from the dangers that threatened them was what David did.[21]

While shepherd vocabulary is widely used of kings in other parts of the Old Testament (and the ancient world more generally[22]), the use of this term by the elders of Israel that day in Hebron was probably influenced more by

David's story and the earlier Biblical history than by more general political vocabulary.

God himself was known as a shepherd. Jacob had spoken of "the God who has been my shepherd all my life long to this day" (Genesis 48:15; cf. 49:24). David himself famously affirmed, "The LORD is my shepherd" (Psalm 23:1), just as he prayed that the Lord would save his people: "Be their shepherd and carry them forever" (Psalm 28:9; see also Psalm 78:71; 80:1; Ecclesiastes 12:11; Isaiah 40:11; Jeremiah 31:10).

Moses had recognized that Israel needed a shepherd. In words remarkably similar to the words of the elders of Israel in Hebron, he asked the Lord to "appoint a man over the congregation who shall go out before them and come in before them, who shall lead them out and bring them in, that the congregation of the LORD may not be as sheep that have no shepherd" (Numbers 27:16, 17).

In days to come, when David's kingdom has collapsed, this promise will be remembered. The prophet Micaiah will say to the wicked King Ahab, "I saw all Israel scattered on the mountains, as sheep that have no shepherd" (1 Kings 22:17; see also Ezekiel 34:5, 8; Zechariah 10:2). Through the prophets of the Old Testament the Lord will promise to provide a shepherd for his people (Jeremiah 3:15; Ezekiel 34:12, 15, 23, 24; Micah 5:4).

The gospel of Jesus Christ brings God's promises concerning David to fulfillment. Indeed as Matthew gives his account of Jesus, the son of David, he quotes the Scriptures concerning the birth of the Christ, combining the text of Micah 5:2 with the precise words of the elders in Hebron: the coming ruler "will shepherd my people Israel" (Matthew 2:6).[23] Jesus recognized the condition of the people: "they were harassed and helpless, like sheep without a shepherd" (Matthew 9:36). He identified himself as the long-awaited shepherd (Matthew 26:31; also John 10:2, 11–16). Christian people today know him as their great and good shepherd (Hebrews 13:20; 1 Peter 2:25; 5:4; Revelation 7:17).

The tribes of Israel coming to David in Hebron wonderfully anticipated what it means for people to come to God's King today. How good it is to be the Lord's people, with such a shepherd!

How They Were Received (v. 3)

This moment in Hebron was remarkable and historic. Before we learn what then happened, the situation already described in verse 1a is reiterated, now making clear that "all the tribes of Israel came to David" by means of their elders: "So all the elders of Israel came to the king at Hebron" (v. 3a).

Having heard what they said to David, it is clear that they had come not just to "David," but to David as "the king."

The last time "all the elders of Israel" appeared together in the story was many years previously when "all the elders of Israel gathered together and came to Samuel at Ramah" to demand that he appoint for them a king (1 Samuel 8:4, 5).[24] That was the beginning of the long and complex story that led to this day when all the elders of Israel came to David, about twenty-five miles south of Ramah, at Hebron.

The repetition of the fact that they came to David "at Hebron" (David did not come to them at Mahanaim) underlines the theme that has dominated so many pages: David did not *take* the leadership of Israel that was about to become his; he *received* it.

"And King David made a covenant with them at Hebron before the LORD" (v. 3b). King David is now given his full royal title (for the second time in the narrative; see 3:31). It was *as king* that he made this covenant. Furthermore *he* made the covenant. That is, the terms were given by him and accepted by the elders, not the other way around.[25]

"Before the LORD" (v. 3) is a phrase that emphasizes the personal presence of the Lord in which some action is taken.[26] Importantly, Saul had been made king "before the LORD" in Gilgal (1 Samuel 11:15). This meant that Saul's kingship was set in the proper relationship to the kingship of God spelled out in Samuel's Gilgal speech (1 Samuel 12).[27] Saul would be king, but on terms and conditions that ensured that the Lord's supremacy over this people was not compromised.[28]

David had earlier agreed to make a covenant with Abner (3:13) and with "all Israel" (3:21). The latter was delayed and hindered by the actions of Joab. However, at last the covenant was enacted. This covenant can be assumed to give expression to the acceptance of David by all the tribes of Israel as their shepherd leader and the acceptance by David of all the tribes of Israel as the Lord's people who are his bone and his flesh. Thus the king and the people of God accepted God's purpose for David. The division caused by the earlier rejection of David by the northern tribes had been overcome. Israel was again one: there was one shepherd, one king. This is the nature of the unity of God's people (see Ezekiel 34:23; 37:24; John 10:16). As all Israel was "one" under King David, Christian believers are "all one in Christ Jesus" (Galatians 3:28).

The agreement was expressed in action: "and they anointed David king over Israel" (v. 3c), just as the men of Judah had anointed him king over the house of Judah about seven years earlier (2:4). The sequence of events that had begun when the Lord "rejected" Saul "from being king over Israel" (1 Samuel 16:1) had now reached its goal. At long last David was "king over Israel" (v. 3). "Israel" here still means the northern tribes, but in reality David was now king over the whole nation. The kingdom had come.

How would it go? That would depend on the goodness, the wisdom, and the power of the king.

How will it go for us? The goodness, the wisdom, and the power of Jesus Christ guarantee that the kingdom of God is secure and good forever.

Part 3

THE KINGDOM
OF DAVID

2 Samuel 5:4—10:19

11

"On Zion, My Holy Hill"

2 SAMUEL 5:4–16

THOSE WHO BELIEVE the promises of God have an extraordinary vision of the future. This view of the future is one of the many ways in which the gospel of Jesus Christ is more powerful than any other understanding of life. Wars, natural and other disasters, sickness and disease, ecological crises, political and economic catastrophes, and a host of other troubles threaten the future for individuals, societies, nations, and sometimes even the whole world. Believers do not despair. We pray, "Your kingdom come"(Matthew 6:10). Christian prayer is an expression of Christian hope. Christian prayer is made possible by Christian hope. And Christian hope rests on the promises of God.

John described this vision:

> Then I saw a new heaven and a new earth, for the first heaven and the first earth had passed away, and the sea was no more. And I saw the holy city, new Jerusalem, coming down out of heaven from God, prepared as a bride adorned for her husband. And I heard a loud voice from the throne saying, "Behold, the dwelling place of God is with man. He will dwell with them, and they will be his people, and God himself will be with them as their God. He will wipe away every tear from their eyes, and death shall be no more, neither shall there be mourning, nor crying, nor pain anymore, for the former things have passed away." (Revelation 21:1–4)

This is our vision, if we believe the promises of God. We know, of course, that the reality will surpass the vision. The human heart is not able to imagine "what God has prepared for those who love him" (1 Corinthians 2:9). But this God-given and therefore profoundly true vision of the promised future is why we pray, "Your kingdom come" (Matthew 6:10).

While there is much to be said about every aspect of this vision,[1] I want to draw your attention to one element: Christian believers look forward to "the holy city, new Jerusalem, coming down out of heaven from God" (Revelation 21:2). Our vision of the future, if it is based on God's promises, is a vision of a city (see Hebrews 11:10, 16; 13:14). The city is Jerusalem. Not *old* Jerusalem, but "*new* Jerusalem" (v. 2).

Jerusalem means many things to different people. The historic city features prominently in the thoughts and affections of Christians and even of Jewish and Muslim people.[2] Among each of these groups (including, perhaps especially, Christians) there is a wide diversity of ideas about Jerusalem and its importance, significance, and future. The conflict between some of these ideas has been part of the complex of factors that have contributed to the social, political, and military turmoil in the vicinity of Jerusalem over the last half-century (and more).[3] The confusion of ideas about Jerusalem has been massive and tragic. Some of this is due to distortions of the Bible's teaching about Jerusalem, often in the form of taking ideas out of their full Biblical context.[4]

Although Jerusalem appears briefly at a number of points in Biblical history prior to King David (and we will take note of these earlier appearances shortly), Jerusalem becomes prominent in the Bible from the time that it became David's royal city. The significance of Jerusalem for David's kingdom is the key to understanding Jerusalem in God's promises. Christians look forward to the *new* Jerusalem because of the significance of the *old* Jerusalem. As we hear the beginning of the main story of Jerusalem, we will understand more clearly what it means to look forward to the new Jerusalem. The point and purpose of hearing about the old Jerusalem is to bring our vision of the new Jerusalem into shaper focus.

Our passage unfolds as follows:

(1) Jerusalem: where David reigned (vv. 4, 5).
(2) Jerusalem: promise and defiance (v. 6).
(3) Jerusalem: the blind and the lame (vv. 7, 8).
(4) Jerusalem: the city of the king (vv. 9–12).
(5) Jerusalem: where David takes . . . (vv. 13–16).

Jerusalem: Where David Reigned (vv. 4, 5)

In Biblical history the account of a king's reign often begins with a summary of the reign in terms of a basic chronology and evaluation (for example, 1 Kings 14:21; 15:1–3, 9–11). Now that David had at last become king of *all*

Israel (5:1–3), our historian provides us with such a summary, supplementing what he told us in 2:11:

> David was thirty years old when he began to reign, and he reigned forty years. At Hebron he reigned over Judah seven years and six months, and at Jerusalem he reigned over all Israel and Judah thirty-three years. (vv. 4, 5)

At about the same age that Jesus would later begin his public life (see Luke 3:23), David became king. The reference is to David's becoming king over Judah in Hebron (2:4). Since Ish-bosheth reigned in Mahanaim for only two years (2:10), he was either made king by Abner toward the end of David's seven and a half years in Hebron (we then know very little of the five years or so before Ish-bosheth's installation), or, assuming he was made king early in David's reign, there may have been a period of up to five years between the end of 2 Samuel 4 (the death of Ish-bosheth) and the beginning of 2 Samuel 5 (when the elders of Israel came to David). I find the former reconstruction more persuasive.[5]

The mention of Jerusalem anticipates the next episode to be recounted. Jerusalem has been mentioned once before in this story in a most surprising place. When David killed Goliath, we were told that he "took the head of the Philistine and brought it to Jerusalem" (1 Samuel 17:54). David's journey to Jerusalem began with the slaying of Goliath. It had been a long time and a difficult road, but we are about to hear how it was that David could bring Goliath's head to Jerusalem[6] and in that same place begin a thirty-three-year reign.

Jerusalem: Promise and Defiance (v. 6)

After the conventional summary, the historical account of David's reign as king of all Israel formally begins in 5:6. David's first recorded act as king of the whole nation is his going up to Jerusalem.[7]

> And the king and his men[8] went to Jerusalem against the Jebusites, the inhabitants of the land, who said to David, "You will not come in here, but the blind and the lame will ward you off"—thinking, "David cannot come in here." (v. 6)

Unlike many of the place names in this narrative (Hebron and Mahanaim are good examples), Jerusalem does not (at this point in Biblical history) carry weighty associations from Israel's historical experience. Certainly it was, even in David's day, an ancient and famous city.[9] It appears to have been only partially and temporarily conquered by the Israelites during the conquest (Joshua 10; 12:10; 15:63; Judges 1:8, 21). Only one event stands out in the Biblical history of Jerusalem prior to David's taking of the city. Centuries earlier Melchizedek, the mysterious priest-king of Salem (that is, Jerusalem), had blessed Abraham and received a tithe from him (Genesis 14:18–20). In due course Melchizedek became the pattern for a promised future priest-king (Psalm 110, especially v. 4). This promise has been fulfilled in Jesus (see Hebrews 6:20—7:28).

We do not know whether the associations with Melchizedek were in David's mind when he decided to go up against Jerusalem. Memories of the experience of Abraham at Salem should not be denied to David, who was living in Abraham's Hebron. However, the wording of 5:6 suggests two other reasons for David's action.

First, Jerusalem was populated by "Jebusites, the inhabitants of the land" (v. 6).[10] "The inhabitants of the land" means the native inhabitants of the land.[11] The phrase appears repeatedly earlier in the history with reference to the peoples whom God promised to drive out before the Israelites and required the Israelites to expel (see Exodus 23:31; Numbers 33:52, 55; Joshua 9:24). It had been a failure of faithfulness on the part of the Israelites that they did not drive out all "the inhabitants of the land" (see Judges 1:32, 33). Earlier David had engaged in extensive deadly raids against "the inhabitants of the land" from his base in Ziklag (1 Samuel 27:8). Therefore David's action against Jerusalem (from *Abraham's* town of Hebron) was probably motivated by the ancient promise of God (originally spoken to Abraham) concerning the land. David was doing what Israel had failed to do and was at the same time acting as the agent of the fulfillment of God's promise. This suggestion is strengthened by the fact that "Jebusites" (v. 6) is a reminder of the promise to Abraham (see Genesis 15:18–21; also Exodus 3:8, 17; 13:5; 23:23; 33:2; 34:11; Deuteronomy 7:1; 20:17; Joshua 3:10; 12:8; 24:11). In this way it is appropriate to think of the city of Jerusalem in terms of God's promise to Abraham. David came to Jerusalem to fulfill that promise.

A second reason for David's action against Jerusalem is suggested by the defiance of the city's people. The city's impressive defenses made them sure that David would not be able to come in. They saw no need for a serious military defense. An army of "the blind and the lame" (v. 6) would be sufficient to keep David out of Jerusalem.[12] David's advance against Jerusalem was therefore directed against explicit insolent rejection of his authority from within the borders of his kingdom. David came to Jerusalem to overthrow such defiance.

The new Jerusalem will be the place where God's promises to Abraham of blessing for the nations reach their ultimate fulfillment (see Revelation 21:24, 26; 22:2). It will be a place where all defiance of God's kingdom is finally done away with (Revelation 21:8, 27).

Jerusalem: The Blind and the Lame (vv. 7, 8)

The narrator wastes no time telling us of David's success. "Nevertheless, David took the stronghold of Zion, that is, the city of David" (v. 7). The confident defiance of the Jebusites was misplaced. They join others in this history who underestimated God's king to their very great cost. David made this city his own—"the city of David" (v. 7). Shortly we will learn what is anticipated here.

"The stronghold" (v. 7) was the city's fortress or citadel, or perhaps the well fortified city itself,[13] located on the southeastern ridge of the later city of Jerusalem. It was this ridge, overlooking the Kidron Valley, that was originally known as "Zion" (v. 7, as also in 1 Kings 8:1).[14]

This is the first reference in the Bible to "Zion" (v. 7). "Zion" will become a profoundly evocative term, particularly in the Psalms and the Prophets.[15] This is partly because the name was taken and applied to the hill on the north side of the city of Solomon's day, where the temple was built. "Mount Zion" came to refer to the Temple Mount, Mount Moriah (Psalm 74:2; 78:68, 69; Isaiah 4:5; Lamentations 2:6, 7). It is understandable that the terms "Zion" and "Mount Zion" then came to mean the city of Jerusalem itself (2 Kings 19:31; Psalm 48:2; 125:1, 2) or its citizens, that is God's people (Psalm 48:11; Isaiah 40:9; 51:16; 52:7). In these various uses of "Zion" the topographical reference is less important than the ideas evoked—God's promises, his king, and his kingdom.[16]

The original Jebusite Zion was surrounded on three sides by steep valleys.[17] The Jebusites had reasons for their confidence. After all, the Israelites had failed to permanently or completely take the city previously (compare Judges 1:8, 21; also Joshua 15:63). How was it that David accomplished what the people had previously been unable to do? The narrator explains:

> And David said on that day, "Whoever would strike the Jebusites, let him get up the water shaft to attack 'the lame and the blind,' who are hated by David's soul." (v. 8a)

Unfortunately this explanation of David's strategy is not entirely clear to us today. The key uncertainty is the word translated "water shaft" (v. 8).[18] This rendering comes from the popular suggestion that David's men gained access to the city by climbing up the water shaft (known today as Warren's Shaft[19]), which leads into the city from the Gihon Spring, down in the Kidron Valley outside the city walls.[20] We must admit, however, that this understanding is not certain (and has some difficulties[21]). The key word may refer to the water supply of the Gihon Spring itself, and the sense of David's command may have been to take control of the city's water supply and so enable its capture without bloodshed.[22] There are a number of other possibilities.[23] This means that we know David took Jerusalem, but it is not clear to us how he did it.

Following the ESV "the blind and the lame" (v. 8) is probably a derogatory reference by David to the Jebusites, who had used the expression in their defiance of him. David's hatred was not a matter of holding a prejudice against disabled people, but rather the hostility of the king toward those who defied his reign: they were, to use their own words, "blind" and "lame." (We note that some time later David famously showed great kindness to the lame son of Jonathan, as we will see in 2 Samuel 9.[24])

As a result of all this there was a saying that persisted to the day of the writer of this history: "Therefore it is said, 'The blind and the lame shall not [or do not[25]] come into the house'" (v. 8b). "The house" (for the writer of this history, at a later time) could be the temple but in this context probably refers to David's palace (see "house" in verse 11).[26] It is possible that "the blind and the lame" (v. 8) is still a reference to the Jebusites and that the saying reflects their exclusion from entering the temple or the palace, in recognition of this day when they had defied the king.[27] The saying, however, without the context of the present story, seems to generalize the reference. It may be that these events were remembered by the exclusion of *all* blind and lame persons from "the house" (v. 8). The exclusion (whatever its extent) was not a God-given matter but a practice reflected in this popular saying.[28]

As we look forward to the new Jerusalem we understand that this aspect of the old Jerusalem will be reversed. It is wonderful to see how Jesus dealt with "the blind and the lame" when he came into the Jerusalem temple: "And *the blind and the lame* came to him in the temple, and he healed them" (Matthew 21:14; cf. Acts 3:1–10).[29] In this Jesus was fulfilling what had been promised through the prophets (see Isaiah 35:5, 6; Jeremiah 31:8; then Matthew 11:5; 15:30, 31; Luke 14:13, 21).

Jerusalem: The City of the King (vv. 9–12)

The story of David's rise from the young shepherd lad in Bethlehem (1 Samuel 16) to king of all Israel has reached its climax.[30] We are invited to pause and observe the new king, secure in his new home. Our attention moves from the city (v. 9) to David (v. 10), then from the city's most important building for the time being (v. 11) to the great king who now dwelt there (v. 12). Jerusalem became important because it became David's city.

Great City (v. 9)

> And David lived in the stronghold and called it the city of David. And David built the city all around from the Millo inward. (v. 9)

In other words, Jerusalem became David's royal city—the city of God's king. David took up residence in "the stronghold of Zion" (v. 7), the fortress on the hill to the southeast. The location of the city as well as its natural topography made it ideal. Although the text makes no direct reference to these features, it is clear that the city, centrally located on the border of Judah and Benjamin (Joshua 15:8), was highly suited for the new king's reign over the whole nation. Since the city had not previously been taken, it belonged to no particular Israelite tribe (although theoretically allocated to Benjamin, Joshua 18:28) and could therefore be associated with David himself (hence "the city of David," v. 7). The building works (fortifications) speak of a king secure and prosperous. The Millo was probably a well-known part of Jerusalem's fortifications.[31] It may refer to "a system of artificial terraces supported by retaining walls with leveled filling, and by other substructures,"[32] uncovered by archaeologists.

Great David (v. 10)

> And David became greater and greater, for the LORD, the God of hosts, was with him. (v. 10)

David's story began with the Lord's choice of a shepherd boy to be his king (1 Samuel 16:1, 12). The most important force determining the course of events was the Lord's presence "with" David (v. 10). We have been reminded of this at a number of points in the story (1 Samuel 16:18; 17:37; 18:12, 14, 28; 20:13; see also 2 Samuel 7:3, 9), but even when it is not explicitly mentioned (as, for example, in 3:1) we must understand that David's life only makes sense when we see his place in *God's* purposes.[33]

"The LORD of hosts" is a title for God that appeared for the first time in the Bible in 1 Samuel 1:3 (then in 1 Samuel 1:11; 4:4; 15:2; 17:45; 2 Samuel 6:2, 18; 7:8, 26, 27). "Hosts" appears to refer to the heavenly powers at the Lord's disposal. The expansion of the title here ("the LORD, the *God of* hosts," v. 10) emphasizes the majesty of the King behind the king.[34]

Great Palace (v. 11)

This sketch of David's greatness and that of his city is not constrained by chronology.[35] The writer is looking back from his vantage point and outlining key highlights. In due course[36] David's fame spread.

> And Hiram king of Tyre sent messengers to David, and cedar trees, also carpenters and masons who built David a house. (v. 11)

Tyre was the most important seaport on the coast of Phoenicia, about 100 miles north of Jerusalem.[37] Apart from one passing reference in Joshua 19:29, this is the first substantial appearance of Tyre in the Bible. In due course, however, Tyre and its king will epitomize human arrogance (see especially Ezekiel 26:1—28:19; also Isaiah 23:1–18; Joel 3:4–8; Amos 1:9, 10; Zechariah 9:2–4; cf. Luke 10:13, 14).

It is likely that Hiram's approach to David occurred after David had subdued the Philistines (5:17–25). The king of Tyre was no doubt grateful to see this neighbor weakened and was eager to secure good relations with the victor, as well as access to trade routes through the territory David now controlled.

How different were the messengers Hiram sent to David in Jerusalem from the series of messengers sent to and from David through his years in Hebron (2:5; 3:12, 14). These messengers came from a foreign king, apparently seeking good relations with the "great" king in Jerusalem. Gifts from the king of Tyre contributed to the building of David's royal "house" (v. 11).

It is probably right to see two sides to Hiram's generosity to David. On the one hand it was a sign of David's greatness (see Psalm 45:12). It was an acknowledgment that the king in Jerusalem was a blessing to the nations! It was a token of David's significance reaching beyond the borders of Israel. On the other hand we should also see a hint of trouble to come. The involvement of Hiram with the king in Jerusalem begins but does not end here. Hiram will still be around in Solomon's day (1 Kings 5:1; 9:11, 12). It is probable that the foreign influences that eventually corrupted Solomon's kingdom included influences from Tyre (see 1 Kings 11:1–8[38]). The whole troublesome story of the kingdom began with Israel's desire to have a king "like the nations" (1 Samuel 8:5, 20). The king of Tyre was just such a king.[39]

Great King (v. 12)

Nonetheless, although there may be hints here of future troubles, the focus of attention is the establishment of God's king in Jerusalem and God's purpose for him.

> And David knew that the LORD had established him king over Israel, and
> that he had exalted his kingdom for the sake of his people Israel. (v. 12)

"David knew" (v. 12). Here is the faith of David. He trusted the promises of God concerning him and knew that the present situation had come about because the Lord had been faithful to these promises. Hannah's prayer had summed up that promise many years previously: "The LORD . . . will give strength to his king and exalt the horn of his anointed" (1 Samuel 2:10). He had done just that. What David knew is summed up in two points.

First, "the LORD had established him king over Israel" (v. 12). An observer of the events that led to David's becoming king over all Israel would see a complex of factors, some of which we have followed through the account in 2 Samuel up to this point. There have been lies, betrayal, murder, ambition, and treachery. However, it was not Abner, Joab, Rechab, or Baanah who established David's kingdom (any more than it was the young Amalekite who brought Saul's crown to David in Ziklag). It was the Lord. And David knew it.

Second, David knew why the Lord had made him a great king: "he had exalted his kingdom [that is, his kingship, his royal rule] *for the sake of his people Israel*" (v. 12).[40] David was not king for *David's* sake. The Lord made David a great king for the good of *his people Israel*. As Samuel had said long ago, "It has pleased the LORD to make you a people for himself" (1 Samuel 12:22). Now it had pleased the Lord to make David king for the good of this people. And David knew it.

Remember God's purpose for "his people Israel" (v. 12). Ultimately it was that "in [them] all the families of the earth shall be blessed" (Genesis 12:3). God made David great in the service of his purpose for his people Israel, a purpose that would ultimately be realized through the person and work of the Son of David of whom the New Testament speaks. He, too, would be one who came to serve, not to be served. For the good of his people he would "give his life as a ransom" (Matthew 20:28).

The importance of Jerusalem is that it is the city of this great king. Old Jerusalem was the city of David, the place where God's king reigned. The Lord says, "I have set my King on Zion, my holy hill" (Psalm 2:6).

New Jerusalem will be the city of Jesus (see Hebrews 12:22, 24; Revelation 14:1; 21:2, 22, 23). We look forward to the new Jerusalem because we look forward to the city where Jesus is the King.

Jerusalem: Where David Takes . . . (vv. 13–16)

However, the greatness of David's kingdom (and therefore of David's city) needs to be qualified. The frank honesty of the Bible's account is often astonishing. Here, at the very point where we have been shown the greatness of David, we are given indications of weaknesses that will one day undermine David's kingdom. The foreign relations represented by Hiram may already have hinted at trouble ahead. But the first words of verse 13 are alarming. "And David *took* . . ."

In the context of the newly established king of all Israel, these words must remind us of the stern warning of Samuel years earlier about "the ways of the king who will reign over you": "he will *take* . . . he will *take* . . . he will *take*" (see 1 Samuel 8:11–17). Samuel (by way of contrast) had defended his own leadership of Israel: he had *not* "taken" (1 Samuel 12:3–5). It is troubling to hear that a summary of one aspect of David's reign in Jerusalem begins, "And David *took* . . ." (v. 13).

> And David took more concubines and wives from Jerusalem, after he came from Hebron, and more sons and daughters were born to David. And these are the names of those who were born to him in Jerusalem: Shammua, Shobab, Nathan, Solomon, Ibhar, Elishua, Nepheg, Japhia, Elishama, Eliada, and Eliphelet. (vv. 13–16)

What David took adds to the disturbing nature of this report: "more concubines and wives" (v. 13). We noticed in 3:2–5 (the list of six sons born to David in the Hebron years) that there was more than a hint of trouble in the multiplication of David's wives. Now the problem is magnified considerably. Although once again the narrator makes no explicit judgment concerning this, the requirement of Deuteronomy 17:17 cannot be forgotten. Already we are beginning to see that great David will fail to be everything that God's king must be.[41]

The mention of "concubines" (*before* "wives,"[42] v. 13) may indicate the narrator's disapproval of "David's proclivity for the trappings of a typical ancient Near Eastern monarch, including a harem."[43] Certainly "concubines" adds to the problematic tone of the plural "wives."[44]

Furthermore his taking these women "from Jerusalem" (v. 13) may indicate that they (or some of them) were Jebusite.[45] It is likely that some of these arrangements had a political dimension, possibly in forging David's relationship with the previous inhabitants of Jerusalem. The seeds of Solomon's downfall (1 Kings 11:1–11) can therefore be seen in David's reign.

The most important name in the list of David's sons born in Jerusalem is

Solomon. Assuming that the list is in the order of birth, Solomon, the fourth son born in Jerusalem, was David's tenth son. Like him, Shammua, Shobab, and Nathan[46] were sons of Bathsheba (called Bath-shua in 1 Chronicles 3:5). The mention of these sons anticipates the great troubles that will follow from David's adultery with Bathsheba (2 Samuel 11, 12).

For several reasons, therefore, this paragraph suggests that old Jerusalem was the place of David's failure as well as his greatness. Just as the Bible will come to look forward to a new and better David, so we who believe God's promises look forward to a new and a better Jerusalem, where God will make "*all things* new" (Revelation 21:5).

Embrace this hope. Delight in this hope. Find comfort in this hope. Because of this hope, do not despair. Pray, "Your kingdom come" (Matthew 6:10).

We do need to understand, however, that the new Jerusalem, like the old, has enemies. The citizens of Jerusalem experience conflict, as we are about to see.

12

"The Nations Rage and the Peoples Plot in Vain"

2 SAMUEL 5:17–25

IT IS NOT POSSIBLE to be a Christian and escape conflict. We are citizens of *Jerusalem.* To be sure, our citizenship is of the Jerusalem *above* (Galatians 4:26; cf. Philippians 3:20), "the *heavenly* Jerusalem" (Hebrews 12:22). It is of utmost importance to understand and insist that the New Jerusalem is not to be defended by us through physical violence (see Ephesians 6:10–20; 2 Corinthians 10:3–6). Nonetheless Jerusalem has always been a center of conflict. It is the city of God's King. Therefore hostility to God and his King is focused there. It used to be the Jerusalem below, the earthly Jerusalem, the city of David. Today the enemies of God's kingdom direct their aggression against the heavenly king and the citizens of his city (cf. Revelation 20:9).[1]

Hostility against God and his King has been a feature of human life since the initial disobedience of Genesis 3. It is the monumental stupidity of the peoples of the world to oppose, resist, and defy God and the king he has set on Zion. This is a major theme of the Book of Psalms, introduced in the opening words of Psalm 2:

> Why do the nations rage
>   and the peoples plot in vain?
> The kings of the earth set themselves,
>   and the rulers take counsel together,
>   against the LORD and against his Anointed, saying,
> "Let us burst their bonds apart
>   and cast away their cords from us." (Psalm 2:1–3)

This hostility reached a peak when "in this city" of Jerusalem the words of Psalm 2 were dramatically realized. Believers who subsequently experienced this continued aggression understood and prayed:

> For truly in this city there were gathered together against your holy servant Jesus, whom you anointed, both Herod and Pontius Pilate, along with the Gentiles [or, nations] and the peoples of Israel . . . (Acts 4:27)

Christian believers today should not be surprised that this hostility is still our experience. There are (as there always have been) formidable voices and threatening powers raging against the Lord and his Christ. We serve him, knowing that the Lord *has* set his King on Zion, and he will "break them with a rod of iron and dash them in pieces like a potter's vessel" (Psalm 2:9; see Revelation 2:27; 12:5; 19:15).

This is precisely what happened when God's king was *first* established in Zion (5:12). In 5:17–25 the Philistines enter the story of God's kingdom once again. They are the enemies of David (v. 20).

The Philistines have been part of this story from the beginning. In 1 Samuel 4 it was the Philistines who defeated the Israelites, captured the ark of the covenant, and caused the death of Eli. In 1 Samuel 5, 6 the Philistines were briefly brought into submission to the Lord in a most remarkable way, with no help from the Israelites. In 1 Samuel 7 the Philistines again threatened the Israelites, who were delivered through the prayers of Samuel. In 1 Samuel 8, when the people asked for a king to "go out before us and fight our battles" (1 Samuel 8:20), the Philistines were no doubt very much in their thoughts. When the Lord sent Samuel to anoint Saul, the promise was, "He shall save my people from the hand of the Philistines" (1 Samuel 9:16). Saul failed to do that (see 1 Samuel 10:5[2]). Indeed Saul's first major act of disobedience (1 Samuel 13) was under the threat of the Philistines. Saul's son Jonathan then showed up his father's failure by a defeat of the Philistines that was, however, "not . . . great" (1 Samuel 14:30). The next appearance of the Philistines was perhaps the most memorable of all. A lad from Bethlehem killed Goliath of Gath, and consequently the Philistines were driven from the land of the Israelites (1 Samuel 17). David continued to give Philistines a hard time (1 Samuel 18:27, 30; 19:8; 23:1–5), until he was forced by Saul's murderous pursuit of him to seek refuge among the Philistines and convince both the Philistines and Saul that he had become an ally of the old enemy (1 Samuel 27; cf. 1 Samuel 21:10–15). This deception was not entirely convincing, and David was excluded from the ranks of the

Philistines when they launched their final assault against Saul (1 Samuel 29), in which Saul died (1 Samuel 31).

The opening chapters of 2 Samuel have been concerned with the aftermath of Saul's death (1:1a). The absence of any further information about the Philistines in these chapters is curious.[3] We must assume that they were a significant factor throughout the events of 1:1—5:12. Their decisive victory at Mount Gilboa resulted in a Philistine occupation of many northern cities (1 Samuel 31:7). Their dominance of the north may have influenced David's going first to the southern town of Hebron (2:1–4). Ish-bosheth's failure to establish himself in Mahanaim may also have had something to do with Philistine supremacy. However, for the narrator the Philistines were in the background and not worth mentioning until David became king of all Israel.

There are two parts to what happened next:

(1) Hearing the news (v. 17).
(2) Reactions to the news (vv. 18–25).

Hearing the News (v. 17)

It was the news of David being made king of the whole nation that triggered a response from the Philistines. News of this response then reached David.

What the Philistines Heard (v. 17a)

When the Philistines heard that David had been anointed king over Israel, all the Philistines went up to search for David. (v. 17a)

The news that reached the ears of the Philistines had been told to us in 5:3. It was gospel-like news: "David has been anointed king" (v. 17). It was like the gospel of Jesus: "Jesus is the Christ." It was good news, but only for those who welcomed it. For others the gospel is terrifying news (see Revelation 14:6, 7). For the Philistines the gospel of David was not good news.

We have noted earlier some imprecision in the chronology of events in this chapter. However, the narrator seems to set two sequences of events beside one another, in parallel, both being consequences of David's being anointed in Hebron as king over Israel (5:3). First we heard how he went and took Jerusalem (5:6–12). Now we learn that (also as a consequence of David's becoming king over Israel) the Philistines went up to search for David (5:17a). The impression given is that these things took place at about the same time.[4]

The news that David had been anointed king over Israel (some twenty miles south of Jerusalem at Hebron) may have caused some confusion among the Philistines. On the one hand, for a long time David had been the leader of numerous Israelite victories over the Philistines. The idea of *David* becoming king over the recently defeated nation may therefore have been disturbing. On the other hand, more recently he had made himself out to be a loyal servant of the Philistine ruler Achish, who trusted him (1 Samuel 27:5, 12). Other Philistine commanders did not share Achish's gullibility (1 Samuel 29). The news that David had been anointed king over Israel therefore meant that either the Philistines had a puppet king who would keep the Israelites under the Philistine thumb or they had a big problem on their hands.

The Philistines concluded that they had a problem on their hands. Even Achish must have now seen through David's duplicity. He had become king over Israel without a word of consultation with his Philistine "master"! Their response to the news was, "all the Philistines [that is, presumably, the whole army] went up to search for David" (v. 17). They could have sent messengers to sound out David's intentions. That was not considered necessary. They sent a much more substantial force with obvious purpose.

For readers of the narrative this purpose is doubly ominous. "To search for David" (v. 17) reminds us of the many chapters of 1 Samuel where we have read of Saul "searching for" (sometimes translated "seeking") David (see 1 Samuel 19:2, 10; 20:1; 22:23; 23:10, 14, 15, 25; 24:2; 25:26, 29; 26:2, 20; 27:1, 4).[5] Saul was now dead, and David was king, but the Philistines were now "seeking" him. This suggests that David had not yet taken up residence in Jerusalem, or at least that the Philistines had not heard that he had.

What David Heard (v. 17b)

News of the Philistine movement reached David. "But David heard of it and went down to the stronghold" (v. 17b). The arrangement of the narrative that we have already noted suggests that David took Jerusalem at about the same time as the Philistines were moving eastward in search of him. We may suppose therefore that David was in Jerusalem by the time he heard of their advance.

The news that the Philistines were approaching in great numbers would have had unambiguous significance for David. Despite his recent deception of Achish, the Philistines had always been David's enemy because they had always been Israel's enemy (most recently recall his words in 1:20). The approach of the Philistine hordes could only have been seen by David as a threat to him and his people.

His response to the news was that he "went down to the stronghold"

(v. 17). If we are right to assume that David was now in Jerusalem, then it seems that he moved into a defensive position in "the stronghold of Zion," mentioned twice a few lines earlier (5:7, 9).[6]

Reactions to the News (vv. 18–25)

The account continues with alternating scenes, showing us the actions of the Philistines and of David.

What the Philistines Did (v. 18)

"Now the Philistines had come and spread out in the Valley of Rephaim" (v. 18). That is what the Philistines did in response to the news of David's kingdom.

The Valley of Rephaim ran southwest of Jerusalem.[7] Its northern end was on the boundary between Judah and Benjamin (Joshua 15:8; 18:16). Perhaps by now they had learned that David was in Jerusalem, and their movement here was strategic preparation for an attack on the city, cutting David off from access to his substantial support in the south.[8]

The valley's name added to the threatening sound of any news of the Philistine presence there that reached David. The "Rephaim" were giants.[9] "Philistines in the Valley of the Giants" would have triggered a powerful memory for David of one terrifying Philistine giant (1 Samuel 17). What did David do in response to the news of the Philistine threat?

What David Did (vv. 19–21)

David's actions were highly significant. He acted as God's king should act.

He Asked (v. 19a)

First, he prayed. "And David inquired of the Lord, 'Shall I go up against the Philistines? Will you give them into my hand?'" (v. 19a).

Precisely as in 2:1, David asked the Lord whether he should "go up" (v. 19). This time it was not to Hebron, to be welcomed as king by the people of Judah, but into battle against the Philistines.[10] God's king does nothing by his own will. In this David was like Jesus, who said, "I can do nothing on my own. As I hear, I judge, and my judgment is just, because I seek not my own will but the will of him who sent me" (John 5:30).

David not only asked the Lord for direction ("Shall I go up . . . ?"), he asked for a promise ("Will you give them . . . ?" v. 19). He would obey God's command and trust his promise.

He Heard (v. 19b)

Second, he received an answer from the Lord. "And the LORD said to David, 'Go up, for I will certainly give the Philistines into your hand'" (v. 19b). As elsewhere, the narrator is much less interested in how David received this answer than in the answer itself. David received the command and the promise he sought. In this he was very different from Saul, who found that the Lord would not answer him (1 Samuel 14:37; 28:6, 15). God answers his king (see Psalm 2:7–9; cf. John 12:49, 50).

He Obeyed (v. 20a)

Third, David obeyed the Lord's command and received what the Lord promised. "And David came to Baal-perazim, and David defeated them there" (v. 20a).

Baal-perazim (the name was not given until after David's victory, v. 20b) was apparently a mountain (see Isaiah 28:21) from which David could attack at least some of the Philistines in the Valley of Rephaim. Since the Philistines were "spread out" in the Valley of Rephaim (v. 18), this was probably a skirmish with a limited number of Philistines. In this concise account we are to understand that David was accompanied by "his men" (see v. 21), the very men with whom he took Jerusalem ("his men" in 5:6).

Without pausing to give details, the narrator tells us, "David defeated them there" (v. 20). That is, as promised, the Lord gave the Philistines into David's hand.

He Remembered (v. 20b)

Fourth, David ensured that this event would be remembered. The mountain was named after it.

> And [David] said, "The LORD has broken through my enemies before me like a breaking flood." Therefore the name of that place is called Baal-perazim. (v. 20b)

God's king had been the agent of the Lord's terrible wrath, bursting forth like a flash flood "before" David (v. 20). This was not to be forgotten, and so David named the mountain where it happened Baal-perazim.[11] "Baal-perazim" means "Lord[12] of breaking through" or "bursting forth." The terminology will be used again in 2 Samuel 6 where David will have a rather more troubling experience of the Lord who breaks out (6:8).

It is noteworthy that just as the king had done the Lord's will, so the

Lord had overthrown *David's* enemies. David's enemies in this context were the Lord's enemies. That is what the Philistines were.

He Triumphed (v. 21)

Fifth, the triumph of David over the Philistines, which was in fact the Lord's victory over *his* enemies, took a particularly interesting form. "And the Philistines left their idols there, and David and his men carried them away" (v. 21).

The idolatry of the Philistines epitomized their corruption. Much earlier they had dared to put the captured "ark of the covenant of the LORD of hosts, who is enthroned on the cherubim" (1 Samuel 4:4) into the house of their idol Dagon (1 Samuel 5:2). They suffered for their presumption; their idols failed them (1 Samuel 5, 6). But they did not learn. Years later, after butchering the body of Saul, they sent it to the house of their idols and put his armor in the temple of Ashtaroth.[13] This was "good news" for the pagans (1 Samuel 31:9, 10). It seemed as though their idols had triumphed. It is fitting that David's decisive victory over the Philistines involved taking away their idols. David and his men carrying away the Philistine idols is a fitting conclusion to the story of the Philistine hostility to Israel that had begun with the Philistines taking the ark of God.[14] The tables had been decisively turned. "Thus, under David, the lost glory of Israel is being restored."[15]

What David Did the Next Time (vv. 22–25)

The victory at Baal-perazim was the beginning of the end for the Philistines. They regrouped and tried again to deal with God's king. "And the Philistines came up yet again and spread out in the Valley of Rephaim" (v. 22). The action, strategy, and intention had not changed (just as the wording of verse 22 has hardly changed from verse 18). What did David do?

He Asked and Heard Again (vv. 23, 24)

David did as he had done before. He prayed to the Lord, and he heard the Lord's reply.

> And when David inquired of the LORD, he said, "You shall not go up; go around to their rear, and come against them opposite the balsam trees.[16] And when you hear the sound of marching in the tops of the balsam trees, then rouse yourself,[17] for then the LORD has gone out before you to strike down the army of the Philistines." (vv. 23, 24)

We assume that David's questions were the same as before (v. 19a). The Lord's answer, however, was not the same. "Go up" (v. 19) became "You shall not go up" (v. 23). In other words, the earlier straightforward attack was not to be repeated. David probably now faced a considerably larger Philistine force.[18] We may assume that David and his men were thoroughly outnumbered. This time the Lord ordered a surprise attack from the rear.

The most interesting element of this was the signal to attack. They would hear "the sound of marching" (v. 24) in the trees. I doubt that this was simply the rustling of leaves in the wind.[19] It was the signal that the Lord himself ("the LORD, the God of hosts," 5:10) had "gone out before you" (v. 24). Long ago the Israelites had asked for a king to "go out before us and fight our battles" (1 Samuel 8:20). This is better. The Lord himself would go out before his king and strike down the enemy.

He Obeyed and Triumphed Again (v. 25)

"And David did as the LORD commanded him, and struck down the Philistines from Geba to Gezer" (v. 25). In obedience to the Lord, the Lord's king defeated his enemies.

"From Geba to Gezer" (v. 25) means that David drove the Philistines not only out of the Valley of Rephaim (southwest of Jerusalem) but also from the area to the north where they had been since the battle of Mount Gilboa (Geba being about six miles north of Jerusalem).[20] This suggests a wider campaign by David against the Philistines than the battle in the Valley of Rephaim. Gezer, twenty miles west of Jerusalem, was in the foothills and close to the Philistine territory of the coastal plain. This was a decisive turning of the tables. The Philistine victory at Mount Gilboa and their occupation of Israel (1 Samuel 31) was over. Indeed, the Philistine presence on Israelite soil since their much earlier victory at Aphek (1 Samuel 4) had at last been brought to an end. By the hand of his servant David the Lord had saved his people Israel from the hand of the Philistines, just as he had promised (see 2 Samuel 3:18; cf. 1 Samuel 9:16). With the enemy defeated and driven out, the way was now clear for David's long-promised kingdom (God's kingdom!) to be established.

The story is remote, ancient, strange to our ears—unless we know that God has again set his King on Zion, his holy hill. Then this story is a revelation. The nations rage still. The peoples plot against the Lord and his Christ. We who belong to him remember the victory of God's king from Mount Zion over the Philistines. It was a taste of the victory that Jesus has won over all the powers of evil on the cross. As we experience the conflict that inevitably comes against the citizens of Jerusalem, what shall we say? "If God is for us [as he was for David and his men], who can be against us?" (Romans 8:31). Obey him. Trust him.

13

"Rejoice with Trembling"

2 SAMUEL 6:1–11

NOTHING COULD BE MORE FOOLISH than a casual attitude toward Jesus Christ. Those who despise him are making a very big mistake. Those who ignore him are just as careless. Those who claim to follow him but take him for granted, caring little about his perfection and power, will one day regret their casual attitude toward the Lord Jesus Christ.

In Christ Jesus "all the fullness of God was pleased to dwell," and "in him the whole fullness of deity dwells bodily" (Colossians 1:19; 2:9). He is the one through whom, for whom, and in whom "all things were created, in heaven and on earth, visible and invisible, whether thrones or dominions or rulers or authorities" (Colossians 1:16). Furthermore, through Jesus Christ, by his death on the cross, God has "reconciled" us to our maker (Colossians 1:22) and defeated all alienation, hostility, and evil in the whole of creation (Colossians 1:20; 2:15). His resurrection from the dead was the beginning of the future that God has promised (Colossians 1:5, 18; 3:3, 4). Nothing is more important than who he is and what he has done.

Therefore he is not answerable to us; we are answerable to him. He is not obliged to us; we are obliged to him. He does not exist to do our will; we exist to do his will. It does not matter whether he pleases us; it matters supremely that we please him. There is no reason at all that he should meet our ideas of right and goodness; we need forgiveness for every failure to be and do what is good and right in his eyes. And all of this is how it should be.

Do you believe that? Are you glad to submit your thoughts, hopes, and expectations to the goodness of Christ Jesus the Lord? As you face the future are you thankful that he is the wise and all-powerful king and you are not?

These questions can too easily be answered glibly.

Part of the preparation that enables us to take Jesus as seriously as we must was the appointment of David as king over God's people Israel about 1,000 years before Jesus came into the world. What happened in 2 Samuel 6 shook David to the core but taught him the terrifying yet wonderful truth that the Lord God is above and beyond human comprehension, evaluation, or control. The most important thing about David's kingdom was that the Lord God was King.

Second Samuel 6 is about the ark of the covenant being brought by David into his city, Jerusalem. This (as we will see) was momentous in significance, but it requires careful attention from us if we are to learn the lessons of this event. Why did David bring up the ark from the place where it had been left for years? We will see that David's first attempt to do this failed in most distressing and tragic circumstances. Why was that? We will subsequently see that when David did joyfully bring the ark into Jerusalem, the rejoicing led to a bitter row. What was that about?

We will follow the story in its two parts. In this chapter we will see David's terrifying failed attempt to bring the ark to the city. In our next chapter we will see his joyous but problematic success.

In the first part of this remarkable story we will see:

(1) A mighty project (vv. 1, 2).
(2) A celebration (vv. 3–5).
(3) A disaster (vv. 6–9).
(4) A project abandoned (vv. 10, 11).

A Mighty Project (vv. 1, 2)

The chapter begins with David engaged in preparations for a major event. Although we are given little by way of direct explanation, the great importance of this project becomes clear when we recall certain things that had happened previously.

> David again gathered all the chosen men of Israel, thirty thousand. And David arose and went with all the people who were with him from[1] Baale-judah to bring up from there the ark of God, which is called by the name of the LORD of hosts who sits enthroned on the cherubim. (vv. 1, 2)

The defeat of the Philistines, and particularly their pursuit "from Geba to Gezer" (5:25), had made it possible for David to undertake this venture, the full and historic significance of which even he could not have been completely aware. David's great victory over the occupying foe had freed him to act without Philistine interference in parts of his kingdom that had, since the battle of Mount Gilboa (1 Samuel 31), been dominated by the enemy presence.

Indeed the double defeat of the Philistines in the Valley of Rephaim, and the capture of their idols (5:17–25), was a striking reversal of the double defeat of the Israelites by the Philistines at Aphek about seventy years previously,[2] when the ark of the covenant had been taken by the enemy (1 Samuel 4:1–11).[3] Then it was said, "The glory has departed from Israel, for the ark of God has been captured" (1 Samuel 4:22). Those troubles had led to Israel demanding to have a king (1 Samuel 8:5). King David was now acting to return "the glory" (1 Samuel 4:22) to Israel.

The Great Gathering (v. 1)

David understood that what he was proposing to do was big.[4] The gathering of the 30,000 "chosen men of Israel" (v. 1) sounds like preparations for a serious battle.[5] "Chosen men" usually refers to troops (Judges 20:15, 16, 34; 2 Chronicles 13:3, 17). On two previous occasions Saul had taken "*three* thousand chosen men of all Israel" (1 Samuel 24:2; 26:2). These were trusted, able fighters whom Saul had engaged in his pursuit of David and his men. David now gathered ten times that number.[6] What was he about to do that called for such a force?

"Again" in verse 1 is a little perplexing. David had not previously gathered all the chosen men of Israel. The recently narrated military actions against the Jebusites and the Philistines involved David and "his men" (5:6, 21), almost certainly a more limited group.[7] The gathering this time was on a grander scale, signifying an even greater enterprise than the taking of Jerusalem or the defeat of the Philistines. Representatives of all Israel were involved. This suggests that "again" points back to 5:1, 3, where "all the tribes of Israel" had first come to David at Hebron.[8] What David was about to do was the most important thing that had happened since that day when he was anointed king over all Israel.

Indeed the crowd that accompanied David was even more extensive than the 30,000 chosen men of Israel. "All the people who were with him" (v. 2a) no doubt also included "his men" (5:6), but in addition (at least representatively) all those who were now identified with David and his kingdom. In verse 5 they will be called "all the house of Israel." What David was about to do was important for "all the people who were *with him*" (v. 2).

The Forgotten Place (v. 2a)

The action began from a location named here Baale-judah (v. 2, meaning "Baals of Judah" or "Lords of Judah"[9]). This was certainly the place elsewhere called Kiriath-jearim[10] ("city of forests").[11] Our narrator has chosen to use what we may suppose was an ancient pagan name ("Baale") for the place, perhaps distinguishing it from other places of that name (this one was in "Judah").[12] This contributes to a sense of obscurity. This was a forgotten place in Israel, despite the most remarkable treasure that was located there.

Baale-judah (that is, Kiriath-jearim) was located about nine miles west of Jerusalem (roughly halfway between Geba and Gezer).[13] This is where the ark had been left some seven decades earlier, following its dramatic time in the possession of the Philistines and after the people of nearby Beth-shemesh had suffered a terrible tragedy in connection with the ark (1 Samuel 5:1—7:2). The ark had been taken by the men of Kiriath-jearim and placed in "the house of Abinadab on the hill" and put in the charge of his son Eleazar (1 Samuel 7:1). No mention has been made of Kiriath-jearim (by that or any other name) through more than seventy years covered by the narrative from 1 Samuel 7:3 to 2 Samuel 6:2. It had been all but forgotten.

The Astonishing Purpose (v. 2b)

David's purpose in taking the vast crowd with him to Baale-judah was "to bring up from there the ark of God" (v. 2). Apart from a reference to the ark accompanying the people of Israel on a particular occasion in the days of Saul (1 Samuel 14:18),[14] the ark has not been mentioned in the narrative since it had been abandoned at Kiriath-jearim after its return from the Philistines. Why did David decide to "bring up from there the ark of God" (v. 2)? What was going through his mind?

The ark was the most important symbol of the relationship between God and his people Israel. That is why it was known as "the ark of *the covenant*" (Numbers 10:33; 14:44; Deuteronomy 10:8; 31:9, 25, 26; Joshua 3:3, 6, 8; Judges 20:27; 1 Samuel 4:3, 4, 5; 2 Samuel 15:24; 1 Kings 3:15; 6:19; etc.). It represented God's promises to his people and their consequential obligations, a relationship summed up in the word "covenant."

The ark was a gold-plated wooden box, approximately three feet, nine inches long by two feet, three inches both wide and high. It had been made in the days of Moses according to God's instructions. It was fitted with gold rings, through which gold-plated wooden poles were placed by which it was to be carried. On top of the ark was a pure gold cover with a solid gold cherub at each end (Exodus 25:10–22; 37:1–9). Inside the ark were the stone tablets on which were engraved the words of the ten commandments, beginning, "I am the LORD your God, who brought you out of the land of Egypt, out of the house of slavery. You shall have no other gods before me . . ." (Exodus 20:2, 3; see also Exodus 25:16, 21; 40:20; Deuteronomy 10:1–5; 1 Kings 8:9; cf. Hebrews 9:4).

This "ark" (v. 2) represented the covenant between the Lord and Israel—God's promise to be their God and their obligation to be his people. In the ark God represented himself to Israel. The neglect of the ark in the days of Saul (cf. 1 Chronicles 13:3) was an expression of Saul's failure to "fear . . . serve . . . obey . . . and . . . follow the LORD" (see 1 Samuel 12:14). Just as David knew where the ark had been left, he no doubt knew the story of how it got there. He certainly knew its central importance for the life of the people of the Lord over whom he was now king. He determined that the ark (and therefore what the ark represented) would be neglected no longer.

The Breathtaking Significance (v. 2c)

The ark is frequently, as here, called simply "the ark of God" (1 Samuel 3:3; 4:11; etc.). However it had a number of other names,[15] which pointed to its astonishing significance. It was "called by the name of the LORD of hosts who sits enthroned on the cherubim" (v. 2b). There are at least four important points here.

First, the ark bore God's "*name*" (v. 2).[16] This indicates that God was the owner of the ark. More that that, God's "name" is his self-revelation. God's people have the privilege and responsibility of knowing God "by . . . name" (see Exodus 6:3). The fact that God is known by a number of names ("Yahweh," "God," "Father," and more[17]) is less important than the fact that God has made known his "name," by which his people may know him and call upon him. The place where the people were to meet with God was the "place where I cause my name to be remembered" (Exodus 20:24), or "the place that the LORD your God will . . . make his name dwell there" (Deuteronomy 12:11). Furthermore God's "name" is his honor and reputation (see Joshua 7:9; 1 Samuel 12:22; Psalm 106:8; Jeremiah 14:21; Ezekiel 20:9, 14, 22; Matthew 6:9). The name of God in both these senses (revelation and reputation) was closely associated with the ark. Symbolically David had set out to bring up from obscurity in Baale-judah *the name of God*.

Second, the name mentioned here is "the LORD of hosts" (v. 2). This reminds us that "David became greater and greater, for *the Lord, the God of hosts*, was with him" (5:10). David's journey to the throne had begun when he defeated Goliath "in the name of *the Lord of hosts*" (1 Samuel 17:45). The God of the heavenly armies was the one whose name David intended to bring up from Baale-judah.

Third, the ark represented God's kingship. He "sits enthroned on the cherubim" (v. 2, see Exodus 25:22; Psalm 80:1; 99:1). The idea appears to be that the Lord is enthroned in Heaven, and on earth the ark is his footstool (1 Chronicles 28:2; cf. Psalm 132:7). The ark was therefore closely associated with the heavenly King who had made David king over his people Israel.

Fourth, the description of the ark here is strongly reminiscent of the very similar description in 1 Samuel 4:4. This is another link between what David was about to do and the events of 1 Samuel 4—7, which had resulted in the ark being put in the place up from which David now intended to bring it. In 1 Samuel 4 the text of Scripture alerted readers to the profound importance of "the ark of the covenant of the LORD of hosts, who is enthroned on the cherubim" (1 Samuel 4:4). The elders of Israel, who were then about to bring it from Shiloh, did not fully understand what they were doing. In a similar way the text in 6:2 points us to the awesome significance of the ark, which David may not yet have fully comprehended.

A Celebration (vv. 3–5)

To understand what happened next we need to be aware that the Lord had long ago given clear instructions to Moses about the way in which the ark was to be moved.[18] It was first to be *covered* with several layers of coverings (Numbers 4:5, 6). It was to be *carried* by the priests, by means of the poles attached to the ark (Exodus 25:13–15; Numbers 4:6, 15; 7:9; Deuteronomy 10:8). "They must not *touch* the holy things [including the ark], lest they die" (Numbers 4:15). "They shall not go in to *look on* the holy things even for a moment, lest they die" (Numbers 4:20).

Careful? (vv. 3, 4)

This is what happened on the day David and the crowds with him came from Baale-judah:

> And they carried the ark of God on a new cart and brought it out of the house of Abinadab, which was on the hill. And Uzzah and Ahio, the sons of Abinadab, were driving the new cart,[19] with the ark of God, and Ahio went before the ark. (vv. 3, 4)

The end of the long period since the ark had been brought *to* "the house of Abinadab on the hill" (1 Samuel 7:1) is marked by an echo of just that phrase. The ark was now being brought *from* "the house of Abinadab, which was on the hill" (2 Samuel 6:3). Its time of obscurity and neglect was over.

We may reasonably suppose that Uzzah and Ahio were priests, like their (grand? [20])father, Abinadab.[21] The scene has the appearance of a careful, respectful, and appropriately dignified procession.

However, if we have in mind God's instructions to Moses, the first thing we notice is that no mention is made of the ark being *covered*. It was therefore probably being carried in full view of everyone. Then the mention of "a new cart" (v. 3) is disturbing if we remember what had happened seventy years earlier. The idea of transporting the ark on "a new cart" came from the pagan Philistine priests and diviners (1 Samuel 6:2, 7). The fact that the ark was transported from Baale-judah in a manner reminiscent of the Philistines' handling of God's ark is troubling, to say the least. The priests were meant to carry the ark by its poles (see 1 Chronicles 15:13).

Joyful (v. 5)

None of these scruples seem to have bothered anyone that day—yet. It was a time for celebration.

> And David and all the house of Israel were celebrating before the Lord, with songs and lyres and harps and tambourines and castanets and cymbals. (v. 5)

To all appearances this was a wonderful occasion. The crowd represented "all the house of Israel" (v. 5), now appropriately seen as a reunited family. Together they were "celebrating" (v. 5). The word suggests happiness and laughter.[22] The source of their joy was the wonder expressed in the procession that was moving from Baale-judah—wonder over *the king* God had given them and *the promises* God had made to his people. If ever Israel had cause for celebration, this day was it. "Before the Lord" (v. 5) is the reality symbolized by the ark. Their joy in the presence of the ark (and all that the ark stood for) was happiness "before the Lord" (v. 5). Their delight was expressed in much music and song.[23]

A Disaster (vv. 6–9)

But it did not last. The laughter and singing was suddenly silenced by a terrible shock that brought the procession and the celebration to an abrupt halt. What happened?

Uzzah's Act (v. 6)

For a brief moment it seemed insignificant.

> And when they came to the threshing floor of Nacon, Uzzah put out his hand to the ark of God and took hold of it, for the oxen stumbled. (v. 6)

The great and noisy procession had not gone far when this apparently minor incident took place. However, the otherwise unknown "threshing floor of Nacon" (v. 6)[24] would forever be remembered because of the bumps in the road just there. A slight stumble[25] by the oxen pulling the new cart, a shudder of the cart itself, a quick response from the priest who was watching the cart's precious load carefully—and all was well. I suspect that you would have had to be watching closely to have even noticed what happened. Thanks to Uzzah's attentive reaction, no harm was done. The ark remained safely on the cart. The procession could continue. So you might think.

The Lord's Anger (v. 7)

No one that day expected or anticipated what then happened.

> And the anger of the LORD was kindled against Uzzah, and God struck him down there because of his error, and he died there beside the ark of God. (v. 7)

The music stopped. The joyful shouts became a trembling silence. The procession changed from an excited, happy parade to a stunned and frightened crowd. There, "beside [literally, with] the ark" (v. 7)[26] was the dead body of Uzzah. What had happened? Why?

Those with long memories (and those who had heard the story) may have immediately thought of what had happened not far away many years ago at Beth-shemesh. It was worse than this. Then seventy[27] men had been struck dead when they looked upon (or into) the ark after its return from the land of the Philistines (1 Samuel 6:19). On that occasion the witnesses understood that this was God's doing, but did not understand why it had happened. They were overwhelmed with fear of the God of the ark. "Who is able to stand before the LORD, this holy God?" they asked (1 Samuel 6:20). That is why the ark had been sent away and left at Kiriath-jearim.

Now Uzzah lay dead beside the ark. This was the Lord's doing. In his anger he struck down Uzzah. It is a horrifying scene. Perhaps the most troubling thing about it is that the text makes almost no attempt to explain *why*

God did this. Why was the Lord's anger kindled? Why did the poor priest have to die? All we are told is "because of his error" (v. 7).[28] What error?

We (the readers) find ourselves in a situation similar to that of the witnesses on that terrible day. Our questions are not answered. Our objections are not satisfied. No doubt we should remember the instructions that God had given to Moses concerning the handling of the ark. These had been largely ignored. However, the text of Scripture at this point does not attempt to justify God's actions to us. There was a reason for what happened ("because of his error," v. 7), but we are not given a fuller explanation.

It is difficult for many people to accept that God does not have to explain himself to us. He is not answerable to us. The reasons for his actions are often hidden from us (see Deuteronomy 29:29). He is not obliged to win our approval. Our reaction to what happened to Uzzah (like the reaction of those who were there) is an excellent indication of whether we believe this.

David's Anger (v. 8)

One person's reaction to what had happened was important enough to be recorded here.

> And David was angry because the LORD had broken out against Uzzah. And that place is called Perez-uzzah to this day. (v. 8)

David's anger is described in similar (although not quite identical) words to the Lord's anger in the previous verse. One subtle difference is that the Lord's anger was directly "against Uzzah" (v. 7). David's anger is not said to be directly against the Lord, but *"because" of* what the Lord had done (v. 8).[29] The difference matters. David hated what had happened, but this did not mean that he hated the Lord. He was deeply troubled by what had happened, but this did not mean that he no longer "knew" God's goodness to him (5:12).

What angered David was that "the LORD had *broken out* against Uzzah." The Hebrew here is a clear echo of 5:20.[30] David had been glad of the Lord's terrifying power when it was directed against his enemies, the Philistines. Then he had named the place after the "Lord of bursting through" ("Baal-perazim," 5:20). It was, however, more troubling when the same terrifying power came against one of his own people. David renamed[31] the threshing floor of Nacon, "Bursting out [against] Uzzah," so ensuring that what happened that day was never forgotten.[32]

David's Fear (v. 9)

David's response to what had happened to Uzzah was similar to the men of Beth-shemesh seventy years earlier.

> And David was afraid of the LORD that day, and he said, "How can the ark of the LORD come to me?" (v. 9)

David did not understand what the Lord had done and therefore what God might do next. The men of Beth-shemesh had asked, "Who is able to stand before the LORD, this holy God?" (1 Samuel 6:20). David's question was essentially the same: "How can the ark of the LORD come to me?"(v. 9).

The question is good. It expresses the opposite of presumption. The person who asks David's question, or the equivalent question of the men of Beth-shemesh, has learned that the Lord God is not under our control or answerable to us. We never fully understand him. We certainly have no control over him. He is the holy God. He is not tame. He really is terrifying.

This may have been the occasion for the composition of Psalm 24,[33] in which David asked a similar question:

> Who shall ascend the hill of the LORD?
>   And who shall stand in his holy place?
> He who has clean hands and a pure heart,
>   who does not lift up his soul to what is false
>   and does not swear deceitfully. (Psalm 24:3, 4)

Understandably David "was afraid of the LORD" (v. 9) that day. This was a proper response, not only to what had happened at Perez-uzzah, but also to who the Lord is (see Psalm 24:1, 2). The Bible teaches that "the fear of the LORD" is the right foundation for human life. It is the recognition of who God is. In particular the king of God's people must "learn to fear the LORD" (Deuteronomy 17:19; see 1 Samuel 12:14). In due course the prophet Isaiah would promise a new king, a descendant of David whose "delight shall be in the fear of the LORD" (Isaiah 11:3). Christian believers are to "walk in the fear of the Lord" (Acts 9:31; cf. 2 Corinthians 5:11).[34]

Fear is not all there is in a proper response to God. Those who know him fear *and* love *and* trust him (Deuteronomy 10:12; Psalm 33:18; 40:3; 115:11). However, we only realize the wonder of this if we truly fear him. Soon David will learn to rejoice as well as fear.[35]

A Project Abandoned (vv. 10, 11)

The men of Beth-shemesh, out of their fear, had sent the ark away to Kiriath-jearim (1 Samuel 6:21). David likewise abandoned his plan to bring the ark up from Baale-Judah.

A Change of Plan (v. 10)

> So David was not willing to take the ark of the LORD into the city of David. But David took it aside to the house of Obed-edom the Gittite. (v. 10)

For the first time we are told (as we might well have guessed) that David's intention had been to bring the ark into Jerusalem, now "the city of David" (v. 10). What had happened to Uzzah, however, changed that. He was no longer "willing" (v. 10) to follow through on this plan. This was not disobedience. The Lord had not told David to bring the ark up, as he had told him to go up to Hebron (2:1) and to attack the Philistines (5:19, 23, 24). This was different. The initiative to bring the ark from Baale-judah was David's. It appeared to be commendable. The death of Uzzah, however, changed David's mind. He could not now see how he and the ark could be together.

Perhaps we should see some degree of presumption in David's earlier plan. Certainly we have noted that the Lord's instructions concerning the ark seem to have been ignored. Any such presumption was now abandoned, along with the plan to bring the ark to Jerusalem.

Just as we have no explanation for the choice, many years previously, of Kiriath-jearim as the place to leave the ark, so the writer gives us no indication of why David chose to put the ark in the house of Obed-edom. No doubt it was nearby and therefore convenient. Was it difficult, after what had happened, to find an Israelite willing to look after the ark? Is that why it was left in the house of a Gittite (that is, a Philistine)?[36] All of these are reasonable suggestions, but the writer does not confirm our suspicions.

A Big Surprise (v. 11)

We are left to imagine the subdued crowd making their way back home. The laughter and singing had died. What an anticlimax! What a letdown! The thousands returned to their families, no doubt perplexed about what to think of the events in which they had participated.

What happened next was as surprising as (though less spectacular than) what had happened to Uzzah.

> And the ark of the LORD remained in the house of Obed-edom the Gittite three months, and the LORD blessed Obed-edom and all his household. (v. 11)

Three months passed. Obed-edom (and we are reminded again that he was a Gittite, a Philistine) did not suffer as Uzzah had. On the contrary, he and "all his household" were "*blessed*" by the Lord (v. 11). What had happened to Uzzah was not the only way in which this holy God acted. In the most surprising place (the house of a Philistine from Gath) his blessing could be known.

It is not necessary for us to know what form that blessing took in those three months. In due course the blessing of God on Obed-edom extended to eight sons and many descendants (see 1 Chronicles 26:4–8). It is enough to realize that the holy God who had his reasons for burning with anger against Uzzah (and he is under no obligation to explain himself to David or to us) chose to bless this foreigner who had no claim on him. We will see the profound effect this had on David in our next chapter.

David was learning to be God's king. He had been right to rejoice before the Lord. But God's king must also fear the Lord (cf. Isaiah 11:2).

As we serve God's King, the great son of David, let the experience of David illuminate our path. In the words of Psalm 2: "Serve the LORD *with fear*, and rejoice *with trembling*" (Psalm 2:11). Do you need to repent of a casual attitude toward God's King?

14

The Joy of Humility and the Misery of Pride

2 SAMUEL 6:12–23

THE ACCOUNT IN 2 SAMUEL 6 of David bringing the ark of the covenant from Kiriath-jearim (or Baale-judah), where it had lain in obscurity for seventy years, to Jerusalem (the city that King David had recently made his own) is one of the Bible's more perplexing stories. As we read this portion of God's Word as Christian believers, we are very conscious of the distance that separates us from David. Whenever we read the Scriptures of the Old Testament it is always important to understand the *difference* that the Lord Jesus Christ has made. This is the key to properly understanding any Old Testament text as it really is—Christian Scripture. Second Samuel 6 is a striking example.

Our King is not the imperfect (though impressive) David, but the Lord Jesus Christ. The presence and promises of God are represented to us not by the ark that bore "the name of the Lord of hosts" (6:2) but by Jesus who bears "the name that is above every name" (Philippians 2:9) and in whom "the whole fullness of deity dwells bodily" (Colossians 2:9). Our King does not reside in the earthly but in the heavenly Jerusalem (Hebrews 12:22, 24).

Far from making 2 Samuel 6 irrelevant to us today, these differences are the key to learning the important lessons of this part of Scripture. As we see David learning to be God's king, we marvel at the perfection of Christ Jesus (Hebrews 5:9; 7:28). As we tremble at the anger of the Lord that burst out against Uzzah (6:7), we shudder at the wrath of God that has been "revealed from heaven against all ungodliness and unrighteousness of men" (Romans 1:18). As we see the foreigner, Obed-edom, "blessed . . . because of the ark

185

of God" (2 Samuel 6:12), we rightly recognize that the blessing of God has been extended to the nations of the world because of Jesus Christ (Galatians 3:14). Superficially 2 Samuel 6 seems strange to us. In fact, however, in these events we find "a shadow of the things to come" (Colossians 2:17)—the kingdom of our Lord Jesus Christ.

Of course, this does not mean that we are immediately *comfortable* with the events of 2 Samuel 6. However, we need to see that our difficulties with this chapter are difficulties with the kingdom of God. This kingdom challenges our ways, our values, and even our morality. Is that not what Jesus did as he proclaimed the gospel of the kingdom, most famously in the so-called Sermon on the Mount (Matthew 5—7)?

After David's first attempt to bring the ark up from Baale-judah (6:1–5), abandoned because of the bursting out of the Lord's anger (6:6–10), a second attempt succeeded, prompted by an outpouring of the Lord's blessing (6:11–19). However, this too was marred by behavior that brought the Lord's displeasure (6:20–23). We turn our attention now to the second attempt and its aftermath, and we will see the strange way in which, in the kingdom of God, there is (1) joy in humility (vv. 12–20a), but (2) misery in pride (vv. 20b–23).

The Joy of Humility (vv. 12–20a)

When David had abandoned his plan to bring the ark up, he had left it in the house of a foreigner named Obed-edom (6:11). Three months passed. We are told little about what happened through those days. I imagine David's confusion. What was he to do about the ark? How could he be king over the Lord's people without proper acknowledgment of the covenant that stood between the Lord and his people? I see him tossing and turning through sleepless nights as the question he had asked on the day that Uzzah died continued to bother him ("How can the ark of the LORD come to me?" [6:9]). I sense the disillusionment of the people who had joined David in the excitement of the procession from Baale-judah ("all the house of Israel," 6:5). So long as they only knew about Uzzah, fear could be their only attitude toward the ark.

David Hears the News (v. 12a)

Then one day some astonishing news reached David.

> And it was told King David, "The LORD has blessed the household of Obed-edom and all that belongs to him, because of the ark of God." (v. 12a)

This was more than a simple report about Obed-edom's experience through the past few months. It was a profound account of the *meaning* of what had happened to him. The message made no mention of what *exactly* had happened to Obed-edom and his household. The emphasis fell entirely on: (a) the character of his experience ("blessed"); (b) the giver of the blessing ("the LORD"); and (c) the reason for the blessing ("because of [on account of] the ark," v. 12).

Certainly this news would have been understood by David as a reversal of what had happened to Uzzah who had experienced the Lord's anger on account of the ark (6:7). As Hannah had proclaimed many years earlier, "The LORD kills *and* brings to life; he brings down to Sheol *and* raises up . . . he brings low *and* he exalts" (1 Samuel 2:6, 7).

Project Renewed (vv. 12b–19)

This news was all that David needed. We may assume that he was longing to resume his earlier plan to bring the ark to Jerusalem. The word about Obed-edom's experience moved him to action.

Some of the details are left to our imagination.[1] The emphasis is almost entirely on the overwhelming joy of the occasion.

With Joy (v. 12b)

> So David went and brought up the ark of God from the house of Obed-edom to the city of David with rejoicing. (v. 12b)

We may assume that a similar crowd was involved as previously (this is confirmed by verse 15 and 1 Chronicles 15:3). However, we should notice that this time there is no mention of "the new cart" or the oxen (2 Samuel 6:3). That wrongheaded aspect of the first attempt to bring the ark was not repeated (this is made explicit in 1 Chronicles 15:13–15). The emphasis of this concise one-sentence summary (which will be elaborated somewhat in verses 13–19) falls on the last word: "rejoicing" (6:12).[2] No doubt we are to understand that this took a similar form to the celebration of verse 5—joyful music and song.

With Trepidation (v. 13)

However, this time it was rejoicing with trembling. "And when those who bore the ark of the LORD had gone six steps, he sacrificed an ox and a fattened animal" (v. 13).

We notice again that the ark was not now on a cart but was being carried. We may assume that "those who bore the ark" (v. 13)[3] were Levites, as they ought to have been (this is confirmed by 1 Chronicles 15:26). More than this, however, any presumption that had been involved in the earlier procession of the ark had gone altogether. This time they moved forward with extreme caution and trepidation. After six steps the procession stopped as an ox and a fattened animal were sacrificed.[4]

At first sight the account seems to suggest that David personally carried out the sacrifices ("*he* sacrificed," 2 Samuel 6:13). This would be surprising. Normally it was priests who did such things. However, this situation was not normal: God's king was ascending to his city with the ark of the covenant. At this point, however, we should probably not read priestly activity by David himself into the account. He was responsible for the sacrifices (he was in charge), but they were probably conducted by the Levites (see 1 Chronicles 15:26).

Although the sacrifices did not involve the tabernacle (as required, for example, in Leviticus 1:3; however, see 1 Samuel 13:9; 14:34, 35), the significance of these sacrifices should be understood from the laws of Leviticus. They were "to make atonement" (Leviticus 1:4).[5] David remembered what had happened to Uzzah "because of his error" (2 Samuel 6:7). The question he asked on that occasion ("How can the ark of the Lord come to me?" v. 9) was now answered: only by atonement being made.

With Humility (vv. 14, 15)

The joy continued, and it was intense. "And David danced before the Lord with all his might"[6] (v. 14a). The striking point in this scene is that "all [the] might" of this great warrior (as David certainly was), this triumphant king of all Israel (which was now undisputed), was directed to dancing "before the Lord" (v. 14). The trappings of pomp and dignity were dropped. Displays of power and prestige were nowhere to be seen. This was not about David. "David danced *before the Lord*" (v. 14).

It was the joy of *humility*; there were no royal robes, no encouragement for the crowd to cheer or bow to David. Indeed "David was wearing a linen ephod" (v. 14b). The significance of this is elusive. On the one hand, a linen ephod was hardly a garment of royal splendor. It was a simple linen item of clothing, probably like an apron. The boy Samuel had worn one during the days of his apprenticeship to Eli (1 Samuel 2:18).[7] It was not the trappings of greatness. If the text implies (as I think it does) that David was wearing *only* a linen ephod, then his deliberate humiliation "before the Lord" (2 Samuel 6:14) is even more obvious. On the other hand, the linen ephod seems to have been a priestly garment (although not prescribed as such by the Law).[8] It was certainly worn by ordinary priests (1 Samuel 22:18). David's linen ephod therefore seems to suggest that his royal status was subordinated here to his role as God's servant and the servant of God's people.[9]

The scene is summed up: "So David and all the house of Israel brought up the ark of the LORD with shouting and with the sound of the horn" (v. 15). Just as in verse 5, this was the king and the whole family of God's people together, rejoicing as they brought the ark of the Lord to Jerusalem.[10]

Another View (v. 16)

As this extraordinary procession approached its destination, the scene shifts for a moment from the jubilant crowd in the street to a window overlooking the scene and one particular observer.

> As the ark of the LORD came into the city of David, Michal the daughter of Saul looked out of the window and saw King David leaping and dancing before the LORD, and she despised him in her heart. (v. 16)

"The ark of the LORD" was coming into "the city of David" (v. 16). That's what was happening. But that is not what Michal saw beneath her window.

Michal is identified not as "the wife of David," but as "the daughter of Saul" (v. 16). This phrase will be repeated in verses 20 and 23. She represents the old, rejected kingdom of her father. She showed herself to be truly "the daughter of Saul" (v. 16).

Years earlier she had loved David (1 Samuel 18:20, 28). Indeed she had put herself in considerable danger in order to enable David (by then her husband) to escape from her father "through the window" of their house (1 Samuel 19:12). During the years of David's absence, as a fugitive from Saul, Michal had been taken from David by her father and given to another (1 Samuel 25:44). More recently David had insisted on her return (2 Samuel 3:13–16). Now Saul's daughter was looking through another window.[11]

What did she see? Not "the ark of the LORD [coming] into the city of David," but "King David leaping and dancing" (6:16). It was undignified. It was embarrassing. She saw the incongruity of "the king" "leaping and dancing." Where was the royal dignity? David's joyful humility before the Lord, Michal saw as conduct unbecoming of a king. "She despised him in her heart" (v. 16). She adopted the attitude that Goliath had once displayed toward David (1 Samuel 17:42) and that certain "worthless fellows" had once shown toward Saul (1 Samuel 10:27), indeed the wicked insolence that Eli and his sons had long ago shown toward the Lord himself (1 Samuel 2:30).[12]

Ironically Michal was contributing to the portrait of God's servant, his chosen one, of whom the prophets would later speak. He will be "one deeply despised, abhorred" (Isaiah 49:7), "despised and rejected" (Isaiah 53:3). He will not, however be "despised or abhorred" by the Lord (Psalm 22:24; cf. 69:33; 102:17). We will hear more from Michal shortly.

The Priest-King (vv. 17–19)

Our attention moves back to the street.

> And they brought in the ark of the LORD and set it in its place, inside the tent that David had pitched for it. And David offered burnt offerings and peace offerings before the LORD. And when David had finished offering the burnt offerings and the peace offerings, he blessed the people in the name of the LORD of hosts and distributed among all the people, the whole multitude of Israel, both men and women, a cake of bread, a portion of meat, and a cake of raisins to each one. Then all the people departed, each to his house. (2 Samuel 6:17–19)

Notice first that the ark was "set . . . in its place" (v. 17). In this way a journey that had begun many years earlier reached its destination. When the Philistines had been forced to send the ark back to Israel some seventy years previously, they had said, "let it return *to its own place*" (1 Samuel 5:11).[13] At last it was "in its place" (2 Samuel 6:17). Indeed, David had pitched a tent for it. This was not the original tabernacle, but a temporary substitute for that structure, which may have been destroyed at some stage by the Philistines.[14] In other words, David did all he could to provide a proper place for the ark, aware of God's instructions concerning it. The narrator endorses his actions by affirming that this was "its place."

Second, "David offered burnt offerings and peace offerings before the LORD" (v. 17). As before, it is likely that David was in charge of the sacrifices, but they were actually conducted by the priests (as implied by 1 Chronicles 16:1). Details concerning the burnt offering are given in Leviticus 1. The main function of the burnt offering was "to atone for man's sin by propitiating God's wrath"; in addition it "could be offered as an act of obedience or thanksgiving."[15] The peace offering is described in Leviticus 3. It was principally "a festival meal," celebrating or expressing "peace" in the fullest sense of peace with God.[16]

Third, David "blessed the people in the name of the LORD of hosts" (2 Samuel 6:18). This, too, may have been actually done by the priests under David's authority (see Leviticus 9:22; Numbers 6:22–27; Deuteronomy

10:8; 21:5). It is also possible that David himself issued this blessing, as his son Solomon would do in a coming day, when the temple was completed (1 Kings 8:55). As the Lord had blessed Obed-edom, the Gittite, and his entire household because of the ark of God (2 Samuel 6:11, 12), so David now blessed all the people who had brought the ark of God to David's city. He blessed them in the name by which the ark was called (6:2), indeed the name in which he had, years before, approached Goliath (1 Samuel 17:45)—"the name of the LORD of hosts [armies]." The blessing was probably a prayer for the safety and security of all God's people. Under this king God will protect his people.

Fourth, David gave the people gifts of food. The emphasis is on the inclusion of everyone in this: "all the people, the whole multitude of Israel, both men and women" (2 Samuel 6:19). This, too, was an expression of the blessing of the people. Under this king God will provide for his people.[17]

In all of this, perhaps indirectly, David was performing priestly functions. It is reminiscent of Melchizedek ("king of righteousness," Hebrews 7:2), the priest-king Abraham had met in Jerusalem (Genesis 14:18–20), and anticipates the promised "priest forever after the order of Melchizedek" (Psalm 110:4), wonderfully realized in our Lord Jesus Christ (Hebrews 5:6; 6:20; 7:17, 21). God's king does not just fight battles—he brings his people to God.

Fifth, the momentous events of that day had come to an end. The people had a king who humbly rejoiced before the Lord and a God who had allowed the ark of his covenant to be brought into David's city. As they "departed, each to his house" (2 Samuel 6:19), we sense the peace and contentment of the situation. David, too, went home to share the blessing with those under his roof: "And David returned to bless his household" (v. 20a). His household would be like the household of Obed-edom—a place of blessing. Central to that blessing was what David embodied that day—the joy of humility before the Lord.

The Misery of Pride (vv. 20b–23)

If that was the end of the story, we could imagine the people back in their homes, gladly aware of the goodness of the kingdom in which they now found themselves, exhausted by a day of joyful celebration. However, within David's own household there was a rather different perspective on the day's events.

Michal's Scorn: What Kind of King! (v. 20b)

> But Michal the daughter of Saul came out to meet David and said, "How the king of Israel honored himself today, uncovering himself today before the eyes of his servants' female servants, as one of the vulgar fellows shamelessly uncovers himself!" (v. 20b)

The woman who had been watching the spectacle "out of the window" (v. 16) was eager to let David know what she thought of what she had seen. Before he reached the house, she came out to meet him.[18] Her voice dripped with sarcasm. She had found David's behavior utterly intolerable. She saw it as "vulgar" (v. 20). Was this the glory of the king of Israel?[19] Half-naked before the servants! What was he thinking?

Michal had a view of the glory of a king, and it was not this. She was indeed "the daughter of Saul" (v. 20). David's kingship was causing her as much difficulty as it had once caused her father. David was a different kind of king with a different kind of glory.

In the heading of this section I have called Michal's outburst "pride."[20] The dignity, power, and splendor of the king were too important to the daughter of Saul. David had put aside these things, joyfully humbling himself "before the LORD" (v. 14). The daughter of Saul could not accept this. To her it was simply uncouth.

The truth is that it was Michal who was uncouth. She described David's behavior as "uncovering himself" (v. 20, that is, "exposing himself"). It was perverse to see David's casting off royal garb in these coarse sexual terms. The removal of royal clothing has been a theme of the story told in 1 Samuel. In the case of Jonathan he was abandoning his claim to the throne in favor of David (1 Samuel 18:4). In the case of Saul the significance was similar, although generally ironic and tragic (see 1 Samuel 17:38; 19:24; 28:8).[21] In like manner David had abandoned his royal dignity "before the LORD" (2 Samuel 6:14), as an act of glad humility. He knew who was the real King (see 5:12). David was making himself nothing, taking the form of a servant. He was not counting his own dignity something to which to cling. Michal was embarrassed. But she could not have been more wrong.

David's Concern: "Before the Lord" (vv. 21, 22)

Listen to David's response:

> And David said to Michal, "It was before the LORD, who chose me above your father and above all his house, to appoint me as prince over Israel, the people of the LORD—and I will celebrate before the LORD. I will make

myself yet more contemptible than this, and I will be abased in your[22] eyes. But by the female servants of whom you have spoken, by them I shall be held in honor." (vv. 21, 22)

"Before the LORD" was David's theme. This is what mattered to him and what the daughter of Saul did not understand. She cared about the status of the king. He understood the grace of the Lord toward him. David was what he was because the Lord had chosen him. Michal's father ("your father," v. 21— this relationship continues to define Michal) was no longer king because the Lord had rejected him. Understanding the Lord's goodness to David made him both joyful and humble. He did not even think of himself as "king" but as "leader" (better than "prince"[23]) over a nation that was not *his* people but "the people of the LORD" (v. 21). David understood that "before the LORD" (v. 21) there was no place for arrogance and show, as though *he* was the glorious one. Do you see the unique character of this joyful humility?

David vowed that he would continue to "celebrate"[24] before the LORD" (v. 21). The Lord's grace toward him would continue to give him joy and turn him away from concern for himself and his own reputation. He would not seek to be great in his own eyes. He would rejoice in the greatness and goodness of God.

In verse 22 there is a small but significant textual problem. The ESV has followed the Septuagint ("in *your* eyes") and made David's words refer to how Michal would regard him: "contemptible." However, the Hebrew has David describing how he would see himself ("in *my* eyes"). Following the Hebrew, a better rendering than "contemptible" is "small," "of little account."[25] This continues (and indeed confirms) the theme of David's humbling himself "before the LORD" (v. 21). He will be "abased"[26] in his own eyes. "It's not about *me*." This is the joy of humility "before *the LORD*."

This humbling of himself before the Lord was expressed by David in a number of the Psalms. For example:

O LORD, my heart is not lifted up;
    my eyes are not raised too high;
I do not occupy myself with things
    too great and too marvelous for me. (Psalm 131:1)

And yet he says, "I shall be held in honor" (v. 22). "Honor" again represents the Hebrew for "glory" (like "honored" in v. 20). The glory of this king will be recognized (cf. Proverbs 29:23; Ezekiel 21:26; Matthew 18:4; 23:12; James 4:6, 10; 1 Peter 5:5, 6), but not by the likes of Saul's daughter. Those who cling to worldly values do not understand the genuine humility of this king. It is the weak in the world, the low and despised in this world, who will honor the humble king (cf. 1 Corinthians 1:26–29).

Michal's Misery (v. 23)

The episode concludes with brief but tragic words. The blessing enjoyed by the household of Obed-edom (2 Samuel 6:11), the people as a whole (v. 18), and David's household in particular (v. 20) was not shared by the daughter of Saul. "And Michal the daughter of Saul had no child to the day of her death" (v. 23). This is almost certainly more than an indication that David and Michal had no more to do with one another.[27] Her childlessness was part of the judgment that had fallen on the house of Saul, who had been rejected by the Lord and who failed to receive the new thing that the Lord was doing in David.[28] The house of David would have no descendants of Saul within it. This is the last we hear of Michal in the book of 2 Samuel.[29] She shared the misery of Hannah at the very beginning of 1 Samuel (see 1 Samuel 1:2b), although she did not share in the happy outcome that was given to Hannah.

The strange events of 2 Samuel 6 show us the most important truth about David's kingdom. Bringing the ark into the city of David was not a political maneuver to bolster his power with some religious trappings. Nor was it an attempt to bring religion under the control of the state. While these and other motives have been read into David's action,[30] the text of the Bible tells us something very different and much more important. David was king "before the LORD" (v. 21). This phrase occurs six times in the chapter (6:5, 14, 16, 17, 21). It means "in the personal presence of and in the sight of the Lord" (literally "to the face of the LORD"). Far from David taking control of religion or using religion for his political purposes, the ark in Jerusalem subordinated David's kingdom to the Lord as King (6:2), whose presence and promises were represented by the ark.

The joy of David's kingdom was therefore the joy of humility before the Lord.[31] The arrogance of human pomp and power had no place here and could not know this joy. It was miserable.

Do you know the joy of God's kingdom? David's kingdom has given way to Jesus' kingdom. But David helps us see Jesus, "who for the joy that was set before him endured the cross, despising the shame" (Hebrews 12:2). The humility of Jesus took him to the cross (Philippians 2:8). There he, too, was stripped of all respectable clothing and was mocked by those who held to worldly power (see Matthew 27:27–31). There he became our priest-king (see Hebrews 5:7–10).

Take care as you serve this King. Take great care of the temptation to grasp honor and dignity and status for yourself. Learn from David (better still, learn from Jesus) the joy of humility before the Lord. It's not about you.

> Have this mind among yourselves, which is yours in Christ Jesus, who, though he was in the form of God, did not count equality with God a thing to be grasped, but emptied himself, by taking the form of a servant . . . he humbled himself by becoming obedient to the point of death, even death on a cross. (Philippians 2:5–8)

Therefore:

> Do nothing from selfish ambition or conceit, but in humility count others more significant than yourselves. Let each of you look not only to his own interests, but also to the interests of others. (Philippians 2:3, 4)

That is the joy of the kingdom of Jesus.

15

The Most Important
Words in the World

2 SAMUEL 7:1–7

A FEW YEARS AGO I was given a volume of great and historic speeches that
have influenced the world in which we live. It contains speeches by Win-
ston Churchill, Nikita Khrushchev, John F. Kennedy, Martin Luther King Jr.,
Nelson Mandela, Richard Nixon, Margaret Thatcher, Barack Obama, and
others. Each speech is impressive. Some are brilliant. I enjoy browsing the
pages and sensing something of the excitement, courage, determination, and
hope these words must have aroused when they were first heard. The volume
is subtitled "The Speeches That Shaped the Modern World."

In 2 Samuel 7 there is a speech that deserves to be in that book. However, it would need to be in a separate section, with its own subtitle: "A
speech that is shaping the history of the world and all eternity."

Unlike all of the speeches that my volume contains, this speech did not
consist of words of human wisdom, courage, optimism, and resolve. Rather,
"the word *of the* Lord came to Nathan" (7:4). This word is shaping the history of the world in which we live and will shape all of eternity more certainly and comprehensively than any human speech.

There are few passages in the entire Bible more important and exciting
than 2 Samuel 7. The chapter has three main sections: verses 1–3: an introduction where we hear about a problem David confronted; verses 4–16: the
word of the Lord that cast a whole new light on David's problem; and verses
17–29: David's response to the word of the Lord. In this chapter we will
consider the introduction and the first part of the message from God:

(1) The situation as David saw it (vv. 1–3).

(2) The situation as the Lord saw it (vv. 4–7).

The Situation as David Saw It (vv. 1–3)

This momentous chapter begins with an understandable misunderstanding. Historical evidence suggests that the situation at the beginning of 2 Samuel 7 was quite late in David's thirty-three year reign in Jerusalem,[1] although it is reasonable to assume that it occurred before the troubles that began with 2 Samuel 11. While the timing is not emphasized by the account, the peaceful situation described in the first verse of this chapter may suggest that the battles listed in 2 Samuel 8 (or most of them) were now over. The events of 2 Samuel 7 are recounted immediately after 2 Samuel 6 for thematic rather than chronological reasons.[2] That is, the ideas of 2 Samuel 7 should be understood in the light of what happened in 2 Samuel 6, even if there was a considerable time gap between the chapters.[3]

Although the words of 7:1 are the narrator's, we should notice that he is describing *David's understanding* of the situation, because the situation as described here was the basis for what David said in verse 2. There were three things that together raised an important issue for David and led to his misunderstanding.

The King in His House (v. 1a)

The first was that David was comfortably settled and secure as king. The chapter begins, "Now when the king lived in his house . . ." (v. 1a). This was the house that had been built by carpenters and masons who had been sent to David by Hiram, king of Tyre, along with a supply of cedar wood (5:11). We know little about this edifice, but the use of cedar suggests some level of opulence. This "house" was David's palace.[4] Appropriately its occupant is called not "David" but "the king" (three times in verses 1–3), underlining his established royal status.

Rest from All His Enemies (v. 1b)

The second relevant aspect of David's situation (as he saw it) was, "the Lord had given him rest from all his surrounding enemies" (v. 1b). This would include the Philistines, whose expulsion from Israelite territory (5:17–25) was the key to the nation's liberation and peace. Most of the victories listed in 8:1–14 had probably also been won (if, as we have suggested, the situation described here was quite late in David's reign).[5] As

David saw it, the external threats had been dealt with. Israel had begun a period of peace.

It is worth pausing to notice the highly significant words used to describe the nation's peace. It was the Lord's doing, not David's achievement (literally, "*the* LORD[6] had caused rest for him"). Furthermore the word "rest" suggests that David saw the situation in terms of God's promises.[7] God "rested" on the seventh day (Exodus 20:11). He promised to give "rest" in the promised land (Exodus 33:14; Deuteronomy 3:20; Joshua 1:13, 15). Indeed he promised "rest from all your enemies around" (Deuteronomy 12:10; 25:19), precisely what is described here.[8]

As David saw it, God's promises to his people had now been very substantially fulfilled. The goal (at least in this respect) had been reached. They had arrived. It is true that Israel had experienced "rest" from their enemies previously (see Joshua 21:44; 22:4; 23:1), but it had been fleeting. The ensuing period of repeated rebellion covered by the book of Judges and then the period of Saul's reign had known no settled time of peace from the surrounding adversaries. At last, however, under King David, Israel was at "rest" again, as the Lord had promised. That, at least, was how David saw it. It seemed as though the promise in Hannah's prayer many years previously had been realized: "The LORD . . . will give strength to his king and exalt the horn of his anointed" (1 Samuel 2:10).

The Ark in a Tent (v. 2)

This situation prompted David to speak of a third aspect of his situation that was causing him concern: "the king said to Nathan the prophet, 'See now, I dwell in a house of cedar, but the ark of God dwells in a tent[9]'" (v. 2).

This is the first time that Nathan has appeared in the record. He will play a vitally important role in the ensuing narrative (see 12:1–15; 1 Kings 1), comparable to Samuel's role with Saul.[10]

David did not ask Nathan a direct question but posed what he saw as an anomaly that we can set out as follows:

> I dwell in a house of cedar,
> but the ark of God dwells in a tent. (2 Samuel 7:2)

The difference between "a house of cedar" and "a tent" was comparable to the difference between "I" ("I" is emphatic in the Hebrew) and "the ark of God" (also emphasized in the Hebrew sentence). The problem was that it was back to front! In the light of the experience recounted in 2 Samuel 6, David clearly saw that what the ark of God represented (the divine King, 6:2b) was more important than himself. He seemed to be questioning the appropriateness of the humble tent for the ark compared to the splendid dwelling for himself. Was this properly honoring the God who had given him so much?

David did not explicitly propose a solution. Did he have something in mind? Was he exploring possibilities? It is fair to assume that he was not thinking of moving into a tent himself to even things up. He seemed to be considering upgrading the accommodation for the ark to something more appropriate. If the king lived in peace in a palace, then surely it was time that the ark of God had a dwelling place that was at least comparable.

We know that in David's world it was common for kings to build temples for their gods. But Saul had not done so, and David was meant to be a king who was *not* like the kings of the nations. It may be understandable (in the light of subsequent events) to say that David was thinking of building a temple, but we should notice that he did not use that word, nor does it occur anywhere in 2 Samuel 7.[11] It almost seems that David (and later God himself) avoided any suggestion that God's king was like the pagan kings who earned the favor of their gods by building temples for them.[12] Just as a "king" in Israel was not like the kings of the nations (and sometimes even the word "king" was therefore avoided[13]), a "temple" in Israel would be so different from the pagan temples that the word itself could be problematic.[14]

It seems that David was thinking through the consequences of the settled permanence of his kingdom having been achieved. What was appropriate for the ark in this situation? Was "the tent that David had pitched for it" (6:17) still suitable? Did it give proper honor to the true King in this kingdom?

A Plan for the Times (v. 3)

Nathan understood David's thinking. "And Nathan said to the king, 'Go, do all that is in your heart, for the LORD is with you'" (v. 3). This was not Nathan speaking *as the prophet*. He had received no word from the Lord on this matter (yet). He expressed his personal view that the king was on to a good and proper idea. He based his advice on the well-established fact that the Lord was with David (see 1 Samuel 16:18; 17:37; 18:12, 14, 28; 2 Samuel 5:10). We notice again, however, that the proposal is vague and undefined. It is as though neither David nor Nathan was clear on precisely what should be done. They just agreed that the present situation (the king in a cedar house, the ark in a tent) was less than satisfactory. *Something* should be done. "Do what seems best to you," Nathan said to David.

The Situation as the Lord Saw It (vv. 4–7)

The best of human beings with the highest motives often get things wrong. This is especially true in our response to God. Frequently it is because we do not properly understand the situation in which we find ourselves. David had initiated bringing the ark up from Kiriath-jearim, which seemed a right and good thing to do (6:1–5). However, something was wrong. God intervened, and the project was delayed (6:6–11). We are unable to see as God sees (cf. 1 Samuel 16:7) and are therefore often incapable by our own abilities to discern the right way. This was also the case with David and Nathan and their concerns about the ark and its tent.

The Word of the Lord (v. 4)

The only way in which they could learn their error was by divine intervention. This time, however, it was not an outburst of God's anger (as in 2 Samuel 6) but a word from God: "But that same night the word of the LORD came to Nathan" (v. 4).

Particularly important revelations from God sometimes came at night (see, for example, 1 Samuel 3; 15:16; cf. 28:8).[15] While it is possible that some of these involved dreams, the night setting seems more to do with the absence of the distractions of daytime activities. In the relative quiet of the night, when Nathan was alone, the word of the Lord came to him in a "vision" (see 7:17).

The fundamental requirement for a king over God's people was that he "listen to the voice of the words of the LORD" (1 Samuel 15:1b AT). Although there had been a number of occasions on which God had given particular directions to David (see 1 Samuel 22:5; 23:2, 4, 11, 12; 2 Samuel 2:1), none of these is referred to as "the word of the LORD came" (7:4). This phrase signals a particularly important message from God.[16] The first part of this message reveals God's very different perspective on the situation of David. The second part (to which we turn in our next chapter) will replace David's vaguely expressed agenda for the situation with the Lord's agenda for all eternity.

Not You, David (v. 5)

The word of the Lord that came that night began, "Go and tell my servant David, 'Thus says the LORD: Would you build me a house to dwell in?'" (v. 5).

We notice immediately the striking way in which the Lord referred to David: "my servant David." In the first three verses of the chapter we have seen him as "the king . . . the king . . . the king." But the Lord did not say, "Go and tell *the king*." He said, "Go and tell *my servant David*" (v. 5). While it is common enough in the language of the Bible for people to be called servants, and particular people servants of the Lord, in this context there is something wonderful about this reference by the Lord to David as "my servant."[17] It recognizes the way in which David had humbled himself "before the LORD" in the previous chapter and at the same time bestows on him a very high status indeed. The status comes not from the word "servant," but from the one whose servant he was.

Nathan was to introduce what he said to David with the phrase (literally translated) "Thus the LORD has said." This expression was the trademark of a prophet.[18] The prophet had a job to do precisely when the Lord had spoken. His job was to speak the words that the Lord had spoken.[19]

The Lord's word to David began with a simple-sounding question: "Would you build me a house to dwell in?" (v. 5). The Lord had understood what was going through David's mind, probably better than David did himself. The king was considering building a more appropriate "house" (to replace the tent) in which to place the ark.

However the Lord did not explicitly mention the ark. In the previous chapter we were told that David was making merry, dancing, leaping, and offering sacrifices "before the LORD" (6:14). That was the reality, although those activities took place *before the ark*. In a similar way the Lord now spoke of the house in which *the ark* might be placed as a dwelling place for *the Lord himself*: "a house [for me] to dwell in" (7:5). Again it is a case of the language speaking directly of the reality symbolized. The ark represented the Lord's presence with his people. The ark dwelling in a "tent" or a "house" therefore represented, in that dwelling, the Lord's own presence.

This way of speaking should sound strange to us. We might not be surprised to hear pagans and idol worshipers speaking of the "houses" for their gods (see 1 Samuel 5:2; 31:9). But as Solomon will pray when, in due course, he does build the house referred to here, "Behold, heaven and the highest heaven cannot contain you; how much less this house that I have built!" (1 Kings 8:27; see also 2 Chronicles 2:6; Isaiah 66:1; Acts 7:48–50; 17:24).

Some have therefore understood the question ("Would you build me a house to dwell in?") to be a rejection by God not just of any *pagan* understanding of temples but of the very idea of such an edifice being built at all.[20] This misses the subtlety of the Lord's words. The emphasis in the question is on the word "you."[21] "Are *you* the one, David, who will build a house for

me to dwell in?" The question implies the answer—"No, David, you are
not the one," rather than "No, David, no such house is to be built." The full
significance of this will only become clear in the second part of the Lord's
message to David, where we will hear that *someone else* will build the house
that David was not to build (see 7:13a).[22]

This is surprising. David was God's own king. He had shown himself to
be faithful and righteous. Why would he not be the one to build this house?

Look Back (vv. 6, 7)

The answer to this question[23] begins by showing David's situation in the
light of God's history with this people. There are two simple but telling
points. First:

> I have not lived in a house since the day I brought up the people of Israel
> from Egypt to this day, but I have been moving about in a tent for my
> dwelling. (v. 6)

From the day the Israelites were rescued, under Moses' leadership, from
slavery in Egypt (Exodus 1–19) to this day, nearly 300 years later,[24] when
David was king in Jerusalem, the tabernacle that had been built in Moses'
day according to the Lord's detailed instructions (Exodus 26; 36:8–38; 40:1–
33) had been where the ark (representing the Lord's presence) was housed.[25]
This portable structure was a tent. It had traveled with the people as they
moved from place to place. Just so the Lord himself had moved with his
people (see Exodus 40:36–38).[26] This was an arrangement that God himself
had prescribed. From the wonder of the exodus through the many occasions
on which the Lord had protected, rescued, and provided for the people of
Israel to this day on which David was concerned about the ark dwelling in a
tent, a tent had been all that God required. Furthermore the very portability
of a tent, in contrast to the stable permanence implied in a "house" (2 Samuel
7:2), was appropriate for a God who moved with his people.

This first point is by no means all that the Lord will say about the idea
of building a "house" (v. 2) for the ark, but it is foundational and important.
God cannot be restricted to any set place as "house" (or temple) might imply.
He came to his suffering people in Egypt and brought them up from there
to the land that he had promised Abraham. He traveled with his people. The
symbol of his presence was never put in a fixed place but in the traveling
tabernacle.

In years to come, long after a temple was built in Jerusalem, this lesson will be dramatically taught again when the people will be driven from this land into exile in Babylon. There, far from the Jerusalem temple, by the Chebar canal the Lord will come to a young priest named Ezekiel in an extraordinary display of his glory and mobility (read Ezekiel 1).

The implication of the Lord's words to David seems to be, "Through these many years I have rescued, protected, and guided Israel without needing a house. Why would you consider building one now?"

The second point was that the Lord had never suggested that this arrangement was inappropriate.

> In all places where I have moved with all the people of Israel, did I speak a word with any of the judges[27] of Israel, whom I commanded to shepherd my people Israel, saying, "Why have you not built me a house of cedar?" (v. 7)

While there were many occasions when the Lord found fault with the people of Israel, not once did he suggest that they should have built a house like David's place ("a house of cedar," v. 7) to replace the tabernacle. Those who preceded David as shepherds of God's people (see 5:2) were never asked to provide such a thing.

The implied question is, "Why, then, would you think that you, David, should now build a house for the ark?"

This is only the first part of the word of the Lord that came to Nathan that night. It lays the foundation for a word that changes everything. The second part will be introduced by a repetition of the instruction to Nathan: "Now, therefore, thus you shall say to my servant David . . ." (7:8a; cf. v. 5a). Then we will hear a promise of God that will shape the rest of human history.

Before we hear those astonishing words, let us be sure that the foundation is firm and clear. Responding rightly to God is the most important thing in life. How easily our instincts and intuitions mislead us. To honor God by building a splendid house for the ark of the covenant seemed right to David in the circumstances as he understood them. But he was wrong. How often Christian people have devised projects (often building projects) that seem to them to be honoring to God. But are they? Do we fully recognize that God does not need our projects? As David had to reflect on the tabernacle-presence of God who moved with his people, we should contemplate the presence of God among us in the person of Jesus (in whom he "tabernacled among us," a rather literal translation of John 1:14). How foolish to think that the God who has done *that* to save his people needs buildings made by us, or any other human help. David needed to understand that God is the one who tells us what he requires. If he did not ask for a house of cedar, why would David imagine that such a thing would please him? What we do to honor God must arise from obedience to his word, not from our instincts and intuitions, however good they seem. The agenda is set by him, not by us. The most important words in the world are the words of God that make known his agenda, as we will see in our next chapter.

16

The Promise

2 SAMUEL 7:8–16

THE BIBLE'S radical and powerful message is not simply that *God exists*, nor merely that he is *the Creator of all that is*. Of course, the Bible does teach these important truths, but if that is all we understand we will remain confused and will not respond to God rightly. Furthermore the Bible is more than an account of *God's particular and purposeful actions in history*, guiding the remarkable course of Israel in the Old Testament and working in the life of Jesus Christ in the New Testament. Again the Bible certainly does tell the remarkable story of God's involvement in the history of the world that he created, but even if we know that record well we may still have missed the heart of the Bible's message and be mistaken in our response to God. To take this line of thinking one step further, it is even inadequate to realize that the Bible is *God's own message* about who he is, his creation of all that is, and his acts in world history. The Bible is God's word to us about all of these things, but it is more than that.

It is possible to understand and believe all of the things that I have mentioned and not yet know what the Bible is really all about. It is a case of missing the forest for the trees. Many church members know quite a lot about the contents of the Bible and even accept what they know to be true, but have not yet come to what the Bible calls faith. What are they missing?

The golden thread that holds the whole Bible together, the central message that makes sense of all the details, is this: *God has promised*. The Bible is valuable for the wealth of information it contains about many things, but the Bible is of ultimate worth because in it *God makes his promise*.

Faith (in the Biblical sense) is not just believing the information the Bible contains. Faith is *believing God's promise*. Of course, this faith believes all that the Bible teaches, but everything in the Bible works together to enable and build *this* faith. The Bible tells us what God has promised, what he has already done in faithfulness to his promise, what he will yet do, and what the implications of his promise are for human life. Unless we see that everything in the Bible is related to God's promise, we miss the point. Once we believe God's promise, the Bible comes to life because we read and listen to grow in our knowledge of the God who promises. Our faith, hope, and love are nourished by God's promise, which comes to us in the words on the pages of the Bible as those words are breathed to us by God's own Spirit, who powerfully convinces us of his faithfulness (this experience is fully comparable with that described in 1 Thessalonians 1:2–5).

I have spoken of God's *promise*. The singular is important. Of course, it is also true that the Bible contains many promises. However, the promises (plural) of God are all expressions or aspects of the one promise. Just as the history, laws, songs, prayers, and teachings are only properly understood when we see how they are connected to God's promise, so the many promises must be seen in relation to the one promise.

What is that one promise? There are various ways to express it. God has promised to "bless" the creation he has made and humankind whom he has made in his image (see Genesis 1:22, 28; 2:3). He has promised to do this through a great nation, descended from Abraham (Genesis 12:1–3; 18:18; 22:18; 26:4; 28:14; see Jeremiah 4:1, 2). The promise has begun to be fulfilled through the death and resurrection of Jesus (Acts 3:25, 26) and as people from every nation are put right with God through faith in Jesus Christ (Galatians 3:7–9). The vision of a great multitude from every nation rejoicing before God's throne points to the final realization of the promise (Revelation 7:9, 10).[1]

God's promise is not only the key for understanding everything in the Bible—it is also fundamental for understanding *everything*. Those who know and believe God's promise see all things in a brilliant new light—life and death, prosperity and suffering, beauty and ugliness, love and hate, hope and despair.

My brief summary of the Bible's presentation of God's promise has jumped too quickly from the early expressions of that promise in the book of Genesis to its fulfillment in Jesus Christ. How is it that the promise to bless the nations of the world through a great nation descended from Abraham was fulfilled in the person of Jesus? Put that another way: how is it that Jesus (one man) fulfills the promise made to Abraham (about a great nation and all the families of the earth)? At the risk of oversimplifying, we can say that the purpose of the Old Testament is to provide the links between the promise we hear in Genesis and the fulfillment announced in the New Testament.

The most important of those links is King David. In this sense David is the central human figure in the Bible: he is the crucial link between Abraham and Jesus. David's place in the unfolding story of the Bible is a decisive step in God's faithfulness to his promise to Abraham. We only understand David (as we will shortly see) in the light of that promise. But then (as we will also see) God reiterated his promise to David in terms that prepare us for its fulfillment in Jesus. Jesus must be understood in the light of God's promise as it was made to David.[2]

I hope that I am not making this sound too complicated. It really isn't. God made his promise to Abraham. He spelled that promise out more fully to David. When we see God's promise to David fulfilled in Jesus, we see how Jesus fulfills the promise to Abraham. It is thrilling to see (as Paul put it in a slightly different context) "the depth of the riches and wisdom and knowledge of God! How unsearchable are his judgments and how inscrutable his ways!" (Romans 11:33).

The crucially important promise God made to David is recorded in 7:8–16 (particularly verses 12–16). Hearing these words was the most important event in David's life. The text before us is one of the most important passages in the whole Bible. After David had become king of the nation of Israel (the nation descended from Abraham, as God had promised; see 5:1–12), after he had at last defeated the enemies of Israel (see 5:17–25), and after he had brought the ark of God into his city (2 Samuel 6), God made his promise to David in terms that would never be forgotten. Although it was still essentially the promise that was first made to Abraham, it was now expressed in such a way that it became clear that the promise involved a king and a kingdom that would last forever. It was this expression of the promise that taught the people who believed it to expect a "Messiah" or "Christ." When the New Testament announces "Jesus is the Christ," it is saying that Jesus is the one who was promised in these words.

We have seen that King David was concerned about properly honoring God when he was securely established as king in Jerusalem. Surely it was not right for the ark of God's covenant with Israel (representing the true King of Israel) to sit in a tent when he was living comfortably in "a house of cedar" (7:1, 2). The word of the Lord that came to Nathan the prophet that night (7:4) and that Nathan was to speak to David made clear that David was not to pursue the plan that was forming in his mind. David was not to build "a house of cedar" (v. 7) for the Lord to dwell in (that is, for the ark, which represented God's presence), to match his own. Whatever David may have thought, this was not what the Lord wanted. It may have seemed like a good idea. But it wasn't, for reasons that the Lord began to explain in the first part of the message heard that night by Nathan (7:5–7).

When David heard those words, I imagine him thinking something like, "That's all very well, but times have changed. The exodus from Egypt (when the ark was first placed in a tent) is now history. The people of Israel are no longer on the move (as we were when the ark traveled with us in the tabernacle). I am settled in my splendid royal house. The nation is secure in the land the Lord has given us. Enemies are no longer a threat to us. A tent for the ark of God may have been appropriate when we were wandering from place to place, but we are not traveling anymore. Thank God, we have arrived! Now we need the Lord to *stay* with us, not *move* with us. Surely a tent is no longer right."

The Lord had more to say to David that would silence such objections. He spoke of:

(1) The Lord's purpose for David (vv. 8–11b).
(2) The Lord's purpose beyond David (vv. 11c–16).

The Lord's Purpose for David (vv. 8–11b)

The second part of the message (spoken first to Nathan the prophet, then to be spoken by him to David) was introduced by a reiteration of the instruction that had been given to Nathan at the beginning of the first part: "Now, therefore, thus you shall say to my servant David, 'Thus says the LORD of hosts'" (v. 8a; cf. 7:5a).

Part Two of the Lord's word for David is a consequence of Part One ("Now, therefore"[3]), in which the Lord reviewed his dealings with Israel since the exodus (7:6) and the fact that he had never suggested that a house should be built for the ark (7:7).

The expansion of God's name to "the LORD *of hosts*" (v. 8) makes what follows even more serious if that were possible. This is the name by which the ark was called (6:2). Since this title was used for the first time in the Old Testament in 1 Samuel 1:3, it has occurred at moments of solemn importance, emphasizing God's sovereignty and power (see 1 Samuel 1:11; 4:4; 15:2; 17:45; 2 Samuel 5:10; 6:2, 18; 7:26, 27). The words that follow focus on the purpose of the Lord of the heavenly armies[4] for David.[5]

David's Past (vv. 8b, 9a)

I took you from the pasture, from following the sheep, that you should be prince over my people Israel. And I have been with you wherever you went and have cut off all your enemies from before you. (vv. 8b, 9a)

It was the Lord of hosts who had been at work in David's life from Bethlehem to Jerusalem. From the time when David used to look after his father's sheep (1 Samuel 16:11; see 17:34–37) and Samuel anointed him to be Israel's ruler[6] (1 Samuel 16:13) to the day this came about (2 Samuel 5:3), all of his accomplishments, especially victories over his enemies, had been due to the Lord's being with him (just as Nathan had said, 7:3). Chief among David's "enemies" were the Philistines (v. 9). Perhaps we should add others who chose to oppose David, even if David refused to be hostile toward them—Saul, Abner, and Ish-bosheth. All who had set themselves against David had been "cut off" (v. 9). This had been the Lord's doing.

"I" in verse 8b is emphatic in exactly the same way as "you" was emphasized in verse 5b. The implication seems to be that the Lord of hosts was the one whose will is accomplished in David's life (notice the repetition of "my servant David," vv. 5, 8a). The idea of building a "house" (v. 2) for the Lord (that is, for the ark) was not for David to initiate. Only the Lord himself could propose such a thing.

David's Future (vv. 9b–11b)

I imagine that when David heard this, he was still rather perplexed. Perhaps he was happy to wait for a word from the Lord before embarking on the building project. Wasn't that why he had raised the matter with Nathan (7:2)? But why didn't the Lord give such a word?

The answer is that although David may have thought that the goal of his life had been reached and God's promises had been fulfilled (7:1), he was mistaken. In verse 9b there is an important shift that takes the argument to its next stage. From reviewing events of the past (vv. 6–9a) the Lord moved to anticipating events that lay in the future.[7] The Lord had not yet finished what he intended to do for and through David. The king may have seen the situation as settled, stable, and finally established (as we heard in 7:1), so that it was time to build a house for the ark, but this was not the case. The journey was not yet completed. In four ways the Lord's promised goal had not yet been reached.

A Name (v. 9b)

First, "I will make for you a great name, like the name of the great ones of the earth" (v. 9b). These words point back to the promise God had made long ago to Abraham: "I will . . . make your name great" (Genesis 12:2). The Lord intended to fulfill that promise by making *David's* name great.[8] To some extent this had already happened (see 1 Samuel 18:30; also 2 Samuel 8:13).

However, the Lord had not finished making a great name for David. There was more to come.

A Place (v. 10a)

Second, "And I will appoint a place for my people Israel and will plant them, so that they may dwell in their own place" (v. 10a). What the Lord promised to do for David was "for the sake of his people Israel" (5:12). Therefore there is a shift from "you" (David) in verse 9b to "them" ("my people Israel") in verses 10, 11a. This time the words echo the song of Moses and the people of Israel at the time of the exodus.

> You will bring them in and plant[9] them on your own mountain,
>   the place,[10] O Lᴏʀᴅ, which you have made for your abode,
>   the sanctuary, O Lord, which your hands have established.
>   (Exodus 15:17)

These words in Exodus were based on God's promise to Abraham. They are poetic language for the establishing of the people in the land[11] that the Lord had promised to Abraham (Genesis 12:1, 7; 13:15, 17; 15:7, 18, 19; 17:8; 24:7; 26:2, 3; 28:4, 13; 35:12; 48:4, 21; 50:24). While the Israelites had lived in this land since the days of Joshua, the promise in 7:10 indicates that the security God promised ("plant") had not yet been fully accomplished (see the use of this metaphor in Psalm 44:2; 80:8; Isaiah 5:2; Jeremiah 2:21; 11:17; 45:4; Ezekiel 17:5; 19:10; Amos 9:15).[12]

Peace (vv. 10b, 11a)

Third, this is confirmed: ". . . and be disturbed no more. And violent men shall afflict them no more, as formerly, from the time that I appointed judges over my people Israel" (2 Samuel 7:10b, 11a). David may have thought that the people's security had been won and that those who had repeatedly oppressed them, since the death of Joshua (as recorded in the books of Judges and 1 Samuel), had been dealt with (7:1). The Lord saw things differently. That goal had not yet been reached. It still lay in the future.

Rest (v. 11b)

Fourth, "And I will give you rest from all your enemies" (v. 11b). The focus turns back to "you" (David).[13] What God had promised, and has just promised again, to do for his people Israel will be accomplished through David.[14] David had thought that the Lord had already given him the promised "rest from all his . . . enemies" (7:1). However, the rest that God promised still lay in the future.[15]

Together these four elements (*great name* for David, *secure place* and *no more affliction* for Israel, *rest* for David) point us back to the promise originally made to Abraham. The Lord's faithfulness to that promise is seen in all that had happened in David's experience (vv. 8, 9a), but there was more to come (vv. 9b–11b). David himself was central to that future.

The implication, in this context, is that this is a further reason that David should not consider building a "house" (v. 2) for the ark. Not only had a tent been appropriate in the past (7:6), but the Lord had never suggested otherwise (7:7), and the Lord is the one who sets the agenda for David, not the other way around (7:8, 9a). There was more the Lord intended to do for and through David before there should be any talk of such a "house" (v. 2).

In other words, the Lord seems to suggest that David's motivation for thinking about building this house arose from a sense of having *arrived* (as 7:1 suggests). But David was mistaken. Perhaps a "house" (v. 2) for the Lord's dwelling would be appropriate when his work was done, just as the Lord "rested" on the seventh day when he had finished "all his work that he had done" in creation (Genesis 2:2). However, the Lord was not yet ready to rest from his work on behalf of his people or from the fulfillment of his promise to Abraham. There was more to be accomplished for Israel. It was not yet time to put the ark in a house.

The Lord's Purpose beyond David (vv. 11c–16)

Furthermore what the Lord would do in faithfulness to his promise to Abraham would not be completed in David's lifetime. To understand his situation, David needed to hear not only about the past (vv. 6–9a), the near future (vv. 9b–11b), but also beyond that (vv. 11c–16). The very great importance of what was about to be said is signaled: "'Moreover, the Lord declares to you . . .'" (v. 11c).[16]

The House the Lord Will Build (v. 11d, 12)

Even if we have been listening carefully and following every word that the Lord has spoken so far, the following words take us by surprise. The word of the Lord that came that night for David had begun with the rhetorical question, "Would *you* build *me* a house to dwell in?"[17] (v. 5b). The various reasons that we have heard for David's not doing this have been leading to this climax, where the original question is turned on its head: "'. . . that *the LORD* will make *you* a house'"[18] (v. 11d).

David already had "a house," and a very fine house it was (7:1). However, the Lord appeared to have no interest whatsoever in David's royal residence. Its cedar panels did not impress him at all. The Lord intended to make for David another house, a different kind of house:[19]

> When your days are fulfilled and you lie down with your fathers, I will raise up your offspring after you, who shall come from your body, and I will establish his kingdom. (v. 12)

This is the "house" that God cared about (v. 11). The house of David was to be not a palace but a royal dynasty. *This* "house" will be made by the Lord. This is how he will make David's name great and also give his people Israel peace and safety. Notice three things about this promise.

First, it points beyond David's lifetime. His days will have run their completed course. He will follow his ancestors who have gone before him. This was always going to be the problem with any human leader. Even the best grew old and died. Indeed it was this very difficulty in the case of Samuel (one of the finest leaders Israel ever had) that had led to the appointment of Saul as Israel's first king (see 1 Samuel 8:4). But Saul, too, had died, and with him his kingdom (see 1:19–27). God's promise to David, however, would not be destroyed by David's death.

Second, the promise focuses on "your offspring" (or "your seed," 2 Samuel 7:12). In this word there is yet another echo of the promise to Abraham, in which this was a key word (see Genesis 12:7; 13:15, 16; 15:4, 5, 18; 17:7, 8, 9, 10, 19; 21:12; 22:17, 18; 24:7, 60; 26:3, 4, 24; 28:4, 13, 14; 32:12; 35:12; 48:4, 19; Exodus 32:13; 33:1; Deuteronomy 1:8; 11:9; 30:19; 34:4; Joshua 24:3; see also Genesis 3:15; 4:25; 9:9). Just as "a great name," "a place," and the "rest" promised to Abraham would be given to and through David (2 Samuel 7:9b–11b), so God's promise concerning Abraham's "seed" would be fulfilled in the "seed" of David (who would also be, of course, the "seed" of Abraham).[20]

"Offspring" (v. 12) or "seed" represents a singular noun in Hebrew that (like the English) can refer to an individual or collectively to a whole line of descendants. On the surface, as the following verse will make clear, the reference is to David's son and heir (as yet unborn, but who will be Solomon, 5:14; 12:24; 1 Kings 2:12). We will see that there are deeper dimensions to the promise as well (cf. Galatians 3:16). The "offspring" of David will not end with Solomon (2 Samuel 7:12).

Third, it would be the kingdom of David's offspring that would be "established" (v. 12; literally, "caused to stand") by the Lord. David may have thought that his own kingdom was already established (as 7:1 implies). Be that as it may, the Lord was concerned for more than the kingdom of David's lifetime. After David's death the Lord would "establish" the kingdom in the hands of his "offspring" or "seed" (see 1 Kings 2:46b).

Here the important word "kingdom" is introduced to this passage. The word has a range of senses in different contexts. Frequently it means "rule" or "reign," that is, "king*ship.*" That seems to be the sense here. The Lord will make the reign of David's offspring secure.[21]

In this way the Lord would be the one who would make "a house" for David (2 Samuel 7:11).

A House That Will Then Be Built (v. 13a)

Surprise follows surprise. In case you were wondering about the "house" (v. 2) that was on David's mind from the beginning of this chapter (the "house" to replace the ark's tent), the Lord ever so briefly (almost in passing[22]) says, of David's offspring, "*He* shall build a house for my name" (v. 13a). Not *you*, David, but *him*.[23]

The Lord therefore answered the question with his message to David on two levels. "Are *you* the one, David, who will build a house for *me* to dwell in?" (7:5b AT). On the one hand the answer is "No. *I* am the one who will make *you* a house" (paraphrase of 7:11d). On the other hand, "As far as the house you have in mind is concerned, David, the answer is also no. Not *you*, but *your offspring* will build a house for my name" (paraphrase of 7:13a).

This is the last we will hear of *this* house in 2 Samuel 7. The "house" (v. 11) that the Lord promised to make for David was much more important. However, notice the new expression for the other house: "a house *for my name*" (v. 13). Various reasons had been advanced as to why David was not to build a house as a dwelling place *for the Lord* (see 7:5b–7). Now that it is acknowledged that such a house will be built by David's offspring, the direct language is modified. The Lord himself would never inhabit a "house" in the way in which pagan gods and their idols may have been imagined to inhabit temples. The Lord's dwelling place is in Heaven (see Deuteronomy 26:15; 1 Kings 8:34, 39, 43, 49; Nehemiah 9:13; Psalm 2:4; 11:4; 33:13, 14; Isaiah 40:22; 63:15; 66:1; Matthew 5:34; 6:1; and especially Acts 7:48, 49). This building would be a house for *his name*. Since the ark was "called by *the name* of the Lord of hosts" (2 Samuel 6:2), a "house for *my name*" (7:13) means "a house for *the ark*." "A house for my name" may also mean that: (1) the Lord would own this house (it would have *his name* on it, so to speak); (2) it would be a place where the Lord would be known (in this house people would call on *his name*); and (3) it would enhance the Lord's reputation and fame (it would, like the ark itself, be known by *his name*).

Just four words (in the Hebrew) are given here to the future "house" that would, in due course, be built by Solomon (1 Kings 5—8). Attention immediately turns back (for the rest of the chapter) to the very different and much more important "house" that the Lord promised to make for David. No more will be said in 2 Samuel 7 about the idea of a house for the ark, with which the chapter began. Indeed that idea will not be mentioned again in this narrative until after David's death (1 Kings 3:1; cf. 2 Samuel 22:7).

The House That Will Last Forever (vv. 13b–16)

The "house" that the Lord had promised to build for David, however, will be of interest for the rest of the Bible. Everything that the Old Testament will say about a Messiah to come (particularly in the books of the prophets and in the Psalms) will look back to this promise. The New Testament message about Jesus proclaims the fulfillment of this promise in him. Here the key elements of that promise are stated clearly.

Eternal Throne (v. 13b)

First, *this* house (the one the Lord will make, not the one that David's offspring will build) will never come to an end: "and I will establish the throne of his kingdom forever" (v. 13b). "The throne of his kingdom" means the king's power to reign. The royal rule of David's offspring will last "forever." This is the "house" that the Lord will make for David.

The Hebrew phrase translated "forever" occurs seven more times in this chapter (v. 13).[24] The idea of permanence implied in the building of a "house" (with which the chapter began, v. 2) is taken to a whole new level in the house that the Lord was promising. In itself the Hebrew expression does not necessarily mean that this kingdom will be eternal.[25] However, the context (especially the next two verses) suggests that the meaning here is that this kingdom will never come to an end.

This kingdom, then, will be different from Saul's kingdom. Although there was a possibility (we might call it a *theoretical* possibility) that "the LORD would have established [Saul's] kingdom over Israel *forever*" (1 Samuel 13:13), this did not happen, because of Saul's disobedience (see 1 Samuel 12:15; 28:18). The promise, however, in 7:13 is that the Lord *will* establish the kingdom of David's offspring forever. What will make David's kingdom different from Saul's?

Father and Son Forever (vv. 14, 15)

The answer comes in the second element of the promise. The eternal stability of this kingdom will be secured by the relationship of the Lord to the king: "I will be to him a father, and he shall be to me a son" (v. 14a). "I" and "he" are emphasized in the Hebrew, stressing the relationship of each to the other.

Christian readers should be patient here. In the first place this is not a *direct* reference to the eternal relationship in the Trinity between God the Son and God the Father. In other words, this promise is not a *prediction* that one day the eternal Son of God the Father will be the King in the line of David. Rather, this is a promise that will be fulfilled at different levels in the centuries following David.

To understand this we need to see how the relationship between the Lord and his people Israel was understood as a Father-son(s) relationship (see Exodus 4:22, 23; Deuteronomy 14:1; 32:6; Psalm 82:6; Isaiah 1:2; 30:1; 63:16; 64:8; Jeremiah 3:22; 31:9, 20; Hosea 1:10; 11:1; Malachi 1:6; 2:10).[26] This was a case of sonship by gracious adoption.[27] It conveyed the idea of Israel being God's chosen people (Deuteronomy 10:15; Isaiah 43:20), who belonged to him (Exodus 19:5; Deuteronomy 7:6; 14:2), and who ought to love and obey him (Deuteronomy 11:13).

Therefore in the first place we should understand the promise in 7:14a like those in the immediate context. The promise made to Abraham and his offspring was now focused on the offspring of David. Just as the offspring of Abraham (namely, Israel) was God's "son," so now the offspring of David (the king of Israel) will be God's "son" (Psalm 2:7; 89:26). In other words (just as we have been hearing in the preceding verses), God's great promises to Abraham concerning Israel are now applied to the king of Israel descended from David. This king will be God's "son" (2 Samuel 7:14)—chosen by God, belonging to him, and bound to love and obey him.

This does not mean that the promise concerning Israel has been forgotten. On the contrary. God will make *Abraham's* name great (Genesis 12:2) by giving *King David* a great name (2 Samuel 7:9). God will give rest to his people *Israel* (Deuteronomy 12:10) by giving rest to *King David* (2 Samuel 7:11). The Lord will do these things by providing David with offspring who will reign forever. God's people will be his "sons" because their king will be God's son (see Matthew 5:9; John 1:12; Romans 8:14, 19; Galatians 3:26).

We may now see, therefore, profound significance in the words of the elders who came to David in Hebron (almost certainly beyond their understanding at the time): "We are your bone and flesh" (5:1). The bond between king and people is such that the people are included in the relationship between the king and God.

In the New Testament the identification of Jesus as the "Son of God" indicates that he is the promised offspring of David, the King (see, for example, Matthew 16:16; Mark 1:1; 14:61; Luke 1:32; John 1:49; 11:27; Acts 13:33; Romans 1:4; Hebrews 1:5; 5:5). Certainly the New Testament teaches us that Jesus was and is the Son of God in a deeper sense as well. How amazing and wonderful that the promised king is now not just God's Son by adoption, but God the eternal Son!

The Old Testament Scriptures thus find their *fulfillment* in the person and work of Jesus Christ proclaimed in the New Testament (2 Corinthians 1:20). However, the fulfillment surpasses the expectations created by the promises (cf. 1 Corinthians 2:9).

Let's return to the promise in 7:14a. In the first place these words pointed to David's son and heir, Solomon. The context ("forever" at the end of the previous verse) shows that they also pointed beyond Solomon to the later descendants of David who would reign in Jerusalem. "He" in the promise does not refer simply to one individual but to each of the "offspring" who would comprise the "house" of David.[28]

The Father-son relationship between the Lord and the king in David's line is the key difference from Saul's kingdom. It is not, in the first place, that the offspring of David will be perfectly obedient or even that they will be better than Saul. However, instances of disobedience will not have the same consequences as they did for Saul's kingdom: "When he commits iniquity, I will discipline him with the rod of men, with the stripes of the sons of men, but my steadfast love will not depart from him, as I took it from Saul, whom I put away from before you" (vv. 14b, 15).

This promise will be worked out in the lives of kings in David's line, starting with David himself. Individual kings (starting with David) will "commit . . . iniquity" (v. 14), and punishment will follow, just as a good human father disciplines his children (cf. Hebrews 12:5–11). The wording of 2 Samuel 7:14b may also suggest that the Lord's discipline will come by human agents ("the rod of men . . . the stripes of the sons of men"). This will not, however, be like the punishment that fell on Saul—the complete rejection of him and his kingdom. David's offspring (the "house" that the Lord will make for David, v. 11) will never be rejected like that. In due course we will see that individual kings in David's line could be condemned, but the promise was that the Lord's "steadfast love will not depart from" the line of David's offspring (v. 15).[29]

We now know that one day there would be a son of David who committed no iniquity (1 Peter 2:22, 23). Of him his Father would say, "This is my beloved Son, with whom I am well pleased" (Matthew 3:17).[30] However, from David to Jesus there was not one other of whom this could be said. They were all disciplined. However, the line of David's offspring was never rejected. The Lord did not go back on his choice, although (as we will see even in David himself) he was sorely provoked.

Eternal Kingdom (v. 16)

The whole message from the Lord for David finishes by returning to the permanence of what was being promised with a twice repeated "forever": "And your house and your kingdom shall be made sure *forever* before me.[31] Your throne shall be established *forever*" (v. 16).

"House," "kingdom," and "throne" are virtually synonyms here. "Your" is singular and refers again to David (v. 16). In his offspring the reign of David will be secure *forever*.

"Made sure" represents a Hebrew word that suggests reliability, trustworthiness, faithfulness, stability (v. 16). The promise was anticipated in the words of Abigail in 1 Samuel 25:28. This idea has been important at several points in the story that the books of Samuel have told. In 1 Samuel 2:35 the Lord promised that he would raise up "a *faithful* priest" and would build him "a sure [*reliable*] house." In 1 Samuel 3:20 Samuel was known as a *trustworthy* "prophet." David had a reputation for *faithfulness* (1 Samuel 22:14; cf. 26:23). Ironically even Achish "*trusted* David" (1 Samuel 27:12). *Faithfulness* is a gift from God that David promised to bring (2:6).[32] The long-anticipated stability, trustworthiness, and faithfulness will come in the royal house of David that will be reliable forever.[33]

There are many different ways in which this promise could now be traced through the pages of the Old Testament. In time David's kingdom was, in fact, destroyed. After Solomon it divided into two kingdoms (1 Kings 12). Each of these was, in turn, devastated by an enemy, first the Assyrians (2 Kings 17), then the Babylonians (2 Kings 25). This was the Lord's doing because the kings and their people "sinned against the LORD their God" (2 Kings 17:7, 19). This was a terrible tragedy and a mighty challenge to those who believed God's promise to David (see, for example, the book of Lamentations; Psalm 89:38–52).

However, through the decline and fall of the kingdom, there were prophets who insisted that the promise of 2 Samuel 7 stood. For example the prophet Isaiah proclaimed the continuing validity of this promise: "There shall come forth a shoot from the stump of Jesse,[34] and a branch from his roots shall bear fruit." "Of the increase of his government and of peace there will be no end, on the throne of David and over his kingdom, to establish it and uphold it with justice and with righteousness from this time forth and forevermore" (Isaiah 11:1; 9:7; see also Psalm 18:50; 89:3, 4, 19–37; 122:5; 132:11, 17; 144:10; Isaiah 16:5; 22:22; 37:35; 55:3; Jeremiah 17:25; 23:5; 30:9; 33:14–26; Ezekiel 34:23, 24; 37:24, 25; Hosea 3:5; Amos 9:11; Zechariah 12:7—13:1).

The New Testament introduces Jesus as "Christ, the son of David, the son of Abraham" (Matthew 1:1). One day Jesus engaged in a searching conversation with his disciples in the region of Caesarea Philippi. He asked them, "Who do you say that I am?" It was Peter who answered, perhaps on behalf of them all, "You are the Christ, the Son of the living God" (Matthew 16:13–16). It is almost certain that Peter had in mind the promise of 7:14, as well as echoes of this promise elsewhere in the Old Testament Scriptures (such as Psalm 2:7). The two aspects of Peter's identification of Jesus come from that context. "The Christ" means the anointed one, like David himself. "The Son of the living God" (Matthew 16:16) identifies Jesus in terms of the promise in 2 Samuel 7:14a. Peter had recognized that Jesus was the promised Messiah, the offspring of David, who was God's Son. In response Jesus affirmed Peter's insight and said, "On this rock *I will build . . .*" (Matthew 16:18). David's son, Solomon, built the temple in Jerusalem, in which the ark of God was placed, but the promise in 2 Samuel 7 found its *fulfillment* in Jesus. He was the offspring of David, in whom the purpose of God would finally reach its end. As promised, this son of David would build a house for the Lord's name. It would not now, however, be a temple in Jerusalem, but ". . . my church" (Matthew 16:18).[35] Those whom Jesus would gather to himself would become a spiritual house, of which the temple built by Solomon was only ever a shadow (see 1 Peter 2:4–8; 2 Corinthians 6:16–18).

In our next chapter we will see something of the impact the word of the Lord that came that night had on David when he heard it. We will need to consider the profound impact these words must have on us. They are words that directly impact our lives. The promised offspring of David (7:12) has come (Matthew 1:1; Acts 13:22, 23; Hebrews 1:5). The eternal kingdom (7:16) has begun (Matthew 4:17, 23; Luke 1:32). "The kingdom of the world has become the kingdom of our Lord and of his Christ, and he shall reign forever and ever" (Revelation 11:15). This news is the gospel we believe and proclaim—the most important words in the world.

17

The King's Prayer

2 SAMUEL 7:17–29

Our Father in heaven, hallowed be your name.
Your kingdom come, your will be done,
on earth as it is in heaven.

MATTHEW 6:9, 10

IT TAKES SOME COURAGE to pray the Lord's Prayer. I do not, of course, mean that it takes courage to *say the words* of the Lord's Prayer. Anyone can do that. But to *pray* the Lord's Prayer is an utterly extraordinary thing to do—to actually want the things we ask for in this prayer, and then to approach God, call him "Father," and ask for these things (Matthew 6:9). Who would dare to do such a thing?

In 2 Samuel 7:17–29 we will hear a prayer that King David prayed. It was very much like the prayer that Jesus taught his disciples. We might call it an anticipation of the Lord's Prayer. We will hear David speak of the "courage" that enabled him to pray as he did (see 7:27b). It is the same courage that enables us to pray the Lord's Prayer.

Consider David's prayer under three headings:

(1) The word of the Lord heard and heeded (vv. 17, 18a).
(2) Praise the Lord! (vv. 18b–24).
(3) Prayer to the Lord (vv. 25–29).

The Word of the Lord Heard and Heeded (v. 17, 18a)

David Heard (v. 17)

The most important thing to understand about King David's prayer is that it was a response to something he heard. As we have listened to the first half of 2 Samuel 7 we have heard what David heard. "The word of the LORD came to Nathan" on that historic night (7:4). As instructed, Nathan spoke the words he heard to David: "In accordance with all these words, and in accordance with all this vision, Nathan spoke to David" (v. 17). This is the key to King David's prayer.

Nathan's role was that of a faithful messenger who passed on "all these words" to David (v. 17; that is, of course, the words recorded in 7:5–16). By this means David heard "the word of the LORD" (7:4). The normal way in which the word of the Lord is heard is by being faithfully passed on from one human being to another. We might think that Nathan's experience of hearing the word of the Lord directly (as we might say) was more extraordinary than David's experience of hearing Nathan speak to him. Not so. The word of the Lord that came to David was the *same* word that had come to Nathan. The reality was the same, and David knew that it was extraordinary. The prayer he prayed proves that.

Nathan's experience is described as "all these words" and also as "all this vision" (v. 17). In other words, "these words" did not come from within Nathan himself—his wisdom, intuition, or subconscious. They came *to* Nathan *from* the Lord in an experience that was external to him—"this vision." That is what he passed on to David. However, we should also be clear that the entire emphasis of the experience lay on the "*words*" that came. Nothing of what Nathan *saw* has been recorded or appears to be of any interest to the Bible writer. Nor is there any suggestion that Nathan passed on to David anything visual. The essential content of "this vision" was "these words." The whole experience is summed up as "the *word* of the LORD came to Nathan" (7:4). The emphasis is on what he *heard*, not on what he saw.[1]

The description of "all these words" as "all this vision" (v. 17) may also have another level of meaning. The words that the Lord spoke to Nathan are so profoundly important that they enable the hearer to "see" the whole world and all of history in a new and brilliant light. In this sense "these words" *constitute* "this vision."

David Heeded (v. 18a)

What did David do when he heard the word of the Lord? "Then King David went in and sat before the LORD . . ." (v. 18a).

At the beginning of this chapter we heard that "the king lived [in Hebrew this is the same word as "sat" in verse 18a] *in his house*" (7:1), his fine house made of cedar. Nearby was a rather more humble dwelling, a tent that David had pitched for the ark of God (7:2; see 6:17). The impact of the word of the Lord upon him began with David moving from his grand house into the tent. He "went in and sat[2] *before the* Lord."

"Before the Lord" is a phrase we heard repeatedly in the previous chapter when David was rejoicing, leaping, dancing, and offering sacrifices *before the ark* (see 6:5, 14, 16, 17, 21). "Before the Lord" described the *reality* of that situation. The truth was that in his actions before the ark, King David was humbly recognizing the one who was the true King. What he did *before the ark* was in actuality "before the Lord" (v. 18).

Now we see the king sitting not in his opulent palace (as in 7:1) but where he belongs—"before the Lord." Even before we hear the words of his prayer, we can see something of the impact the word of the Lord had on the king. No longer did he see his "house of cedar" and the "tent" in which the ark of God dwelt in the same way as previously (7:2). The word of the Lord quite literally moved him from one to the other.

The rest of the chapter consists of the words David then spoke to the Lord. King David's prayer put into words the impact that the word of the Lord had on him. As we listen we will learn that we can only pray a prayer like this (and the Lord's Prayer is a prayer like this) if the word of the Lord has had the same impact on us.

King David's prayer has two parts. First he looks back at what the Lord had done (vv. 18b–24; cf. vv. 5–9a). These are words of praise. Second, he looks to the future (vv. 25–29; cf. vv. 9b–16). These are words of believing prayer.

Praise the Lord! (vv. 18b–24)

In the language of the Bible (especially the Psalms), to praise God means to declare *what he has done* and *what he is like*. Praise does not have to involve music. The essential thing is that the great deeds of the Lord as well as his power and goodness are made known. Such speech is praise.[3]

David's words, in response to hearing the word of the Lord, began with praise. First he spoke of what the Lord had done (vv. 18b–21), then of what the Lord (who had done these things) is like (vv. 22–24).

What the Lord Has Done (vv. 18b–21)

Amazing Grace—So Far (v. 18b)

David was amazed not only at what the Lord had done, but that he had done these things *for him*. He said, "Who am I, O Lord GOD, and what is my house, that you have brought me thus far?" (v. 18b).

"You have brought me thus far" (v. 18) responds to the Lord's words in 7:8, 9a.[4] The Lord had taken him from his shepherding work in Bethlehem to make him leader in Jerusalem over his people Israel. The Lord had been with him and had cut off all his enemies. "Who am I," David said, "that you should do all that for me?"

True praise can only come from a person who is humbled by what the Lord has done. John Newton's famous hymn comes from an experience like David's in this respect. "Amazing grace . . . that saved *a wretch like me*." The grace of God is astonishing precisely because it has been shown to people like David (and like us, cf. Romans 5:6–8). All who know God's goodness toward them will echo David's words, "Who am I?" (compare David's words in Psalm 8:4; 144:3).

Furthermore, David asked, "What is my house?" (2 Samuel 7:18).[5] He meant, of course, his family, in particular his descendants of whom the Lord had spoken ("the LORD will make you a house," 7:11). However, there is a delightful double entendre here. This chapter began with David's house ("his house," 7:1a). David, now seated in the tent "before the LORD" (v. 18), surely knew that "his house" (v. 1) of cedar was unimportant, just as he and his descendants were unworthy of all that the Lord had done for them.

David addressed God with a rather unusual phrase: "O Lord GOD" (more literally "my Lord Yahweh"[6]). The same expression occurs seven (possibly eight[7]) times through this prayer, but nowhere else in the books of Samuel. "My Lord Yahweh" is David's answer to the Lord's words, "my servant David" (7:5, 8). David recognized that the privilege of being Yahweh's servant lay in the fact that Yahweh was his Lord. Furthermore "my Lord Yahweh" was the very expression used by Abraham in his response to God's promise (Genesis 15:2, 8; but nowhere else in the book of Genesis).[8] This may have reflected David's awareness that the Lord's words to him were an extension of his promise to Abraham.[9]

More Amazing Grace—To Come (v. 19)

What the Lord had done for David "thus far" was astonishing in David's eyes (v. 18). However, it was even more astonishing that the Lord saw these things differently: "And yet this was a small thing in your eyes, O Lord God" (v. 19a). David knew that, remarkable as God's kindness toward him had been, in the Lord's eyes it was but the beginning, and a small beginning at that, when considered alongside what was to come. David had heard the Lord's promise: "You have spoken also of your servant's house for a great while to come . . ." (v. 19b). He was referring, of course, to the Lord's words in 7:11d–16. Not only had the Lord done great things for David, but his promise had assured that this grace would continue to be enjoyed by the descendants of David far into the future.

Ten times in this prayer David will identify himself as "your servant." This (like "my Lord Yahweh") was in response to God's great kindness in calling him "my servant David" (3:18; 7:5, 8).[10] In this David recognized that he had been granted a very great honor; yet it was an honor that lay not in David himself, but in the one whose "servant" he had become. Only Abraham, Moses, and Caleb had previously been called by the Lord "my servant" (Genesis 26:24; Numbers 12:7; 14:24; Joshua 1:2, 7).

David's grasp of the significance of the remarkable promise that the Lord had spoken to him is expressed enigmatically but profoundly: "and this is instruction for mankind, O Lord God!" (v. 19c). This brief exclamation expresses David's far-reaching understanding of the promise he had heard.[11]

David realized that this word of the Lord was not simply for him personally, nor was it restricted in its significance to his promised line of descendants, nor even to the nation of Israel. It concerned "mankind" (v. 19). The Hebrew is *adam*, the name of the first human, and the word for the whole human race ("humanity"). David understood that the words he had heard from Nathan were, like the promise that had been made to Abraham, an affirmation of the Lord's creation purpose to bless *adam*, mankind (Genesis 1:28). The promise to Abraham was that through his offspring, the great nation of Israel, blessing would reach all the families of the earth (Genesis 12:1–3). David now understood that this would happen through his own promised offspring, whose kingdom the Lord will establish forever. The Lord's words concerning David's house in the future were therefore for "mankind" (2 Samuel 7:19).

He called the Lord's promise (literally) "the *torah* of mankind." The Hebrew word *torah* almost always refers to divine instruction, especially the Law that God gave through Moses (see Psalm 19:7–11). Through Moses the Lord had given the Torah for Israel—his Law. In his words to David he had given the Torah for mankind—his promise. Amazing grace!

Being Known and Knowing (vv. 20, 21)

This left David speechless. "And what more can David say to you?" (v. 20a). He was not *literally* speechless (as this remarkable prayer shows). However, he was deeply aware of the inadequacy of *his* words to appropriately respond to the astonishing words he had heard from the Lord.

We may be reminded (as so often through these pages) of Hannah's prayer many years previously: "Talk no more so very proudly, let not arrogance come from your mouth" (1 Samuel 2:3a). The reason for this humbled speechlessness in Hannah's prayer was: "for the LORD is a God of knowledge, and by him actions are weighed" (1 Samuel 2:3b). The value and importance of everything (and everyone) is dependent on the Lord's knowledge. As the Lord knows a person, so that person is. Therefore the Lord's words matter infinitely more than any human words, certainly any human words that dare to be proud or arrogant.

David understood this. The reason he had nothing worthy to say was the Lord's knowledge of him: "For you know your servant, O Lord GOD!" (v. 20b). The Lord's "knowledge" of David was something far deeper than knowledge of facts and information about him. It included the Lord's great purpose for David (cf. Psalm 139:1–6).[12] Indeed God's purpose for David *was* his knowledge of David: "Because of your promise, and according to your own heart, you have brought about all this greatness, to make your servant know it[13]" (v. 21).

Notice the movement from "you know your servant" (v. 20b) to "your servant know[s]" (v. 21d). God's knowledge comes first and is expressed in his promise (literally "your word," v. 21a), which corresponds to his own will ("your own heart," v. 21b). This word coming to David is a great act of God ("all this greatness," v. 21c), which causes David to "know" the heart of God (v. 21d). Notice four important details here.

First, after all this, what did David "know" (v. 21)? Glance back at 5:12. Then "David *knew* that the LORD had established him king over Israel, and that he had exalted his kingdom for the sake of his people Israel." That was the start of it. But we have already heard that in the Lord's eyes this was "a small thing" (v. 19a). David now knew more than this.

Second, the "*small* thing"(v. 19) was surpassed by "all this *greatness*" (v. 21). What the Lord had now "brought about" (v. 21; literally "done") was to speak his promise (v. 19b). This involved "a *great* name" (v. 9c) for David and blessing for mankind (v. 19c). David's knowledge was caused by the greatness of God's act of revelation.[14]

Third, "all this greatness" (v. 21) had nothing whatsoever to do with

David's worthiness or importance. It came from God himself: "according to your own heart" (v. 21). The Lord's great purpose, in his promise to David, for Abraham, Israel, and the whole world arose from within himself. This is a wonderful expression of God's gracious sovereignty and freedom in all things. He did not choose Israel because they were a more impressive nation than others, but simply because he chose to love them (see Deuteronomy 7:7, 8). Likewise he did not choose David because of some qualities in that man, but simply because he chose to set his heart on David.[15] Of course, David's knowledge of what the Lord had done deeply affected him. But that is the point. The very great qualities of David as a man of God (the author of most of the Psalms) are a *consequence* of God's grace toward him, not the reason for it. Ultimately the difference between David and Saul was that the Lord showed grace to David that he did not show to Saul (see 7:14, 15), for reasons that lie hidden in God's own heart.[16]

Fourth, the Lord's *word* ("your promise" [v. 21] is literally "your word") is the effective cause or reason for what the Lord had now done.[17] That is, the Lord had *now* spoken this very great promise to David (v. 19b) "because of" (v. 21) the promise he had made earlier, specifically his word to Abraham.

David's words so far have spoken of what the Lord had done, especially in speaking his promise to David. In this way David praised the Lord. I have little doubt that David spoke these words to the Lord publicly. It is our privilege to join those who heard them. When we hear *what the Lord has done*, it leads to amazement at *what the Lord is like*. As David's words of praise continue he leads us along that path.

What the Lord Is Like (vv. 22–24)

The Greatness of the Lord (v. 22)

> Therefore you are great, O LORD God. For there is none like you, and there is no God besides you, according to all that we have heard with our ears. (v. 22)

There is a wonderful logic to praise. We know what God is like because of what he has done. "Therefore" makes this connection (v. 22).

The first conclusion to draw from the Lord's extraordinary word (his astonishing purpose for David, Israel, and all mankind) is, "you are great, O LORD God" (v. 22). The greatness he has *done* (in speaking this promise, v. 21c) displays how great he *is*.

The second conclusion is, "there is none like you, and there is no God besides you." David knew what Hannah knew. "There is none holy like the

LORD: for there is none besides you; there is no rock like our God" (1 Samuel 2:2). The God who had answered Hannah's prayer with the birth of Samuel had continued to be faithful to his great purpose for his people (and for the whole world) in the word of the Lord that had come to David. That is why David knew what Hannah knew.

The emphasis on *the word* of the Lord is underlined with the effective cause of David's knowledge of the Lord's unique greatness: "according to all that we have heard with our ears" (v. 22). In an important way David's experience was like ours. We know the Lord's greatness because of his *word* (v. 21a). "[F]aith comes from *hearing*" (Romans 10:17).

The Greatness of the Lord's People (vv. 23, 24)

Since the greatness of the Lord is known in his word concerning his purposes, God's unique greatness entails the uniqueness of his people who are at the center of those purposes. So David's thought moved back to reflect again on the greatness of what the Lord had done.

> And who is like your people Israel, the one nation on earth whom God went to redeem to be his people, making himself a name and doing for them great and awesome things[18] by driving out before your people, whom you redeemed for yourself from Egypt, a nation and its gods? And you established for yourself your people Israel to be your people forever. And you, O LORD, became their God. (vv. 23, 24)

David's praise had begun with the humble question, "Who am I?" (v. 18). The implied answer was that David was an unworthy man chosen by the Lord to serve him. Now he asked, with similar amazement, "[W]ho is like your people Israel?" The implied answer is that just as none is like the Lord (v. 22), none is like the Lord's people. The reason is that, unworthy though they were, they were a people chosen by the Lord to serve him. These two verses are rich in their reflections on the wonderful uniqueness of the people of God.

First, Israel was "your people" (v. 23a), and the Lord was "their God" (v. 24b). These ideas frame verses 23 and 24. The people belonged to the Lord, and they served him. This was Israel's privileged identity (see Exodus 6:7; Leviticus 26:12).

Second, there was only "one nation on earth" of whom this was true (2 Samuel 7:23; see Deuteronomy 4:7, 32–35). No claim to greatness (military, economic, cultural, or political) could match Israel's unique place in the nations of the world. In this way Israel was the "great nation" promised to

Abraham (Genesis 12:2; 18:18; 21:18; 46:3; cf. Exodus 19:6; Deuteronomy 4:6, 8; 26:5).

Third, the event that demonstrated their unique identity as the Lord's people more than any other was the exodus from Egypt. This event was not the beginning of this relationship. The beginning was God's promise to Abraham (see Exodus 2:24, 25; 3:7, 10; 5:1, 23; 7:4, 16; etc.). However "God went[19] to redeem [them] *to be his people,*" to make the promise a reality (2 Samuel 7:23; see especially Exodus 6:7; 19:4–6).

Fourth, there was a twofold purpose in what the Lord did when he redeemed Israel from Egypt.[20] On the one hand it was to make "himself a name." The Lord had promised to make David a "great *name*" and that his offspring would build a house "for [the Lord's] *name*" (7:9, 13). The whole Bible story moves toward *the name* of God being known through the people he makes his own (see 1 Samuel 12:22; also Matthew 6:9; 28:19; Acts 9:15; Romans 1:5; 9:17; 15:9; Philippians 2:9; 1 Timothy 6:1; Hebrews 13:15; Revelation 15:4). On the other hand, the Lord's purpose was to do "great and awesome things" for his people (2 Samuel 7:23). These things were acts of judgment against "a nation [Egypt] and its gods" (v. 23), or (more literally) "nations[21] [Egypt and the nations of Canaan] and each one's gods."

Fifth, David's contemporaries must understand that they were included in what the Lord did for his people back in the days of Moses and Joshua. Where the ESV (presumably for reasons of English style) has "for them," the Hebrew text has "for you [plural]" (v. 23).[22] This probably reflects the fact that the prayer was deliberately uttered publicly. While as a whole it was addressed to the Lord, the human hearers were not ignored, and therefore the prayer could include words directly addressed to them.[23] As they heard David praise God, they were to understand that both the Lord's great and awesome deeds of the past and the promise he had now made concerning the future kingdom were "for you."

Sixth, this continuity of past, present, and future is emphasized. The Lord has "established" his people "forever" (v. 24). "Established" and "forever" are echoes from the word of the Lord that David had heard from Nathan. David understood that the promise to establish *the kingdom of his offspring* forever (7:12, 13, 16) was the way in which the Lord would establish *his people* forever.[24]

The joy of praising the Lord, so obvious in David's words here, arises from knowing the reality of which the words of praise speak. Such praise always invites others to learn how great and good the Lord is and therefore to join in the praise.

Prayer to the Lord (vv. 25–29)

Just as we have seen something of the logic of praise (declaring what God has done leads to declaring what he is like), we now see the wonderful link between praise and prayer (in the narrower sense of making requests). How does a person who praises the Lord (knowing his greatness and goodness) pray to the Lord?

David's Prayer (vv. 25, 26)

Listen to David's prayer and see how it is shaped by his praise.

"Do as You Have Spoken" (v. 25)

David's prayer consisted of only one request:

> And now, O LORD God, confirm forever the word that you have spoken concerning your servant and concerning his house, and do as you have spoken. (v. 25)

"And now" introduces a conclusion from what has just been said.[25] The following prayer is based on the preceding words of praise.

The earnestness of David's one request is obvious in its repeated expression: "confirm forever the word that you have spoken" and "do as you have spoken" (v. 25). David's prayer was that the Lord would do what he had promised to do. In this way it was an anticipation of the prayer Jesus taught his disciples: "Your kingdom come" (Matthew 6:10).

The word of the Lord that Nathan spoke to David had affected him deeply. This word had created a longing in David's heart. God's promise was so good! What did David long for more than anything else? Nothing but what God had promised.

This (like the Lord's Prayer) is the kind of prayer that can only be prayed by a person who knows what God has promised and believes that it is good. In other words, *prayer* like this only arises from *praise* like David's. That is why the prayer is so full of confidence. David was not caught up with his own concerns, ideas, desires, or ambitions. His prayer was inspired by the word of the Lord that he had heard.

"Hallowed Be Your Name" (v. 26)

> And your name will be magnified [literally, made great] forever, saying, "The LORD of hosts is God over Israel," and the house of your servant David will be established before you. (2 Samuel 7:26)

David recognized that the goodness of God toward him, Israel, and mankind was not the whole story. Perhaps he had heard about Samuel's historic speech at Gilgal, where he had explained why the Lord would not abandon the people of Israel despite their repeated rejections of him, culminating in their demand for a king like the nations. Samuel had said:

> [T]he LORD will not forsake his people, for his great name's sake, because it has pleased the LORD to make you a people for himself. (1 Samuel 12:22)

When the Lord establishes the kingdom of David, people will say, "The LORD of hosts is God over Israel" (2 Samuel 7:26). In this way the name[26] of God will be made great. God's great goodness toward his people has this greater purpose—to display his greatness to the nations of the world and even beyond that.

When Jesus taught his disciples to pray for the kingdom of God to come, they were to pray "[H]allowed be *your name*" (Matthew 6:9). This idea is close to David's prayer. The kingdom Jesus promised is the fulfillment of the kingdom for which David was praying.

In due course the Apostle Paul explained that God called him to preach the gospel of his Son "for the sake of *his name* among all the nations" (Romans 1:5). This is the realization of David's prayer. The kingdom of David's offspring is the kingdom of Jesus Christ. God has realized his eternal purpose in Christ Jesus our Lord, so that through the assembly of God's people ("the church"), called together by the gospel, the "manifold wisdom of God might now be made known to the rulers and authorities in the heavenly places" (Ephesians 3:7–11).

David's Confidence to Pray (vv. 27, 28)

What a prayer David prayed! It was as remarkable as the prayer Christians pray today: "Our Father in heaven, hallowed be your name. Your kingdom come, your will be done, on earth as it is in heaven" (Matthew 6:9, 10). If such prayers are not exercises in fanciful wishful thinking, how is it possible to responsibly and seriously pray like this? David was clear:

> For you, O LORD of hosts, the God of Israel, have made this revelation to your servant, saying, "I will build you a house." Therefore your servant has found courage to pray this prayer to you. And now, O Lord GOD, you are God, and your words are true, and you have promised this good thing to your servant. (vv. 27, 28)

David "found courage" (v. 27; literally "found his heart") to pray this prayer because the Lord had spoken to him. "Made this revelation to your servant" (v. 27) is literally "uncovered the ear of your servant." David prayed like this because he had *heard* the word of the Lord. He knew that (1) the Lord who had spoken was truly *God* (literally, "you are he, the God"); (2) the Lord's words were *true* (literally, "*will* be truth" because they were words of promise); and (3) what the Lord promised was *good* (see 1 Samuel 25:30). Because the Lord had uncovered David's ears to hear God's true, good word, the king prayed as he prayed.

Just so it will be those whose ears the Lord uncovers to hear the gospel of Jesus Christ (the news that the promise to David finds fulfillment in him) who will pray, "Our Father in heaven, hallowed be your name. Your kingdom come . . ." (Matthew 6:9, 10).

David's Prayer: "Bless" (v. 29)

David concluded his prayer by summing up his request and introducing to his prayer the important language of "bless" and "blessing."

> Now therefore may it please you to bless the house of your servant, so that it may continue forever before you. For you, O Lord God, have spoken, and with your blessing shall the house of your servant be blessed forever. (v. 29)

Some time earlier, when David had brought the ark of God up to Jerusalem, the "household" (literally "house") of Obed-edom had been "*blessed . . . because of the ark*" (6:11, 12), and David had *blessed* his own household (6:20). The word that the Lord had now spoken, however, moved the idea of "blessing" to another level. In the context of David's prayer and the word of the Lord that he had heard, the "blessing" for which he now prayed was the "blessing" of the Lord's great promise (7:29). It was, as God had said to Abraham:

> I will make of you a great nation, and I will bless you and make your name great, so that you will be a blessing. I will bless those who bless you, and him who dishonors you I will curse, and in you all the families of the earth shall be blessed. (Genesis 12:2, 3)

This promise would be fulfilled through David's "house" (v. 16; see Psalm 72:17). The gospel of Jesus Christ is the news that in him the blessing promised to Abraham, and prayed for by David, has come to the nations of the world (Galatians 3:14). Hear this gospel, and believe it, and you will have the courage to pray the Lord's Prayer.

18

"I Will Make the Nations Your Heritage"

2 SAMUEL 8:1-6

IN 2 SAMUEL 7 we have heard some of the most important words ever heard in the history of the world—God's promise about his coming kingdom. In 2 Samuel 8 we will see a sketch of David's remarkable kingdom that in many ways anticipated the promised kingdom. The opening words of 2 Samuel 8 ("After this") should not be taken as strictly chronological.[1] The chapter includes events that took place before David became king (the defeat of the Amalekites, v. 12; see 1:1) and events from later in his reign (the Ammonites, v. 12; see 2 Samuel 10—12). "After this" (8:1) marks a *thematic* connection with the preceding chapter. Chapter 8 outlines what happened as a consequence of the promises made to David in chapter 7.

Particularly important is the promise, "I will appoint a place for my people Israel and will plant them, so that they may dwell in their own place and be disturbed no more. And violent men shall afflict them no more, as formerly . . ." (7:10). The "place" was the land God had promised Abraham (Genesis 12:1–3, 7). It extended from the River Nile in the south to the Euphrates in the north, from the Great Sea (the Mediterranean) in the west to the desert east of the Jordan valley (see Genesis 15:18; also Numbers 34:1–15; Deuteronomy 1:7; 11:24; Joshua 1:4). Until David became king, this promise was only ever partially realized. In the course of this chapter we will see how the kingdom of David extended to the west (v. 1), to the east (v. 2), to the north (vv. 3, 5), and to the south (8:13, 14). Throughout this area enemies were "subdued" so that they threatened Israel no longer. Under David God's great promise reached a new level of fulfillment. That is the theme of this chapter.

The problem with establishing God's kingdom is that this kingdom has enemies. In the case of David there were enemies in all directions. However, the Lord gave David victory over them all (vv. 6b, 14b). It was remarkable. The Philistines to the west (v. 1), the Moabites to the east (v. 2), Zobar to the far north (vv. 3, 4), the people of Damascus to the nearer north (vv. 5, 6), and the Edomites to the south (8:14) were all soundly "defeated" by David.[2] In each case the narrator records the victory and describes the consequences that followed. We need to pause and appreciate that each of these victories was an extraordinary act of God's goodness. The enemies of God's king were enemies of God's good purposes. Their defeat was necessary if God's kingdom of righteousness was to be established. It was a demonstration that God is able to save his king and his people from every enemy that threatens them.

Philistines (v. 1)

The Philistines occupied much of the coastal plain to the west of Israel's heartland.[3] According to Genesis 10:14 they came from a branch among the descendants of Ham and his son Egypt. They were therefore as ethnically distant from the Israelites as the Egyptians and the Canaanites. The Philistines come to prominence in Biblical history in the days of the judges (Judges 3:3). By the time of Samson they had become the most persistent enemies of the people of Israel (Judges 13—16[4]). In the days of Samuel they defeated Israel and captured the ark of the covenant, but were subsequently humbled by God's heavy hand (1 Samuel 4:10, 11; 5:6, 11) and subdued through Samuel's prayers (1 Samuel 7:7–14). They soon recovered, however, and the threat they posed was a big part of the motivation behind the Israelite demand for a king, "that we also may be like all the nations, and that our king may judge us and go out before us and fight our battles" (1 Samuel 8:20; see 1 Samuel 9:16b). The king they were given (Saul) never did manage to deliver Israel from the Philistine threat,[5] but a youth named David was launched into public prominence by his astonishing felling of the greatest Philistine of them all, Goliath of Gath (1 Samuel 17). Since that day David repeatedly fought against the Philistines, invariably prevailing (1 Samuel 18:6, 30; 19:8; 23:1–5). Twice he actually moved to Philistine territory, deceiving the enemy in different ways (1 Samuel 21:10–15; 27:1–12). In their final battle against King Saul, the Philistines triumphed (1 Samuel 31) and occupied much of Israel's territory. The promise of deliverance from this oppression had been a powerful motivation for the northern tribes to accept David as their king (see 3:17, 18).

Victory (v. 1a)

David's double defeat of the Philistines in the vicinity of Jerusalem after he had begun his reign from that city has been recounted in 5:17–25. This appears to have led to their subjugation in their own territory. All of this is now recorded as the first item in the official summary of David's great kingdom: "David defeated the Philistines and subdued them" (v. 1a). David did what Saul had been appointed to do (1 Samuel 9:16).

Defeating Israel's enemies is what God's king did. It is what Saul had failed to do. Second Samuel began with a reference to David "striking down" (same verb in Hebrew as "defeated" here) the Amalekites (1:1), another enemy Saul had failed to deal with adequately (1 Samuel 15; 28:18). Under David the greatest contemporary adversary of God's people was at last overcome. The last reference to the Philistines being "subdued" was 1 Samuel 7:13, when Samuel had led Israel. Since then the Philistines were far from "subdued." Only under King David were they again put in their place. David completed the work he had begun years earlier when, as a lad, he had killed Goliath.

The idea of enemies being "subdued" by a leader raised up by God to save his people from them is something of a refrain in the book of Judges (Judges 4:23; 11:33). When the enemy was "subdued," the land enjoyed "rest" (Judges 3:30; 8:28). What had been temporarily achieved from time to time under the judges was now accomplished in a more permanent sense under King David. Israel would be "disturbed no more" by the Philistines (see 2 Samuel 7:10).

The Hebrew word translated "subdued" (8:1) suggests humiliation.[6] In a positive sense it can refer to humbling oneself before God in repentance (see Leviticus 26:41; 1 Kings 21:29; 2 Kings 22:19; 2 Chronicles 7:14; 12:6, 7, 12; 30:11; 32:26; 33:12, 19, 23; 34:27; 36:12). Those, however, who refuse to humble themselves before the Lord will be "humbled" by him ("bring . . . low" in Job 40:12; cf. Isaiah 25:5). The "subduing" of the Philistines is therefore a fitting fulfillment of Hannah's prayer: "The bows of the mighty are broken . . . the LORD . . . brings down to Sheol . . . he brings low . . . the adversaries of the LORD shall be broken to pieces. . . . The LORD will judge the ends of the earth; he will give strength to his king and exalt the horn of his anointed" (1 Samuel 2:4–10).

The Philistines "subdued" before King David anticipate the day when "at the name of Jesus *every* knee [will] bow, in heaven and on earth and under the earth" (Philippians 2:10). We are asking for nothing less when we pray, "Your kingdom come" (Matthew 6:10).

Consequences (v. 1b)

As a consequence of David's decisive victory over the Philistines, "David took Metheg-ammah out of the hand of the Philistines" (v. 1b). This translation suggests that "Metheg-ammah" was the name of an otherwise unknown city. It is difficult to understand why this particular victory would be singled out for mention here. It seems more likely that the Hebrew "metheg-ammah" is a figurative expression meaning "the bridle of the mother city."[7] From the parallel account in 1 Chronicles 18:1 we may deduce that the "mother city" of the Philistines was Gath. "Taking the bridle" is a metaphor for taking control. The Philistines were apparently now under David's direct power. Unlike the other nations about to be mentioned, they were not simply vassals who had to pay tribute. Their chief city was now ruled by David.[8]

Moab (v. 2)

The Moabites, whose territory lay southeast of Jerusalem on the other side of the Dead Sea,[9] play a very different role in Biblical history from the Philistines. They were the descendants of Moab, a son of Abraham's nephew, Lot (conceived in rather unfortunate circumstances, Genesis 19:36, 37). The Moabites were therefore relatively close kinsmen to the Israelites.[10] However, the Moabites had persistently expressed hostility to the Israelites. In the days of Moses, on the journey from Egypt to the promised land, the Israelites had sought safe passage through Moabite territory, but were refused (an act that was not forgotten, Judges 11:17). Moab's king, Balak, unsuccessfully attempted to have Israel cursed by the prophet Balaam (Numbers 22—24), which was also long remembered (Joshua 24:9). Contrary to Balak's plan, Balaam prophesied the defeat of Moab:

> A star shall come out of Jacob,
>   and a scepter shall rise out of Israel;
> it shall crush the forehead of Moab . . . (Numbers 24:17)

In 2 Samuel 8 we learn that this "star" or "scepter" was David, and we hear the fulfillment of Balaam's prophecy.

On another occasion Moabite women seduced Israelite men and lured them into idolatry (Numbers 25; see Psalm 106:28; Hosea 9:10).

The Moabites' hostility toward the Israelites was such that they were explicitly excluded from the assembly of God's people (Deuteronomy 23:3–6). Their animosity continued into the period of the judges (Judges 3:12–30; cf. 1 Samuel 12:9).

However, there was a remarkable exception. A Moabite woman named Ruth joined the Israelites and accepted Israel's God (Ruth 1:4, 16). She was David's great grandmother (see Ruth 4:13–22). This probably explains the help David received from the king of Moab in his days on the run from Saul (1 Samuel 22:3, 4), although that may also have been a case of "the enemy of my enemy is my friend" (see 1 Samuel 14:47).[11]

Victory (v. 2a)

It seems that whatever friendly relations David had once personally enjoyed with Moab, the enmity between Israel and Moab continued. David dealt with this enemy as he had dealt with the Philistines: "he defeated Moab" (v. 2a). We know nothing more of the circumstances of this conflict.

Consequences (v. 2b)

David's treatment of the defeated Moabites was severe.

> [A]nd he measured them with a line, making them lie down on the ground.
> Two lines he measured to be put to death, and one full line to be spared.
> (v. 2b)

This is difficult. David executed fully two-thirds of the captured Moabites, strangely measured out with a rope. When we read of such terrible violence, especially in the pages of the Old Testament, we need to respond carefully.

First, we should understand that a sense of abhorrence at violence and slaughter like this is right. God himself has no pleasure in the death of anyone (Ezekiel 18:23, 32). While the Bible is honest in its record of such horrors as this, no one should delight in the suffering. God doesn't.

Second, when the Bible recounts a violent episode such as this, it does not *necessarily* follow that David's actions are approved. David was not a perfect king. Unlike the Lord Jesus, we cannot be confident that all David did was right. Like David, Jesus will act in judgment, but unlike David, Jesus will be the perfectly righteous judge (see John 16:8; Acts 17:31; 24:25; Romans 2:5; 2 Thessalonians 1:5; 2 Timothy 4:8; Revelation 19:11).

However, a third point must be made. Our task as humble Bible readers is to learn *from the text of Scripture*, not to make our own independent moral judgments of what we find there.[12] In the context of the generally positive presentation of David's reign in 2 Samuel 8, we need to see that in this case David's actions against the Moabites seem to be approved. Calvin captures the tone of the text: "the stringency which David exercised against the Moabites ought not to be considered cruelty, but to be the just judgement of God, since they had abused his long patience and had mocked him."[13] Rather than mounting our moral high horse and condemning David's action, we should recognize that the righteousness and justice of God's kingdom includes his judgment on all rebellion against him. In his mercy this judgment may be held back for a time, giving opportunity for repentance (Romans 2:4). But, as was the case with the Moabites, the day will come when God will "judge the world in righteousness" (Acts 17:31). Let us not abuse the patience of God by failing to heed the warnings of the gospel concerning the righteous judgment to come (2 Thessalonians 1:5–10). What happened to the Moabites should serve as such a warning.

Mercy was shown to a third of the captured Moabites. No reason is given. Shall we then accuse David of injustice? To quote Paul in a similar context, "By no means! For [God] says to Moses, 'I will have mercy on whom I have mercy, and I will have compassion on whom I have compassion'" (Romans 9:14, 15).

The outcome was that the surviving Moabites became David's subjects. "And the Moabites became servants to David and brought tribute" (v. 2c). The Hebrew word translated "tribute" is used for sacrificial "offerings" made to God (1 Samuel 2:17, 29; 3:14; 26:19; but note also "present" in 1 Samuel 10:27). They may not have been *willing* subjects, but in the end God's king will prevail (again "every knee [will] bow," Philippians 2:10).[14]

Zobah (vv. 3, 4)

Zobah was a powerful Aramean kingdom[15] well to the north of Israel, beyond Damascus, probably emerging as a power in the region during the eleventh century BC.[16] This is only the second mention of Zobah in the Bible,[17] although the conflict referred to in verse 3 probably took place later than the one we will hear about in 2 Samuel 10,[18] where Hadadezer's earlier wide sphere of influence, even beyond the Euphrates River, is recognized (see 10:16).[19]

Victory (v. 3)

Hadadezer was a "king of Zobah." Ironically his name means "Hadad is [my] help." Hadad was an ancient pagan deity, a storm-god whose name means

"The one who smashes." He did not prove to be much "help" to the one who bore his name when confronted with King David: "David also defeated Hadadezer the son of Rehob, king of Zobah, as he went to restore his power[20] at the river Euphrates[21]" (v. 3).

Hadadezer had clashed with David earlier, in a conflict that will be described in 10:15–19. This had involved "Arameans [esv, Syrians] who were beyond the Euphrates" (10:16). They were soundly defeated by David on that occasion. This is probably the background to Hadadezer going "to restore his power at the river Euphrates" (8:3). The events of 8:3–6 may then have occurred between 10:19 and 11:1.[22] For a second time, then, David defeated Hadadezer.[23]

David's victory over Hadadezer extended his influence northward and eastward at least toward the Euphrates. The promise to Abraham was being fulfilled.

Consequences (v. 4)

David's actions after his victory over Hadadezer are summarized:

> And David took from him 1,700 horsemen, and 20,000 foot soldiers. And David hamstrung all the chariot horses but left enough for 100 chariots. (v. 4)

In the earlier conflict involving Hadadezer, David had killed a greater number than this (10:18).[24] But Hadadezer had not learned the lesson. This time David "took" the captured troops (8:4). Some, no doubt, were killed; others may have been incorporated into the Israelite forces as mercenaries. Hamstringing horses was what the Israelites had done previously, at the Lord's command, to disable the enemy's chariotry (Joshua 11:6–9).[25]

But what are we to make of David sparing enough horses "for 100 chariots" (2 Samuel 8:4)? Israel did not yet use chariots. Indeed "trust in chariots" was understood by David himself as contrary to "trust in the name of the Lord our God" (Psalm 20:7; see 2 Kings 18:24 where Hezekiah's trust in chariots is linked to trust in Egypt; cf. Isaiah 31:1; 2 Kings 19:23 where Sennacherib's trust in chariots is linked to mocking the Lord). One of the requirements for a king in Israel was that "he must not acquire many horses for himself" (Deuteronomy 17:16). Furthermore, one of the features of the undesirable kingship of which Samuel had spoken (when the Israelites had first demanded to have a king "like all the nations," 1 Samuel 8:5, 20) was the possession of chariots (1 Samuel 8:11, 12).

Chariots were commonly used by Israel's enemies (Deuteronomy 20:1; Joshua 17:16–18; Judges 1:19; 4:3; 1 Samuel 13:5; 2 Samuel 1:6; Jeremiah 46:9; 47:3; 50:37; 51:21; Ezekiel 23:24; 26:7; 39:20; cf. Revelation 18:13). The Egyptians had employed chariots against Israel, but they and their chariots had suffered an extraordinary never-to-be-forgotten defeat by God's power (Exodus 14:5–9, 23–25; 15:4, 19; Deuteronomy 11:4; Joshua 24:6; Isaiah 43:17).

As far as we know it was David's rebel son, Absalom, who first introduced the use of chariots in Israel (15:1), followed by another delinquent, Adonijah (1 Kings 1:5). Solomon developed chariotry on a large scale (1 Kings 4:26; 9:19, 22; 10:26) and became a trader in chariots (1 Kings 10:29). Subsequently chariots were commonly used by Israelite and Judean kings (1 Kings 12:18; 16:9; 18:44; 22:34, 35, 38; 2 Kings 8:21; 9:16, 21, 24, 27, 28; 10:15, 16; 13:7; 23:30). However, Josiah's reforms involved burning chariots (2 Kings 23:11).

In general terms, trust in chariots was a sign of Israel's turning from trust in the Lord (Psalm 20:7). Isaiah's condemnation of apostate Israel includes, "there is no end to their chariots" (Isaiah 2:7). These chariots will be no defense against the Lord's judgment (Isaiah 22:18). The Lord "will destroy your chariots" (Micah 5:10; cf. Zechariah 9:10). When the Lord "makes wars cease to the end of the earth," he will burn "the chariots with fire" (Psalm 46:9).

It seems reasonable, then, to be more than a little disturbed at the comment about David saving enough horses for 100 chariots. Was he intending to experiment with this strange military hardware? Is there a hint here that David's trust in the Lord was not perfect?[26] Probably, although we have no evidence that the experiment was carried through.

Damascus (vv. 5, 6a)

The Aramean kingdom immediately to the north of Israel (between Israel and Hadadezer's Aram-Zobah further to the north) was Aram-Damascus (represented in the ESV here by "the Syrians of Damascus"). Aram-Damascus was apparently a vassal state (or possibly an ally) of the powerful Hadadezer and so provided military support to their overlord in his struggle with David.

Victory (v. 5)

And when the Syrians [Hebrew, Aram] of Damascus came to help Hadadezer king of Zobah, David struck down 22,000 men of the Syrians [Hebrew, in Aram]. (v. 5)

The irony is pointed. We noted that Hadadezer's name means "[The god] Hadad is [my] help." But Hadad had been no help! And so the people of Damascus must come to "help." They proved to be of no more "help" than the useless god they all trusted. David struck them down in even greater numbers than he had taken from Hadadezer himself.

Consequences (v. 6a)

The consequences of David's victory over the Arameans of Damascus were unambiguous. The enemies of King David had to submit to his rule.

> Then David put garrisons[27] in Aram of Damascus, and the Syrians [Hebrew, Aram] became servants to David and brought tribute. (v. 6a)

Just like the Moabites (v. 2), the people of Damascus submitted to David's rule (they became his "servants"), and they "brought tribute" (v. 6). Willingly or otherwise every knee will bow to God's king and give him the honor due to him.

Summary (v. 6b)

The situation in every direction throughout the land that has been sketched in verses 1–6a is now summarized: "And the LORD gave victory to David wherever he went" (v. 6b). The Lord had promised, "I will give you rest from all your enemies" (7:11). In another place the Lord promised his king, "I will make the nations your heritage" (Psalm 2:8). That is exactly what he did.

"Gave victory to" (2 Samuel 8:6) is, more literally, "saved." The Lord "saved" David from every threat and danger. The Lord was indeed with David wherever he went (cf. 7:9). No wonder David learned to pray:

> Save me, O my God!
> For you strike all my enemies on the cheek;
> you break the teeth of the wicked. (Psalm 3:7)

The defeat of the enemies of God's king is not only inevitable because God's king is *God's* king, it is also necessary. Only with the overthrow of the enemies will God's kingdom come. Because the Lord saved David from his enemies, David was able to save his people from those same enemies. This is what God's kingdom is like. It is a kingdom of safety from the enemies.

Jesus is able to save his people from their enemies, even from death, because God saved him from death (see Hebrews 5:7). The kingdom of Jesus is a kingdom of safety from our enemies, even from death.

19

A Kingdom of Justice and Righteousness

2 SAMUEL 8:7–18

But let justice roll down like waters,
and righteousness like an
ever-flowing stream.

AMOS 5:24

THIS WAS THE CALL OF GOD to a people who had wandered far from his ways. Theirs had become a community in which the rich oppressed the poor (Amos 2:7), the powerful took advantage of the weak (Amos 4:1), and the privileged trampled on the underprivileged (Amos 5:11; 8:4). In other words, it was a society that had become like all other nations in the world. To be sure there are variations in the degree to which human communities suffer from injustices and unrighteousness, but in every human society there are those who long for freedom from wrongs.

Mind you, those who cry out most desperately for freedom do not always know how to replace a tyrannical regime with something better. Too often the world has seen a dreadful government overthrown, only to be replaced by something not much better, or even worse. Sometimes the power vacuum is filled by anarchy, which can only be brought under control by a new tyranny, often backed by military force. The solution to injustice and unrighteousness in human communities is far from simple.

What does the Bible have to say to a world where too many societies suffer in these ways? Certainly there is the news that God cares about justice and righteousness in human communities (see Psalm 33:5; 89:14; 97:2; 99:4; Jeremiah 9:24). Those who take God seriously must take this seriously (see Psalm 15; Ezekiel 18:5–9).

But the Bible has more to say than this. At about the same time as Amos proclaimed God's call for justice and righteousness (it was the eighth century BC), the prophet Isaiah promised that a king would come who would rule with justice and righteousness:

> For to us a child is born,
> to us a son is given. . . .
> Of the increase of his government and of peace
> there will be no end,
> on the throne of David and over his kingdom,
> to establish it and to uphold it
> with justice and with righteousness
> from this time forth and forevermore.
> (Isaiah 9:6, 7; cf. Jeremiah 23:5; 33:15)

We have seen that this king had been promised more than 150 years earlier, in the days of David. He would be a descendant of David (hence "on the throne of David," Isaiah 9:7), whose kingdom the Lord will establish forever (7:12–17).

The gospel of Jesus Christ announces the fulfillment of these promises. Our Lord Jesus Christ is the perfectly righteous one (see Acts 3:14; 7:52; 22:14; 2 Timothy 4:8; 1 Peter 3:18; 1 John 2:1, 29). The kingdom of God, which he has inaugurated and will one day finally establish, is a kingdom of righteousness (Romans 14:17). This is the kingdom and the righteousness we are to "seek first" (Matthew 6:33). When Christians today pray, "Your kingdom come" (Matthew 6:10), we are praying for justice to roll down like waters and righteousness like an ever-flowing stream. The ultimate answer to the injustices and other wrongs of human societies is the gospel of our Lord Jesus Christ, the news of God's kingdom.

Those who are wealthy, powerful, or otherwise privileged in this world are often less sympathetic to the longing for justice and righteousness. The reason is simple. Too often their advantaged position depends on the injustices and disadvantages that others suffer. As Jesus said, "How difficult it is for those who have wealth to enter the kingdom of God! For it is easier for a camel to go through the eye of a needle than for a rich person to enter the kingdom of God" (Luke 18:24, 25).

However, Jesus also said that those who truly "hunger and thirst for righteousness . . . shall be satisfied," for the promised kingdom "is at hand" (Matthew 5:6; 4:17).

The kingdom of David, 1,000 years before Jesus was born, anticipated the promised kingdom of perfect justice and righteousness and gave us a glimpse of what it will be like. The eighth chapter of 2 Samuel presents us with a summary sketch of David's kingdom.[1] "David administered justice and equity [or righteousness[2]] to all his people" (8:15b). While his was certainly not a perfect kingdom (as we will see), it did display in a preliminary, anticipatory way the nature of God's kingdom and gives us a preview of what the kingdom of God is like. It was a kingdom characterized by justice and righteousness (although perhaps not yet rolling down like waters and an ever-flowing stream).

What does the Bible mean when it promises a kingdom of "justice and righteousness" (v. 15)? In 2 Samuel 8 we see that David's kingdom of justice and righteousness involved:

(1) Victory wherever he went (vv. 1–6).
(2) The wealth of the nations brought to Jerusalem (vv. 7–12).
(3) A great name for the king (vv. 13, 14).
(4) Justice and righteousness for all the people (vv. 15–18).

Each of these is an aspect of the justice and righteousness of David's kingdom and anticipates the justice and righteousness of the kingdom of our Lord Jesus Christ. In our previous chapter we saw David's victories over the nations who threatened or opposed his kingdom of justice and righteousness. We come now to three other displays of the justice and righteousness of this kingdom.

The Wealth of the Nations Brought to Jerusalem (vv. 7–12)

Powerful nations glory in their wealth. They trust in their riches. Even today nations tend to be ranked in terms of their prosperity. The wealth of the nations defeated by David was brought to Jerusalem and "dedicated to the LORD" (v. 11).

The Wealth of Hadadezer (vv. 7, 8)

We hear first about the wealth of Hadadezer.

> And David took the shields of gold that were carried by the servants of Hadadezer and brought them to Jerusalem. And from Betah and from Berothai,[3] cities of Hadadezer, King David took very much bronze. (vv. 7, 8)

There may be a certain ambiguity at this stage as we watch David take these objects of gold and bronze from Hadadezer. Did he bring them to Jerusalem for his own aggrandizement?[4] It will soon become clear that this was not the case.

David's actions anticipated something greater. It would be spoken of by the prophets many years after King David's time. "The wealth of the nations shall come to you," promised Isaiah (Isaiah 60:5, 11; 61:6). Later still Haggai proclaimed God's word:

> And I will shake all nations, so that the treasures of all nations shall come in, and I will fill this house with glory, says the LORD of hosts. The silver is mine, and the gold is mine, declares the LORD of hosts. The latter glory of this house shall be greater than the former, says the LORD of hosts. And in this place I will give peace, declares the LORD of hosts. (Haggai 2:7–9; cf. Zechariah 14:14)

When the Magi brought "their treasures" to Bethlehem and gave gifts of gold, frankincense, and myrrh to the infant Jesus, the fulfillment of these promises was signaled (compare Matthew 2:11 and Isaiah 60:6). We look forward to the day when the kings of the earth will bring their glory into the New Jerusalem, where Jesus will reign forever (see Revelation 21:24, 26).

All of this we rightly see anticipated as David brought the gold and bronze of Hadadezer to Jerusalem.

The Wealth of Toi (vv. 9, 10)

We are now introduced to another northern king whose reaction to King David was very different from the Philistines, the Moabites, Hadadezer, and the people of Damascus earlier in the chapter.

> When Toi king of Hamath heard that David had defeated the whole army of Hadadezer, Toi sent his son Joram to King David, to ask about his health and to bless him because he had fought against Hadadezer and defeated him, for Hadadezer had often been at war with Toi. And Joram brought with him articles of silver, of gold, and of bronze. (vv. 9, 10)

Hamath was a city to the north of Hadadezer's kingdom of Zobar.[5] Its origins were Canaanite (Genesis 10:18). It is often mentioned in reference to the northern boundary of the promised land[6] (Numbers 13:21; 34:8; Joshua 13:5; Judges 3:3; 1 Kings 8:65; 2 Kings 14:25; 1 Chronicles 13:5; 2 Chronicles 7:8; Ezekiel 47:15–17, 20; 48:1; Amos 6:14; Zechariah 9:2). At this time Toi, the king of Hamath, had been suffering aggression from his southern neighbor, the powerful Hadadezer. News of David's defeat of Hadadezer was welcomed by Toi. What a wise man! His deadly enemy had been crushed. He had the sense to seek good relations with David. He sent his son[7] to seek peace[8] with King David (note the full title for David) and to "bless" (that is, congratulate) him.

Toi was a model of what the kings of the earth ought to do when faced with the Lord's anointed King.

> Now therefore, O kings, be wise;
>   be warned, O rulers of the earth.
> Serve the LORD with fear,
>   and rejoice with trembling.
> Kiss the Son,
>   lest he be angry, and you perish in the way,
>   for his wrath is quickly kindled.
> Blessed are all who take refuge in him. (Psalm 2:10–12)

That is what the king of Hamath did. It is not necessary to face God's King as an enemy. Those who do will certainly be overthrown, but those who seek peace with him, as did Toi, will certainly find it.

Toi sent, by the hand of his son, further contributions to the wealth that was accumulating in Jerusalem. The wealth of the nations comes not only by confiscation from defeated nations, but also as willing gifts from those who gladly submit to God's king.

The Wealth of All the Nations (vv. 11, 12)

What was the purpose of this accumulating wealth? Importantly we are told:

> These also King David dedicated to the LORD, together with the silver and gold that he dedicated from all the nations he subdued, from Edom [Hebrew, Aram],[9] Moab, the Ammonites, the Philistines, Amalek, and from the spoil of Hadadezer the son of Rehob, king of Zobah. (vv. 11, 12)

These riches taken from defeated enemies and given by willing friends were not the usual spoils of war, to puff up the conqueror. They were "dedicated [or consecrated] to the LORD" (v. 11). Eventually this means that the treasures gathered will be for "the house of the LORD" to be built by David's son (see 1 Kings 7:51; cf. 1 Chronicles 22:2–5).[10]

A Great Name for the King (vv. 13, 14)

The Lord had promised David, "I will make for you a great name" (7:9). We noted that this was a reaffirmation of the much earlier promise to Abraham,

"I will . . . make your name great" (Genesis 12:2). Now we hear that David received a great name.

> And David made a name for himself when he returned from striking down 18,000 Edomites [Hebrew, Aram] in the Valley of Salt. Then he put garrisons in Edom; throughout all Edom he put garrisons, and all the Edomites became David's servants. (vv. 13, 14a)

Some have suggested that David *making* a name *for himself* suggests that this was something quite different from what the Lord had promised as a *gift*. Was this "name" (v. 13) an autonomous achievement by David, implying that he was getting too big for his boots?[11] This is unlikely.[12] God's gifts do not necessarily exclude human agency. "David defeated . . ." in verses 1, 2, 3, and 5 is entirely consistent with "the LORD gave victory to David" in verses 6, 14. Just so, when David "made a name" (v. 13), anyone who has heard the Lord's promise to him (7:9) should recognize that behind David's activity was the faithfulness of God to his promise.

David's fame is associated with a particular victory in "the Valley of Salt" (8:13). This is not a known location, but for obvious reasons is often assumed to be somewhere near the Dead Sea. This, in addition to the references to Edom in verse 14, has encouraged many commentators and translators to emend the Hebrew "Aram" to "Edom[ites]."[13] In Hebrew these two words are very similar and could easily be confused. Edom was southeast of the Dead Sea and may well have had a valley known as the Valley of Salt, while Aram refers to a wide area well to the north and some distance from the Dead Sea. At the same time much attention has been given in this context to David's victories over Arameans, and we do not know that this "Valley of Salt" was near the Dead Sea.

Whether the victory that led to David's fame was over Arameans or Edomites, it is clear that he did gain control of Edom (v. 14), thus extending his influence well to the south,[14] just as he had extended it to the north (v. 6).

Of all the nations mentioned in this chapter, the Edomites were the closest relatives of the Israelites. They were the descendants of Jacob's brother Esau (Genesis 36:1–17). Despite these links of kinship (or because of them) the Edomites had refused to grant the Israelites safe passage through their land in the days of Moses (Numbers 20:14–21). This severe act of unkindness was remembered (Judges 11:17, 18), and hostilities continued through the following years.[15] Some time later Balaam prophesied the victory now recorded in 2 Samuel 8:

> Edom shall be dispossessed;
>   Seir also, his enemies, shall be dispossessed.
>   Israel is doing valiantly.
> And one from Jacob shall exercise dominion
>   and destroy the survivors of cities! (Numbers 24:18, 19)

Saul had fought with the Edomites (1 Samuel 14:47), but had at least one ruthless Edomite among his servants (1 Samuel 21:7). David's conquest of Edom was further fulfillment of the Lord's promises.

Just as David gained a "name" by his God-given victories (2 Samuel 8:13), so Jesus has been given "the name that is above every name" (Philippians 2:9).

This section concludes with the reminder that stood at the end of the previous section: "And the LORD gave victory to David wherever he went" (2 Samuel 8:14b). The wording is identical to verse 6b, thus providing something like a refrain to the chapter. The chapter is about the Lord "saving" his anointed king. The salvation of the king "wherever he went" (v. 14) made possible his reign of justice and righteousness, the subject of the fourth and final section of the chapter.

Justice and Righteousness for All the People (vv. 15–18)

There has been a repeated emphasis throughout this chapter on the comprehensiveness of David's rule. This is conveyed with the recurring word "all"[16] as well as the wide geographical area covered by the chapter. We have noted that this area corresponds to the extensiveness of the promise that had been made to Abraham.

David's Reign (v. 15)

It is fitting, therefore to sum up the chapter: "So David reigned [or was king] over *all* Israel" (v. 15a). His reign entailed victory over all those who opposed his rule and threatened his people, peace with those who welcomed his rule, and the wealth of those nations being turned to the service of the Lord rather than the glory of men who opposed God's kingdom.

This state of affairs is described as follows: "And David administered [literally, did] justice and equity [or, righteousness][17] to [or for] all his people" (v. 15b). It is difficult to overstate the significance of this statement. What we are seeing in 2 Samuel 8 is a summary of David's reign of "justice and righteousness" (v. 15).

This is the first of many occurrences in the Bible of the phrase "justice and righteousness." Once previously the same two words have been used together in reverse order. God had said of Abraham, "I have chosen him, that he may command his children and his household after him to keep the way of the LORD by doing *righteousness and justice*, so that the LORD may bring to Abraham what he has promised him" (Genesis 18:19).[18] In King David this promise of God reached a remarkable fulfillment. He "did justice and righteousness for all his people" (2 Samuel 8:15). Subsequent to David's reign the phrase "justice and righteousness" repeatedly represents:

(a) What can be expected from the (promised) king in David's line (see 1 Kings 10:9; Isaiah 9:7; 32:16; Jeremiah 22:3, 15; 23:5; 33:15; Ezekiel 45:9).

(b) What can be expected from God himself (Job 37:23; Psalm 33:5; 99:4; 103:6; Isaiah 33:5; Jeremiah 4:2; 9:24).

(c) What is lacking when the people are no longer enjoying the goodness of God's kingdom (Isaiah 59:9, 14; Amos 5:7).

(d) What God requires in the behavior of his people (Proverbs 21:3; Ezekiel 18:5, 19, 21, 27; 33:14, 16, 19; Amos 5:24).[19]

"Justice and righteousness" should probably not be understood as two distinct concepts, but as a wonderful reality rightly described by these two words: it is "justice" that is "righteous." This sounds redundant in English, where "justice" and "righteousness" are almost synonyms. The Hebrew is a little more subtle.

"Justice" represents a word that has played an important role in the story of the books of Samuel. Perhaps with a note of irony 1 Samuel 2:13 spoke of the perverse "justice" (ESV, "custom") of the priests with the people in the days of Eli. This was decidedly unrighteous "justice." Samuel's sons turned out to be no better than Eli's. They "perverted justice" (1 Samuel 8:3). When the people then demanded a king "like all the nations" (1 Samuel 8:5, 20), Samuel solemnly warned them that the "justice" (ESV, "ways") of such a king would be the same kind of "justice" that Eli's and Samuel's sons had delivered (1 Samuel 8:9, 11). Then when Saul was appointed as their king, Samuel spelled out the "justice of the kingdom" (ESV, "rights and duties of the kingship"), that is, what was required of a king over God's people (1 Samuel 10:25). Later David's dealings with various groups was called "justice" (ESV, "custom" in 1 Samuel 27:11, "rule" in 1 Samuel 30:25).[20] Now we learn that King David did justice that was *righteousness* for all his people.

"Righteousness" also represents a Hebrew word that is not exactly captured by the English noun. It is more than a moral principle. It is actions and behavior that are "right" and that put things "right" in the situation and relationships envisaged.[21] "Righteousness" is a major theme of the Bible. God himself is righteous: he acts to put things right. His acts to save his people, which include acts of judgment against their enemies and acts of undeserved love toward Israel, can be called "righteousnesses" (ESV, "the righteous deeds of the LORD" in 1 Samuel 12:7; cf. Isaiah 56:1).[22] Eventually the righteousness of God is revealed in the gospel of Jesus Christ (Romans 1:17). This means that his wrath is revealed against all unrighteousness (Romans 1:18) and that he has displayed his righteousness in the way in which he has acted to save sinners (Romans 3:26).

David's kingdom of justice and righteousness was a remarkable phenomenon. To get a sense of what this king was like, read David's promise concerning his reign in Psalm 101. His was an anticipation of the kingdom of Jesus, where the ultimate enemy is defeated, the wealth of the nations will be brought to the New Jerusalem, and the King has been given a name that is above every name.

David's Ministers (vv. 16–18a)

This just and righteous kingdom was ordered.[23]

> Joab the son of Zeruiah was over the army, and Jehoshaphat the son of Ahilud was recorder, and Zadok the son of Ahitub and Ahimelech the son of Abiathar were priests, and Seraiah was secretary, and Benaiah the son of Jehoiada was over the Cherethites and the Pelethites . . . (vv. 16–18a)

Joab, of course, we have met before (first in 2:13). He and his brothers have played a significant role in David's story. Joab will be part of that story until after David's death, although David never forgot his ruthlessness (see 1 Kings 2:5, 6). After David's death Joab backed the wrong side in the tussle for the kingship and was executed by Solomon (1 Kings 1:7, 18, 19; 2:22, 28–35).

Little is known of the Jehoshaphat ("the LORD judges") who was David's "recorder" (2 Samuel 8:16). He still held this office under Solomon (1 Kings 4:3). The "recorder"[24] may have been the official in charge of public records[25] or one who brought state business to the king's notice.[26]

This is the first mention of Zadok ("righteous"). According to 1 Chronicles 6:1–8, 50–53 he was a descendant of Aaron's third son, Eleazar.[27] He will be an important figure in David's story, particularly during Absalom's rebellion. In due course Zadok will be a key supporter of Solomon as David's rightful successor (1 Kings 1:8, 38, 39).

It appears that Abiathar's son, Ahimelech, was named after his grandfather who, at the cost of his and many other lives, had assisted David in the days of Saul (1 Samuel 21:1–9). Abiathar had been the only survivor of Saul's subsequent massacre of the priests at Nob (1 Samuel 22:20), and he had then served David well (see 1 Samuel 22:20–23; 23:6, 9; 30:7). He continued to serve King David, along with Zadok (15:24, 29, 35; 17:15; 19:11; 20:25). Second Samuel 8:17 informs us that Abiathar's son also served as priest alongside Zadok, although we hear nothing more of this son in 2 Samuel.[28]

The two priests named represent two priestly families. Their lineage goes back to two sons of Aaron. Zadok was descended from Eleazar, Ahimelech from Ithamar (1 Chronicles 24:3). The latter was the line to which Eli had belonged. Many years earlier the demise of the house of Eli had been prophesied (1 Samuel 2:31–34). This happened in stages. Eli's sons, Hophni and Phinehas, died in battle (1 Samuel 4:11). All other priests of Eli's house, save one, were slaughtered by Saul (1 Samuel 22:19, 20). That one, Abiathar, would later be banished by Solomon, in final fulfillment of the prophecy (1 Kings 2:27). The prophecy had included a promise that the Lord would "raise up for myself a faithful priest, who shall do according to what is in my heart and in my mind. And I will build him a sure house, and he shall go in and out before my anointed forever [literally, all the days]" (1 Samuel 2:35). Zadok will be one part of the fulfillment of this promise (again see 1 Kings 2:26, 27).[29]

Seraiah ("the Lord prevails") served as royal secretary in David's kingdom (v. 17b). The "secretary" was an important figure in the kingdom. He played a significant role in public affairs. We may think of him as both the king's private secretary and secretary of state, responsible for all correspondence, internal and external, and (later) for the temple collections (2 Kings 12:10).[30]

Benaiah ("the Lord builds") was a mighty warrior whom David set over his bodyguard (23:20–23). "The Cherethites and the Pelethites" (v. 18a) appears, therefore, to refer to David's bodyguard. It has been suggested that they were foreigners (perhaps of Cretan and Philistine origin respectively) in the personal service of David. They were impressively loyal to him (see 15:18; 20:7) and to his son Solomon (1 Kings 1:38, 44). After David's death we hear no more of them. Benaiah, who was over them, would later be a loyal servant of Solomon and the executioner of Adonijah, Joab, and Shimei (1 Kings 2:25, 34, 46). Solomon made him commander of his army (1 Kings 2:35; 4:4).

David's kingdom of justice and righteousness was well-ordered. We may note that the Lord Jesus Christ brings good order to the lives of those who trust in him (1 Corinthians 14:40; Colossians 2:5).

David's Sons (v. 18b)

The final note of this chapter is a considerable puzzle: ". . . and David's sons were priests" (v. 18b). With no further comment we must assume that the writer intended this comment to raise, but not necessarily answer, questions.

The statement at the end of this broad-brush sketch of David's kingdom of justice and righteousness draws our attention to "David's sons" (v. 18). On the one hand the future of David's kingdom would obviously depend on a successor. Interest in David's kingdom therefore naturally involves an interest in David's sons. On the other hand the promise of God, which was the foundation of David's kingdom, had a particular interest in a particular son of David. God had promised, "*He* shall build a house for my name, and I will establish the throne of *his* kingdom forever" (7:13).

However, in relatively recent history human leadership of the people of Israel had failed precisely because of the failure of the leaders' sons. Eli's sons had been corrupt rogues (1 Samuel 2:12–17). Samuel's sons had been no better (1 Samuel 8:1–3, 5).[31] What would David's sons be like?

"David's sons were priests" (2 Samuel 8:18).[32] If we have been conditioned to worry about the sons of Israel's leaders, this statement will stir those concerns. Does it mean that they presumed to make themselves priests (like King Uzziah many years later, 2 Chronicles 26:16–18)? We might notice that two of David's sons did in fact perform priestly actions (sacrifices) in the context of rebellion against David (Absalom in 15:12 and Adonijah in 1 Kings 1:9, 19). While the words at the end of 2 Samuel 8 can hardly be alluding to these actions, a reader familiar with the way in which the story will unfold may recognize a hint of the trouble to come in the statement, "and David's sons were priests."[33]

However, at this stage it is no more than a hint. Like the comment in 8:4 about chariots, this may be seen, with the benefit of hindsight, as an early suggestion that all was not entirely right in the remarkable kingdom of David.[34] The world will have to wait for Jesus Christ. Only with him will the kingdom of perfect and permanent justice and righteousness come.

20

The Kindness of the King

2 SAMUEL 9

THE KINGDOM OF GOD is unlike any human society. It is a kingdom of perfect justice and righteousness. While David's kingdom was not perfect (far from it, as we shall see), in his reign something of the character of the kingdom of God was on display. King David "did justice and righteousness for all his people" (8:15 AT).

We have seen that David's kingdom of justice and righteousness was powerful and prevailed over all opposition (8:1–6), as the kingdom of God ultimately will do (Revelation 19:11–16). In David's kingdom the wealth of the nations was "dedicated to the LORD" (8:7–12), just as it will finally be returned to its true owner and creator (Revelation 21:26). As God's chosen king, David's name became great (8:13), just as Jesus has been given a great name (Philippians 2:9; Revelation 19:13, 16). David administered an ordered kingdom (8:16–18), just as everything will be in its right place in God's kingdom (see the orderliness of John's vision in Revelation 21:9–21).

All of this is wonderful, but perhaps it should not be surprising when we consider that the God behind both David's kingdom and the kingdom of his beloved son, Jesus Christ, is the creator and sustainer of all things whose orderly ways are presented magnificently in the opening chapter of the Bible (Genesis 1).

However, what we are about to see in 2 Samuel 9 is astonishing. It is not what most of us would expect in a kingdom of "justice and righteousness."

In 2 Samuel 9 we see the *kindness* of King David (vv. 1, 7), which is described at one point as "the kindness of God" (v. 3). This chapter presents a particular instance of "David doing justice and righteousness for all his people" (8:15 AT).[1] David showed extraordinary kindness to one who could have been his enemy. In this David's kingdom again displayed a very important characteristic of the kingdom of God. God's kingdom is a kingdom of kindness to those who were once enemies (Romans 5:8, 10; Colossians 1:21, 22).

The surprising story of King David's kindness unfolds in seven stages, with the king's promise at the center.

(1) Kindness promised (v. 1)
    (2) Kindness initiated (vv. 2–4)
        (3) Kindness doubted (vv. 5, 6)
            (4) Kindness assured (v. 7)
        (5) Kindness questioned (v. 8)
    (6) Kindness given (vv. 9–11)
(7) Kindness experienced (vv. 12, 13)

Kindness Promised (v. 1)

Some years had passed since David became king of Israel.[2] The Biblical historian has no doubt passed over many things that David said and did through those years. He has given us a general picture of growing security, prosperity, reputation, and good order in chapter 8. The particular incident he now chooses to recount begins with David asking a surprising question:

> And David said, "Is there still anyone left of the house of Saul, that I may show him kindness for Jonathan's sake?" (v. 1)

These are the first recorded words of King David since his thankful prayer in 7:18–29 in response to the great promise of 7:1–17. The question he asked was not addressed to anyone in particular, but expressed a concern that was on his heart.

What prompted David to ask this after he had been king for perhaps a decade or more?[3]

On the one hand, by this time key people "of the house of Saul" (9:1) and their supporters had died. We have heard of the deaths of Saul himself (1:1), his son Jonathan (1:4), 360 of "the house of Saul" at the battle of Gibeon (2:31; cf. 3:1), Abner (3:27), and Saul's last surviving son, Ish-bosheth (4:7). The record is clear that David himself had no involvement in any of these deaths. However, it is understandable that he may have wondered, in those circumstances, "Is there still anyone left of the house of Saul?"[4] But what did David intend to do with any surviving member of Saul's household?

We cannot forget that in Saul's eyes David had become his bitterest enemy (see 1 Samuel 18:29; 19:17; and then 21:10). After Saul's death, his son Ish-bosheth became David's rival, claiming to be king over all Israel

(2:8, 9). There had then been a long period of "war between the house of Saul and the house of David" (3:1). It would be no surprise if David was concerned that "anyone left of the house of Saul" (9:1) might be a threat to him and his kingdom. His inquiry could have been motivated by an intention to eliminate any such threat.

But it wasn't. Many years earlier David had made certain promises to the then King Saul and to Saul's son Jonathan. On the one hand he had acceded to Saul's request: "Swear to me . . . by the LORD that you will not cut off my offspring after me, and that you will not destroy my name out of my father's house" (1 Samuel 24:21, 22). The record so far in 2 Samuel testifies to David's faithfulness to that oath: he played no part in the deaths of any of the house of Saul. On the other hand he had bound himself more solemnly still by a covenant to Saul's son, Jonathan (see 1 Samuel 18:1–4; 20:16, 17, 42; 23:18). Jonathan had foreseen this day when David would reign securely over all Israel and made the following request:

> If I am still alive, show me the steadfast love of the LORD, that I may not die; and do not cut off your steadfast love from my house forever, when the LORD cuts off every one of the enemies of David from the face of the earth. (1 Samuel 20:14, 15)

David did not forget the love by which he had sworn this oath to Jonathan (1 Samuel 20:17). Jonathan was not "still alive" (1 Samuel 20:14), but the day had come when the Lord had, so to speak, "cut off every one of the enemies of David" (see 8:1–14). David's question in 9:1, therefore, was "for Jonathan's sake."

The key word in 9:1 is translated "kindness." It is the same word Jonathan had used when he said, "Show me the *steadfast love* of the LORD" (1 Samuel 20:14). It refers to extraordinary acts of kindness, "meeting an extreme need, outside the normal run of perceived duty, and arising from personal affection or pure goodness."[5] David spoke, therefore, of surprising, unexpected kindness—unexpected, that is, were it not for the promise that David had remarkably made to Jonathan.[6]

"Kindness" has featured at several key points in David's story so far. It was important in David's relationship to Jonathan, particularly (as we have seen) in 1 Samuel 20. Remember that Jonathan was, on the one hand, the crown prince who was first in line to inherit Saul's kingdom. On the other hand Jonathan was the first to recognize and welcome David as God's chosen king, to whom he gladly surrendered his inheritance (see 1 Samuel 18:1–4). When David found his life in danger from Saul, he sought and received kindness from Jonathan (1 Samuel 20:8, literally, "do kindness"). In turn Jonathan asked David to "do kindness" (ESV, "show . . . steadfast love") with him when he became king (1 Samuel 20:14, 15).

When David became king over the tribe of Judah, he commended the people of Jabesh-gilead for the "kindness" (ESV, "loyalty") they had shown to Saul and anticipated that the Lord himself would likewise "do kindness" (ESV, "show steadfast love") with them. David promised that he himself would be the agent of this "good" (2:5, 6). In other words, David's initial presentation of himself to the people of the north was as one who would do "kindness," the very kindness of God.

In God's great promise concerning David and his house, the Lord promised that his own "kindness" (ESV, "steadfast love") will never depart from the son of David whose kingdom will therefore be established forever (7:15).

Thus David's question in 9:1 about any survivors from the house of Saul, to whom he could show kindness "for Jonathan's sake," indicates: (a) David's faithfulness to his word to Jonathan (this was a king who kept his promises); (b) the kind of king he intended to be (this was a king who showed kindness); (c) something of the very character of God (this king was like God himself in his kindness).

Kindness Initiated (vv. 2–4)

David's question became known, at least in the circles close to David. Steps were taken to find the answer. A man who had served in Saul's household was identified and brought to David to assist in the inquiries. He found himself interrogated by the king.

> Now there was a servant of the house of Saul whose name was Ziba, and they called him to David. And the king said to him, "Are you Ziba?" And he said, "I am your servant." (v. 2)

Ziba had probably been a senior servant in Saul's household. We learn a little later that he had a large family and some twenty servants of his own (v. 10). He will reappear in our story in two further scenes (16:1–4; 19:25–30). In due course we will have questions about his character. At this stage we simply note that this (former) "servant of the house of Saul" presents himself to David as "your servant" (9:2).[7] We know nothing more about his change of allegiance, but it is reasonable to assume that he had joined with "all the tribes of Israel" when they made David their king (5:1–3).

Throughout the account of David's conversations with Ziba, David is called "the king." This is what Ziba was acknowledging with his words, "Your servant" (v. 2).

The king addressed Ziba with the question that had been on his mind.

> And the king said, "Is there not still someone of the house of Saul, that I may show the kindness of God to him?" (v. 3a)

He did not refer to Jonathan this time, presumably because his promise to Jonathan was known only to David. Strikingly, however, the kindness he intended to show is described as "the kindness of God" (v. 3).

Jonathan had spoken of "the kindness [ESV, "steadfast love"] *of the LORD*" in his request to David in 1 Samuel 20:14. This is what he asked David to do for him if he were still alive when David became king. David now intended to fulfill that request by showing "the kindness of God" (v. 3).

This should also be understood in the light of David's earlier approach to the people of Jabesh-gilead, when David had said, "May the LORD show kindness and faithfulness to you. And I am the one who will do *this good* to you" (2:6 AT). David seems to have been aware that in his kindness as king he was the agent of God's own kindness.[8]

It was Ziba's reply to the king that brought Jonathan's name into this conversation.

> Ziba said to the king, "There is still a son of Jonathan; he is crippled in his feet." (v. 3b)

It would seem that Ziba either believed David's promise of kindness or he feared the king sufficiently to betray his former master's grandson. On the surface Ziba was acting as the "servant" of David he now claimed to be (v. 2). However, doubts about his motives will be raised when he appears again later in the story.

Much later in this book we will learn that Ziba was not telling David the whole truth. There were other surviving members of Saul's family (21:8). Why they were not mentioned here (or, indeed, by the narrator in 4:4) is not explained. The impression given both to David (and to the reader at this stage) is that this son of Jonathan was the only one left of Saul's household.

Ziba chose to tell the king just one thing about this son of Jonathan: he was "crippled in his feet" (9:3). It is reasonable to assume that both the existence of this son of Jonathan and his disability were news to David. However, readers of 2 Samuel have heard about him in some detail previously (4:4).

There we were told how he came to be "crippled in his feet"[9] when he was five years old and that his name was Mephibosheth.

Ziba may have highlighted the handicap of Jonathan's son in order to assure David that he was not a potential threat to David's throne[10] (as his uncle, Ish-bosheth, had been, 2:8, 9). However, we (the readers) can hardly miss the fact that David was informed of this son of Jonathan in terms that showed his need of "kindness" (9:1).

The king was determined to "show . . . kindness" (v. 1) to this newly discovered and obviously needy son of Jonathan. "The king said to him, 'Where is he?' And Ziba said to the king, 'He is in the house of Machir the son of Ammiel, at Lo-debar'" (v. 4).

Lo-debar was a location on the east side of the Jordan River, possibly not far from Mahanaim.[11] Machir, the son of Ammiel, was presumably a person with the means and the inclination to look after and provide refuge to the helpless grandson of Saul. He may still have been a Saul loyalist. The events that are about to unfold may have caused a change of heart in Machir, because later we will see him using his resources to help David when he was in need (17:27–29). Was he won over by the kindness of this king?

Kindness Doubted (vv. 5, 6)

David wasted no time. He sent for this survivor of the house of Saul and brought him from his hiding place. "Then King David sent and brought him from the house of Machir the son of Ammiel, at Lo-debar" (v. 5).

It must have been terrifying for the young, disabled man to be taken from his caregiver in Lo-debar and brought all the way to Jerusalem, to the king who had been his grandfather's bitter enemy. While the king's men may not have used force to bring him, I doubt that the poor refugee felt he had any choice in the matter.

He is named for the first time in this episode as he came to the king, and his family connections are clearly stated: "And Mephibosheth the son of Jonathan, son of Saul, came to David" (v. 6a)—wondering, no doubt, what would become of him. He had only been five years old when his father and grandfather had died (4:4). Presumably he knew nothing about David's promise to Jonathan.

We can picture him trembling with fear as he "fell on his face and paid homage" (v. 6b). Ziba had not felt the need to grovel so. But the cripple, with considerable difficulty and even agony, bowed to the ground before King David, almost certainly fearful that he might not rise again alive.

Mephibosheth had no reason to expect the "kindness" of which David had spoken (v. 1). Certainly he had no claim on this king, who (from Mephibosheth's point of view) had every reason to regard him as his enemy.

As he lay there prostrated before the king, shaking and afraid, he must have been utterly astonished to hear the king's voice. "And David said, 'Mephibosheth!'" (v. 6c). I have no doubt that there was kindness in David's voice. This may be subtly suggested by the way in which the speaker is not called "the king" or even "King David," but simply and personally "David." David addressed the son of the man he had so greatly loved (see 1:26).

David's word changed everything for Mephibosheth. When he responded, it was with new and surprising confidence. "And he answered, 'Behold, I am your servant'" (v. 6d).[12] That is, he submitted to David as his king.

Kindness Assured (v. 7)

The kindness indicated in David's first word to Mephibosheth was then expressed unambiguously in a wonderful promise that stands at the center of the narrative.[13]

"And David said to him, 'Do not fear'" (v. 7a). In the Bible extraordinary promises are often preceded by these assuring words (see, for example, 1 Samuel 12:20; 22:23; 23:17[14]). The promises of the Bible come to those who have powerful reasons to be afraid. The promises, however, give greater reason not to fear. That is the case here. There were ample reasons for Mephibosheth to be afraid of David. David's promise had the power to quiet his fears.

"[F]or I will show you kindness" (v. 7b). The Hebrew is more emphatic: "I will *surely* show you kindness." What was promised is not what was expected (at least by Mephibosheth). The promise opened a new possibility that did not exist before—*kindness* from the king!

As we have seen, the reason for this promised kindness had to do with a commitment David had made before Mephibosheth had been born. Mephibosheth did nothing to deserve this kindness. The promise had a basis and purpose that did not depend on Mephibosheth. It was "for the sake of your father Jonathan" (v. 7c, cf. v. 1). It is not unusual for promises in the Bible to be "for the sake of" something greater than and beyond the one who receives the promised kindness. The Lord promised not to forsake his people Israel "*for his great name's sake*" (1 Samuel 12:22). He exalted David's kingdom "*for the sake of* his people Israel" (5:12). David understood that the Lord had revealed his great purposes to David "*for the sake of* your word" (7:21 AT). In a similar way it was David's covenant with Jonathan that stood behind his promise to Mephibosheth. David's kingdom would be one in which those with reason to be his enemies (like Jonathan and Mephibosheth) would receive kindness if only they (like Jonathan and now Mephibosheth) received him as their king.

The kindness David promised was expressed in two gifts to Mephibosheth. First, "I will restore to you all the land of Saul your father" (v. 7d). "Land" (perhaps better, "fields") did not mean the land over which Saul had ruled, but the personal private land possessed by the former king, his farmlands. These would be fully restored to Saul's grandson. He would suffer no loss in David's kingdom.

Second, and perhaps even more importantly, "you shall eat at my table always" (v. 7e). To eat at the king's table was a special privilege and signified the king's particular favor (cf. 1 Kings 2:7; 18:19). There would always be a place at David's table for Mephibosheth.[15]

The promise of David to this potential enemy wonderfully anticipates the gospel of Jesus Christ, which, as always, brings the fullness of God's gracious kingdom. As David said "Do not fear" to Mephibosheth (2 Samuel 9:7), the angel said to the shepherds:

> Fear not, for behold, I bring you good news of great joy that will be for all the people. For unto you is born this day in the city of David a Savior, who is Christ the Lord. (Luke 2:10, 11)

As David promised kindness (the kindness of God) to Mephibosheth, "the goodness and loving kindness of God our Savior [has] appeared" in Jesus Christ (Titus 3:4).

As David ensured that Mephibosheth did not lose out by becoming a servant of David, so Jesus said:

> And everyone who has left houses or brothers or sisters or father or mother or children or lands, for my name's sake, will receive a hundredfold and will inherit eternal life. (Matthew 19:29)

As David welcomed Mephibosheth to his table "always" (2 Samuel 9:7), so Jesus said, "people will come from east and west, and from north and south, and recline at table in the kingdom of God" (Luke 13:29; cf. Psalm 23:5, 6).

Kindness Questioned (v. 8)

Understandably Mephibosheth found David's promise difficult to believe.

> And he paid homage and said, "What is your servant, that you should show regard for a dead dog such as I?" (v. 8)

Still trembling, the crippled young man again bowed low before the king. The scene corresponds to verse 6, but is transformed by the promise that had now been heard. The kindness of God's king was astonishing. It certainly could not be accounted for by reference to the insignificant and unworthy recipient. Years earlier David had likened himself to "a dead dog" (1 Samuel 24:14). The image suggests insignificance and powerlessness. The king's kindness was utterly unexpected by Mephibosheth. "How can this be?" he essentially asked.

Kindness Given (vv. 9–11)

The kindness of the king was put into effect through instructions to Ziba (thus corresponding in this balanced narrative to the earlier conversation with Saul's old servant in verses 2–4).

> Then the king called Ziba, Saul's servant, and said to him, "All that belonged to Saul and to all his house I have given to your master's grandson.[16] And you and your sons and your servants shall till the land for him and shall bring in the produce, that your master's grandson may have bread to eat. But Mephibosheth your master's grandson shall always eat at my table." (vv. 9, 10a)

This may mean that Mephibosheth's farmlands would provide the food he would eat at the king's table, in which case we should remember both that the farmlands were the king's gift to him and that the privilege of eating at the king's table was considerably more than the provision of a free meal.[17] On the other hand it is possible that the farmlands produced Mephibosheth's day-to-day provisions, while his regular place at David's table was not for every single meal. Either way King David was "doing" the kindness that he had promised.

As an aside the narrator informs us that Ziba himself was a man of considerable means. "Now Ziba had fifteen sons and twenty servants" (v. 10b). We may conclude that he had been a senior figure in the household of Saul (or just possibly that he had managed to do very well through the demise of the house of Saul). We notice, however, that Ziba, with his substantial household, had not taken responsibility for the care of his master's crippled son. It is reasonable to wonder whether Ziba may have been something of an opportunist who saw no reason to maintain his loyalty to the house of Saul once its fortunes had collapsed.

We may, therefore, have reason to suspect that Ziba's submission to David was not entirely without guile.[18] But for the time being he said what was expected: "Then Ziba said to the king, 'According to all that my lord the king commands his servant, so will your servant do'" (v. 11a).

The consequence was that David's kindness intended in verse 1, proposed in verse 3, and promised in verse 7 was actually given to Mephibosheth. "So Mephibosheth ate at David's table,[19] like one of the king's sons" (v. 11b). A place at the king's table was the epitome of the promised kindness and implies the other aspects of it as well.

Kindness Experienced (vv. 12, 13)

This story of King David's kindness toward Mephibosheth concludes by describing directly Mephibosheth's experience.

First we learn that Mephibosheth had a son. "And Mephibosheth had a young son, whose name was Mica" (v. 12a). We presume that this information was (or soon became) known to David. This son represented a future for the house of Saul. David's kindness was therefore utterly extraordinary. It was not simply an act of benevolence toward a cripple whose condition made him no threat to David's kingdom. David's goodness toward Mephibosheth ensured the survival of Saul's line.[20] It was, in other words, precisely what he had sworn to Saul and to Jonathan (see 1 Samuel 20:15; 24:21). David was faithful.

Second, "And all who lived in Ziba's house became Mephibosheth's servants" (v. 12b). This included, we may presume, Ziba himself. If our suspicions about Ziba are valid, then Mephibosheth was restored to the position Ziba had undermined.

Third, "So Mephibosheth lived in Jerusalem" (v. 13a). He took up residence in the city of David. No longer was he hiding from the new king in remote Lo-debar. On the contrary, he took his place at the very center of the kingdom of David.

Fourth, indeed "he ate always at the king's table" (v. 13b). For the fourth time this remarkable point is made (see vv. 7, 10, 11). Mephibosheth, grandson of Saul, was elevated to the most privileged position in David's kingdom. He enjoyed the intimacy of table fellowship with the king.

Finally, we are reminded, "Now he was lame in both his feet" (v. 13c). In this last line of the story a word that had featured in an earlier episode is introduced. When David had taken Jerusalem from the Jebusites, he had referred to these enemies as "the *lame* and the blind, who are hated by David's soul." This incident had resulted in the saying, "The blind and the *lame* shall not come into the house" (5:8).

Whatever that saying may have meant, the present incident shows that

David's kingdom of justice and righteousness involved kindness toward this lame man. He was welcomed, not excluded; honored, not despised.

Years after David the prophets in Israel will look forward to a day when what happened for Mephibosheth will be surpassed for many more who are "lame" (both literally and metaphorically). "Then," proclaimed Isaiah, "shall the lame man leap like a deer" (Isaiah 35:6; cf. 33:23). Among the great company whom the Lord will gather there will be "the lame" (Jeremiah 31:8; cf. Micah 4:6, 7). The fulfillment of these promises in the presence of Jesus were signs that he was the long-anticipated son of David who would finally bring God's kingdom (see Matthew 11:2–6; 15:30, 31; Luke 14:13, 21).

The justice and righteousness of God's kingdom involves kindness to enemies, even lame enemies.

21

Those Who Despise the Kindness of the King

2 SAMUEL 10

WE EXPERIENCE GOD'S kindness every moment of our lives. Every breath we take and each beat of our heart is a gift from our maker. There are so many expressions of his kindness every day that no one could number them. How slow we are to recognize the magnitude of his goodness toward us! Add to this the wonder that his righteous judgment "against all ungodliness and unrighteousness of men" (Romans 1:18) has not yet fallen on us, and we ought to see that his forbearance and patience are extraordinary. Each moment that we are spared from God's wrath is an experience of the riches of his kindness.

Many people "presume on the riches of his kindness and forbearance and patience." Far from being full of thankfulness for God's goodness, their hearts are hard toward him, and they arrogantly refuse to acknowledge him. In this way they despise his kindness.

In his letter to the Romans the Apostle Paul poses the following question:

> Do you presume on [or despise[1]] the riches of [God's] kindness and forbearance and patience, not knowing that God's kindness is meant to lead you to repentance? (Romans 2:4)

In other words, God's kindness (which we experience constantly) has a purpose—to lead us to turn to him in repentance. This is a very serious matter. Paul goes on to explain what those who show contempt for God's kindness are really doing.

But because of your hard and impenitent heart you are storing up wrath for yourself on the day of wrath when God's righteous judgment will be revealed. (Romans 2:5)

David, as we have seen, was a king who showed the kindness of God (see 9:3). In this respect his kingdom anticipated (in a shadowy and imperfect way) the character of the kingdom of God that is now being proclaimed throughout the whole world (Matthew 24:14). In Jesus Christ "the *kindness* and love of God our Savior appeared" (Titus 3:4 NIV).

The kindness of King David, which was extended to Mephibosheth in 2 Samuel 9, is also the theme of 2 Samuel 10. This time, however, the kindness of the king was despised, and those who despised it suffered the consequences. As we hear the story, we will see what a terrible thing it is to show contempt for the kindness of God's king.

Second Samuel 10 is also the beginning of a new section in the story of David's kingdom.[2] The account of David's dealing with the Ammonites that begins here continues to the end of 2 Samuel 12 and provides the setting for the notorious events that will be recounted in chapter 11. In due course the events of 2 Samuel 10 will become the background for that episode, intensifying its shocking impact. At this stage we focus on the background events themselves.

Kindness Despised (vv. 1–5)

David's Surprising Kindness (vv. 1, 2)

The occasion for the story about to be told was the death of a foreign king. "After this the king of the Ammonites died, and Hanun his son reigned in his place" (v. 1).

The opening phrase ("After this") is less of a chronological indicator than it seems in English. The events in this chapter almost certainly took place prior to those recounted in 8:3–12.[3]

The king who had died was Nahash. He had played a role in Israel's history once before, in the early days of King Saul. He was a cruel tyrant who threatened dreadful violence against the people of Jabesh-gilead (see 1 Samuel 11:1, 2). Furthermore his people, the Ammonites, had a long history of hostility toward the people of Israel.[4]

In the world of the Old Testament the death of a king often created a period of instability as his successor established his power. The death of Nahash could therefore have afforded David the opportunity to subjugate a long-time enemy of his people. We would not be surprised to read that

David acted to crush the new king before he had a firm grip on the reins of power.

That is not what happened. "And David said, 'I will deal loyally [better, show kindness[5]] with Hanun the son of Nahash, as his father dealt loyally [showed kindness] with me'" (v. 2a). This is a complete surprise. The new king of the Ammonites is to experience the same characteristic of King David as Jonathan's son, Mephibosheth—*kindness*!

David's remarkable proposal was connected in some way[6] with another surprise. Hanun's father, the infamous Nahash, had (said David) "dealt kindly" to David. We can only guess what David meant. Nahash and his army had been soundly defeated by Saul and driven from Israel's territory (see 1 Samuel 11:11; 14:47). When David became Saul's hated enemy, it is possible that Nahash, on some occasion(s) unknown to us, provided him with protection or assistance. This is less perplexing than it may seem when we remember that David did receive such support from the Philistines (1 Samuel 27:1–4).[7]

Whatever the "kindness" was that Nahash had shown to David, it did not follow that David necessarily owed anything to Nahash's son. Nonetheless David intended to show "kindness" to Hanun.

David initiated his first act of kindness to the new king. "So David sent by his servants to console [Hanun] concerning his father" (v. 2b). David's kindness was expressed in sympathy, a word of comfort, to the son whose father had died.

As David "sent" his servants to carry out his intentions, we see him acting as king (v. 2). The comfort offered was from David himself, to be delivered (literally) "by the hand of his servants." Of course, David could not know how his gracious action would be received. His intentions should not be judged by the outcome, but by their inherent goodness.[8]

The scene now shifts from David (presumably in Jerusalem) to the east, across the Jordan River, to the land of the Ammonites. "And David's servants came into the land of the Ammonites" (v. 2c).[9] As we picture the servants of David arriving in this foreign land, bringing (so to speak) the kindness of King David, we might recall the promise of God that lies behind the whole Bible story, that through the seed of Abraham blessing will come to the nations (see Genesis 12:3; 18:18; 22:18; 26:4; cf. Psalm 72:17; Galatians 3:8). As David's servants came into the land of the Ammonites, this promise was poised for a small-scale realization.

But it did not happen.

Hanun's Despicable Act (vv. 3, 4)

> But the princes of the Ammonites said to Hanun their lord, "Do you think, because David has sent comforters to you, that he is honoring your father? Has not David sent his servants to you to search the city and to spy it out and to overthrow it?" (v. 3)

"The princes of the Ammonites" (v. 3) were probably military men ("commanders").[10] They chose to interpret David's goodness as duplicitous. They displayed an attitude that poisons too many human relationships. Distrust prevents us from seeing good intentions for what they are. We are prone to suspicion. Sometimes, of course, suspicion is justified, but when it makes us incapable of seeing the goodness of someone else's words, actions, or intentions much harm is caused.[11] Here this common human failing of distrust was more serious still. They were despising the kindness of God's king.

We know (because the narrator has told us as much) that David *was* honoring Hanun's father by sending these comforters to him. His action was transparently honest. However, the Ammonite commanders saw a nonexistent hostile intention: "to search the city and to spy it out and to overthrow it."

The city about which they were so concerned was, no doubt, their royal capital Rabbah (see 11:1; 12:26), about forty-three miles northeast of Jerusalem.[12] Rabbah was outside the territory allotted to the Israelites in the days of Joshua.[13]

The suspicion of the commanders won the day, and King David's offer of kindness to the Ammonite king was met with humiliating rejection.

> So Hanun took David's servants and shaved off half the beard of each and cut off their garments in the middle, at their hips, and sent them away. (v. 4)

The young Ammonite king accepted the cynicism of his military chiefs. Instead of welcoming the bearers of King David's kindness, he abused them. A man's beard represented his dignity (see Leviticus 19:27; 21:5).[14] To shave it expressed sorrow and mourning (Isaiah 15:2; Jeremiah 41:5; 48:37; cf. Ezekiel 5:1; Ezra 9:3). To have it forcibly shaved by another was deeply humiliating, an indignity similar to flogging[15] (cf. Isaiah 7:20). In this case Hanun added injury to the insult by shaving *half* the beard (presumably vertically), thus making them look ridiculous and drawing attention to their disgrace.

To this indignity was added another. Their clothes were cut off "in the middle." Whether this means that they were cut in half vertically, making them look ludicrously (and literally) half-naked[16] or that the garments were cut in the middle leaving them naked from the waist down[17] is not clear and matters little. The indignity and humiliation are obvious, even if only partly appreciated by modern readers.[18]

Hanun proved to be a true son of his father, not in regard to whatever kindness Nahash may have once shown to David, but in his violently despising the people of Israel (see 1 Samuel 11:2). David had "sent" an expression of kindness and compassion to Hanun (v. 2). In response Hanun "sent" the representatives of King David away in their embarrassing and shameful state—an expression of hostile scorn and ridicule. Thus King Hanun despised the kindness of King David.

David's Kindness (v. 5)

We can picture the servants of David making their way slowly back home, no doubt seeking to avoid the derision and mockery of those who saw them. However, they were seen, and news of what had happened soon reached King David, whose kindness was now extended to his faithful but humiliated servants.

> When it was told David, he sent to meet them, for the men were greatly ashamed. And the king said, "Remain at Jericho until your beards have grown and then return." (v. 5)

For the second time in the story King David "sent." The implication is that, as before, he sent messengers,[19] this time to express the kindness of the king to his "greatly ashamed" servants (v. 5).

The shame of the servants expresses the overturning of David's purpose by the Ammonites. Although they denied it, David had acted to give "honor" (v. 3). The Ammonites turned honor to shame.[20]

In turn King David met the ashamed ones (by his messengers) and provided for the restoration of their honor. They were to stay at Jericho (near where they would have crossed the Jordan River on their way back to Jerusalem).[21] The king would wait for them until their beards had grown (replacement clothes no doubt being a simpler matter). No more humiliation. Such was the kindness of this king.

Hostilities Begin: Stage One (vv. 6–14)

We have heard nothing yet of David's reaction to Hanun's aggressive repudiation of his kindness. At this stage David did nothing. Like God himself, on this occasion King David was "slow to anger" (cf. Exodus 34:6; Numbers 14:18; Psalm 86:15; Proverbs 16:32; James 1:19).

What the Ammonites Saw (v. 6)

But the Ammonites realized the enormity of what they had done. "When the Ammonites saw that they had become a stench to David . . ." (v. 6a). This was the Ammonites' view of the situation. The vivid language expresses a deep hatred and hostility that they "saw" (see, for example, 1 Samuel 13:4; 27:12; 2 Samuel 16:21[22]). We are not told that this *was* David's reaction to what the Ammonites had done, just that they "saw" it that way.

They recognized the seriousness of what they had done, but not in order to take steps to put matters right. On the contrary, they decided to go all out or quit: ". . . the Ammonites sent and hired the Syrians of Beth-rehob, and the Syrians of Zobah, 20,000 foot soldiers, and the king of Maacah with 1,000 men, and the men of Tob, 12,000 men" (v. 6b).

It did not occur to the Ammonites to throw themselves on the kindness of King David, to seek his pardon. In their case the kindness and patience of the king did not lead to repentance (cf. Romans 2:4). The only course of action considered was to strengthen themselves *against* him.[23]

They sought to establish a coalition of forces. "The Syrians[24] of Beth-rehob" were a northern Aramaean kingdom with Rehob (or Beth-rehob) as its capital (2 Samuel 10:6).[25] We have heard of "the Syrians of Zobah" (v. 6) in 8:3. Their king was Hadadezer (about whom we will hear more shortly), and their territory lay further to the north.[26] From these two regions the Ammonites hired 20,000 foot soldiers.[27] Furthermore they engaged another thousand from the king of Maacah (another region north of Israel's territory, but south of Beth-rehob[28]) and 12,000 from Tob (probably forty miles or so northeast of Rabbah[29]).

David had made no move against the Ammonites. Either they still imagined (with no evidence) that he had hostile intentions against them and so were preparing a defense, or they were preparing to continue their aggression by initiating hostilities. As things unfold the latter seems to have been the case.

What David Heard (v. 7)

David's effective and efficient intelligence network brought him news of what was happening. "And when David heard of it, he sent Joab and all the host of the mighty men" (v. 7).

For the third time in this episode King David "sent" (v. 7). This time he did not send messengers of his kindness (as in verses 2 and 5) but an army. The move was defensive. No destination is indicated. In effect David put the army on standby.

Joab, David's feisty military commander (8:16), has not appeared in the story since the tensions with David over his murder of Abner (see 3:26–31). Despite those tensions, Joab was still David's top military man, perhaps because of his outstanding abilities, but possibly also because of his forceful character that David never managed to master.

"All the host [or army] of the mighty men" introduces us to David's "mighty men" (10:7; see 23:8). They were the strong and powerful soldiers who made up David's army. "The mighty men" had an earned reputation for greatness, usually (as here) in military activities.[30] We might recall that "the mighty" of Saul had fallen (1:19, 21, 22, 25, 27) and that the Lord himself breaks the bows of "the mighty" (1 Samuel 2:4). However, we reasonably expect that *King David's* mighty men will be a force to be reckoned with.

David "sent" his army (2 Samuel 10:7). He did not accompany them (as he had done previously; see, most recently, 5:17–25; 8:1–14). At this stage, however, we should probably understand that David still had no hostile intentions against the Ammonites. Joab's mission was deterrence (as we will see). It was not necessary for the king to always accompany his army (see, for example, 2:13).[31]

What the Ammonites Did (v. 8)

> And the Ammonites came out and drew up in battle array at the entrance of the gate, and the Syrians of Zobah and of Rehob and the men of Tob and Maacah were by themselves in the open country. (v. 8)

The Ammonites and their allies proceeded with their hostile intentions. The Ammonite army, having been assembled in the capital, Rabbah, appeared at the gate of that city, clearly ready to advance and do battle with the king they had offended.[32] The auxiliary troops they had recruited from surrounding nations had taken up a separate position, in the open country, presumably to the south of Rabbah, near Medeba.[33]

What Joab Saw and What Joab Did (vv. 9, 10)

The account is concise and omits unnecessary details. Somehow the battle deployment of the Ammonite coalition became known to Joab. "When Joab saw that the battle was set against him both in front and in the rear . . ."

(v. 9a). Either a report had reached him or he had moved into the Ammonite territory and saw the situation for himself. If he were to approach Rabbah from the south, then armies were positioned both directly in front (that is, the Ammonite troops drawn up for battle at the entrance to the city) and behind (that is, the mercenaries gathered further south).

Joab was an astute tactician. ". . . he chose some of the best men of Israel and arrayed them against the Syrians. The rest of his men he put in the charge of Abishai his brother, and he arrayed them against the Ammonites" (vv. 9b, 10). Thus Joab would lead a contingent of crack troops to the south and confront the mercenaries in the open country, while his brother Abishai would lead the rest of the army against the Ammonites at Rabbah.[34]

What Joab Said (vv. 11, 12)

Joab spoke to Abishai. The space given to his words in this concise narrative is striking. Joab had many faults, but here his words illuminate the whole episode. Perhaps, as we often find in the Bible, this man spoke more truly than he understood—or even believed in his heart. That is beside the point. The narrator does not here invite us to assess Joab's character, but to hear what he said.

First, he explained the strategy. "And he said, 'If the Syrians are too strong for me, then you[35] shall help me [literally, you shall become my salvation[36]], but if the Ammonites are too strong for you, then I will come and help you [literally, I will come to save[37] you]'" (v. 11). Joab was expecting the strategy to work and lead to the "salvation" of the Israelites from their enemies.

Second, he therefore called on Abishai to be strong: "Be of good courage [literally, be strong[38]], and let us be courageous [literally, let us be strong] . . ." (v. 12a). The Ammonites and their allies may prove to be strong, but Joab and his brother would respond with a strength of their own.

Third, there was a purpose to their courage, an intended beneficiary of their strength: ". . . for our people, and for the cities of our God" (v. 12b). Joab was confident that he and his brother could find the strength to save their people. We begin to see the basis for this confidence when the towns and cities in which these people lived are called "the cities of our God" (v. 12). They were God's people, living in the places that God had given them (cf. Deuteronomy 6:10; 13:12; 20:16; Psalm 69:35; Isaiah 40:9).

Fourth, Joab's confidence was based on his knowledge of God: ". . . and may the Lord do [or, the Lord will do][39] what seems good to him" (v. 12c).

Joab's confidence was not that he knew in advance *what* the Lord would do, but he did know that the Lord would do (literally) "the good in his eyes."[40]

Joab's words to Abishai stand at the heart of this chapter. He makes the only direct reference to God in the whole chapter,[41] and what he said illuminates the whole episode. The words are a wonderful expression of faith in God. Faith is knowing that the Lord is good and that he does what is good. What is good is decided by God, not us.[42] But with this faith we can face any enemy, any situation, any threat with a strength that comes from this faith. As we walk honestly before God, doing what he approves, he will give us strength that surpasses whatever power confronts us (cf. Romans 8:31–39).

What Happened (v. 13)

Events now unfolded quickly. First we follow Joab southward as he confronted the foreign forces the Ammonites had hired. "So Joab and the people who were with him drew near to battle against the Syrians, and they fled before him" (v. 13). As far as we can tell he needed no support from Abishai. The victory was swift and complete. Apparently no blood was shed. The enemy fled (cf. 1 Samuel 17:51; 19:8).

What the Ammonites Saw (v. 14a)

The scene shifts quickly to the city of Rabbah, where the Ammonites learned of the route of their allies. "And when the Ammonites saw that the Syrians fled, they likewise fled before Abishai and entered the city" (v. 14a). That is, they withdrew behind the city walls, abandoning (for now) the aggressive intentions with which they had assembled in verse 8. Again we hear of no bloodshed.

These events are to be seen in the light of Joab's faith. The Lord had indeed done "what seem[ed] good to him" (v. 12).

The Outcome—for Now (v. 14b)

Again the scene moves, this time back to where this episode had begun: "Then Joab returned from fighting against the Ammonites and came to Jerusalem" (v. 14b). It is possible that Joab withdrew from further action against Rabbah because the winter had set in, making a prolonged siege difficult.[43] However, remembering how these events began (with David's expression of goodwill toward the new Ammonite king) and how the aggression was initiated by the Ammonites, it is more likely that Joab withdrew simply because the threat had receded. David's (and therefore Joab's) actions against the Ammonites and their allies were defensive.

Hostilities Continue: Stage Two (vv. 15–19)

The aggressors, however, were not prepared to abandon their hostilities for long.

What the Syrians Saw (v. 15)

"But when the Syrians saw that they had been defeated by Israel, they gathered themselves together" (v. 15). The foreign mercenaries realized that Israel had humiliated them. One course of action could have been to accept the defeat and return to their own lands. After all, this had not begun as their fight. But that did not happen. The dishonor of their defeat had made it their fight. So they "regrouped" (NIV) and took action intended to undo the disgrace.

What the Syrians Did (v. 16)

The lead was taken by Hadadezer, the king of Zobah (see v. 6 and 8:3), the most powerful of all the Aramaean kings, who held some kind of sway over all of them (see v. 19). His influence extended beyond the Euphrates River. From there he gathered reinforcements.

> And Hadadezer sent and brought out the Syrians who were beyond the Euphrates.[44] They came to Helam, with Shobach the commander of the army of Hadadezer at their head. (v. 16)

The location of Helam is not certainly known, but a site about forty miles east of the Sea of Galilee fits the available evidence.[45] This was well to the north of Rabbah and the previous hostilities, a suitable place to prepare secretly for a renewed assault on Israel, this time with an expanded army. And Hadadezer put his own general in charge. His name was Shobach.[46]

What David Heard (v. 17a)

Secrets were hard to keep from King David. His intelligence network did its work again, and David soon heard of the renewed threat gathering at Helam. He wasted no time.

> And when it was told David, he gathered all Israel together and crossed the Jordan and came to Helam. (v. 17a)

This time David did not send Joab (as in verse 7). The king himself led the whole army of Israel (representing the entire nation, hence "all Israel," v. 17) across the Jordan River to the place where Hadadezer's expanded forces were getting ready. David's personal involvement signals that things had changed.

What Happened (vv. 17b, 18)

The Syrians arrayed themselves against David and fought with him. And the Syrians fled before Israel, and David killed of the Syrians the men of 700 chariots, and 40,000 horsemen, and wounded Shobach the commander of their army, so that he died there. (vv. 17b, 18)

The aggressive initiative still came from Hadadezer's forces. They were, however, decisively defeated by the fighters under King David's command. This time blood was shed. A lot. Verse 18 may suggest that David himself inflicted the fatal wound on Shobach (although it may equally mean that this was done by those under David's command[47]). Be that as it may, the victory was David's. This was part of the story we heard in 2 Samuel 8. "The LORD gave victory to David wherever he went" (8:6, 14).

What the Kings Saw (v. 19a)

The earlier defeat at the hands of Joab had led the Syrians, under Hadadezer's leadership, to regroup and strengthen their position in order to reverse the humiliation (v. 15). Their defeat at the hands of David produced a different response.[48]

And when all the kings who were servants of Hadadezer saw that they had been defeated by Israel, they made peace with Israel and became subject to [literally, served] them. (v. 19a)

The servants of Hadadezer became servants of Israel. Those who had been recruited to help the Ammonites against King David "made peace" with David (v. 19). The obvious difference between the earlier defeat and this one is the direct involvement of David. Consistent with the kindness he expressed at the beginning of this affair (v. 2) David had been slow to act against the Ammonites and their allies. His initial action had been only a show of force that (we may reasonably surmise) by divine intervention had frightened the enemy to withdraw. However, persistent aggression had led to a violent confrontation with King David himself. At that point every knee was forced to bow to Israel's king.

The Outcome (v. 19b)

But what about the Ammonites themselves, who had caused all the trouble by despising the kindness of the king? It will be some time before we hear what happened to them (see 11:1; 12:26–31). At this point we simply learn that the Ammonites were now on their own: "So the Syrians were afraid to save the Ammonites anymore" (v. 19b). The Ammonites had assembled powerful forces to defy and oppose the king who had been kind and patient with them. Those forces failed them. The foolish wickedness of despising the kindness of God's king is clear to those with eyes to see.

It could have been very different. If only the Ammonites had welcomed David's kindness . . . If only they had sought his pardon for their abuse of his kindness while there was still time . . .

Be warned. God's kindness toward us, which we experience every day we live, is meant to lead us to repentance (Romans 2:4). Let us see that our response to the kindness of King Jesus is not like those foolish Ammonites. Let us gladly receive our kind and patient King with thankfulness and joy.

Part 4

THE FAILURE
OF DAVID

2 Samuel 11—20

22

The Disaster

2 SAMUEL 11:1–5

ONE OF THE MOST difficult lessons for human beings to learn is that we are not up to the task of ruling the world. Again and again we are deceived into hoping that a new leader, government, political system, economic program, foreign policy, or *something* will provide the answers that the world and its communities need. The disappointments that inevitably follow do not seem to have the power to teach us that the resources of humanity are simply inadequate to resolve the dilemmas of humanity.

This does not mean that we are incapable of doing *anything* worthwhile. It is clear that people of goodwill can achieve much. There are many examples of human suffering being alleviated by actions, decisions, policies, inventions, and initiatives taken by men and women whose commitment and abilities are impressive and wonderful. Every such effort is worthwhile. Thank God for doctors, scientists, politicians, and many others who do good. We should pray for them, encourage them, and support them. Those of us who have opportunity to do such good work should know that it is valuable.

But the inadequacy of what we can do is (or should be) obvious. The good we manage to do is patchy and partial. On a global scale poverty may be reduced, but will it ever be eliminated? Certain injustices may be addressed, but will there ever be a community in which no one is treated unfairly? Some diseases may be cured, but will sickness ever be eradicated? Does anyone realistically hope for a world in which lies are no longer told, conflict between people is unknown, greed no longer drives the economy, selfishness no longer dominates human behavior? Do we even dare to dream of a world in which trust is universal, peace is everywhere, all relationships are harmonious, generosity has displaced avarice, and kindness is the mark of all human interactions?

The strange thing is that the unreality of such a dream is matched by its desirability. Who would not want such a world, if only it were possible?

When we pray "Your kingdom come," we are praying for such a world (Matthew 6:10; see, for example, Revelation 21:3, 4). However, the prayer is realistic precisely because it is a *prayer*, not a dream. It is based on God's promise, not on human optimism. This means that our hope for such a world does not rest on the potential of human beings to bring it about. When we believe God's promise, we are trusting *him*, believing that he is good, wise, and powerful enough to do what he has promised (cf. Romans 4:21).

In earlier pages of 2 Samuel, as David's kingdom was being established, we saw something of the impotence of human efforts to bring in his kingdom. In different ways Joab and Abner (2 Samuel 2) and Rechab and Baanah (2 Samuel 4), whatever their intentions, did more harm than good. Only the king God had chosen for himself (1 Samuel 16:1) was good, wise, and powerful enough to establish a kingdom of justice and righteousness (8:15). He achieved that only because "the Lord, the God of hosts, was with him" (5:10) and "the Lord gave victory to David wherever he went" (8:6, 14; cf. 1 Samuel 18:12, 14, 28). This king and his kingdom were God's gift.

In 2 Samuel 11 we hear the devastating news that even King David failed. His failure was spectacular and terrible. All that we have heard of David, since he first appeared in the pages of this history in 1 Samuel 16, has been impressive. He was, undoubtedly, one of the greatest and best men ever to have lived. Occasionally we have seen hints that he was (as we say) "only human" (see, for example, the fact of his multiple wives in 3:2–5; 5:13 or his possible experiment with chariots in 8:4). However, these rare blemishes have hardly dimmed the glowing picture we have been given of a man and a king who was righteous and faithful (see 1 Samuel 26:23), kind and good (see 2:6; 9:3; 10:2), as well as successful in all he did (8:15). The goodness and the success of this king were inseparable because David was *God's* king, and David's kingdom was *God's* kingdom.

The problem was that David, despite all that God gave him and did for him, was a flawed human being, like all of us. The shock of his fall is intensified by the genuine greatness that we have seen in him. In Biblical history 2 Samuel 11 is comparable to Genesis 3—the fall of Adam. In the disaster of King David we see the damaged and weak human nature we share with him.

We are not up to the task of ruling the world for the same reason that David proved inadequate to rule God's kingdom.

Second Samuel 11 is the turning point of the story of David and his kingdom, just as Genesis 3 was the turning point for the human race. Things will never be the same again. While the story told in this chapter is rightly famous, its massive significance is rarely appreciated.[1] Here we will consider the beginning of the story.

Setting the Scene (v. 1)

The military conflicts of 2 Samuel 10 provide the background to what happened.[2] Those events have shown us (yet again) something of the noble character (10:2), compassionate heart (10:5), and powerful strength (10:18) of King David. The Syrian coalition that had formed to assist the Ammonites in their aggression against David had been crushed (10:19). The Ammonites themselves had retreated to the shelter of their capital city, Rabbah (10:14), although their hostility toward King David was yet to be decisively dealt with. Second Samuel 11 begins with King David at the height of his greatness.

When Was It? (v. 1a, b)

"In the spring of the year" (v. 1a) is literally, "At the return of the year." It may have been spring, but the text does not say so. Rather "the return of the year" means that a year had passed since the hostilities with the Ammonites had begun (2 Samuel 10).[3] We noted that the conflict that had begun a year earlier may have been interrupted by the onset of winter, although a more likely explanation for Joab's (premature?) return to Jerusalem (10:14) was simply that his mission was defensive and had been accomplished. With "the return of the year," however, the campaign was about to be resumed.

There are three further difficulties with the translation of the next phrase, "the time when kings go out to battle" (v. 1b). First, it is possible that the word "kings" should be "messengers."[4] Second, the Hebrew does not have the words "to battle." Third, the text does not seem to refer to kings (or messengers) in general, but to "*the* kings" (or "*the* messengers").[5] This seems to be a reference to the kings (or the messengers) of the previous chapter. It was the same time of year that the Syrian kings (10:8) or possibly David's messengers (10:2) had gone out. The course of events that had begun a year earlier was about to be resumed: "And at the return of the year, at the time that the kings [or messengers] had gone out . . ." (v. 1a, b AT).[6]

What Was Going on? (v. 1c, d)

At this time "David sent Joab, and his servants with him, and all Israel" (v. 1c). This was the resumption of the campaign that had concluded a year or so earlier with Joab's withdrawal from Rabbah and return to Jerusalem (10:14). The reason for the resumption is not stated. The implication is that, unlike the servants of Hadadezer, the Ammonites still refused to "make peace with Israel" (see 10:19).

There is no surprise in Joab being sent to complete the task he had so effectively begun a year earlier. David sent Joab again, just as he had sent him earlier (see 10:7). In this context David's "servants" were his soldiers, the whole army representing the entire nation. "[A]ll Israel" was now at war with the Ammonites.[7]

The authority of the king is expressed in the word "sent" (11:1). The story about to unfold will involve much "sending."[8] As David had earlier "sent" a message of kindness (10:2), now he "sent" his army to deal with those who persisted in despising his kindness.

Briefly we follow Joab and his men. As usual they were effective: "And they ravaged[9] the Ammonites and besieged Rabbah" (v. 1d). There is a story to be told here. We will have to wait, however, until 12:26–31 to hear about the siege of Rabbah and the outcome. In the meantime there is another, much more important story to be told. It is about what happened in Jerusalem while the army was surrounding the Ammonite capital. The scene shifts, therefore, quickly back to Jerusalem.

And What Was King David Doing? (v. 1e)

"But David remained at [or in] Jerusalem" (v. 1e). There is a certain emphasis in the Hebrew sentence on *"But David."* The story about to unfold will not be about Joab and the troops at Rabbah. Our attention is firmly brought back to Jerusalem, where David "remained."

Of course, David had remained in Jerusalem before. When he had sent the messengers to Rabbah with his message of kindness a year or more earlier, we assume that David remained in Jerusalem (10:2). When he had sent messengers to comfort these same messengers after their humiliation, apparently David remained in Jerusalem (10:5). Indeed when David had previously sent Joab out in response to the Ammonite threat, he (presumably) remained in Jerusalem (10:7).[10]

This piece of information that had previously not been important enough to mention is now starkly stated. *"But David* remained in Jerusalem" (11:1).

The verb could be translated "was sitting." What interest can there possibly be in the king seated in his city (when far more exciting things were happening forty miles to the east at Rabbah)?

Great King David's Disaster (vv. 2–5)

It was a remarkably simple sequence of events. But it was a disaster greater than anything that might happen at Rabbah. The story is told with astonishing matter-of-fact directness. We are told what happened, but we are left to wonder how and why.

"It happened, late one afternoon, when David arose from his couch and was walking on the roof of the king's house . . ." (v. 2a). On this day, as the sun was sinking low in the sky over Jerusalem,[11] our attention is drawn to the king. His circumstances made a stark contrast to the troops ravaging the Ammonites and besieging Rabbah. As they were engaged in that life-and-death struggle, David had been resting on his bed. Now he stretched and took a stroll on the flat roof of the palace (see 7:2), enjoying the cool evening air. The scene is relaxed, casual, and calm.

And safe. It is reassuring to realize that this great and good king (as we have undoubtedly seen him to be, particularly in chapters 8, 9, and 10) was far from the dangers of the battlefield—safe in the city that protected him (see 5:9, 10; cf. 21:17).

But the sequence of events that then began to unfold will show us that the king was not safe. The power that brought David down was not an external enemy. King David was not safe from himself. The walls of Jerusalem were no protection against his own deep flaws.

He Saw (v. 2b)

The disaster began with something he glimpsed as he strolled high above the other buildings around his palace: "he saw from the roof a woman bathing; and the woman was very beautiful" (v. 2b). The Hebrew emphasizes that she was very beautiful *to look at*. This was David's point of view as his eyes lit on the naked woman. Literally, "the woman was very good to see!"[12]

There is no suggestion that the woman was acting provocatively.[13] We will learn shortly that her bathing was in fact emphatically proper. There is no reason at all to think that she was indiscreet. It was the elevation of David's palace that made her visible from that height ("he saw *from the roof*," v. 2). We may reasonably suppose that her place of bathing was otherwise private and was probably some distance from the palace.

Furthermore, at this point we have seen nothing reprehensible in David's conduct. The chance sighting of a beautiful naked woman was hardly a crime. Indeed we might anticipate, from all we have learned of David's character, that this will prove to be another occasion in which he displayed his surprising kindness and goodness, as he had toward the vulnerable Mephibosheth (2 Samuel 9) and many others.

We all know what David should have done. He should have averted his gaze and got on with something else (cf. Job 31:1). We also know what David should not have done. He should not have continued to look at the woman and foster lustful thoughts (see Numbers 15:39; Matthew 5:28).

Since Adam and Eve disobeyed God in the garden of Eden human nakedness has been problematic (see Genesis 2:25 and then 3:7, 10, 11). As our natures have been corrupted by our rejection of God, our sexual desires have been distorted. The self-centeredness that is expressed in defiance of God has turned the goodness of sex (for the purposes for which God created it) into something selfish. We now find it very difficult to direct our sexual desires as they were intended—namely, the self-giving union of a man and a woman in marriage and the procreation of children in the security of a loving family. Instead sex has been turned into a selfish pleasure to be *taken* rather than *given*. As in other aspects of life, we all find it very difficult indeed to escape from selfishness in our sexual desires and behavior. The power of our sexual natures (powerful because of their remarkable purpose) makes this a challenging aspect of life for us all. In this King David was like us all.

He Sought (v. 3)

What did King David do? "And David sent and inquired about the woman" (v. 3a). He did not turn his attention *away* from the woman he had seen. On the contrary he used his royal authority ("sent") and directed his attention to her.[14]

Perhaps he "sent" a trusted personal servant to make discreet inquiries. Perhaps he was less careful. We do not know. We do know the information he received: "And one said, 'Is not this[15] Bathsheba, the daughter of Eliam, the wife of Uriah the Hittite?'" (v. 3b).

David learned three things about the beautiful woman he had seen from his rooftop. First, her name was Bathsheba. There may be irony in the fact that one possible meaning of her name is "daughter of an oath." What was about to happen would make a mockery of the world of oath-keeping. Be that as it may, with the name "the woman" became known to David as a particular person, "Bathsheba."

Second, she was the daughter of Eliam. On the reasonable assumption that this Eliam was the son of Ahithophel, then he was one of David's "mighty men" (23:34),[16] and Bathsheba was the granddaughter of David's esteemed counselor (see 16:23). Bathsheba, then, belonged to a family that was close to David's court.[17] Although Ahithophel will later betray David (15:12, 31; 16:15), that turn of events may well have been prompted by the events we are about to witness. At the time when David saw Bathsheba from his roof, the indications are that she belonged to a family who loyally served the king.

Third, and most importantly, the woman David had seen from his rooftop was "the wife of Uriah the Hittite" (11:3). She was married. Her husband, Uriah, was probably a resident alien[18] who was nonetheless a loyal servant to King David (like Ahimelech the Hittite, 1 Samuel 26:6). He, like his father-in-law, was one of David's "mighty men" (23:39). His name (probably meaning "Yahweh is my light") suggests that Uriah's Hittite ancestry may have been quite distant. At an earlier time the Hittites had been a powerful people in the region,[19] but at the time of David the Hittites were just a number of small states to the north of Israel.[20] As we will see in the course of 2 Samuel 11, "Uriah the Hittite" was a man who took Israel's God seriously—more seriously, indeed, than did King David on this occasion.

David knew what we will learn only in verse 6, namely that Uriah was among the servants of David who had been sent with Joab to battle with the Ammonites. The woman's husband was out of town.

What David should now have done is even clearer than before. God's Law was unambiguous: "You shall not covet your neighbor's wife" (Exodus 20:17) and "[Y]ou shall not commit adultery" (Exodus 20:14). Everything that David had learned about "the woman" he had seen should have told him that his interest in her must go no further (2 Samuel 11:3).

He Took (v. 4)

So what did King David then do? Again he asserted his royal authority. "So David *sent* messengers" (v. 4a). How different this was from the messengers David had sent the previous year (see 10:1, 2). They had carried a word of great kindness and goodness to a foreigner and a potential enemy. David's messengers now went to a nearby house of a family who had shown nothing but friendship and loyal service to David. What the messengers brought to that household was very different from kindness and goodness.

In three stark, sharply expressed clauses we are told what David used his messengers to do.

And he "took her" (v. 4b). One word in Hebrew conveys the forcefulness of David's action. It may not have been physically violent. It may simply have been the power of his position that was wielded. Either way David "took" her.

Many years earlier Samuel had warned the people of Israel about a king who "takes" (see 1 Samuel 8:11–17). A king who "takes" is a king "like all the nations" (1 Samuel 8:5), which is precisely what David had been chosen *not* to be (1 Samuel 13:14; 15:28; 16:1).[21] At this moment David, who for so long had refused to *take* power, but waited patiently for it to be *given* to him, fell from his greatness. He "took" Bathsheba (2 Samuel 11:4). His capacity for "kindness," so wonderfully displayed in earlier episodes (2:6; 9:1; 10:2), had been overtaken by something very different.

"[A]nd she came to him" (v. 4c). The two Hebrew words give no suggestion that she had any choice in the matter.[22] After all, her husband was away. The king had sent a number of his men to take her. It is unlikely that the king's intentions were explicitly revealed. How could she have refused the royal summons?

"[A]nd he lay with her" (v. 4d). Two Hebrew words now conclude the remarkably brief account of this disastrous sequence of events. It is now clear that David had broken God's Law. He had coveted his neighbor's wife. Now he had taken what he coveted and committed adultery with her. He returned to the bed from which he had innocently risen a little earlier (v. 2), no longer innocent.

The extraordinary brevity of the account is brutal: He "sent," he "took," she "came," he "lay." We hear of no conversation between them, no expressions of affection. We are told nothing about the emotions or the thoughts of either person. All we see are the acts.

And we are stunned. Is this the same man who had repeatedly resisted great temptations with words like, "The LORD forbid that I should do this thing . . ." (1 Samuel 24:6; cf. 26:11) and "The LORD rewards every man for his righteousness and his faithfulness" (1 Samuel 26:23)? Is this the one who expressed outrage at the wrongdoings of others (1:14, 16; 3:28, 39; 4:10, 11)? Is this the king who extended kindness and goodness to those who would have least expected it (2:6; 9:1; 10:2)? As David himself said in a different context and with a different meaning, "How the mighty have fallen!" (1:19, 25, 27).

We have many questions that the text before us refuses to answer. Can we account for David's out-of-character actions in any way? Was he under unusual stress? Were there difficulties at home? Did he feel unappreciated?

Was he suffering a midlife crisis? Did he struggle at all with the temptation?[23] We may wonder whether Bathsheba offered any resistance at all. Or was she complicit? Was she even more enthusiastic than that? Did she encourage him?

None of these questions can be answered because none of them is of any interest to the Bible writer. They are all eclipsed by the fact of what David did and his definite responsibility for his actions. The mighty had indeed fallen!

The questions we want to ask are understandable because as we witness David's fall we are all too aware that we share the weakness of his human nature. Whether or not we have fallen just as David fell, we understand his action. We sympathize. Given the circumstances and opportunity we can imagine ourselves doing what David did.

The account of what David did contains a number of subtle reminders in vocabulary and ideas of what happened in the garden of Eden: "So when the woman *saw . . . good . . .* a delight to the eyes . . . to be desired . . . she *took . . .* and ate" (Genesis 3:6). In like manner, David *saw* a woman . . . she was *good* to see . . . he desired her . . . and he *took* her . . . and lay with her. David did what Adam and Eve did. He was ruled by his desires rather than by God's good word.

Are you wondering what all the fuss (of my last few paragraphs) is about? Many people today, at least in the Western world, have embraced what they call sexual freedom. This generally means freedom to act sexually in any way we may desire, with any person we may choose. The only proviso is that no one should be coerced against his or her will, and no one should be hurt. But that is (for many) the only accepted boundary to sexual behavior. Provided, therefore, that Bathsheba freely consented (which may or may not have been the case), and provided that David did not use the power of his position to coerce her consent (that's a bit harder to believe), and provided he did not hurt her (we simply do not know about that), many today would ask, "What harm was done?"

Before these events have run their course we will all see that a great deal of harm was done. But it is worth noting that our world is terribly deceived in this matter of "sexual freedom." As understood these days, this idea robs sex of its profound and wonderful purposefulness. Our sexual natures are a gift from our Creator for the purpose of binding together a man and a woman in lifelong marriage and for the birth of children in that context. The boundaries that God places on our sexual behavior are there to protect the wonderful and powerful purpose of sex. True sexual freedom is when sex is freed from self-centered lust and is able to accomplish its brilliant (and unselfish) purpose.

In due course we will hear the very last sentence of this chapter: "The thing that David had done was evil in the eyes of the LORD" (11:27b AT). Although those words apply to more than his act of adultery, they certainly do apply there. What David had done was very wrong indeed.

At this point in the account we are given a surprising piece of information, rightly put in parentheses by our translation: "(Now she had been purifying herself [literally, making herself holy] from her uncleanness.)" (v. 4e). As we often find in Biblical narratives, an important piece of information has been held back until it is needed. This is an explanation of Bathsheba's bathing earlier on.[24] Far from being a matter of immodesty, her bathing was a matter of holiness. The laws of the book of Leviticus defined various states in life as "unclean." This was part of a life-sized symbolic system under which Israelites were to learn that God is holy and requires holiness of his people.[25] One of those states was a woman's monthly menstrual period (see Leviticus 15:19–30). Bathsheba's bathing had been a ritual cleansing following her period.

The vital relevance of this information will be clear shortly. However, before we get to that point, notice the contrast between the woman who was pursuing *holiness* (in this peculiar Old Testament way) and King David who pursued *wickedness*.

The act of adultery was over. David's lust had been satisfied. He had taken what he had coveted. "Then she returned to her house" (v. 4f).

That might have been the end of the matter. Whether or not David had further plans for this little affair, I am sure he thought that Bathsheba's returning home concluded things, at least for now. Whether or not he felt remorse or guilt we are not told. It does not matter. He had every reason to think that he had taken and there need be no consequences.

But he was wrong.

There Were Consequences (v. 5)

Several weeks passed. We hear nothing of the shame, guilt, or other emotions that either David or Bathsheba may have experienced. The time is passed over without comment, except for the briefest possible statement of the immediate consequence of what had happened: "And the woman conceived . . ." (v. 5a).

The relevance of the information just given about her recent menstrual period is now devastatingly clear. Her pregnancy did not pre-date David's act of adultery. The paternity of the child she conceived is beyond doubt.

Strikingly the narrator refrains from using Bathsheba's name. She is "the woman" (v. 5). That is how David had seen her at the beginning (see vv. 2, 3). Is the narrator reflecting David's continued refusal to treat "the woman" as the person, Bathsheba? To David was she still "the woman"?

Now it was Bathsheba's turn to send: "and she sent and told David, 'I am pregnant'" (v. 5b). These are the only recorded words of Bathsheba in 2 Samuel 11. The news from Bathsheba shatters the illusion that David was in control of events.[26]

All this "sending" implies a distance between David's and Bathsheba's places. We know it was not a great distance physically (her house was, unfortunately, within clear eyesight from the palace). There was, however, the great social "distance" between the king and his subjects. From this distance Bathsheba waited. The initiative (as always) lay with the king.

Before we hear what the king did in response to the shattering news, we should pause and reflect on the lessons of what we have heard so far.

It is certainly right for us to reflect on the moral lessons of this incident. If a great and good man like David can fall morally as spectacularly as this, then we must all acknowledge the danger that we are to ourselves. Like David, safety from external threats does not secure us from the flaws of our fallen nature. We are all capable of crossing proper moral boundaries for the sake of shortsighted and selfish desires. Those of us in positions of any kind of power must pay particular attention here. We very easily use power over others, not to serve, but to "take."

This applies to many aspects of life, but it applies particularly to sexual behavior. The boundaries of sexual morality given to us in the Bible are not to be despised or disregarded. They are for our good. They protect true sexual freedom. Witness David's folly, and take whatever steps are needed for you to "flee from sexual immorality" (1 Corinthians 6:18). Again, those with power to exert must take special care.

But if that is all there is to be said, then we are in trouble. Our difficulties come into focus when we listen to the words of Jesus:

> You have heard that it was said, "You shall not commit adultery." But I say to you that everyone who looks at a woman with lustful intent has already committed adultery with her in his heart. (Matthew 5:27, 28)

Perhaps Jesus had David in mind. Even if we have not participated in conduct like King David's, we share his deeper flaws. Our hearts, like his, are impure. The words of James also aptly fit the experience of King David:

> But each person is tempted when he is lured and enticed by his own desire. Then desire when it has conceived gives birth to sin, and sin when it is fully grown brings forth death. (James 1:14, 15)

If a great and good man like King David can be destroyed (and we will see that this is not saying too much) by his own weaknesses, then what hope can there be for any of us?

The story of David's fall has a further important dimension that points us to the extraordinary answer to this question. God had promised that David's kingdom would be established forever (7:16). How can that be when David has proved to be such a flawed human being, just like each of us? How can his kingdom really be God's kingdom? How can *this* man really "do justice and righteousness for all his people" (8:15 AT)?

The answer is that God's kingdom will be the kingdom of a *son* of David (7:12, 13). The New Testament message is that this "son of David" has come (Matthew 1:1). The remarkable thing about him is that, unlike David (and unlike the rest of us), he was "without sin" (Hebrews 4:15; cf. 2 Corinthians 5:21). "He committed no sin, neither was deceit found in his mouth" (1 Peter 2:22). He is in every way "pure" (1 John 3:3), "holy, innocent, unstained, separated from sinners" (Hebrews 7:26). Unlike David (and unlike the rest of us) he was entirely obedient to God (Philippians 2:8; cf. Matthew 3:17). The consequences of David's sin, like that of Adam, were massive (as we shall see). Just so, the consequences of Jesus Christ's obedience are huge for all of us (see Romans 5:18, 19).

Like David we are not up to the task of ruling ourselves, let alone ruling the world. Thank God for Jesus! In him we find forgiveness and safety from enemies far greater than any physical threat. By his death for our sins and his resurrection to new life, "you have been set free from sin and have become slaves of God, [and] the fruit you get leads to sanctification and its end, eternal life" (Romans 6:22).

And so we pray "*Your* kingdom come!" *and* "Lead us not into temptation, but deliver us from evil" (Matthew 6:10, 13).

23

The Deceitful Heart

2 SAMUEL 11:6–13

The heart is deceitful above all things,
and desperately sick; who can understand it?

JEREMIAH 17:9

For from within, out of the heart of man, come
evil thoughts, sexual immorality, theft, murder,
adultery, coveting, wickedness, deceit, sensuality,
envy, slander, pride, foolishness. All these evil things
come from within, and they defile a person.

MARK 7:21–23

None is righteous, no, not one.

ROMANS 3:10

THE BIBLE HAS A BLEAK VIEW of human nature. Our hearts deceive us. We fail to see ourselves as we really are (profoundly unrighteous, desperately weak, and extremely foolish). We prefer a more positive, optimistic view of human nature. But when God does not have his rightful place in our understanding of life and the world, we have a terribly distorted vision (Romans 1:28). Furthermore we are deceived into thinking that we are not deceived. We cannot see the seriousness of our defiance of God. We "suppress the truth" (Romans 1:18), while imagining that we are people of integrity. We become captives to our own sinfulness (Romans 1:28), while being deluded into thinking that we are in control of our lives. What hope is there for us? What hope is there for the world if the Bible's diagnosis of human nature is true?

Second Samuel 11 is the account of the time when it became clear that the even great King David had a heart that was "deceitful above all things, and desperately sick" (Jeremiah 17:9). We have heard how, in the apparent safety and security of his royal city (2 Samuel 11:1), David allowed his own selfish desires to rule him (11:2, 3). He "took" Bathsheba, knowing she was the wife of Uriah the Hittite, and committed adultery with her (11:4). Then, just when he must have thought that he had gotten away with it, a message came from Bathsheba: "I am pregnant" (11:5).

What was to be done?

One course of action could have been for David to humble himself, acknowledge what he had done, and take responsibility for the consequences of his crime. Admittedly that would be a lot to ask, since Israel's God-given law carried the death penalty for what David had done (Leviticus 20:10; Deuteronomy 22:22). We do not know whether or not the full force of the Law would have been applied in this situation.[1] That is beside the point. There had been numerous occasions when David had risked his life to do what is right. That was when he trusted God (see, for example, his eloquent speech in 1 Samuel 26:22–24).

Plan A (vv. 6–11)

David had always been quick to devise clever strategies to deal with awkward situations (see, for example, 1 Samuel 21:10–15). He now employed this skill to deal with the situation his foolishness had created. He initiated what we will call "Plan A."[2]

Decisive Action (v. 6)

Boldly David asserted his royal power and again "sent": "So David sent word to Joab, 'Send me Uriah the Hittite'" (v. 6a). We now learn what David had known all along. Uriah was among those who had been "sent" (v. 1) by the king to fight, under the command of Joab, against the Ammonites. They were at this very time engaged in a siege of Rabbah, the Ammonite capital, some forty miles east of Jerusalem (11:1). The king now ordered Joab to "send" (v. 6) Uriah back to Jerusalem.

There is no reason to think that David's message to Joab would have aroused suspicion. The king was (one might have thought) keen to hear how the campaign was going. If anyone (including Uriah) had wondered, "Why Uriah?" the answer might have been, "Why not?" A king can have his reasons. This king certainly did.

The story of David up to this point has contained many astonishing examples of his selfless goodness and numerous occasions on which he has acted kindly toward potential enemies, even at cost to himself. When we hear that he had Uriah sent back to Jerusalem, we might expect that David was now going to put things right. His indiscretion with Bathsheba may have been a momentary lapse in this otherwise upright and noble character. When Uriah returns, perhaps David will confess his act of adultery, seek Uriah's forgiveness, and somehow make amends for what he had done. There is plenty in the record of David's life to suggest that he was capable of such an honest, courageous, and humble response to what he had done. That his immediate response to the news of Bathsheba's pregnancy was to summon Uriah may raise our hopes that David had come to his right mind and was about to do the right thing.

Before we follow the events that David's summons set in motion (and learn just how David intended to sort out the mess his indiscretion had got him into), let's look a little more closely at the situation in Jerusalem.

The king's night with Bathsheba was not a very well kept secret. There was at least one person who had made inquiries for the king about the beautiful woman's identity (11:3). There was a group of messengers (how many?) whom David sent to bring her to him (11:4). There was at least one other person who carried the news of Bathsheba's pregnancy back to the king (11:5). It takes very little imagination to see how the king's little fling would almost certainly have been gossiped around the palace, and probably more widely.[3] The king must have known that the matter could not be kept secret.

Therefore, sending for Uriah involved the very definite possibility that the soldier would hear the rumors before he met with David. Certainly summoning Uriah to Jerusalem would be a strange thing to do if David intended to keep the matter a secret from Uriah. It was a bold move. But David was a man used to taking risks.

The commander in the field received the king's message and, naturally, promptly obeyed. "And Joab sent Uriah to David" (v. 6b). As earlier in the story the "sending" (three times in verse 6!) suggests the distance between the sender and the destination. This time it is not only the forty miles or so from Rabbah to Jerusalem. There is also the distance between the apparent peace and quiet of Jerusalem and the situation at the battlefront. As Uriah was "sent" from the dangerous situation at Rabbah, he came to the quiet safety of Jerusalem. Or so it must have initially felt.

A Clever Deception? (vv. 7, 8)

Uriah came to David (v. 7a), just as Bathsheba had done (see the similar wording in 11:4)! Our first impression of Uriah is of an obedient servant of the king.

Did anyone speak to him before he met with the king? Did he hear any of the whispers that were being passed around Jerusalem? We are not told. The narrator keeps us in the dark about this, just as David could not have known whether or not Uriah yet suspected anything.

The conversation began. "When Uriah came to him, David asked how Joab was doing and how the people were doing and how the war was going" (v. 7). David attempted to make the situation seem as normal as possible. The king wanted news from the battlefront, as would have been expected. Literally he asked about the "peace" (Hebrew, shalom, "being whole, intact, prosperity, peace"[4]) of Joab, the people, and the war. Shalom (three times in verse 7) is a subject that should concern a good king.[5] But notice that David did not ask about the shalom of Uriah, which he had so wickedly violated.

We know that these questions were not David's real concern. Indeed the narrator does not report Uriah's answers to David's opening questions. We do not hear them, just as David was not interested in them.[6] He had brought Uriah here for a very different purpose. How long they talked, we do not know. What they said was of no importance because it had nothing to do with the reason Uriah had been brought back to Jerusalem. All we hear is the very end of the conversation, because that is when David played his card. "Then David said to Uriah, 'Go down to your house and wash your feet'" (v. 8a).

Instead of an honest, humble confession of what he had done, David concluded the interview with an almost trivial directive. So it was intended to seem.

It sounded innocent. The soldier had been away from home for some time. He had suffered the privations of war. How fortunate that he had been chosen to report back to the king, with the opportunity for a short break in the comfort of his home. The king concluded his interview with the soldier by kindly giving him permission to enjoy his brief break. The king who had earned a reputation for extraordinary kindness (9:1; 10:2) appeared to be living up to his name.

But as we listen we begin to see David's duplicity. It comes as a shock, but the hypocrisy of David's feigned interest in the welfare of his troops, and in Uriah's relaxation, is stunning. "Go down to your house" (11:8)—that is, of course, the house to which Bathsheba had returned ("her house," 11:4). "Go down to your house" means "Go down to Bathsheba." Did Uriah hear this as a kind word from the king? Or had he learned enough to see something of what we see? If Uriah spent the night with Bathsheba, then who would know that the child to be born was not Uriah's?

In this complex situation, where David was playing a clever but complicated game, "Wash your feet" (v. 8) likewise carries levels of meaning. On the surface it is what a traveler would do after the long dusty walk from Rabbah. But the idea of washing feet suggests the other comforts of relaxation and home. It is even possible to hear "wash your feet" as a veiled euphemism for the sexual relations David wanted Uriah to have with his wife (cf. Exodus 4:25; Deuteronomy 28:57; Isaiah 7:20).[7] Perhaps the narrator wants us to notice that what David wanted Uriah to do ("wash") is just what David had seen from his roof (the same Hebrew word is translated "bathing" in 11:2).[8]

So much for our expectations that David had summoned Uriah in order to now do the right thing. David wanted a cover-up. He seems to have cared little what Uriah might learn from the Jerusalem gossip. So long as David could plausibly deny what people were saying (and linking Bathsheba's pregnancy to Uriah's visit was the key to that), he would be satisfied.

If Uriah suspected David's duplicity, he did not show it (at least initially). He did what an obedient servant of the king would be expected to do when dismissed: "And Uriah went out of the king's house . . ." (v. 8b). The king's plan seemed to be working. Uriah was on his way.

David took a further step to confirm his pretended goodwill toward Uriah: "and there followed him a present from the king" (v. 8c). This was probably a gift of food to provide for a sumptuous meal for Uriah to share with his wife.[9]

As the evening of Uriah's first day in Jerusalem fell, the king had every reason to think that his plan was on track. He had seen no indication that Uriah was suspicious. His deception had succeeded. So it must have seemed.

The Failure of Plan A (vv. 9–11)

The narrator allows us (for a moment) to share David's perspective. Verse 9 begins (literally), "And Uriah lay . . ." This is an exact echo of verse 4: "and he [David] *lay* with her [Bathsheba]"! For a moment we are led to expect (as David hoped) that Uriah did what David had done. Just for an instant we may think that Uriah had heard nothing of David's secret.

But immediately we hear that Uriah "lay" not with his wife but "at the door of the king's house with all the servants of his lord, and did not go down to his house" (v. 9)! Suddenly we suspect that Uriah knew more than he was letting on. The most obvious explanation for his remarkable restraint that night is that he *had* heard something of what had occurred. We cannot yet be sure of this. But at this stage it seems likely.[10]

Notice the irony in the description of what Uriah did. Uriah still regarded David as "his lord" and counted himself among David's "servants" at the same time as he was acting (deliberately or otherwise) to frustrate the king's scheme. As he joined "all the servants of his lord" he was in fact defying the king's word ("Go down to your house," v. 8; he "did *not* go down to his house," v. 9).

David, as always, had his informants. He soon (the next morning?) learned that, contrary to his expectations (and hopes), "Uriah did not go down to his house" (v. 10a).[11] Like us (the readers of this story), David must have realized that Uriah's strange behavior could mean that he had learned David's not-so-well-kept secret. David needed to know whether this was so. He summoned Uriah to a second interview. "David said to Uriah, 'Have you not come from a journey?[12] Why did you not go down to your house?'" (v. 10b). David wanted to know the explanation for Uriah not doing what one would expect anyone to do in his circumstances (not to mention the fact that the king had told him to do it). Although David did his best to make his question sound innocent, it must have seemed at least curious that the king cared at all whether or not one of his servants had spent the night at his own home.

Uriah's response to David was extraordinary.

> Uriah said to David, "The ark and Israel and Judah dwell in booths,[13] and my lord Joab and the servants of my lord are camping in the open field. Shall I then go to my house, to eat and to drink and to lie with my wife? As you live, and as your soul lives, I will not do this thing." (v. 11)

As readers we are made to share David's dilemma. We do not know whether Uriah was speaking honestly and with an innocent naïveté about the situation or was carefully, cleverly, and brilliantly issuing an implied but severe rebuke to the king. We do not know (just as David did not know) whether Uriah's words simply expressed his noble character or whether behind them was his knowledge of David's secret. We (like David) therefore listen to what Uriah said at two levels.

The first thing we hear from Uriah is, "The ark" (v. 11), referring to the ark of the covenant that has played such a significant role in the history recorded in the books of Samuel,[14] most recently when David had brought the ark to Jerusalem (2 Samuel 6) and had sought to build a "house" for it (7:1–3). Indeed it had previously been David who was concerned about the inappropriateness of his grand accommodation when the ark "dwells in a tent" (7:1). Now Uriah the Hittite expressed a similar conviction.

On the surface Uriah's first word indicated that Uriah the Hittite was a believer in the Lord and his covenant with Israel. Uriah presented himself to David not simply as a foreigner ("Hittite"), but as one who acknowledged the Lord. He knew and apparently cared about "the ark."

But was there more to this remarkable reference to "the ark"? Was it intended to remind the king of the terms of the covenant represented by the ark? After all, inside the ark were the tablets on which were inscribed the Ten Commandments (Deuteronomy 10:5). The ark contained these words from God: "[Y]ou shall not covet your neighbor's wife"; "You shall not commit adultery" (Exodus 20:17, 14). Did Uriah know that his first word to the king pointed to the command of God that the king had broken?

The second thing we hear is Uriah's reference to the army in which he served as "Israel and Judah" (2 Samuel 11:11). Though his ancestry was Hittite, Uriah identified himself with God's own people over whom David was king (cf. 5:5). He was not simply a mercenary. He had joined and served God's people.

But again, was this intended to indicate that the one whose wife David had coveted and taken was not simply a foreigner? David had taken his "neighbor's" wife (Exodus 20:17). Uriah belonged to the covenant community. David's sin was all the more heinous if it was committed, not against an enemy (a "Hittite"), but against a brother (albeit one by adoption, so to speak).

The third thing we hear is the point that Uriah made about "the ark and Israel and Judah": they were dwelling "in booths" (2 Samuel 11:11). This may not have been literally the case, since the ark was housed "in a tent" (7:2). A "booth" was a shelter constructed from branches thick with foliage that provided temporary and insubstantial protection from the heat of the day (see Jonah 4:5; Isaiah 1:8).[15] Such, Uriah said, was the situation at the battlefront for the ark and the army. Life was rough and precarious.

Uriah's obvious point was the inappropriate contrast between that situation and the potential indulgence of going to his house "to eat and to drink and to lie with my wife" (2 Samuel 11:11).[16] The circumstances of "the ark and Israel and Judah" magnified the reprehensible indulgence of the king's conduct as he "remained at Jerusalem" (11:1). "To lie with my wife" (v. 11) is what David himself *had* done!

The fourth element in Uriah's remarkable speech reiterated, in different words, the circumstances at the front line: "my lord Joab and the servants of my lord are camping in the open field" (v. 11). Here Uriah presented himself as a loyal servant of his commanding officer (Joab was his "lord"), and hence he, like the rest of the army, was a loyal servant of David (the second "my lord" should be understood as referring to David[17]).

Was this, too, a pointed reminder that the one whom David had so wickedly betrayed had at the time been faithfully serving his king and his king's commander?

The fifth striking expression from Uriah was his description, in the form of a question, of what he would not contemplate doing in these circumstances: "Shall I[18] then go to my house, to eat and to drink and to lie with my wife?" (v. 11). Was there a hint that Uriah understood that "to lie with my wife" was what David really wanted him to do? In other circumstances, of course, Uriah would be perfectly entitled to do all these things. The legitimacy of such enjoyment is underlined by "*my* wife." But were those very words chosen to implicitly accuse David? In any circumstances what David had done was wrong, and he knew it. Bathsheba had been introduced to him as "the wife of Uriah the Hittite" (11:3). And he *did* lay with her (11:4).

The sixth and final thing we hear from Uriah is an oath: "As you live, and as your soul lives, I will not do this thing." At one level these sound like noble words, honoring the king's life (on which he swears his oath) and declaring with utter clarity that he will not do "this thing," which would involve a compromise of his dedication to his king, his commander, his people, and even his God (represented here by the ark). Taking his words at face value, the dignity and integrity of this man are astonishing. This was virtue beyond the call of duty.

Or was it? For those with ears to hear, the wording of the oath in Hebrew suggests that what is at stake in "this thing" was David's life, the life of David's soul. Literally Uriah said to David, "Your life and the life of your soul if I will do this thing." Was Uriah aware that David had urged him to do "this thing" precisely to *save* David's life (perhaps literally, if the requirements of the Law were strictly applied)? Uriah's stunning oath declared that doing "this thing" was as weighty as "your life and the life of your soul." Was this an amazing instance of a man who spoke more truly than he knew? Or did Uriah know more than he dared to openly admit?

Like David, we cannot know with certainty the answers to those crucial questions. From a practical point of view it made little difference. Either Uriah's noble character or his wily cunning (or both, for they are not mutually exclusive) had caused David's Plan A to fail. Uriah had not gone down to his house, slept with his wife, and given David a cover for his adultery. Furthermore he had no intention of doing so in a time frame that would suit David's scurrilous purpose. His speech also left no room for David to press the matter without revealing his hidden agenda.[19]

If David had ears to hear, he did not need to know the motives behind Uriah's speech to hear the implied rebuke. Here was a further opportunity for the king to come to his senses and try to make amends for his failure.[20] But there is no indication that Uriah's words touched David's conscience.

Plan B (vv. 12, 13)

David's heart deceived him into thinking that there were better options than repentance. He promptly embarked on Plan B.

Another Clever Deception? (vv. 12, 13a)

"Then David said to Uriah, 'Remain here today also, and tomorrow I will send you back'" (v. 12a). David did not argue with Uriah. Indeed he gave the impression of accepting his explanation and therefore respecting his principled conduct. The king did not have to give any reason for his instruction to Uriah to stay another day. Various legitimate reasons are conceivable. Perhaps the king was preparing a message he wanted taken back to the battlefield. The real reason is obvious to us, and it may have been plain to Uriah. David wanted more time to solve the problem his sin had caused.

We still do not really know, as David did not know (although our suspicions have surely been raised), whether Uriah suspected anything. Nonetheless he was obedient to his king. "So Uriah remained in Jerusalem that day and the next" (v. 12b). This sentence sums up Uriah's three-day stay in Jerusalem.[21] Like David (11:1), Uriah "remained in Jerusalem." However, Uriah's conduct in Jerusalem was very different from David's.

Returning to Day 2, we learn how David followed up the ominous conversation with Uriah. "And David invited him, and he ate in his presence and drank, so that he made him drunk" (v. 13a).

What Uriah refused to do in his own house ("eat and . . . drink and . . . lie with my wife," v. 11), David required him to do in the king's house, with the exception that "lie with my wife" was replaced with David making Uriah drunk.[22] David was responsible for this last aspect of the meal.

How different is the ignominy of this scene from the goodness of the superficially similar occasion when Mephibosheth had been invited to the king's table (9:13).

We do not know whether David's intentions were as transparent to Uriah as they are to us (although we may well be thinking by now that this fellow was not as simple as he might have liked to appear). David obviously wanted Uriah's drunkenness to lead to a lowering of his noble standards expressed in verse 11. David wanted Uriah to go down to his house and lie with his wife.

The Failure of Plan B (v. 13b)

For a brief moment the narrator again holds us in suspense. He tells us what happened that night in terms that lead us to think (for a moment) that David's scheme may have worked: "And in the evening he went out to lie on his couch . . ." (v. 13b). With his wife? No. ". . . with the servants of his lord" (v. 13c). The pointed irony of this account continues. In the very act that frustrated David's shameful intentions, David was still "his lord," and Uriah still regarded himself as one of David's "servants." Just as on the previous night, "he did not go down to his house" (v. 13d).[23] As he had sworn by David's life, he did "not do this thing" (v. 11). Uriah drunk was better than David sober![24]

Through these three days David had shown himself to be deceived by his own wickedness. Having disregarded the Law of God and the love of neighbor, he gave no thought to the seriousness of what he had done. He cared only about avoiding public shame and whatever might have followed from the public exposure of his crime. As he was frustrated in his attempted cover-up by Uriah's integrity or ingenuity (or both), we are right to perceive the hidden hand of God thwarting his attempts to make evil have no consequences.

We do not know what would have happened if David had trusted God and come clean, confessed his wrongdoing, and accepted responsibility for the consequences. Nor did he. But doing what is right is not about being in control of what then happens. It is about trusting God (cf. Psalm 37:3; Proverbs 3:5–8; 1 Peter 4:19). On this occasion David did not trust God, and he did not do what was right. The absence of any direct reference to the Lord in 2 Samuel 11 (until the last sentence) reflects David's own disregard for God through these days. King that he was, he attempted to take control of the course of events himself. His deceitful heart deluded him into thinking that (a) he had the wisdom and power to protect himself from the consequences of his wickedness, and (b) the only consequences that mattered had to do with his behavior becoming known publicly. The delusion depended on disregarding God.

Let us beware of putting our consciences to sleep, as David seems to have done. When we have done wrong, immediate acknowledgment and willingness to bear the shame is a far wiser path than a foolish attempt at cover-up that will never work in the long run. The God whose hand was at work in David's world is at work in ours and will finally bring every deed to account (see Ecclesiastes 12:14; Matthew 12:36; Romans 14:12; 1 Peter 4:5).

There is, however, more than this here. As we see David's deceitful, sick heart, we not only recognize that our own hearts share the same disease but also remember that King David (yes, this weak, deceitful, and deceiving King David) had been given a promise by God:

> When your days are fulfilled and you lie down with your fathers, I will raise up your offspring after you, who shall come from your body, and I will establish his kingdom. . . . And your house and your kingdom shall be made sure forever before me. Your throne shall be established forever. (7:12, 16)

As we read King David's story we must never forget the promise that stands behind it. As we witness the failings of David, who was too like all of us, the promise may seem more and more remarkable. But the One who made this promise is faithful and true. The great mystery of the life of David is how this promise could ever come to pass, how God's faithfulness could ever overcome the unfaithfulness of even the best human beings.

The answer is the gospel of the Lord Jesus Christ, the son of David. He, like David and the rest of us, experienced human weakness and temptation. But he was not deceived, and he did not fail (Hebrews 4:15). As we consider the failures of David, we will do well to heed the call of the Apostle Paul:

> Remember Jesus Christ, risen from the dead, the offspring of David, as preached in my gospel. (2 Timothy 2:8)

24

The Murderer

2 SAMUEL 11:14–27

IN THE EPIC HISTORY recorded in the books of Samuel, the failure of human leaders has been an overarching theme. In 1 Samuel we see, most dramatically of all, the failure of Saul. Despite his apparent potential (1 Samuel 10:23, 24), considerable abilities (seen, for example, in 1 Samuel 11:11), and substantial accomplishments (summarized in 1 Samuel 14:47, 48), Saul was a disaster as king of God's people. He failed to "listen to the words of the Lord" (1 Samuel 15:1). Power in the hands of such a man eventually did more harm than good.

The tragic story of Saul provides the backdrop for the story of a very different man. But what made him different? David was chosen by God for God's own purposes (1 Samuel 13:14; 16:1). The Lord was with him (1 Samuel 18:12, 14, 28). Indeed "David became greater and greater, *for the Lord, the God of hosts, was with him*" (5:10). That is why David proved to be "better" than Saul (1 Samuel 15:28).

The difference between Saul and David was that David had a place in God's heart that Saul did not (1 Samuel 13:14[1]). David was the recipient of God's grace in a way that Saul was not. David's greatness and goodness was a consequence of, not the reason for, God's choice of him. God's choice of David, and his gracious purpose for him, was eventually made clear in the momentous promise that Nathan passed on to David (7:4–17).

The events recorded in 2 Samuel 11 demonstrate once and for all that David, in himself, was no better than Saul. Power, in the hands of David, became an instrument for indulgent, self-serving abuse of others. He fancied the wife of Uriah the Hittite, and so he took her. When he learned that she was pregnant, he embarked on a cover-up. His relatively simple Plan A failed

(11:6–9), as did his more scurrilous Plan B (11:10–13). The king's schemes were foiled by the apparent integrity, and possibly the ingenuity, of Uriah, the faithful servant he had wronged.

The deceitfulness of the human heart that we thought about in our last chapter, and saw displayed in David's misguided attempts to evade taking responsibility for his crime, includes the delusion that our sinfulness can be contained. We regard certain behavior as of little consequence. As one thing leads to another, we find it easy to underestimate our wrongdoing. David looked at the beautiful, naked woman (11:2). What harm can there be in a look? He made inquiries about her (11:3). What's wrong with knowing who she is? He sent for her (11:4a). Why not meet the lady? He had sex with her (11:4b). Her husband was away. No one need know. What harm was done? Inconveniently she fell pregnant (11:5). The easiest thing for all concerned would be to arrange things so that everyone, including her husband, would think the child was his. The deception would hurt nobody and would save a lot of trouble.

Unfortunately (for David, whose thoughts I have been trying to imagine in the preceding paragraph), he failed in his attempts to arrange things. If only Uriah had been a little more cooperative, a little less principled, a little easier to manipulate. David was now in a difficult spot. It wasn't his fault (I imagine him thinking). He had tried to deal with the problem in a low-cost way by which no one would be hurt. Uriah, who could have been the solution, was now the problem. David had no choice. The situation was becoming desperate. A desperate measure was called for.

Plan C (vv. 14, 15)

The third day (since Uriah had come back to Jerusalem at David's summons) dawned. It was time for Uriah to return to the battlefront (11:12). The king had settled on a third plan. It was daring in the extreme, but if it worked, then David's difficulties would be resolved. "In the morning David wrote a letter to Joab and sent it by the hand of Uriah" (v. 14). Once again the king "sent"; this time it was a message put in writing.

If Uriah knew nothing of David's problem (which by now we have come to doubt, but like David we do not know for sure), then he would think that the letter contained the king's response to the news Uriah had brought about the state of the war (11:7), perhaps royal words of encouragement, possibly fresh orders for the commander. It may have been a little unusual for the message to be sent in writing. Of the many messages sent back and forth in these chapters, no other is said to have been written (although some may have been). However, a letter sent from a king to his commander by the hand of a trusted messenger would not normally arouse suspicion.

Momentarily the contents of this letter are not revealed to us, just as the bearer of the letter did not know what it contained.

As Uriah leaves the city of Jerusalem, the king's letter in his hand, on his way back to his commander and his fellow troops at the front line, the narrator lets us in on the secret: "In the letter [David] wrote,[2] 'Set[3] Uriah in the forefront of the hardest fighting, and then draw back from him, that he may be struck down, and die'" (v. 15).

I hope that you are horrified. The lustful glance from his rooftop just a few weeks earlier had now led to a murder plot. One step after another David had not trusted God and done what was right. Now he was initiating the deliberate execution of an innocent man to protect himself. This great king who in better days had refused to shed blood to defend himself (see 1 Samuel 24:6, 12; 25:33, 34; 26:9–11, 23, 24) and who had condemned in the strongest terms those who had presumed to do so on his behalf (1 Samuel 24:7; 2 Samuel 1:14–16; 3:28, 29, 37, 39; 4:9–11) now resorted to a shameful murder conspiracy to cover up his own crime.

The risk involved in sending this secret letter (effectively Uriah's death warrant) by Uriah's hand was considerable, especially if David (like us) suspected that Uriah had heard some of the latest Jerusalem gossip. Perhaps the risk was mitigated by (a) the fact that the letter would have been sealed, (b) the possibility that Uriah could not read, and (c) the evident integrity of this faithful servant of the king that had been so strikingly displayed in the interviews (and the man's conduct) over the last three days. David's plan depended on his letter being confidentially delivered. Such was Uriah's character that David trusted him with this!

The plan itself has the marks of being hastily conceived. David clearly wanted the killing of Uriah to look like an unfortunate but not unusual casualty of war. Otherwise he could have commanded Joab simply to kill the man. Joab had shown himself more than capable of executing anyone he thought was a threat to his king (see 3:27; cf. Joab's brother in 1 Samuel 26:9). But how was Joab supposed to arrange for the army, with the single exception of Uriah, to suddenly withdraw from the battlefront? How could this be done without arousing suspicion? How could Joab explain this plan to the troops without someone alerting Uriah? David's eagerness to deal with Uriah had clouded his usual good sense.

The objective, however, was clear. If Uriah had come to know about David's act of adultery, then the accusation would be silenced by his death.

If Uriah was still ignorant of David's offense against him, then his death would ensure that he never found out. Either way Bathsheba's pregnancy could be ascribed to a dead Uriah without fear of contradiction.

The "Success" of Plan C (Improved by Joab) (vv. 16, 17)

We follow Uriah back to the front line of the conflict with the Ammonites, which is where this chapter of 2 Samuel began. While the sordid events of David's personal life had been unfolding in Jerusalem (lust, adultery, deception, and attempted cover-up), the action of more obvious national importance had been taking place in the vicinity of the Ammonite city of Rabbah. Joab and his men had "ravaged the Ammonites and besieged Rabbah" (11:1). When Uriah reported back to his commander, letter in hand, "Joab was besieging[4] the city . . ." (v. 16a).

Joab was a loyal general, highly competent, but headstrong and determined. He had always acted in what he considered to be the best interests of David's kingdom, but his actions had not always pleased David. Some years earlier, as David was carefully and graciously making peace with Saul's old commander, Abner (3:20, 21), Joab had decided that Abner could not be trusted and killed him (3:22–30). David was furious. But the action was characteristic of Joab and his brothers (see 3:39).

When Joab received the king's letter from Uriah's hand, he wasted no time in acting on David's instructions, but characteristically he made some improvements to the king's plan.

In response to the order he had now received from David, Joab "assigned Uriah to the place where he knew there were valiant men" (v. 16b). Joab "knew" things that others did not know.[5] He "knew" where the strongest enemy soldiers were. That's where he put Uriah. The account is concise. Filling in the picture, we are to imagine that there were parts of the city that were more strongly defended than others. The strength of the Ammonite forces was concentrated in one place more than others. That is where Uriah was stationed.

So far Joab was enacting the king's directive fairly precisely ("Set Uriah in the forefront of the hardest fighting," v. 15). He placed Uriah where the hardest fighting could be anticipated.

Apparently putting Uriah in place was accompanied by some other provocative action. The contingent to which Uriah had been assigned may have made some kind of advance on the city, precisely at its strongest point. Perhaps they made themselves appear vulnerable. In some way Joab provoked a response from the city at what he "knew" (v. 16) to be its strongest point.

The Ammonites wasted no time in seizing the advantage (whatever it was) that Joab had delivered to them. "And the men of the city came out and fought with Joab" (v. 17a). The Ammonite "valiant men" advanced out of the city and engaged the Israelites who, under Joab's command, had been exposed to the Ammonites' strength.

"And some of the servants of David among the people fell" (v. 17b). A number of Joab's men died that day. The text emphasizes that those who died were "servants of David."[6] They fell because of a strategically reckless plan. There must have been questions asked. Joab was no fool. He had an earned reputation for strategic skill. Why had he ordered such an irresponsible maneuver? Why had he needlessly sacrificed the lives of his men?

He was, of course, implementing David's command. He was also improving on it. David had ordered a premature withdrawal of the troops, leaving Uriah alone, stranded, and vulnerable. Joab's action might be judged to be strategically foolish. But at least it camouflaged the murder it contained. What David really wanted was accomplished. Among those who fell that day was the one who was a problem for David: "Uriah the Hittite also died" (v. 17c). Questions may have been asked about Joab's strategic judgment, but he had managed to avoid the most dangerous question: "Why Uriah?" Uriah "also" died. He was just one of a number.

Those who fell that day, including Uriah, were "servants of David" (v. 17). To protect the king from the consequences of his crime, a number of those who served him were sacrificed. The "innocent" gaze from the palace roof (11:2) had led (step by step) to multiple innocent deaths. Could anyone still think that the beginning of this sequence of events was a small thing? We will soon see someone who did.

Good News (?) for David (vv. 18–24)

The narrator has a way of summing up a sequence of events and then going back and filling in details. What happened next is summarized: "Then Joab sent and told David all the news about the fighting [literally, all the things of the war]" (v. 18). That, of course, in normal circumstances is what Joab would be expected to do. It is what he (and Uriah) may have thought he was doing when he sent Uriah back to David earlier. But on this occasion very little was as it seemed.

How to Turn Bad News into Good News (vv. 18–21)

The messenger would, no doubt, have been puzzled that his commander was so eager to send back news to the king of his botched assault on the city.

Indeed, the messenger may have been worried at how the king would receive this news. David had a reputation for severe treatment toward certain persons who had thought they were bringing him good news that he in fact judged to be bad news (see 1:2–16; 3:28, 29; 4:5–12). To all appearances this messenger was the bearer of *bad* news, news of a costly, reckless, and pointless loss of Israelite lives. The king would not be pleased.

Joab had anticipated this concern and had briefed the messenger, not with the truth, but with words to use should the king be unhappy with the news he brought. Joab's speech to the messenger was (it seems) rather animated: "And he instructed[7] the messenger, 'When you have finished telling all the news about the fighting [literally, all the things of the war] to the king, then, if the king's anger rises, and if he says to you . . .'" (vv. 19, 20a).

The following speech suggests that Joab was in an agitated state. He was not, of course, literally *anticipating* exactly what David would say.[8] He was *imagining*, and acting out, the king's response. Perhaps he mimicked the king's manner and voice—furious and shouting. In this Joab was expressing his own view of the disastrous maneuver that had cost so many lives, and as we listen we learn more about what actually happened than the narrator has yet told us. "Why did you go so near the city to fight?" (v. 20b), Joab imagined David asking. Joab would only imagine the king asking this question if that is in fact what happened. In verse 17 the narrator only told us, "the men of the city came out and fought." Now we learn that the fighting somehow involved the Israelite forces approaching the city walls. In a siege the army outside the city has the advantage of time. Eventually the inhabitants of the city may grow desperate and be forced to come out from the shelter of the city walls and engage the enemy on his terms. The sieging army forfeits their advantage if they approach the city walls. Joab knew that. He knew that David knew that. Of course the king would ask, "Why did you do it?"

"Did you not know that they would shoot from the wall?" (v. 20c), Joab then imagined the king asking. Of course Joab knew that. The reason a sieging army would normally keep its distance from the city walls was precisely this. From the height of the wall the inhabitants of the city had a decisive advantage if an enemy were foolish enough to approach within the range of archers or other weapons.

Again in verse 17 we did not hear about archers shooting from the city wall. We now deduce that is what happened. That is why the Ammonites prevailed. Joab knew that what he had done was, from the point of view of military strategy, suicidal. He knew that David knew that too.

Indeed there was a well-known case study. Any military man in Israel worth his salt would know the story of what had happened more than a century previously at Thebez.[9] Abimelech was a son of the famous judge Gideon. After Gideon's death Abimelech murdered his brothers and had himself declared king (Judges 9:5, 6). It was a shameful episode in Israel's history. However, Abimelech met his end when he foolishly tried to set fire to a tower in which the citizens of Thebez had taken refuge from him. Abimelech was mortally wounded when a woman dropped a millstone[10] from the tower roof, crushing Abimelech under its force. Fearing a reputation for being killed by a woman, in his last breath Abimelech ordered his armor-bearer to finish him off. (See Judges 9:50–54.) There could not be a more powerful lesson in the foolishness of approaching too close to a wall that protected an enemy. And so Joab imagined David asking, "Who killed Abimelech the son of Jerubbesheth[11]? Did not a woman cast an upper millstone on him from the wall, so that he died at Thebez?" (v. 21a).

What did Joab know? Had the rumors circulating in Jerusalem reached him? Perhaps Uriah himself had spoken of things he had heard in Jerusalem. Did Joab know that behind the tragedy at Rabbah, like the disaster that fell on Abimelech, there was a woman? Was he at all troubled by the fact that the example he cited (in his imagination of what David might say) was in fact an act of divine judgment on "the evil of Abimelech" (see Judges 9:56)? We cannot know clearly what was in Joab's mind, but his strange speech to the messenger suggests that what he had done (on David's order) troubled him. The all-important question, the answer to which only he and David knew, was, "Why did you go so near the wall?" (v. 21b).

The secret behind the debacle at Rabbah, however, explained everything. The success of the plan is what Joab needed to communicate to David. He therefore told the messenger how he should respond to David's anger at the news he brought: "then you shall say, 'Your servant Uriah the Hittite is dead also'" (v. 21c).

We cannot know what the messenger made of this strange speech, especially its last words. Did he suspect anything of the truth? Had he heard rumors? Or did he think that the news about Uriah would be of interest to the king simply because Uriah had so recently visited the king?

The News Delivered (vv. 22–24)

We follow the messenger as he arrived in Jerusalem, without knowing the answers to our questions. "So the messenger went and came and told David all that Joab had sent him to tell" (v. 22).

Indeed he did, but like his commander, this messenger was prepared to be a little flexible in the way in which he chose to carry out his superior's instructions. Aware (as Joab had anticipated) that a simple report of the debacle would probably incur the king's anger, the messenger took it upon himself to give his report in such a way that the questions Joab anticipated David would ask were answered without the king asking them. The Ammonites, he said, "gained an advantage over us" (v. 23a), presumably by taking the Israelites by surprise when they "came out against us in the field" (v. 23b), perhaps in an unexpected pre-dawn attack. But the Israelite response seemed to be effective: "we drove them back to the entrance of the gate" (v. 23c), the gate in the wall of the city. On the reasonable assumption that the messenger was telling the truth, we now learn how the Israelite force came to be close to the city wall. It was their effort to drive the Ammonites back into the city that brought the Israelites too near. The confusion and excitement of the fighting briefly camouflaged the foolishness of Joab's orders to pursue the Ammonites "to the entrance of the gate" (v. 23).

Unfortunately for the Israelite contingent, there were archers ready on the city wall. "Then the archers shot at your servants from the wall" (v. 24a), as the Israelites were drawn within range of the arrows. There were casualties. "Some of the king's servants are dead" (v. 24b). These included (the messenger finished his report by noting) "your servant Uriah the Hittite [who] is dead also" (v. 24c).

If the messenger suspected the truth, he was smart enough to conceal the fact. He mentioned Uriah because Joab had told him to, but he did not hint that his reason went beyond the fact that Uriah was David's servant (who had, of course, recently visited the king).[12] Indeed by going to some trouble to explain (or explain away) the debacle, we (with David) get the impression that the messenger did not know that the news of Uriah's death was all that the king needed (or wanted) to hear.

David's Response (v. 25)

The messenger waited for the king's response. Would he explode with rage at such uncharacteristic incompetence on the part of his general? Would he be overcome with grief at the pointless loss of life? Would the messenger be required to carry back to Joab a rebuke from his king?

Imagine the relief when the king responded calmly, even gently. "David said to the messenger, 'Thus shall you say to Joab, "Do not let this matter displease you . . ."'" (v. 25a). That is the gist of what he said, but literally the king's message to Joab was, "Do not let this thing be evil in your eyes."

David's deceitful heart had now blinded him to the evil of what he had done. His conscience was seared. *Uriah has been murdered—other servants of David were sacrificed—but don't see this thing as evil, Joab, because your king does not see it as evil!*

David had become morally bankrupt. In due course the Bible writers will tell us in various ways that a basic requirement of God's king is the ability to discern good and evil (14:17; 1 Kings 3:9; cf. Hebrews 5:14). The prophet Isaiah will condemn "those who call evil good and good evil" (Isaiah 5:20; cf. Malachi 2:17; Romans 16:19). David was now refusing to see the evil thing that he had done as evil. The contrast with David's lament over the deaths of Saul and Jonathan is bewildering (1:17–27). David was no longer the great and good man he had been.

With astonishing and callous cynicism he pretended that what had happened was no more than the unfortunate unpredictability of war: ". . . for the sword devours now one and now another" (v. 25b). David's advice to Joab was to put "this matter" behind him and get on with the war: "Strengthen your attack against the city and overthrow it" (v. 25c). Far from any word of rebuke from the king, he told the messenger to "encourage him" (v. 25d).

The Aftermath (vv. 26, 27a)

It had worked! David's difficulties were over. Thanks to the ingenuity of Joab, it had worked better than David had planned. The conspiracy had been sufficiently disguised in a confused military operation that no awkward questions need arise. Any rumors circulating in Jerusalem could be plausibly denied. The one obstacle to David's covering his crime was out of the way. It was time to move on.

For the Wife of Uriah (v. 26)

We have heard nothing about Bathsheba since she sent the ominous news to David of her pregnancy (11:5). From what the narrator has been prepared to tell us, it seems that she had nothing to do with David's schemes. She had complied with the king's wishes at the beginning, but it is difficult to see how she could have refused. He was the king. He then did not need or seek her help in arranging the cover-up. When she learned of her husband's death, whatever she may have suspected, we have no reason to think that she learned the truth. "When the wife of Uriah heard that Uriah her husband was dead, she lamented over her husband" (v. 26). That is all we are told. Unlike David, she grieved Uriah's death.

Note, however, that the narrator insists on calling her "the wife of Uriah," emphasizing this by calling Uriah "her husband" (v. 26). David may have put these facts behind him. But we are not allowed to forget them.

For David (v. 27a)

David had one more move to make. He completed the concealment of his crimes as soon as the customary period for Bathsheba's mourning was finished. For the last time in this episode, the king "sent": "And when the mourning was over, David sent and brought her to his house, and she became his wife and bore him a son" (v. 27a).

We can imagine David thinking, "All's well that ends well." It had ended well (for David). David could claim the boy he had fathered as his own. And surely that was the end of the matter.

Something David Overlooked (v. 27b)

Except for one thing. Unusually in the life of David everything that happened since that evening when David spied Bathsheba bathing had occurred without any reference to God.[13]

However, as always, the Lord had been watching. The account of what happened with David, Bathsheba, and Uriah concludes with the devastating closing statement, "But the thing that David had done displeased the LORD" (v. 27b). Literally the narrator's closing words echo David's message to Joab in verse 25. David had said, "Do not let *this thing* be *evil in your eyes*" (AT). The account closes with, "But *the thing* that David had done was *evil in the eyes of the LORD*" (AT). It may not have been "evil" in the eyes of Joab or of David. But "evil" it was. The Lord himself saw it as such.

David's efforts at a cover-up may have momentarily seemed successful. But they were ridiculous. We may deceive ourselves about our evil thoughts, words, and deeds. But evil cannot be hidden from God! What consequences will flow from the fact that the Lord had seen all that David did and had seen it as it was—evil?

Before we turn the page and begin to see what those consequences were, let us pause and reflect on what we have heard in 2 Samuel 11. What do you make of this story? It is one of the ugliest stories you will find anywhere. It is the story of a callous brute with the conscience of a brick wall! If we had heard the story on the television news, we might have shaken our heads and said, "There are some rotten people in this world! Makes you sick, doesn't it?

What is the world coming to?" We might have comforted ourselves that we are not like this dreadful man and forgotten about it.

But we cannot do that because we have not heard this story on a television news program. We have heard it from the Bible! I will put it simply like this: *God* has told us this story. Why?

In the first place it is reasonable to understand that this story is here in God's Word as a demonstration to us of human nature and human sinfulness. David was not the worst man to ever have lived. Quite the contrary. He was, as we have seen, a great man. One of the greatest. And yet even David fell to a level as low as this.

That is a solemn and astounding lesson to us all. No matter how upright and noble a person might be, there is in human nature an inherent rottenness that can always come out, given the circumstances. Do I dare to say in my heart that I would never act like David? Do I think in my heart that I am inherently good and not a brute like David? Then this story might wake me up to reality. There is in the human nature we all share a far greater capacity for evil than we usually think. That is serious! Its full seriousness is only made explicit in the last sentence of the chapter: "The thing David did was evil in the eyes of the LORD."

Let us see that in God's eyes wrong is wrong, sin is sin. In our day it will do us good to take that in and understand it in the very area dealt with here, sexual morality.

But there is something more. This is not just a story of human sinfulness—it is a story of *David's* sinfulness. That is what is especially disturbing about this story. The man we have seen commit adultery and murder was *God's chosen one*! Is that not extraordinary?

The Lord, in whose eyes what David had done was evil, had promised to establish David's kingdom forever (7:16). What will now become of the Lord's promise? Could the Lord be expected to keep his promise now that David had so spectacularly forgotten the Lord? That is the question that is raised by the events of 2 Samuel 11.

Is it possible that as we read the story of David's wickedness, we are at the same time reading the story of God accomplishing his purposes? Can you believe that? Don't you feel in your bones that God's kingdom on earth must be advanced by *good* people (people more like us), not men like David?

If that is how we think then, quite simply, we are mistaken. The facts of history are against us. You might think, after hearing this story, that David, the adulterer and murderer, marked a very low point in the Old Testament. In fact he marks the high point! The promises that God made to David—that through David's line God would establish a kingdom that would last for all eternity—were never to be forgotten.

Was that because of what a saint David was? Certainly not. It was because of what a great God God is.

In due course the Old Testament prophets brought the assurance that the Lord *will* keep his promise despite the failings of David (see, for example, Isaiah 9:6, 7; 11:1–9; Amos 9:11–15). The grace of the Lord is even more spectacular than the failure of David. As we read the later parts of the Old Testament, we see that the promises of God given to David became the basis for a great spirit of expectancy, the hope of Israel. The prophets much later in the Old Testament insisted that God would keep his sure promises to David.

The events of this chapter are remembered in the first page of the New Testament, where we learn that the ancestry of Jesus includes "the wife of Uriah" (Matthew 1:6). Jesus is the son of David who was "promised beforehand . . . in the holy Scriptures. . . . [He has been] declared to be the Son of God in power . . . by his resurrection from the dead, Jesus Christ our Lord" (Romans 1:2–4).

When we pray, as he taught us, "Your kingdom come" (Matthew 6:10), we do so with confidence because we have seen the Lord's spectacular grace. When we pray "Your kingdom come," we know that God's kingdom advances not by human goodness, cleverness, or power but despite human sinfulness, foolishness, and weakness. God himself is the one who will do this. Rejoice in this news!

25

Shattered by the Word of God

2 SAMUEL 12:1–15

HAVE YOU EVER BEEN SHATTERED by the word of God? Some of us have become so familiar with the word of God (or at least we think it is familiar to us) that God's word never disturbs us. We read our Bibles, perhaps we study our Bibles, we listen to Bible talks, and life goes on. But we would not say that the word of God had *shattered* us.

In 2 Samuel 12 we hear about one of the most important occasions in world history when a man was shattered by the word of God. The man was King David. The circumstances were those that we have been following in our last three chapters. The king had not used his position and power (as he had previously) for "doing justice and righteousness for all his people" (8:15 AT), but rather to commit adultery and arrange a murder to cover it up. Like too many humans given a position of power, he forgot the one to whom he was accountable. He used his position not to serve those entrusted to his care, but to assert his own self-serving desires, to abuse and harm others, to benefit and protect himself.

David deluded himself (and did his best to delude others) into thinking that he had done nothing wrong (11:25). However, the last line of 2 Samuel 11 casts a true light on "the thing that David had done": it was "evil in the eyes of the LORD" (11:27b AT).

There is no mention of the Lord in chapter 11 until that last sentence, reflecting in the narrative David's own lack of attention to God. It is true that God has not appeared in the narrative since chapter 8,[1] but in chapters 9, 10 he seems to be "with" David, as he had been since that day when young

David was anointed in Bethlehem (see 1 Samuel 16:13, 18; 18:12, 14, 28; 2 Samuel 5:10; 8:6b, 14b). The Lord had blessed David richly, just as David had prayed (7:29) and as the Lord had promised (7:16). As a consequence David had become a great and good king. In 2 Samuel 11 all this changed. What will happen now that David's actions were "evil in the eyes of the LORD" (AT)?

Some time passed (almost a year, or perhaps a little more[2]) after David committed his crimes. With the benefit of hindsight, David would later reflect on this time:

> For when I kept silent, my bones wasted away
>   through my groaning all day long.
> For day and night your hand was heavy upon me;
>   my strength was dried up as by the heat of summer. (Psalm 32:3, 4)[3]

At what he must have judged to be just the right time "the LORD sent Nathan to David" (v. 1a). After all the "sending" in chapter 11,[4] this was the most significant sending of them all. It would change everything.

We met "Nathan the prophet" in 7:2. He was the one who conveyed the Lord's mighty promise to David in 7:4–17. Nathan is a reminder of that extraordinary promise. Now the Lord (in whose eyes David's recent actions were evil) sent Nathan to David again.

A Situation (vv. 1b–4)

Nathan, obedient prophet that he was, came to David (v. 1b). He began to speak. He brought a situation before the king. The story is so well-known that we easily forget that David did not yet know its true nature. An important role for a king was to administer justice among his people (as the judges had done before there was a king, 1 Samuel 7:15–17; see 2 Samuel 8:15; cf. 14:1–20). It seemed that Nathan had brought a case for the king to consider.[5]

Introduction (v. 1b–3a)

> There were two men in a certain city, the one rich and the other poor. The rich man had very many flocks and herds, but the poor man had nothing but one little ewe lamb, which he had bought. (vv. 1b–3a)

The two men were neighbors. Their circumstances were very different—one rich, the other poor. The rich man's possessions ("very many flocks and herds") he simply "had" (v. 2). He was fortunate. The poor man's only possession ("one little ewe lamb") he had "bought" (v. 3).

The Poor Man's Wealth (v. 3b)

However, the poor man delighted in his "one" possession.

> And he brought it up, and it grew up with him and with his children.[6] It used to eat of his morsel and drink from his cup and lie in his arms, and it was like a daughter to him. (v. 3b)

His was a happy home life, rich in kindness and relationships, and the little ewe lamb was just like a loved member of the family. Notice three important aspects of this scene. First, the poor man's home life was characterized by different forms of *giving*. The poor man gave of his food, drink, and affection. Shortly we will see someone else who *takes*. Second, the delightful and innocent intimacy of the poor man with his little ewe lamb is described in terms ("lie in his arms," v. 3[7]) that will soon be used to describe sexual intimacy between a man and a woman (see v. 8[8]). Third, the ewe lamb was like a "daughter" (v. 3; Hebrew, *bath*) to him. Shortly we will realize that the lamb was like another *bath*: *Bath*sheba![9]

These subtleties were not noticed (at this stage) by David, but they were certainly deliberate elements in this brilliantly crafted story. As we listen we may also hear other echoes from the previous chapter. "Eat," "drink," and "lie" were the three luxuries of domestic bliss that Uriah had refused to enjoy (11:11). This was the very language that Uriah had chosen to describe his own home life in happier times!

At this stage, however, David was simply hearing about a poor man who was nonetheless contented and happy in the warmth of his home life.

The Rich Man's Poverty (v. 4)

This happy situation had been shattered by something that happened in the other man's life.

> Now there came a traveler to the rich man, and he was unwilling to take one of his own flock or herd to prepare for the guest who had come to him, but he took the poor man's lamb and prepared it for the man who had come to him. (v. 4)

Again there are aspects of the narrative here that will soon take on great significance. First, the visitor "came" (the verb occurs three times in this single sentence) to the rich man, creating the circumstances for his crime. In the previous chapter Bathsheba and then Uriah "came" to David, and their coming created the situations in which David acted so wickedly (11:4, 7).[10]

Second, we now see the man who "took" (v. 4). The rich man thought it would be a "pity"[11] to "take" anything from his own vast flocks and herds (that would be giving). So he "took" the little ewe lamb that belonged to the poor man. Soon we (and David) will be forced to recall that the king "took" Bathsheba (11:4). Third, the rich man not only took the ewe lamb, he killed it (this action being hidden under the expression "prepared it," v. 4).

It is "a tale of cynicism, selfishness, destruction, and greed,"[12] and deliberately so, of course. This rich man behaved like Nabal,[13] and remember what happened to him (1 Samuel 25)! This was the kind of behavior that would one day become a theme in the preaching of prophets in Israel.[14] There is absolutely no moral ambiguity in the situation as it is presented. The only question is, what should be done? What does justice demand?

A Judgment (vv. 5, 6)

King David, apparently regarding the story as a report of an actual incident, adopted his role as judge.

> Then David's anger was greatly kindled against the man, and he said to Nathan, "As the LORD lives, the man who has done this deserves to die, and he shall restore the lamb fourfold, because he did this thing, and because he had no pity." (vv. 5, 6)

The outburst from David takes us by surprise. Through the turbulent events of the previous chapter we have seen no display of emotion from him (unless we count the lust with which it all began). He was disturbingly calm and calculating, even when Joab anticipated that he might become angry (cf. 11:20, 25). But now there is nothing calm or calculating about his judgment on the rich man and his conduct. David invoked the name of God. This is the first time that David seems to have thought of the Lord for some time. By the living God he pronounced the death sentence on the rich man.

The trouble is, despicable as the rich man's conduct was, it was not a capital offense. He had stolen and killed a lamb. For that the Law required fourfold restitution (see Exodus 22:1), not death. David knew the requirement of the Law and pronounced that verdict accordingly, but *before* that he pronounced the death sentence, saying literally, "a son of death[15] is the man who has done this."

There are two problems with David's judicial conduct. The first is that it was unbalanced. This was not what justice called for. It was what David's anger called for. Without indulging in psychoanalysis, it seems reasonable to deduce that David was a troubled man. Was he overcompensating for his accusing conscience by lashing out at the wickedness of another? The second problem, of course, was the dazzling hypocrisy of David's furious judgment. The judge was himself a criminal whose deeds *did* deserve death.[16]

David's words contain a surprising hint (to us readers) of what is to come. The double verdict (death and fourfold restoration) is supported by a double indictment. On the one hand "because he did *this thing*" (v. 6) reminds us of the way in which David's own crime has been called "this thing" (11:25 AT; ESV, "this matter"). On the other hand, "because he had no pity" sounds like a very good description of David's ruthless scheme to "take" Bathsheba and to murder Uriah.[17] The doubling of the judgment anticipates the double judgment that was about to fall on David.

The Shattering Word of the Lord (vv. 7–12)

Gotcha! (v. 7a)

In one of the most dramatic moments in the history of the world (when you know what was at stake), the prophet Nathan faced the king whom the Lord had chosen and pronounced two devastating words (in the original): "Nathan said to David, '*You* are the man!'" (v. 7a). The two words pass judgment on the sequence of events that had begun with another two-word message (in the original): "I am pregnant" (11:5).[18]

Nathan's two shattering words began the most difficult hour of David's life.[19] With brutal force Nathan confronted David. The situation on which the king had pronounced his furious verdict was his own situation. The story was not a report about someone else's crime; it was a mirror revealing David's own wickedness. The rich man in Nathan's story was David. His flocks and herds were David's considerable possessions, particularly his numerous wives. The poor man was Uriah. The lamb was Bathsheba. David had taken Bathsheba (11:4). He had killed Uriah (11:15).[20] "*You* are the man!"

Without waiting for David's response to his shocking two words, Nathan proceeded to bring, now in a somewhat more formal way, the word of God that he had been sent to speak to David. It begins with a preamble, setting out the possessions "the rich man" had and where they had come from. There follows a two-part indictment and pronouncement of punishment. The first part concerns the act of murder, the second the adultery.[21]

Preamble (vv. 7b, 8)

Thus says the LORD, the God of Israel, "I anointed you king over Israel, and I delivered you out of the hand of Saul. And I gave you your master's house and your master's wives into your arms and gave you the house of Israel and of Judah. And if this were too little, I would add to you as much more." (vv. 7b, 8)

David's crime was a matter of national importance, to say the least. The words he was about to hear were therefore from "the God *of Israel*" (v. 7). Since Israel was God's own chosen people, the matter had an even wider significance.

David had previously heard a message with a preamble similar to this on a very different occasion. On the night Nathan had told David God's great promise concerning his kingdom, he had begun with a recital of what God had done for David (7:8–11), which introduced the promise concerning what God would yet do. Now he heard again of God's remarkable grace toward him.

The word "I" is emphatic in its first two occurrences in 12:7b–8: "*I* anointed you . . . delivered you . . . gave [to] you . . . gave [to] you . . ." David had experienced God as one who "gave" and "gave" to him. All that he had and all that he was had been God's gift.[22] And the Lord's bounteous generosity to David had not come to an end. The last sentence of verse 8 could be paraphrased, "If this isn't enough, then David must say so, and he'll get more."[23]

This is the rich man who "had very many flocks and herds" (v. 2) in Nathan's story. The God who "gave" (v. 8) so much to David now asked why he had so wickedly "taken."

Part 1: Murderer (vv. 9, 10a)

The first part of the accusation focuses on the murder of Uriah, the later (but greater) of David's crimes.

Indictment (v. 9)

> Why have you despised the word of the LORD, to do what is evil in his sight? You have struck down Uriah the Hittite with the sword and have taken his wife to be your wife and have killed him with the sword of the Ammonites. (v. 9)

The indictment begins not with the crime itself but with the evil heart that the crime revealed. David had "despised the word of the LORD" (v. 9). This could be a general reference to the word of God that included, for example, the Law (and the commandments about coveting, adultery, and murder). Certainly David had "despised" God's word in this sense when he willfully disregarded its requirements. But in this context "the word of the LORD" almost certainly refers to the promise that the Lord had made to David, alluded to in verses 7, 8.[24] In his wickedness he had despised the extraordinary promise of God. He had despised the grace of God.

"Despised" (v. 9) is a strong word, and a key word in the twofold indictment of David (it is repeated in verse 10b). At the beginning of the story told in the books of Samuel we heard God say, "those who honor me I will honor, and those who despise me shall be lightly esteemed" (1 Samuel 2:30). This was why the house of Eli fell under the heavy hand of God's judgment. To hear that David has "despised" the word of the Lord is ominous. In the unfolding story we have seen the "worthless fellows" who "despised" Saul (1 Samuel 10:27), Goliath who "disdained" (same Hebrew word) David (1 Samuel 17:42), and Michal who also "despised" David in her heart (6:16). It is devastating to hear that David, like the terrible sons of Eli, was now accused of despising the Lord and his word.

Before hearing this word David was, no doubt, not conscious of despising the Lord. But he did so by doing "what is evil in his sight" (see 11:27b AT). The ultimate seriousness of David's crime lay in what lay behind it. The crime was the *evidence* for the even more profound offence of despising the word of the Lord.

This evidence was that David had "struck down" Uriah, "taken" his wife, and "killed" him (12:9). Two references to the violence against Uriah framed a reference to the theft that killing Uriah was intended to hide.[25] The emphasis is on how "the rich man" had treated "the poor man" (v. 4).[26] In this David had despised the word of the Lord who had given him so much.

Punishment (v. 10a)

The indictment could not be disputed. The pronouncement of punishment followed: "Now therefore the sword shall never depart from your house"[27] (v. 10a).

On the one hand, the punishment corresponds to the immediate crime. "The sword" that will "never depart" from David's house corresponds to the "sword"[28] with which David had Uriah killed. On the other hand, the punishment corresponds to the deeper crime. David's "house" was at the heart of "the word of the LORD" that he had despised ("house" is the key word of 2 Samuel 7, occurring fifteen times in the chapter, ten of which refer to David's dynasty).

Could this be the moment at which the great promise concerning David's "house" would be forfeited? Is this the Lord's rejection of David, just as he had rejected Saul (who had "rejected the word of the LORD," 1 Samuel 15:23)?

There is a difference. The word of the Lord that Saul rejected was a command (1 Samuel 15:2, 3). Saul's kingship had been established with a warning about obedience: "if you will not obey the voice of the LORD, but rebel against the commandment of the LORD, then the hand of the LORD will be against you and your king" (1 Samuel 12:15). The word of the Lord that David had despised was a promise, and that promise included: "When he commits iniquity, I will discipline him . . . but my steadfast love will not depart from him, as I took it from Saul . . ." (7:14, 15). What would happen to the one who had despised this promise?

Part 2: Adulterer (vv. 10b–12)

Before we can answer that question we must hear the second part of what "the LORD, the God of Israel" (v. 7) had to say to David that day. The focus shifts from the murder to the adultery.

Indictment (v. 10b, c)

The second indictment is stated more briefly than the first, but has the same two elements: ". . . because[29] you have despised me and have taken the wife of Uriah the Hittite to be your wife . . ."[30] (v. 10b, c). To despise the Lord's word is to despise the Lord himself. This, again, was the ultimate seriousness of what David had done. The evidence this time was that he had committed adultery with ("taken") the wife of Uriah.[31]

Punishment (vv. 11, 12)

Again the indictment could not be challenged, and so punishment was pronounced.

> Thus says the LORD, "Behold, I will raise up evil against you out of your own house. And I will take your wives before your eyes and give them to your neighbor, and he shall lie with your wives in the sight of this sun. For you did it secretly, but I will do this thing before all Israel and before the sun." (vv. 11, 12)

As in the previous pronouncement (v. 10a), the punishment corresponded, at one level, to the immediate crime. The Lord will "take" David's wives (just as David had "taken" Bathsheba) and "give" them to a "neighbor" (just as the rich man had been a neighbor of the poor man, and Uriah had been a neighbor of David) (v. 11). However, unlike David's secret, hidden wickedness (at night), which he went to extreme lengths to keep hidden, "this thing" will be done "before the sun." It will be in the open, "before all Israel" (v. 12).

At a deeper and even more important level the punishment again fits the still darker crime of despising the Lord. The focus of the punishment will be the very "house" the Lord had promised to bless (7:16, 29). Indeed, as the Lord had promised to "raise up" David's offspring who would become David's "house" (7:11, 12), now "I will *raise up* evil against you out of your own house" (12:11). As the Lord had promised to establish David's house for the sake of "Israel" (7:8, 23–27), now the humiliation of David will take place "before all Israel" (12:12).

We are also reminded again of the rejection of Saul. The Lord tore Saul's kingdom from him and "gave" it to a "neighbor" (1 Samuel 15:28). That neighbor turned out to be, of course, David. Now the Lord will "give" David's wives (representing his household) to a "neighbor."

The rest of the book of 2 Samuel (and also the books of 1 and 2 Kings) will tell the terrible story anticipated in these two pronouncements of punishment. David's "house" will be deeply troubled by violence for the rest of his life and for generations to come (through to the end of 2 Kings). Much evil will arise from David's house, beginning with the rape of his daughter Tamar by her half-brother Amnon (13:1–14). The "neighbor" will turn out to be another of David's sons, Absalom (see 16:21, 22).

As David heard Nathan that day, this terrible future confronted him in the word of the Lord.

Shattered (v. 13a)

At long last David was broken. "David said to Nathan, 'I have sinned against the LORD'" (v. 13a). Again the original has just two words. Some time later David expanded those two words into Psalm 51, which profoundly expresses all that these two words imply.

The brevity of the confession (as we hear it here) should discourage efforts to evaluate the *quality* of David's response to the word of the Lord.[32] The word of the Lord did its work on David. His confession was no more than the echo from his own heart of the word of the Lord that had been spoken to him. "I have sinned" corresponded to the indictments. "Against the LORD" confirmed the wrong that lay behind his crimes, his despising the Lord and his word (v. 13).

We should be slow to give David *credit* for this response. This man, after all this time, after all the damage he had done, after showing no remorse at all, was at last shattered by the word of God. The wonder is that the word of the Lord could bring about this response in him. Nothing else could.

Grace with Consequences (vv. 13b–15)

The most astounding words in this chapter were now heard by David. "And Nathan said to David, 'The LORD also[33] has put away your sin; you shall not die'" (v. 13b).

Here is the scandal of the grace of God. How is it possible, indeed how is it right, that God would "put away" the sin of David (v. 13)? It is not as though David had any excuse. He, of all people, knew exactly what he was doing. Nor can we pretend that what he did was harmless. People died! And yet the Lord who had seen it all, in whose eyes it had been "evil" (v. 9), who sent Nathan to tell David what the God of Israel says, "put away" David's sin (v. 13). This means that the Lord would not hold David's sin against him.

The "putting away" of David's sin meant that he would not bear the penalty that he deserved and that he had, in his earlier furious outburst, unwittingly pronounced on his crime. "You shall *not* die" (v. 13).

This did not mean that David's sin had no consequences. Indeed the terrible things pronounced in verses 10–12 all happened in due course. What did not happen is what happened to Saul: the Lord's steadfast love did not depart from David, just as the Lord had promised (7:15). The Lord did not reject David (cf. 1 Samuel 15:23).

However, the terrible consequences of David's crimes began with the son who had been born out of the adultery: "Nevertheless, because by this deed you have caused the enemies of the LORD[34] to utterly scorn, the child who is born to you shall die" (v. 14 AT). God's chosen king had given the enemies of God grounds to mock. In days to come the Apostle Paul will say of God's chosen people (citing the prophet Isaiah), "The name of God is blasphemed among the Gentiles because of you" (Romans 2:24; cf. Isaiah 52:5). For the sake of his name, the Lord would not allow David's sin to determine the future. The child born out of David's adultery would die.

No one should be untroubled by this pronouncement. How terrible that David's wickedness should be responsible for the death of the child! And this was God's doing? Indeed it was. I do not have comfortable answers to the questions and objections that we all want to raise. Nor do I want to silence them, and we will be thinking further about this in our next chapter. However, I do want to say that we should be slow to pass self-righteous judgments on God's ways. We do not necessarily understand what God does, but the one who knows all things is righteous in all his ways.[35] This reality is greater and more reliable than our discomfort.

The word of the Lord had been delivered to David. The prophet's job was done. "Then Nathan went to his house" (v. 15a). The word of the Lord came to pass: "And the LORD afflicted the child that Uriah's wife bore to David, and he became sick" (v. 15b).

These ominous words impress on us how serious sin is. King David's sin was like all human sin. It had consequences. We cannot always understand the consequences, and there are certainly times when we hate the consequences. We will be thinking further on this matter in our next chapter. Here we should understand that the word of God exposes us all as sinners. "You are the man" (v. 7). "You are the woman."

Only when we understand the reality and seriousness of sin are we ready to wonder at God's grace. He "put away" David's sin (v. 13). David's sin did not do all the damage that it could have done, but only because God was gracious. It did not destroy God's good purposes. *And for that reason* we are privileged to know the Son of David, who was named Jesus, "for he will save his people from their sins" (Matthew 1:21).

26

Restoration

2 SAMUEL 12:16–31

GOD IS POWERFUL. Of course he is. He is also good. There are times when we are deeply conscious of this. Perhaps a prayer has been remarkably answered. Or we pause to marvel at the astonishing wonder of creation. Or we see God's providential hand in some situation, bringing something good out of a potential disaster. Or we reflect on the spectacular adventure of being human. In so many ways the products of the power and goodness of God surround us.

Our problem is that we are also surrounded by too much that challenges our confidence that God is powerful and good. Too often we feel that our prayers are not heard. Too many natural disasters wreak havoc. It is not uncommon for a disaster to come out of something potentially good. And let's not get started on the contradictions in human nature: it's not all a wonderful adventure.

It is not possible to make sense of all this just by observing life and thinking about it. The Bible's message is that: (1) The whole world (and everything else for that matter) has been created by God and is ruled over by him. That is why we see so much that reminds us of his power and goodness. (2) What God has created has been deeply distorted by human sin (rejection of God), the consequences of which have been cosmic. That is why there is so much that is not good. There is an alienation between the Creator and his creation. (3) God is not yet finished with his creation. His promise to establish his kingdom forever is a promise to *restore* the goodness and beauty of all things. (4) We can know all this because the work of reconciliation has begun, and God has made known what he is doing. That is why he has given us the Bible.

The death and resurrection of Jesus Christ is central to God's purpose to restore all things. Through Jesus' death on the cross the problem of human sin was decisively addressed (Colossians 2:14), and the power of evil was "disarmed" (Colossians 2:15). His resurrection from the dead was the beginning of the reconciliation of all things (Colossians 1:18). And this work of reconciliation and restoration is going on now. "He has delivered us from the dominion of darkness and transferred us to the kingdom of his beloved Son, in whom we have redemption, the forgiveness of sins" (Colossians 1:13, 14).

Christian people therefore experience the power and goodness of God as they taste the restoration that the kingdom of Jesus Christ brings. This restoration is what Paul rejoiced to see in the Colossian believers: "your good order and the firmness of your faith in Christ" (Colossians 2:5).

Therefore, among the many ways in which we see the power and goodness of God, none is greater than the death and resurrection of Jesus. We see and experience the restoring power of God in our own lives and the lives of those around us who are changed by Jesus' death and resurrection. We see wholesome and unselfish sexual behavior replace sexual immorality and impurity; kind and generous speech instead of anger, malice, and slander; humble, forgiving, and loving patience where there was once arrogance and resentment (see Colossians 3:1–17). We are witnessing the power that raised Jesus Christ from the dead at work in human lives. It is the power and goodness of God that is putting the whole creation back together. It is astonishing and wonderful—and not to be taken for granted.

In the life of King David all this was anticipated. The power and goodness of God was at work in David's kingdom, and there too it was astonishing and wonderful. It needed to be. The promise of God's kingdom (7:12–16) became difficult to believe when the weakness and wickedness of King David became apparent (2 Samuel 11). He committed adultery. To cover it up he had the woman's husband murdered. Then he married the widow and claimed the son who was born from the adultery. And this was God's king!

What did God do? First, he saw it all. David's cover-up did not conceal his crimes from the Lord (11:27b). Second, the Lord sent Nathan the prophet to David to confront David with his crime and its consequences (12:1–12).

This much is what God had done when Saul had disobeyed him. Then the Lord had sent Samuel to confront Saul with what he had done and pronounce the consequences (1 Samuel 15:10–29).

All of this is very important. God's kingdom will not tolerate wickedness (cf. Revelation 21:8). But in David's case there was something more astonishing still. When David was brought to his knees by the word of the Lord and confessed his sin, he was told, "The LORD . . . has put away your sin;

you shall not die" (12:13).[1] David's sin did not destroy everything (as Saul's had done). The Lord himself dealt with David's sin. What would that mean?

David's crimes still had consequences. Terrible consequences. But David's sin did not thwart the power and goodness of God. The promises were sure.

The first terrible consequence of what David had done was that the child born from his adultery would die (12:14). It was as though "The LORD had laid on another the consequences of his sin" (2 Samuel 12:13 AT). But as the child fell ill (12:15), we wonder how God's promise (which was all about a son of David, 7:12) could possibly survive the consequences of David's wickedness.

David's Surprising Behavior (vv. 16–20)

The first thing we see is that David himself was a changed man. His behavior perplexed and troubled those around him, and it surprises us. The only explanation for the difference between David in 2 Samuel 11 and in 12:16–31 is the impact of the word of the Lord that Nathan had spoken to him in 12:1–14. Consider carefully what David did.

What David Did before the Child Died (vv. 16, 17)

As the child lay stricken with illness, "David[2] . . . sought God on behalf of the child" (v. 16a). The man who had disregarded God for too long and done so much evil as a consequence at last "sought God" (v. 16). That is, he prayed. The man who for too long had acted only in self-interest at last cared about someone else: he sought God "on behalf of the child."

In normal circumstances this might not surprise us. Many parents of critically ill children have prayed to God for their little ones. But these were not normal circumstances. The sickness of this child was no ordinary illness, and the father who prayed felt more (though not less) than a parent's natural love for his child.

Consider, first, that the boy was ill because "the LORD afflicted the child" (v. 15). David had been told that this was because of the dishonor that his crimes had brought on God's name (see our earlier discussion of verse 14). David knew that his son's sickness had to do with God's disapproval of what he had done. It was therefore a humbled David who "sought God on behalf of the child" (v. 16). It was as though he said, "Lord, my son is suffering because of me. Have mercy on me, and so have mercy on him."[3] How different from the man who took Bathsheba and murdered her husband!

Second, if David understood (as I think he did) that the child's death was in some sense to be a substitute for his own deserved death (see vv. 13, 14), David's prayer may have implied a willingness to die himself rather than the child. Was the man who had arranged a murder to save himself now willing to die to save another? He was a changed man!

Third, Nathan's visit to David must have reminded the king of the promises God had made to him. God's word through Nathan, "The LORD . . . has put away your sin" (12:13), had confirmed God's gracious goodwill toward him. David "sought God on behalf of the child" (v. 16), knowing that God was gracious toward him. That is what changed him.

Fourth, we should see the child (as David almost certainly saw him) in the light of God's promise: "I will raise up your offspring after you, who shall come from your body, and I will establish his kingdom" (7:12). David's prayer on behalf of his son was in the context of God's promise concerning his offspring.

It is particularly striking that David "sought" (v. 16) the God who had just pronounced terrible consequences for his crimes that involved the life of the child. The severe judgment of God did not make him unapproachable as far as David was concerned. On the contrary, the grace of God that "put away" David's sin gave David the confidence to seek him. A little later David will explain his prayer in his own words.

The earnestness of David's prayer on behalf of the child was obvious: "David fasted and went in [to his house] and lay all night on the ground" (v. 16b). The Hebrew suggests that this is what David did each night while the child's life hung in the balance.[4]

"And the elders of his house stood beside him, to raise him from the ground, but he would not, nor did he eat food with them" (v. 17). David's behavior was such that his trusted servants[5] became concerned for him. However, he was not willing to be distracted from his prayers for the child, even in order to eat. This went on for seven days.

Ironically during these seven days David's behavior reminds us of Uriah,[6] who had refused the pleasures of normal life out of faithfulness to God and his people (11:11). Uriah's faithfulness had cost him his life at David's hand. At last, however, David had become like Uriah.

The Child's Death (vv. 18, 19)

> On the seventh day the child died. And the servants of David were afraid to tell him that the child was dead, for they said, "Behold, while the child was yet alive, we spoke to him, and he did not listen to us. How then can we say to him the child is dead? He may do himself some harm." (v. 18)

Seven days was often the period for mourning after a death (for example, Genesis 50:10; 1 Samuel 31:13). David's seven days of seeking the Lord *before* the child's death looked like a period of mourning. The servants were fearful, therefore, of what might happen *after* the child died. "He may do himself some harm" (2 Samuel 12:18) is literally, "He may do evil." While the translation may capture their meaning,[7] the text reminds us that David had indeed recently done great "evil" (v. 9), and it was the evil he had done that had led to this child's death. Did the servants perhaps remember what had happened to Saul when "an evil [ESV, harmful] spirit from the LORD tormented him" (1 Samuel 16:14, 15, 16, 23; 18:10; 19:9)? Did they fear for more than David's own welfare?[8] In any case they dared not tell David of the child's death.

However, David was alert.

> But when David saw that his servants were whispering together, David understood that the child was dead. And David said to his servants, "Is the child dead?" They said, "He is dead." (v. 19)

Death dominates the scene. Six times in two verses we have heard that the child is *dead*. The terrible bleak reality is unavoidable. David's earnest prayers had not averted the announced judgment. Like the servants we wait to see what the grieving father will do now.

What David Did After the Child Died (v. 20)

> Then David arose from the earth and washed and anointed himself and changed his clothes. And he went into the house of the LORD and worshiped. He then went to his own house. And when he asked, they set food before him, and he ate. (v. 20)

The change in David's behavior was hardly what his servants had expected. He resumed the activities of normal life.[9] This included going into "the house of the LORD" (not the temple, of course, but some less substantial structure; see 1 Samuel 1:7), where he "worshiped" (2 Samuel 12:20; the word refers to humbly bowing down deeply before a superior). David resembled Job, whose response to his terrible losses was equally striking.

> Then Job arose and tore his robe and shaved his head and fell on the ground and worshiped. And he said, "Naked I came from my mother's womb, and

naked shall I return. The LORD gave, and the LORD has taken away; blessed
be the name of the LORD." (Job 1:20, 21)

What Was He Doing? (vv. 21–23)

Such behavior was not normal. The servants were perplexed. "Then his servants said to him, 'What is this thing that you have done? You fasted and
wept for the child while he was alive; but when the child died, you arose and
ate food'" (v. 21). David's conduct seemed to be the reverse of what made
sense. He appeared to mourn for the child *before* he died, but *after* he died
(when grief would be expected) David abandoned his weeping and returned
to his life.

David explained his behavior:

> He said, "While the child was still alive, I fasted and wept, for I said, 'Who
> knows whether the LORD will be gracious to me, that the child may live?'
> But now he is dead. Why should I fast? Can I bring him back again? I shall
> go to him, but he will not return to me." (vv. 22, 23)

David's behavior before the child died was based on the possibilities of
God's grace toward David. David did not know what God, in his kindness,
might do. As far as he knew, the Lord may have permitted the child to live.
That is why David "sought God on behalf of the child" (v. 16).

It is important to notice that David's prayer for his child did not involve
knowing what God would do. He prayed because God had been gracious to
him, but not because he knew in this particular matter whether God would or
would not grant his request.[10]

After the death of the child, God's will was known. David knew that his
prayers would not now bring the child back. David understood the finality
of death. The possibility that had led him to pray was now gone. The time
would come when David would die, as his son had now died. But the child
who had died would not return to his father.

David's quiet acceptance of the death of his child suggests contentment with God's wisdom and trust in his goodness.[11] He was a remarkably
changed man!

A Restored Household (vv. 24, 25)

The biggest surprises of the whole affair are yet to be told. While David's
crimes, though forgiven, still had consequences, it is even more astonishing
to see the consequences of his sin being "put away" (v. 13). The first of these
consequences was that God blessed David's marriage to Bathsheba.

Comfort (v. 24a)

The positive description of David and Bathsheba begins: "Then David comforted his wife, Bathsheba" (v. 24a). For the first time since she appeared in the story, Bathsheba is not called "the wife of Uriah" (11:3). She is now called "[David's] wife."[12]

For the first time in the narrative David began to treat her as his wife: he "comforted" her (12:24). There had been no mention of comfort from David when Bathsheba had mourned the death of Uriah (11:26). But now "David comforted his wife" (12:24).

This is very difficult for us to comprehend. Did David now come clean and admit to Bathsheba his own role in her first husband's death? I am sure he did. Did he explain that her child had died because he had so dishonored God's name? He must have done so. How was it possible for *this* man to be a *comfort* to his wife? How could that happen?

It was a miracle of grace. The Lord really had "put away" David's sin (v. 13). Only so was it possible for David's marriage to Bathsheba now to be unaffected by David's sin. It really had been "put away"!

A Son! (v. 24b)

The description of David's restored life continues: "and [he] went in to her and lay with her, and she bore a son, and he [or, she][13] called his name Solomon" (v. 24b). There was now nothing illegitimate about David's relationship with Bathsheba. How can that be right? Does this mean that David actually benefited, in the long run, from his wrongdoing? The difficult-for-us-to-grasp answer is, no: he benefited from God's grace. The Lord really did *"put away"* his sin (v. 13).

From this marriage a son was born. This son was named (probably by Bathsheba) Solomon. The name suggests the Hebrew word *shalom*, peace. David had cynically spoken with Uriah about "peace" (the word appears three times in the Hebrew of 11:7). How was it possible for Bathsheba to give such a name to the child born out of the turbulent and terrible events that led to this? She must have believed that the Lord really had put away David's sin.[14]

Loved by the Lord (vv. 24c, 25)

The hints that this marriage and this child now had God's approval are confirmed: "And the LORD loved him [Solomon] and sent a message by Nathan the prophet. So he called[15] his name Jedidiah, because of the LORD" (vv. 24c, 25).

Of all the surprises in this astonishing story, this is the greatest. Previously David had been the one "loved" (1 Samuel 16:21; 18:1, 16, 20, 22, 28; 20:17). While the Lord's love for David through those years is clearly implied, up until now it is not mentioned explicitly in the narrative. But the Lord loved *Solomon*! David's marriage to Bathsheba was blessed by the Lord! This is almost incomprehensible to us. How could a marriage with such a beginning as this one receive God's favor? The answer, just as difficult for us to comprehend, is that the Lord *really did* put away David's sin. He no longer took it into account in his dealings with David. His grace really is amazing.

The Lord's love for Solomon suggests that the Lord had set his love on Solomon as David's successor, just as the Lord had set his heart on David (1 Samuel 13:14; 2 Samuel 7:21). In this history Solomon will not be mentioned again until 1 Kings 1:10.

A Restored King (vv. 26–31)

The last part of the chapter is probably a flashback.[16] The siege of Rabbah had begun before (or at about the same time) as David had first caught sight of Bathsheba from the palace roof (11:1, 2) and had been the setting in which Uriah was killed (11:16). The restoration of David as a victorious king in the events we are about to follow suggests that they occurred after David's confession of his sin and the news that the Lord had "put away" his sin (12:13). However, they may have occurred before the birth of Solomon.[17]

Another Message from Joab (vv. 26–28)

> Now Joab fought against Rabbah of the Ammonites and took the royal city. And Joab sent messengers to David and said, "I have fought against Rabbah; moreover, I have taken the city of waters. Now then gather the rest of the people together and encamp against the city and take it, lest I take the city and it be called by my name." (vv. 26–28)

Joab continues to amaze (and there is much more amazement to come from David's commander). His loyalty to David, while impetuous at times and always self-assured, was boundless. The fight for the city was near to its successful conclusion. "The city of waters" (v. 27) may refer to the fortifications protecting the city's water supply.[18] With that under Joab's control the city itself would not hold out much longer.

Joab was concerned to see that the victory brought honor to his king rather than to himself. Was Joab aware that David's reputation was in some danger from recent events in Jerusalem? Did he see a need for some positive (not to mention distracting) publicity? Possibly. Whatever his reasons, he called on David (he almost commanded him) to come and lead the final assault.

The Victorious King (vv. 29–31a)

"So David gathered all the people together and went to Rabbah and fought against it and took it" (v. 29). This was the last great war of David's life.[19] It was remarkable that he was restored to something like his former greatness, but (as we will see) it did not last.

Briefly, however, we should appreciate this victory over those who had despised and rejected his kindness (2 Samuel 10). "And he took the crown of their king from his head. The weight of it was a talent of gold, and in it was a precious stone, and it was placed on David's head" (v. 30a). There may be some hyperbole here. Taken literally a crown weighing "a talent of gold" (v. 30) would be about sixty-five pounds.[20] This may have been how heavy it *looked*.[21] "And he brought out the spoil of the city, a very great amount" (v. 30b). This was like the great victories listed in 2 Samuel 8. Although we are not told that "the LORD gave victory to David" (8:6) on this occasion, it is reasonable to see the situation in those terms.

> And he brought out the people who were in it and set them to labor with saws and iron picks and iron axes and made them toil at the brick kilns. And thus he did to all the cities of the Ammonites. (v. 31a)

Unfortunately, the meaning of the first sentence here is not clear, and the ESV (and other modern translations) have taken an easier option.[22] A quite literal rendering, preserving the ambiguity, is:

> And he brought forth the people that were therein, and put them under saws, and under harrows of iron, and under axes of iron, and made them pass through the brickkiln. (v. 31a RV)

This seems to refer to very harsh and cruel treatment of the Ammonites by David.[23] Was this justice for Ammonite atrocities we do not know about? Or was King David, the now flawed leader, losing a sense of proportion?

Back to Jerusalem (v. 31b)

The extraordinary sequence of events that began in 11:1 and because of which David's kingdom was never the same again conclude: "Then David and all the people returned to Jerusalem" (v. 31b).

We will soon see that a sense of foreboding is not out of place. Great troubles lay ahead for David and his kingdom, troubles flowing from his own wickedness. But at this point the amazing thing is that the king and his people "returned to Jerusalem" (v. 31). They were safe (for now). David was still king (for now).

David's restoration as a man and as king was remarkable. It was not perfect, and it was not complete. But it was enough to point us to the kingdom of God in which all things will be put back in their proper order. That is what the death of Jesus was about (see Colossians 1:20). At the very heart of the restoration of all things is the forgiveness of sins (Colossians 1:14; 2:13; 3:13). The Lord Jesus Christ restores people who come to him, just as he will one day gloriously restore all things.

27

Like Father, Like Son

2 SAMUEL 13:1–22

HERE'S A TERRIFYING THOUGHT: the faults and failings of parents are often reproduced in their children. Good looks and intelligence are not the only things that are passed on from one generation to the next. We who are parents shape our children in many ways, in our own image. Sometimes we take pride in that. But it is a terrifying thought.

I wonder if that is why there is almost always some degree of tension and conflict within families. Is it the case that friction between parents and children often has to do with how like their parents the children are turning out to be rather than how different? And too often the parents do not like what they see in the chips off the old blocks.

As one wise Christian teacher put it many years ago (so allow for the quaintness of the English to our ears), "Godly parents have often been afflicted with wicked children; grace does not run in the blood, but corruption does."[1] Whatever qualifications you might like to put on a statement like that, there is truth in it. Of course, it is not mechanical. It is not *inevitable* that my children will display all my faults. But it is highly likely that they will be affected by them. And it is not an excuse. I cannot blame my parents for my own faults. However, it is not too much to say that it is terrible to realize that the flaws in my character, the failures of my discipline, and the foibles of my bad habits can easily appear in my children—it takes no effort or planning. Like father, like son can be a terrifying thought.

In 13:1–22 we find one of the most disturbing stories in the whole Bible. It is a story that will affect some readers deeply. One of its most disturbing aspects (more disturbing than might at first appear) is that it is a story of like father, like son.

There are five main characters in the story we are about to read. First, there was *David*. By now we know David quite well. He is the main human character in the book of 2 Samuel. He was God's chosen king over the Lord's chosen people, Israel. A promise had been made to this king by God: "Your house and your kingdom shall be made sure forever before me. Your throne shall be established forever" (7:16). But we have been somewhat disillusioned with David. He was an adulterer and a murderer.

Second, in 2 Samuel 13 we will meet *Amnon*, David's eldest son (3:2). When we meet Amnon, we cannot help recalling God's word to David in 7:12: "When your days are fulfilled and you lie down with your fathers, I will raise up your offspring after you, who shall come from your body, and I will establish his kingdom." Amnon was at this time the most obvious candidate to inherit David's throne.

Third, we will also meet another son of David, *Absalom*. Absalom was apparently the second oldest surviving son of David. An older brother seems to have died young (see 3:3). Absalom was by this time the son second in line to the throne. Amnon and Absalom were both David's sons but had different mothers. They were half-brothers.

The fourth character to mention is *Tamar*. She was David's daughter and Absalom's sister. She was, therefore, Amnon's half-sister.

A fifth relatively minor character in the story is *Jonadab*. He was a son of David's brother, Shimeah. He was therefore David's nephew and Amnon's and Absalom's cousin. He is described in the story as a "friend" of Amnon (v. 3).

The story is carefully and brilliantly told, building to its terrible turning point and then the aftermath.[2] It is a story that moves from "love" in verse 1 to hatred in verse 22. It unfolds as follows:

A. Amnon's "love" for Tamar (vv. 1, 2)
    B. The intervention of Jonadab (vv. 3–5)
        C. Tamar's arrival (vv. 6–9a)
            D. Amnon's servants ordered to leave (v. 9b)
                E. Amnon's demand and Tamar's objection (vv. 10–14a)
                    F. The violation (vv. 14b, 15a)
                E. Amnon's demand and Tamar's objection (vv. 15b, 16)
            D. Amnon's servant recalled (v. 17)
        C. Tamar's departure (vv. 18, 19)
    B. The intervention of Absalom (v. 20)
A. Absalom's hatred of Amnon (vv. 21, 22)[3]

Amnon's "Love" for Tamar (vv. 1, 2)

The story begins: "Now[4] Absalom, David's son, had a beautiful sister, whose name was Tamar. And after a time Amnon, David's son, loved her" (v. 1).

"Loved" was Amnon's word for his feelings toward Tamar, as we will hear shortly. But he was deluded. What he felt was not "love," it was desire. They are not the same thing. What Amnon felt was exactly what his father had felt when he had seen, from his rooftop, the beautiful Bathsheba bathing.

Amnon was no better at dealing with his feelings than was his father. His desire played on him, as sexual desire can do when allowed. He was sick with his frustration: "And Amnon was so tormented that he made himself ill because of his sister Tamar, for she was a virgin, and it seemed impossible to Amnon to do anything to her" (v. 2).

The thing he wanted "to do . . . to her" is all too obvious.[5] The barrier to his desire is less clear. "She was a virgin" is stated as a reason ("for") for Amnon's torment (v. 2). Was it that her virginity made her all the more desirable to him (the word translated "virgin" means a young woman of marriageable age, sexually mature, rather than necessarily "virgin" as such[6])? Or was her virginity the reason that his desire was frustrated?[7] Incest (including half-sisters) was explicitly forbidden in the Law (see Leviticus 18:9, 11; 20:17; Deuteronomy 27:22). We can assume that readers of this story are expected to know this. But did Amnon care about God's Law?[8] We are simply told that what Amnon wanted "seemed impossible" to him (v. 2). From his subsequent behavior we may doubt that this was just a moral problem for Amnon. More probably he could not see how Tamar could be persuaded to cooperate.

The Intervention of Jonadab (vv. 3–5)

It so happened that Amnon had a "friend":[9] "But Amnon had a friend, whose name was Jonadab, the son of Shimeah, David's brother. And Jonadab was a very crafty man" (v. 3). Jonadab was clever. The text says literally in verse 3 that he was "very wise." He was certainly observant enough to notice that his cousin was troubled.

"And he said to him, 'O son of the king, why are you so haggard morning after morning? Will you not tell me?'" (v. 4a). In other words, "You are the king's son! Why on earth are you looking so wretched?" Jonadab wanted to help.

"Amnon said to him, 'I love Tamar, my brother Absalom's sister'" (v. 4b). For Amnon the problem was that Tamar was "my brother Absalom's sister."[10] Presumably he did not add these words in order to identify which Tamar he was talking about! Jonadab knew who Tamar was. "My brother Absalom's sister" (v. 4) identifies the cause of Amnon's frustration. It was her relationship to his brother that made it "impossible" for him "to do anything to her" (v. 2).[11]

If Jonadab were really wise (and if he were a true friend), he would have given Amnon the kind of advice you can find in that book of real wisdom, Proverbs (such as Proverbs 5:20–23).

Instead he gave Amnon a plan by which he could overcome the palace protocols and any other awkwardness so he could be alone with Tamar.

> Jonadab said to him, "Lie down on your bed and pretend to be ill. And when your father[12] comes to see you, say to him, 'Let my sister Tamar come and give me bread to eat, and prepare the food in my sight, that I may see it and eat it from her hand.'" (v. 5)

Perhaps Jonadab should not be blamed for all that ensued, particularly the violence. He may have concocted a devious plan to get the two alone together, but no more. However, Jonadab's complicity in Amnon's crime should not be underestimated.[13] He knew what Amnon wanted, and he told him how he could get it. Clever man that he was, he was probably well aware of the sexual overtones of his words to the ears of the sexually tormented Amnon. "Lie down" (v. 5) is the verb that will shortly be used for sexual intercourse (vv. 11, 14). And what might "eat from her hand" (v. 5) have suggested to Amnon's obsessed mind? Amnon will use this same phrase as a cloak for what he wants from Tamar (see vv. 6, 10). The best we can say of Jonadab at this stage is that he employed his skills to assist the prince.[14]

Tamar's Arrival (vv. 6–9a)

Amnon took up Jonadab's crafty scheme with enthusiasm, and perhaps a bolder purpose than his cousin intended.

> So Amnon lay down and pretended to be ill. And when the king came to see him, Amnon said to the king, "Please let my sister Tamar come and make a couple of cakes in my sight, that I may eat from her hand." (v. 6)

Amnon's embellishment on Jonadab's proposed words probably betrays (to us) his obsession. He wants Tamar to "make two heart cakes" (it is difficult to translate the subtleties of the Hebrew into English, but both the verb and the noun have a root that also means "heart").[15]

We get a glimpse here of David's excessive indulgence of his sons.[16] It was as though Amnon's wish was David's command!

> Then David sent home to Tamar, saying, "Go to your brother Amnon's house and prepare food for him." So Tamar went to her brother Amnon's house, where he was lying down. And she took dough and kneaded it and

made cakes in his sight and baked the cakes. And she took the pan and emptied it out before him, but he refused to eat. (vv. 7–9a)

Everything suggests that Tamar was unaware of what was going on in Amnon's mind. Her immediate response to her father's instruction and her earnest devotion to the preparation of food for Amnon indicate her innocence, even her sisterly care for her apparently ill brother. The first unexpected development was Amnon's refusal to eat.

Amnon's Servants Ordered to Leave (v. 9b)

The second unexpected development (from Tamar's point of view) was a command from Amnon to clear the room: "And Amnon said, 'Send out everyone from me.' So everyone went out from him" (v. 9b).

The scheme had worked. Amnon was with Tamar, alone. What now?

Amnon's Demand and Tamar's Objection (vv. 10–14a)

Still Tamar seemed to suspect nothing.

> Then Amnon said to Tamar, "Bring the food into the chamber, that I may eat from your hand." And Tamar took the cakes she had made and brought them into the chamber to Amnon her brother. (v. 10)

In the privacy of his "chamber" (presumably bedroom), out of earshot of any lingering servants, Amnon threw off the deception and made his demand. "But when she brought them near him to eat, he took hold of her and said to her, 'Come, lie with me, my sister'" (v. 11). Words that have had an apparently innocent meaning so far in this story become, in Amnon's mouth, something else. Three times we have heard about Amnon "lying" on his bed (feigning illness) (vv. 5, 6, 8). The demand, "*Lie* with me" (v. 11) discarded the pretense and any appearance of innocence.[17] Tamar has been called Amnon's and Absalom's "sister" five times (vv. 1, 2, 4, 5, 6), but now "my sister" (v. 11) takes an erotic connotation.[18]

In the strongest terms Tamar objected.

> She answered him, "No, my brother, do not violate me, for such a thing is not done in Israel; do not do this outrageous thing. As for me, where could I carry my shame? And as for you, you would be as one of the outrageous fools in Israel. Now therefore, please speak to the king, for he will not withhold me from you." (vv. 12, 13)

Hear her protest. *Such a thing is not done in Israel. God's people do not act like this! Don't do it, Amnon. It is wicked! It is wrong, Amnon! Don't do*

*it. Think about the effect on me! Don't do it! Think about the effect on you!
You will reduce yourself to the level of a wicked fool.*[19] *Don't do it!* She even
suggested that if Amnon asked the king, the king would allow him to marry
her. This may have been a last desperate ploy to distract him. God's Law
certainly forbade a marriage between Amnon and Tamar. Perhaps she realized that God's Law meant little to Amnon at this moment.[20] Perhaps she was
suggesting that the king could make exceptions![21]

The irony of Tamar's powerful words is, of course, that the kind of thing
that "is not done in Israel" (v. 12) had recently been done by Israel's king. As
Tamar's speech warns Amnon, it also shows up David's act of lust.[22]

Her protest was to no avail: "But he would not listen to her . . ." (v. 14a).
It is a mark of the fool that he refuses to listen to wise advice (cf. Proverbs
1:7, 22; 12:15; 23:9). Amnon showed himself to be such a fool.

The Violation (vv. 14b, 15a)

At the center of this terrible story is the violent horror: "and being stronger
than she, he violated her and lay with her" (v. 14b). Physical strength prevailed. Any possible doubt about Tamar's role in this assault is removed.
"Violated" is a word that speaks of humiliation, oppression, and subjugation.[23] It refers to Amnon's physical overpowering of Tamar against her will.
There was a fight. Even the expression "lay with her" is made more assertive
by the omission of "with" in the original.[24] There was no "with" in what
Amnon did to Tamar! "He . . . lay her" means "he raped her."[25] The language
is brutal and brief, as was the act.

Amnon discovered, to his own and to Tamar's terrible loss, the deceitfulness of temptation, particularly sexual temptation. Only a little while ago
he had said to Jonadab, "I love Tamar" (v. 4). What were his feelings now
toward Tamar?

> Then Amnon hated her with very great hatred, so that the hatred with which
> he hated her was greater than the love with which he had loved her. (v. 15a)

What had been called "love" was turned, by the violation of the sexual
assault, into hatred. The psychological insight in this sentence is profound.[26]
Our sexual natures are powerful and capable of powerful good when they
are expressed according to their God-given purpose, but are also capable
of powerful and deceptive harm when our sexual desires and behavior are
perverted from their good purpose. What Amnon thought was "love" suddenly became hate through the sexual violation of the "loved" one. Did he

now blame his victim for attracting him into the trouble that he now knew he faced?[27]

Just as the first half of the story followed the course of the so-called "love" to its terrible climax, the second half of the story now traces the out-working of even greater hatred. But the consequences of Amnon's moment of lust will take seven years to unravel (see 13:23, 38; 14:28).[28]

Amnon's Demand and Tamar's Objection (vv. 15b, 16)

"And Amnon said to her, 'Get up! Go!'" (v. 15b). His words were brutal and rough. Before he had said, "Come" (v. 11). Now he said, "Go!" Before he had said, "Lie with me" (v. 11). Now he said, "Get up!"[29] The selfishness of his violation of Tamar had unmasked his delusion that he "loved" her. He could not bear to have her in his presence any longer. To see her was to see his own shameful self-obsession.[30] He therefore demanded that she get out.

Again Tamar protested at Amnon's demand. "But she said to him, 'No, my brother,[31] for this wrong in sending me away is greater than the other that you did to me'" (v. 16a). By "greater" she may have simply meant that it makes matters even worse. She may also have envisaged the life of desolation (see v. 20) to which Amnon was now sending her.[32]

The violent act had done nothing to improve Amnon's listening skills. In words almost identical to verse 14a, the narrator tells us, "But he would not listen to her" (v. 16b). Amnon was still a fool.

Amnon's Servant Recalled (v. 17)

One of the servants who had been ordered to leave in verse 9 was now re-called and drawn into Amnon's despicable conduct. "He called the young man who served him and said, 'Put [literally, send] this woman out of my presence and bolt the door after her'" (v. 17). Amnon's disgust, which ought to have been directed at himself, was turned on Tamar. "This woman" is a single syllable in Hebrew. He does not even use the word for "woman." "Send *this* out of my presence." He had used her and now disposed of the trash. The door must be bolted to protect him from her! The bolted door may even have been meant to give the impression that she had made a shameful advance to him.[33]

It is good to remind ourselves why this incident (and incidents like it) are so hideous. It is because of the level of abuse involved. What is so abused is meant to be so good. A brother and a sister should care for each other. Here that good thing was violently abused. Sex, and the power of sexual desire, is meant for the strengthening of love and commitment and unselfishness in a marriage. Here that good thing was abused into its opposite—hatred, rejection, pure and brutal selfishness. The greater the good, the greater the potential for evil in its abuse. This is horrible.

Tamar's Departure (vv. 18, 19)

In contrast to the unsuspecting and kind arrival of Tamar in verses 8, 9a, we now hear of her wretched departure.

In an aside we are reminded of Tamar's former standing as a "virgin daughter of the king": "Now she was wearing a long robe with sleeves,[34] for thus were the virgin daughters of the king dressed" (v. 18a). Her flowing garments signified her position. Her status as a "virgin" had been a problem for Amnon (v. 2). He had changed that. Her position as a daughter of the king ought to have made her safe. Amnon had paid no regard to that either.

The servant did as he was told. "So his servant put her out and bolted the door after her" (v. 18b). Amnon no longer had to endure the presence of the one who had witnessed and suffered his monstrous depravity.

It was pathetic and tragic to behold: "And Tamar put ashes on her head and tore the long robe that she wore. And she laid her hand on her head and went away, crying aloud as she went" (v. 19). She ripped up the robe that represented all that had been trashed by Amnon. She was a picture of utter misery.

The Intervention of Absalom[35] (v. 20)

Either Tamar made her way to the house of her full-brother Absalom or Absalom found her as she was making her wretched way from Amnon's place. The details do not matter. Absalom guessed what had happened. Her appearance, tears, and dejection told him that she had been harmed. "And her brother Absalom said to her, 'Has Amnon your brother been with you?'" (v. 20a). Absalom did not need to spell out what he meant by "been with you."[36] It speaks volumes about Amnon's reputation that Absalom immediately suspected that he had raped his sister.

Perhaps the weeping woman nodded her head or by some other gesture confirmed Absalom's suspicions. He then said to her, "Now hold your peace, my sister" (v. 20b). On the one hand these words were, no doubt, designed to calm her crying. More than that, however, Absalom was almost certainly assuring Tamar that she need not deal with this matter herself. She would not need to make a complaint or a protest.[37] The reason for that will emerge in the second half of 2 Samuel 13.

When Absalom added, "He is your brother" (v. 20c), I am sure (especially in the light of subsequent events) that he was not appealing to family solidarity or sisterly feelings. More probably he was indicating that Amnon would be difficult to deal with. He was the prince and a much-loved son of his father (see 13:37c, 39). Absalom was not confident that David could be trusted to deal with Amnon as he deserved.[38]

Therefore when Absalom said, "Do not take this[39] to heart"[40] (v. 20d), these were not empty, unsympathetic words. Absalom was in effect taking the matter into *his* heart.[41]

These words did not resolve anything, but it meant that Tamar was safe with her protector. "So Tamar lived, a desolate[42] woman, in her brother Absalom's house" (v. 20e). Tamar lived withdrawn from the company of others, hidden away in her brother's house.

This is the last we see of Tamar in the Bible.[43] What became of her through the violent events that were unleashed by what she suffered we simply do not know. Her withdrawal from the community is reflected in her withdrawal from the Biblical narrative.

Absalom's Hatred of Amnon (vv. 21, 22)

The episode that began with Amnon's supposed "love" concludes with the king's anger and, more importantly, Absalom's dangerous hatred.

David's reaction resembled his reaction to Nathan's story about the rich man and the poor man (see 12:5)—he was furious. "When King David heard of all these things, he was very angry" (v. 21). But this time he did not pronounce the death sentence on the culprit. Did David too clearly see himself in the actions of his son, without this time needing the help of Nathan? One ancient version[44] of this text adds the words, "but he did not curb the spirit of his son Amnon; he favoured him because he was his firstborn." If those words are not original, a scribe has simply added what is already there between the lines. David was furious, but he did nothing.[45] He reminds us of old Eli, at the beginning of 1 Samuel, who failed to curb the wickedness of his sons (1 Samuel 3:13).

Through this episode Tamar is identified as Absalom's sister (vv. 1, 4, 20, 22) or Amnon's (half) sister (vv. 2, 5, 6, 11), but not as David's daughter. It was her relationship to her brothers that presented the obstacle to Amnon's desires (vv. 2, 4), not the protection of her father. The very fact that David could be used as the agent in Jonadab's successful plan suggests that the king was not going to be an obstacle to his son's wickedness. And he wasn't.

Absalom's reaction to what had happened was ominous. "But Absalom spoke to Amnon neither good nor bad, for Absalom hated Amnon, because he had violated his sister Tamar" (v. 22). Absalom's hatred will have terrible consequences that will come close to destroying David and his kingdom. That is the story that will occupy the rest of the book of 2 Samuel.

Before we begin to follow those consequences let's pause and ask why this shocking story has been told. Since we have read it in the Bible, it is right for us to ask, why has God told us this story? This isn't television, where sordid stories of sexual and other violence have become entertainment. What does it say about our world that stories like this have become the stuff of entertainment and big business? But this is God's Word, and all Scripture is *profitable* (2 Timothy 3:16). Our question is, what profit is this story intended to give?

At one level it is very obvious. Unpleasant as it may be, look at this story and learn its obvious lessons. Look at this particularly ugly example of what sin can do to people. Look at how deceptive temptation, particularly sexual temptation, can be. Look at how deaf Amnon was to reason in his determination to satisfy his desire. Look at the misery it brought to everyone. Look. And learn. This is God's world. We are God's creatures. Defy God's ways, and terrible damage will be done—to ourselves and to others. I have no doubt that God has told us this story so that we will look and learn.

Very soon we will see David's family torn apart by the hatred unleashed in this terrible episode. Has there ever been a family so wrecked by hatred and violence as David's family? Will you tell me it has nothing whatsoever to do with the fact that David was an adulterer and a murderer?

Fathers, mothers, look and learn. If you care for your children (and God knows, David cared for his, to a fault), then guard your own integrity, uprightness, truthfulness, and character. Go further if you will. Look at how the earlier wickedness of David seems to have produced a weakness. He loved his sons, but he seemed powerless to curb *their* waywardness.

But once again there is another level at which we must learn. In the bigger story that 2 Samuel is telling us, what we have seen is that the son Amnon was all too much like his father David. Remember those words in 7:12: "When your days are fulfilled and you lie down with your fathers, I will raise up your offspring after you, who shall come from your body." Amnon was David's offspring. It doesn't give you much hope for the future, does it, if God's purpose is to make a son of *David* his king. What kind of king would this man be?

This story, you see, should make us puzzled. There is a deep problem here. The children of flawed people are flawed. They do not get better and better. David not only failed himself, but his son turned out to be no better. Indeed, he was worse. That is the problem with human leadership. Even great and good leaders can have terrible sons (even Samuel's sons were as bad as Eli's, 1 Samuel 2:12; 8:3). If that is the case, what hope is there for God's kingdom? What hope is there for humanity?

It hardly helps (although it is important) to realize that what we have witnessed in this episode is the beginning of the trouble that had been prophesied for David's house as a consequence of his adultery and murder (see 12:10–12). What hope can there be if God's promise is tied to this fractured family?

The Scriptures are not meant to be merely "profitable" for general life lessons, but they are also "able to make you wise for salvation through faith in Christ Jesus" (2 Timothy 3:15, 16). As we hear this story of a son of David, Amnon, we are amazed that God's promise concerning his kingdom has nonetheless been fulfilled. The ultimate son of David has come who did not inherit his father David's flaws and failures. He has come to call us all into a kingdom where corruption, even like that of Amnon, can be washed clean.

> Or do you not know that the unrighteous will not inherit the kingdom of God? Do not be deceived: neither the sexually immoral, nor idolaters, nor adulterers, nor men who practice homosexuality, nor thieves, nor the greedy, nor drunkards, nor revilers, nor swindlers will inherit the kingdom of God. And such were some of you. But you were washed, you were sanctified, you were justified in the name of the Lord Jesus Christ and by the Spirit of our God. (1 Corinthians 6:9–11)

28

Vengeance and the Kingdom

2 SAMUEL 13:23–39

O Lᴏʀᴅ, God of vengeance,
O God of vengeance, shine forth!

PSALM 94:1

THIS IS A PRAYER for the coming of God's kingdom. The King is the Judge. He will deal justly and rightly with all evil. Many people today find this shocking. Do Christian people really believe in a God who takes *vengeance*? Indeed we do, and it is a wonderful and powerful truth.

One of the terrible consequences of human sinfulness is that we humans are very bad at dealing with sinfulness. We rarely get vengeance right. Vengeance means a punishment that is inflicted in return for a wrong. Those who are shocked at the idea of a God who takes vengeance are still likely to want something done about a person who hurts, cheats, or robs them. But *what* should be done? If a culprit is punished to satisfy the rage of the victim, it will probably be excessive and therefore unjust. If the rage of the victim is ignored, then the perpetrator may be dealt with too gently.

No one really wants a world where wickedness goes unpunished. Even criminals want vengeance taken on someone who wrongs *them*.

In the course of our lives we all suffer from the sinfulness of others, just as others suffer in various ways from our sinfulness. The resulting desire to hurt someone who has hurt us can be very strong. But is it *right*? It can, of course, be expressed in subtle ways. "I will never speak to so-and-so again" might not sound like much of a punishment, but it is *intended* to be! In our hands vengeance becomes another expression of our own sinfulness,

351

foolishness, and weakness. One reason that God has provided the world with governing authorities is that we cannot individually be trusted to get vengeance right (see Romans 13:4b). The trouble is that the governing authorities can also be incompetent, prejudiced, or corrupt.

It is therefore very important to know that God says, "Vengeance is mine, I will repay, says the Lord" (Romans 12:19b, citing Deuteronomy 32:35; see also 1 Thessalonians 4:6; Hebrews 10:30). Those who believe God's promise do not need to avenge themselves (see Romans 12:19a). We know that, unlike us, God gets vengeance right. That is a powerful reason to pray, "Your kingdom come" (Matthew 6:10).

As David's kingdom suffered the consequences of his sinfulness (in his acts of adultery and murder), the problem of human vengeance was dramatically displayed. As David's son Amnon followed in his father's footsteps and raped his half-sister Tamar, the problem of vengeance was raised. What was to be done about this outrage?

For two years *nothing* was done. Tamar lived as a "desolate woman" in her other (full) brother's house (13:20; cf. v. 23). King David, who had been "very angry" (13:21), did nothing. Tamar's full-brother Absalom, who cared about his sister and hated Amnon for what he had done, did nothing (13:22). But once we see what Absalom did do, after two years of patient waiting (v. 23), we will want to cry out for *God's* kingdom to come. Absalom's vengeance solved nothing and in due course threatened to destroy the kingdom of David. We need something better than Absalom!

This episode has three parts:

(1) Absalom's activity: the murder of Amnon (vv. 23–29).
(2) David's passivity: mourning for Amnon (vv. 30–36).
(3) But what about Absalom? (vv. 37–39).

Absalom's Activity: The Murder of Amnon (vv. 23–29)

A Summary (v. 23)

The episode begins (as we often find in Biblical narrative) with a concise summary of the incident that is about to be recounted in more detail: "After two full years Absalom had sheep-shearers at Baal-hazor, which is near Ephraim, and Absalom invited all the king's sons" (v. 23).

What happened during those "two full years"[1] is passed over in silence precisely because *nothing* happened. That is, nothing significant happened. After two years David's anger may have abated. But Absalom's hatred quietly burned (as we will soon see).

The incident about to unfold took place some distance from Jerusalem. Baal-hazor was about fifteen miles north-northeast of the capital, near the town (rather than the tribal territory) of Ephraim.[2]

The occasion was the annual sheep-shearing feast. "Absalom had a sheep-shearing" may be a better way to translate this.[3] The first impression we are given is that the terrible events of two years previously may have been put behind the family. We might wonder what had become of Tamar, but Absalom seemed to be getting on with life. We might imagine (for a moment) that Absalom took this opportunity to express his goodwill toward his family. He invited "all the king's sons" to his celebration (v. 23). Happy days were here again. That is the impression we get because it is the impression that Absalom wanted to give.

The mention of "the king's sons" (v. 23) reminds us of the twofold "David's son" in 13:1, referring to Amnon and Absalom. "All" the sons of David included Amnon. We are also reminded that the great promise of God that stands behind these pages concerned a son of David (7:12–16). The importance of these reminders will soon become clear.

Absalom's Conversation with the King (vv. 24–27)

In truth Absalom had been biding his time. As the sheep-shearing feast approached he had carefully (we could say, cunningly) approached his father, the king, suggesting that this year's feast be a big one.[4] "And Absalom came[5] to the king and said, 'Behold, your servant has sheepshearers [better, has a sheep-shearing]. Please let the king and his servants go with your servant'" (v. 24). The request probably sounded generous but absurd. The words were impeccably respectful ("your servant," "please"). But "the king and his servants" represented the whole of David's court. Absalom seems to have begun his negotiations with his father on terms he knew very well his father would decline.

He was right. "But the king said to Absalom, 'No, my son, let us not all go, lest we be burdensome to you[6]'" (v. 25a). David's words were also respectful and proper ("my son"[7]). *It would be too much! I couldn't possibly allow you to go to such expense and trouble.* Mind you, David did not reject Absalom's invitation entirely. It was just "all" of us that would be too much.

Absalom persisted with the manipulative conversation. It was going well for him. It was important to his plan that the king felt uncomfortable at declining his son's kind invitation. "He pressed him, but he would not go but gave him his blessing" (v. 25b). Absalom gave every impression that he really wanted the king and his servants to come. David wished him well with the feast but was still unwilling to attend himself, presumably for the reasons already given.

It was time for Absalom to offer a compromise. This was the dangerous bit. "Then Absalom said, 'If not, please let my brother Amnon go with us'" (v. 26a). Absalom had ingeniously concocted an almost believable reason to invite his older half-brother to the feast. He was the crown prince. If David himself was unwilling to come (which Absalom had banked on), then why not allow his eldest son to represent him?

This was the most precarious moment in the conversation. Although two years had passed, David could not have forgotten what Amnon had done. Absalom's refusal to speak to Amnon (13:22), presumably for these two years, would hardly have gone unnoticed. What could possibly have brought about this sudden brotherly friendliness on Absalom's part toward the previously hated brother?

David hesitated. "And the king said to him, 'Why should he go with you?'" (v. 26b). Not quite a refusal, but cautious reluctance. David clearly suspected that something might not be quite right here. David knew that Absalom had very good reason for his hatred of Amnon. Why should David allow Absalom access to Amnon?

Absalom was ready. "But Absalom pressed him . . ." (v. 27a). Just as before,[8] Absalom urged the king to grant his request, this time disguising his focus on Amnon by extending the invitation not to the whole court this time, but to "all the king's sons" (v. 23). Absalom overcame David's reluctance. He carefully argued his case ". . . and he sent Amnon and all the king's sons with him"[9] (v. 27b AT).

What appeared to David as a compromise, and a safe one at that, was almost certainly exactly what Absalom had planned all along. As readers of the story, we have been given a sense of Absalom's intentions by being told in advance where the conversation was heading (v. 23).

For a second time one of David's sons had manipulated the king into being the agent who brought two of his children together with disastrous consequences. Amnon had duped David into sending Tamar to him (13:6, 7). Now Absalom had hoodwinked his father into sending Amnon to Baal-hazor. Absalom had skillfully ensured that Amnon had little choice. The king *sent* him to Baal-hazor.

This is the second of eight times that we will hear the phrase "the king's sons" in this episode. Until verse 35 it will be "*all* the king's sons." The phrase is weighty in significance. "The king's sons" represented the future of David's house.

Absalom's Revenge (vv. 28, 29)

Absalom's scheme was coming together perfectly. He had just one more piece to put in place. Before the guests arrived he called together his own "lads"[10] in Baal-hazor and issued his instructions.

> Then Absalom commanded his servants, "Mark when Amnon's heart is merry with wine, and when I say to you, 'Strike Amnon,' then kill him. Do not fear; have I not commanded you? Be courageous and be valiant." (v. 28)

This is chilling. Absalom's clarity of purpose and calm authority is unnerving. He addressed his young men as though he was the commander of soldiers about to attack the enemy.[11] At the center of the speech is the operational command: "kill him" (v. 28). Leading up to that are the detailed instructions. *Keep your eye on Amnon. Listen for my signal.* The command itself is then supported by words of encouragement that sound strangely like God's own words of encouragement to his people before an engagement with their enemies (compare Joshua 1:9). Absalom's words not only accept full responsibility for the proposed action,[12] they make it sound like an act of honor. No doubt that is how Absalom saw it.

We are spared a detailed description of the deed itself. We are simply told, "So the servants of Absalom [Absalom's lads] did to Amnon as Absalom had commanded" (v. 29a).

The earlier actions of David were disturbingly reflected in the actions of his sons. As David's surrender to his illicit sexual desires led eventually to a murder, so now Amnon's different (but too similar) giving in to his lust has led to another killing. David's two crimes were reproduced in his two sons. They were indeed chips off the old block.[13]

While we imagine the horror of the bloody scene, those who witnessed it were terrified. "Then all the king's sons arose, and each mounted his mule[14] and fled" (v. 29b). For the third time we hear "all the kings sons." As they fled for their lives, it must have seemed that the future of the house of David was indeed in jeopardy.

David's Passivity: Mourning for Amnon (vv. 30–38)

As the king's sons were fleeing from Baal-hazor, and before they arrived safely back in Jerusalem, we are taken back to the capital where there were remarkable developments.

What David Heard First: A False Rumor (vv. 30, 31)

Somehow David heard a confused report of what had happened at Baal-hazor. "While they were on the way, news came to David, 'Absalom has struck down all the king's sons, and not one of them is left'" (v. 30). The "news" was more a rumor than anything official.[15] Unless the fleeing princes took a roundabout route, it is difficult to see how this story could have originated in Baal-hazor. How could it have reached Jerusalem *before* the escapees? This was not an actual report of the event that had somehow become confused in transmission. Rather it was court gossip of what some *thought* Absalom had done.

Like much gossip, it was expressed in terms that sounded authoritative. Gossipers usually claim to *know* much more than they do. Indeed the rumor took the form of a report of a military incident.[16] "Struck down" (v. 30) is a word used for killing in battles and the like.[17] "Not one of them is left" (v. 30) is the kind of thing that one says about an overwhelming conquest.[18]

The fact that this rumor circulated so quickly in David's court and apparently reached the king's ears before anyone had returned from Baal-hazor suggests to a high degree the tension and suspicion in these circles concerning Absalom's intentions for his sheep-shearing feast. No doubt the Amnon-Tamar affair two years earlier was well-known. Absalom's brooding bitterness toward Amnon was no secret. Was it also known that Absalom had personal ambitions (which will become public soon enough)? Such thoughts would form a potent brew. Shortly we will see there was probably another strong ingredient in the rumor mill that was David's court. Someone guessed that Absalom had brought all of his brothers to Baal-hazor for a wholesale slaughter. The guess became a conviction. The conviction became a rumor. And the rumor reached David's ears.[19]

Astonishingly, David immediately believed what he heard. "Then the king arose and tore his garments and lay on the earth. And all his servants who were standing by tore their garments" (v. 31). David was disturbingly quick to believe that his son had murdered all his brothers. He did not, as on a previous occasion, ask questions to test the validity of what he heard (see 1:5). David's readiness to believe this horrifying news tells us a great deal about David's own suspicions behind his earlier question, "Why should he go with you?" (v. 26b). "All his servants who were standing by" (v. 31) were just as ready as the king to believe this dreadful thing. The vehement display of abject grief looks like an outburst of pent-up fearful anticipation.

What David Heard Next: Jonadab's "Wise" Counsel (vv. 32, 33)

There was just one person there who was not caught up in the grieving. It was Jonadab, the man who had played a crucial role in the earlier trouble of Amnon and Tamar. Jonadab now appeared to know far too much about what had happened at Baal-hazor.

> But Jonadab the son of Shimeah, David's brother, said, "Let not my lord suppose that they have killed all the young men, the king's sons, for Amnon alone is dead. For by the command of Absalom this has been determined from the day he violated his sister Tamar. Now therefore let not my lord the king so take it to heart as to suppose that all the king's sons are dead, for Amnon alone is dead." (vv. 32, 33)

When Jonadab appeared previously, we were told that he was "very wise" (ESV, "very crafty," 13:3). However, it would take more than wisdom to know what Jonadab seems to have known. He knew that there had been a murder, that it had been committed by a group ("they"), that Amnon was the only victim, and that Absalom's command was behind it, and he knew Absalom's thoughts about the matter over the past two years. This was more than "shrewd discernment."[20] The only possible explanation for Jonadab's detailed and accurate knowledge of what had happened at Baal-hazor before anyone had come from there with news is that he had learned of Absalom's plans earlier, presumably from Absalom himself.[21] This suggests that Jonadab had been a confidant to Absalom, just as he had been to Amnon earlier. Indeed it now seems likely that the plan itself may have been concocted by Jonadab, or at least with his assistance, just as he had devised the scheme that brought Amnon and Tamar together. Jonadab had a lot to answer for!

His words to King David in verse 32 were carefully chosen.[22] Of course, he displayed appropriate deference ("my lord"). Referring to the king's sons as "the young men" ("the lads") showed empathy with David's concern for his boys.[23] He did not immediately implicate Absalom, but spoke of "they." Even the news of Amnon's death was given the most positive possible spin: "Amnon *alone* is dead," still without reference to his killing or his killer(s). At the center of Jonadab's speech is an explanation. This was a thing "determined" since the day Amnon raped Tamar.[24] Absalom is identified as the person responsible, but the necessity of his action is emphasized because of Amnon's atrocity. Jonadab then repeats his consolation to the king: David should not take what he had heard to heart. The rumor was false. Only one of the king's sons was dead.

Jonadab needed his considerable "wisdom" to make this dangerous speech. It reveals that Jonadab knew of Absalom's intentions all along (just as he had known Amnon's intentions previously). Would David turn on him now and hold him to account for his silence? Perhaps Jonadab knew there would soon be such turmoil in the king's household that there would be little opportunity for any attention to be given to him.

What David Saw: The Truth (vv. 34–36)

Momentarily we are taken back to Baal-hazor and informed that "Absalom fled" (v. 34a). This important fact will be repeated twice before the chapter closes. We presume that Absalom fled shortly after the king's sons (v. 29)[25] and therefore at about the same time as David was hearing the various versions of what had happened. Absalom, of course, did not flee with "all the king's sons" (v. 29). In fact he went in the opposite direction (v. 37). Just as David was hearing about the assassination, the culprit took himself well beyond the king's reach.

Meanwhile back in Jerusalem a young man who was on lookout duty saw an approaching but as yet unidentifiable crowd. "And the young man who kept the watch lifted up his eyes and looked, and behold, many people were coming from the road behind him by the side of the mountain" (v. 34b). The description of where they were coming from is not entirely clear, but that matters little.[26] When the approaching mob was reported to the king and his company, Jonadab knew immediately who they were. "And Jonadab said to the king, 'Behold, the king's sons[27] have come; as your servant said, so it has come about'" (v. 35). *See? I was right!* Jonadab banked on the relief and grief of that moment preventing David from asking obvious questions about *how* he was right.

And, of course, he *was* right: "And as soon as he had finished speaking, behold, the king's sons came and lifted up their voice and wept. And the king also and all his servants wept very bitterly" (v. 36).

The king's worst expectations, which had been so quickly believed a little earlier and led to the outpouring of grief, had not been realized. But nevertheless something terrible had happened. David's firstborn son was dead,[28] at the hand of his third son. David's house had become a house deeply and bitterly divided against itself (cf. Matthew 12:25).

What about Absalom? (vv. 37–39)

The episode closes with two glimpses of Absalom and two painful glances at David.

Where Absalom Went (v. 37a)

First we follow Absalom to see where he went. "But Absalom fled and went to Talmai the son of Ammihud, king of Geshur" (v. 37a). Talmai was Absalom's maternal grandfather (3:3). His kingdom of Geshur was east of the Jordan River and to the north, beyond David's jurisdiction.[29] Did Absalom seek refuge there because he feared that his father would take action against him, even though he had not done anything about Amnon? Or did Absalom have other reasons to withdraw from David's kingdom for a while? Time will tell.

And David . . . (v. 37b)

Meanwhile, "David mourned for his son day after day" (v. 37b). The obvious meaning is that it was Amnon over whom David mourned. But was he also grieving for his other lost son?[30] "Day after day" is literally "all the days." David mourned for his son for the rest of his life.

How Long Absalom Was Away (v. 38)

Absalom's sojourn in Geshur was shorter than David's mourning, but it was long enough. "So Absalom fled and went to Geshur, and was there three years" (v. 38). What happened after those three years will occupy the rest of 2 Samuel.

And David . . . (v. 39)

The chapter closes with an unfortunately difficult verse. The ESV and most other English versions suggest that David came through his grief for Amnon, coming to terms with his death, and began to miss Absalom. "And the spirit of the king longed to go out to Absalom, because he was comforted about Amnon, since he was dead" (v. 39).[31]

The Hebrew of this sentence is ambiguous, but it does not seem to indicate that David was *longing for* Absalom. Perhaps the ambiguity is appropriate. David's emotions were almost certainly in turmoil. He loved his sons (see his grief at the false report that they had all been killed in verse 31 and at the realization that Amnon was in fact dead in verses 36, 37, and especially at the later death of Absalom, 18:33). But he was furious at what Amnon had done to Tamar (13:21). However, he took no action against Amnon. He had been worried about Absalom's request to send Amnon to his feast (v. 26), but had been unable to refuse him. Now Absalom had killed Amnon, and Absalom had fled. David "mourned for his son" (Amnon) for the rest of his life (v. 37). What were his feelings toward Absalom? Verse 39 is perhaps best translated, "And this [the circumstances described in verse 38] held the king back from marching out against Absalom, but he mourned over Amnon, because he was dead."[32] David was (on this understanding) furious with Absalom, just as he had been with Amnon. Once again, however, he did not take action, this time because Absalom had taken himself beyond King David's reach.

The shortcomings of David's kingdom are on display again. But do not be deluded into thinking that any other human society does any better. It is a very serious thing to pray, "Your kingdom come" (Matthew 6:10) because we are asking God to sort out vengeance in his way, not ours. God's way involves forgiveness. Some will not like that. God's way also involves "vengeance on those who do not know God and on those who do not obey the gospel of our Lord Jesus" (2 Thessalonians 1:8). Are you sure you want to pray for God's kingdom to come?

29

Foolish Schemes

2 SAMUEL 14

JOAB WAS ONE OF THOSE PEOPLE who are absolutely sure that they know what needs to be done and fully confident that they are the ones who are able to do what needs to be done. Do you know the type? They are not rare. One of the causes of conflict in nations, communities, organizations, and even families is different people with different ideas about what should be done, each persuaded that he or she knows best.

We are not thinking here about people with obviously bad motives. Joab wanted to disentangle the troubles that had come on King David, his family, and his kingdom. He wanted to put things right. He wanted to help. At least I am sure that is how he saw it.

The problem is that the mess that results from human sin is intractable. The difficulties in which people find themselves, ranging from international issues to family dysfunctions, are almost always harder to deal with than the self-confident would-be saviors suppose. Their schemes are only rarely successful, and what success they achieve hardly ever lasts. That was certainly so for the domineering Joab.

In 2 Samuel 14 we find that Joab, David, and Absalom each devise schemes to deal with the troubles that had come on David's kingdom. Each scheme made sense, but each scheme only succeeded in making matters worse. The failure of these schemes shows us what a mess David's kingdom had become and how the most able, confident, and determined schemes devised by assertive and self-assured men did not provide solutions. On the contrary, Joab's clever scheme (vv. 1–20), David's compromising scheme (vv. 21–24), and Absalom's determined scheme (vv. 25–33) unintentionally prepared the way for the near destruction of David's kingdom.

Joab's Clever Scheme (vv. 1–20)

Joab's scheme occupies most of the chapter. His was a clever scheme. The detail in which the story is told displays its cleverness.

The Problem Joab Saw (v. 1)

Joab's scheme was devised in order to sort out at least some of the mess that Absalom's murder of his brother had caused for David and his kingdom. Three years had passed since that dreadful day (13:38). The ESV suggests that the problem was that David longed to have Absalom back, but for some reason (pride, protocol, ongoing anger at what Absalom had done?) the king had not been willing to initiate Absalom's return to Jerusalem. "Now Joab the son of Zeruiah knew that the king's heart went out to Absalom" (v. 1).

This translation has been influenced by the rendering of the preceding sentence (13:39; see the earlier discussion of this verse), but the Hebrew probably suggests the opposite meaning: "Now Joab the son of Zeruiah knew that the king's heart was *against* Absalom" (v. 1 AT).[1]

Joab's reentry to the story is marked by the reminder of his pedigree. Of course, we know that Joab was "the son of Zeruiah" (1 Samuel 26:6; 2 Samuel 2:13, 18; 3:39; 8:16), but he has not appeared in the narrative since the defeat of Rabbah (12:27). His standing with the king is important for the story about to unfold. "The son of Zeruiah" reminds us again that he was David's nephew (see 1 Chronicles 2:16).

Joab saw David's ongoing antagonism toward Absalom as a problem. Since Absalom was now the heir to the throne, his banishment from the kingdom would certainly cause problems when the succession became an issue. Furthermore, as we will see in due course, Absalom was popular. A public rift between the king and this son could be dangerous for David himself and for the security of his throne.

It is reasonable to suppose that it was thoughts along these lines that motivated Joab to devise a way of bringing Absalom back to Jerusalem and securing the heir to the throne and the harmony of David's kingdom. It is unlikely that Joab was motivated (at least consciously) by a personal agenda.[2] He cared passionately about David's kingdom and was confident that he knew what needed to be done. However, he understood that it would not be a simple matter to bring David and his son together again.

The Plot Joab Devised (vv. 2, 3)

> And Joab sent to Tekoa and brought from there a wise woman and said to her, "Pretend to be a mourner and put on mourning garments. Do not anoint

yourself with oil, but behave like a woman who has been mourning many days for the dead. Go to the king and speak thus to him." So Joab put the words in her mouth. (vv. 2, 3)

Tekoa was about ten miles south of Jerusalem.[3] The woman he brought from there had a reputation for wisdom. We know little more about her than that she was "wise" (v. 2). Perhaps she was like a counselor who was consulted by people with problems. She may have had some role in giving advice to officials in her community. What mattered for Joab's purposes was that she was clever with words and David did not know her.

It is hardly encouraging when we remember the last person in this story who was described as "wise." That was Jonadab (ESV, "crafty," 13:3), whose "wisdom" had made possible Amnon's rape and who may even have had a hand in Absalom's murder plan. What will this "wise" woman do?

She was to be Joab's agent in the plot he had devised. It involved a deception. She was to dress up and behave as a woman who had been in mourning for "many days" (v. 2). In the Hebrew there is a clear echo of the description of David's morning "day after day" in 13:37. The woman was to appear before the king in the guise of his own state.

Joab gave her careful instructions. He "put the words in her mouth" (v. 3). As the Lord had sent Nathan to David earlier to speak the words of the Lord to the king (12:1, 7), Joab sent the woman from Tekoa to speak the words of Joab to the king.[4] It was not quite the same!

At this stage the narrator has not disclosed Joab's plan. As we listen to the ensuing conversation between the woman and the king, we have a slight advantage over David. We know that she was pretending, and we know that it was Joab's idea. However, we do not yet know what she (and Joab) hoped to accomplish, except that it probably had to do with Absalom.

The Clever Conversation That Did It (vv. 4, 5a)

What follows is "the longest as well as the richest and most complex conversation in the books of Samuel."[5] It began with all the appearances of a distressed citizen seeking help from her king.

> When the woman of Tekoa came[6] to the king, she fell on her face to the ground and paid homage and said, "Save me, O king." And the king said to her, "What is your trouble?" (vv. 4, 5a)

If we wonder how the woman could gain access to the king like this, the answer is surely that Joab was more than capable of arranging such things.

Furthermore, dealing with grievances such as hers was one of the king's duties (a duty that Absalom will exploit for his own purposes in due course, 15:2–6).[7] Her opening words, "Save me, O king," indicated that she was in trouble of some kind and that she was looking to the king to deliver her from a threatening situation (14:4).

Stage 1: A Distressing Situation (vv. 5b–11)

With the king's permission (and with Joab's coaching) the woman explained her supposed distressing situation. She began, "Alas, I am a widow; my husband is dead" (v. 5b). Her appearance, clothing, and manner (v. 2) reinforced this claim. The loss of her husband, however, was only the beginning of her troubles. She continued, "And your servant had two sons, and they quarreled with one another in the field. There was no one to separate them, and one struck the other and killed him" (v. 6). Her story is reminiscent of Cain who quarreled with his brother Abel and killed him (Genesis 4:1–16). Cain was banished, but was protected from any who would attack him. As the woman's story continued, we hear further echoes of Cain and Abel.

> And now the whole clan has risen against your servant, and they say, "Give up the man who struck his brother, that we may put him to death for the life of his brother whom he killed." And so they would destroy[8] the heir also. Thus they would quench my coal that is left and leave to my husband neither name nor remnant on the face of the earth. (v. 7)

The woman's wider family (or clan), she said, was seeking vengeance for the blood of the brother who had been killed. They might have argued that God's Law required this (see Exodus 21:12). The woman, however, indicated four mitigating factors. The first was that, as she described it, the death was not premeditated murder. The surviving brother had not cunningly planned to kill his brother. It happened in the heat of a quarrel. Even God's Law allows for mercy in such a case and makes a distinction between murder and manslaughter (see Exodus 21:13, 14). The second point she made (with little subtlety) was that the family was not really interested in justice. They wanted to get their hands on the inheritance: "They would destroy the heir also." The third plank in her appeal to the king was a frank plea for compassion. Her surviving son was "my coal that is left," the only remaining source of light and warmth in her life (2 Samuel 14:7). Her final point was that her dead husband's name and posterity would be eliminated if the only surviving son were to die.

The woman's (that is, Joab's) story had been carefully created, much like Nathan's story about the poor man and the rich man (12:1–4). There were enough parallels with David's situation for the purpose of this scheme, but these were disguised. The accidental killing in a quarrel was rather different from Absalom's cunning plan to kill Amnon, which was, of course, justified in Absalom's view because of Amnon's rape of Tamar. Furthermore, it is not clear that anyone wanted Absalom killed because of Amnon's death (as the family wanted the woman's son killed). David's anger with Absalom did not go that far.

As previously when Nathan had told of the fictitious situation that called for justice, David took the story at face value. However, with all that was on his mind he appeared to give her case little thought. Almost dismissively he said to her, "Go to your house, and I[9] will give orders concerning you" (v. 8).

In normal circumstances that would have concluded the matter. What more could be asked for than an assurance from the king that he would deal with your problem?

For reasons that will come to light shortly, the woman was not satisfied with the vagueness of the king's promise. "I will give orders concerning you" (v. 8). What orders? Was the king persuaded of her case? Would he support her against the wishes of the family? Was he refusing to take sides? He had, after all, only heard one side of the story. Was he avoiding a more decisive pronouncement in case the boy really did deserve to die and the family was right? "I will give orders concerning you" was not the response the woman (and Joab) needed from the king.

The woman decided to boldly press her case. "On me be the guilt, my lord the king, and on my father's house; let the king and his throne be guiltless" (v. 9). Her meaning was, if the king is concerned that there may be something wrong in allowing the bloodshed to go unpunished, let the guilt fall on me and my family, not on the king.[10] She was taking full responsibility for any possible omission or distortion in her story that might have given the king cause to be cautious (which is a bit rich, given that the whole tale was a fiction).

"The king said, 'If anyone says anything to you, bring him to me, and he shall never touch you again'" (v. 10). The king was moved to side more emphatically with the woman. No one would be allowed to raise this matter again with her or they would have King David to deal with.

I imagine (but it is only my imagination) the king now turning away. He had no more time to spend on this simple matter. He would tell someone (maybe Joab!) to see that the woman and her son were not troubled anymore. Another case resolved by the king's authority.

But this woman did not thank the king and quietly depart. She was not yet satisfied. The king's word was not yet enough for her. He had not mentioned her son. He had not unambiguously taken her side. With astonishing audacity she said, "Please let the king invoke the LORD your God, that the avenger of blood kill no more, and my son be not destroyed" (v. 11a). With these words she seems to acknowledge that the family had a case. "The avenger of blood" (v. 11) was recognized in God's Law as one who had the right or responsibility (in certain circumstances) to put to death the murderer of a relative (see Numbers 35:16–29; Deuteronomy 19:4–13; Joshua 20:1–9).[11] The woman was appealing to the king to swear by the name of the Lord that this would not be allowed in her son's case.

The king seemed to be moved by the woman's passionate persistence. He said to her, "As the LORD lives, not one hair of your son shall fall to the ground" (v. 11b). Unambiguously and with an oath the king decided in the woman's favor. The sworn decision had not come as quickly as it had following Nathan's story (see 12:5), but it was just as clear.[12] David was fully committed, on oath, to the woman's cause. That surely was the end of the matter.

Actually it was only the end of the first round of this clever conversation, as it had been devised by Joab. The woman had brilliantly and with considerable nerve brought this first stage to the desired conclusion. But just as David must have thought he was free from the persistent widow, she started again.

Stage 2: Another Distressing Situation (vv. 12–17)

"Then the woman said, 'Please let your servant speak a word to my lord the king'" (v. 12a). Ever so carefully she sought the king's permission to raise another matter. By this time the woman seems to have captured the king's interest. Was it her unusual boldness? Or her passionate pleading? Or perhaps it was her compelling story. Whatever it was, the king (perhaps with a sigh) said, "Speak" (v. 12b). With that one word David opened the way for the woman to say what she had really come to say.

> And the woman said, "Why then have you planned such a thing against the people of God? For in giving this decision the king convicts himself, inasmuch as the king does not bring his banished one home again. We must all die; we are like water spilled on the ground, which cannot be gathered up again. But God will not take away life, and he devises means so that the banished one will not remain an outcast." (vv. 13, 14)

As we will see shortly, the woman had not dropped her pretense of being a troubled widow.[13] She pretended to raise the king's own situation as another circumstance that called for similar compassion from the king.

While her words were extremely daring, they were carefully chosen (with the earlier help of Joab, of course). She did not mention Absalom's name, but effectively accused the king of a double standard that was unacceptable.

She made four points. First, David had "planned such a thing against the people of God" (v. 13). I suspect that David wondered for a moment what on earth this woman was talking about. He may well have immediately regretted granting her permission to speak further. What did she mean by "such a thing" (v. 13)? She meant, of course, that David had done something similar to the wrong that he had just righted by his decision in her favor. But she added that what David had done was against "the people of God" (v. 13). This rare expression (Judges 20:2 is the only other occurrence in the Old Testament) is striking. It raised the stakes of the conversation considerably. The woman had shrewdly brought "the LORD your God" into the conclusion of the first stage of the conversation with the king and made the king swear by the life of the Lord (v. 11). Now she said the king had planned something against the interests of "the people of God," something therefore more serious than her own family troubles.

We know that she was expressing Joab's view of things. We can now infer that he saw David's continued antagonism toward Absalom (v. 1) as something potentially damaging to Israel as God's people. Precisely what he feared is not stated, but it is likely that the shrewd Joab could see the possibility of civil war if the problem of Absalom was not resolved.

The second point of the woman's bold speech was that the decision the king had just made about her troubles applied to the king's own situation. "For in giving this decision the king convicts himself" (v. 13). This is not quite as forthright as Nathan's "You are the man!" (12:7), but the upshot is the same.[14] Although Nathan was accusing David of the grave crimes of adultery and murder and the woman was alleging only harmful thoughts and plans, both of these failures were more serious than they might appear. The former was "against the LORD" (12:13), the latter was "against the people of God" (14:13).

David's compassionate decision in favor of the woman being self-condemnatory is less obvious than his furious condemnation of the rich man in Nathan's story. He had given his protection to the widow's possibly guilty son. I doubt that David yet understood what this woman was getting at.

For her third point, she dropped the allusive language and stated the problem plainly: "the king does not bring his banished one home again" (v. 13). Without actually uttering Absalom's name (that may have been too dangerous), she identified the matter of concern. It was not something that the king had done. It was something he had *not* done. He had not brought his banished son back. He had not shown to his own son the compassion that he had shown to hers. If it was right for him to do so in her case, it was all the more important in the case of his "banished one," because the welfare of the people of God was at stake.

Describing Absalom as the king's "banished one" (v. 13) puts the responsibility for Absalom's living in Geshur for three years (13:38) on David. This may have been a bit unfair to David. Absalom had fled to Geshur after killing Amnon. David had nothing to do with it. In fact David had done precisely nothing about Absalom, just as he earlier did nothing about Amnon. And that, of course, was the woman's (Joab's) point. David had done nothing to bring Absalom back, and so he had in effect banished him.

The woman's fourth point is a rather enigmatic statement about death's finality and God's ways. On the one hand, "We must all die" (v. 14). Death is irreversible, like "water spilled on the ground" (v. 14), which oozes away and cannot be collected again.[15] She may have been implying that David's crippling mourning over Amnon's death (13:37, 39) would not bring him back. David had understood this earlier, when his first son born to Bathsheba had died (see 12:22, 23). On the other hand, "God will not take away life" (v. 14). This, of course, is not strictly true (see 1 Samuel 2:6). The woman was stating the general truth that God is a life-*giver* (compare Job 33:4; Acts 17:25; Romans 4:17; 1 Timothy 6:13; cf. Ezekiel 18:32). Consistent with this, God "devises means" to restore the "outcast" (v. 14), unlike David who had "planned" (v. 13, same Hebrew word) not to bring his banished one back.

Remembering that the woman was speaking words given to her by Joab, she was reminding the king of his own experience. He had been an outcast in the days of Saul. God had not allowed that situation to be permanent.

The woman had courageously brought the matter that concerned her instructor (Joab) before the king. She now quickly retreated behind her disguise as a troubled widow, pretending that the matter just mentioned was a secondary afterthought. Her main concern was her own family difficulties:

> Now I have come to say this to my lord the king because the people have made me afraid, and your servant thought, "I will speak to the king; it may be that the king will perform the request of his servant. For the king will hear and deliver his servant from the hand of the man who would destroy me and my son together from the heritage of God." And your servant

thought, "The word of my lord the king will set me at rest," for my lord the king is like the angel of God to discern good and evil. The LORD your God be with you! (vv. 15–17)

Although flattery and subservience returned to her manner and she spoke now only of her own circumstances, she brilliantly kept alluding to the king's situation that she had just exposed. By referring to her family now as "the people" (v. 15), she suggested a connection with "the people of God" (v. 13) in the king's case. By suggesting that what was at stake for her was "the heritage of God" (v. 16),[16] she indicated that an heir was the focus of both her situation and that of the king. Even her reference to "rest" as the desired outcome of the king's decision in her case reminds us (and may have been intended to remind David) of what God had promised him (7:11).

The extravagant language likening the king to "the angel of God" (v. 17) may be softened a little when we recognize that the Hebrew word translated "angel" can mean, more simply, "messenger."[17] The reference, then, was to David's ability to "discern[18] good and evil," like a messenger of God (v. 17). There is irony here, because Joab's whole scheme had only been devised because he thought that he knew better than David what needed to be done. The whole point of the exercise was to bring the king to see the error of his ways.

The woman's closing flourish ("The LORD your God be with you!" v. 17) reminds us that this was precisely what made David the great king that he had been (5:10).

The woman from Tekoa had delivered a brilliant, manipulative speech. She had confronted the king with the issue of the moment. He had not silenced her. He had listened. She and Joab made a great team. All that remained was to see how the king would react to it all.

Stage 3: Unmasked (vv. 18–20)

In the third stage of the conversation, David took control of the agenda (although we may suspect that even this part of the conversation had been anticipated and wanted by Joab).

Then the king answered the woman, "Do not hide from me anything I ask you." And the woman said, "Let my lord the king speak." The king said, "Is the hand of Joab with you in all this?" The woman answered and said, "As surely as you live, my lord the king, one cannot turn to the right hand or to the left from anything that my lord the king has said. It was your servant Joab who commanded me; it was he who put all these words in the mouth of your servant. In order to change the course of things your servant Joab did this. But my lord has wisdom like the wisdom of the angel of God to know all things that are on the earth."[19] (vv. 18–20)

In a surprising reversal of roles, the woman gave David permission to speak! There had been some truth in the woman's flattery. David was discerning and rightly suspected that "the hand of Joab" was behind the strange conversation he had just endured (v. 19). It is, of course, possible that Joab had raised the matter of Absalom with David over the past three years, and so David knew Joab's view of the matter. The woman was so direct in her admission that Joab was behind the whole thing that we may reasonably suspect that the king's realization here, at the end of the conversation, was part of Joab's scheme all along.[20] Joab was the kind of man who had such confidence in his own judgment that he did not need to conceal it. He may well have thought that the king's realization that the woman was Joab's agent would increase the pressure on the king to do what he needed (in Joab's view) to do.

The woman frankly told the king why Joab had done it: "in order to change the course of things" (v. 20). Joab wanted to turn things around. In Joab's view things needed to be turned around. If the king maintained his present course (with respect to Absalom), disaster loomed. That is why Joab had taken matters in hand.

David's Scheme to Avoid the Issue (vv. 21–24)

We are left to imagine the woman departing from the king's presence and Joab being summoned. Perhaps he was waiting just outside the door. He had yet to learn (as do we) whether his scheme had been successful.

Permission: Joab's Success (vv. 21–23)

The king expressed no displeasure with Joab's scheme. On the contrary, "Then the king said to Joab, 'Behold now, I grant this; go, bring back the young man Absalom'" (v. 21). In this context "the young man" sounds like an expression of David's affection for his son, and perhaps at that moment it was.[21]

Joab was delighted. "And Joab fell on his face to the ground and paid homage and blessed the king. And Joab said, 'Today your servant knows that I have found favor in your sight, my lord the king, in that the king has granted the request of his servant'" (v. 22). He wasted no time in bringing his scheme to what seemed to be a successful conclusion. "So Joab arose and went to Geshur and brought Absalom to Jerusalem" (v. 23).

Restriction: Joab's Failure (v. 24)

However, Joab had made a major miscalculation. He had underestimated the king's hostility toward Absalom. Joab's brilliant scheme to turn things around for David's kingdom foundered on David's own scheme to keep his son Absalom at a distance. "And the king said, 'Let him dwell apart in his own house; he is not to come into my presence [literally, my face he shall not see]'" (v. 24a). Joab may have turned things around, but the king turned them around again.[22] "So Absalom lived apart in his own house and did not come into the king's presence [literally, did not see the king's face]" (v. 24b).

What David hoped to accomplish is far from clear, just as it was probably unclear to him. The situation was terribly messy. It could be argued that what Absalom had done in killing Amnon was justified and ought not to be held against him. He had done what David, as the custodian of justice in the land, should have seen to. It was not exactly manslaughter (as in the woman's story of her two sons), but was it really murder? David could not bring himself to treat Absalom either as a murderer (and therefore have him executed) or an innocent (and therefore welcome him back). David's scheme was designed to avoid the issue. If Absalom could be kept away from the king, the king could (once again) avoid the difficult task of deciding what should be done about his son. David's scheme frustrated Joab's scheme but hardly improved the situation.

The intricate detail with which we have been shown Joab's brilliant scheme and the Tekoite woman's ingenious execution of it makes this outcome massively disappointing. The mess in David's kingdom was not sorted out, even by the efforts of the great and able Joab. The kingdom was in deeper trouble than even Joab had seen.

Absalom's Determined Scheme (vv. 25–33)

The problem that Joab had gone to so much effort to solve was Absalom. Far from solving the problem, however, Joab's scheme (when frustrated by David's scheme) had intensified the problem.

Our attention now turns to Absalom. Absalom will dominate the next four chapters of 2 Samuel. Joab had been right to fear terrible consequences from Absalom's banishment. But he had not been able to avert the looming catastrophe. Absalom had his own schemes.

Absalom the Beautiful (vv. 25–27)

Before we hear about Absalom's response to the situation in which he now found himself, the narrator gives us a closer look at the man who will overshadow the following pages. He was a beautiful man and he knew it. "Now in all Israel there was no one so much to be praised for his handsome appearance as Absalom" (v. 25a). He had the good looks David had enjoyed as a boy (1 Samuel 16:12) and that his sister Tamar had (13:1).[23] This had made him something of a celebrity in Israel. He may have been shunned by the king, but in all Israel he was (literally) "greatly praised."

The careful reader of the books of Samuel should be more than a little concerned at this emphasis on Absalom's appearance. Remember Saul ("There was not a man among the people of Israel more handsome than he. From his shoulders upward he was taller than any of the people," 1 Samuel 9:2).[24] It is hardly encouraging to find Absalom reminding us of Saul![25]

The narrator may therefore have his tongue firmly in his cheek as he tells us, "From the sole of his foot to the crown of his head there was no blemish in him" (v. 25b). He was perfect! At least his body was. The vocabulary may remind us of the requirements of the book of Leviticus for priests and sacrifices that had to be without "blemish" (Leviticus 21:17, 18, 21, 23; 22:20, 21, 25). What a young man this was!

And he delighted in his beauty. "And when he cut the hair of his head (for at the end of every year he used to cut it; when it was heavy on him, he cut it), he weighed the hair of his head, two hundred shekels by the king's weight" (v. 26). Although we cannot be sure what "the king's weight" was, 200 shekels sounds like a lot of hair.[26] The description is probably exaggerated, perhaps reflecting Absalom's own perception of his magnificent virility. While his mass of hair may remind us of Samson (Judges 16), as will his actions shortly, his preoccupation with his magnificent hair verges on narcissism. A celebrity indeed! How ironic that David had been tricked into saying of the woman's son (who represented Absalom), "As the LORD lives, not one hair of your son shall fall to the ground" (v. 11)! Further irony awaits us in the story of this young man and his head of hair (see 18:9).

This portrait of the vanity of the prince prepares us for the terrible story that will soon unfold. It is very much about a young man's ego.

Before the action begins, we are told one more thing about Absalom: "There were born to Absalom three sons, and one daughter whose name was Tamar. She was a beautiful woman" (v. 27). Absalom's three sons are mentioned to complete the account of his family, but they are beside the point (they are not even named). Indeed they may have died young, since in 18:18 we hear that Absalom had no son.[27] Be that as it may, the focus here is on the beautiful daughter of the beautiful father, whom he named after his loved (and beautiful) sister (13:1).[28] In this way we are gently reminded of the tragic violence that stands behind the story about to unfold. Absalom never forgot Tamar.

Absalom the Frustrated (vv. 28, 29)

Having presented the important portrait of Absalom we return to the situation that was described in verse 14b and learn that it went on for some time: "So Absalom lived two full years in Jerusalem, without coming into the king's presence" (v. 28). It was a long time, and Absalom felt each day (literally "two years of days"). Five years had now passed since he had fled on the day of the fateful sheep-shearing feast (13:38). Absalom grew impatient with the humiliation of his exclusion from any contact with his father. It was time for Absalom to do something about his situation. It was time for Absalom's scheme.

He knew enough to realize that the one man who could get through to his father was Joab. "Then Absalom sent for Joab, to send him to the king, but Joab would not come to him" (v. 29a). Joab, for his part, seems to have accepted David's decision with regard to Absalom. He had underestimated David's antagonism toward Absalom but would not make that mistake again. Certainly Joab had no intention of siding with Absalom *against* the king. He refused Absalom's summons. "And [Absalom] sent a second time, but Joab would not come" (v. 29b). Joab was not going to be a pawn in anyone's game, certainly not Absalom's. Momentarily Absalom's scheme was frustrated by Joab's intransigence.

Absalom the Determined (vv. 30–32)

But Absalom was a man used to getting what he wanted and was always prepared to do whatever it takes to achieve that end. "Then he said to his servants, 'See, Joab's field is next to mine, and he has barley there; go and set it on fire.' So Absalom's servants set the field on fire" (v. 30). He reminds us once again of Samson who captured the attention of the Philistines with a similar trick (see Judges 15:4–8). Absalom certainly got Joab's attention. "Then Joab arose and went to Absalom at his house and said to him, 'Why have your servants set my field on fire?'" (v. 31).

> Absalom answered Joab, "Behold, I sent word to you, 'Come here, that I may send you to the king, to ask, "Why have I come from Geshur? It would be better for me to be there still." Now therefore let me go into the presence of the king, and if there is guilt in me, let him put me to death.'" (v. 32)

The situation was intolerable to Absalom. Either he was guilty, in which case he would have been better off in Geshur, or he was innocent, in which case this exclusion from the king's presence was inexcusable. The king had allowed him to return. So was he innocent or guilty? The king cannot have it both ways.

Of course, Absalom was not denying responsibility for Amnon's death. In his mind, however, this was not a matter of "guilt." David had left Amnon's crime unpunished. That is the only reason Absalom had to take vengeance into his own hands.[29]

Absalom: The Son Who Got His Way (v. 33)

The chapter concludes with the success of Absalom's scheme.

> Then Joab went to the king and told him, and he summoned Absalom. So he came to the king and bowed himself on his face to the ground before the king, and the king kissed Absalom. (v. 33)

We notice, however, that Absalom came to "the king" (not to "David" or "his father"). He approached like a servant rather than a son.[30] There was no weeping (as one might expect at such a reunion after years of estrangement).[31] There were not even any words spoken (at least none are recorded). This was an awkward meeting. Even the king's kiss looks more royal and official than paternal.[32]

As the next episode in the story will show, this resolution (such as it was) failed to satisfy Absalom. His scheme to restore things to the way they had been before the terrible events of the last decade, like Joab's scheme to guard the kingdom and David's scheme to avoid the issues, failed.

Four chapters of 2 Samuel (chapters 11—14) have taken us through ten years or so. It had now been two years since Absalom had been brought back to Jerusalem (14:28), five years since Absalom had killed Amnon (13:38), seven years since Amnon had raped Tamar (13:23), and about ten years since David had committed adultery with Bathsheba and had Uriah killed (assuming two or three years, which is no more than a guess, between those events and the Amnon/Tamar atrocity). For ten years human sin had embroiled David's family and kingdom in more trouble than they ever faced from external enemies. The consequences of David's sins declared by Nathan (12:10–12) were being felt.

As every effort to make things better seemed only to make things worse, we could wonder whether God had given them up (cf. Romans 1:24, 26, 28). Where was the grace of God to be seen in all this mess?

Certainly not in the clever, compromising, or determined schemes of the human participants in the tangled situation. God's grace was in the promise he had made to establish David's kingdom forever (7:16). It will certainly take One greater than David, not to mention Joab or Absalom, to sort out the mess that human sin makes.

That is what Jesus Christ has done by the blood of his cross (see Colossians 1:20).

30

Politics and Power

2 SAMUEL 15:1–12

*A dispute also arose among [the disciples of Jesus], as
to which of them was to be regarded as the greatest.
And he said to them, "The kings of the Gentiles
exercise lordship over them, and those in authority
over them are called benefactors. But not so with
you. Rather, let the greatest among you become as
the youngest, and the leader as one who serves. For
who is the greater, one who reclines at table or one
who serves? Is it not the one who reclines at table?
But I am among you as the one who serves."*

LUKE 22:24–27

THE PURSUIT OF GREATNESS by humans typically involves displays of power
and pomp, fame and fortune, privileges and benefits. Jesus Christ introduced
a radically different understanding of greatness. "I am among you as the one
who serves," he said (Luke 22:27). Greatness in the kingdom of God is measured by the greatness of the King. Therefore the kingdom of God belongs
not to those who seek power, fame, and privilege for themselves, but to those
who are childlike in their powerlessness and dependence (Luke 18:16, 17).

Do you believe that? We need to understand that the pursuit of worldly
greatness is profoundly inconsistent with faith in Jesus Christ. Such ambitions represent an *alternative* to the way of Jesus Christ. This is not a
lesson easily learned. The cult of celebrity has not been abolished from

Christian churches. We have a way to go in heeding our King's word: "Not so with you" (Luke 22:26).

David's kingdom had, for a little while, embodied something of the greatness of the kingdom of God. David had been a king who served (see, for example, 2 Samuel 2:6; 8:15; 9:1, 7; 10:2). For a long time he had refused to *take* power (see especially 1 Samuel 24, 26). But things had changed. David had *taken* Bathsheba, and he had *taken* her husband's life (2 Samuel 11). Remarkably the Lord had "put away" David's sin (12:13b), but there were still consequences (12:10–12). David's kingdom would never be the same again.

The Lord (through the prophet Nathan) had told David, "I will raise up evil against you out of your own house" (12:11). The evil that came out of David's house (Amnon's rape of Tamar and Absalom's killing of Amnon were the start) must be seen as consequences of David's crimes. His sons' behavior terrifyingly resonated with their father's—sexual violation and deadly violence. David himself appears to have become incapable of curbing his sons, weakened it would seem by his own failures. Their wicked acts disturbed, even angered him, but he (like old Eli and old Samuel many years before, 1 Samuel 2:23–25; 8:3) was not able to contain the cancer that had begun to attack his kingdom from within. David understood (as numerous Psalms show) that the Lord's hand was behind his troubles (see, for example, Psalm 6:1; 10:1; 13:1; 22:1; 38:2[1]), just as Nathan had said.

Second Samuel 15—19 tells the story of how all this became the greatest threat the kingdom of David ever experienced. It is the account of Absalom,[2] David's oldest surviving son,[3] who had been brought back to Jerusalem and formally (although awkwardly) reconciled to his father five years after he had killed his older brother (14:33). Absalom's challenge to David's kingdom was the antithesis of the kingdom of God as it has now been revealed in Jesus Christ and as it had briefly been seen in David's kingdom. In Absalom we see worldly ambition pitted against the kingdom of David. The kingdom of David, weakened by David's own failures, was almost destroyed. There are important lessons here about the power and greatness that humans too often desire and admire. As we follow Absalom's rise to this kind of greatness, and as we see the apparent weakness of the kingdom of David, we will learn that true greatness is not like Absalom.

The story of Absalom's "rise" begins with two scenes:

(1) Politics Absalom-style (vv. 1–6).
(2) Taking power Absalom's way (vv. 7–12).

Politics Absalom-Style (vv. 1–6)

"After this"[4] (v. 1a) suggests on the one hand that the scene we are about to witness took shape not long after the formal reinstatement of Absalom in Jerusalem with the king's official endorsement (14:33). On the other hand, "After this" indicates that the behavior of Absalom about to be described was without excuse. He had been accepted back into the kingdom of David. He was no longer excluded by the king. All this would have entailed his being recognized as the heir apparent to David's throne.[5] Responsibility for what would soon happen lay squarely with Absalom.[6]

The Politics of Pomp (v. 1)

The reinstated prince took steps to develop his image. "After this Absalom got himself a chariot and horses, and fifty men to run before him" (v. 1). None of this had any practical purpose except to make Absalom look important. In particular chariots were of little use in the mountainous terrain around Jerusalem. But in the streets of Jerusalem the magnificent young prince must have made a grand impression as he paraded with an escort of fifty men running ahead of the small cavalry and the classy chariot that carried his royal highness.

As far as we know this was the first time that a chariot had been seen in the streets of Jerusalem. We noticed earlier that chariots were typically the equipment of Israel's enemies and that "trust in chariots" was what people did when they did not "trust . . . in the LORD" (Psalm 20:7; see the discussion of 2 Samuel 8:4). When Samuel had warned the people of Israel many years previously about the dangers of having a king "like all the nations," he had emphasized that such a king would have chariots and horsemen to run before his chariots (1 Samuel 8:5, 11). Absalom's introduction of a chariot to the streets of Jerusalem was worse than pompous and pretentious. He had begun to display an alternative kind of power and greatness. There was more than a hint of his intention to usurp his father.[7]

We recognize in Absalom's street parades what we might call the politics of pomp. Jesus warned against those who love drawing attention to themselves by ostentatious clothing and conspicuous displays of grandeur (Luke 20:46). Those who want to be great still play this game; power-dressing and other attempts to *look* great are part of the pursuit of worldly greatness. The problem is that we are all too easily taken in by the politics of pomp, being impressed by such outward displays. The words of Jesus should ring in our ears: "It shall not be so among you" (Mark 10:43).

What did David think about Absalom's exhibitions of royal magnificence? We are not told. It will become clear that he didn't *do* anything about it. Ironically the woman from Tekoa had flattered David, saying that he had wisdom "to know all things that are in the land" (14:20 AT). We reasonably wonder whether he had any idea of the threat that was beginning to emerge under his very nose.[8]

The Politics of Promises (vv. 2–4)

The street parades were accompanied by something even more sinister. Absalom perceived a way of fostering discontent in David's kingdom and positioning himself in the minds of the people as the potential answer to their unhappiness. It was the politics of promises.

"And Absalom used to rise early and stand beside the way of the gate" (v. 2a), that is, by the road leading to the city gate.[9] The city gate was a place where (among other things) disputes or complaints could be brought for adjudication (see Deuteronomy 21:19; 22:15; Joshua 20:4; Ruth 4:1, 11; 2 Samuel 19:8; Job 5:4; 29:7; Psalm 127:5; Proverbs 22:22; Isaiah 29:21; Amos 5:12, 15; cf. 2 Samuel 18:4, 24, 33).[10] Absalom made a habit of taking up a position, early in the day, where he could intercept any who were approaching the gate with an issue to be resolved.

"And when any man had a dispute to come before the king for judgment, Absalom would call to him and say, 'From what city are you?'" (v. 2b). Absalom targeted those who were bringing their cases for a decision by the king. An example of such a case was brought by the woman from Tekoa (14:4–11), although her story was, of course, fabricated. Whenever such a person came along, the prince engaged him (or presumably her) in the kind of conversation that a ruler might expect to initiate with his subjects ("And where are you from?").

A "dispute" (15:2)[11] was a case generally brought by a private individual who was seeking redress for some wrong. What the plaintiff would be seeking was "justice" ("judgment," v. 2 ESV) from the king. David's kingdom had been characterized by the "justice" he did for all his people (8:15).[12] It was right that the people should look to their king for "justice."

The person bringing their case to the gate would reply to Absalom, "Your servant is of such and such a tribe in Israel" (v. 2c). The reply does not exactly match the question, but this part of the conversation was not important. It was simply intended to give Absalom the opportunity to say, "See, your claims are good and right" (v. 3a). This was precisely what the complainant wanted to hear and no doubt in many cases feared he might not hear. Is there any surer way for a powerful person to win the support of people than by giving the impression he is on their side? The brief sketch we are given here suggests that Absalom did not bother hearing what their claims were before declaring them good and right! He adopted the pose of an all-knowing superior who could tell, just by meeting a person, that he or she was in the right. Absalom did not tell *anyone* that he or she was in the wrong.

The insincerity of such words is familiar to all of us who have listened to the promises in a modern election campaign. How often have you heard a candidate for office inform members of the public that he cannot agree with them, their grievances are not justified, their complaints are unreasonable? Not often, if ever, is my guess.

"There is no problem with your complaint," Absalom would essentially assure each litigant. "Your chances of receiving justice, however, are slim." Why? Because "there is no man designated by the king to hear you" (v. 3b). *The problem is with the government. The king clearly does not care enough about you to provide the resources needed to get your case heard and dealt with.*[13]

We cannot tell to what degree Absalom's criticism of David's administration of justice was valid. After all, the woman from Tekoa had her case heard by the king himself (but she did have Joab to arrange things for her). Had David's capacity for doing justice and righteousness for all his people (8:15) been compromised by his recent troubles? Quite possibly. However, Absalom was almost certainly overstating (if not making up) the problem for his own purposes.[14]

We may again be struck by how familiar such political tactics are to us. Those aspiring to positions of power rarely acknowledge that those currently in power are doing a good job, even when they really are. Creating and feeding discontent with those who stand in the way of your ambitions is a common political ploy.

The point of all this, of course, was to make the solution to everyone's problems obvious. "Then Absalom would say, 'Oh that I were judge in the land! Then every man with a dispute or cause might come to me,[15] and I would give him justice'" (v. 4). He did not, of course, say, "Oh that I were king!" That would have been dangerous. He simply wanted to be the one who brought these poor people the justice they all deserved.[16] In Israel a "judge" was more (though not less) than a judicial figure (v. 4). He put things right in Israel.[17] The "judge in the land" these days was the king (v. 4). Absalom was certainly not entertaining the idea of returning to the old days when a judge (like Samuel) was not a king (1 Samuel 7:15–17). When the people had demanded a king in the days of Samuel, they wanted "a *king* to judge us" (1 Samuel 8:5, 6, 20). Without putting it in so many words, Absalom was sowing the idea that the hope for justice in the land lay in a new source of justice, namely King Absalom rather than King David.

We need to understand that "I would give [them] justice" does not quite mean what it sounds like in English (2 Samuel 15:4). The sense is, "I would declare in their favor."[18] What a promise! Every litigant would get the decision he or she wanted. The impossibility of all judicial decisions being favorable to everyone did not constrain Absalom in his undertaking any more than the modern politician who promises to lower taxes, increase entitlements, and balance the budget.

The politics of promises pretends to be concerned for the needs or desires of each individual. The promises are shaped by their yearnings. The truth is that Absalom had no interest whatsoever for the individuals he worked over. He wanted the support of the crowd and promised whatever it took to get the individuals on board.[19] Sound familiar?

The Politics of Pleasing (v. 5)

Absalom's political campaign was crowned by a strategy of charm. "And whenever a man came near to pay homage to him, he would put out his hand and take hold of him and kiss him" (v. 5).

A very careful reader of this story might notice that "he would . . . take hold of him" repeats the wording of 13:11, where Amnon "took hold of" Tamar in order to violate her.[20] Certainly the expression suggests this was an act of Absalom's strength imposed on a weaker party. More obviously his "kiss" is a remarkable repetition of what the king had recently done to him (14:33). Absalom was behaving like the king! Perhaps the evident falseness of Absalom's kiss suggests (retrospectively) that there may have been insincerity in David's gesture.[21]

It Worked! (v. 6)

The remarkable thing about Absalom-style politics is that it works. It did for him. "Thus Absalom did to all of Israel who came to the king for judgment. So Absalom stole the hearts of the men of Israel" (v. 6). Absalom worked on "all of Israel" with his strategy to arouse the affection and support of the people. Just in case we readers are as gullible as the people, the narrator describes what Absalom achieved in terms that evaluate his success. He "stole the hearts" of the people of Israel (v. 6). It was a deception.[22] Politics Absalom-style can succeed, but those who fall for it have been duped.

Taking Power Absalom's Way (vv. 7–12)

Absalom's campaign to "steal" the hearts of the people of Israel went on for four years (v. 7).[23] He had already shown himself a man who could wait for the right time to carry out his long-harbored intentions. For two full years after Amnon's rape of Tamar he had seethed with hatred toward his half-brother before carrying out the well-planned execution at Baal-hazor (13:23, 28). Now four years passed after the prince had been reinstated by the king (14:33). During this time Absalom had been active in the manner described in verses 1–6. If David noticed the prince's subversive activity, he did not take any action, nor did the matter seem to concern him.

Deceiving David (vv. 7–9)

The time came when Absalom was ready to move into action. As he had done previously (13:24), he approached the king with an innocent-sounding request.

> And at the end of four years Absalom said to the king, "Please let me go and pay my vow, which I have vowed to the Lord, in Hebron. For your servant vowed a vow while I lived at Geshur in Aram, saying, 'If the Lord will indeed bring me back to Jerusalem, then I will offer worship to the Lord.'" (vv. 7, 8)

Having witnessed Absalom's previous carefully timed conversation with the king in 13:24–27 we know that the prince must be plotting something under this cloak of piety. As previously, Absalom's request to David involved an activity away from Jerusalem, out of the king's sight. This time it was to be in Hebron, nineteen miles south-southeast of Jerusalem. The immediate significance of Hebron to Absalom was that he was born there (3:2, 3). This may have been sufficient explanation for his desire to "pay [his] vow" there rather than in Jerusalem (15:7).[24] However, Hebron was also the city where David had, at the Lord's direction, first been anointed king (2:1, 4). Hebron was Abraham's town and therefore linked David's kingship to the promises that God had made to Abraham.[25] Hebron was David's first royal city, before it was displaced by Jerusalem. We would be right to suspect that when Absalom proposed going to Hebron, he had more in mind than a visit to his place of birth.[26]

As in his previous scheming conversation with the king, Absalom had concocted a plausible reason for the trip from Jerusalem. This time it was not a sheep-shearing feast but a religious festivity of some kind. The details are not given, nor did David inquire. The story was that during his three-year exile in Geshur (13:38) the young man had struck a bargain with the Lord. If the Lord would bring him back to Jerusalem (presumably that meant being reinstated as the king's son, now his eldest), then Absalom would "offer worship to the LORD" (15:8). The Hebrew could be literally translated "serve the LORD," probably meaning in this context to offer a sacrifice (see v. 12).[27] However, the literal meaning of the expression should be noticed. It was a lie. Absalom had no intention of being a servant to anyone. His outward expressions of submission to his father and king were hardly sincere (14:33). If Absalom made a vow in Geshur, we can be sure it was quite different from the one he now claimed. He may have sworn (but not to the Lord) that he would avenge himself, displace his father, and banish him to exile.[28] The feigned piety of this speech to David is the last time we hear Absalom mention God.

In the earlier conversation with David about the sheep-shearing feast, David had been cautious, and at least a little suspicious. Not so now. "The king said to him, 'Go in peace'" (v. 9a). These would be the very last words that David would ever say to his son Absalom. The bitter irony is palpable. "Go *in peace* [Hebrew, *shalom*]" opened the way for Absalom to go to war!

The irony is intensified when we notice that David had named this son Ab*salom* ("Father [presumably meaning God] is peace"), and the city in which this ominous conversation took place was Jeru*salem* ("city of peace"[29]). Furthermore the son who would eventually become king after David (as Absalom was hoping to do) had been named Solomon (another name based on the word for "peace").[30]

David trusted Absalom. In this he was less wise than the Tekoite woman had said he was. He failed to discern evil, and he did not understand what was happening in the land (see 14:17, 20).

The way was clear for Absalom to enact his plans. "So he arose and went to Hebron" (v. 9b).

Secret Support (v. 10)

Just as in his previous conspiracy, Absalom had a well-formed plan. Again it involved instructions for those who would implement his scheme to await his signal and then to do the deed. "Absalom sent secret messengers throughout all the tribes of Israel, saying, 'As soon as you hear the sound of the trumpet, then say, "Absalom is king at Hebron!"'" (v. 10).

The "secret messengers" were literally "spies" (as in 1 Samuel 26:4; 2 Samuel 10:3). They were more than "messengers." We may suppose that they ascertained the attitudes of the people before carrying out their commission where they could count on support.[31]

Absalom's skill in bringing things to this state is astonishing. Over four years he had apparently garnered support "throughout all the tribes of Israel" (15:10) and prepared the whole nation for a coup, without arousing David's suspicions.

Convincing Cover (v. 11)

In the earlier plot Absalom had covered his real intentions by taking along a crowd who knew nothing of his plans (13:27). He employed the same trick again. "With Absalom went two hundred men from Jerusalem who were invited guests, and they went in their innocence and knew nothing" (v. 11).

It is clear that despite widespread support throughout the land (v. 10), the plot had been kept secret from most people in Jerusalem. The crowd of innocents would have dispelled any lingering suspicions about the prince's intentions.

A Clever Collaborator (v. 12a)

There was one final stroke of genius to be put in place. In his last secretive scheme it is almost certain that Absalom enlisted the assistance of a "wise" collaborator (13:3; ESV, "crafty") in the person of Jonadab (see 13:32, 33). This time he not only recruited a clever advisor, but in the process weakened David. "And while Absalom was offering the sacrifices,[32] he sent for[33] Ahithophel the Gilonite, David's counselor, from his city Giloh" (v. 12a).

We will learn in due course that Ahithophel[34] was a remarkably clever man, esteemed very highly by those who sought his counsel (see 16:23). If Ahithophel was Bathsheba's grandfather,[35] it seems likely (although we are not told in as many words) that David's treatment of his granddaughter (not to mention her husband) had turned Ahithophel against the king. Absalom had seized this opportunity with both hands.

The location of Giloh is not known, although a site about five miles north-northwest of Hebron has been suggested, while others propose a location to the southwest of Hebron.[36] The important point is that Ahithophel, David's counselor, had conveniently got himself out of Jerusalem to his hometown, from which he could more easily be summoned by Absalom.[37] In other words, it seems clear that Ahithophel (like Jonadab before him) had been involved in Absalom's scheming for some time and had in all probability helped him formulate the plan.

It Worked (v. 12b)

"And the conspiracy grew strong, and the people with Absalom kept increasing" (v. 12b). The narrator calls it a "conspiracy." The sense of this word (and the related verb) can be seen in Saul's suspicions about Jonathan and David (1 Samuel 22:8, 13). The words usually refer to plots to depose or kill a reigning king and usurp his throne.[38] Absalom was leading a treasonous plot against the kingdom of David.

As the conspiracy gained strength, the disasters that Nathan had announced as consequences of David's crimes began to overwhelm King David. Certainly we may suppose that he was weakened by his own failures. In earlier and better days it is difficult to imagine a plot like Absalom's getting off the ground. But it is important to see that David's kingdom was not threatened by someone "better" than him (as Saul's had been, 1 Samuel 15:28). On the contrary, Absalom represented the very opposite of the one whom David had previously foreshadowed—the one who came "to serve, and to give his life as a ransom for many" (Matthew 20:28).

As we watch the ways of Absalom (beautiful, charming, grand, popular, pleasing, clever, deceiving, and ruthless), let us hear the words of Jesus: "It shall not be so among you" (Matthew 20:26).

31

The Darkest Day

2 SAMUEL 15:13–31

When Jesus had spoken these words,
he went out with his disciples across the
brook Kidron, where there was a garden,
which he and his disciples entered.

JOHN 18:1

SO THE DARKEST DAY in the history of the world began. It was well into the night, probably the small hours of the morning (see John 13:30). Jesus went out with his disciples from the city of Jerusalem, crossed the brook Kidron (in the valley on the east side of the city), and climbed to the Garden of Gethsemane on the Mount of Olives, on the other side of the Kidron Valley.[1] Within twenty-four hours Jesus would be dead.

Each of the Gospels recounts this short but excruciating walk from the city to the mountain (Matthew 26:30; Mark 14:26; Luke 22:39; John 18:1), where Jesus prayed, "My Father, if it be possible, let this cup pass from me; nevertheless, not as I will, but as you will" (Matthew 26:39; Mark 14:36; Luke 22:42). The dark and dangerous clouds of deadly opposition to Jesus had been gathering for some time. Jesus had spoken to his disciples repeatedly about the violent death he would soon suffer at the hands of those who hated him, if only they had ears to hear. There on the Mount of Olives his betrayer's hand would soon be shown (Matthew 26:46; Mark 14:42; Luke 22:47, 48; John 18:2, 3). In a short time he would be denied (Matthew 26:69–75; Mark 14:66–72; Luke 22:54–62; John 18:15–18, 25–27), abused (Matthew 26:67, 68; Mark 14:65; Luke 22:63; John 19:1), mocked (Matthew

27:27–31; Mark 15:16–20; Luke 23:36, 37; John 19:2, 3), and condemned to death (Matthew 27:26; Mark 15:15; Luke 23:23, 24; John 19:16).

It was the darkest of days for all who had hoped that "he was the one to redeem Israel" (Luke 24:21), the long-promised son of David whose kingdom would be the kingdom of God. It was a day of humiliation and shame for Jesus and devastating disillusionment for those who had followed him.

Centuries earlier King David had left Jerusalem accompanied by those who were with him, crossed the Kidron Valley, and climbed the Mount of Olives. It was (I think) his darkest day. In that momentous short walk across the Kidron Valley, King David anticipated the footsteps of Jesus about 1,000 years later. As Jesus led his disciples out of the city and across to the Mount of Olives, he was following in the footsteps of King David. The sufferings of David anticipated and illuminated the sufferings of the Son of David.[2]

The dark and dangerous clouds that led to David's departure from Jerusalem had been gathering for some time. The trouble had begun with David's sin in 2 Samuel 11. Although the Lord had "put away" that sin (12:13), there were terrible consequences. These led to David's son Absalom gathering popular support (by dubious means) and having himself acclaimed as king (15:1–12). This is where we pick up the story, but as we follow David we will find ourselves thinking about Jesus and his replication (the correct word is "fulfillment") of David's experience.

Our passage begins and ends with a message reaching David about the troubles that had arisen.[3] The news forced David to flee from Jerusalem.

    (1) Message 1: Absalom's threat (vv. 13–15).
    (2) Stage 1: Out of Jerusalem (vv. 16–22).
    (3) Stage 2: Across the brook Kidron (vv. 23–29).
    (4) Stage 3: Up the Mount of Olives (v. 30).
    (5) Message 2: Ahithophel's betrayal (v. 31).

Message 1: Absalom's Threat (vv. 13–15)

"And a messenger[4] came to David, saying, 'The hearts of the men of Israel have gone after Absalom'" (v. 13). The informant may have been one of the 200 guests Absalom had taken with him from Jerusalem to Hebron (15:11). The news he brought echoes what we have already been told in 15:6b, 12b. "The men of Israel" sounds like the vast majority of the people (v. 13).[5] This, at least, was how it seemed to the informant.

It is surprising how little the informant needed to say to convey the crisis. If Absalom had been known to be a loyal son and prince, then news of his great popularity with all the people would not be alarming. It is clear, however, that the news that Absalom had won the affections of the people of Israel meant that David had lost them. Everyone (including, it would seem, David) had known for some time that Absalom had set himself against King David.[6] And everyone (certainly including King David) knew what Absalom was capable of.

David immediately understood the seriousness of the news.

> Then David said to all his servants who were with him at Jerusalem, "Arise, and let us flee, or else there will be no escape for us from Absalom. Go quickly, lest he overtake us quickly and bring down ruin on us and strike the city with the edge of the sword." (v. 14)

So much for the prince who had promised "justice" for all (15:4) and who had left Jerusalem with words of "peace" from David (15:9).

The strategic sense of David's prompt decision is clear. If Absalom had the massive support that had been suggested, then remaining within the city walls would be dangerous. David knew about besieging a city (11:1, 25; 12:29). Furthermore, David could not have been sure at this stage whether Jerusalem contained supporters (or potential supporters) of Absalom. That was very likely since most of the 200 innocents who had gone to Hebron seemed to have been caught up in the coup. It is striking, however, that David so quickly concluded (correctly) that Absalom had become a dangerous and violent enemy from whom he and those "with him" desperately needed to "escape" (15:14).

With these words we recognize that David was about to become a fugitive again. It was back to the days before he became king when he and those with him "fled" from Saul.[7] More recently it was Absalom who had "fled" (13:34, 37, 38). The tables had been dramatically turned.

"All his servants who were with him at Jerusalem" (15:14) included at least his household and a number of military contingents whom we will see shortly.

David's fleeing from Jerusalem was enormously significant. What would become of him? What would become of his kingdom? It appeared that all was lost. At about this time David prayed:

> O Lord, how many are my foes!
>   Many are rising against me;
> many are saying of my soul,
>   there is no salvation for him in God. (Psalm 3:1, 2)[8]

At the same time, the "evil" (ESV, "ruin," v. 14) that Absalom threatened to bring down on David and those with him was the "evil" that the Lord had said he would raise up "out of your [David's] own house" (12:11). In turn this was on account of the thing that David had done that was "evil" in the eyes of the Lord (11:27 AT). "The sword" with which Absalom now threatened to strike the city was "the sword" that the Lord had declared would "never depart from your house" (12:10). David knew (as his words and conduct would soon show) that the disaster that had come upon him was *both* the wicked work of Absalom *and* the righteousness of God (cf. Acts 2:23).

As we hear David's words, "Arise, and let us flee" (2 Samuel 15:14), we should be reminded of the words of Jesus to his disciples centuries later: "Rise, let us go from here" (John 14:31).[9] Jesus knew that he was about to do what David had done. His experience would be the fulfillment of what was anticipated in David's story. The differences will be as important as the similarities.

David's swift and decisive response to the crisis may take us by surprise. Since his great failure in 2 Samuel 11 he had repeatedly failed to respond effectively to growing troubles. At last, however, the old David seemed to be back, albeit David the fugitive again.

David found that although the hearts of the men of Israel had gone after Absalom, his servants who were with him in Jerusalem were faithful. "And the king's servants said to the king, 'Behold, your servants are ready to do whatever my lord the king decides'" (v. 15). They at least still regarded him as their "lord" and "king." The bold assertion of their commitment to the king reminds us, on the one hand, of Peter's declaration of loyalty to Jesus (John 13:37), which he failed to keep. On the other hand, the general failure of the disciples of Jesus to stand with him in his great hour of need (Matthew 26:31; John 16:32) makes a disturbing contrast to the servants of David.

Stage 1: Out of Jerusalem (vv. 16–22)

The Departure (vv. 16–18)

"So the king went out, and all his household after him" (v. 16a). "After him" is a rather striking expression in Hebrew, literally "in his feet." It suggests their closeness to him and the completeness of their obedience.[10] At the same time this procession "on foot" makes a rather stark and depressing contrast to the picture we have been given of Absalom in his chariot in 15:1. There was no pomp in David's departure from Jerusalem.

Notice that David left Jerusalem with "all his household" (v. 16). "Household" and "house" are the same word in Hebrew. As we watch David's "house" depart from Jerusalem, we may remember with puzzlement the Lord's promise of 7:16: "Your *house* and your kingdom shall be made sure forever before me." What had become of that promise? Had David's sin destroyed what God had promised?

Just as we are wondering about these questions, we are surprised to read, "And the king left ten concubines to keep the house" (v. 16b). We will not discuss the vexed questions raised by David's concubines here. We have heard about them before (see 5:13).[11] The surprise here is that David left these women in Jerusalem "to keep the house." This measure will have disastrous consequences (see 16:21, 22; 20:3; cf. 12:11), but that was not David's intention. It seems as though he was making preparations for his return to Jerusalem.[12] Furthermore, his words indicate that in some sense at least a house of David continued in Jerusalem, even when "all his household" had departed (15:16). Would he, then, return?

The account of the departure resumes: "And the king went out, and all the people after him [literally again, in his feet]" (v. 17a). Since these words are precisely parallel to verse 16, "all the people" includes "all his household," but is probably a much bigger group, including many military men (see v. 18 and 16:6). When they reached the outskirts of the city, "they halted at the last house"[13] (v. 17b).

This pause in the urgent flight from Jerusalem, as they were about to leave the city behind, is full of pathos. As they stand there at the edge of the city there is the opportunity for them (and us) to reflect for a moment on the king's departure from "the city of David" (5:7). How different from the day he triumphantly took the city (5:6–10)! What a contrast to the day he joyfully brought the ark of God into the city (6:12–15)! How far he had come from the days in which he and his men returned to Jerusalem in victory over all their enemies (8:7; 10:14; 12:31). In Jerusalem David's kindness had triumphed with the grandson of his old enemy Saul (9:13). Now David and his household paused at "the last house" as they left the city behind (15:17).

The pause at the city's limits turned the exodus into a "march-past" of the king's faithful servants and soldiers.[14] "And all his servants passed by[15] him, and all the Cherethites, and all the Pelethites, and all the six hundred Gittites who had followed him[16] from Gath, passed on before the king" (v. 18). We heard about the Cherethites and Pelethites in 8:18, where we noted that they appear to have been foreigners who constituted David's bodyguard. The Gittites are a surprise (although we did meet Obed-edom the Gittite in 6:10). They appear to be a contingent of Philistines who joined themselves to David during his desperate sixteen months in Gath (1 Samuel 27).[17] This remarkable testimony to the magnetism of David is a token of what he might have been. In due course the prophets will speak of a day when "all the nations shall flow" to Mount Zion (Isaiah 2:2). In David there had been a small anticipation of that day. Indeed these foreigners were more faithful to him than were most of his own people (cf. Matthew 8:10).[18]

The movement of David and those accompanying him is repeatedly described in this chapter with a Hebrew verb meaning to "pass by" or "cross over." It occurs nine times between verses 18 and 33. The same verb occurs twenty-two times in Joshua 3, 4, where it refers to the crossing of the Jordan and the entry of the people of Israel *into* the promised land. In this way David's departure from Jerusalem is made to sound like a reversal of the entry into the land. The gift was being lost.

Ittai the Gittite (vv. 19–22)

David addressed the leader of the contingent of Gittites:[19]

> Then the king said to Ittai the Gittite, "Why do you also go with us? Go back and stay with the king, for you are a foreigner and also an exile from your home. You came only yesterday, and shall I today make you wander about with us, since I go I know not where? Go back and take your brothers with you, and may the LORD show steadfast love and faithfulness to you." But Ittai answered the king, "As the LORD lives, and as my lord the king lives, wherever my lord the king shall be, whether for death or for life, there also will your servant be." And David said to Ittai, "Go then, pass on." So Ittai the Gittite passed on with all his men and all the little ones who were with him. (vv. 19–22)

Although David's words were addressed to Ittai,[20] he included the 600 Gittites ("your brothers," v. 20) in what he said. These foreigners, already exiles from their homeland and relatively recent adherents of King David, had no obligation to join him in his exile. It would be understandable (and no hard feelings as far as David was concerned) if they stayed in the safety of Jerusalem and threw in their lot with the new king (Absalom). Ittai, however, was utterly committed to sticking with his "lord the king" (v. 21). Along with his 600 men and their families, Ittai continued with the procession of those who were joining David in his exile. We will look more closely at Ittai's encounter with David in our next chapter.

Stage 2: Across the Brook Kidron (vv. 23–29)

The second stage of David's departure was his crossing of the valley on the east side of the city. The stream in that valley marked a boundary. Crossing it took David and those who were with him beyond the city of Jerusalem.

The Crossing (v. 23)

> And all the land wept aloud as all the people passed by, and the king crossed the brook Kidron, and all the people passed on toward the wilderness. (v. 23)

The significance of this crossing was felt by all who witnessed or heard about it. "All the land was weeping with a great voice" (AT). Even those who were not part of the great crowd of refugees understood that something terrible was taking place. David's extraordinary kingdom was crumbling. The great king (see 5:10) had become a fugitive again. It was the reversal of the great crossing that had marked the beginning of Israel's life in this land that the Lord had given them.[21] The loss was unbearable. The land itself, God's gift to his people Israel (Joshua 1:2), cried out (so to speak) at the sadness of what was happening. Israel was rejecting her king.

"The brook Kidron" marked a boundary on the east side of Jerusalem (2 Samuel 15:23; see 1 Kings 2:37; 2 Kings 23:4, 6; cf. Jeremiah 31:40). In later times it became the site of much that was cast out of Jerusalem (see 1 Kings 15:13; 2 Kings 23:4, 6, 12). Later readers could be expected to see the poignancy in David's crossing "the brook Kidron" as he was cast out of the city.[22]

The only reference to "the brook Kidron" in the New Testament is John 18:1 where we read of Jesus and his disciples crossing "the brook Kidron." The reference appears to be a deliberate allusion to the account of David's departure from Jerusalem.[23] The great Son of David walked (so to speak) in David's footsteps and likewise was rejected by "his own people" (John 1:11).

The evocative symbolism of the scene is capped by the words "toward the wilderness" (v. 23). This may refer to "the northern part of the desert of Judah, through which the road to Jericho and the Jordan lay."[24] More importantly "the wilderness" reminds us of that period of Israel's history when they had no land, no "place" of security (7:10)—the wilderness wanderings in the days of Moses. Nothing could suggest the end of David's kingdom and the loss of all it represented more vividly than this procession of David and his people "toward the wilderness."[25]

Zadok and Abiathar (vv. 24–29)

As this solemn procession was moving out of the city and across the valley, there was another astonishing reminder of the day long ago when the Israelites had crossed *into* the promised land.

> And Abiathar came up, and behold, Zadok came also with all the Levites, bearing the ark of the covenant of God. And they set down the ark of God until the people had all passed out of the city.[26] (v. 24)

The ark of the covenant of God, which David had so dramatically brought into Jerusalem (2 Samuel 6), had much earlier played a crucial role when the people had crossed the Jordan and entered the promised land (see Joshua 3:6, 11, 17, etc.). Zadok and the Levites[27] seem to have assumed (understandably) that where King David goes, there the ark must go.[28]

However, David insisted that the ark of God must not be part of his departure from the city. "Then the king said to Zadok, 'Carry the ark of God back into the city'" (v. 25a). David seemed to understand that the ark of the covenant of God, representing the promises of God, belonged in the city.[29] If David trusted the promises of God, he expected to return to Jerusalem.

This is the faith he expressed:

> If I find favor in the eyes of the LORD, he will bring me back and let me see both it and his dwelling place. But if he says, "I have no pleasure in you," behold, here I am, let him do to me what seems good to him. (vv. 25b, 26)

Uncertainty about what the future held was tied to an absolute surrender to the will of God. Whether or not David would again join the ark in Jerusalem was a matter for the Lord. It was not for David to take the ark with him.

David's longing was to "see both it and his [or its] dwelling place" (v. 25). This hope of David became expressed in a number of psalms (for example, Psalm 23:6; 27:4). And yet this was his faith: "Let [the LORD] do to me what seems good to him" (v. 26). This is true faith: to trust ultimately in the goodness and wisdom of God, whatever that might involve.

Did Jesus remember these words of David when he prayed (not far from this spot), "Father, if you are willing, remove this cup from me. Nevertheless, not my will, but yours, be done" (Luke 22:42)?

David's words received no response from Zadok. Therefore David took matters further.

The king also said to Zadok the priest, "Are you not a seer?[30] Go back to the city in peace, with your two sons, Ahimaaz your son, and Jonathan the son of Abiathar. See, I will wait at the fords of the wilderness until word comes from you to inform me." (vv. 27, 28)

David's utter trust in God did not make him passive.[31] David would work for what he believed to be right. He began to put in place a scheme. Key players in the scheme would be the two priests and their two sons. The scheme depended on these four being inside the city. They would provide David with vital intelligence. David would wait for word from them at the places where the Jordan could be crossed on the way to the wilderness further east.[32]

David's faith (which required the ark to be returned to the city) and his plan (which required the priests and their sons to be in the city) worked together. Both aspects were carried out. On the one hand, "So Zadok and Abiathar carried the ark of God back to Jerusalem" (v. 29a). On the other hand, "they remained there" (v. 29b).

Stage 3: Up the Mount of Olives (v. 30)

The final stage of the procession from the city was overwhelming for all concerned.

But David went up the ascent of the Mount of Olives,[33] weeping as he went, barefoot and with his head covered.[34] And all the people who were with him covered their heads, and they went up, weeping as they went. (v. 30)

Tears flowed that day as the king and his people climbed the Mount of Olives, on the other side of the Kidron Valley. David led the expressions of sorrow, despair, shame, and humiliation. This was surely David's darkest day.

Message 2: Ahithophel's Betrayal (v. 31)

Our passage began with David receiving the news of Absalom's rise. It closes with a second informant bringing news to David: "And it was told David, 'Ahithophel is among the conspirators with Absalom'" (v. 31a).

Just when it seemed that things could get no worse, David heard that his most valued advisor, the wise and trusted Ahithophel, had betrayed him (see 16:23). With the support of "the men of Israel" (v. 13) and the counsel of Ahithophel, Absalom's success must have seemed all but certain.

What could David do? He prayed. "And David said, 'O Lord, please turn the counsel of Ahithophel into foolishness'" (v. 31b). We hear again the sentiment that will find full expression in many psalms. Specifically Psalm 41:9 has often been understood as a reference to Ahithophel and his treachery:[35]

> Even my close friend in whom I trusted,
>   who ate my bread, has lifted his heel against me.

Jesus applied these very words to Judas, the one who betrayed him (John 13:18).

As we see David's darkest day, let us appreciate afresh the Son of David whose sufferings were anticipated in David's sufferings, but whose sufferings (unlike David's) had nothing to do with his own sin and everything to do with ours. He understood that he "must suffer many things and be rejected by the elders and chief priests and scribes, and be killed" (Luke 9:22).

Those who join Jesus Christ must join him in his sufferings (as Ittai joined David and as Zadok served David). We are "fellow heirs with Christ, provided we suffer with him in order that we may also be glorified with him" (Romans 8:17).

32

People Who Met David

2 SAMUEL 15:19—16:14

THE GOSPELS OF THE NEW TESTAMENT that tell the story of the life, death, and resurrection of Jesus Christ include numerous examples of people who met Jesus. In each case the impact of Jesus on the person concerned and his or her response to him invites me (and every reader) to identify with the person who met Jesus and reflect on the impact that Jesus has on me and my response to him. Who can forget Levi the tax collector (Mark 2), Jairus and his daughter (Mark 5), the Syrophoenician woman (Mark 7), the rich young ruler (Mark 10), blind Bartimaeus (Mark 10), Nicodemus (John 3), the woman of Samaria (John 4), the woman caught in adultery (John 8), the man born blind (John 9), Lazarus, Martha, and Mary (John 11), Pontius Pilate (John 18), and many, many more?

These encounters with Jesus are powerful features of the Gospels. Without them the Gospels would be unrecognizable. They teach us that the kingdom of God is not an abstract idea but a personal reality: the King speaks to individuals in their need, weakness, guilt, ignorance, and suffering, or in their prosperity, power, self-righteousness, arrogance, and complacency. He heals, forgives, teaches, delivers, and humbles those who listen to him, believe him, and come to him. The kingdom of God is about the King *and his people*. There is certainly more to the kingdom of God than this, but not less.

In this, as in many other ways, the kingdom of David was an anticipation of the kingdom of Jesus Christ. The story of David's flight from Jerusalem is punctuated by incidents that we might call "people who met David." The importance of each of these encounters lies in how King David dealt with the person concerned and the person's response to the king.

As we follow David leaving Jerusalem, crossing the Kidron Valley, climbing the Mount of Olives and heading east toward the wilderness, we witness six encounters with King David.[1]

(1) Ittai, who stayed with David (15:19–22).
(2) Zadok and Abiathar, who served David (15:24–29).
(3) Hushai, who was David's friend (15:32–37).
(4) Ziba, who appeared to be on David's side (16:1–4).
(5) Shimei, who cursed David (16:5–8).
(6) Abishai, who got it wrong (16:9–14).

Ittai, Who Stayed with David (15:19–22)

In our previous chapter we saw the circumstances in which Ittai, the leader of 600 Gittites, came before the king as David paused at the last house on the outskirts of Jerusalem (15:17, 18). In the crowds who were passing before the king, David singled out Ittai and spoke to him.

> Then the king said to Ittai the Gittite, "Why do you also go with us? Go back and stay with the king, for you are a foreigner and also an exile from your home. You came only yesterday, and shall I today make you wander about with us, since I go I know not where? Go back and take your brothers with you, and may the LORD show steadfast love and faithfulness to you [or, Go back and take your brothers with you. Steadfast love and faithfulness!]."[2] (vv. 19, 20)

We noted the gist of David's speech to Ittai in our last chapter. Six particular points are noteworthy. First, David saw a significant similarity between the circumstances he now faced and the past experience of the Gittites. They were exiles. He was about to become an exile, "going wherever I am going" (v. 20 AT). The comparison is highlighted by the repeated emphatic Hebrew pronouns "you" (in v. 19) and "I" (in v. 20).[3]

Second, "an exile from your home" (v. 19) is literally "an exile with respect to your *place*." The wording reminds us of the promise that the Lord had made concerning David and his people: "I will appoint a *place* for my people Israel" (7:10). By his departure from Jerusalem David had become an exile from his "place," just as Ittai and his men had from theirs.

However, third, the similarity of their circumstances was a reason, said David, for Ittai and the Gittites *not* to go "with us." They were already exiles. It did not seem right for them to be expected to become exiles from their exile!

Nonetheless, fourth, when David said "with us" (v. 19), there was a wordplay on Ittai's name, which sounds like the Hebrew for "with me."[4] The name suggests loyalty and companionship. David was indicating that in these circumstances Ittai and his fellow Gittites did not need to live up to Ittai's name.

Fifth, David surprisingly referred to Absalom as "the king" (v. 19).[5] This was not irony, nor was it suggesting that Absalom's kingship was legitimate. It was an acknowledgment of political reality. If Absalom had been acclaimed king (15:10), and if he were to take the now undefended city of Jerusalem from which David had fled, then he would in fact be king.

Sixth, David expressed his goodwill toward Ittai and his men in fulsome terms—"steadfast love and faithfulness" (v. 20), or "kindness and truth." This was David's commitment to the Gittites. "Kindness" had characterized David at his best (2:5, 6; 9:1; 10:2). He would be true to his word.

For his part, however, Ittai (presumably speaking for both himself and his men) was devoted to serving only one king, and that was David.

> But Ittai answered the king, "As the LORD lives, and as my lord the king lives, wherever my lord the king shall be, whether for death or for life, there also will your servant be." (v. 21)

This was an astonishing declaration. This Philistine from Gath (like Uriah the Hittite earlier) had become a man who acknowledged the Lord God of Israel. Furthermore, his acknowledgment of God was tied to his acknowledgment of King David (twice called "my lord the king"). "I belong just as closely to you as you do to God," he seemed to say.[6] In life or in death, Ittai's place was with his king (cf. Philippians 1:19–24).

Ittai ("With Me") was a model disciple. David could have said, "Truly, I tell you, with no one in Israel have I found such faith" (Matthew 8:10). What he did say was, "Go then, pass on" (v. 22a). David welcomed this devoted foreigner into his kingdom, albeit a kingdom under threat and facing exile. Ittai, his men, and their families accepted the invitation. "So Ittai the Gittite passed on with all his men and all the little ones[7] who were with him" (v. 22b). Altogether they would have numbered several thousand.[8]

Zadok and Abithar, Who Served David (15:24–29)

As the procession was crossing the brook Kidron, there was a second important encounter, this time with the priests Zadok and Abiathar (15:24–29). We considered this episode in our last chapter. Here we notice how these two men served their king, but not by staying with him, like Ittai. They returned to what would soon be enemy territory, at great risk to themselves, to do whatever David asked of them.

Hushai, Who Was David's Friend (15:32–37)

The third encounter occurred as David reached the summit of the Mount of Olives.

Hushai's Well-Timed Arrival at the Mountain (v. 32)

> While David was coming to the summit, where God was worshiped, behold, Hushai the Archite came to meet him with his coat torn and dirt on his head. (v. 32)

As David reached the top of the Mount of Olives, there would have been a clear view of the city of Jerusalem, some 200 feet below and behind him.[9] The spot is enigmatically described as "where God was worshiped" (v. 32). Exactly what these words refer to is not clear. They could mean "where he (that is, David) was in the habit of worshipping God."[10] The word translated "worship" refers simply to the physical action of bowing down and by implication the recognition and honor given by this act to the one before whom it is done (see examples in 1 Samuel 15:25, 30, 31; 20:41; 24:8; 25:23, 41; 28:14; 2 Samuel 1:2; 9:6, 8; 14:4, 22, 33; 15:5; 16:4; 18:21, 28; 24:20). Here it is possible that we are being told that the summit of the Mount of Olives was a place where David would come to pray. It is further possible that this is why it was Jesus' custom to come to the Mount of Olives (Luke 22:39; cf. 21:37; John 8:1; 18:2). In this, as in so many ways, he was "the son of David."

As David was approaching this place of prayer, the answer to his most recent prayer (15:31) came to meet him.[11] That is what Hushai the Archite will turn out to be.

The evidence suggests that the Archites were a Benjaminite family (Joshua 16:2).[12] This would mean that Hushai belonged to Saul's tribe. He makes a stark contrast to another Benjaminite we will meet shortly.

Hushai shared fully in the despair and sadness that overwhelmed all of those who were leaving Jerusalem with David (15:30). His torn clothes and dirt on his head were genuine signs of grief (cf. 1:2).

David's Prayer and David's Plan (vv. 33–36)

Having prayed that the Lord would turn the counsel of Ahithophel into foolishness (15:31), David immediately recognized Hushai as the possible answer to his prayers.

> David said to him, "If you go on with me, you will be a burden to me. But if you return to the city and say to Absalom, 'I will be your servant, O king;

as I have been your father's servant in time past, so now I will be your servant,' then you will defeat for me the counsel of Ahithophel." (vv. 33, 34)

There is no tension or contradiction in Biblical thought between asking *the Lord* to cause something to happen and then working hard to make that very thing come about. The sovereignty of God (on which our prayers depend) does not undermine human responsibility and initiative. Quite the opposite. David worked to accomplish precisely what he asked the Lord to do. When David's scheme succeeded, the narrator is perfectly clear that it was *the Lord's* doing (see 17:14b).

Hushai was probably an old man. In the fugitive life that David was facing, Hushai's presence would be "a burden" (15:33). How much more useful he could be if he stayed in Jerusalem and pretended to switch his allegiance to Absalom; then, in a way yet to be worked out, Hushai would be in a position to undermine the famously brilliant advice that Ahithophel would give to the usurper. David could not foresee what opportunity Hushai might have to do this. Hushai would have to respond to the situation as it developed. Only the end goal was clear: to "defeat for me the counsel of Ahithophel" (v. 34).

That was the plan. Carrying it out might be trickier. However, Hushai would not be alone, and it so happened that David had already set up a network for Hushai to communicate back to David. This had been accomplished just before the climb up the Mount of Olives, when Zadok and Abiathar had met with David (15:24–29).

> Are not Zadok and Abiathar the priests with you there? So whatever you hear from the king's house, tell it to Zadok and Abiathar the priests. Behold, their two sons are with them there, Ahimaaz, Zadok's son, and Jonathan, Abiathar's son, and by them you shall send to me everything you hear. (vv. 35, 36)

There were four people in Jerusalem whom Hushai could trust—because David trusted them.

Hushai's Well-Timed Arrival in Jerusalem (v. 37)

Like Zadok and Abiathar, Hushai did not hesitate to embrace the dangerous mission given to him by David, and he arrived back in the city in the nick of time. "So Hushai, David's friend, came into the city, just as Absalom was entering Jerusalem" (v. 37). The Hebrew probably suggests that Hushai reached the city just a little before Absalom.[13] Perhaps we should imagine this giving him just enough time to clean himself up and put on some fresh clothes.

The timing of Hushai's arrival in Jerusalem also indicates that David escaped in the nick of time. Had Absalom reached the city only a short time earlier, David and his entourage would have been visible on the Mount of Olives. Presumably the time that it took Hushai to descend the mountain and enter the city allowed David and those with him to get over to the other side of the summit and therefore out of sight from the city.[14]

At this point Hushai is called "David's friend" (v. 37). It is often conjectured that this may refer to an official position—"the friend of the king," a close confidant and advisor to the king (cf. 1 Kings 4:5).[15] This is beside the point here.[16] Hushai was David's "friend" in every sense of the word,[17] and his conduct in the coming days will prove it.

Ziba, Who Appeared to Be on David's Side (16:1–4)

As David and those accompanying him moved beyond the summit to the Mount of Olives and therefore out of sight from the city (with no time to spare), a fourth meeting took place.

He Appeared to Be Generous (vv. 1, 2)

> When David had passed a little beyond the summit, Ziba the servant of Mephibosheth met him, with a couple of donkeys saddled, bearing two hundred loaves of bread, a hundred bunches of raisins, a hundred of summer fruits, and a skin of wine. (16:1)

I confess that the skepticism suggested in the headings I have used in this section ("*appeared* to be . . .") comes partly from the wisdom of hindsight, after reading the rest of the story (if you, too, want to cheat, glance ahead to 19:24–30). However, we did wonder about the transparency of this man when we first met him in 2 Samuel 9. There he was introduced as "a servant of the house of Saul," who presented himself to David as "your servant" (9:2), but we saw reasons to wonder about his motives. Therefore, even without reading ahead we might be cautious about his display of generosity.

However, we must admit that Ziba's performance was impressive. The "couple of donkeys" (v. 1) might have in fact been "a string of donkeys" (NIV).[18] They carried a substantial quantity of provisions. In the urgent departure from Jerusalem (15:14), the thousands who were fleeing with David probably had little time to gather much by way of supplies.

However, David seemed to have some doubts. "And the king said to Ziba, 'Why have you brought these?'" (v. 2a). The literal wording of the question is less precise that that: "What are you doing with these things?" It was a question about whether these things belonged to Ziba and his right to be bringing them.[19] Remember that Ziba had been appointed by David to look after the lands that he had given to Mephibosheth (9:10). Had Ziba run off with a load of Mephibosheth's produce? David, it seems, had doubts similar to ours about Ziba.

> Ziba answered, "The donkeys are for the king's household to ride on, the bread and summer fruit for the young men to eat, and the wine for those who faint in the wilderness to drink." (v. 2b)

Ziba did not answer the question David had asked (adding to our suspicions), but rather spoke of the use to which he hoped the things would be put. David and his family had left Jerusalem on foot. The donkeys would provide not only some respite from walking, but also a measure of dignity to the royals. The food would, of course, be welcome. With the wine Ziba recognized the hardships that lay ahead. They were heading for "the wilderness" (see 15:23, 28), where people faint and grow weary (see 16:14). Ziba was thoughtful, considerate, and generous. Or was he?

He Appeared to Be Loyal (v. 3)

David had a follow-up question. "And the king said, 'And where is your master's son?'" (v. 3a). "Your master" was, of course, Saul.[20] Ziba had never been required by David to relinquish his role as "a servant of the house of Saul." On the contrary (see 9:2, 9, 10). "Your master's son" was Saul's grandson, Mephibosheth.[21] If David had his doubts about the honesty of Ziba's generous gifts, then this question was pointed: "And where is the owner of what you are so generously giving us?"[22]

This gave Ziba the perfect opportunity (for which he was almost certainly looking) to present himself as a loyal servant of David at this time of so much treachery. "Ziba said to the king, 'Behold, he remains in Jerusalem, for he said, "Today the house of Israel will give me back the kingdom of my father"'" (v. 3b).

The first part of Ziba's reply was undoubtedly true. Indeed, "he remains in Jerusalem" (v. 3) exactly reproduces the last we have heard about Mephibosheth in 9:13.[23] However, Ziba added that the reason Mephibosheth had stayed in the city now was a hope that the present crisis would lead to the kingdom returning to the house of Saul. The implausibility of this hope is beside the point. Ziba was suggesting that Mephibosheth (unlike Ziba!) had not repaid David's kindness with loyalty to David.

In due course we will see that Ziba was lying (19:24).

He Appeared to Be Grateful (v. 4)

It is a sign of just how distressed he was that David believed Ziba's slander without further inquiry. "Then the king said to Ziba, 'Behold, all that belonged to Mephibosheth is now yours'" (v. 4a). This, we might suspect, was Ziba's plan all along. In due course such suspicions will be confirmed (19:24–30). Here we note that David was taken in by Ziba's performance. David was deceived. Perhaps he was also foolish in failing to ask further questions (contrast 1:1–16).

Ziba concluded his act with a flourish. "And Ziba said, 'I pay homage; let me ever find favor in your sight, my lord the king'" (v. 4b). "Pay homage" represents the same Hebrew word translated "worshiped" in 15:32 and refers to bowing down before a superior. It is worth noting that in the earlier episode (2 Samuel 9) Mephibosheth repeatedly "paid homage" to David (9:6, 8), but Ziba did not. Now that he had benefited greatly from deceiving the king, he at last bowed before him.

Shimei, Who Cursed David (16:5–8)

As David and his people moved further from the city, now on the lower slopes of the Mount of Olives, they encountered a dramatic corroboration of Ziba's claim that the house of Saul was rising against David.

They came to Bahurim, about one and a half miles northeast of Jerusalem.[24] This was where, years earlier, the miserable, weeping Paltiel had been forced to abandon his wife Michal as she was being taken to David (see 3:16). Bahurim again became a place of weeping as the tearful fugitives continued on their way from Jerusalem toward the Jordan valley.[25]

> When King David came to Bahurim, there came out a man of the family of the house of Saul, whose name was Shimei, the son of Gera, and as he came he cursed continually. (v. 5)

For the first time since the troubles between David and Absalom began (13:21), the narrator uses the full title "King David." We should be perfectly clear that whatever was happening to David, whatever danger he was in, however precarious his reign had become, he had not been rejected by God, as had Saul (see 7:15). He was still *King David*. It was this reality that the man who came out from Bahurim defied.

His name was Shimei. What he did on this day was to determine the rest of his life. He will appear again in the history when David returns to Jerusalem (19:16–23), near the end of David's life (1 Kings 2:8, 9), and early in

Solomon's reign (1 Kings 2:36–46). On each occasion what he did on this day will be remembered.

Shimei belonged to the wider family of Saul; in other words, he was from the tribe of Benjamin. His father, Gera, had a good Benjaminite name (see Genesis 46:21).

Shimei was mad with rage. At the sight of David he burst into a tirade of curses. His vile words were supported with violent actions.

> And he threw stones at David and at all the servants of King David, and all the people and all the mighty men were on his right hand and on his left. (v. 6)

The description (like the scene) is confusing. If it weren't so serious it would be comical. The furious fellow was shouting abuse and hurling stones at King David (note the full title again) and the great throng of people around him, including his "mighty men" (valiant warriors). The text may mean that the mighty men were protecting David on both sides, or it could mean that the crazy man was hurling the rocks with both hands: "from his right hand and from his left."[26] Either way this one man was hardly a real threat (at least physically) to the horde surrounding David.

His words were more dangerous than the stones.

> And Shimei said as he cursed, "Get out, get out, you man of blood, you worthless man! The LORD has avenged on you all the blood of the house of Saul, in whose place you have reigned, and the LORD has given the kingdom into the hand of your son Absalom. See, your evil is on you,[27] for you are a man of blood." (vv. 7, 8)

"Get out, get out" (v. 7) were stinging words because that is exactly what the king was doing—getting out of Jerusalem. The power of Shimei's words lay in the interpretation he put on David's departure.

He called him a "man of blood" (v. 7)—that is, a man who had shed blood,[28] a murderer. He added, "You worthless man!" (v. 7; literally, "man of worthlessness"). In the story told in 1 Samuel there were a number of "worthless men." The dreadful sons of Eli were so described (1 Samuel 2:12); likewise some fellows who did not believe in King Saul (1 Samuel 10:27), the fool Nabal (1 Samuel 25:17, 25), and a number of those who had attached themselves to David in the early days (1 Samuel 30:22).[29] To describe David in these terms was an ultimate insult.

The irony is that we (the readers of this history) know that David *had* been a murderer. We might even have been prepared to call him a "worthless man" as we saw how he behaved with Bathsheba and Uriah. However, that is not what Shimei had in mind.

Shimei saw Absalom's present rebellion as the Lord's vengeance on David for "all the blood of the house of Saul" (v. 8). Almost certainly Shimei represented the views of many others, especially among those who had been close to Saul. When we remember that David had been with the Philistines (1 Samuel 27) who had (in effect) killed Saul and his sons, including Jonathan, we can understand rumors that he had something to do with their deaths. Perhaps that is why the historian went to such lengths to demonstrate that David had nothing at all to do with those tragedies and that he lamented them (1:17–27). Similarly, it is easy to see how David could be thought to have had a hand in the deaths of Abner (3:27) and Ish-bosheth (4:6). Again the historian has been at pains to prove David's innocence in these matters (3:28, 37; 4:9–11). But Shimei was convinced that the rumors were the truth.

Again there is bitter irony here. None of Shimei's charges were true, and yet we know that, for quite different reasons, the Lord's hand *was* behind the troubles that had come on David's kingdom. The Lord had said, "I will raise up evil against you out of your own house" (12:11). We know, and David knew, that this is what had happened. However, what Shimei completely missed was the Lord's grace toward David. God had promised that David's kingdom would be established forever (7:16), and he had "put away" David's sin (12:13). Shimei had no idea what the Lord was doing!

Abishai, Who Got It Wrong (16:9–14)

As Shimei raved on, hurling curses and rocks at David and those with him, one of David's people had a suggestion.

The Abishai Solution (v. 9)

> Then Abishai the son of Zeruiah said to the king, "Why should this dead dog curse my lord the king? Let me go over and take off his head." (v. 9)

Abishai shared with his brother Joab the impulsive determination we have seen repeatedly from these sons of David's sister, Zeruiah (1 Samuel 26:6–9; 2 Samuel 2:24; 3:30; see 1 Chronicles 2:16). He had a simple solution to the nuisance of Shimei. Removing his head should settle him down.

Abishai's contempt for Shimei is captured in the words, "this dead dog" (16:9). Useless trash, he might have said.[30]

The David Correction (vv. 10–12)

David's reply to Abishai gives us the clearest insight so far into his own view of the whole situation.

> But the king said, "What have I to do with you, you sons of Zeruiah? If he is cursing because the LORD has said to him, 'Curse David,' who then shall say, 'Why have you done so?'" And David said to Abishai and to all his servants, "Behold, my own son seeks my life; how much more now may this Benjaminite! Leave him alone, and let him curse, for the LORD has told him to. It may be that the LORD will look on the wrong done to me [or, my iniquity],[31] and that the LORD will repay me with good for his cursing today." (vv. 10–12)

"You sons of Zeruiah" (v. 10) suggests that Joab may have joined his brother in proposing the quick solution to the noisy problem. (This is the first indication of the important fact that Joab was still with David.) However, the ways of Abishai and Joab were not the ways of David.[32] David rightly understood the situation in the light of the Lord's word to him about the consequences of his sins (12:11). He did not, of course, mean that Shimei was consciously cursing him in obedience to a command he had actually heard from the Lord. On the contrary, Shimei's own actions and motivations were wrong (as he himself will later admit, 19:19). However, David could see the Lord's purpose in it. This is a very important part of the Bible's teaching about the sovereignty of God and evil. Evil never thwarts God's good purposes. Neither is evil ever justified because it is used by God for good. But the Lord is able to take evil and with it to achieve good (see Genesis 50:20; Acts 2:23). David understood that he was to receive the curses of Shimei in the light of God's purpose, not of Shimei's hatred. "Not what I will, but what you will" is what he meant (compare Mark 14:36). He was "prepared to let the cursing go unanswered, not as an admission of guilt but as an act of faith."[33] He knew that "those who suffer according to God's will entrust their souls to a faithful Creator while doing good" (1 Peter 4:19).

Indeed the abuse coming from Shimei was a small thing to David, when his "own son" was seeking his life (2 Samuel 16:11). "My own son" is literally "my son who came out from my belly." David was echoing precisely the promise the Lord had given him: "I will raise up your offspring after you, *who shall come out from your belly*" (7:12 AT). If this son, about whom the Lord had promised so much, was now seeking David's life, the curses of the crazy Shimei were a minor matter.

Most important of all, David's acceptance of the Lord's will was not a matter of stoic resignation. He did not know how and he did not know when, but he hoped expectantly that he would receive "good" from the Lord. That much of verse 12 is clear. This expectation had been expressed in David's words to Zadok in 15:25. Of course, it was a hope that depended on God's grace ("If I find favor in the eyes of the LORD . . ."). That is what "It may be . . . that the LORD will . . ." means here. Nonetheless it is clear that David knew God's grace toward him.

The first part of verse 12 is more difficult. The Hebrew says, "It may be that the LORD will look on the wrong done to me [or, my iniquity or guilt] . . ." Because of the awkwardness of expecting the Lord to look on his wickedness and repay him with "good," various alternatives have been proposed (the ESV is an example). The Hebrew text itself has a marginal alternative meaning "on my eye," understood to mean "on my tears." Along the same lines, the ancient versions have "on my affliction."[34] But the awkwardness of the Hebrew is precisely what David had come to know of God's grace toward him.[35] The cursing David endured from Shimei was indeed a consequence of his iniquity. But the Lord who had seen his iniquity will in due course return good to David in place of the cursing. That is the grace on which David depended.

Abishai's understandable response to the furious abuse of his king serves to highlight the extraordinarily different perspective that the grace of God, when known, brings to life. That was the perspective of King David. It is the perspective that can say, "Father, forgive them, for they know not what they do" (Luke 23:34).

And David Continued on His Way (vv. 13, 14)

So David and his men went on the road, while Shimei went along on the hillside opposite him and cursed as he went and threw stones at him and flung dust. And the king, and all the people who were with him, arrived weary [at the Jordan].[36] And there he refreshed himself. (vv. 13, 14)

Shimei's cursing continued, from what he probably judged to be a safe distance along the hillside. David and all those with him arrived at last, probably at the Jordan River. It had been exhausting, emotionally as well as physically. In the relative safety of the Jordan valley they rested. The king refreshed himself, perhaps with some of the wine that Ziba had supplied.

Look back at these people who met David. Ittai, the model disciple, only wanted to be "with" his king (cf. John 6:68). Zadok and Abiathar were willing to risk their lives to serve their king (cf. Philippians 1:21). Hushai was David's friend (cf. John 15:14, 15). Ziba made a show of his devotion to the king, but it was false (cf. Luke 21:4). Shimei abused the king (cf. John 19:15). Abishai thought that he could help his king by violence (cf. John 18:10).

Take time to reflect on these people who met David. It is not difficult to see similarities with people who met Jesus. It is good for us to consider ways in which we are (or should be) like and unlike these people who met the king.

33

The Friend and the Traitor

2 SAMUEL 16:15–23

IT IS A WONDERFUL THING to be a friend of the King, especially when the King is Jesus Christ. No other friendship is the same as being a friend of Jesus. This friendship cannot be casual. The privilege is immense, and it must be taken with the utmost seriousness. The King has enemies. His friends will therefore have enemies. A friend of the King cannot be a friend of the King's enemies.

On the night that Jesus made the journey out of Jerusalem, across the Kidron Valley, and up the Mount of Olives (John 18:1), he spoke at length with his disciples. One of his themes was friendship.

> This is my commandment, that you love one another as I have loved you. Greater love has no one than this, that someone lay down his life for his friends. You are my friends if you do what I command you. No longer do I call you servants, for the servant does not know what his master is doing; but I have called you friends, for all that I have heard from my Father I have made known to you. (John 15:12–15)

Of course, the friends of Jesus do what he commands them. But being a "friend" of Jesus is better than being a "servant" because of what Jesus shares with his friends (John 15:15). He discloses to his friends what his Father has disclosed to him. In this way, remarkably, Jesus' friends enjoy his trust.

As the disciples of Jesus remembered that momentous night, the words of Jesus would have been very precious. "You are my *friends*" (John 15:14).

As we have seen, the events of that night had deep connections with the experience of King David about 1,000 years earlier as he made the same journey that Jesus made. There was a man who was known as David's "friend"

411

(2 Samuel 15:37). David trusted him, and he did what David commanded him. I would not be surprised if Jesus had Hushai the Archite in mind when he said to his disciples, "You are my friends" (John 15:14).

On that same night Jesus also spoke about a traitor who, he said, would be the fulfillment of Psalm 41:9: "He who ate my bread has lifted his heel against me" (John 13:18). Jesus was speaking of Judas Iscariot who that very night betrayed him (John 13:21–30; 18:2–5).

This is another indication that Jesus was conscious of the profound connection between the events of that night and the long-past experience of King David. Psalm 41 is a psalm of King David. If (as is likely) the psalm was composed with reference to David's flight from Absalom (see the superscription of Psalm 3), then the traitor of whom David spoke was almost certainly Ahithophel.[1] Ahithophel had been David's trusted adviser who, for reasons we have guessed at but have not been told, had gone over to support Absalom in his rebellion against his father's kingdom (15:12, 31).

The kingdom of David and the kingdom of Jesus Christ had friends and traitors. As we watch the conduct of Hushai, David's friend, and Ahithophel, who betrayed him, we should examine our own hearts and behavior. Are we friends of the King?

We have followed David and those with him as they went out from Jerusalem, across the Kidron Valley, up the Mount of Olives, and on toward the wilderness east of the Jordan River. At the summit of the Mount of Olives David had met Hushai and sent him back into Jerusalem in order to "defeat for me the counsel of Ahithophel" (15:34). Hushai reached the city "just as Absalom was entering Jerusalem" (15:37). The narrative followed David on his eastward journey in 16:1–14, but in verse 15 takes us back to Jerusalem, shortly after Hushai had arrived.

The Traitor's Arrival (v. 15)

"Now Absalom and all the people, the men of Israel, came [or, had come][2] to Jerusalem, and Ahithophel with him" (v. 15). "All the people" were those who had joined Absalom when the trumpet had sounded throughout all the tribes of Israel, summoning the nation to acclaim Absalom as king (15:10). This would at least include fighting men. Absalom came to Jerusalem with a considerable force.

"*All the people*, the men of Israel" (16:15) coming into Jerusalem with Absalom contrast with David "and *all the people* who were with him" arriving "weary" at their destination, as far as possible from Jerusalem in the previous verse (v. 14). There is no suggestion that Absalom and his company were "weary" (v. 14). They did not need to "refresh" themselves, as David did (v. 14). The pressure was all on David.

The critical factor in Absalom's favor was not superior numbers (although his people must have substantially outnumbered David's), but one particular supporter. "Ahithophel [was] with him." Before long we will see what a formidable advantage this gave to Absalom. However, the mention of Ahithophel's name reminds us of David's prayer (to "turn the counsel of Ahithophel into foolishness," 15:31) and Hushai's mission (to "defeat for [David] the counsel of Ahithophel," 15:34). Only if the Lord answered David's prayer and Hushai was successful in his task (which were one and the same thing) could David and his kingdom survive.

The Friend's Friendship (vv. 16–19)

Our eyes are therefore now on Hushai, who is reintroduced to the narrative from the perspective of Absalom, who of course knew nothing of the conversation with David earlier (15:32–36). "And when Hushai the Archite, David's friend, came to Absalom, Hushai said to Absalom, 'Long live the king! Long live the king!'" (v. 16).

Imagine Absalom's surprise. He would have noticed that many people had left Jerusalem. David was obviously not there. He met no resistance as he entered the city, laying claim to the throne. Then who should appear before him but Hushai the Archite, the well-known friend of David? If Ahithophel had a reason to turn against David (as we have surmised)—a reason that Absalom may have exploited—that was not the case with Hushai. His reputation as "David's friend" was untarnished (15:37). The last person Absalom expected to see still in Jerusalem was Hushai the Archite.

Absalom did not know what we know. Since we have heard the conversation that took place at the summit of the Mount of Olives, we know that Hushai was there in Jerusalem *because* he was David's friend. Unknown to Absalom, but clear to us, Hushai was in Jerusalem *as* David's friend.

Hushai took the initiative. Before Absalom could say a word, Hushai exclaimed, "Long live the king! Long live the king!" (16:16). It tells us something about Absalom's effrontery that he understood these words as an unambiguous reference to himself. He had been acclaimed king in Hebron (15:10). He had stolen the hearts of the men of Israel (15:6). David had fled, and Absalom had come unchallenged into Jerusalem. Of course he was "the king."[3]

But we know better. Hushai was still "David's friend" (15:37). The king he hoped would "live" was not Absalom, but the old king, David.[4] Hushai did *not* say "Long live King Absalom!"[5] The irony is that in the very act of appearing to celebrate Absalom as king, Hushai was already working to save King David's life.[6]

Absalom (believing that the acclamation applied to him) was astonished. "And Absalom said to Hushai, 'Is this your loyalty [or kindness] to your friend? Why did you not go with your friend?'" (v. 17). Absalom saw Hushai's presence in Jerusalem and what he said as a contradiction of his friendship to David.

There is irony in Absalom's words. "Kindness" (v. 17; ESV, "loyalty") has been a very important word characterizing King David (see 15:20, ESV, "steadfast love"). It is a word that normally refers to the compassionate acts of a superior to an inferior. So when Absalom suggested that Hushai should have shown "kindness" to David, he was implicitly subordinating David to Hushai. For Absalom, David was no longer the *king*. Furthermore, Absalom spoke of David being Hushai's friend rather than Hushai being David's friend. This reversal of roles was another subtle stripping David of his kingly status. David was *Hushai's* "friend" who needed *Hushai's* "kindness."

If I have the honor of being a "friend" of the king, that does not mean that I would dare refer to the king as "*my* friend." This friendship is not a mutual relationship between equals. He is always my king. In the books of Samuel this is related to the fact that while many people are said to "love" David, David is never said to "love" others. Too much should not be read into this. It does not mean that David did not in any sense "love" or that he was not in any sense a "friend." The language just reflects the fact that relationships with the king are not symmetrical. (I will still sing, "What a friend we have in Jesus," but understanding that the Bible, for good reason, does not put it like that.)

At the same time, what Absalom said to Hushai probably expressed his genuine perplexity at finding Hushai in Jerusalem. It is not what he expected. He probably could hardly believe his luck!

In order to confirm Absalom's misunderstanding of the situation Hushai continued with his double speak.

> And Hushai said to Absalom, "No, for whom the LORD and this people and all the men of Israel have chosen, his I will be, and with him I will remain. And again, whom should I serve? Should it not be his son? As I have served your father,[7] so I will serve[8] you." (vv. 18, 19)

The deception is brilliant. It worked because of Absalom's arrogant presumption. Hushai did not say that he had switched his allegiance (like

Ahithophel), but his words would be taken that way by anyone who thought like Absalom. Everything he said, however, had another meaning.

Even his "No" must have meant to Absalom, "No, David is not (as you put it) my 'friend.'" However, Hushai's real meaning was, "No, I have not (as you think) betrayed my 'friend.'"

Hushai's insistence that he will belong to the one "whom the LORD . . . has chosen" (v. 18)[9] must have been taken by Absalom as a remarkable endorsement of his aspirations. Absalom had not been so bold as to make that claim, but I am sure he did not mind at all if someone else (especially Hushai) made it for him. However, for Hushai the one "whom the LORD has chosen" would always be David.[10]

The reference to the one whom "this people and all the men of Israel have chosen" obviously meant Absalom, if you heard it with Absalom's ears. Had he not stolen their hearts (15:6, 13) and been acclaimed king "throughout all the tribes of Israel" (15:10)? However, Hushai had a longer memory and knew that "all the tribes of Israel" through "all the elders of Israel" had "anointed *David* king over Israel" (5:1, 3).

Therefore when Hushai said, "With him I will remain" (16:18). Absalom understood it as a pledge of loyalty to him as the new chosen one. Hushai's secret meaning, however, was that his heart and soul would always be "with" David.

Hushai had a second argument[11] to advance, the true meaning of which was even more carefully disguised. "Whom should I serve?" (v. 19). He emphasized the word "I" and carefully introduced the language that David had instructed him to use (see the three uses of an emphatic "I" and "servant" in 15:34). This was the question that the present crisis presented for Hushai. "Whom should *I* serve?"

Hushai pretended to answer his question with a rhetorical question: "Should it not be [before] his son?" And no doubt that is how Absalom heard it. But Hushai cleverly avoided the question about *whom* he would serve with this further question about *where* he would serve. He would indeed serve "before" David's son. That is what *David* had told him to do (15:34)!

Then the brilliant speech was capped with what, to Absalom, must have sounded like a complete swap of commitment from David to Absalom: "As I have served [before] your father, so I will serve [be before] you." What more could Absalom ask? With the benefit of what we know, however, we can understand Hushai's words to mean, "Before you, Absalom, I will be as I have always been, serving your father."[12]

Hushai's speech is superb. The omission of the names "David" and

"Absalom" was critical to his careful ambiguity. No only did he effectively hoodwink Absalom (which was accomplished because Absalom's own narcissism interpreted the words), but he actually expressed the reality of his friendship toward David. He would always belong to the one whom the Lord had chosen. Wherever he was, he would be "with" David (16:17). He would serve King David, even in the presence of David's enemy. Hushai was indeed David's "friend" (v. 17).

The Traitor's Treachery (vv. 20–22)

Absalom was satisfied with what he had (mis)heard from Hushai. It was time now to get on with the task at hand, namely, taking over David's kingdom. "Then Absalom said to Ahithophel, 'Give your counsel. What shall we do?'" (v. 20).

Although Absalom spoke to Ahithophel, he curiously used a plural verb (not apparent in the English "Give" and "your," but obvious in Hebrew). Had Absalom been so impressed with Hushai's speech that he included the newcomer in the request for advice?[13] Perhaps. The surprising thing is that Absalom did not know what to do next. "What do we do now?"

On an earlier occasion, in a similar situation of uncertainty with the future of the kingdom unclear, the one whom the Lord really had chosen "inquired of the LORD" (2:1). Not so Absalom. He asked Ahithophel.

Ahithophel's reply takes your breath away.

> Ahithophel said to Absalom, "Go in to your father's concubines, whom he has left to keep the house, and all Israel will hear that you have made yourself a stench to your father, and the hands of all who are with you will be strengthened." (v. 21)

Ahithophel did not hesitate. His instructions to Absalom were clear, direct, unambiguous, and absolutely outrageous. David had left ten concubines in Jerusalem "to keep the house" (15:16). It is difficult to imagine anything more calculated to offend, disrespect, and hurt David than Ahithophel's cool (cold-blooded would be more accurate) counsel that Absalom have sex with each of his father's concubines. It was not simply that such an act would be understood as a claim to David's throne (cf. Abner taking Saul's concubine in 3:7).[14] Absalom had already claimed to be king. It was the father-son relationship that made the advice in this case particularly crude. It involved what God's Law called "uncovering his father's nakedness" (Leviticus 18:8; 20:11; Deuteronomy 22:30; 27:20; cf. Genesis

9:23; Ezekiel 22:10). It was "an irreversible act of the utmost provocation comparable even to rape."[15]

But it was not stupid. Ahithophel knew that nothing would make the breach between Absalom and David more definite and irreparable than this. There may have been a degree of self-interest in this. After all, if by some means Absalom and David were reconciled, Ahithophel's future would not be bright. Furthermore, once Absalom's course was made irreversible, those who had committed themselves to him would know that there was no turning back. There would be no place for halfhearted commitment. Ahithophel's advice was coldly calculated to serve the conspiracy.

And so it happened. Absalom asked no questions, nor did he hesitate to do what Ahithophel so brutally recommended. "So they pitched a tent for Absalom on the roof. And Absalom went in to his father's concubines in the sight of all Israel" (v. 22). The contemptible acts took place inside the tent. "In the sight of all Israel" should not therefore be taken literally. But "all Israel" knew what Absalom had done. It was public.

But did you notice where it happened? "On the roof" (v. 22)—the very same roof where the tragic sequence of events, in which David's kingdom was now embroiled, began. It was the very roof from which David had spied Bathsheba (11:2). Absalom's disgraceful deed was a consequence of David's disgraceful deed, just as the more recent rape of Tamar by Absalom's brother (13:1–22) was a dreadful reminder of what David had done.

The Traitor's Power (v. 23)

We have seen Hushai, the friend, and Ahithophel, the traitor. At this stage it seems clear where the advantage lay. The ruthless Ahithophel was clearly in control of events. It is difficult to imagine that Hushai (for all his clever talk) could "defeat . . . the counsel of Ahithophel" (15:34). This impression is confirmed in the last verse of the chapter:

> Now in those days the counsel that Ahithophel gave was as if one consulted the word of God; so was all the counsel of Ahithophel esteemed, both by David and by Absalom. (v. 23)

Ahithophel's counsel was powerful. It accomplished its purposes—just like the word of God. Both David and Absalom knew that.

The irony is that Ahithophel's counsel actually did accomplish the purpose of the word of God! Ahithophel's counsel was wicked and contemptible. Absalom's unquestioning acceptance of Ahithophel's advice was inexcusable. And yet behind this evil was the hand of the Lord, achieving his purpose.

In the mysterious way in which God takes evil and employs it to achieve his purposes, this evil act by Absalom was at the same time the Lord's doing. He had said:

> Behold, I will raise up evil against you out of your own house. And I will take your wives before your eyes and give them to your neighbor, and he shall lie with your wives in the sight of this sun. For you did it secretly, but I will do this thing before all Israel and before the sun. (12:11, 12)

On the roof of David's house, this word of the Lord had come to pass. The "neighbor" was David's son, on whom the promise of *blessing* should have rested (7:12). But no reader of this history should miss the fact that the Lord's hand was behind it all.

We do not yet know how, but we should be confident that God's good purpose for David's kingdom will prevail.

It can be terrifying to be a friend of the King. But no matter how chilling the attacks on his kingdom may be, you can be sure that the friends of the King will prevail.

34

The Plan That
Really Matters

2 SAMUEL 17

IT IS DIFFICULT TO BE WISE. As we make decisions, big and small, how can we find *wisdom*? Those of us who have made foolish decisions and suffered the consequences (and who hasn't?) may ask, "How can I learn to be more wise?" Is it a matter of experience? Some people become wiser as the years go by. But some don't. Is it a matter of education? Some well-educated people are wise. But many are not. Is it a matter of luck? Are some people wise and some people fools, just as some are tall and some are short?

It is important to be wise. In every area of life we want and need wisdom. No one wants to make a foolish investment or a stupid purchase or form an unwise friendship or embark on a silly career choice or show poor judgment or give others imprudent advice. By definition a foolish decision is one that we will sooner or later regret.

Living life well has a lot to do with wisdom. The difficult thing for all of us is that what is wise and what is foolish often only become clear when it is too late. We call this the wisdom of hindsight. The wisdom of hindsight is usually the realization that something that seemed wise at the time has turned out to be disastrous. The wisdom of hindsight is of little practical value. We need the wisdom of foresight, which is a bit more difficult. This is the problem. Wisdom is a kind of foresight. It involves seeing the consequences of a decision, a choice, or an action. Since none of us can see very far into the future with much accuracy, it is difficult to be wise.

This is a major theme in the Bible. "Where shall wisdom be found?" asks the author of the book of Job in a wonderful poem exploring this human

419

dilemma (Job 28). Indeed the purpose of becoming familiar with the Bible is "to make you wise" (2 Timothy 3:15). The Bible does this by teaching us about God. The beginning and foundation of wisdom is taking God seriously (what the Bible often calls "the fear of the LORD," Job 28:28; Psalm 111:10; Proverbs 1:7). That is because God is the one who knows and determines the future. Trusting *him* is always wise.

The most important thing that the Bible teaches us about God is that he has a plan for the future. Our plans, decisions, choices, and judgments can seem to be wise and right, but God's plan will prevail (see Proverbs 14:12; 16:25). We do not know every detail of God's plan, but we can know what he has promised. When we take God's promises seriously, we understand that even the most impressive human plans are unreliable. Certainly human plans that disregard, despise, or oppose God's promises are foolish, no matter how brilliant they seem.

Our problem with all this is that human plans can be very impressive indeed. Karl Marx had a plan for the world that persuaded many, as did Adolf Hitler. With the wisdom of hindsight the foolishness of these plans may be clear, but that did not help those who really did think that one or other of these plans would be the future. We are less clear about contemporary human plans that will one day be seen to be foolish.

If you had lived in the days of Jesus' earthly life, the plans of those who were determined to destroy him and his cause would have seemed very impressive indeed. Those in the religious establishment in Jerusalem, with all their learning and tradition, plotted to do away with him. They managed to enlist the power of the Roman government. They were determined to have him killed and bring an end to his teaching about "the kingdom of God" (Matthew 6:33). If you had been there and you had to choose, it would not have seemed wise to stand with Jesus. But (if I may put it like this) you are reading this commentary today because the plans to destroy Jesus and his cause failed. The gospel of the kingdom of God, the news that Jesus is the King, continues to be heard throughout the whole world. The plans to destroy him were foolish, like all plans today to extinguish the Christian faith. The plan that really matters is God's plan.

Jesus wanted his disciples to be wiser than they were about the plots to destroy him. If only they had believed the Scriptures (see Luke 24:25–27). If they had, they would have remembered what happened to the powerful and impressive plan to destroy King David.

The architect of that plan was Ahithophel, the esteemed counselor who had once advised King David, but had now defected to the usurper Absalom.

Absalom had arrived in Jerusalem to claim the throne. David had fled from the city, across the Kidron Valley, over the Mount of Olives, and on to the Jordan River. Ahithophel had advised Absalom to make the rift from his father public and irreversible, which Absalom had done (16:20–22). It was time for Ahithophel to reveal his plan to destroy David and his kingdom.

We will see:

(1) Ahithophel's plan to destroy David (vv. 1–4).
(2) Hushai's alternative "plan" (vv. 5–14a).
(3) The plan that really mattered (v. 14b).
(4) "To defeat the good counsel of Ahithophel" (vv. 15–23).
(5) Readiness for the battle (vv. 24–29).

Ahithophel's Plan to Destroy David (vv. 1–4)

Ahithophel's Plan (vv. 1–3)

> Moreover, Ahithophel said to Absalom, "Let me choose twelve thousand men, and I will arise and pursue David tonight. I will come upon him while he is weary and discouraged and throw him into a panic, and all the people who are with him will flee. I will strike down only the king, and I will bring all the people back to you as a bride comes home to her husband. You seek the life of only one man, and all the people will be at peace."[1] (vv. 1–3)

Like his initial advice to Absalom (16:21), this was careful, calculated, and concise. Ahithophel had thought things through. He had a clear six-point plan. It was brilliant.

Point 1: Ahithophel himself should lead the troops on this expedition ("Let *me* choose . . . *I* will arise . . . *I* will come . . . *I* will strike . . . *I* will bring . . . ," 17:1–3). There was no need to expose Absalom to the dangers of this night raid. We do not know whether Ahithophel had doubts about Absalom's ability as a military commander, but he was obviously confident of his own. More pertinently, Ahithophel's plan avoided any difficulty that could arise if the son had to confront his father.

Point 2: He would assemble a contingent of men who would represent all Israel ("*twelve* thousand," v. 1). He may have intended to choose a "thousand" from each of the twelve tribes of Israel. This would symbolically involve the whole nation in the overthrow of David and prepare the ground for reuniting the nation after the event.[2]

We have noted previously that the Hebrew word for "thousand" often seems to refer to a military group of unspecified size, which may have been much smaller than a thousand. The number must have been such that

Ahithophel could have assembled them there in Jerusalem within a matter of hours.

Point 3: It was important to move against David as soon as possible. It had to be "tonight" (v. 1). The strategic advantage of immediate action was crucial to Ahithophel's plan.

The night of which Ahithophel spoke was the evening of the same day that news of Absalom's rebellion had reached David in Jerusalem (15:13). All that had happened since then had taken place within that day. David and his company had fled twenty miles or so to the east, where they were resting (16:14). David's friend, Hushai, had been sent back into Jerusalem by David just before Absalom arrived in the city (15:37). It was presumably the afternoon when a tent was pitched on the palace roof for Absalom to commit his outrage (16:22).[3] Ahithophel's plan was to strike before the night of that day was over.

The night suited Ahithophel's plan. He wanted David to die in obscurity, witnessed by as few as possible.[4] The darkness was also fitting at another level. It was a dark plan. Centuries later, when Judas went out to initiate his plan to destroy Jesus, the account carefully notes, "And it was night" (John 13:30).

Point 4: The purpose of this sudden strike was to throw David and those with him into "a panic," which would not be difficult because they were "weary and discouraged" (2 Samuel 17:2).[5] It would not have been difficult for Ahithophel to learn some of the details about David's departure from Jerusalem. The sorrow and despair had been very public (15:23, 30). Word of the abuse that had been hurled at David as he passed Bahurim (16:5–8, 13) may well have reached some back in Jerusalem. In any case it would not have been difficult to accurately guess the condition of the fugitives that night (16:14). Ahithophel intended to take full advantage of the weariness and despondency of the enemy. In his judgment an immediate attack with a superior force would send them fleeing in all directions.

Point 5: This would give Ahithophel the opportunity to kill David without further unnecessary bloodshed. If Ahithophel was Bathsheba's grandfather (as we have earlier surmised), there may have been a personal agenda here. If so, his desire for vengeance was remarkably controlled. He was planning to kill David in such a way that collateral damage was kept to an absolute minimum. This was a careful, calculated plan, not vengeful violence.

At this point Ahithophel referred to David as "the king" (17:2) because the chief significance of this assassination was political, not personal. It was the death of the monarch that would secure the succession of David's son.[6]

Point 6: Ahithophel believed that once David was dead, it would be a simple matter to bring his supporters over to Absalom, who was, after all, David's son and heir. Indeed the reunification of the whole nation under Absalom was the purpose of the elimination of David. There was to be no revenge taken on those who had stayed with David. The goal was "peace" for all the people.[7]

The Reception of Ahithophel's Plan (v. 4)

It was a very impressive plan. Ahithophel's reputation for wise advice was clearly deserved. It is difficult to see how this plan could have failed. It was measured and meticulous. If the goal was to secure Absalom as king and the nation at peace, Ahithophel had worked out the way in which that could be achieved.

Those who heard the plan could see its strength. "And the advice [literally, word] seemed right in the eyes of Absalom and all the elders of Israel" (v. 4). We do not know how large was the group of "all the elders of Israel" (v. 4), but they were regarded as an adequate representation of the whole nation. The expression "all the elders of Israel" appears only three times in the books of Samuel: when they demanded a king (1 Samuel 8:4, 5), when they anointed David as king over Israel (5:3), and here, where they decided to destroy the king God had given them.

However, shortly we will see that the narrator himself agreed with their view of Ahithophel's advice (v. 14b). It *was* good advice, judged by the circumstances and by the purpose for which it was given.

Hushai's Alternative "Plan" (vv. 5–14a)

However, Ahithophel's plan reminds us (the readers) of two important things that happened earlier but were unknown to Ahithophel and Absalom. The first is David's prayer: "O Lord, please turn the counsel of Ahithophel into foolishness" (15:31). Ahithophel's counsel, at this stage, looks nothing like "foolishness." The second is that David had sent his friend Hushai back into Jerusalem to "defeat for me the counsel of Ahithophel" (15:34). Now that we have heard the counsel of Ahithophel, it is not clear how it could be defeated.

What Absalom said next was the turning point of his rebellion and the beginning of both the answer to David's prayer and the realization of his plan. "Then Absalom said, 'Call Hushai the Archite also, and let us hear what he has to say'" (v. 5).

For some reason Absalom wanted a second opinion. Perhaps that seemed sensible. A great deal was at stake. Perhaps, too, the proud young man was uneasy with a plan that had no active role for him. Ahithophel's plan was all about what Ahithophel would do. "What about me?" If that was Absalom's thought, perhaps he still had in mind the flattering words (as he had heard them) spoken earlier that day by Hushai (16:16–19).[8] Whatever reasons Absalom may have had, we can see the hand of the one to whom David had prayed behind this turn of events.

All the more so when we hear that Absalom made Hushai's task a lot easier than it might have been. "And when Hushai came to Absalom, Absalom said to him, 'Thus has Ahithophel spoken; shall we do as he says? If not, you speak'" (v. 6). Thanks to Absalom, Hushai knew exactly what he was up against. He was handed the opportunity to undermine Ahithophel's plan, and he grabbed it with both hands.

The "Problem" with Ahithophel's Plan (vv. 7–10)

"Then Hushai said to Absalom, 'This time the counsel that Ahithophel has given is not good'" (v. 7). This was a bold way to start, given Ahithophel's unrivaled reputation (16:23). However, Hushai acknowledged this by saying "This time," meaning "This once." Even Ahithophel cannot be expected to be right all the time. On this one occasion, Hushai said, Ahithophel had given advice that was "not good."

I am sure Hushai now had everyone's attention. It is not clear whether Ahithophel was still present. If he was, he was not given the opportunity to speak. It seems more likely that he had withdrawn immediately after his advice had been unanimously accepted. In any case Hushai's opening pronouncement was not challenged. He proceeded to explain the problems that made Ahithophel's advice "not good" on this occasion (vv. 8–10) before advancing his alternative "plan" (vv. 11–13).

> Hushai said, "You know that your father and his men are mighty men, and that they are enraged, like a bear robbed of her cubs in the field. Besides, your father is expert in war; he will not spend the night with the people. Behold, even now he has hidden himself in one of the pits or in some other place. And as soon as some of the people fall at the first attack, whoever hears it will say, 'There has been a slaughter among the people who follow Absalom.' Then even the valiant man, whose heart is like the heart of a lion, will utterly melt with fear, for all Israel knows that your father is a mighty man, and that those who are with him are valiant men." (vv. 8–10)

Unlike Ahithophel's straightforward, honest counsel, Hushai employed every manipulative and deceptive trick at his disposal. His speech used flattery and flowery language, designed to distract Absalom from the genius of Ahithophel's plan. Ahithophel's *plan* was brilliant. Hushai's *speech* was brilliant.[9]

Hushai undermined the six points of Ahithophel's advice with a mixture of flattery, fear, and rhetoric.

His first word was "you" (v. 8; unusually emphatic in the Hebrew sentence). This was no doubt music to Absalom's ears. Ahithophel's advice had begun "Let me" and only referred to Absalom at the end, in an entirely passive role. Hushai's speech sounded better to a proud young man's ears from the first word. Ahithophel's Point 1 was undercut.

Hushai's first sentence was gently flattering and subtly challenged Ahithophel's right to be involved at all. *"You* know . . ." *I appreciate your asking my advice, Absalom, but you don't need me to tell you about your father's strength.* "You know" implied that Ahithophel did not know. *The problem with Ahithophel's' advic*e, said Hushai, *is that he doesn't seem to know what you know very well, Absalom.* Ahithophel's Point 1 was effectively demolished.

Hushai proceeded to use his rhetorical skill to stir up and play on the fears of Absalom and those who had joined him. David was a formidable opponent. He and his men had defeated every adversary who had ever been foolish enough to take them on. Ever since Goliath crashed to the ground, no one had outwitted or overpowered David and his men. They were "mighty men" (v. 8). Would Ahithophel's hastily assembled "twelve thousand men" (v. 1; which may have numbered only a few hundred) really have any hope? Ahithophel's Point 2 was looking shaky.

Ahithophel's plan depended on David being "weary and discouraged" (v. 2). *You know better, Absalom. You know that they are "enraged" (or "embittered"). Do you really think it is a good idea to take on David enraged? Do you think the haste of Ahithophel's plan is wise, Absalom? You know that David will be "like a bear robbed of her cubs in the field." Not a good idea, Absalom.* Ahithophel's Points 3 and 4 were suddenly rather less convincing.

Furthermore, Ahithophel's plan was not well thought through. *He has not taken into account your father's great experience as a man of war, Absalom. Do you really think that David would spend the night with the people, where he could easily be found? Ahithophel has overlooked the obvious fact that David would have found a hiding place. We don't know where ("in one of the pits or in some other place"), but that is the point! Ahithophel will not take him by surprise. More likely David will spring an ambush on Ahithophel!* So much for Ahithophel's Point 5.

And what do you think will happen then? As soon as some blood is shed, word will spread. And everyone will assume that there has been a slaughter among your people, Absalom. That is what always happens to those who attack your father. Then where will we be? The bravest, lion-like men in Israel will tremble with fear. Ahithophel will not bring all the people back to you, Absalom (Point 6 in Ahithophel's plan). *It cannot be that simple. For like you, "all Israel knows" the might of your father and his men.*

Hushai's speech did not use facts but played on Absalom's fears (which were stirred up), his pride (which was stroked), and the power of language to manipulate the imagination. His purpose was to make Ahithophel's plan no longer seem "right" but rather "not good" (vv. 4, 7).[10] Hushai used the power of language to deceive.

Hushai's "Plan" (vv. 11–13)

Hushai had an alternative "plan," the purpose of which was to achieve the opposite of its stated goal. Hushai's true purpose was to give David time to escape from any attack that might come from Absalom's forces. The essential point that he had to defeat in Ahithophel's good advice was Point 3: to move against David as soon as possible.

> But my counsel is that all Israel be gathered to you, from Dan to Beersheba, as the sand by the sea for multitude, and that you go to battle in person. So we shall come upon him in some place where he is to be found, and we shall light upon him as the dew falls on the ground, and of him and all the men with him not one will be left. If he withdraws into a city, then all Israel will bring ropes to that city, and we shall drag it into the valley, until not even a pebble is to be found there. (vv. 11–13)

Point 1: Absalom, *you* are the one who must lead your people in this glorious battle. You must "go to battle in person" (v. 11). Ahithophel's plan did not give you your proper place.

Point 2: Assemble to yourself, Absalom, a mighty force from "all Israel" (v. 11).[11] Ahithophel's plan was not only too small for the task at hand; it was small-minded. This is a time, Absalom, for a grand and glorious historic act.

"From Dan [north of Lake Galilee] to Beersheba [to the south]" (v. 11) was a way of describing the full extent of Israel's land (see Judges 20:1; 1 Samuel 3:20; 2 Samuel 3:10; 24:2, 15; 1 Kings 4:25; 1 Chronicles 21:2; 2 Chronicles 30:5).[12] "As the sand by the sea" is an allusion to God's promises concerning this nation (2 Samuel 17:11; see Genesis 32:12; 1 Kings

4:20; Hosea 1:10). Hushai made his proposed course of action sound like one of the great events of Israel's history.

Point 3: If we do this properly (unstated: and take the necessary time to prepare), then we will be the ones who will come upon David. He will not ambush us (as Hushai had implied would happen under Ahithophel's plan). We[13] will fall upon him.

Hushai draws again on his rhetoric. "As the dew falls on the ground" suggests a silent but vast and inevitable event (2 Samuel 17:12). There will be no escape, just as nothing is untouched by the morning dew.[14] This will be far more effective, and much less risky than Ahithophel's proposed quick, surgical strike.

Point 4: Ahithophel's plan, even if it succeeded, would only destroy David. Hushai's plan will ensure that "of him and all the men with him not one will be left" (v. 12). Absalom would have his revenge not only on his father but on all who had remained with David. There would be no remaining opposition to Absalom's claims. How much more effective than Ahithophel's little plan!

Point 5: Hushai painted a vivid picture of the power of his proposal. Not even a city would be able to protect David from the forces that would be arrayed against him. The image of "all Israel" (v. 13) dragging a city on a hill down into the valley with ropes is a grandiose representation of a successful siege, where military might and machinery demolishes and destroys the defenses. The representation is designed, on the one hand, to show that taking David will not be easy and, on the other hand, to portray the irresistible power that the whole nation could summon (again unstated: if only we take a bit more time).

The Reception of Hushai's "Plan" (v. 14a)

Ahithophel's simple and honest advice was given in forty-two Hebrew words. Hushai's deceptive alternative took 129 words. The greater number of words, not the quality of the advice, won the day. "And Absalom and all the men of Israel said, 'The counsel of Hushai the Archite is better than the counsel of Ahithophel'" (v. 14a). The Hebrew suggests that this is what Absalom said, and "all the men of Israel" agreed with him.[15] "All the men of Israel" means the "all elders of Israel" who had previously endorsed Ahithophel's advice (v. 4).

The Plan That Really Mattered (v. 14b)

At this point, in the midst of so many words offering so much advice, the narrator places a statement that is more important than anything else that anyone has said.[16] He uses just fourteen words (in Hebrew): "For[17] the LORD had ordained to defeat the good counsel of Ahithophel, so that the LORD might bring harm upon Absalom" (v. 14b).

In other words, the Lord answered David's prayer (15:31), but the Lord's purpose in doing so was his own: to "bring harm [or evil] upon Absalom" (17:14). The Lord was acting in judgment on Absalom.

This is one of many examples in the Bible of the sovereignty of God (which is absolute—nothing occurs outside his control) and human responsibility (which is real—humans are genuinely accountable to God for what they do). What Absalom had done was from one point of view the Lord's doing (12:11). At the same time Absalom was fully responsible, and the Lord dealt with him accordingly. No explanation that compromises the sovereignty of God or reduces human responsibility is true according to the Bible. The fact that our minds cannot understand how this can be is beside the point. It is sufficient for us to know that it is so and that it is good that it is so.

However, it does mean that the plan that really matters is God's plan. His is the plan that will come to pass. Ahithophel's plan seemed "right" (17:4). Indeed our narrator calls it "good counsel" (v. 14), not in a moral sense, but meaning that it was just the right advice for the purpose of destroying David and his kingdom. For that purpose it was Hushai's counsel that was "not good" (v. 7). The problem was that the Lord's plan was to *establish* David's kingdom (7:16). That is (ultimately) why Hushai's advice prevailed. The Lord answered David's prayer not by actually making Ahithophel's advice foolish, but by making it appear foolish to Absalom, through the clever words of Hushai.[18]

To "Defeat . . . the Counsel of Ahithophel" (vv. 15–23)

Suddenly the scene changes from the meeting of Hushai with Absalom and the elders of Israel to somewhere else in the city. The immediacy of the scene change supports the impression that Hushai wasted no time. In contrast to the verbose and time-consuming speech before Absalom, the narrative now reports urgent and rapid action. Hushai hurried to find Zadok and Abiathar.

Hushai's Real Plan Activated (vv. 15–17)

Then Hushai said to Zadok and Abiathar the priests, "Thus and so did Ahithophel counsel Absalom and the elders of Israel, and thus and so have

I counseled. Now therefore send quickly and tell David, 'Do not stay to-night at the fords of the wilderness, but by all means pass over, lest the king and all the people who are with him be swallowed up.'"[19] (vv. 15, 16)

David had sent the priests, Zadok and Abiathar, back into Jerusalem with their two sons in order to be his eyes and ears in the city. David was waiting at the Jordan River crossing until he received word from them (15:25–29). David had told Hushai about this little intelligence network (15:35, 36).

So Hushai now outlined to the priests the two competing plans that had been presented to Absalom by himself and Ahithophel. He did not say that his plan had been favored, almost certainly because he could not be sure that the decision to accept his advice was final. What if Ahithophel was given the chance to show the holes in Hushai's arguments?[20] There was no time to waste. "Send *quickly* and tell David" (17:16).

The hidden purpose of Hushai's earlier speech now becomes plain. He was buying time for David and the people with him to escape across the Jordan, putting them at least out of the immediate reach of Absalom's people.

The arrangement for getting information to David had been carefully put together, as the narrator now explains:

Now Jonathan and Ahimaaz were waiting at En-rogel. A female servant was to go and tell them, and they were to go and tell King David, for they were not to be seen entering the city. (v. 17)

En-rogel was surprisingly fittingly named. A possible meaning is "Well of the spy."[21] It was about 300 yards south of the city near where the north-south Kidron Valley meets the west-east Hinnom Valley.[22] There the priests' sons waited. They must not be seen coming and going from the city, or suspicions would be aroused. An inconspicuous female servant had been recruited (who may have been assumed to be fetching water from the well at En-rogel) to carry messages from inside the city to the lads, who would then slip away to pass on the information to David. That was the plan.

The story is told with the usual brevity of Biblical narrative, leaving interesting but unimportant details to be filled in by the reader's imagination. We are not yet told whether Hushai's message had reached the boys at En-rogel. We are just told how the scheme was supposed to work.

Hushai's Real Plan Endangered (vv. 18–20)

Like all human schemes, this one had a weakness. Someone saw the boys waiting at En-rogel. Their identity (sons of the priests who had served King

David) and their location (outside the city; why were they not inside the city with everyone else?) raised a suspicion in the mind of another young man. We are simply told, "But a young man saw them and told Absalom" (v. 18a).

Suddenly Hushai's real plan (to gain time for David to escape) was in jeopardy. If the chain of communication to David was broken or, worse, if the whole spy network was exposed, then Hushai's warning could not reach David, and perhaps Hushai's treachery (from Absalom's point of view) would be exposed. It is a moment of high suspense. Ahithophel's plan could be back on track.

Somehow the boys at En-rogel realized that their cover had been blown. The young man who saw them may himself have acted in a way that alarmed the boys. They did not wait around.

> So both of them went away quickly and came to the house of a man at Bahurim, who had a well in his courtyard. And they went down into it. And the woman took and spread a covering over the well's mouth and scattered grain on it, and nothing was known of it. (vv. 18b, 19)

"Quickly" corresponds to Hushai's instruction (v. 16), but the boys were now not running for their king but for their lives (or so it seems). There was a known David-sympathizer in Bahurim. He provided them with a hiding place in his well. His wife helped by covering the well and spreading out grain on the covering, as though it were drying in what must have been by now the late afternoon sun.

Earlier that day David had passed this way. Bahurim was the place from which Shimei had emerged with his vigorous tirade of abuse (16:5). It was not, therefore, an obviously safe place for suspected servants of David to hide. The lives of the boys and, it would seem, the future of David and his kingdom was as precarious as their hiding place in the well.

> When Absalom's servants came to the woman at the house, they said, "Where are Ahimaaz and Jonathan?" And the woman said to them, "They have gone over the brook of water." And when they had sought and could not find them, they returned to Jerusalem. (v. 20)

Absalom's men had no trouble, it seems, following the boys as far as Bahurim. There were probably plenty of witnesses willing to report the two lads running across the valley and over the hills. They tracked them to the very house in which they were hiding. But the woman of the house lied to them and sent them searching over "the brook of water" (v. 20). This would not have been the Jordan, but some other local watercourse. Of course, the trail went cold. No one had seen two lads on the run. Absalom's men gave up the chase and returned to Jerusalem. I am sure they had no idea how much was at stake that day or they would not have stopped searching so soon.

As we follow the story we are made more anxious still because it is difficult for us to see how Hushai's message can possibly reach the boys (and then David) now.

Hushai's Real Plan Accomplished (vv. 21, 22)

Only at this point does the narrator relieve some of the tension of the story by letting us know that Hushai's message *had* been passed on from Zadok and Abiathar, presumably via the female servant, to the boys at En-rogel. We now realize that it may have been the exchange between the female servant and the boys that had been witnessed and led to the hurried escape.

> After they had gone, the men came up out of the well, and went and told King David. They said to David, "Arise, and go quickly over the water, for thus and so has Ahithophel counseled against you." Then David arose, and all the people who were with him, and they crossed the Jordan. By daybreak not one was left who had not crossed the Jordan. (vv. 21, 22)

This is the third time we have heard "quickly" (see vv. 16, 18). Everything hung on the speed with which David received Hushai's message and acted on it. David acted without delay. He and his people crossed the Jordan River under the cover of darkness.

As the new day dawned, the dangers of the previous night faded. Just as Hushai had imaginatively pictured no one of David and those with him being left (alive) (v. 12), so in fact by daybreak "not one was left" (v. 22) on the wrong side of the Jordan. The dark night of Ahithophel's plans (v. 1) was over. The light of the future for David and his kingdom had dawned.[23]

Ahithophel Destroyed (v. 23)

Ahithophel's brilliant plan had been thwarted. David's prayer had been answered. It remains to note Ahithophel's tragic end.

> When Ahithophel saw that his counsel was not followed, he saddled his donkey and went off home to his own city. He set his house in order and hanged himself, and he died and was buried in the tomb of his father. (v. 23)

There is more detail here than is needed. Ahithophel is not the main interest of the story we are following, but the narrator seems to want us to take note of Ahithophel. If our supposition is correct that Ahithophel was Bathsheba's grandfather and that his motivation for abandoning David and going over to Absalom was at least partly outrage at David's behavior in his adultery with Bathsheba and the subsequent murder of Uriah, then the Bible's treatment of Ahithophel is illuminated. He is not presented as a wicked man. Indeed his stature as a wise advisor is unparalleled (16:23). He may have wanted David to fall (for understandable reasons), but he did not allow his rage to spill over to others (note "only the king" in 17:2).

Even Ahithophel's end was marked by careful dignity. He saw the consequences when "his counsel was not followed" (v. 23). It seems that he waited through the night, perhaps weighing up all the options.[24] He did not panic. We are told of the saddling of his donkey and his journey to his own city, Giloh (15:12). Although the location is not known, the sites suggested are in the vicinity of Hebron and therefore some distance from Jerusalem. There, as appears to have been his methodical way, he set his affairs in order and then hanged himself. In a way that honors his memory we are told that Ahithophel "was buried in the tomb of his father" (17:23).

The honesty and objectivity of the Bible can be astonishing. There is no doubt that Ahithophel was on the wrong side of history. He was wrong to choose Absalom over David. But we need to see that this is not because David was a better man than Absalom. It was because God had chosen David, and Absalom had risen up against God's king. If our suppositions about Ahithophel's motives are correct, then Ahithophel was not wicked to be outraged at David's behavior. The Lord himself was outraged at David's behavior (12:7–12). Ahithophel deserves respect for despising David's crimes. Ahithophel's great and tragic failure was (it would seem) a failure to accept the grace of God that was extended to David and the purpose of God to establish his kingdom through such a man as David. Ahithophel's plans, whatever may have been good about them, were opposed to the Lord's plan and were therefore doomed to failure.

There are striking parallels between Ahithophel and the man who betrayed Jesus. However, Judas does not come off well by the comparison. Judas betrayed the one who "committed no sin, neither was deceit found in his mouth" (1 Peter 2:22). Judas did it for money (Matthew 26:15; see John 12:6). Judas, like Ahithophel, hanged himself when the consequences of what he had done dawned on him (Matthew 27:5), but no Bible writer seems to sympathize with, let alone respect Judas.

Readiness for the Battle (vv. 24–29)

The chapter concludes with two paragraphs that set the scene for the conflict to be reported in 2 Samuel 18. Both paragraphs begin with the fact that "David came to Mahanaim" (vv. 24a, 27a), about a thirty-mile march from the Jordan River crossing.[25]

Mahanaim (meaning "two camps") had been the center from which Ishbosheth had attempted to rule "all Israel" (2:8) after David had become king over the house of Judah in Hebron. There was bitter irony in David's fleeing from Absalom in Jerusalem to Mahanaim. Israel was again "two camps." The unity of the nation had been shattered again by the rejection of the Lord's anointed king.

Absalom's Forces (vv. 24b–26)

> And Absalom crossed the Jordan with all the men of Israel.[26] Now Absalom had set Amasa over the army instead of Joab. Amasa was the son of a man named Ithra the Ishmaelite,[27] who had married Abigal[28] the daughter of Nahash, sister of Zeruiah, Joab's mother. And Israel and Absalom encamped in the land of Gilead. (vv. 24b–26)

Absalom was clearly following some version of Hushai's advice earlier on, since he was in charge of the advance. We are not told whether he had gathered men "from Dan to Beersheba" as Hushai had counseled (v. 11), nor how much time passed before Absalom crossed the Jordan. How large a force he had mustered is unclear. While it no doubt fell short of the hyperbole of Hushai's counsel, it is very likely to have exceeded the size of the forces available to David.

It has been hinted that Joab was with David (see 16:10). He was certainly not with Absalom, since Absalom appointed Amasa "instead of Joab" (17:25). That is not something that would have happened without trouble if Joab had been around. The details about Amasa tell us that he was a nephew of David and a cousin of Joab and draw our attention to a man who will play an important role in the events about to unfold.

The expression "Israel and Absalom" (v. 26) emphasizes that the nation as a whole had now rejected King David.[29] Encamped in Gilead (referring broadly to the land east of the Jordan[30]) was the nation who had chosen another king.

David's Supporters (vv. 27–29)

However, even in Mahanaim, once the center of hostility to David's kingdom, David did not lack devotees. The chapter closes by taking us back to David's arrival there:

> When David came to Mahanaim, Shobi the son of Nahash from Rabbah of the Ammonites, and Machir the son of Ammiel from Lo-debar, and Barzillai the Gileadite from Rogelim, brought beds, basins, and earthen vessels, wheat, barley, flour, parched grain, beans and lentils,[31] honey and curds and sheep and cheese from the herd, for David and the people with him to eat, for they said, "The people are hungry and weary and thirsty in the wilderness." (vv. 27–29)

These followers of David are an interesting collection. Shobi the Ammonite was a brother of Hanun, who had despised the kindness of King David, leading to a terrible war (see 10:2ff.). There must be an interesting story (unfortunately now lost) about how Shobi became a supporter of David, the king who conquered his home city of Rabbah (12:29). It is very likely that it had something to do with David's attempt to show kindness to his family. Machir had provided shelter to Saul's son, Mephibosheth, and may therefore be assumed to have once been a supporter of Saul (see 9:4). It is reasonable to assume that he, too, had been won over to King David by the king's kindness, in this case toward his ward. Barzillai was an old man who, like the other two, came from east of the Jordan River. This is the first time he has appeared in the narrative, but we will meet him again in due course and will learn that he was very wealthy and devoted to David. The king, for his part, showed kindness to this faithful follower (see 19:31–39).

These three brought an astonishing array of provisions to the refugees in Mahanaim. The gifts were testimony not only to their support for David and those with him, but also to the condition of these exiles—"hungry and weary and thirsty" (17:29). They were "in the wilderness" in more than the ordinary physical sense. In Israel's history "the wilderness" was the place of wandering and rejection (Numbers 14:25; Deuteronomy 1:40; 2:1; cf. Matthew 4:1[32]).

God had answered David's prayer to frustrate the counsel of Ahithophel. David had not been destroyed, as he could have been, on the night of his escape from Jerusalem. However, it is far from clear how these exhausted outcasts will survive conflict with "Israel and Absalom" encamped nearby in Gilead (2 Samuel 17:26).

As we leave David and his people resting and regaining their strength at Mahanaim, it is worth asking, who in this chapter has been wise? Those who opposed or disregarded God's plan (v. 14b) were the foolish ones. For all his brilliance Ahithophel was foolish. So, of course, was Absalom. Indeed all those who were drawn to follow Absalom (apparently most of the nation) were foolish.

Centuries later Jesus "came to his own, and his own people did not receive him" (John 1:11). What blind foolishness (cf. Matthew 23:17)!

We do not know how, but we should know that those like Shobi, Machir, and Barzillai who welcomed King David will sooner or later prove to have been the wise ones.

Likewise with Jesus: "But to all who did receive him, who believed in his name, he gave the right to become children of God" (John 1:12).

35

When Love and Justice
Do Not Meet

2 SAMUEL 18

WHICH PRINCIPLE WOULD YOU PREFER to prevail in human relationships—love or justice? I suspect that your answer to that question is, "It all depends." There are times when we would like love to triumph over justice (particularly when we ourselves are the ones in trouble with justice). At other times it does not seem right for the claims of justice to be outweighed by compassion. As I write this there is yet another debate in the local media in my part of the world about an apparently lenient sentence passed on a young man who committed a terrible crime. The judge is said to have taken various factors into account that led him not to apply the full force of the law. Was the judge too soft? Was justice done? Can justice show compassion?

We often experience an insoluble tension between justice and love. At the risk of an oversimplification of complex issues, the difficult political tensions between so-called right-wing and left-wing political views often seem to be an expression of this tension. Right-wing views tend to care about righteousness, justice, and ensuring that people get what they deserve. Left-wing views tend to emphasize compassion and kindness and helping people in ways they do not deserve. This caricature will not please many who identify themselves with either side of the political divide. My point is that we often find ourselves having to choose to prioritize justice (and related ideas like truth, law, and responsibility) over love (and such things as compassion, kindness, forgiveness, and generosity), or the other way around.

In a world deeply affected by human sin, there is no avoiding the tension. It is an aspect of the fallenness of the world that love and justice do not meet. If there were no sin, there would be no tension. In the garden of Eden there was no contradiction between love and justice. But it is a deeply distressing aspect of life in our world. Parents with troublesome sons or daughters can agonize over this. Their love for their children is strong and true. But is it right to try to protect them from the consequences of their bad, perhaps criminal behavior? How can love and justice meet?

When we pray, "Your kingdom come" (Matthew 6:10), we are praying to one who is perfect in his love (1 John 4:8, 16) *and* pure in his justice (Romans 3:26; 1 John 1:9). Perhaps the greatest wonder of the kingdom for which we pray is that love and justice are in perfect harmony. This is the profound mystery of the death and resurrection of Jesus Christ. In these events justice was done *and* love triumphed. Neither was compromised. Members of this kingdom must be people of justice *and* love. We cannot be right-wing conservatives who lack compassion. Nor can we be left-wing radicals who care only about freedom from restraint. In this world this will always be difficult. How earnestly we must pray, "Your kingdom come."

David's kingdom, centuries before the Lord Jesus Christ, did not solve this problem. In David's kingdom the demands of justice and the claims of love were in irreconcilable contradiction. This was most clearly displayed in the conflict with David's son, Absalom, who was attempting to destroy David and take over his kingdom. We are about to see David's intense love for his son. But what about justice? It was a situation in which love and justice failed to meet.

We will see:

(1) Preparations for the battle (vv. 1–5).
(2) The battle (vv. 6–18).
(3) The gospel of justice (vv. 19–32).
(4) No meeting of justice and love (v. 33).

Preparations for the Battle (vv. 1–5)

The situation at the end of 2 Samuel 17 had Absalom and his substantial army (referred to as "all the men of Israel," v. 24) camped somewhere on the east side of the Jordan, under the command of Amasa (17:24–26). David and those who had remained faithful to him (referred to as "the people with him," v. 22) were in the city of Mahanaim, exhausted and famished, but provided for by the surprising generosity of locals (17:27–29).

We are not told how much time passed between the end of 2 Samuel 17 and the beginning of 2 Samuel 18. It may have been a day or two. Thanks to the success of Hushai's deceptive advice to Absalom (17:11–13), David and his followers were given time to rest and recuperate from their arduous forced march from Jerusalem to Mahanaim.

The King's Men Ordered (vv. 1, 2a)

There was, however, a job to be done. The escape from Jerusalem in the nick of time, the successful crossing of the Jordan, and the surprising welcome they found in Mahanaim had done nothing to deal with the threat to David and his kingdom that Absalom had instigated. It was time for David to grasp the initiative.

He organized "the men who were with him" into an army.[1] "Then David mustered the men who were with him and set over them commanders of thousands and commanders of hundreds" (v. 1). In contexts such as these the Hebrew for "thousands" and "hundreds" seems to be language for military units, without necessarily indicating their size. We could think of "thousands" as regiments and "hundreds" as companies.

The army so organized was sent out as three divisions[2] under three well known commanders. "And David sent out the army, one third under the command of Joab,[3] one third under the command of Abishai the son of Zeruiah, Joab's brother, and one third under the command of Ittai the Gittite" (v. 2a). No doubt the senior commander was Joab, and it is reasonable to assume that besides being on top of his own division he was over the army as a whole (see 8:16), although the army was now much diminished in size. Amasa now commanded for Absalom many of the troops who had once been under Joab's command (17:25). However, Joab's overall command of David's army will be important as events unfold. Joab had been a loyal, if often difficult-to-handle supporter of David's kingdom since the days when David was on the run from Saul (1 Samuel 26:6). Joab was an astute, self-confident activist for David's kingdom, with his own ways of doing things (see 2:13; 3:26, 27). He had recently taken the initiative in a failed attempt to reconcile Absalom and David (2 Samuel 14).

Abishai was Joab's headstrong brother, sharing Joab's aggressive loyalty to David's kingdom (1 Samuel 26:6–9; 2 Samuel 2:24; 3:30; 16:9). He had worked successfully before in military operations with Joab (2 Samuel 10:9, 10).

The surprise in David's arrangement of the army was the appointment of Ittai the Gittite (a Philistine!) as the commander of one of the divisions. Since Ittai was (it seems) the leader of at least 600 Gittites (as well as possibly "all the Cherethites, and all the Pelethites," 15:18), the division he commanded may have been made up largely of foreigners who had, like Ittai himself, become faithful servants of David (see 15:18–22).

The army may by now have been supplemented by many supporters from east of the Jordan (of whom Shobi, Machir, and Barzillai had been representative, 17:27). David "sent out" this army (v. 2). Much detail is omitted, at least some of which the reader is expected to fill in. It seems that David had learned that Absalom had crossed the Jordan (was the same intelligence network still operating?). He "sent out" the army to confront his foes (see Psalm 3:1).

The King's Worth Acknowledged (vv. 2b–4a)

Surprisingly in this chapter, which is all about war, several conversations are reported in great detail. We are expected to listen carefully. The words spoken are at least as important as the actions.

The first of these conversations began when "the king said to the men, 'I myself will also go out with you'" (v. 2b). David did not always accompany his men into battle (10:7; 11:1), but there were many occasions when he did (5:17–25; 8:1–8; 10:17; 12:29). The conflict with Absalom was the most important and difficult in David's life. The importance of the king leading the remnant of his people in this confrontation was obvious to David.[4]

However, the people had a different perspective.

> But the men said, "You shall not go out. For if we flee, they will not care about us. If half of us die, they will not care about us. But you[5] are worth ten thousand of us. Therefore it is better that you send us help from the city." (v. 3)

It is just possible that "ten thousand of us" is an indication of the approximate size of the army that had now been put together.[6] The point, however, is that the people recognized the importance of their king. The kingdom depended on the king. For the sake of the kingdom, the life of the king mattered more than all of their lives.

This was the very opposite of the advice with which Hushai had deceived Absalom (17:11). The recommendation of David's men accorded with the good advice that Ahithophel had given (17:1). The arrogant young Absalom had found the flattery of Hushai more attractive than the sound counsel of Ahithophel. That is why Absalom was now with his troops, seeking to find and destroy David and his people (see 17:12).

David's people understood that it would be far better for their king to support them from the shelter of the city of Mahanaim, perhaps by sending auxiliary troops when needed,[7] or perhaps just by the encouragement of knowing that he was safe.

David (unlike Absalom earlier) was prepared to accept this good advice. "The king said to them, 'Whatever seems best to you I will do'" (18:4a).

The King's Men Advance (v. 4b)

Therefore the army, by companies and regiments, marched out of the city of Mahanaim under King David's watchful eye. "So the king stood at the side of the gate, while all the army marched out by hundreds and by thousands" (v. 4b). In human terms the kingdom of David depended on this advancing army. Out there somewhere a much greater numerical force was waiting (see 17:11). The outcome of the conflict would determine the future for David's kingdom.

The procession that day was rather different from the one that had marched past King David a few days earlier, when David had halted at the last house on the outskirts of Jerusalem (15:17, 18). Then they had been fleeing for their lives, overwhelmed with sorrow (15:23, 30). Now the army was intent on action. The time for tears had passed (for now).

The procession that day was also very different from the way in which Absalom used to stand by the city gate (15:2ff.), as David stood now by a different city gate. Absalom had been hard at work undermining his father's kingdom and stealing the hearts of the people with his empty promises. David now stood by the gate of Mahanaim, anxious about where this procession would lead.

The King's Love Spoken (v. 5)

His anxiety was less about the victory that his troops sought than his love for the one against whom they were advancing. In a brief flashback, we hear David's love for Absalom put into words of command to his divisional commanders: "And the king ordered Joab and Abishai and Ittai, 'Deal gently for my sake with the young man Absalom'" (18:5a).

It was "the king" who spoke, but his words were a father's words. Absalom was a traitor and a killer who deserved to die. That would be justice. But he was a son whom his father loved. Love demanded gentleness, not because Absalom deserved gentleness, but "for [the] sake" of the father who loved him, who always saw him as "the young man Absalom" (v. 5; see also 14:21; 18:29, 32).

The demands of justice and the requirements of love were in terrible conflict. From the point of view of justice, David's words sound sentimental and weak. The king must surely, above all, "do justice and righteousness for all his people" (8:15 AT). But David's love for Absalom would not be subordinated to the demands of justice. "Deal gently for my sake with the young man Absalom."

These words from David were witnessed by "all the people": "And all the people heard when the king gave orders to all the commanders about Absalom" (v. 5b).

The Battle (vv. 6–18)

There may have been a longer campaign than the text indicates. The Biblical historian was only interested in the outcome and moves quickly to that point. It is possible (as we will see in a moment) that David's forces drove Absalom's army back across the Jordan prior to the confrontation that is about to be described. The narrative focuses on what matters most to the writer.

The Big Picture: A Great Defeat (vv. 6–8)

> So the army went out into the field against Israel, and the battle was fought in the forest of Ephraim. And the men of Israel were defeated there by the servants of David, and the loss there was great on that day, twenty thousand men. The battle spread over the face of all the country,[8] and the forest devoured more people that day than the sword. (vv. 6–8)

The enemy whom David's army confronted is called, simply, "Israel" in verse 6. The nation as a whole had rejected their king. The problem with that was that he was not simply *their* king, he was the Lord's anointed.

This was the decisive battle, but it may not have been the only one. If "the forest of Ephraim" (v. 6) was in the territory of the tribe of Ephraim (which, of course, is what it sounds like), then somehow this battle took place back on the west side of the Jordan.[9] In that case there may have been a number of earlier encounters between the forces of David and Absalom that resulted in the latter being driven back across the Jordan. However, it is also possible that the name "forest of Ephraim" is not a sure guide to its location. The "forest" was probably a thickly wooded region of rough terrain, with ravines, marshes, cliffs, and so on.[10]

The record may not be clear about the location of this battle, but it is very clear about the outcome. "The men of Israel were defeated there by the servants of David" (v. 7). Again it is striking that Absalom's side is called, literally, "the people of Israel." They suffered the heavy loss of 20,000—

twice the number that the people with David had said their king was worth (v. 3), perhaps twice the number of people fighting for David.

With some hyperbole we are told that the battle spread over the whole land. With similar overstatement, "all the land" (exactly the same expression in 15:23) was said to have "wept" as David departed from Jerusalem. Now it was as though the land itself turned against the people to whom it had been given by the Lord (Genesis 12:7; Exodus 6:4; Leviticus 14:34; Numbers 14:8; Deuteronomy 1:8; Joshua 1:6; Judges 2:1; 1 Kings 8:34[11]). "The forest devoured more people that day than the sword" (2 Samuel 18:8). That is, there were more fatal accidents in the wild undergrowth and treacherous terrain than were killed in actual combat.

The Crucial Incident: Justice for Absalom (vv. 9–18)

The battle and its outcome have been reported briefly. The great interest of the writer is, however, in one crucial incident. At much greater length he now reports what happened to Absalom.

Absalom's "Capture" (v. 9)

"And Absalom happened to meet the servants of David" (v. 9a). We know what lay behind this "chance" event—the Lord's purpose to "bring harm upon Absalom" (17:14). How Absalom found himself confronted by David's men is now explained in detail. "Absalom was riding on his mule" (18:9b). Absalom maintained his regal pretensions to the end. The royal mode of transport (see 2 Samuel 13:29; 1 Kings 1:33, 38, 44) carried him even in the battle. It is likely that he was fleeing from David's troops who were gaining the upper hand. In his haste, perhaps as he glanced back at his pursuers, "the mule went under the thick branches of a great oak,[12] and his head caught fast in the oak, and he was suspended between heaven and earth, while the mule that was under him went on" (2 Samuel 18:9c).

The description makes no reference to Absalom's famous hair (14:26), although later interpreters have often guessed that the symbol of Absalom's conceit played a role in his downfall. The image of Absalom's hair tangled in the tree branches and dangling him in the air is evocative but not quite given to us by the text. More probably "he was caught by the neck in the fork of two boughs,"[13] which then held him firmly, suspending him above the ground as the mule continued on its way.

In this humiliating way Absalom lost the kingdom. As he dangled there "between heaven and earth" (18:9), he was helpless and powerless. The symbol of his royal aspirations (the mule) went on without him. As with so many others that day, "the forest" captured him (v. 8).

Joab's Resolve (vv. 10–14a)

That is how Absalom "happened" to meet the servants of David (v. 9). The incident was witnessed by one man, who promptly reported it to his commander. "And a certain man saw it and told Joab, 'Behold, I saw Absalom hanging in an oak'" (v. 10).

Joab could hardly believe his ears. "Joab said to the man who told him, 'What, you saw him!'" (v. 11a). Literally Joab mimicked the man's own words: "Behold, you saw!" *And that is all you did? What possessed you to "see" and do nothing?* "'Why then did you not strike him there to the ground?'" (v. 11b). An opportunity like that is not to be passed up. Indeed, "I would have been glad to give you ten pieces of silver and a belt" (v. 11c)—a monetary reward along with a hero's emblem.[14]

Joab knew that not only did Absalom deserve to die, but the kingdom would not be secured again under David as long as the incorrigible prince lived. Joab knew what justice (in the full sense of putting things right) demanded.

The man had a different perspective from Joab's.

> But the man said to Joab, "Even if I felt in my hand the weight of a thousand pieces of silver, I would not reach out my hand against the king's son, for in our hearing the king commanded you and Abishai and Ittai, 'For my sake protect the young man Absalom.' On the other hand, if I had dealt treacherously against his life (and there is nothing hidden from the king), then you yourself would have stood aloof." (vv. 12, 13)

A reward one hundred times that offered by Joab would not have persuaded this man to do Joab's will. His perspective is captured in the words he used to describe Absalom: "the king's son" (v. 12). It was the words he had heard from *the father* that were etched on this man's consciousness. This man would not act against the father's love for his son.

No doubt the man feared King David ("there is nothing hidden from the king") more than he feared Joab. Nonetheless, we should notice that, in his view, to strike Absalom would be to act "treacherously" (v. 13; literally, "to do a lie"). Everyone had heard David's command concerning Absalom (v. 5). No one had objected. The silence was implicit acceptance of David's words. To harm Absalom would therefore be to enact a lie.

Furthermore, the man knew his commander. He did not expect any support from Joab in the event that he had ignored the king's words. Joab would have been glad of the outcome, but would have had no concern for the consequences for the man who did it.

This last stinging word against Joab's character was too true to be answered. "Joab said, 'I will not waste time like this with you'"[15] (v. 14a).

Absalom's Death (vv. 14b–17)

Joab promptly took the matter into his own hands. Finding Absalom was apparently no problem. The man's report had no doubt been fuller than recorded here. "And [Joab] took three javelins in his hand and thrust them into the heart of Absalom while he was still alive in the oak" (v. 14b). "Javelins" translates a word that can mean "stick," "rod" (7:14), or "spear" (23:21). "Three" sticks may have been meant to represent the three divisions of the army (v. 2). They were all involved in this action.

It is possible that Joab used these implements to push Absalom in the chest ("heart," 18:14) to dislodge him from the tree, leaving the execution to the ten lads who carried out their task thoroughly: "And ten young men, Joab's armor-bearers, surrounded Absalom and struck him and killed him" (v. 15).

As far as Joab was concerned this was "mission accomplished." Just as Ahithophel, when he advised Absalom, sought to minimize bloodshed (17:2), so Joab brought hostilities to an end as soon as Absalom had fallen. "Then Joab blew the trumpet, and the troops came back from pursuing Israel, for Joab restrained them" (v. 16). The last phrase could mean "for Joab spared the people" (that is, the people of "Israel" who had been following Absalom). Joab, like Ahithophel, did not pursue vengeance on the followers of the rival king once he had been brought down (see 17:2, 3). The concern of each, in his own way, was for the kingdom.

Absalom was given a hasty and ignominious burial. "And they took Absalom and threw him into a great pit in the forest and raised over him a very great heap of stones" (v. 17a). This was a burial fit for a sinner (like Achan, Joshua 7:26) or an enemy (like the king of Ai, Joshua 8:29). The pile of stones (in these three cases) stood as a reminder of what happens to those who set themselves against the Lord and his purposes for his people.

"And all Israel fled every one to his own home" (v. 17b)—literally, "to his tent," the reference perhaps being to their field camp (see 17:26; cf. 11:11) rather than to their homes. The war was over.

Absalom's Memory (v. 18)

A final note on the young man who was responsible for the uprising is given.

> Now Absalom in his lifetime had taken and set up for himself the pillar that is in the King's Valley, for he said, "I have no son to keep my name in remembrance." He called the pillar after his own name, and it is called Absalom's monument to this day. (v. 18)

The three sons mentioned in 14:27 must have died young (which is probably why, unusually, their names are not given[16]). Truly great men or women are not usually obsessed with how history will remember them. History does remember them precisely because they were not self-absorbed. I am sure there are exceptions to this generalization, but Absalom was one of those men who wanted to be great and wanted to be remembered as great. Rather than earn a reputation for greatness, he built a monument to himself. Saul had done something like this a long time earlier (1 Samuel 15:12). Like Saul's edifice, Absalom's pillar was "for himself" (2 Samuel 18:18). The location spoke of his ambition: "the King's Valley" (see Genesis 14:17[17]), possibly a part of the Kidron Valley to the east of Jerusalem.[18] The monument was still standing at the time of the writing of this account.[19] The point, however, is that "Absalom's monument" is a less fitting memorial than the pile of stones marking his grave. He did not die as a hero, much less a king. He died a rebel and an enemy.

Joab was a complex person. Even David had difficulty knowing what to make of the sons of Zeruiah (see 3:39). Assessing Joab's action in killing Absalom requires more than a simple "right" or "wrong." Joab had a deep sense of justice (hence 3:30), which he did not allow to spill over into unnecessary bloodletting (hence 2:28; 18:16; 20:20, 21). From David's point of view Joab's sense of justice was often misplaced, as when he killed Abner (again see 3:39). From Joab's point of view, David's love for Absalom was a dangerous weakness (like his making peace with Abner, 3:24, 25). Joab acted for the sake of David's kingdom, as he saw it. In the death of Absalom justice triumphed over love. If David had his way, love would have triumphed over justice.

The Gospel of Justice (vv. 19–32)

The death of Absalom and the defeat of those who had followed him was an event of immense importance. For those who had remained faithful to David the victory was "good news."

The Messengers (vv. 19–23)

It was the kind of news that a young man like Ahimaaz was keen to take to David. He made his request to Joab: "Then Ahimaaz the son of Zadok said, 'Let me run and carry news to the king'" (v. 19a). Ahimaaz had risked his life already (perhaps more than once) to take news to David from the friends of David within Absalom's circle (17:17–21). For Ahimaaz it would be a privilege to carry the news that it had all been worthwhile.[20]

"Carry news" is gospel language. The New Testament uses the corresponding Greek vocabulary for "preach the gospel."[21] A gospel is momentous news; it is not simply "good news." Sometimes and for some people it is very bad news indeed. Typically this language refers to news of a great victory or triumph. This may be good news for some, but very bad news for those defeated.[22] Ahimaaz wanted to take the gospel of Absalom's defeat to the king. He evidently considered it an honor to be the bearer of such news.

The news (as Ahimaaz understood it) was "that the LORD has delivered [King David] from the hand of his enemies" (v. 19b). "Delivered" is the language of justice—"judged" in the Biblical sense of "to bring justice to a situation," "to put things right."[23] Absalom's defeat was (on this understanding) justice for King David. The rebel had been *justly* overthrown, and the one who was *rightly* king was restored.

Joab was wiser that Ahimaaz. "And Joab said to him, 'You are not to carry news today. You may carry news another day, but today you shall carry no news, because the king's son is dead'"[24] (v. 20). This was not the day for Ahimaaz to be a gospel man. Joab understood what David's perspective would be. The event that Ahimaaz understood as "the LORD has delivered [King David] from the hand of his enemies" (v. 19) was, from David's point of view, "the king's son is dead" (v. 20). Though justice had prevailed, love had lost.

Joab chose a different messenger. "Then Joab said to the[25] Cushite,[26] 'Go, tell the king what you have seen'" (v. 21a). This Cushite was yet another foreigner who had attached himself to King David. Cush was a territory south of Egypt belonging to the descendants of a son of Ham (Genesis 10:6).[27] Joab sent the Cushite to report to the king "what you have seen" (2 Samuel 18:21). Joab used none of the gospel language. Nor did he interpret the event as "justice." He wanted the king to hear from an eyewitness a straightforward account of what had happened. "The Cushite bowed before Joab, and ran" (v. 21b).

Ahimaaz's desire to be part of the announcement to the king was not easily silenced. "Then Ahimaaz the son of Zadok said again to Joab, 'Come what may, let me also run after the Cushite'" (v. 22a). He wanted to be part of this historic event (as he saw it). Joab adopted a fatherly tone. "And Joab said, 'Why will you run, my son, seeing that you will have no reward for the news?'" (v. 22b). Contrary to Ahimaaz's understanding, Joab knew that the news would not be welcomed by David. Ahimaaz's eagerness was not wise.

But the young man's determination was irrepressible, and Joab yielded. "'Come what may,' he said,[28] 'I will run.' So [Joab] said to him, 'Run'" (v. 23a). The head start given to the Cushite probably assured Joab that David would receive the news from him before Ahimaaz reached Mahanaim.

However, "Ahimaaz ran by the way of the plain, and outran the Cushite" (v. 23b). The point is clear, even if the details elude us. Ahimaaz chose a route that enabled him to beat the Cushite to their common destination, Mahanaim. If the forest of Ephraim was on the west side of the Jordan, then Ahimaaz may have taken a more direct route across the plain of the Jordan than the Cushite.[29] If the forest was east of the river, then Ahimaaz may have taken a longer but faster route by a detour along part of the Jordan valley, while the Cushite took the more direct but slower way straight across the mountains.[30]

The Waiting Father (vv. 24–27)

The scene shifts to Mahanaim as David waited anxiously to hear what had happened. "Now David was sitting between the two gates" (v. 24a). These would have been the outer and inner gates of the walled city, between which there was a space where David was seated. No doubt he had been there some time.

David had a man climb onto the wall above the outer gate to scan the horizon for anything that might signal news. At last he saw something. ". . . and when he lifted up his eyes and looked, he saw a man running alone" (v. 24b).

"The watchman called out and told the king. And the king said, 'If he is alone, there is news[31] in his mouth'" (v. 25a). Why else would a man be running alone toward the city? We wait, as David waited: the man "drew nearer and nearer" (v. 25b).

Before the man reached the city, "the watchman saw another man running. And the watchman called to the gate and said, 'See, another man running alone!' The king said, 'He also brings news'" (v. 26). The king was, no doubt, puzzled at *two* messengers approaching the city. The watchman, eager to be as helpful as possible, observed, "I think the running of the first is like the running of Ahimaaz the son of Zadok" (v. 27a). The king was encouraged. "And the king said, 'He is a good man and comes with good news'" (v. 27b).[32] In this context "a good man" probably refers to Ahimaaz's faithfulness to King David.[33] David (perhaps with more than a little wishful thinking) concluded that such a "good" man would be bringing "good" news.

The Gospel That Was Not Good News (vv. 28–32)

Before he got to the king, Ahimaaz shouted, "*Shalom*" ("All is well," v. 28a). "*Shalom*" was the last word that David had spoken to Absalom ("peace," 15:9). Seconds later Ahimaaz reached David. "And he bowed before the king with his face to the earth and said, 'Blessed be the LORD your God, who has delivered up the men who raised their hand against my lord the king'" (v. 28b).

The news Ahimaaz brought to King David was the general news of the victory that had been won (v. 7). This was what he had been so keen to announce to the king. The king, however, wanted more particular news. "And the king said, 'Is it well with the young man Absalom?'" (v. 29a). David wanted to know about the *shalom* of Absalom.

Ahimaaz's reply is a surprise. "Ahimaaz answered, 'When Joab sent the king's servant, your servant, I saw a great commotion, but I do not know what it was'" (v. 29b). If we believe Ahimaaz (and there is no reason why we should not[34]), then he did not know about the killing of Absalom, which had been done by Joab with his ten armor-bearers (vv. 14, 15). Ahimaaz had heard the victory trumpet blast (v. 16), but was not party to the death and burial of Absalom. It is typical of Biblical narrative that this crucial fact has been kept from us until now. Now we can understand Ahimaaz's eagerness to carry the news. He knew David's command to spare Absalom (v. 5), but he did not know that Joab had overridden the king's order. If Ahimaaz did not know about Absalom's death, that provides a fuller explanation for Joab's insistence that the Cushite carry the news (because, as we are about to hear, the Cushite did know).

David accepted what Ahimaaz had said, but was keen to hear the man who was still approaching. "And the king said, 'Turn aside and stand here.' So [Ahimaaz] turned aside and stood still" (v. 30).

At last the Cushite arrived. "And behold, the Cushite came, and the Cushite said, 'Good news for my lord the king! For the LORD has delivered you [done you justice[35]] this day from the hand of all who rose up against you'" (v. 31). Like Ahimaaz, the Cushite spoke, first, of the general victory.

But the king had another concern. "The king said to the Cushite, 'Is it well with the young man Absalom?'" (v. 32a). The Cushite knew what Ahimaaz at least claimed not to know. "And the Cushite answered, 'May the enemies of my lord the king and all who rise up against you for evil be like that young man'" (v. 32b). The language was diplomatic but unambiguous. Perhaps the Cushite was among the ten young men who participated in the killing of Absalom (v. 15). We may now at least deduce that he was a witness to the event (see v. 21).

Justice and Love Did Not Meet (v. 33)

David's reaction to the news is described in one of the most moving verses in the entire Bible:

> And the king was deeply moved and went up to the chamber over the gate and wept. And as he went, he said, "O my son Absalom, my son, my son Absalom! Would I had died instead of you, O Absalom, my son, my son!"
> (v. 33)

There have been many attempts to interpret David's grief. The distress of David, the father, is obvious. But should this be judged a weakness in David the king? Joab thought so, as we will see in the next chapter.

This much is clear: David loved Absalom. But David was unable to save Absalom from the consequences of his rebellion. Joab saw that justice won. Politically Joab was almost certainly right. But politics is not everything. David had experienced God's grace when he had behaved as wickedly as Absalom (12:13). Can it be right to dismiss David's love for his son as weakness? I do not think so.[36]

This episode in the history of David's kingdom is a powerful display of the problem that David's kingdom could not resolve. The king himself was a sinner, as were his sons and his subjects. In particular Absalom was a rebel. Justice demanded one thing. David's love for Absalom longed for something else. Remarkably, David's helpless cry anticipated the solution that would one day be provided. "Would I had died instead of you," David wept (18:33). I do not imagine that David was conscious of the significance of these words. However, when the great son of David eventually came, he came to die *instead of* his enemies—"a ransom *instead of* many," as he said (Matthew 20:28 AT).

> For while we were still weak, at the right time Christ died for the ungodly. For one will scarcely die for a righteous person—though perhaps for a

good person one would dare even to die—but God shows his love for us in that while we were still sinners, Christ died for us. Since, therefore, we have now been justified by his blood, much more shall we be saved by him from the wrath of God. For if while we were enemies we were reconciled to God by the death of his Son, much more, now that we are reconciled, shall we be saved by his life. More than that, we also rejoice in God through our Lord Jesus Christ, through whom we have now received reconciliation. (Romans 5:6–11)

The gospel of Jesus Christ is news of justice and love—justice satisfied by the one who loved us, so that God is "just and the justifier of the one who has faith in Jesus" (Romans 3:26).

36

The Return of the King

2 SAMUEL 19

WHEN CHRISTIAN BELIEVERS PRAY for the kingdom of God, we are praying for the return of our King, the Lord Jesus Christ. On the night before his execution Jesus promised his disciples that he would "come again" (see John 14:3, 18, 28; 16:16, 22). We have seen how that night was, in important ways, like the darkest day in King David's life, when he was rejected by his own people (the nation of Israel) and fled from Jerusalem across the Jordan River and into the wilderness. The parallels between the experiences of Jesus and David also highlight the differences. In particular we have seen that the victory David eventually won over his enemies was problematic. Specifically David's love for Absalom could not save the rebel son from the "justice" of Joab. In contrast, the victory won by Jesus in his death and resurrection was something only God could do. Jesus won his victory by dying instead of his enemies (Romans 5:10), as David had wished he could do for Absalom (18:33). At the cross love and justice did meet.

As we follow David's return as king to Jerusalem, after the victory over Absalom and his rebellion, we will consider the promise of our King to "come again" (John 14:3). It is important to understand that this promise of Jesus has already been substantially (but not finally) fulfilled.

Jesus did "come again" to his disciples on the third day after his death. He was raised from death and came to his astonished disciples. This was the return of the King, just as he had promised. They saw him and touched him, and he spoke with them (see, for example, John 20:19–29). His return was to be proclaimed to the whole world by those who saw him (Luke 24:48; Acts 3:15; 5:32; 10:39, 41; 13:31).

However, there was more to Jesus' promise to "come again" (John 14:3) than his appearances to the disciples over the forty days between his resurrection and his ascension to Heaven (Acts 1:3, 9). Jesus promised, "If anyone loves me, he will keep my word, and my Father will love him, and *we will come to him and make our home with him*" (John 14:23). He was talking about the Holy Spirit (John 14:26). This is the return of the King known to every Christian believer. It is the presence of Jesus by his Spirit in the lives of believers in which we rejoice (Romans 8:9–11).

There is more still. The return of our King in all his glory is still a future event. When he ascended to Heaven, the disciples were told, "This Jesus, who was taken up from you into heaven, will come in the same way as you saw him go into heaven" (Acts 1:11). The New Testament describes this still future return of Jesus as the "revelation" or "unveiling" of Jesus Christ. In other words, it will be the open and undeniable manifestation of something that is already true, something that has already happened. Jesus is Lord today. He has begun to reign. He has won the victory. We are waiting for that reality to be "revealed" (Luke 17:30; 2 Thessalonians 1:7; 1 Peter 1:7, 13; 4:13). On that day every knee will bow, and every mouth will confess the truth that "Jesus Christ is Lord, to the glory of God the Father" (Philippians 2:11).

The return of King David is recounted in 2 Samuel 19. In important ways it was a disappointment. The return of Jesus is not. We will see that:

(1) Love and justice collide (vv. 1–8a).
(2) Repentance is complicated (vv. 8b–14).
(3) The king will return (vv. 15–43).

Love and Justice Collide (vv. 1–8a)

There was a problem with the victory King David's men had won over Absalom. The king loved Absalom. The cost of the victory had been Absalom's death. The victory (or justice in the Biblical sense of things being put right) was therefore not received with joy by David in Mahanaim, but with grief (18:33).

The King's Love (vv. 1–4)

For this reason the king's love for Absalom became a difficulty. Joab (who had been responsible for the victory by executing Absalom) was informed, "Behold, the king is weeping and mourning for Absalom" (v. 1). Joab knew David too well to be surprised by this news. But it was a problem, as the narrator explains:

So the victory that day was turned into mourning for all the people, for the people heard that day, "The king is grieving for his son." And the people stole into the city that day as people steal in who are ashamed when they flee in battle. (vv. 2, 3)

"That day" (strikingly repeated three times in verses 2, 3) of "victory" (literally "salvation") became a day of sadness, not just for the king, but for "all the people" (that is, the people who had remained faithful to David). The king's grief made those who had served him "ashamed" (v. 3). They had risked their own lives for their king. Now they were made to feel that they had acted against him. They came into the city not like the victors they were but like thieves (compare "stole" and "steal" in verse 3 with the same word in 15:6).

These people had wept with their king earlier, as together they climbed the Mount of Olives and fled from Jerusalem (15:30). But that was different. Then they were sharing his sorrow at the loss of the kingdom. Now they were humiliated. Their victory was the cause of their king's grief.

David's anguish is described again. "The king covered his face, and the king cried with a loud voice, 'O my son Absalom, O Absalom, my son, my son!'" (v. 4). The king's grief was inconsolable. His love for Absalom had been great.

Joab's Justice (vv. 5–7)
Joab saw the problem and, as was his way, took it upon himself to deal with it. He confronted the king with his improper conduct (as Joab saw it).

> Then Joab came into the house to the king and said, "You have today covered with shame the faces of all your servants, who have this day saved your life and the lives of your sons and your daughters and the lives of your wives and your concubines. . . ." (v. 5)

These were harsh words. The basic charge was that David had mistreated his servants terribly. They had saved his life (and the lives of his entire household). Instead of the praise and thanks they might reasonably have expected, they found the king they served withdrawn and in mourning *because of what they had done for him*. He had made them ashamed of serving him.

Boldly Joab turned up the heat by attributing David's treatment of his people to perversity: ". . . because you love those who hate you and hate those who love you" (v. 6a). This was a dreadful caricature with a grain of truth. Absalom clearly hated his father, while David just as clearly loved his son. David's servants obviously loved their king. In Joab's judgment, David's mistreatment of them amounted to hatred. This was an unfair exaggeration, but it reasonably represented the perceptions of those who had fought for King David.

Joab was not finished. "For you have made it clear today that commanders and servants are nothing to you" (v. 6b). Again this was unfair, but it was true that David's grief had so overwhelmed him that he was giving no attention to his faithful subjects and what they had done for him.

Joab capped his rebuke with this allegation: "for today I know that if Absalom were alive and all of us were dead today, then you would be pleased" (v. 6c). Joab was angry. He understood the politics. If Absalom had lived and had been given the opportunity, David's servants would have all been killed.[1] According to Joab, David's behavior was telling everyone that he would have preferred that outcome. Is that any way for a king to treat his people?

Joab told David what he must do: "Now therefore arise, go out and speak kindly to your servants" (v. 7a). David had to show that he loved his servants who had proven their love for him.[2]

Joab warned David of the consequences that would follow if the king failed to do what Joab was telling him:

> [F]or I swear by the LORD, if you do not go, not a man will stay with you this night, and this will be worse for you than all the evil that has come upon you from your youth until now. (v. 7b)

This was more a warning than a threat.[3] Although Joab was furious with David, he seems to have been predicting the inevitable political consequences of David's contempt (as he saw it) for his people rather than threatening to bring those consequences about. The people with David had been utterly committed to their king until now. If David did not act to reverse his disgraceful behavior toward them, then it would all be over before morning. And the result would be worse than anything David had previously known. "All the evil that has come upon you from your youth until now" (v. 7) suggests the years as a fugitive from Saul as well as these more recent days when it seemed that Absalom had stolen the kingdom.

What should we think of Joab's forceful speech? Was he right? Was he wise? Should he perhaps have shown a little sympathy for the grieving father? Or was the situation as serious as he obviously thought, so that there was no room for indulging David's sentimentality? Is sentimentality a fair assessment of David's grief? Was his love for Absalom more indulgent than honorable?

Opinions are likely to differ on these questions. The truth is that David's love for Absalom was not able to save the rebel from Joab's justice, and Joab's sense of justice had no space for David's love for his son. The situation was impossible.

A Resolution? (v. 8a)

David listened to Joab. He did what he could.

> Then the king arose and took his seat in the gate. And the people were all told, "Behold, the king is sitting in the gate." And all the people came before the king. (v. 8a)

There is no mention of David speaking to the people,[4] as Joab had demanded. Perhaps in his sorrow that was beyond him. Nonetheless he allowed the people to see him. The scene was hardly joyful. But the people had their king again. He was no longer withdrawn from them.

It was a resolution of sorts there in Mahanaim between David and his faithful supporters. But what next? Would the victory won by David's men translate into the restoration of the kingdom? How would that come about? Much was still uncertain. It was a little like the death of Jesus—victory led to mourning, and it was difficult to see how Jesus could really return as king (cf. Luke 24:21).

Repentance Is Complicated (vv. 8b–14)

From the somber scene in Mahanaim we are taken back to the situation more widely throughout the land. "Now Israel had fled every man to his own home" (v. 8b). "Israel" here refers to those from the northern tribes whose hearts had gone after Absalom (15:13). As a consequence of Absalom's death they had fled (18:17).[5]

Israel's Deliberations (vv. 9, 10)

The death of the pretender focused the minds of those who had been seduced by him (15:6). Absalom's glamor and promises were dead and buried. The hopes and dreams the people had attached to him were dashed, and their worthlessness was now clear. At last the people remembered David, the king they had rejected.

> And all the people were arguing throughout all the tribes of Israel, saying, "The king delivered us from the hand of our enemies and saved us from the hand of the Philistines, and now he has fled out of the land from

> Absalom. But Absalom, whom we anointed over us, is dead in battle.
> Now therefore why do you say nothing about bringing the king back?"
> (vv. 9, 10)

The Hebrew word for "arguing" can suggest a kind of legal dispute (v. 9). It may therefore have been an argument about the legal obligations of the people. Years earlier King David had made a covenant with the elders of Israel (5:3). It is likely that there had been a similar formal agreement made with Absalom, "whom we anointed over us" (19:10). There is no other reference to this "anointing." It probably happened at Hebron (see 15:10; cf. 5:3) and was understood by the people involved to supersede the covenant with David. The question under dispute may have been whether, now that Absalom was dead, the covenant with David could be revived, or had the arrangement with Absalom abolished it?

We only hear one side of the argument—in effect that David had always been their savior. This had been central to the understanding of "all the tribes of Israel" (5:1) years earlier when they had come to David in Hebron to anoint him as their king. "It was you who led out and brought in Israel," they had said (5:2). Remembering this, at least some now saw that it was to their loss that he had "fled out of the land" (19:9). Their anointing of Absalom had been a terrible, foolish mistake. That much was clear now that Absalom was dead. The rejection of their savior-king must therefore now be reversed. It was time to bring their king back. The repeated references to David as "the king" by the people making this argument presupposes the conclusion. They knew that their rightful king was David.

The other side of the argument does not need to be heard, presumably because the narrator had no sympathy for it. The argument that is stated represents the mind that at least some of the people reached.

David's Encouragement (vv. 11–13)

David received word from "all Israel" (the northern tribes) of this change of heart, although it was probably not unanimous. However, "all Israel" did not include the southern tribe of Judah, David's own tribe. Absalom's rebellion had been launched in Judah (at Hebron, 15:10). When David received word from the northern tribes, he sent his own message to the elders of Judah.

> And King David sent this message to Zadok and Abiathar the priests: "Say to the elders of Judah, 'Why should you be the last to bring the king back to his house, when the word of all Israel has come to the king?[6] You are my brothers; you are my bone and my flesh. Why then should you be the

last to bring back the king?' And say to Amasa, 'Are you not my bone and my flesh? God do so to me and more also, if you are not commander of my army from now on in place of Joab.'" (vv. 11–13)

David used the two priests who had served him so well as spies in Jerusalem (15:24–29; 17:15, 16). Presumably they were still in Jerusalem. They could be trusted as David's ambassadors to the elders of Judah.

The message that David sent via the trusted priests urged the elders of Judah to do what "all Israel" had done (v. 11). Earlier Judah had been the first to receive David as king (2:4). "The tribes of Israel" only came later, and after much trouble (5:1–3). David did not want his return to be the reverse of that.

David's message to the elders of Judah is sometimes misunderstood as divisive.[7] Perhaps some of his contemporaries took it that way. It was not David, however, who created the distinction between those who had decided to bring the king back and those who had not. His message was intended to bring Judah and Israel together again.

When he said, "You are my brothers; you are my bone and my flesh" (v. 12), he was not favoring his closer relationship to his own tribe over the northerners, but was rather drawing attention to the identity of relationship that both Judah and the northern tribes had with him. It was the northern tribes who had earlier said, "we are your bone and flesh" (5:1). In our earlier discussion we saw that this statement was weighty in meaning. It was (among other things) a vivid assertion that they belonged to David as his "body." Now David used the same language to lay claim to the people of Judah: they, too, were his "body."[8] They should not lag behind their northern brothers in bringing back their king.

The problem that both the northern tribes and the people of Judah faced was whether David would take reprisals against them for the rebellion. David's surprising word to Amasa signaled that retribution was not on his agenda. Amasa had been appointed commander of the army by Absalom (17:25). David maintained Absalom's appointment. Was this David's revenge on Joab for the death of Absalom?[9] Possibly.[10] But the promise to Amasa (a fellow member of Judah) had the more immediate function of assuring the people of Judah of David's post-rebellion generosity.[11] Furthermore, David seems to have promised Amasa the overall command of the whole army (in place of Joab), but we may assume (and it will later be confirmed, 20:7) that Joab retained his command of the "one third" established by David in 18:2.

Judah's Decision (v. 14)

David's appeal to the people of Judah was effective. "And he swayed the heart of all the men of Judah as one man, so that they sent word to the king, 'Return, both you and all your servants'" (v. 14).

David's message to the elders of Judah was like the gospel—a call to return to the King and to welcome the return of the King.

The Return of the King (vv. 15–43)

David's journey back to Jerusalem, and back to the kingship, retraced the path he had taken as he fled from Absalom, having lost the kingdom. The key word that occurred nine times in 15:18–33 (meaning "pass by" or "cross over"), referring to David's flight eastward across the Jordan, is used fifteen times in 19:15–41 in connection with his return in the opposite direction.[12] We noted earlier that this was the word used repeatedly in Joshua 3, 4 in connection with the entry of the people into the promised land in the days of Joshua. David was reentering the land. His exile in the wilderness was over.

To the Jordan (v. 15)

The narrative is detailed. First we follow the king as he retraced his steps from Mahanaim west to the Jordan River. "So the king came back to the Jordan" (v. 15a). Depending on the route taken, this could have been a journey of fifty miles or so.[13]

This gave time for news of the king's movements to reach the people of Judah. True to their word, they came (the elders representing the rest?) to welcome the king back: "and Judah came to Gilgal to meet the king and to bring the king over the Jordan" (v. 15b). Gilgal was one of those places rich with historical associations. It was on the west side of the Jordan, in the valley, not far from Jericho.[14] In the context of a new crossing of the Jordan, we should be reminded that Gilgal was the first resting place for the Israelites when they entered the promised land in the days of Joshua. It was the place where Israel's life in the land God had given them began (see Joshua 5:10–12).[15] It was an appropriate place for a new beginning. More recently, however, Gilgal had been the place where Samuel had called on the people to "renew the kingdom" (1 Samuel 11:14, 15). It was an appropriate place for the kingdom to be "renewed" once again. However, Gilgal was also the place of Saul's initial failure as king (1 Samuel 13:8–15) and the place where Samuel had confronted him over his great and decisive failure (1 Samuel 15:12–33). Gilgal was the place where Saul was rejected and where the first promise of a "better" king had been made (1 Samuel 13:14; 15:28). It was, therefore, an appropriate place to come to welcome that king back.

People Who Met David Again (vv. 16–40a)

David was on the east side of the Jordan, and the people of Judah were at Gilgal. At this point a number of the people who had met David as the fugitive king some time earlier met him again as he returned to renew the kingdom. For some the change in David's circumstances led to a great change in their stance toward him.

Shimei Who Sought Mercy (vv. 16–23)

The first to meet King David was Shimei, the man who had so boldly shouted violent curses at David as he passed Bahurim (16:5–8). With him was Ziba, who (a little earlier, just past the summit of the Mount of Olives) had brought impressive gifts to ingratiate himself with David (16:1–4).

> And Shimei the son of Gera, the Benjaminite, from Bahurim, hurried to come down with the men of Judah to meet King David. And with him were a thousand men from Benjamin. And Ziba the servant of the house of Saul, with his fifteen sons and his twenty servants, rushed down to the Jordan before the king, and they crossed the ford to bring over the king's household and to do his pleasure. (vv. 16–18a)

Shimei was being as careful now as he had been careless before. The Benjaminite came down "with the men of Judah" (v. 16). He joined the company that had come to welcome King David. The "thousand men from Benjamin" (v. 17) who came with Shimei were an impressive display of a change of heart from Saul's own tribe. Ziba, who had also once been loyal to Saul, rushed down to (or, into[16]) the river. It seems that both Ziba and Shimei, with at least some of their entourages, hurried across the Jordan to meet David in order to escort him back.

These two men seem to have been excessively eager to sort out their standing with David, each for his own reasons. Each had in his own way made a major miscalculation, not expecting David to survive the rebellion.[17] David's surprising return had overturned their world. They were anxious to ensure their security in the renewed kingdom of David. First we hear Shimei's plea for mercy.

> And Shimei the son of Gera fell down before the king, as he was about to cross the Jordan, and said to the king, "Let not my lord hold me guilty or

remember how your servant did wrong on the day my lord the king left Jerusalem. Do not let the king take it to heart. For your servant knows that I have sinned. Therefore, behold, I have come this day, the first of all the house of Joseph to come down to meet my lord the king." (vv. 18b–20)

How different from the furious man who earlier had hurled stones and curses at the apparently defeated king! Now we see him stumbling up out of the Jordan River and falling down in abject submission before the returning king, begging for mercy.

It is tempting to regard Shimei's "repentance" with cynicism. His change of heart seems very convenient. It is doubtful that Shimei would ever have regarded his behavior on the day that David left Jerusalem as "wrong" (v. 19) if David had not returned as king. Shimei's repentance appears to have been thoroughly self-serving.[18]

Such skepticism about Shimei's motives is understandable. The haste with which he made himself "the first of all the house of Joseph" (v. 20)[19] to come to welcome King David back hardly proves his sincerity. But the problem is that if repentance depended on pure motives, repentance would never be effective. When David had uttered exactly the same word that he now heard from Shimei ("I have sinned," 12:13a), it was obvious that his repentance did not arise freely. He had to be forcefully confronted with his wickedness. Nonetheless David's repentance found grace: "The LORD . . . has put away your sin" (12:13b).

Abishai was not inclined to be moved by Shimei's plea for mercy. "Abishai the son of Zeruiah answered, 'Shall not Shimei be put to death for this, because he cursed the LORD's anointed?'" (v. 21). At least this son of Zeruiah was consistent (see 1 Samuel 26:8; 2 Samuel 16:9).

David rejected Abishai's vengeance and treated Shimei (at least for the time being) with the kind of grace he had himself experienced.

But David said, "What have I to do with you, you sons of Zeruiah, that you should this day be as an adversary to me? Shall anyone be put to death in Israel this day? For do I not know that I am this day king over Israel?" And the king said to Shimei, "You shall not die." And the king gave him his oath. (vv. 22, 23)

The Hebrew for "adversary" is *satan*. Elsewhere in the Bible this becomes the name Satan, but here it refers to one "whose business is to entice and accuse a man."[20] Abishai's way of vengeance was not David's way—at least not on "this day" (v. 22; cf. 1 Samuel 11:13). However, this was not the end of Shimei's story (see 1 Kings 2:8, 9, 36–46).

Those who beg for mercy from the returning Lord Jesus will find kindness greater than Shimei could know.

Mephibosheth Who Mourned and Was Comforted (vv. 24–30)

Shimei had been accompanied by Ziba. It was, however, Ziba's master (9:9, 10), the grandson of Saul, whose approach to King David is described next. "And Mephibosheth the son of Saul came down to meet the king" (v. 24a). Since he was lame in both feet (9:13), this would have taken some effort. The narrator describes Mephibosheth's appearance and the reason for it: "He had neither taken care of his feet nor trimmed his beard nor washed his clothes, from the day the king departed until the day he came back in safety" (v. 24b). Immediately we realize that the account that Ziba had given David of Mephibosheth's treachery (16:3) was a lie. Mephibosheth had been deeply distraught by David's troubles rather than hoping to benefit from them.

The conversation that took place between David and Mephibosheth probably occurred later, when both David and Mephibosheth had returned to Jerusalem.[21] It is recorded here to complete the account of Mephibosheth's encounter with the king:

> And when he came to Jerusalem to meet the king, the king said to him, "Why did you not go with me, Mephibosheth?" He answered, "My lord, O king, my servant deceived me, for your servant said to him, 'I will saddle a donkey for myself, that I may ride on it and go with the king.' For your servant is lame. He has slandered your servant to my lord the king. But my lord the king is like the angel of God; do therefore what seems good to you. For all my father's house were but men doomed to death before my lord the king, but you set your servant among those who eat at your table. What further right have I, then, to cry to the king?" And the king said to him, "Why speak any more of your affairs? I have decided: you and Ziba shall divide the land." And Mephibosheth said to the king, "Oh, let him take it all, since my lord the king has come safely home." (vv. 25–30)

Recalling Ziba's assertion that Mephibosheth had stayed in Jerusalem because he hoped that Absalom's revolt would bring the kingdom (that had once been his grandfather's) back to him (16:3), David asked Mephibosheth directly why he had not gone with him from Jerusalem. Mephibosheth's answer indicated that Ziba had refused to help his lame master saddle and mount the donkey that would carry him with David. Instead, as we heard earlier, Ziba went out to David himself with loads of provisions and told his slanderous lie about Mephibosheth. David had responded by passing all of Mephibosheth's possessions over to Ziba (16:1–4).

Mephibosheth came to David, confident that the king would discern right from wrong ("the king is like the angel [or messenger] of God") and glad to submit to King David's will ("what seems good to you," v. 27). Mephibosheth was a man who had already experienced the kindness of David (2 Samuel 9). He understood that he had no "right" to ask the king for anything (v. 28). He was content that the king had returned.

David's response sounds abrupt. His decision to divide the land (reversing his earlier decision, 16:4) means either that he could not decide who was telling the truth (and perhaps was not inclined to bother finding out) or he decided to acknowledge Ziba's generosity and overlook the lie. Either way Mephibosheth cared only that his lord and king had returned. For that reason his mourning turned to joy.

Like Mephibosheth, those who have experienced the kindness of the greater Son of David know that they have no "right" to ask for anything. They find contentment and joy in knowing that their King is coming back to reign perfectly forever (see 1 Thessalonians 1:10).

Barzillai Who Wanted No More (vv. 31–40a)

Barzillai, a resident of the region east of the Jordan (Gilead), had brought help to David when he had reached Mahanaim hungry, weary, and thirsty (17:27–29). This faithful servant of the king now came to support David's return. "Now Barzillai the Gileadite had come down from Rogelim, and he went on with the king to the Jordan, to escort him over the Jordan" (v. 31). The precise location of Rogelim is no longer known, but it was somewhere in the hills (Barzillai "had come down," v. 31) east of the Jordan River, probably not far from Mahanaim.

Like the lame Mephibosheth, it was no small thing for Barzillai to make his way to King David at the Jordan. "Barzillai was a very aged man, eighty years old" (v. 32a). His earlier generosity toward David and his people (17:27–29) had been the beginning of his kindness toward David out of his considerable resources. "He had provided the king with food while he stayed at Mahanaim, for he was a very wealthy man" (v. 32b). Now he was eager to support the return of the king.

For his part David appreciated all that the old man had done for him and hoped to return the kindness. "And the king said to Barzillai, 'Come over with me, and I will provide for you with me in Jerusalem'" (v. 33).

Barzillai did not need to be repaid. His speech to the king is a model of contentment with his lot, happy to know that his king had returned.

> But Barzillai said to the king, "How many years have I still to live, that I should go up with the king to Jerusalem? I am this day eighty years old. Can I discern what is pleasant and what is not? Can your servant taste what he eats or what he drinks? Can I still listen to the voice of singing men and singing women? Why then should your servant be an added burden to my lord the king? Your servant will go a little way over the Jordan with the king. Why should the king repay me with such a reward? Please let your servant return, that I may die in my own city near the grave of my father and my mother. But here is your servant Chimham. Let him go over with my lord the king, and do for him whatever seems good to you." (vv. 34–37)

At his age Barzillai was content to return to his home. The delights of the senses meant little to him now. He only wanted the privilege of accompanying his king "a little way over the Jordan" (v. 36). In his place he asked David to take Chimham (probably a son of Barzillai, see 1 Kings 2:7) and let him enjoy the kindness of the king.

David acceded to Barzillai's request. "And the king answered, 'Chimham shall go over with me, and I will do for him whatever seems good to you, and all that you desire of me I will do for you'" (v. 38). Subtly David indicated that Barzillai's wishes, not David's, would determine how Chimham was treated ("whatever seems good to *you*").

> Then all the people went over the Jordan, and the king went over. And the king kissed Barzillai and blessed him, and he returned to his own home. The king went on to Gilgal, and Chimham went on with him. (vv. 39, 40a)

The king was on his way. Like the Israelites many years earlier he crossed the Jordan River and came to Gilgal (Joshua 4:19).

The King's People (vv. 40b–43)

However, a closer look at the scene reveals that the renewed kingdom of David was fragile. We are taken back to look again at the crossing of the Jordan, this time noticing the larger groups of people who were there: "All the people of Judah, and also half the people of Israel, brought the king on his way" (v. 40b). "Brought the king on his way" is more literally "caused the king to cross over"—that is, to cross over the Jordan. We are not to imagine that this literally involved "all the people of Judah, and also half the people of Israel" (v. 40). It would have been representatives of these populations (presumably elders) who accompanied the king as he crossed the Jordan.

There is a contrast here: "*all* the people of Judah," but only "*half* the people of Israel" were represented (v. 40). Although word had reached David from "all Israel" (v. 11), it seems that the conclusion of their "arguing" (vv. 9, 10) may not have been unanimous. It soon became clear that King David's return did not succeed in uniting the people.

"All the men of Israel" (literally, "every man of Israel"[22]) had a complaint.

> Then all the men of Israel came to the king and said to the king, "Why have our brothers the men of Judah stolen you away and brought the king and his household over the Jordan, and all David's men with him?" (v. 41)

This "all" may be all those who were there, that is, the "half" of verse 40, or it may represent a complaint from the wider population than those who had come to bring the king over the river. Their grievance sounds like the very thing that David had attempted to avoid by urging the elders of Judah not to be "last" to bring the king back (v. 12). The people of Judah were recognized as "our brothers" but had not acted as brothers. They had acted independently and "stolen" David for themselves (v. 41).[23] From what we know the protest seems ill-founded. There were plenty of representatives of the non-Judah tribes included in David's return so far (Shimei, Mephibosheth, Ziba, Barzillai, and then "half the people of Israel," v. 40). It seems unfair for the people of Israel to blame anyone but themselves if they were only partially represented at the king's return.

It was not David who responded to the complaint, but "all the men of Judah" (literally, "each man of Judah").

> All the men of Judah answered the men of Israel, "Because the king is our close relative. Why then are you angry over this matter? Have we eaten at all at the king's expense? Or has he given us any gift?" (v. 42)

The response was partly provocative and partly conciliatory. On the one hand the people of Judah asserted their close relationship to David ("our close relative," v. 42). If they were claiming a closer relationship to David than the other tribes, then this was hardly helpful (see the claim of "all the tribes of Israel" in 5:1). However, the people of Judah insisted that they had not received any privileged treatment from the king. The people of Israel had no reason to be angry.

This did not settle things down.

> And the men of Israel answered the men of Judah, "We have ten shares in the king, and in David also we have more than you. Why then did you despise us? Were we not the first to speak of bringing back our king?" (v. 43a)

The northern tribes asserted superiority. They were ten tribes; Judah was one. They therefore had a greater investment in the kingship than Judah did. They had also been first to speak of bringing back the king. This may have been true, but was it relevant?

The argument raged. The men of Judah had the better of the argument. "But the words of the men of Judah were fiercer than the words of the men of Israel" (v. 43b). "Fiercer" may be better rendered "more weighty." This appears to be the narrator's judgment.[24] It is clear that the return of King David did not unite the people. There were still deep divisions in his kingdom.[25]

One of the greatest accomplishments of the Lord Jesus Christ, in his extraordinary victory and his reign as king, has been to unite his people. He prayed for this on the night before his death (John 17:11, 22). We who belong to him are "all one in Christ Jesus" (Galatians 3:28). The return of our King has accomplished and will accomplish what David's return was not able to bring about, as we will see dramatically in 2 Samuel 20.

37

An Unstable Kingdom

2 SAMUEL 20

THERE IS INSTABILITY in all human organizations, institutions, communities, and nations. That is, the structures we create to support, protect, and enrich human life are not safe. They can collapse and cause much suffering. This is true of everything we build—from roads, bridges, and buildings to economic, legal, and administrative systems.

Ultimately this instability is a consequence of human sinfulness. Sometimes that is obvious. Human greed can cause the failure of an economic system despite the "sound" theory on which it was built. Human hatred can lead to violence and war, despite the best efforts of a body like the United Nations. Human hard-heartedness can allow the vulnerable to suffer unnecessarily, despite the hard work of charitable organizations or governments. Human carelessness can result in the collapse of a building despite the existence of building codes. It is not difficult to cite numerous contemporary examples of such things even in the so-called "stable democracies" in which many of us live. In many less secure parts of the world instability dominates life.

The Bible tells us that this is not how life is meant to be. God is stable. A little later in 2 Samuel we will hear David sing:

> The LORD is my rock and my fortress and my deliverer,
>   my God, my rock, in whom I take refuge,
> my shield, and the horn of my salvation,
>   my stronghold and my refuge,
>   my savior; you save me from violence. (22:2, 3)

David knew that God never collapses; he does not let us down or fail us. The hope of the world is the kingdom of *God*, in which God's perfect will

will be done. The Bible's remarkable message is that God has promised to establish his kingdom forever. The gospel of Jesus Christ is a call to come into that kingdom now by receiving its King.

As we have been following the Bible's account of the kingdom of David, 1,000 years before Jesus Christ, we have seen two aspects to David's kingdom. On the one hand God chose David and made him king of his Old Testament people, Israel. God's promise to establish his kingdom forever was clearly and explicitly made to David. The king in God's promised kingdom would be a son of David (see 7:12–16). David's own kingdom displayed something of the character of God's promised kingdom. "David reigned over all Israel and did justice and righteousness for all his people" (8:15 AT). At its best David's kingdom was astonishing. It provided a glimpse of the promised kingdom of God.

On the other hand David's kingdom was not the promised kingdom. David himself was deeply flawed (like all of us). His failings made his kingdom unstable. He was not wise, powerful, or good enough to establish a permanent kingdom of goodness, love, and justice. His kingdom eventually displayed the weakness of all human communities.

As we come to the end of the story of David's kingdom in the books of Samuel (there is an important epilogue to the story in 2 Samuel 21—24, but 2 Samuel 20 concludes the account of David's rise, fall, and restoration), we see this second aspect of his kingdom displayed. At the end of the story, what we see in David's restored kingdom is:

(1) Rebellion again (vv. 1, 2).
(2) Sadness confirmed (v. 3).
(3) The futile search for stability (vv. 4–22).
(4) An unstable kingdom (vv. 23–26).

Rebellion Again (vv. 1, 2)

Now there happened to be there a worthless man, whose name was Sheba, the son of Bichri, a Benjaminite. And he blew the trumpet and said,

> "We have no portion in David,
> and we have no inheritance in the son of Jesse;
> every man to his tents, O Israel!" (v. 1)

Despite the chapter division the scene has not shifted. A man from Saul's own tribe of Benjamin (like Shimei, 19:16) was "there" (20:1), that is, in the vicinity of Gilgal where the dispute of 19:41–43 had taken place. He was "a worthless man" (v. 1). This vivid description ("man of *belial*") has been applied to a number of characters in the books of Samuel. The Hebrew word *belial* is harsh and is associated with death, wickedness, and rebellion.[1] Hannah had insisted that she was *not* a "daughter of *belial*" (1 Samuel 1:16). The sons of Eli definitely were "sons of *belial*" (1 Samuel 2:12). Certain "sons of *belial*" despised King Saul (1 Samuel 10:27). Nabal was another "son of *belial*" (1 Samuel 25:17, 25). Some of David's own followers were "men of *belial*" (1 Samuel 30:22). Most recently Shimei had cursed David as "a man of *belial*" (16:7).

This man's name was Sheba, and he was "the son of Bichri" (v. 1). This character is mentioned eight times in the Hebrew of 2 Samuel 20; each time he is called "Sheba the son of Bichri."[2] Bichri may have been the name of Sheba's father or of a clan to which he belonged (suggested by the ESV in verse 14, "the Bichrites").[3]

This troublemaker attempted to lead the discontented people of Israel (the northern tribes) to secede from David. Absalom's rebellion had sought to remove David as king. This was a call to the nation to withdraw from his sway.

The basis for Sheba's call was the opposite of what the men of Israel had claimed in 19:43 (not to mention 5:1). "We have no portion in David" (20:1) means "we have no share in his kingdom."[4] The claim was that there was nothing in David's kingdom *for them*. "We have no inheritance" (v. 1) elevates the protest, because "inheritance" is a word for God's gift to Israel (specifically the land, see Deuteronomy 4:21, 38) and also for Israel as God's own people (Deuteronomy 4:20; 9:26). Sheba's message was that the people of Israel would not find that which was rightly theirs (as God's gift) in connection with "the son of Jesse" (2 Samuel 20:1). As it had been on the lips of Saul, "son of Jesse" was a disparaging way of referring to David (1 Samuel 20:27, 30, 31; 22:7, 8, 13).

Sheba was calling "Israel" to leave David ("every man to his tents," 2 Samuel 20:1), effectively seceding from David's kingdom.[5]

Sheba's call was heeded by those who heard it. "So all the men of Israel withdrew[6] from David and followed Sheba the son of Bichri" (v. 2a). The people of Judah were galvanized by the departure of the northerners. "But the men of Judah followed their king steadfastly from the Jordan to Jerusalem" (v. 2b). They clung to their king[7] as he at last returned to Jerusalem.

The fragility of David's kingdom is seen in the initial response to Sheba's call. David returned to Jerusalem with only a small part of his kingdom intact. The situation was as in the early chapters of 2 Samuel, where only

Judah acknowledged David's kingship and the potential for ongoing conflict with the north was ever present. David's restored kingdom was far from stable.

Sadness Confirmed (v. 3)

David's return to Jerusalem was not a happy occasion in other ways too. When he came to his house he discovered (if he had not heard previously) what Absalom had done to his ten concubines whom he had left in Jerusalem "to keep the house" (see 15:16; 16:21, 22). David knew that this terrible event had in fact been a consequence of his own wickedness (12:11, 12). The sadness of it all is deeply moving.

> And David came to his house at Jerusalem. And the king took the ten concubines whom he had left to care for the house and put them in a house under guard and provided for them, but did not go in to them. So they were shut up until the day of their death, living as if in widowhood. (v. 3)

We will not discuss again here the matter of David having concubines (see our discussions of 3:7; 5:13). David put these women, who had been violated by Absalom, "in a house under guard" (20:3). This was probably to protect them rather than to imprison them.[8] David saw that they were adequately provided for.[9] He did not, therefore, cast them out. He maintained his responsibility for their welfare. However, he had no further sexual relations with them. Was this David's way of trying to distance himself from his earlier practice of having concubines?[10] If so, we notice how sinful behavior (if we may so characterize the practice in the light of Deuteronomy 17:17) does harm, even in the undoing of it. The sadness of the last sentence of verse 3 is immense. These women were "shut up" (or "restricted") for the rest of their lives, probably referring to their situation of "widowhood of one still living."[11]

These sad women represent something important about David's kingdom now. It was a kingdom that suffered the consequences of sinful men. David himself was responsible for the sadness of these women. So was Absalom. David was not the kind of king who could wipe away their tears.

The Futile Search for Stability (vv. 4–22)

First Attempt: Amasa (vv. 4, 5)

We return to the problem of Sheba's rebellion. David called his nephew Amasa, the man Absalom had appointed as overall commander of the army

(17:25), whom David had promised to keep on in place of Joab (19:13). "Then the king said to Amasa, 'Call the men of Judah together to me within three days, and be here yourself'" (v. 4). David's unstated intention was (as we will soon see) to take urgent military action against Sheba. Amasa obeyed David's command, but did not manage to meet the timetable. "So Amasa went to summon Judah, but he delayed beyond the set time that had been appointed him" (v. 5). The reasons for Amasa's delay are not important (he may have met resistance among the men of Judah, possibly because, as Absalom's former commander they did not trust him[12] or simply because the time frame was so short[13]). The urgency of the task at hand forced David to seek an alternative.

Second Attempt: Abishai (vv. 6, 7)

David did not turn to Joab, his other nephew, who (as far as we know) had not yet been formally replaced as overall commander of the army and in any case was presumably still the commander of his division (18:2). It is likely that the king's relationship with Joab was frosty (since by now Joab had certainly heard of David's intention to replace him in the top job, and David had surely heard about Joab's role in Absalom's death).

David chose to entrust the mission to Joab's brother (therefore another nephew of David), Abishai.

> And David said to Abishai, "Now Sheba the son of Bichri will do us more harm than Absalom. Take your lord's servants and pursue him, lest he get himself to fortified cities and escape from us." And there went out after him Joab's men and the Cherethites and the Pelethites, and all the mighty men. They went out from Jerusalem to pursue Sheba the son of Bichri. (vv. 6, 7)

Sheba's rebellion was, in David's mind, a sequel to Absalom's. If successful, the permanent harm to David's kingdom would be greater than that done by Absalom's failed but nonetheless damaging uprising. The urgency of the mission for David had to do with reaching Sheba before he found a secure hiding place, under the protection of a well-fortified city.[14] Abishai's task was to "pursue him" (v. 6) to prevent such an escape, seeing the possibility of further trouble from Sheba in the future.

Abishai led out a force made up of the Cherethites and the Pelethites (see 8:18; 15:18) and "all the mighty men" (v. 7; see 10:7; 16:6; 17:8). The surprise is that the troops who went out with Abishai included a contingent called "Joab's men" (v. 7). This would be the division under Joab's command

(18:2). Why did "Joab's men" go out with Abishai rather than "Abishai's men"? And where was Joab himself?

In a moment we will see that Joab, true to character, had no intention of allowing himself to be sidelined, even by his king. Abishai went out as the king commanded, but it was Joab's division that he took, and Joab was with them (as we will see). Abishai did not obstruct his brother, but seems to have allowed him, as was his way, to take the lead. It is a fair guess that the involvement of Joab and his men was Joab's idea and unknown to David.

This substantial force, ostensibly under the command of Abishai, "went out from Jerusalem to pursue Sheba the son of Bichri" (v. 7).

The "Success" of Joab (vv. 8–22)

It soon becomes clear that the man in charge was in fact Joab. Joab, as always, had his own way of securing David's kingdom. It was not David's way. Joab had executed Abner when David wanted to make peace with him (3:26–39). He had killed Absalom when David wanted his son spared (18:9–15). He had no patience with David's grief over Absalom's death (19:5, 6). Joab always wanted to secure David's kingdom by means of muscle and sword. He knew no other way. He now did it again. Unknown to David, it was Joab who went out with Abishai and the troops to do more than find Sheba.

Joab Killed Amasa (vv. 8–13)

The men under Joab/Abishai's command came to Gibeon, about five miles northwest of Jerusalem. Gibeon was the site of the early confrontation between the northern tribes who had made Ish-bosheth their king and the servants of King David led by Joab (2:12–32).[15] On that occasion initial attempts at diplomacy had led to a bloody battle in which Joab's brother Asahel had been killed. It was a place with bitter memories, particularly for Joab.

"When they were at the great stone that is in Gibeon, Amasa came to meet them" (v. 8a). "The great stone" was probably a landmark well-known to the historian and his early readers, although it is no longer identifiable. The Hebrew does not suggest (as the English could) that Amasa deliberately came to "the great stone . . . in Gibeon" in order to meet with "them" (v. 8). Literally it simply says, "Amasa came before them." We do not know whether the meeting was prearranged somehow or accidental or even a deliberate interception of one party by the other.

The crucial thing is who was there. For the first time the narrator tells us explicitly that Joab was there and provides an unusually detailed description of his uniform. "Now Joab was wearing a soldier's garment, and over it was a belt with a sword in its sheath fastened on his thigh, and as he went forward it fell out" (v. 8b). The belt was a status symbol (see 2 Samuel 18:11; 1 Kings 2:5). Joab was present with "Joab's men," and he was in charge, he was armed, and he was dangerous. "As he went forward it fell out" (v. 8) probably refers to a swift movement by which Joab's "sword" (probably a dagger) swiftly "fell" from its scabbard into Joab's hand.[16]

Joab pretended warm friendliness, even affection, toward his cousin. "And Joab said to Amasa, 'Is it well with you, my brother?' And Joab took Amasa by the beard with his right hand to kiss him" (v. 9). "Is it well . . . ?" represents the Hebrew word *shalom* ("peace"). We have heard this word before in connection with the work of Joab. It had been a key word leading up to Joab's murder of Abner (3:21–23). David had used the word in his treacherous dealing with Uriah (11:7) that led to Uriah's death at Joab's hand. Once again Joab's intentions were anything but "peace" for Amasa.

As Joab's right hand feigned an expression of love, its real work was to distract Amasa from Joab's other hand.

> But Amasa did not observe the sword that was in Joab's hand. So Joab struck him with it in the stomach and spilled his entrails to the ground without striking a second blow, and he died. (v. 10a)

Joab was an efficient killer. Abner (3:27), Uriah (11:16, 17), Absalom (18:14, 15), and now Amasa had been violently killed directly or indirectly by Joab's hand. For the second time he had now taken out the commander of Israel's army who had made "peace" with King David. This was not forgotten. In years to come David will instruct his son Solomon to ensure that "peace" is taken from Joab for these two acts (see 1 Kings 2:5, 6).

For the time being, however, the prospect of Joab's being replaced by Amasa was averted. David's sidelining of Joab was effectively frustrated. Joab was in charge again. The ruthlessness of Joab's murder of Amasa is chilling. The pursuit of Sheba resumed (now clearly under Joab's command) as if nothing had happened. "Then Joab and Abishai his brother pursued Sheba the son of Bichri" (v. 10b).[17]

Actually it was not quite as simple as that.[18] The brutal killing of Amasa stunned everyone. The king's goodwill toward Amasa was no secret. His intention to replace Joab with Amasa had been announced (19:13). How would the troops, who were after all *David's* men, react to Joab's astonishing insubordination? One of Joab's lads (on Joab's instruction, no doubt)

stood beside the bloody corpse of Amasa and declared that there was no conflict of loyalty. "And one of Joab's young men took his stand by Amasa and
said, 'Whoever favors Joab, and whoever is for David, let him follow Joab'"
(v. 11). *To "favor" Joab is to be "for David" and vice versa. If you belong
to David, you will "follow Joab."* By this audacious proclamation Joab was
insisting that what he had done was in the service of David. That, no doubt,
was his judgment. The king had been foolish to entrust the command of the
army to Amasa "in place of Joab" (19:13). Joab knew better and had put
things right. As always, no matter how much he departed from David's will
and David's ways, Joab was sure that he was serving David and his kingdom.

This time it was not easy to persuade the troops. The sight of Amasa's bleed-
ing body stopped people in their tracks. "And Amasa lay wallowing in his blood
in the highway. And anyone who came by, seeing him, stopped" (v. 12a). The
solution was simple, if gruesome: "And when the man saw that all the people
stopped, he carried Amasa out of the highway into the field and threw a garment
over him" (v. 12b). That did the trick. The idea that following Joab was the same
thing as following David was easier to believe when Amasa's slaughtered body
was out of sight. And so "when he was taken out of the highway, all the people
went on after Joab to pursue Sheba the son of Bichri" (v. 13).

Joab Defeated Sheba (vv. 14–22a)

The scene shifts, and we follow Sheba, briefly filling in what had happened
since verse 2a: "And Sheba[19] passed through all the tribes of Israel to Abel of
Beth-maacah, and all the Bichrites[20] assembled and followed him in" (v. 14).

It seems that Sheba had not been highly successful. He had initially
persuaded "all the men of Israel" to withdraw from David (v. 2a), but by the
time he reached the city of Abel to the far north, only the family clan of this
"son of Bichri" ("all the Bichrites") was following him (v. 14).

Abel Beth-maacah was 100 miles or so north from the locations in the
story so far (Gilgal, Jerusalem, and Gibeon) and twenty-five miles north of
the Sea of Galilee.[21] Sheba had taken himself as far as he could from King
David's reach. This was not, however, beyond the reach of the determined
Joab, who was now firmly in charge of the pursuit. By some means they
found out where Sheba was. "And all the men who were with Joab[22] came
and besieged him in Abel of Beth-maacah. They cast up a mound against
the city, and it stood against the rampart, and they were battering the wall to
throw it down" (v. 15).

Joab was once again doing things his way. He had experience with besieging cities (11:1; 12:26). If he had to destroy the city of Abel to remove

the threat of Sheba (who by now was not much of a threat), then so be it. The power of the battering ram was Joab's way.

However, things unfolded differently. Ironically it was a woman who, in effect, took charge. "Then a wise woman called from the city, 'Listen! Listen! Tell Joab, "Come here, that I may speak to you"'" (v. 16). Earlier Joab had used a "wise woman" in his attempt to reconcile David to Absalom (see 14:2). Now another "wise woman" took the initiative to save her city from the destructive forces of Joab. The negotiation, probably from the top of the city wall, is described in unusual detail, and we are left in no doubt that the woman's skills justified her reputation as "wise."[23]

The assault on the city paused as Joab responded to the woman's call. "And he came near her, and the woman said, 'Are you Joab?' He answered, 'I am.' Then she said to him, 'Listen to the words of your servant.' And he answered, 'I am listening'" (v. 17). She was careful and respectful ("your servant," v. 17). Joab's response is surprising. "I am listening" (v. 17) almost means "I am ready to obey you."[24]

The woman presented her case. First she pointed out the reputation of her city. "Then she said, 'They used to say in former times, "Let them but ask counsel at Abel," and so they settled a matter'" (v. 18). The woman may have played a leading role in the counseling services for which Abel had long been famous. Was Joab aware of the high regard in which this city was held as he pounded the walls with his weapons?

Second, she went on, "I am one of those who are peaceable and faithful in Israel" (v. 19a). "I" is emphatic, but she was speaking (as the plurals suggest) as a representative of the inhabitants of the city.[25] They were not troublemakers, but "peaceable and faithful."

Third, in contrast, "You seek to destroy a city that is a mother in Israel" (v. 19b). "You" is emphatic. How could it be right for Joab, whose name means "the Lord is Father," to bring death (as the Hebrew for "destroy" suggests) to a city who means so much to Israel that she is a "mother"?

Fourth, "Why will you swallow up[26] the heritage of the LORD?" (v. 19c). "The heritage of the LORD" means the people of Israel as the Lord's inalienable possession (see 1 Samuel 10:1; 26:19; 2 Samuel 21:3).[27] Joab's assault on this city, the woman implied, was an attack against the Lord himself.

The woman's forthright speech found its mark. The powerful Joab was forced to back down from his assault on the city. "Joab answered, 'Far be it from me, far be it, that I should swallow up or destroy!'" (v. 20). This, of course, is the same Joab who had never hesitated to "swallow up or destroy" when that was what he considered necessary. Violence was a means he readily employed to accomplish his ends. His words sound hollow, especially as only moments earlier he had his forces battering the city wall to throw it down.

Remarkably, however, the wise woman's words brought Joab to a more proportionate action. He continued, "That is not true [referring to the woman's accusing words]. But a man of the hill country of Ephraim,[28] called Sheba the son of Bichri, has lifted up his hand against King David. Give up him alone, and I will withdraw from the city" (v. 21a). Joab still saw himself as serving the interests of King David. The irony is palpable. If Sheba had "lifted up his hand against King David" (v. 21), what had Joab just done in slaughtering the man David had chosen to command his army?

To save her city the woman was pleased to satisfy Joab's requirement. "And the woman said to Joab, 'Behold, his head shall be thrown to you over the wall'" (v. 21).

She proved true to her word. "Then the woman went to all the people in her wisdom. And they cut off the head of Sheba the son of Bichri and threw it out to Joab" (v. 22a). It seems that we were right to suppose that she was a leader in the city. "Her wisdom"—that is her practical counsel for the situation—was accepted by "all the people," who proceeded to arrange the beheading of the unfortunate Sheba and the delivery of his head to Joab (v. 22).

Joab Won (v. 22b)

Joab had prevailed. Again. By force of personality and arms he had taken control. All was well again, as far as Joab was concerned. "So he blew the trumpet, and they dispersed from the city, every man to his home. And Joab returned to Jerusalem to the king" (v. 22b).

I am not at all sure how pleased David would have been to see him. David's kingdom was secure again, in a manner of speaking. It was secure on Joab's terms, not David's. Against the king's will Absalom and Amasa were dead. Contrary to David's declared intention, Joab was in command of the army. If David's kingdom depended on Joab's ways, how secure was it?

An Unstable Kingdom (vv. 23–26)

The chapter, and the account of the restoration of the kingdom, concludes with a list of office-bearers in David's kingdom. The paragraph is very similar to 8:15–18. The differences, however, are striking. It is worth setting out the two paragraphs side by side to highlight these.

2 Samuel 8:15–18 (slightly rearranged[29])	2 Samuel 20:23–26
So David reigned over all Israel. And David administered justice and equity to all his people.	
Joab the son of Zeruiah was over the army,	Now Joab was in command of all the army of Israel;
and Benaiah the son of Jehoiada was over the Cherethites and the Pelethites,	and Benaiah the son of Jehoiada was in command of the Cherethites and the Pelethites;
	and Adoram was in charge of the forced labor;
and Jehoshaphat the son of Ahilud was recorder,	and Jehoshaphat the son of Ahilud was the recorder;
and Seraiah was secretary,	and Sheva was secretary;
and Zadok the son of Ahitub and Ahimelech the son of Abiathar were priests,	and Zadok and Abiathar were priests;
and David's sons were priests.	and Ira the Jairite was also David's priest.

Notice three striking points of comparison. First, there is nothing corresponding to 8:15 in 2 Samuel 20. David was now struggling to reign over "all Israel," but it was far from clear that "justice and equity" (or "justice and righteousness") prevailed in David's kingdom. The words of 8:15 no longer described David's kingdom.

Second, Joab was *still* over the army. That may have seemed right in 2 Samuel 8, but now it was a sign of the compromise of David's kingdom. Joab was in command *despite* the intention of King David. Furthermore Joab's power is emphasized with "the army" (8:16) expanded to "all the army of Israel" (20:23).[30]

Third, David now had someone named Adoram (elsewhere called Adoniram) "in charge of the forced labor." This was a new development, and hardly a positive one. "The forced labor" (v. 24) was some kind of slavery, probably working on building projects (cf. Deuteronomy 20:11). In due course forced labor included Israelites and contributed to the eventual division of the kingdom (see 1 Kings 4:6; 5:14; 12:4, 18).

Other differences between the two paragraphs are of less consequence. Sheva had replaced Seraiah as secretary (or were these two versions of the same name?[31]). Abiathar is mentioned in the place where his son Ahimelech stood in 8:17. Both father and son seem to have served as priests. Corresponding to the perplexing reference to David's sons as priests (8:18), we find that "Ira the Jairite was also David's priest" (20:26). Ira was probably a descendant of Jair, the son of Manasseh, who took certain villages on the east side of the Jordan (Numbers 32:41; Deuteronomy 3:14; Joshua 13:30).

He was not, therefore, a Levite. We know no more about his role as "David's priest."

The list of officials that in 2 Samuel 8 had been testimony to the order, justice, and righteousness of David's kingdom is in 2 Samuel 20 merely a description of the externals that had been recovered. It was no longer the remarkable kingdom it had been. The consequences of David's sin had undermined the goodness of his kingdom, and Joab's brutal force could not retrieve it. David's kingdom had become too like the kingdoms of this world, held together by the likes of Joab. This is a somber moment in Biblical history. David's kingdom will, in fact, never recover.

And yet the hope of the world is the promise that God made to David. The gospel of our Lord Jesus Christ announces the day when "the kingdom of the world has become the kingdom of our Lord and of his Christ, and he shall reign forever and ever" (Revelation 11:15). We who have come to Jesus Christ are "receiving a kingdom that cannot be shaken" (Hebrews 12:28). In this kingdom, to which we belong and for which we are waiting, there is no place for underhanded ways like the ways of Joab. This kingdom cannot be built by cunning, deceit, or brute force (see 2 Corinthians 4:2). Church politicians, take note! This kingdom is a matter of "righteousness and peace and joy in the Holy Spirit" (Romans 14:17).

Epilogue

THE KINGDOM OF DAVID AND THE KINGDOM OF GOD

2 Samuel 21—24

38

A Problem in
David's Kingdom:
God's Wrath, Part 1

2 SAMUEL 21:1–14

CHAPTERS 21—24 OF 2 SAMUEL form an epilogue to the books of Samuel.[1] This carefully arranged material presents us with important perspectives on the kingdom of David, the kingdom of God, and the relationship between them. These chapters look back over the whole period of David's reign (and earlier). The text is not arranged chronologically but thematically. We can characterize this arrangement as follows:[2]

> 21:1–14 A problem in David's kingdom: God's wrath, part 1.
>> 21:15–22 The strength of David's kingdom: his mighty men, part 1.
>>> 22:1–51 The hope of David's kingdom: the Lord's promise, part 1.
>>> 23:1–7 The hope of David's kingdom: the Lord's promise, part 2.
>> 23:8–39 The strength of David's kingdom: his mighty men, part 2.
> 24:1–25 A problem in David's kingdom: God's wrath, part 2.

The first section of the epilogue (21:1–14) tells of a terrible sequence of events from an unspecified time during David's reign. It is one of the Bible's most difficult stories. It is not so much difficult to understand as difficult to hear and accept. Although the main action involves a relatively small number of people, it is an account of immense personal suffering, unimaginable grief, and what feels like intolerable unfairness. It is a story that will cause most sensitive readers to wonder what is going on. Our greatest difficulty is God's role in what happened.

The emotions, perplexity, and disquiet that most of us will feel as we follow this story are not new to us. Even those fortunate enough to have never experienced great atrocities have heard about them. The cruelties of war, the atrocities of child abuse, the suffering of poverty—these and so many other horrors appear almost daily on our television news broadcasts. Whenever we pause to take seriously any one of these events (which we too rarely do), the immense tragic sadness is overwhelming. Most of us do not think much about these things because it is just too hard. But the toughest questions are about how and why God allows such things to happen.

Very often it is the horror of human suffering (and so much of it) that is given as the reason when a thoughtful person refuses to believe in God. An impossible contradiction is felt between an all-powerful God who is supposed to be good and the unbearable things that occur under his supposed eye.

Answers are not simple. The denial of God's existence is a simple but hardly helpful answer. Atheism "solves" the problem of evil by replacing it with the problem of goodness. If there is no God, then goodness is a matter of opinion. You have "solved" the problem of suffering and sadness by denying it is a problem. If there is no God, and if goodness is a matter of opinion, then the awful suffering of which we have been thinking is just a fact, not really a problem.

A more realistic answer has to face uncomfortable truths. One of them is the righteous wrath of God. We would all like God to be comfortable. He is not. He is good, but his goodness is not determined by ideas that we find cozy. God's goodness is actually terrifying.

Let's turn to the first part of the epilogue to the books of Samuel and carefully consider the horrors that are presented there. We will hear about:

(1) The famine (vv. 1, 2).
(2) The conversation (vv. 3–6).
(3) The execution (vv. 7–9).
(4) The surprise (vv. 10–14).

The Famine (vv. 1, 2)

The Observable Facts (v. 1a)

The story begins at a difficult time in David's kingdom. "Now there was a famine in the days of David for three years, year after year" (v. 1a). "In the days of David" means in the days of David's reign over Israel (therefore not before 2 Samuel 5). However, a three-year famine is not mentioned anywhere in the record of David's reign in 2 Samuel 5—20. The appearance of Mephibosheth in 21:7 narrows down the time frame slightly. The famine must have been after the events of 2 Samuel 9.[3]

Precisely when the famine occurred is unimportant. The focus is on the hardship it brought. For three whole years ("year after year") food was in short supply. Harvests failed. People were hungry.

It was what we call a natural disaster. Like floods, bushfires, and earthquakes, there may be prudent measures that a society can take to mitigate the suffering caused by such calamities, but there is nothing we can do to avert them altogether. We cannot control these catastrophes. This famine was certainly beyond David's power.

Behind the Observable Facts (vv. 1b, c, 2)

However, David knew the one who did have power over such things. Therefore "David sought the face of the LORD" (v. 1b). The expression "to seek the face of" suggests a person seeking an audience with a ruler.[4] Here the king came before the King. By the end of this story we will learn that David prayed to God for the land that was suffering from this famine ("the plea for the land," v. 14). He may also have asked the Lord whether there was a reason for the famine.

It is important for us to understand that the reason for any particular terrible event or situation in the world may be unknowable to us. This is one lesson from the book of Job. There was a reason for Job's suffering, revealed to readers of the book in chapters 1, 2, but Job and the other personalities in the book never learn of this. It is possible to trust that God has his reasons without knowing what those reasons are. Eventually Job learned to trust God like that (Job 42:1–6).

However, on this occasion when David prayed, the Lord told him the reason for the famine.[5] "And the LORD said, 'There is bloodguilt on Saul and on his house, because he put the Gibeonites to death'" (2 Samuel 20:1c).

Here our difficulties with this story begin. The Lord's word to David clearly implied that there was a connection between "bloodguilt" (v. 1)[6] and the famine now being suffered by the people throughout David's kingdom. The "bloodguilt" is explained in terms of something that Saul had done. He had killed certain Gibeonites. In a moment we will learn that there was a particular issue with the Gibeonites. Before we hear about that let us carefully note the difficulty we have with the idea that Saul's deed should bring "bloodguilt" on his "house" (his family in a wide sense; see "house of Saul" in 3:1, 6, 8, 10; 9:1, 2, 3; 16:5, 8) and that this should somehow be causally connected to the suffering of people long after Saul's death, this famine "in the days of David" (20:1).

Our problems are magnified by the fact that this is how the Lord saw the situation. King Saul's deed had terrible consequences for his whole family and for the nation because of God's view of what Saul did. They suffered what can rightly be called God's wrath because of King Saul's action against the Gibeonites. How can that be right? We will return to that question.

However, King David did not ask that question. We might wonder whether he understood something that we do not. Instead David arranged to have a very important conversation. "So the king called the Gibeonites and spoke to them" (v. 2a).

Before we listen to that conversation, the narrator fills in some of the background. First, who were the Gibeonites? They were the original inhabitants of Gibeon, a town that has featured prominently twice in the books of Samuel.[7] Gibeon was the site of the battle between Ish-bosheth's men under Abner and David's men under Joab when only the tribe of Judah had accepted David as king (2:12–28). Much later Gibeon was where Joab killed Amasa (20:8–10). While the mention of the Gibeonites here may remind us of these two events, the original people of Gibeon played no role in either. "Now the Gibeonites were not of the people of Israel but of the remnant of the Amorites" (v. 2b). That is, the Gibeonites were survivors from the indigenous Canaanite peoples who had been displaced when the Lord gave the promised land to the people of Israel.[8]

How had the Gibeonites survived the Israelite conquest? Briefly, "the people of Israel had sworn to spare them" (v. 2c). The circumstances of this unusual arrangement are recounted in Joshua 9:3–27. The Gibeonites had, with good reason, feared the conquering Israelites and had tricked them into thinking that they were not occupants of Canaan, but from a distant country. The people of Israel failed to "ask counsel from the LORD" about this, and Joshua made peace with the Gibeonites and a covenant to let them live (Joshua 9:14, 15). When the Israelites discovered the deception, they considered themselves nonetheless to be bound by the oath they had sworn "by the LORD, the God of Israel" (Joshua 9:19, 20). Whatever we might think about the Gibeonites' deception, they were right to fear the Israelites who were the instrument of the Lord's judgment on the "the iniquity of the Amorites" (see Genesis 15:16). They were also right not to join the kings who "gathered together as one to fight against Joshua and Israel" (Joshua 9:2). As a consequence they received mercy and were permitted to live safely among the Israelites.

Despite this King Saul "had sought to strike them down in his zeal for the people of Israel and Judah" (v. 2b). Saul's zeal had led him to a number of terribly misguided actions. Most of those we know about occurred because of his zeal for his own position and his furious jealousy of David's popularity and success (see, for example, 1 Samuel 22:18, 19). Perhaps in Saul's mind this was "zeal for the people of Israel and Judah" (2 Samuel 20:2). His actions against the Gibeonites were not included in the earlier record of Saul's reign, perhaps because of the focus there on the relationship between Saul and David. Now we learn that Saul had disregarded the oath that had been sworn to the Gibeonites and killed an unknown number of them.[9] Whatever Saul imagined his motivation was, this action incurred the wrath of God (as anticipated in Joshua 9:20).

Having heard from the Lord what was behind the famine, David summoned the Gibeonites (presumably this was the leaders of the Gibeonites who had survived Saul's purge) and spoke with them.

The Conversation (vv. 3–6)

David's Inquiry (v. 3)

> And David said to the Gibeonites, "What shall I do for you? And how shall I make atonement, that you may bless the heritage of the LORD?" (v. 3)

Notice that although the Lord had told David that Saul's slaughter of the Gibeonites was behind the famine, the Lord did not tell David what to do about it. David set about working out what was to be done by consulting the victims. This implicitly acknowledged the oath that Saul had disregarded.

David wanted to "make atonement" (v. 3). Here this loaded term probably means both to satisfy the justified grievance of the Gibeonites and to "make amends" (JB) for the wrong done to them.[10]

The outcome David sought was that the Gibeonites would "bless" the people and land of Israel, "the heritage of the LORD" (v. 3). This would bring the Gibeonites within the promise God made to Abraham ("I will bless those who bless you," Genesis 12:3) and so restore the "peace" made with the Gibeonites by Joshua.

The Gibeonites' Evasion (v. 4a)

> The Gibeonites said to him, "It is not a matter of silver or gold between us and Saul or his house; neither is it for us to put any man to death in Israel." (v. 4a)

Understandably the Gibeonites were cautious in their response to King Saul's successor. They made no demand. They did not want monetary compensation. The offense was not one that could or should be dealt with so easily (cf. Numbers 35:31). On the other hand, the Gibeonites recognized that they had no right to take the life of any Israelite.

David's Promise (v. 4b)

David took the last point in the Gibeonites' response as an indication of what they really expected. "And he said, 'What do you say that I shall do for you?'" (v. 4b). This was in effect a promise from David to do whatever they were asking.[11]

The Gibeonites' Proposal (vv. 5, 6a)

The Gibeonites now spoke more freely and spelled out what they considered would "atone" for the atrocities that Saul had committed against them.

> They said to the king, "The man who consumed us and planned to destroy us, so that we should have no place in all the territory of Israel, let seven of his sons be given to us, so that we may hang them before the LORD at Gibeah of Saul, the chosen of the LORD." (vv. 5, 6a)

What Saul had done ("consumed us"), what he intended ("to destroy us"), and what he was hoping to achieve ("that we should have no place in all the territory of Israel") are described without using Saul's name. He is "the man" who carried out this atrocity.

What the Gibeonites proposed in order to "make atonement" (v. 3) for this outrage is the central horror of this story. Seven "sons" (v. 6; literally, "men from his sons," meaning male descendants) of Saul were to be handed over to the Gibeonites. Seven is probably deliberately symbolic (as well as literal) of the whole house of Saul.[12] The Gibeonites proposed that they would "hang" these seven (v. 6). There is debate about the precise means of execution indicated by the Hebrew word here. Some suggest "impale"[13] or even "crucify."[14] It makes little difference. These seven descendants of Saul were to be put to death in a public execution.

This would happen, said the Gibeonites, "before the LORD" (v. 6). This would not be an act of vengeance on their part, but a judicial act, like Samuel's execution of Agag "before the LORD" (1 Samuel 15:33). The Lord would be witness to it and would, the Gibeonites seemed sure, approve.

They chose the location for the killing—Saul's hometown of Gibeah

(1 Samuel 10:26; 11:4; 14:2; 15:34; 22:6; 23:19; 26:1). With bitter sarcasm, now that his name had been used, they added, "the chosen of the LORD" (2 Samuel 21:6).

This is what the Gibeonites proposed as "atonement" (v. 3) for the horrors that Saul had carried out against them, in breach of the covenant that had been made between the peoples of Gibeon and Israel. We should observe carefully that the proposal did not come from the Lord. This fact does not solve the deep difficulties of this story, but should nonetheless be noted.

David's Agreement (v. 6b)

The discomfort we feel at what was being proposed is intensified when we hear David's response. "And the king said, 'I will give them'" (v. 6b). There are no grounds for the suggestion sometimes made that David agreed to this course of action in order to eliminate potential rivals to his throne.[15] However, neither is David's acquiescence presented as an act of obedience to a word from the Lord.

The Execution (vv. 7–9)

Before we hear the terrible details of the execution being carried out, the narrator notes how David, in contrast to Saul, honored an oath that had been made earlier.

Mephibosheth (v. 7)

> But the king spared Mephibosheth, the son of Saul's son Jonathan, because of the oath of the LORD that was between them, between David and Jonathan the son of Saul. (v. 7)

The story of David's kindness to Mephibosheth in 2 Samuel 9 has this brief sequel. At a terrible time, when descendants of Saul were to be killed, David remembered his promise to Mephibosheth's father, Saul's son Jonathan, and saw that he was protected. We presume that Mephibosheth lived out the rest of his days under the kindness of King David.

Although it is likely that the encounter with David in 19:24 occurred after these events, this is the last we hear of Mephibosheth in the Bible (we will hear of another man by the same name in the next verse).

The Execution (vv. 8, 9)

Verse 7 is only a brief respite to the horrors of this story. We now witness the carrying out of the wishes of the Gibeonites.

> The king took the two sons of Rizpah the daughter of Aiah, whom she bore
> to Saul, Armoni and Mephibosheth; and the five sons of Merab[16] the daugh-
> ter of Saul, whom she bore to Adriel the son of Barzillai the Meholathite;[17]
> and he gave them into the hands of the Gibeonites, and they hanged them
> on the mountain before the LORD, and the seven of them perished together.
> They were put to death in the first days of harvest, at the beginning of bar-
> ley harvest. (vv. 8, 9)

Two sons from one family and five from another were handed over to
the Gibeonites. The mother of the two, Rizpah, was introduced in 3:7, where
we were told that she had been Saul's concubine. On that occasion she was
at the center of a row between Saul's son Ish-bosheth and his military commander, Abner.

Now we discover that Rizpah had two sons by Saul. These would have
been half-brothers to Jonathan. We are left to wonder what may have been
behind Jonathan's naming his son, Mephibosheth, after one of these. We
might guess that these two sons, born in Saul's lifetime, were by now at least
young men. We know nothing more about them.

In addition David delivered to the Gibeonites five grandsons of Saul,
sons of Saul's daughter Merab, who were also possibly adults by this time.
These five are not named.

The Gibeonites did to these seven "sons" of Saul precisely what they
had proposed. We must allow this terrible event to be as terrible as it was.
The narrator takes the time to tell us where they were killed ("on the mountain"), the judicial nature of the execution (it was "before the LORD"), how
they died (they "perished together"[18]), and when it was ("the first days of
harvest, at the beginning of barley harvest," v. 9). We should take time to
feel the horror of it.

It is curious that the time of the execution should be identified in terms
of a "harvest" (v. 9). It may have been the *time* of the beginning of the barley
harvest, but since there was a famine in the land, we may presume that there
was little or no barley being harvested. Barley harvest was in April.[19]

The Surprise (vv. 10–14)

That could have been the end of the story, but just as we are feeling the horror
of the executions, we are forced to watch the scene even more closely by a
surprising development.

Rizpah (v. 10)

One of the mothers did something extraordinary.

> Then Rizpah the daughter of Aiah took sackcloth and spread it for herself
> on the rock, from the beginning of harvest until rain fell upon them from
> the heavens. And she did not allow the birds of the air to come upon them
> by day, or the beasts of the field by night. (v. 10)

The horror of what Rizpah did defies description. For a long time Rizpah placed herself in a pure hell.[20] The autumn rains (if that is what is meant) came in October-November. For those months she watched over the decaying bodies of her two sons and the other five, protecting them, day and night, from predators. She used the cloth of mourners either to lie on[21] or as a shade from the hot sun[22] as she prevented the bodies being further desecrated. Rizpah's devotion magnifies the horror of the story if we can cope with allowing our imaginations to dwell on what she did.

David and the House of Saul (vv. 11–14a)

Eventually David heard about what Rizpah was doing. He was moved to do something less gruesome but equally remarkable.

> When David was told what Rizpah the daughter of Aiah, the concubine
> of Saul, had done, David went and took the bones of Saul and the bones
> of his son Jonathan from the men of Jabesh-gilead, who had stolen them
> from the public square of Beth-shan, where the Philistines had hanged
> them, on the day the Philistines killed Saul on Gilboa. And he brought up
> from there the bones of Saul and the bones of his son Jonathan; and they
> gathered the bones of those who were hanged. And they buried the bones
> of Saul and his son Jonathan in the land of Benjamin in Zela, in the tomb
> of Kish his father. And they did all that the king commanded. (vv. 11–14a)

The men of Jabesh-gilead, some fifty miles northeast of Jerusalem on the east side of the Jordan,[23] had been the first from the northern tribes to be approached by David after the people of Judah had made him king (2:4–7). David had praised them then for what they had done in the events referred to here (see 1 Samuel 31:11–13). After all that had happened between David and the house of Saul, David now returned to the honor he had shown toward Saul and Jonathan in the lament that stands near the beginning of this book (1:17–27). Now this honor was expressed by arranging a proper burial for the seven executed sons of Saul along with the bones of Saul and Jonathan in the family tomb in Zela, in the territory of Saul's tribe, Benjamin.[24]

The compassion and dignity (could we even say love?) displayed by Rizpah and then David in their different ways make a stark contrast to the violence and horror that we have witnessed. At least these last actions of the mother and the king seem right and proper in the circumstances. It's the circumstances that trouble us.

Answered Prayer (v. 14b)

The episode concludes with the simple but vital note, "And after that God responded to the plea for the land" (v. 14b). The rains came. The famine was over.

As we reflect on this intensely disturbing story, I want to suggest we resist the urge to resolve its problems neatly. I do not believe that can be done. Nor does the story invite us to approve or condemn the actions that are most perplexing—David's approach to the Gibeonites, their proposed solution, David's agreement to do what they asked, and the carrying out of these things. These things happened, and the narrative does not denounce them, nor does it present these things as required by God.

What, then, are we to make of this disturbing portion of Scripture? I have three suggestions.

First, feel the sadness and horror of this story—a story of suffering from beginning to end. Although the narrator does not dwell on the hardships of the famine, these would have been terrible. People were dying of starvation. That's what happens in a famine—parents are unable to feed their children, the weak are unable to obtain food that stronger neighbors may have been able to scrounge. The Gibeonites had suffered from King Saul's treacherous massacre of many of their people. We do not need details of what Saul did to know that the suffering was great and continued in the grief of the survivors. And the execution of seven of Saul's sons and grandsons was no less terrible, even though the number involved was smaller. The suffering of the families of these boys or men, especially their mothers, must be added to this catalog of pain. The sight of Rizpah and what she did in her grief is unbearable.

All of this was in some way a consequence of Saul's sin. We do not understand the connections. It is complicated. But God has not so arranged the world that the only person who suffers when someone sins is the sinner. Others get hurt also. Perhaps we wish it were otherwise, but it is not. This is a reality we live with every day. Indeed it is difficult to think of a sin that does not in some way hurt others. Of course, we are all sinners, and we are not in a position to complain that it is unjust for us to suffer because of the sins of someone else. What about those who suffer because of our sins?

This situation, where sin leads to suffering, sometimes on a large scale, is because of the righteous wrath of God (see Romans 1:18–32). As we reflect on 21:1–14, I am suggesting that we should take time to see how immensely sad it all is.

Second, see and appreciate the inadequacy of King David to deal with the problem of God's wrath. David's attempt to deal with the consequences of Saul's sin horrifies us. Perhaps his subsequent effort to give those who had been executed a decent burial was an attempt to make up for what he had done.

If you do not listen to the story carefully, you could think that the deaths of Saul's sons was *God's* requirement in recompense for Saul's slaughter of the Gibeonites. That is not what the text tells us. Indeed it is clear that the Lord did not answer the prayer for the land *until after David had shown compassion and honor* toward Saul, Jonathan, and the seven who had been executed. God answered the prayer for the land when and how he chose to do so, not because of something King David did.

The difficulty we have in making sense of the events should impress upon us the inadequacy of David's kingdom to deal with the problem of the wrath of God.

Third, hear the gospel of Jesus Christ.

> [W]hile we were still weak, at the right time Christ died for the ungodly. For one will scarcely die for a righteous person—though perhaps for a good person one would dare even to die—but God shows his love for us in that while we were still sinners, Christ died for us. Since, therefore, we have now been justified by his blood, much more shall we be saved by him from the wrath of God. For if while we were enemies we were reconciled to God by the death of his Son, much more, now that we are reconciled, shall we be saved by his life. More than that, we also rejoice in God through our Lord Jesus Christ, through whom we have now received reconciliation. (Romans 5:6–11)

Jesus is the King who is able to save us from the wrath of God—"whom God put forward as a propitiation by his blood, to be received by faith" (Romans 3:25). He was fully and effectively "the atoning sacrifice" for the sins of the whole world (cf. 1 John 2:2 NIV). The greatest problem for the kingdom of David is no longer a problem in the kingdom of the son of David, Jesus. But as we have felt the horror of the events in the days of David, we should not take lightly the cost at which we have been saved from God's wrath. The horror of the death of Jesus on the cross is beyond description. The consequences are unfathomable: we are saved from the wrath of God.

We will return to this vital theme in 2 Samuel 24, the corresponding section of the epilogue.

39

The Strength of
David's Kingdom:
His Mighty Men, Part 1

2 SAMUEL 21:15–22

HAVING SEEN THE PROBLEM that the kingdom of David was never able to fully and effectively address (the wrath of God), the second section of the epilogue to the books of Samuel provides four snapshots of the strength of David's kingdom.

We must not underestimate the extraordinary strength of King David. From the day on which he was first noticed by the public, when as a lad he brought down the Philistine giant Goliath (1 Samuel 17), King David had defended and protected his people from their enemies (see 2 Samuel 8). Of course, the record in the books of Samuel is clear on one fundamental point: David was victorious *because the Lord was with him* (see, for example, 1 Samuel 17:37, 46, 47; 2 Samuel 8:6b, 14b).

As we look at the snapshots of the power of David's kingdom in 21:15–22, we will consider two observations. First, we will see once again that the victories of David and his servants were remarkable. The enemies were very powerful. In this the kingdom of David anticipated the King who has given us victory over enemies greater than those defeated by David. We look at the victories of David and say, "[T]hanks be to God, who gives *us* the victory through our Lord Jesus Christ" (1 Corinthians 15:57).

Second, as an *anticipation* of the kingdom of our Lord Jesus Christ, there were inadequacies in the kingdom of David. David had weaknesses.

These help us see the greatness of the King whose kingdom is even more powerful than the kingdom of David.

We will see:

(1) The kingdom at war: David weary (v. 15).
(2) Snapshot 1: Ishbi-benob (vv. 16, 17).
(3) Snapshot 2: Saph (v. 18).
(4) Snapshot 3: Goliath(?) (v. 19).
(5) Snapshot 4: The man of strife (vv. 20, 21).
(6) The victories of David (v. 22).

The Kingdom at War: David Weary (v. 15)

The section (and the first snapshot) is introduced by describing a situation that had arisen many times through David's reign (and earlier through Saul's reign): "There was war again between the Philistines and Israel" (v. 15a). The Hebrew sentence indicates that it was the Philistines who were at war with Israel. The Philistines were the aggressors.

The Philistine threat was in the background of the entire period of Israel's history covered by the books of Samuel. They first appeared in 1 Samuel 4, when Israel suffered a terrible defeat and the ark of the covenant was captured. It took the prayers of Samuel and the intervention of the Lord to defeat them in those days (1 Samuel 7:10, 11, 13, 14). However, the threat emerged again, and when Samuel was old it was part of the motivation of the people's demand for a king to "go out before us and fight our battles" (1 Samuel 8:20). The Lord gave them Saul with the clear commission to "save my people from the hand of the Philistines" (1 Samuel 9:16). Saul neglected this commission (that is the implication of the narrative in 1 Samuel 10:1–10[1]). It was Saul's son Jonathan who did what his father had failed to do (1 Samuel 13:3; 14:1–46). However, the threat persisted throughout Saul's reign: "There was hard fighting against the Philistines all the days of Saul" (1 Samuel 14:52). The next major victory over this enemy came when the young David killed Goliath (1 Samuel 17). This was the beginning of many battles in which David consistently crushed the Philistines (1 Samuel 18:27, 30; 19:8; 23:1–5). Remarkably David twice sought refuge from Saul in the land of the Philistines (1 Samuel 21:10–15; 27:1–12), each time deceiving the enemy. It was the Philistines who finally brought Saul down. He died in his final clash with the old enemy (1 Samuel 31). The people's hope for deliverance from the Philistines now rested on David (see 3:18). This hope was vindicated shortly after David became Israel's king (5:17–25; 8:1). Later, after the people had rejected David, it was the memory of how he had saved them from the Philistines that brought them to a change of mind (19:9).

The conflict referred to in 21:15a could have occurred at almost any time through David's reign, but there are hints that it may have been in his later days, possibly after Absalom's rebellion.

David's response to the Philistine threat is no surprise: "David went down together with his servants, and they fought against the Philistines" (v. 15b). He "went down," presumably from Jerusalem, in the Judean hills, westward to the coastal plain, or perhaps the foothills, toward the territory of the Philistines.

The next thing we expect to hear is something like, "And David defeated the Philistines and subdued them" (as, for example, in 8:1). Instead the narrator tells us, "And David grew weary" (v. 15c). This reminds us of the weariness of David in the days of his exile as he fled from Absalom (16:14; 17:2, 29). Weariness does not mean defeat (the same word is used in 1 Samuel 14:31, ESV, "faint"), but it does suggest weakness and limited capacity to continue the fight.

This may suggest that the years were taking their toll on King David.[2] How long would he be able to continue to protect his people from their enemies?

Snapshot 1: Ishbi-benob (vv. 16, 17)

One particular Philistine decided to take advantage of David's weakness. His name was Ishbi-benob ("his dwelling is on the height"[3]), and he was "one of the descendants of the giants [Hebrew, *raphah*]" (v. 16a). This phrase recurs with minor variations in verses 18, 20, 22, suggesting an important idea through this passage. Unfortunately, the Hebrew is difficult.[4] It probably means that this individual (and the others so described) was a descendant of Rapha (cf. NIV), the ancestor of the Rephaim. While there is uncertainty about the identity and history of the Rephaim, there are indications that they were a people reputed for their gigantic size.[5] It is possible that several different groups who were unusually tall received this designation and that the term acquired a general sense, "giant."

The Rephaim were mentioned in one of David's earlier clashes with the Philistines "in the Valley of Rephaim [Giants?]" (5:18). The term probably suggests a formidable adversary, a reminder of the first Philistine David had encountered, Goliath.

Indeed there was more about this warrior that reminds us of Goliath. His "spear[6] weighed three hundred shekels of bronze, and [he] was armed with a new sword[7]" (v. 16b). His spear, weighing about eight pounds, was half the weight of Goliath's (1 Samuel 17:7) but was nonetheless intimidating.

This heavily armed hulk of a man "thought to kill David" (v. 16c). The Hebrew may suggest that he announced this intention.[8] No doubt he hoped to take advantage of David's weariness.

The David who had once brought down the giant Goliath single-handedly (so to speak, for it was, of course, the Lord who gave the Philistine into David's hand, 1 Samuel 17:47) now needed help. "But Abishai the son of Zeruiah came to his aid and attacked the Philistine and killed him" (v. 17a). How would David cope without the sons of Zeruiah? I suspect that the sons of Zeruiah sometimes wondered the same thing. Abishai did exactly what David had once done to Goliath (1 Samuel 17:50).[9]

However, David's vulnerability was now recognized as a serious matter. "Then David's men swore to him,[10] 'You shall no longer go out with us to battle, lest you quench the lamp of Israel'" (v. 17b). David's immense significance for the people of Israel is captured in this striking expression, "the lamp of Israel." As the Lord's anointed king, David had brought light into the darkness that Israel had sometimes endured. As the Lord himself was David's lamp (22:29), so David was "the lamp of Israel" (cf. Psalm 132:17; 1 Kings 15:4). Indeed the dark days with which the books of Samuel began included a reference to a lamp: "The lamp of God had not yet gone out" (1 Samuel 3:3). This seemed to suggest that the Lord had not abandoned his troubled people. Now, near the end of the story, we hear the people's fear that "the lamp of Israel" might be snuffed out if David were to continue to lead them into battle (2 Samuel 21:17).

There had been a time when David was victorious "wherever he went" (8:6, 14). David's men had no confidence that this would still be the case ("no longer"). David's weakness would be responsible for the extinguishing of Israel's lamp ("lest *you* quench . . .," v. 17).

This concern had been expressed in different terms when David's men were up against Absalom's coup (18:3). This suggests again that the snapshot given here may come from the days after that rebellion.

Snapshot 2: Saph (v. 18)

The second snapshot is more briefly presented.

> After this[11] there was again war with the Philistines at Gob. Then Sibbecai the Hushathite struck down Saph, who was one of the descendants of the giants. (v. 18)

Gob was probably a small place somewhere near Gezer (since the location of this incident is given as Gezer in 1 Chronicles 20:4). This was about twenty miles west of Jerusalem, in the foothills and close to the Philistine territory of the coastal plain, where David had driven the Philistines early in his reign (5:25).[12] Conflict again with the Philistines in this vicinity is a reminder of those stronger days of David's kingdom.

Again the focus is on one large Philistine, another "one of the descendants of the giants" (v. 18; exactly the same phrase as in verse 16). This one was named Saph, and he was slain by a Hushathite (from the town of Hushah in Judah, about four miles west of Bethlehem[13]) named Sibbecai. He was one of David's "mighty men" (1 Chronicles 11:29) and a commander of one of his military divisions (1 Chronicles 27:11).

In this scene there is no mention of David. Presumably the recorded deed of Sibbecai was part of a wider victory over the Philistines, but what role, if any, was played by David we do not know.

Snapshot 3: Goliath (?) (v. 19)

The third snapshot is similarly brief but has generated much debate, because here we do not simply have reminders of David's original Philistine foe but his name, along with an apparent contradiction of the well-known account of David's triumph over Goliath.

> And there was again war with the Philistines at Gob, and Elhanan the son of Jaare-oregim, the Bethlehemite, struck down Goliath the Gittite, the shaft of whose spear was like a weaver's beam. (v. 19)

The obvious problem is that 1 Samuel 17 has recounted in great detail how *David* killed Goliath the Gittite (see 1 Samuel 17:4, 23, 50), the shaft of whose spear was like a weaver's beam (see 1 Samuel 17: 7[14]). To confuse matters further, the text corresponding to 21:19 in 1 Chronicles says that Elhanan "struck down Lahmi, the brother of Goliath the Gittite" (1 Chronicles 20:5). The statement, as it stands, in 21:19 appears to contradict both 1 Samuel 17 and 1 Chronicles 20.

There are two approaches to such puzzles that should be avoided. The first is to be too confident that an apparent contradiction is in fact a contradiction. Too often skeptical readers of the Bible (not to mention skeptical Bible scholars) are impatient with those who search for an explanation that resolves an apparent contradiction. Those of us who receive the Bible as God's word to us are eager to understand the truth and are open to the idea that an apparent contradiction is only apparent. On the other hand, we should be honest about the problem and not pretend it away. It is reasonable to evaluate the likelihood of explanations and refuse to simply accept an argument because it removes the problem.

The simplest (and I think the most probable) solution in the case of 21:19 is that there have been a number of accidental errors in the transmission of this text. It is possible that the original text was close to what we now find in 1 Chronicles 20:5[15] and that therefore Elhanan killed Goliath's brother who, unremarkably, was also a powerful giant equipped with similar weapons to Goliath.[16]

The problem should not distract us from this third snapshot of David's kingdom. It was yet another "war with the Philistines at Gob" (v. 19; identical wording to verse 18a). This town near the border between Israelite and Philistine territory was, unsurprisingly, the setting for a number of the skirmishes between these two adversaries.

Once again the presentation here focuses on one incident in the war, possibly the decisive moment or turning point.

The hero of this incident was named Elhanan. Apart from this episode (also recounted in 1 Chronicles 20:5), this Elhanan does not appear elsewhere in Biblical history.[17] There is some uncertainty about his father's name (probably Jair) and whether he was in fact from Bethlehem.[18] These small difficulties are of little substance.

As for the Philistine whom Elhanan killed (probably Goliath the Gittite's *brother*), we know from verse 22 that he was yet another "one of the descendants of the giants" (2 Samuel 21:18).

In itself this snapshot is very similar to the previous one. There was yet another victory in David's name over a formidable foe. David himself, however, is again not mentioned.

Snapshot 4: The Man of Strife (vv. 20, 21)

The fourth snapshot of the strength of David's kingdom is a little more detailed than the previous two.

> And there was again war at Gath, where there was a man of great stature [or, strife],[19] who had six fingers on each hand, and six toes on each foot, twenty-four in number, and he also was descended from the giants. And when he taunted Israel, Jonathan the son of Shimei, David's brother, struck him down. (vv. 20, 21)

This time the conflict was about ten miles south of the site of the previous two scenes and inside Philistine territory. Gath was one of the Philistine towns. Most famously it was Goliath's town, as we have just been reminded. Gath has featured prominently at a number of other points in the books of Samuel (see 1 Samuel 5:8; 21:10; 27:2; 2 Samuel 15:18).[20] This was yet another Israelite/Philistine war.

Again our attention is drawn to one particular Philistine, a fourth one "descended from the giants" (as in vv. 16, 18, 22). The description "a man of great strife" (AT) suggests expertise in derision and agitation. This fourth giant is not named. Instead his physical peculiarity is described in unusual detail—twelve fingers and twelve toes. This feature, no doubt, enhanced his fearsome and frightening appearance.

We are reminded yet again of David's famous confrontation with Goliath when we hear that "he taunted Israel" (v. 21). That is what Goliath did.[21] Like Goliath his taunting was silenced. Unlike Goliath it was not David but one of his nephews who brought down the twenty-four-digit giant.

There is a connection here with the beginning of David's story. David's brother Shimei (or Shammah) was one of those not chosen by the Lord on the day that Samuel came to Bethlehem to anoint David (1 Samuel 16:9). His son Jonathan was the hero on this day.

The Victories of David (v. 22)

The four brief snapshots are now summed up: "These four were descended from the giants in Gath, and they fell by the hand of David and by the hand of his servants" (v. 22). Such was the strength of David's kingdom. On one hand each of these victories was remarkable. Each could have been told with the same drama and thrills as David's victory over Goliath in 1 Samuel 17. If the stories were told in more extended detail, there is little doubt that the implied truth would have been stated each time: it was the Lord who gave the Philistine giants into the hands of David's servants.

The kingdom of our Lord Jesus Christ is the fulfillment of the kingdom of David. As servants of King Jesus we are given victory over our gigantic enemies—the evil one, sin, and death (cf. Romans 16:20).

However, the Lord Jesus Christ is not absent from the fray as King David was in each of these scenes. The victories were won in David's name, but this section makes a point of the fact that David was weary and probably aging, and it was not safe to have him "go out with us to battle, lest you quench the lamp of Israel" (v. 17). Jesus is the light of the world (John 8:12; 9:5), and there is no possibility of this light ever being quenched. As we serve him, we know that the light shines in the darkness, and the darkness will never overcome it (cf. John 1:5).

40

The Hope of David's Kingdom: The Lord's Promise, Part 1

2 SAMUEL 22

PEOPLE WHO KNOW THE GOODNESS AND THE GREATNESS of the true and living God have something worth having. Now there's an understatement! Such people spend their whole lives learning more and more the immense value of knowing God. There are times when we forget, neglect, or otherwise overlook the treasure that we have been given. That is always foolish. Perhaps as you read these words you realize that you need to see more clearly how wonderful our God is and how good it is to belong to him.

At the center of the epilogue to the books of Samuel (2 Samuel 21—24) are two extraordinary poems (2 Samuel 22 and 23:1–7). The first is a "song" that King David addressed to God: "And David spoke to the Lord the words of this song on the day when the Lord delivered him from the hand of all his enemies, and from the hand of Saul" (v. 1).[1] The song expresses and explains his astonishment at the goodness and greatness of his experience of the God who had chosen him to be his king. The song reappears in the pages of the Bible as Psalm 18.[2]

As we hear David's song, we should remember four things about the books of Samuel that will help us appreciate this brilliant poem.

First, at the beginning of 1 Samuel there was another remarkable poem (1 Samuel 2:1–10). It was a prayer prayed by Hannah, the mother of Samuel, long before David was born.[3] That prayer concluded:

The Lord will judge the ends of the earth; he will give strength to his king and exalt the horn of his anointed. (1 Samuel 2:10b)

The books of Samuel have told the long story of "his king" and the fulfillment of Hannah's words. David's song, near the end of 2 Samuel, contains many echoes of Hannah's prayer. It celebrates the fact that Hannah's prayer was fulfilled. As we hear David's song, remember Hannah's prayer.[4]

Second, God's purpose for "his king" was eventually made known in a promise that God made to David (7:8–16). The promise was, "I will raise up your offspring after you. . . . And your house and your kingdom shall be made sure forever before me. Your throne shall be established forever" (7:12, 16). As we hear David's song, remember God's promise to him.

Third, the story of David, at least from 1 Samuel 16 to 2 Samuel 10, has repeatedly shown that God's promise to him and God's goodness toward him made him a great and good king (for example, see 1 Samuel 24:17–19; 26:23; 2 Samuel 2:6; 7:18–22, 28; 8:15; 9:1; 10:2). As we hear David's song, remember the stories of his goodness and greatness because "the Lord, the God of hosts, was with him" (5:10).

Fourth, ever since David's adultery with Bathsheba and his murder of her husband, his inadequacy as God's king has been seen. Furthermore his sons were a disaster. Remember Amnon and Absalom! Something greater and better than David (and his sons) was needed if God's promised kingdom was to be established. As we hear David's song, we cannot forget that his goodness and greatness were not good or great enough. The immediately preceding section of the epilogue (21:15–22) has shown us that for all the accomplishments of David's kingdom there was a limit to his capacity. "David grew weary" (21:15).

The song has four parts of uneven length, which can be described as follows:

(1) A God worth having (vv. 2–4).
(2) A God who powerfully saves his king (vv. 5–20).
(3) A God of righteousness (vv. 21–31).
(4) A God who gives strength to his king (vv. 32–46).
(5) A God worth having (vv. 47–51).[5]

A God Worth Having (vv. 2–4)

The Lord is my rock and my fortress and my deliverer,
    my God, my rock, in whom I take refuge,
my shield, and the horn of my salvation,
    my stronghold and my refuge,

> my savior; you save me from violence.
> I call upon the Lᴏʀᴅ, who is worthy to be praised,
>   and I am saved from my enemies. (vv. 2–4)

David's song begins with clear echoes of Hannah's prayer many years earlier.[6] What Hannah had known, David had come to know too. He employs a barrage of images to convey one truth: his God makes him *safe*. The Lord is a "rock" sheltering David from danger, a strong and secure "fortress," a "shield" protecting from spears and swords, a "stronghold" (that is, a place high above the dangers and threats), a place of "refuge" (vv. 2, 3). These images fill out the wonderful word "savior" (v. 3). That is what God is.

The point of David's exuberant words is that this is personal. He is "*my* rock," "*my* fortress," "*my* shield," "*my* stronghold," "*my* refuge," "*my* savior." "You save *me*." "*I* am saved" (vv. 2–4).

For David, knowing God was not about being religious or giving existence meaning or adding a spiritual dimension to life. It was about being safe from real and threatening dangers. These dangers are represented in his opening this song with two expressions—"violence" and "my enemies" (vv. 3, 4). His experience of God was: "I call upon the Lᴏʀᴅ . . . and I am saved from my enemies" (v. 4). This is how the Lord was "my rock," "the horn of my salvation" (vv. 2, 3).[7]

We who have read the story of David's life know what he is talking about. David had many violent enemies who wanted to destroy him. There was Goliath and the Philistines. More threatening still was Saul. More recently his own son Absalom had declared war on David. In many remarkable ways, on numerous occasions, the Lord had saved David from violence.

That is why David regarded the Lord as "worthy to be praised" (v. 4). That is, his goodness and greatness should be made known—which is precisely what David's song does. He is a God worth talking about.

These opening lines of David's song are words that those of us who belong to God can also utter. In various ways our God answers our prayers too, and we can point to troubles of various kinds from which God has delivered us. It is brilliant that we can say with David, "The Lᴏʀᴅ is *my* rock" (v. 2). But in the first place this song is about *David's* experience. There is something special about how God dealt with the one he had chosen to be his king, as we will soon hear.

A God Who Powerfully Saves His King (vv. 5–20)

The second major section of the song gives the reasons ("For," v. 5) that David could speak so exuberantly about the Lord. He makes three points.

First, he speaks of the troubles that threatened to destroy him (vv. 5–7). Second, we hear a long and unusual description of God that shows him to be more than a match for David's troubles (vv. 8–16). And third, he describes the deliverance he had experienced from his difficulties (vv. 17–20)

The Threat of Destruction (vv. 5–7)

> For the waves of death encompassed me,
>   the torrents of destruction assailed me;
> the cords of Sheol entangled me;
>   the snares of death confronted me.
>
> In my distress I called upon the LORD;
>   to my God I called.
> From his temple he heard my voice,
>   and my cry came to his ears. (vv. 5–7)

This is a poetic description of the many occasions when David's life was threatened. The particulars are overlooked as the threat is pictured, first, as a raging flood threatening to overwhelm him, then as an animal trap threatening to ensnare him. The forces assailing him were "death," "destruction," "Sheol" (a Hebrew name for the place of the dead),[8] and (again) "death" (vv. 5, 6).

The language is extreme because David was not thinking of minor difficulties to be overcome, small problems to be solved. He was threatened with utter destruction. Whether it was Goliath, Saul, or any number of others, their objective was nothing less than David's death and the annihilation of his kingdom (or the prospect of his kingdom).

Most of us have experienced something like this. Perhaps in our rather comfortable and peaceful age we do not feel this so acutely or frequently. But even for us there are times when we feel that chaos threatens to undo our lives; we can no longer cope with the pressures that are on us, we are afraid that everything is going to collapse around us or the bottom is about to fall out of our lives. And of course, like David, we are all confronted by death. We know what David was talking about, even if, perhaps, many of us do not know it as intensely and as often as he did.

David's testimony is, "In my distress I called upon the LORD. . . . From his temple [here that means "from Heaven"] he heard my voice, and my cry came to his ears" (v. 7).

Perhaps you can echo David's testimony here. Is this what you have done when trouble threatens to overwhelm you? Have you called upon the Lord? Have there been occasions when you know that the Lord has heard your desperate cry? Again, however, we must listen to David speak of his experience as God's king.

A God Greater Than the Threat of Destruction (vv. 8–16)

David was aware that this experience of calling out to God in his distress and his cry coming to the Lord's ears was earth-shattering in its significance, because the God on whom he called is greater—far, far greater—than the forces that threatened to destroy him.

In verses 8–16 he launches into a piece of poetry that most of us will find strange, especially if poetry is not our thing. It is an attempt to show us in images and pictures something of the astonishing significance of the fact that there is a God in Heaven who heard the cry of David in his distress. In these verses we hear nothing about David. It is all about the God upon whom he called.

His Anger (vv. 8, 9)

> Then the earth reeled and rocked;
>> the foundations of the heavens trembled
>> and quaked, because he was angry.
> Smoke went up from his nostrils,
>> and devouring fire from his mouth;
>> glowing coals flamed forth from him. (vv. 8, 9)

The picture begins with this reminder of what happened when God met with his people at Mount Sinai in the days of Moses—the shaking of the earth, smoke, and fire (see Exodus 19:16). But there is something else here. The words in the center of this subsection sum it up: "because he was angry" (2 Samuel 22:8). If God is angry, then the whole of creation should tremble. What will happen if God is angry?

He was not angry, of course, because David cried out to him. He was angry because his king, his chosen one, was threatened with destruction. It was the "violence" of verse 3, the "enemies" of verse 4, "the waves of death" and "the torrents of destruction" of verse 5, "the chords of Sheol" and "the snares of death" of verse 6, and the king's "distress" of verse 7 that aroused the Lord's anger.

People sometimes object to the idea that God can be angry. And yet that is one of the most wonderful things about God. I do not mean that I understand it. Of course I don't. But it is *good news* that God is angry about violence and hatred and death and destruction, about cancer and war, about starvation and cruelty. Would you rather that God didn't care?

His Approach (vv. 10, 11)

> He bowed the heavens and came down;
>> thick darkness was under his feet.
> He rode on a cherub and flew;
>> he was seen on the wings of the wind. (vv. 10, 11)

The picture is vivid and poetic. Imagine the Lord pulling back the curtains of Heaven. "Thick darkness" is his carpet (v. 10). He is borne by angels. The reality pictured is profound: "He . . . came down" (v. 10).

In other words (for those of us who think less poetically), when God's king cried out to him, God did not only hear in Heaven, he was not just angry, he *did* something "down" here.

His Dwelling (vv. 12, 13)

> He made darkness around him his canopy,
>> thick clouds, a gathering of water.
> Out of the brightness before him
>> coals of fire flamed forth. (vv. 12, 13)

At the center of the description of the God who is greater than the threats against his king (vv. 8–16) there is this brief pause in the action. Here is pictured (as much as human language and imagery can manage) God's heavenly dwelling. The "darkness" (v. 12) suggests that he cannot be seen by us. His dwelling is beyond our reach. How astonishing, then, that he heard the cry of David! And "brightness" went out from him so that "coals of fire" were kindled (v. 13).[9] These were the coals of his anger we saw in verse 9.

His Approach (vv. 14, 15)

> The Lord thundered from heaven,
>> and the Most High uttered his voice.
> And he sent out arrows and scattered them;
>> lightning, and routed them. (vv. 14, 15)

We return to God's coming down (v. 10). Of course, any picture of this God coming down will be dramatic—because his coming down *is* dramatic. His coming is first described as a furious, terrifying shout thundering from Heaven, then as a warrior using lightning as his arrows.

Did you notice who is now included in the picture? "Them" (twice in v. 15[10]) refers to the enemies we heard about back in verse 4.[11] They were the ones God "came down" (v. 10) from Heaven to deal with.

His Anger (v. 16)

> Then the channels of the sea were seen;
>   the foundations of the world were laid bare,
> at the rebuke of the LORD,
>   at the blast of the breath of his nostrils. (v. 16)

This takes us back to where this section began—God's anger. Again his anger is shown (in this picture language) as shaking the whole world.

One effect of this long section of vivid but strange imagery is to suggest that when David cried out to the Lord from his distress, something happened comparable to that day in the time of Moses when God appeared on Mount Sinai after rescuing his people from Egypt (see Exodus 19).

What happened is described in the following lines.

Deliverance (vv. 17–20)

> He sent from on high, he took me;
>   he drew me out of many waters.
> He rescued me from my strong enemy,
>   from those who hated me,
>   for they were too mighty for me.
> They confronted me in the day of my calamity,
>   but the LORD was my support.
> He brought me out into a broad place;
>   he rescued me, because he delighted in me. (vv. 17–20)

The "me" of the song (David, of course) reappears for the first time since verse 7 ("my"). Indeed the story of the song is now picked up from where it left off after verse 7 for the important excursus about God in verses 8–16. David had "called" to God, and his cry was "heard" (v. 7). Now God "sent from on high," "took me,"[12] and "drew me out of many waters" (v. 17).

Since we have been reminded of Mount Sinai in the days of Moses in verses 8–16, it is very likely that David chose the phrase "he drew me out of many waters" (v. 17) carefully. The verb translated here "drew out" sounds like "Moses." It occurs in only one other place in the Old Testament, namely Exodus 2:10,[13] where the daughter of Pharaoh gave Moses his name, "Because," she said, "I *drew him out* of the water." David's experiences of escaping from the many threats to his life were remarkable enough. But David seems to be suggesting that they were comparable to what the Lord did in the days of Moses, when Moses himself was rescued from the waters of the Nile, then led the people of Israel in their rescue from slavery in Egypt and their encounter with God at Mount Sinai. Indeed David's portrayal of his own experience seems to suggest that it surpassed what happened in the days of the exodus: "He drew me out of *many* waters" (v. 17).

Furthermore, when David says, "He brought me out into a *broad place*" (v. 20), he again seems to be echoing the exodus experience. At the bush that was not burning (often erroneously called "the burning bush") God said to Moses:

> I have come down[14] to deliver them out of the hand of the Egyptians and to bring them up out of that land to a good and *broad*[15] land, a land flowing with milk and honey. (Exodus 3:8)

A "broad" place is a place of freedom from bondage and oppression.[16] David saw his own liberation in terms that remind us again of the exodus.

The experiences David was referring to are those recounted in the pages of the books of Samuel. They were military victories (sometimes, but not always, against the odds) and other threatening situations from which David escaped with his life. In this sense they were "ordinary" events. Only rarely was there anything obviously miraculous or supernatural. But David saw things more truly. When he defeated "my strong enemy" or escaped from "those who hated me," David knew this was God's doing (2 Samuel 22:18). "*He* rescued me . . . *the* LORD was my support. . . . *he* rescued me" (vv. 18–20).

On the one hand this was because "they were too mighty for me" (v. 18). Sometimes that had been obvious, like the day on which David as a youth had confronted Goliath (1 Samuel 17). David explains that he survived such threats not because he was wily and cunning (though he was), nor because he became a brilliant military strategist (which he did), nor because he was just lucky (although again and again things happened just in time to save his skin). No, says David, the truth was that it was the Lord who rescued him.

On the other hand David understood that the Lord did this "because he delighted in me" (v. 20).[17] This leads us into the most surprising, puzzling, but also most important central section of David's song.

A God of Righteousness (vv. 21–31)

The King's Righteousness (vv. 21–25)

> The LORD dealt with me according to my righteousness;
>   according to the cleanness of my hands he rewarded me.
> For I have kept the ways of the LORD
>   and have not wickedly departed from my God.
> For all his rules were before me,
>   and from his statutes I did not turn aside.

I was blameless before him,
　　and I kept myself from guilt.
And the LORD has rewarded me according to my righteousness,
　　according to my cleanness in his sight. (vv. 21–25)

If David's poetic description of God in verses 8–16 sounded strange to our ears, his description of himself in verses 21–25 sounds bizarre, but for different reasons. We have no difficulty understanding *what* he is saying; our problem is how he can possibly mean it.

Verses 21 and 25 form a frame around this astonishing section of the song, asserting that the Lord's dealings with David (about which we have been hearing) corresponded to his "righteousness," "the cleanness of my hands," indeed his "cleanness in [God's] sight." I am using the rather vague expression *corresponded to* deliberately, because the Hebrew is not quite as clear as the English translation that what God did was a "reward" for David, a payment he *deserved* because of his "righteousness."[18]

This hardly solves the problem, but before we consider how it was possible for David to speak in this way and just what he meant by it, notice how he elaborated what he meant by his "righteousness" and "cleanness" in verses 22–24. His life, he said, followed "the ways of the LORD," guided by "his rules," "his statutes." He did not "wickedly depart" from his God. He was, he said, "blameless," not just in his own eyes, but "before *him*."

What can David possibly mean by this outrageous (as it sounds to us) section of his song? Was he really saying that he was so good that God owed him the many rescues he had experienced? Was he claiming that, unlike the rest of us, he was not a sinner? That is what it sounds like. But, as so often in the Bible, the puzzling nature of what is said invites us to think more deeply.

Perhaps the first thing to be said is that the Bible writer who placed this song of David at this point in his history was not an idiot. He knew that we would read it after we had read the full and frank accounts of David's faults. He knew that this song would be read by people who knew very well that David was an adulterer and a murderer (among other things). No one reading David's words in their context in the books of Samuel could possibly just take them at face value. We have to ask, how was it possible for an adulterer and murderer (and the rest) to speak as David spoke in verses 21–25?[19] This is the question the Bible writer himself has forced on us.

The second thing to say is that what David said here should not be explained away by suggesting he did not really mean it as absolutely as it sounds. It is often argued that David is simply claiming that he never really abandoned his faith in God. Despite the terrible things he did, at least he did not "wickedly depart" (v. 22) from his God. When he sinned, he repented.[20] But that is *not* what David said.

In my judgment there are two keys to understanding how this murderer and adulterer could speak so eloquently of his "righteousness" and the "cleanness of [his] hands" (v. 21; hands that we all know had blood on them).

The first key is simple to understand but difficult for us to take as seriously as we must. After David's adultery with Bathsheba and the murder of her husband, the prophet Nathan told David, "The LORD has . . . put away your sin" (12:13). We (the readers of the books of Samuel) may still remember David's sin and pin it on him. Remarkably, the Lord does not. Concerning these very acts, David prayed:

Wash me thoroughly from my iniquity,
  and cleanse me from my sin! . . .

Purge me with hyssop, and I shall be clean;
  wash me, and I shall be whiter than snow. (Psalm 51:2, 7)

The point is not that he was "righteous" because he prayed in this way. He was "clean" because *God* washed him and cleansed him from his sin. It is what *God* did (not what *David* did) that made him "whiter than snow" (Psalm 51:7). He did not (any longer) have blood on his hands!

The second key is that God forgave David's sin because of God's commitment to David, not because of David's commitment to God (see 7:14, 15). Indeed David was able to pray Psalm 51 because of the Lord's "steadfast love" and "abundant mercy" toward him (Psalm 51:1). This is what "he delighted in me" (v. 20) ultimately means.

This grace of God in which David's life was lived certainly shaped his behavior. Again and again we have been impressed by the genuine goodness of this man. The words of verses 21–25 do describe much of what we have seen of David's life. His evil actions do not undermine the fruit of God's grace in his life precisely because his wicked deeds have been forgiven, taken away, washed clean. David can describe his life without reference to his failures, not because he is self-righteous, but because he is deeply aware that God had done what Nathan told him God had done: "The LORD has . . . put away your sin" (2 Samuel 12:13). What puzzles us is that David sees his life as God sees his life.[21]

Verses 21–25 are then asserting that the Lord dealt with David as a forgiven, cleansed man. His "righteousness" that once was mixed with much unrighteousness has been washed clean. This, David now says, is what God is like.

God's Righteousness (vv. 26, 27)

With the merciful[22] you show yourself merciful;
    with the blameless man[23] you show yourself blameless;
with the purified you deal purely,
    and with the crooked you make yourself seem tortuous.[24] (vv. 26, 27)

These lines are the very center of David's song.[25] This is about God's righteousness. Superficially David seems to be saying that God rewards good people and punishes bad people. However, we are forced to think more deeply, not because we impose a doctrinal system that we have learned somewhere else in the text, but because these are *David's* words, and we have read the story of David's life. God had mercy on David when David had shown *no* mercy to Uriah. God dealt "purely" (v. 27) with David when he was *anything but* pure. There is more to God's righteousness than may at first appear.

There may be a hint in the phrase "the purified" (v. 27).[26] The people with whom God shows himself "merciful" and "blameless" and deals "purely" are those who *have been purified* and are *therefore* "blameless" and "merciful" (vv. 26, 27).

This may raise more questions than it answers, but David's song seems to be saying that God does not "come down" and "rescue" indiscriminately. Only the cleansed ones, who are *therefore* merciful, blameless, and pure, are dealt with like that by the Lord. That is what God is like.

What God Does for His King and His People (vv. 28–31)

You save a humble people,
    but your eyes are on the haughty to bring them down.
For you are my lamp, O Lord,
    and my God lightens my darkness.
For by you I can run against a troop,
    and by my God I can leap over a wall.
This God—his way is perfect;
    the word of the Lord proves true;
    he is a shield for all those who take refuge in him. (vv. 28–31)

As Hannah understood in her prayer (see 1 Samuel 2:4–9), this God turns the world upside down. When he gets involved, it is not "the haughty" (v. 28), the high and mighty ones, the ones who have reasons to be arrogant, who will be the winners. The Lord saves people who need saving.[27]

Because this God is David's "rock" (v. 32), he does not live his life in the darkness of fear and ignorance. The Lord is his "lamp" (v. 29). With his God he is made strong.

What a God he is! Perfect! When David says, "the word of the LORD proves true" (v. 31), he may be speaking in general terms (everything that God says proves true), but he is surely thinking particularly of God's word of promise to him (most fully in 2 Samuel 7). The God who made such sure promises to his king and who has been true to those promises is not only "a shield" to David (see v. 3), he is likewise "for all those who take refuge in him" (v. 31).

A God Who Gives Strength to His King (vv. 32–46)

The song has one more big idea to bring to us. It is that this God who had delivered David so many times from the dangers he faced (vv. 17–20) did so for a purpose. He intended him to be a great king.

God and David (vv. 32–37)

> For who is God, but the LORD?
> And who is a rock, except our God?
> This God is my strong refuge
> and has made my way blameless.
> He made my feet like the feet of a deer
> and set me secure on the heights.
> He trains my hands for war,
> so that my arms can bend a bow of bronze.
> You have given me the shield of your salvation,
> and your gentleness[28] made me great.
> You gave a wide place[29] for my steps under me,
> and my feet did not slip. (vv. 32–37)

David is repeating—because it is worth repeating—what God has been to him. But did you notice verse 33b? God "has made my way blameless." It sounds as though we have correctly understood those puzzling statements about David's innocence. It is the Lord, not David, who *made him* blameless.

But now David adds that God had made him a great warrior. Not only had he been rescued from the enemies who threatened to destroy him, but the tables had now been turned.

A Victorious King (vv. 38–43)

> I pursued my enemies and destroyed them,
> and did not turn back until they were consumed.

> I consumed them; I thrust them through, so that they did not rise;
>> they fell under my feet.
> For you equipped me with strength for the battle;
>> you made those who rise against me sink under me.
> You made my enemies turn their backs to me,
>> those who hated me, and I destroyed them.
> They looked, but there was none to save;
>> they cried to the LORD, but he did not answer them.
> I beat them fine as the dust of the earth;
>> I crushed them and stamped them down like the mire of the streets.
>> (vv. 38–43)

The king had become the agent of God's anger against the violent enemies who threatened destruction. They will not prevail. They will be overthrown by the Lord's king.

Notice verse 42. The great difference between David and his enemies is that when David called, the Lord heard and acted to save him. When these enemies look, there is no one to save them. Even when they cry to the Lord, there is no answer. They are on the wrong side.

A Great King (vv. 44–46)

The main body of David's song ends with a description of the outcome of all this. God's king will be one before whom every knee will bow.

> You delivered me from strife with my people;[30]
>> you kept me as the head of the nations;
>> people whom I had not known served me.
> Foreigners came cringing to me;
>> as soon as they heard of me, they obeyed me.
> Foreigners lost heart
>> and came trembling out of their fortresses. (vv. 44–46)

This king will rule the world. His rule will extend to all nations.

Before we hear the closing lines of David's song, let me remind you that David, at the very height of his power, only ruled over a small Middle Eastern empire. Was he getting just a little carried away with himself in this song? "The head of the nations" (v. 44)? Who is he kidding?

This is not megalomania. It is David understanding what God had promised. The promises were not fully realized in David's own lifetime, but as the promise said, there would be a son of David in whom it would be realized.

This song of David makes sense fully when we realize that the one it really fits is Jesus Christ. He is the son of David who is everything that David failed to be. Like David he was threatened with destruction. This culminated in the cross. Like David he called upon God his Father in his distress, and the Father rescued him from his strong enemy by raising him from the dead. He is the perfectly righteous, blameless, pure one. He is the Lord to whom all authority in Heaven and earth has been given. The news of his kingdom is going into the nations of the world. He will overthrow all who make themselves enemies of his kingdom.

A God Worth Having (vv. 47–51)

David's song concludes on the note with which it began, focusing in the closing lines on the hope of David's kingdom, the promise of the living God who is his rock:

> The LORD lives, and blessed be my rock,
>   and exalted be my God, the rock of my salvation,
> the God who gave me vengeance
>   and brought down peoples under me,
> who brought me out from my enemies;
>   you exalted me above those who rose against me;
>   you delivered me from men of violence.
> For this I will praise you, O LORD, among the nations,
>   and sing praises to your name.
> Great salvation he brings to his king,
>   and shows steadfast love to his anointed,
>   to David and his offspring forever. (vv. 47–51)

"His king" and "his anointed" (v. 51; Messiah or Christ) point us back to the last words of the last two lines of Hannah's prayer. Hannah had said that "The LORD . . . will give strength to *his king* and exalt the horn [the power] of *his anointed*" (1 Samuel 2:10). The story told in the books of Samuel testifies that the Lord has done just that, and this testimony is summed up now in David's song.

The hope of David's kingdom is the Lord's promise concerning "his offspring" (v. 51; cf. 7:12). Ultimately Jesus is the "offspring" of David referred to in the last line of this song (see Matthew 1:1; Acts 2:30, 31; 13:22, 23; Romans 1:3; 2 Timothy 2:8; Revelation 22:16). The way to have David's wonderful God as your God today is to have Jesus as your King.

41

The Hope of David's Kingdom: The Lord's Promise, Part 2

2 SAMUEL 23:1–7

LIFE IS UNBEARABLE WITHOUT HOPE. Our motivation to live depends on a belief that there is something to live for. To be without hope is to be overtaken by despair. While the thoughts we have about the future are often dim ("*something* good will surely happen"), or desperate ("something good *has to* happen"), or deluded ("reality is something I prefer not to think about"), without some kind of hope it is difficult to carry on. There is an industry devoted to manufacturing hopes for those of us who are having trouble forming our own. It is called advertising.

One of life's worst experiences is losing hope. A tragedy, a failure, a disaster, or a disappointment can make the future seem empty or, worse, terrifying. If you have come through such an experience, you will know that somehow you have come to believe in the future again. Of course, your confidence may be shaky and uncertain, but some kind of positive belief about the future is essential for healthy human life.

The Bible teaches us that the proper way for human beings to have hope is to know God. God is described as "the God of hope," and those who know God are meant to "abound in hope."

> May the God of hope fill you with all joy and peace in believing, so that by the power of the Holy Spirit you may abound in hope. (Romans 15:13)

Many in today's world desperately need to find this hope. We live in a time when the future looks grim for many. We are constantly being told the uncomfortable truth of disastrous consequences that are coming from our damaged environment. As political leaders seem unable to agree on action, what will the future hold? Consider the explosion of the human population of the world: one billion in 1800, two billion by 1900, four billion by 1980, six billion by 2000, over seven billion as I write these words toward the end of 2013. How long can this go on? Also the threat of war has not receded. It is difficult to see how the world's financial system will survive the present crises. It is not hard to paint a bleak picture of the future. It is easy for individuals to be overwhelmed with a sense of despair. It is as important as ever to understand that *the way to have hope is to know God*.

This hope is not complacency ("instead of worrying, I just don't care"), nor is it optimism ("every cloud has a silver lining"). The hope of which the Bible speaks comes "by the power of the Holy Spirit" (Romans 15:13). The power of the Holy Spirit is the power of God's promise.

Do you know this hope? Does this hope shape your life?

In many and various ways the books of Samuel have taught us to pray, "Your kingdom come" (Matthew 6:10). That prayer is the drumbeat of a life that abounds in hope by the power of the Holy Spirit. In 2 Samuel 23:1–7 we find the message of the books of Samuel brought into sharp focus. As we hear these words, may God's promise by the power of the Holy Spirit fill you with joy, peace, and abundant hope.

The passage is the second of the two magnificent poems that stand at the center of the epilogue to the books of Samuel (2 Samuel 21—24). It is much shorter than the first and yet is very powerful. The introduction to these few lines is itself arresting: "Now these are the last words of David" (v. 1a). Even before we hear these words the historian has indicated their weighty significance. After all we have heard about David, we now come to his "last words." The account of David's life has been one of the greatest stories ever told. From the day that Samuel visited him as a lad in Bethlehem (1 Samuel 16:1–13), we have followed the extraordinary accomplishments of his life as well as the terrible suffering that he endured. We have seen the impressive goodness of this king as well as the despicable wickedness into which he fell. We have seen the powerful and good kingdom of justice and righteousness that he established and the rather compromised kingdom that David led in the years following his notorious crimes with Bathsheba and Uriah. Now we come to "the last words of David" (2 Samuel 23:1).

What exactly does that mean? On the one hand, it seems unlikely that these were literally the last words to come from David's mouth in his lifetime. We do not know when the poem was composed, but there is no reason to insist that it must have been, for example, after 1 Kings 2:2–9, the last recorded words spoken by David before his death. On the other hand, the suggestion that "words" here has an elevated sense, meaning carefully composed words, poetry (rather than ordinary speech),[1] seems inadequate. Rather these "last words of David" are the words that sum up his life. These are the words that David put at the end of his life (2 Samuel 23:1). They are, so to speak, David's "last will and testament."[2] Here, in David's own words, is the key to understanding the life of this great king.

"The last words of David" (v. 1) might be compared to similar words from other great figures of Biblical history toward the end of their lives, such as Jacob (Genesis 49:1–27) and Moses (Deuteronomy 33:1–29). At the end of their lives each of these spoke of the future in terms shaped by the promise God had given and that they believed. Likewise the "last words of David" are words of prophecy determined by the promise of God.

The poem has five short sections:

(1) David, God's king (v. 1b–e).
(2) What God said to David (vv. 2, 3a, b).
(3) The word of God (vv. 3c–5a).
(4) God's covenant with David (v. 5b–e).
(5) The enemies of God and his king (vv. 6, 7).[3]

Within this structure (1) and (5) are opposites (God's king and the alternatives to him); (2) and (4) correspond (God's dealings with David); and (3) stands at the center of the poem in both position and importance.

David, God's King (v. 1b–e)

Contrary to the punctuation in the ESV, "the last words of David" (v. 1) begin with his own introduction, in which he calls these words an "oracle" and makes four statements about himself (in the third person).[4]

Son of Jesse (v. 1b)

He begins, "The oracle of David, the son of Jesse" (v. 1b). "Oracle" is a weighty word usually used with reference to a declaration from God.[5] It will soon become clear that David understood this oracle to be God's own word.

However, the focus of the first four lines of the poem is on David's own identity. First, by calling himself "the son of Jesse" he points to his humble

origins (cf. 1 Samuel 16:18).[6] The expression here does not carry the pe-
jorative connotations that it did on a number of occasions in the story (see
1 Samuel 20:27, 30, 31; 22:7, 8, 9, 13; 25:10; 2 Samuel 20:1), but should
nonetheless remind us of the beginning of David's story, the lad from Bethlehem, the youngest son who watched over his father's sheep (1 Samuel
16:11; 17:34). As "the son of Jesse" David's origins gave him no claim to
greatness (2 Samuel 23:1).

Raised on High (v. 1c)

However, second, this son of Jesse was "the man who was raised on high"
(v. 1c). Here the Hebrew word for "man" suggests strength and is particularly used in the Old Testament for a man who trusts and fears God.[7] David's
greatness, however, did not come from his being a "man" in this sense, but in
his being "raised on high." The NIV has "exalted by the Most High."[8] There
is no substantial difference between these translations, since the one who
"raised" David was clearly the Lord.

Here we are reminded of the day that David asked the Lord, "Shall I *go
up* into any of the cities of Judah?" and the Lord answered, "Go up" (2:1).
That was the beginning of David's elevation to kingship. He went up to Hebron where he became king over the tribe of Judah (2:4). In due course he
became king over all Israel (5:3) and made the city of Jerusalem his royal
city (5:6, 7). There "David became greater and greater, for the LORD, the God
of hosts, was with him" (5:10). Furthermore the Lord "*exalted* his kingdom
for the sake of his people Israel" (5:12). Indeed, when David looked at his
life through the lens of God's promises to him, he saw himself and his kingdom elevated higher than was ever realized in his historical experience: "you
kept me as the head of the nations . . . you exalted me above those who rose
against me" (2 Samuel 22:44, 49).

Anointed by God (v. 1d)

However, David was more than a great man. He was, third, "the anointed
[*messiah*] of the God of Jacob" (v. 1d). This picks up the reference at the end
of the previous chapter to "his anointed" (22:51) and points us back to Hannah's prayer, in which she said that the Lord will "exalt the horn [power] of
his anointed" (1 Samuel 2:10b).

Historically we are reminded of the day in Bethlehem when Samuel
"anointed him. . . . And the Spirit of the LORD rushed upon David from that
day forward" (1 Samuel 16:13). Samuel's action was in obedience to the

Lord's word (1 Samuel 16:1). Furthermore Samuel anointed the one who was already "the LORD's anointed," that is, the one the Lord had "chosen" (see 1 Samuel 16:6, 8–10 in context). David's anointing therefore points us to David as the "man after [God's] own heart" (1 Samuel 13:14), that is, the man on whom God set his heart according to his own purpose (cf. 7:21). David's greatness lay in God's purpose for him.

We must not lose sight of the fact that this was "the God of Jacob." This phrase has two senses, both of which are important here. On the one hand, Jacob (also named Israel, Genesis 32:28; 35:10) was the father of the nation. God had made great promises to Jacob (see Genesis 35:11, 12). These were the promises that God had made to Jacob's grandfather, Abraham (first in Genesis 12:1–3). God's promises to Jacob included, "kings shall come from your own body" (Genesis 35:11; cf. 17:6, 16). The "God of *Jacob*" chose and anointed David in accordance with his promises to Jacob (2 Samuel 23:1). David was one of the promised kings descended from Jacob.

On the other hand, Jacob is an alternative name for the nation Israel. In faithfulness to his promises to Jacob (the man) God had blessed his descendants, and they had become Jacob the nation. They were God's chosen people, whom he had promised to bless and make into a great nation and through them bring blessing to all the families of the earth (Genesis 12:1–3). The God of this people had anointed David as king *for the sake of his people* (cf. 5:12), in accordance with his purposes for this people.

The Songs of Israel (v. 1e)

The fourth designation that David applied to himself is a surprise. The traditional translation, "the sweet psalmist of Israel" (v. 1e ESV, RSV), points to David as the composer/singer of Israel's psalms (that is, songs). If that is what the phrase means, it reminds us of the two remarkable compositions of David recorded in 2 Samuel—the lament over the deaths of Saul and Jonathan (1:17–27) and the song of praise that precedes our present passage (2 Samuel 22). These are two of the many songs composed by David, many of which are included in the book of Psalms. David is aptly described as "the sweet psalmist of Israel."

However, there is an alternative (and in my opinion preferable) translation: "the hero of Israel's songs" (v. 1e NIV; cf. ESV margin, "the favorite of the songs of Israel").[9] If this is the meaning, then the fourth line is more obviously climactic. In Israel's songs David was recognized to be "the anointed of the God of Jacob" who had been "raised on high" (2 Samuel 23:1). This was true—and famously so—from the day he returned from striking down

Goliath (see 1 Samuel 18:7; 21:11; 29:5). It is particularly true in the great book of Israel's songs, the Psalms. In Psalm 2 we hear the Lord say, "I have set my King on Zion, my holy hill" (Psalm 2:6). That was David. Psalm 3 is a prayer calling on the Lord to save David from his many foes, a prayer that was answered (Psalm 3:4). The "I" of the Psalms is usually (although not always) rightly understood to be David.[10]

In the songs of Israel (particularly the book of Psalms) we find a rich understanding of "the LORD and . . . his anointed" (Psalm 2:2). An obvious example is Psalm 18 (that is, 2 Samuel 22), where we heard a great deal about God's king. The one of whom Israel sings is the one whose "last words" we are about to hear (23:1).

God Spoke to David (vv. 2, 3a, b)

The second section of the poem, where David begins to speak in the first person, consists of another four lines, which elaborate on the term "oracle" (v. 1a, b). The word on David's tongue was the Lord's "word" (v. 2), a word that God had spoken to David (v. 3a, b).

The Spirit and the Word (v. 2a, b)

> The Spirit of the LORD speaks by me;
> his word is on my tongue (v. 2).

The God of the Bible speaks. Frequently he has spoken through human agents, sometimes called prophets. Here David asserts that he is such an agent. The "Spirit" of the Lord is his "breath" (as the Hebrew word is translated in, for example, 22:16). This is what theologians call an anthropomorphism (language that applies characteristics of a human person to God, such as the arm, mouth, ear, or nostrils of the Lord). Just as human words are carried by the person's "breath," so, when David speaks by "the breath of the LORD," then it is *his* (the Lord's) word that is on David's tongue. In this context the word of God and the Spirit of God cannot be separated, any more than the words I speak can be separated from my breath.[11]

What is "his word" that is on David's tongue as the breath of the Lord speaks by him (23:2)? In 7:21 David called God's promise he had heard from Nathan "your word" (ESV, "your promise"). The word spoken *to* David (7:4–16) and the word spoken *by* David are (as we will see) the same word of God.

The God and Rock (v. 3a, b)

Before we hear that word we are reminded of the God whose word it is.

> The God of Israel has spoken;
>> the Rock of Israel has said to me . . . (v. 3a, b)

"The God of Israel" echoes "the God of Jacob" in verse 1d and carries the same two levels of meaning. God spoke to David in accordance with his promises to Jacob and for the sake of his people Israel. This God had been David's "rock," "the rock of [his] salvation" (22:3, 32, 47). He is likewise "the Rock of Israel" (23:3).

The first eight lines of this short poem have been preparatory. The effect is to magnify the importance of what we are now to hear.

The Word of God (vv. 3c–5a)

At the center of the poem are six lines in which we hear what God said to David and now says by David. Two lines present the substance of this word of God with stark brevity. Three lines then reflect on the goodness of it. Finally a single line connects this astonishing word with David's "house."

A Ruler (v. 3c, d)

The most important two lines of the whole poem are vividly pithy in Hebrew. This is generally lost in English versions. Here is a fairly literal translation:

> A ruler over humankind—a righteous one!
>> A ruler [in] the fear of God! (v. 3c, d AT)

In context this must be heard as an announcement or a promise.[12] It is a simple restatement of the essence of "the word of the LORD" that had come to David through Nathan (7:4). There are four aspects of this word of God that we should appreciate.

First, "ruler" represents a Hebrew word that occurs nowhere else in the books of Samuel. It is a word that focuses less on the person of the ruler (than does the word "king," for example) and more on the rule itself, as we will see in the following lines.[13]

Second, the rule will be over humankind (Hebrew, *adam*). Just as David had understood the promise in 2 Samuel 7 to be "instruction for mankind [*adam*]" (7:19), so David speaks here of a ruler whose dominion will embrace humanity.

Third, this ruler will be "righteous." The human race has had many rulers. Rarely could their rule be characterized by this word. A righteous ruler is one who does what is *right* by those he rules. David's kingdom had been (if only briefly) a kingdom of "righteousness" (8:15, ESV, "equity"). However, since the Bathsheba/Uriah affair, "righteous" is not the word that first comes to mind to describe David and his rule.

Fourth, the announced ruler will be characterized by "the fear of God" (23:3; cf. 1 Samuel 12:14, 24). This means that his rule will be in full accord with God's rule.

With these succinct words we hear the promise of a ruler who will establish *God's* kingdom. The goodness of this rule is beyond imagining, but something of what it is like is now described.

The Goodness of His Rule (v. 4)

The three lines of verse 4 are difficult to translate, the Hebrew poetry being delightfully elusive. The picture, however, is clear.

> [H]e dawns on them like the morning light,
>> like the sun shining forth on a cloudless morning,
>> like rain that makes grass to sprout from the earth. (v. 4)

The promised ruler is likened to the brilliance of the sun rising on a cloudless morning. His rule is like the sun's warmth joined with the rain, bringing forth abundant and lush growth. It is a picture of blessing in terms reminiscent of Genesis 1.[14]

It is a wonderful picture. It is a delightful dream. But is there any reason to think that it is more than that?

Where Is This Ruler to be Found? (v. 5a)

A big part of the power of the Bible's message is that the word of God has been accompanied by the works of God. In other words, the Bible does not simply contain ideas. The Bible sets the promises of God in the history of what God has done in faithfulness to his promises. In New Testament terms the news that Jesus is Lord is accompanied by the historical testimony to his resurrection from death: "We are witnesses to these things" (Acts 5:32).

In just the same way the promise of a righteous ruler is given concrete expression by David: "For does not my house stand so with God?" (v. 5a). Indeed the certainty of the promise seems to be supported ("For") by this reference to the standing of David's house with God.

This reminds us that God's promise had come to a concrete realization in David's own kingdom. As we have heard in verse 1, the son of Jesse was "raised on high, the anointed of the God of Jacob" and was the hero of Israel's songs. Certainly by this stage of our reading of the history we have come to understand that David's kingdom was inadequate and could only be a shadow of the good things to come (cf. Colossians 2:17; Hebrews 10:1). The justice and righteousness of David's kingdom (8:15) did not last. However, what God did achieve through David, in accordance with his great promises to Abraham, Isaac, and Jacob and for the sake of his people, should not be forgotten. It was remarkable and gives historic and objective substance to the promise.[15]

More particularly David's reference to his "house" (dynasty) clearly points us back to the promise of 2 Samuel 7: "the LORD will make you a house. And your house and your kingdom shall be made sure forever before me. Your throne shall be established forever" (7:11, 16). The terms in which the Lord's promise was given there made clear that the kingdom would be established through a son of David, "his offspring" (22:51). The promised righteous ruler and the promised son of David are one and the same (cf. Micah 5:2).

God's Covenant with David (v. 5b–e)

The fourth section of David's poem returns to the subject of the second section, namely, that the God of Israel had spoken to him.

The Covenant (v. 5b, c)

God's word to David is now described as the making of a covenant.

> For he has made with me an everlasting covenant,
> ordered in all things and secure. (v. 5b, c)

There is a certain unavoidable circularity to the argument. The standing of David's house with God is based on ("For") the covenant (that is, the promise) the Lord had made, which is in turn made sure by the experience of David's house.

Our earlier understanding is confirmed. The "word" spoken by God to and through David was the promise of 2 Samuel 7. For the first time this is now called a "covenant" (see also 2 Chronicles 13:5; 21:7; Psalm 89:3, 28, 34, 39; Jeremiah 33:21). It was an "everlasting" covenant (23:5) because it was about a kingdom to be established "forever" (7:13, 16). It was "ordered in all things and secure" (23:5), which sounds like legal terminology for everything being in order and certain.[16]

The Certainty (v. 5c, d)

This is followed up (another "For") with the certainty of God's good purposes toward David.

> For will he not cause to prosper
>> all my help and my desire? (v. 5c, d)

Like the grass that sprouts under the sun and rain (v. 4), so David's "help" (or "salvation"[17]) and his "desire" will be brought to bloom.

Here is a man with hope! These "last words of David" (v. 1) must have come at least toward the end of his life. His confidence about the future was formed and nourished by God's promise.

The Enemies of God and His King (vv. 6, 7)

The poem concludes with a reflection on the alternative to the hope offered in David's last words.

> But worthless men are all like thorns that are thrown away,
>> for they cannot be taken with the hand;
> but the man who touches them
>> arms himself with iron and the shaft of a spear,
>> and they are utterly consumed with fire. (vv. 6, 7)

"Worthless men" (literally "worthlessness") have appeared a number of times in our narrative, most recently "a worthless man" named Sheba (20:1). They are the opposite and the opponents of righteousness and the fear of God. Like thorns they are both dangerous and useless. They must be dealt with forcefully. Their proper end is destruction. This picture of the enemies of God and of his king and the judgment that will fall on them is an unavoidable aspect of the promise of a righteous ruler who will rule in the fear of God.

"The last words of David" are gospel words (23:1). The hope of the world and the hope every person needs is the promise of the kingdom of God. Jesus Christ is the promised righteous one (1 John 2:1). As you trust in him, may the God of hope fill you with joy, peace, and hope by the power of the Holy Spirit (Romans 15:13).

42

The Strength of David's Kingdom: His Mighty Men, Part 2

2 SAMUEL 23:8–39

EVERY HUMAN ACHIEVEMENT is eventually disappointing. The greatest human accomplishments are impressive, at least to us fellow humans who admire them. Leading scientists make remarkable discoveries and enable extraordinary, previously unimaginable things to be done. Top athletes continue to perform feats that no human before them has achieved. Great leaders can make a difference. And so on. Of course we ought to respect and honor those who do great things. But we know that human achievements always fall short of meeting the greatest needs, the deepest longings, and the most challenging problems of human societies and individuals.

The inadequacy of human achievements, even when measured by human standards, is magnified when we consider God's view of our accomplishments. Not only do we ultimately fail to satisfy human ideals and dreams— we fall far short of doing God's perfect will.

When we pray, "Your kingdom come" (Matthew 6:10) we are asking God to do more than humans can achieve. We are asking for the goodness of God's will to be done. We are longing for the day when there will be no more disappointment, no more regrets, no more pain, no more tears (cf. Revelation 21:4).

King David's kingdom was, on the one hand, a human kingdom. As we look back over the historical record of his kingdom, we can see that it was eventually disappointing. On the other hand, David's kingdom was an anticipation of God's kingdom. The Lord was with David in very remarkable ways, so that as we have looked at David's kingdom we have seen something of what God's kingdom will be like.

In 23:8–39 we have a part of the Bible that (at first sight) may seem unpromising. There are many names, most of which are otherwise unknown. Perhaps because of the obscurity of some of the information in this chapter, there seem to be an unusual number of places where the text is uncertain.[1] It would be easy to get lost in the details and the problems. However, the passage provides important perspectives on David's kingdom and helps us see why we need something more than humans can attain.

In the epilogue to the books of Samuel (2 Samuel 21—24), this passage corresponds to and supplements what we have heard in 21:15–22. We will see:

(1) Great human accomplishments in perspective (vv. 8–12).
(2) Great human devotion in perspective (vv. 13–17).
(3) More great human accomplishments (vv. 18–23).
(4) The problem with human heroes (vv. 24–39).

Great Human Accomplishments in Perspective (vv. 8–12)

We begin with three men in David's kingdom who accomplished great things. "These are the names of the mighty men whom David had . . ." (v. 8a). David had many "mighty men" (10:7; 16:6; 17:8; 20:7), and David himself was known as a "mighty man" (the Hebrew word is applied to David in 1 Samuel 16:18; 2 Samuel 17:10; 23:1).[2] While the term could well be applied to the other great ones mentioned in the whole passage before us, there were three who were outstanding, and these are the subject of verses 8–12.[3]

Josheb-basshebeth (v. 8b–d)

The first was "Josheb-basshebeth a Tahchemonite" (v. 8b). There is uncertainty about this man's name, and "Tahchemonite" is an obscure, otherwise unknown term (cf. 1 Chronicles 11:11). He was, however, "chief [literally "head"] of the three" (v. 8c).

His greatest claim to fame (no doubt among other exploits) was: "He wielded his spear against eight hundred whom he killed at one time" (v. 8d). That is all we know about this extraordinary feat of courage, skill, and strength. The brevity of the record should not obscure the magnitude of what he did. The full story would be thrilling to hear. The 800 he killed were probably (but not certainly) Philistines, on one of the many occasions when David's men fought with their western aggressive neighbor.

Rightly this mighty man was remembered for what he did. It was a great human accomplishment.

Eleazar (vv. 9, 10)

"And next to him among the three mighty men was Eleazar[4] the son of Dodo,[5] son of Ahohi[6]" (v. 9a). Eleazar's most famous deed is recorded in a little more detail.

> He was with David when they defied the Philistines who were gathered there for battle, and the men of Israel withdrew. He rose and struck down the Philistines until his hand was weary, and his hand clung to the sword. And the LORD brought about a great victory that day, and the men returned after him only to strip the slain. (vv. 9b, 10)

This was yet another conflict with the Philistines. It could have occurred at almost any time in David's public life. The Philistines had drawn up for an attack. David and his men "defied" the Philistines (v. 9). This probably means that they mocked them, tormenting and provoking them, as Goliath had once done to the Israelites (the same word is used in 1 Samuel 17:10, 25, 26, 36, 45; cf. ESV "taunted" in 21:21).

The taunting was effective and aroused the Philistines sufficiently for the Israelites to withdraw. This may have been tactical. As the incensed Philistines pursued the Israelites (into the hills?), were they being deliberately led into a trap?

It is tantalizing to have no more detail of how Eleazar, single-handedly it seems, struck down a huge number of Philistines. It was clearly a great and memorable display of strength and audacity. The narrator focuses dramatically on Eleazar's sword-wielding "hand." It grew "weary," but gripped his sword and would not let go of its blood-splattered, viselike grip until the terrible job was done (2 Samuel 23:10).

Eventually the Israelite troops returned to the scene of the battle, but "only to strip the slain" (v. 10). The victory had been won by one amazing fighter. Eleazar was remembered. And so he should have been. What an accomplishment!

Shammah (vv. 11, 12)

Meet the third member of this heroic trio: "And next to [Eleazar] was Shammah, the son of Agee[7] the Hararite[8]" (v. 11a). Like his fellows, Shammah had a great deed that was remembered.

> The Philistines gathered together at Lehi, where there was a plot of ground full of lentils, and the men fled from the Philistines. But he took his stand in the midst of the plot and defended it and struck down the Philistines, and the LORD worked a great victory. (vv. 11b, 12)

Lehi was apparently situated in the foothills of Judah near the territory of the Philistines.[9] Lehi had been raided by the Philistines in the days of Samson (Judges 15:9), resulting in Samson being handed over to the Philistines there and 1,000 Philistines being struck down by him (Judges 15:14, 15). God also provided water for Samson from a famous rock at Lehi (Judges 15:19). In other words, Lehi was a place long associated with a great hero of Israel and his dealings with the Philistines.

On this occasion, many years later in the days of King David, the Philistines again threatened Lehi. They had their eyes on the crops in a particular field: "a plot of ground full of lentils" (2 Samuel 23:11). The Philistines came in sufficient numbers and with enough aggression to cause the locals to flee for their lives. It looked as though the bumper harvest of lentils would be simple for the Philistines to filch.

They had not counted on Shammah, a worthy successor to Samson if ever there was one. Samson had struck down a thousand Philistines in Lehi with "a fresh jawbone of a donkey" (Judges 15:15). We do not know what weapon Shammah used, but it had a similar effect. He defeated the Philistines and saved the field and its crop.

These three exceptional heroes had certainly earned the designation "mighty men" (2 Samuel 23:8). Their accomplishments were in the never-to-be-forgotten category.

We have, however, passed over the most important words in this description of David's most outstanding three champions. Twice we are told, "The LORD brought about a great victory" (vv. 10, 12).[10] In other words these great accomplishments by Josheb-basshebeth, Eleazar, and Shammah were more than they seemed. They may have looked like outstanding feats of human strength, ingenuity, and courage. They were more than that. They were saving acts of God.[11] The Lord gave the might, skill, and daring by which these deeds were accomplished. He may have acted in other ways as well to ensure that the enemies of David and his kingdom were defeated.

The point is that these particular human accomplishments were more than that. The greatness and importance of what happened really lies in what the Lord was doing. Indeed the true measure of all human achievements is how they relate to what God is doing. So much of the time humans accomplish what they think are great things in defiance of God. They are like the builders of the tower of Babel (Genesis 11:1–9; cf. Revelation 18). Only when our achievements and our activities serve the kingdom of God do they have any lasting value. "Unless the LORD builds the house, those who build it labor in vain" (Psalm 127:1). The kingdom of God—that is, the rule of God by his anointed king—puts the greatness of all human accomplishments in perspective.

Great Human Devotion in Perspective (vv. 13–17)

The second section of our passage tells a remarkable story about another "three mighty men" (2 Samuel 23:9) and their breathtaking devotion to King David. Has a king ever had more dedicated subjects than these three men were to David? David's astonishing response to their devotion was one of the most memorable things he ever did.

The men are described as "three of the thirty chief men" (v. 13a). There was a group of David's mighty men known as "the thirty" (see vv. 18, 19, 23, 24). The name seems to have applied, whether the number was actually thirty or not (see v. 39b). No doubt the group expanded and contracted in membership over time.

It was "three of the thirty" who "went down and came about harvest time to David at the cave of Adullam" (v. 13b). It is possible that this was in David's early days, before he was king, when he was on the run from Saul. He had spent a significant time in the cave of Adullam (1 Samuel 22:1–5). It is also possible that the present incident occurred much later than that, when the Philistines came into the Valley of Rephaim in response to the news that David had become king of Israel (5:17, 18).[12] It is also possible (I think probable) that the episode before us took place at some other time in David's life, unknown to us, involving an otherwise unrecorded engagement with the Philistines.

Adullam was roughly twenty miles southwest from Jerusalem, in the foothills of Judah, about ten miles southeast of the Philistine town of Gath.[13] The cave may have been part of a fortified area ("the stronghold," v. 14; cf. 1 Samuel 22:5; 24:22).

David was in the cave "when a band of Philistines was encamped in the Valley of Rephaim" (v. 13c), as they did on at least one other occasion either before or after this incident (assuming 5:17–25 was a different occasion). Further details of the interaction between David and the Philistines on this occasion are not given. The concern of the narrative is with something else.

"David was then in the stronghold, and the garrison of the Philistines[14] was then at Bethlehem" (v. 14). A Philistine presence in the Valley of Rephaim and Bethlehem suggests a significant incursion into Israelite territory. Perhaps (as in the previous episode) they were intent on raiding Israelite harvests.

In this situation David was overcome with a surprising desire. "And David said longingly [literally, desired and said], 'Oh, that someone would give me water to drink from the well of Bethlehem that is by the gate!'" (v. 15). It was fifteen miles or more from Adullam to Bethlehem. There were enemy soldiers in the way. David's words were not meant literally, but he was expressing a deep longing.[15] In the dangers he was facing and the many troubles his life had brought him, he was thinking of his hometown, his life there as a boy. Though not without its dangers (see 1 Samuel 17:34, 35), those had been simple days. I am not sure that it was such nostalgia that overcame David. There was, however, a wistful longing for an experience of his childhood. How good it would be to drink again from Bethlehem's well!

The astonishing turn of events came when the three men who had come to him at the cave heard David's musings, and although I doubt that they thought he meant what he said literally, they decided that they would do something extraordinary. "Then the three mighty men broke through the camp of the Philistines and drew water out of the well of Bethlehem that was by the gate and carried and brought it to David" (v. 16a). It would have been remarkable enough if the men had used stealth and secretly managed to procure some of the Bethlehem water under the cover of darkness. But they "broke through" the Philistine lines (v. 16). The language suggests a violent and forceful entry into the town.[16] The recklessness is alarming, but speaks volumes of the devotion that David's men had to their master. This action showed that they would do *anything* for him. There are few moments in David's life that show us the love he inspired in his followers more powerfully than this one. His brave men would have been understandably pleased with what they had done, and no doubt eager to see David's reaction as they presented him with their gift and told him how they had acquired it.

David's response to what the three had done was so deeply profound that it defies rational explanation. "But he would not drink of it" (v. 16b). The reason? David considered the water that had been obtained by such an act to be too precious for something as trivial as his own refreshment.[17] To the amazement of all, "He poured it out to the LORD" (v. 16c; cf. 1 Samuel 7:6). The deep significance of David's action is seen in the words "to the LORD." Without those words the action of pouring out the water brought to him at such cost and with such love could have been seen as an appalling insult. It could have been understood as a rejection of the gift, despising the sacrifice with which it had been obtained. But no one misunderstood David's action along such lines because they heard what he said.

David explained, "Far be it from me, O LORD, that I should do this. Shall I drink the blood of the men who went at the risk of their lives?" (v. 17a). David honored the devotion of these three men more than they could have anticipated. What mattered to him was not the water itself, but the extraordinary sacrificial love they had shown to him. For David the water, obtained at such a cost, represented the *blood* of his men. David would not use such devotion for his own physical nourishment. It was something that had to be given to God.

We sense that there is something magnificent here, even if it is not easy to put into words. David gave what these men had done *to the Lord*. It was as though he was saying that such devotion, love, and sacrifice really belongs to God. We must be careful with the kind of adulation and commitment we give to our fellow humans (or expect from them). In this case, of course, these men were devoted to God's king and therefore (whether they fully understood it or not) to God himself. That, however, seems to be the point that David vividly demonstrated by giving the fruits of their devotion to the one to whom their devotion truly belonged.

The episode concludes, "Therefore he would not drink it. These things the three mighty men did" (v. 17b). It was one of David's finest moments. Here was a king who was the very opposite of the king Samuel had feared many years earlier, when he warned that a king would "take . . . take . . . take" (1 Samuel 8:10–18). David turned great human devotion from himself to the Lord.

More Great Human Accomplishments (vv. 18–23)

The third section of our passage introduces two further great men who served David faithfully and effectively. These two add more details to the picture we are being given of the strength of David's kingdom.

Abishai (vv. 18, 19)

> Now Abishai, the brother of Joab, the son of Zeruiah, was chief of the thirty.[18] And he wielded his spear against three hundred men and killed them and won a name beside the three. He was the most renowned of the thirty and became their commander, but he did not attain to the three. (vv. 18, 19)

David's nephew, Abishai, has been a prominent person in the story of David's life. In the early days it was Abishai who offered to eliminate Saul for

David (1 Samuel 26:8). Later Abishai had assisted his brother Joab in pursuing and eventually killing Abner in revenge for the death of their brother Asahel (2:24; 3:30). Abishai, true to character, had offered to silence the curses of Shimei by removing his head (16:9; cf. 19:21). David had put this bold though impetuous soldier in command of one third of his army (18:2). Indeed like other men in this passage Abishai had saved David's life, probably more than once (21:17). We are not surprised to find him mentioned here as a leader of leaders.

Abishai's great feat recorded here was similar to that of Josheb-basshebeth, on a smaller but nonetheless amazing scale. His accomplishment was great, but (the historian notes) it did not qualify him to join "the three" (23:18).

Benaiah (vv. 20–23)

> And Benaiah the son of Jehoiada was a valiant man of Kabzeel, a doer of great deeds. He struck down two ariels of Moab. He also went down and struck down a lion in a pit on a day when snow had fallen. And he struck down an Egyptian, a handsome man. The Egyptian had a spear in his hand, but Benaiah went down to him with a staff and snatched the spear out of the Egyptian's hand and killed him with his own spear. These things did Benaiah the son of Jehoiada, and won a name beside the three mighty men. He was renowned among the thirty, but he did not attain to the three. And David set him over his bodyguard. (vv. 20–23)

Benaiah has not played as prominent a role in the history as Abishai, but he has been mentioned previously in his capacity as commander of the Cherethites and the Pelethites (8:18; 20:23).[19] Here we learn that he was from Kabzeel, a town in southern Judah (Joshua 15:21) and that he was "a doer of great deeds" (2 Samuel 23:20). Three of these deeds are briefly described. The first is puzzling simply because we do not know what an "ariel" was (v. 20).[20] However, striking two of them down was a great deed! The second was the killing of a lion in challenging circumstances.[21] David had done something similar in his youth (1 Samuel 17:34–37). The third "great deed" is described in more detail. It was the defeat of an Egyptian of impressive appearance.[22] Benaiah was armed only with a staff, but he disarmed the Egyptian and finished him off with his own spear. With these (and no doubt other) deeds Benaiah won a reputation (although, like Abishai, he was not included in "the three," v. 23). David's confidence in Benaiah was such that he set him over his bodyguard,[23] a role David had played for Saul (1 Samuel 22:14).

Before we come to the final section of our passage, let us notice that the overwhelming picture we are given of the strength of David's kingdom, through the presentation of these mighty men and their exploits, is violent. Those were, of course, violent times. David and his kingdom were constantly under threat from ferocious enemies. David's "mighty men" are celebrated here because of their strength and ability in overcoming violence with violence (2 Samuel 23:8).

This picture of David's kingdom is deeply unsatisfying. Certainly we can appreciate that it was better for David and his kingdom that the Philistines were defeated rather than victorious. But this was not a kingdom of peace. This fell far short of God's promise to David and his people, "that they may dwell in their own place and be disturbed no more. And violent men shall afflict them no more, as formerly. . . . And I will give you rest from all your enemies" (7:10, 11).

Long after David's lifetime the prophets insisted that God's promise stood firm. A king would come whose kingdom would surpass David's kingdom. It would be everything that David's kingdom failed to be.

> For to us a child is born,
>   to us a son is given;
> and the government shall be upon his shoulder,
>   and his name shall be called
> Wonderful Counselor, Mighty God,
>   Everlasting Father, Prince of Peace.
> Of the increase of his government and of peace
>   there will be no end,
> on the throne of David and over his kingdom,
>   to establish it and to uphold it
> with justice and with righteousness
>   from this time forth and forevermore.
> The zeal of the LORD of hosts will do this. (Isaiah 9:6, 7)

The birth of Jesus was announced with the following proclamation:

> For unto you is born this day in the city of David a Savior, who is Christ the Lord. . . . Glory to God in the highest, and on earth peace among those with whom he is pleased! (Luke 2:11, 14)

The Problem with Human Heroes (vv. 24–39)

Our passage concludes with a list of names of "the thirty" (2 Samuel 23:24). We are told at the end of the list that there were actually "thirty-seven" (v. 39), which appears to include "the three" of verses 8–12 and Abishai and Benaiah (vv. 18–23) as well as the thirty-two listed in verses 24–39.[24] The group, no doubt, varied in composition and size over time.

> Asahel the brother of Joab was one of the thirty; Elhanan the son of Dodo of Bethlehem, Shammah of Harod, Elika of Harod, Helez the Paltite, Ira the son of Ikkesh of Tekoa, Abiezer of Anathoth, Mebunnai the Hushathite, Zalmon the Ahohite, Maharai of Netophah, Heleb the son of Baanah of Netophah, Ittai the son of Ribai of Gibeah of the people of Benjamin, Benaiah of Pirathon, Hiddai of the brooks of Gaash, Abi-albon the Arbathite, Azmaveth of Bahurim, Eliahba the Shaalbonite, the sons of Jashen, Jonathan, Shammah the Hararite, Ahiam the son of Sharar the Hararite, Eliphelet the son of Ahasbai of Maacah, Eliam the son of Ahithophel of Gilo, Hezro of Carmel, Paarai the Arbite, Igal the son of Nathan of Zobah, Bani the Gadite, Zelek the Ammonite, Naharai of Beeroth, the armor-bearer of Joab the son of Zeruiah, Ira the Ithrite, Gareb the Ithrite, Uriah the Hittite: thirty-seven in all. (vv. 24–39)

Three points are worth noting.[25] The first is that Asahel, brother of Joab and Abishai, begins the list. Asahel was killed by Abner in the battle of Gibeon (2:23). This suggests that "the thirty" (23:24) were a recognized group from the earliest days of David's reign, perhaps from the days when David was on the run from Saul. They may have been a kind of army council, assisting David in framing plans and policies.[26]

The second point to note is that Joab, though mentioned in 23:18, 24, and 37, is not included in "the thirty" (v. 24). This may simply be because he was over the whole army and therefore not numbered among this group. However, the sidelining of Joab in the chapter may remind us of the tensions and difficulties between David and his senior military man.

The third point, however, is (in my opinion) most important of all. The last name in the list of "the thirty" (v. 24) cannot fail to catch our attention: "Uriah the Hittite" (v. 39). This sketch of David's kingdom and the strength it enjoyed through David's "mighty men" ends on a somber note. All of the mighty men in our passage may have been devoted, courageous, faithful, and great servants of David. David, however, murdered one of them. Furthermore verse 34 mentions Eliam, the father of Bathsheba (11:3), and his father Ahithophel. This reminder of David's adultery and the unraveling of his family and kingdom that ensued points to the greatest weakness of David's kingdom—David himself.

The mighty kingdom of David with his "mighty men" (23:8) and their heroic deeds contains much that should cause us to appreciate the kingdom ruled by the Prince of Peace. Let us pray daily, "Your kingdom come" (Matthew 6:10).

43

A Problem in David's Kingdom: God's Wrath, Part 2

2 SAMUEL 24

There is therefore now no condemnation
for those who are in Christ Jesus.

ROMANS 8:1

"NO CONDEMNATION" means no condemnation *before God*. The remarkable words of Romans 8:1 are only possible in the New Testament. No Old Testament writer could have said, "There is therefore now no condemnation."

Israel, in particular the kingdom of David, was an astonishing historical phenomenon. The books of Samuel tell a crucial part of the story. King David was one of the greatest men to have ever lived, and his kingdom (at its best) displayed outstanding qualities (see 8:15). But King David could not save his people from the most serious problem of the human race—the righteous wrath of God against all human ungodliness and unrighteousness (Romans 1:18). "No condemnation" was *not* the case for those who were in David's kingdom.

The final chapter of 2 Samuel returns to the difficult subject of the wrath of God. This was the theme of the first part of the epilogue to the books of Samuel (21:1–14), where we saw David's inability to deal adequately with the reality of God's wrath. This aspect of David and his kingdom is so important that it is the subject with which the books of Samuel conclude.

This closing chapter recounts a sequence of events (some of them deeply perplexing) that bring before us again the reality of God's righteous wrath.

(1) The wrath of God and the numbering of the people (vv. 1–9).
(2) The wrath of God and the pestilence on Israel (vv. 10–15).
(3) The wrath of God and the mercy of God (vv. 16–19).
(4) The wrath of God and atonement (verses 20–25).

The Wrath of God and the Numbering of the People (vv. 1–9)

The Perplexing Wrath of God (v. 1)

> Again the anger of the LORD was kindled against Israel, and he incited David against them, saying, "Go, number Israel and Judah."[1] (v. 1)

The opening sentence of the chapter bristles with difficult questions, some of which we cannot answer; but others must be considered.

We cannot know precisely when this occurred, except that it was while David was king. There is a reasonable argument that it was probably in the latter days of his reign.[2] "Again" suggests at least one earlier occasion on which "the anger of the LORD was kindled against Israel" (v. 1). The most obvious earlier occasion is 21:1–14, and that is probably what the narrator had in mind.[3] However, we should remember that the anger of the Lord had burned on other occasions (see 6:7).[4]

We also cannot know the reason for the Lord's anger on this occasion. In 21:1 the Lord had told David about the "bloodguilt on Saul." That raised further questions, but at least it identified an offense. In 2 Samuel 24 there is no explanation for the Lord's anger. That suggests we do not need to know *why* the Lord's anger was kindled, but it is very important for us to understand *that* the Lord's anger was aroused against Israel before any of the events of this chapter took place. There certainly was a reason. The Bible is consistently clear that God's wrath is always righteous; it is never unjustified (see Psalm 145:17).[5] On this occasion, however, the reason for God's wrath is beside the point.

The information in verse 1 is made known to us (the readers) although it was not known (at this stage) to any of the human participants in the following narrative. No one yet knew that the Lord's anger had been kindled against Israel.

What the Lord did in his anger (unknown to any of the human characters) is a puzzle that reverberates through the whole chapter. "He incited David against [Israel]" (2 Samuel 24:1). David was to be the unwitting agent of the Lord's anger against Israel.[6] The parallel between "against Israel" and "against them" in this verse clearly indicates that what David was to do would hurt Israel.

Surprisingly the account of these things in 1 Chronicles 21:1 says, "Satan . . . incited David."[7] There is no contradiction, however, when we understand that even Satan serves the Lord's purposes. Putting the texts together we can say that the Lord used Satan as his agent in inciting David to be the agent of his anger against Israel.[8]

Before we consider what the Lord incited David to do (or, in 1 Chronicles 21:1 terms, what the Lord used Satan to incite David to do), we should understand that the Lord is able to use both good and evil human acts for his purposes without in any way diminishing human responsibility for the deeds themselves. There are a number of outstanding examples of this general truth. In Genesis 50:20 Joseph said to his brothers who had intended to kill him, "As for you, you meant evil against me, but God meant it for good." Their actions were evil, but God was involved bringing good out of the evil. More dramatically still, Peter said of the crucifixion of Jesus, "[T]his Jesus, delivered up according to the definite plan and foreknowledge of God, you crucified and killed by the hands of lawless men" (Acts 2:23). The killing of Jesus was a wicked act, for which "you" and "lawless men" were fully responsible. Yet it was also "according to the definite plan and foreknowledge of God." Divine sovereignty does not diminish human responsibility; neither does human responsibility diminish divine sovereignty. The Lord had his purpose in what he incited David to do, without compromising David's responsibility for what he did.

What did the Lord incite David to do? "Go, number Israel and Judah" (2 Samuel 24:1). In the context of the whole chapter, I strongly suspect that these words were not actually heard by David, either through a prophet or by any other means. The quoted words indicate what the Lord "incited" David to do, not what he *commanded* David to do. The difference may seem slight, but in due course it will be clear that David did not see numbering the people as something that the Lord had *commanded* him to do. From David's point of view it was his idea, for which he rightly took full responsibility (as we will see).

It is not obvious why numbering the nation would be "against them" (v. 1). In our experience a census is, on the whole, benign. In a modern democracy privacy is generally respected, and the purpose of the exercise is normally for the good of the people. However, in the ancient world a census could have various unwelcome purposes including taxation and military conscription.[9] A ruler's numbering his people could certainly be ominous, as it was 1,000 years later when Caesar Augustus ordered a census of the whole Roman world (Luke 2:1).

However, it remains puzzling that the consequence of the Lord's anger being kindled against Israel was that David was stirred up to conduct a census.

The Contentious Command of the King (vv. 2–4a)

David (presumably unaware of the Lord's hand in this) instructed Joab to carry out his wish.

> So the king said to Joab, the commander of the army, who was with him, "Go through all the tribes of Israel, from Dan to Beersheba, and number[10] the people, that I may know the number of the people." (v. 2)

It is ominous that it was Joab who was instructed to carry out the census. Was this because military force might be required to ensure the people's compliance?

The extent of the exercise was to be comprehensive. It was to include "all the tribes of Israel" from Dan in the far north to Beersheba in the south (v. 2).[11]

David's statement of the purpose of the census is elusive: "that I may know the number of the people" (v. 2). He did not say why he wanted or needed to "know the number of the people." Did he simply want to delight in how many subjects served him? Or did he have some practical purpose for this knowledge?

It was not unusual for Joab to think that his own ideas were better than his king's (remember Abner and Absalom!). On this occasion he didn't have an alternative, but questioned the wisdom of the king's proposal.

> But Joab said to the king, "May the LORD your God add to the people a hundred times as many as they are, while the eyes of my lord the king still see it, but why does my lord the king delight in this thing?" (v. 3)

What was Joab's objection? He obviously thought that the king should *not* "delight in this thing."[12] But why? On the surface he declared his confidence that the Lord would so multiply the number of the people in David's own lifetime that numbering the people was pointless. A census would soon be out-of-date if one believed the Lord's promises! Furthermore, was he suggesting that if David trusted God, there was no need to number the people? Beneath the surface (there was usually something beneath the surface with Joab) Joab probably understood that David's census would arouse resentment and would serve no useful purpose.[13]

However, on this occasion David had his way. "But the king's word prevailed against Joab and the commanders of the army" (v. 4a). David's instructions had been directed to a wider group of military men than Joab. It seems that they had agreed with Joab's objection, but David's word (literally) "was strong over them." The objection was overruled.

The Numbering of the People (vv. 4b–9)

"So Joab and the commanders of the army went out from the presence of the king to number the people of Israel" (v. 4b). There follows an account of their itinerary.

> They crossed the Jordan and began from Aroer,[14] and from the city that is in the middle of the valley, toward Gad and on to Jazer. Then they came to Gilead, and to Kadesh in the land of the Hittites;[15] and they came to Dan, and from Dan they went around to Sidon, and came to the fortress of Tyre and to all the cities of the Hivites and Canaanites; and they went out to the Negeb of Judah at Beersheba. So when they had gone through all the land, they came to Jerusalem at the end of nine months and twenty days. (vv. 5–8)

The territory covered did not include lands David had conquered, but involved a circuit of the land of the tribes of Israel. The route began on the east of the Jordan at Aroer on the southern boundary of Israel's eastern territory (Deuteronomy 2:36). It then went north and northwest, eventually reaching Sidon on the Mediterranean coast. It then proceeded southward and then east to Beersheba.[16]

The project took nearly ten months to complete. Joab and his men returned to Jerusalem and brought the results to the king.

> And Joab gave the sum of the numbering of the people to the king: in Israel there were 800,000 valiant men who drew the sword, and the men of Judah were 500,000. (v. 9)

These numbers are very high, implying a total population of at least six million in the land.[17] However, we have noted a number of times that the Hebrew word for "thousand" was also used for a military unit. It has been suggested that such units were quite small (one proposal is five to fourteen men per unit[18]). This would result in more probable numbers.[19]

The terms in which the report was brought to the king reveal that at least one purpose of the numbering was to ascertain the nation's military capability. Why David wanted this information remains unstated. However, what happened next will reveal that his intentions were problematic.

It is still not clear how David's numbering the people (whatever his motives) was to be used by the Lord "against Israel" (v. 1).

The Wrath of God and the Pestilence on Israel (vv. 10–15)

David's Confession (v. 10)

Verse 10 is the most perplexing development in this puzzling sequence of events.

> But David's heart struck him after he had numbered the people. And David said to the LORD, "I have sinned greatly in what I have done. But now, O LORD, please take away the iniquity of your servant, for I have done very foolishly." (v. 10)

We have no reason to think that numbering the people *in itself* was a sin.[20] However, either the circumstances or the intention of this census caused David a serious attack of conscience.[21] Did the census express a failure by David to trust the Lord and his promises (cf. 1 Samuel 14:6)? Or was the census an act of arrogant pride, giving King David something to boast about? Or had David formulated personal military ambitions without regard to the Lord's will?[22] It is probably important to see that the narrator does not tell us *what* it was about David's census that caused his heart to strike him as it did. The various suggestions may all be possibilities, but the details of the offense are again not important.

Just as we do not know what offense Israel had committed to kindle the Lord's anger (v. 1), so now we do not need to know the details of what David had done. The important point is that the king now knew himself to be what we know the people also were—sinners against the Lord.

David responded to his troubled conscience by speaking to the Lord. This can be a very difficult thing to do. Israel had not done this. Sin tends to harden the heart against God, blinding us to the one we have offended and the riches of his mercy.

David had learned of God's grace through profound experience. Remember his confession on an earlier occasion, after he had sinned very greatly? "I have sinned against the LORD." Remember the word he heard from the Lord's prophet on that occasion? "The LORD . . . has put away your sin" (12:13). Now David confessed his sin as he had before: "I have sinned greatly in what I have done" (24:10). And he asked the Lord to do what he had done before: "But now, O LORD, please take away[23] the iniquity of your servant"

(v. 10). David acknowledged that what he had done (like all sin really) was very stupid: "for I have done very foolishly" (v. 10).[24]

The Word of the Lord (vv. 11–13)

We might expect that David would now receive a gracious word from the Lord, as he had on the previous occasion (although his sin then still had terrible consequences). But this time things were more complicated. Remember that the episode began with the fact that the Lord's anger had been kindled against Israel. David's census, whatever his personal and sinful intentions may have been, had another purpose—the outworking of the Lord's anger against Israel.

The word of the Lord did come, but it was not what David had hoped for.

> And when David arose in the morning, the word of the LORD came to the prophet Gad, David's seer, saying, "Go and say to David, 'Thus says the LORD, Three things I offer you. Choose one of them, that I may do it to you.'" (vv. 11, 12)

David had probably spent the whole night in prayer (v. 10). It was when he "arose in the morning" (v. 11) that the Lord answered him.

The prophet Gad had been around for a long time. Although he appeared only once previously in the books of Samuel (1 Samuel 22:5), we now learn that he was "David's seer" (2 Samuel 24:11). This suggests an ongoing relationship with David (probably since his days on the run from Saul) and that he was a means by which David received revelations from God. This was one of the more important revelations.

The narrative unfolds with considerable suspense. First we hear that Gad was to go to David and invite him to choose one of three things that the Lord would then "do it to [or for] you" (v. 12). For a moment we might expect that David was being told to choose between three blessings.

Only when Gad reached David are we permitted to hear what the three things were.

> So Gad came to David and told him, and said to him, "Shall three[25] years of famine come to you in your land? Or will you flee three months before your foes while they pursue you? Or shall there be three days' pestilence in your land? Now consider, and decide what answer I shall return to him who sent me." (v. 13)

The "three things" were punishments, not blessings—years of famine, months of a losing war, or days of pestilence. Presumably the decreasing periods of time were being matched by increasing horrors and suffering.

These three options should not be seen simply as punishments for whatever offense David committed by his census. Indeed David personally did not suffer (although, of course, as king he shared in the suffering of his people). Rather, the census was the means by which the Lord brought a punishment on Israel for the offense that had kindled his anger at the beginning of this episode (v. 1).

Gad insisted that David consider carefully and make a decision that the prophet would report back to the Lord ("him who sent me," v. 13).

Why did the Lord involve David in this unusual way? Why didn't he send one of his punishments (chosen by him) as soon as his anger was kindled against Israel (v. 1)? We do not have answers to these questions, just as we often cannot answer "why?" questions about God's ways today (cf. Romans 9:20). However, we can observe that one effect of what the Lord did (and the way in which he did it) was to involve King David in the judgment of his people and to demonstrate that King David the sinner was not able to save his people from the wrath of God.

What good news it is that a greater King has now come! "God did not send his Son into the world to condemn the world, but in order that the world might be saved through him" (John 3:17).

David's Faith (v. 14)

David was out of his depth.

> Then David said to Gad, "I am in great distress. Let us fall into the hand of the LORD, for his mercy is great; but let me not fall into the hand of man."
> (2 Samuel 24:14)

We can sympathize with David's distress. What a dreadful decision was being asked of him. His response was not a clear choice. Was he excluding the second option because that would be to "fall into the hand of man" (v. 14)? Had he forgotten that it was the Lord who had repeatedly given him victory over his enemies (8:14, etc.)? Was he excluding the first two options because famine would make the people dependent on those who had access to food? Again, the experience of 21:1–14 shows that the Lord controls famine.

I prefer to understand David's words here as an expression of faith in God in the midst of his confused distress. He did not make a clear choice. He couldn't. But he wanted himself and his people ("us") to fall into the Lord's hands, "for his mercy is great" (24:14). The only hope for anyone against whom the Lord's anger has been kindled is the mercy of the Lord. David knew that much.

The Reality of God's Wrath (v. 15)

> So the LORD sent a pestilence on Israel from the morning until the appointed time. And there died of the people from Dan to Beersheba 70,000 men. (v. 15)

If our understanding of David's words in verse 14 is correct, it was the Lord who chose the punishment. It was terrible. A dreadful infectious disease (possibly bubonic plague) broke out in Israel that very morning.[26] It continued wreaking havoc "until the appointed time" (v. 15). This striking phrase emphasizes that the pestilence was under the Lord's control. It began when he "sent" it, and it continued until the "time" he had "appointed." The big surprise is going to be that "the appointed time" was probably not at the end of three days (v. 13) but significantly sooner (v. 16).

Before we object to this severe punishment, remember that we do not know what offense had kindled the Lord's anger. We are therefore hardly in a position to judge the punishment as excessive. Indeed the severity of the punishment tells us that the offense must have been great in the Lord's eyes.

Again, if our understanding of the numbers in verse 9 is correct, then it is likely that "70,000" (v. 15) really means seventy military units, possibly in the order of 700 men in all. Be that as it may, the anger of the Lord (v. 1) was real and had terrible consequences in Israel that day throughout the whole land ("from Dan to Beersheba," v. 15).

The Wrath of God and the Mercy of God (vv. 16–19)

The plague that the Lord "sent" (v. 15) is described in verse 16 in terms of an "angel" (the word also means "messenger") who was the Lord's agent in bringing this terrible judgment. This "messenger" was no doubt acting behind the scenes as far as most observers of the catastrophe were concerned, but his presence and activity were known to God and became clear to David.

The Mystery of God's Mercy (v. 16)

The Lord did not allow the plague he had sent to do as much damage as it might have done.

> And when the angel stretched out his hand toward Jerusalem to destroy it, the LORD relented from the calamity and said to the angel who was working

destruction among the people, "It is enough; now stay your hand." And the angel of the LORD was by the threshing floor of Araunah the Jebusite. (v. 16)

In this strange scene it was when the messenger "stretched out his hand toward *Jerusalem*" that the Lord stopped the destruction. The implication seems to be that this was before the destruction had run its course (the three days of v. 13). Jerusalem represents God's promises. The ark of the covenant was there (2 Samuel 6). It was "the city of David" (5:9), to whom the Lord had promised a kingdom that would be established forever (7:16). The Lord was (as always) faithful to his promises and therefore had mercy for the sake of his great name (cf. 1 Samuel 12:22). The messenger was commanded to stop his terrible work.

The Lord takes no delight in the death and destruction that wickedness brings (cf. Ezekiel 18:32). While the Lord's relenting must not be understood in human terms, neither must it be emptied of its force (see the same word with the same difficulties in 1 Samuel 15:11, 35, where the ESV has "regret"[27]). The Lord is "merciful and gracious, slow to anger" (Exodus 34:6; Psalm 103:8). He delights to have mercy and is grieved at sin and its consequences. On this day, when the destruction threatened Jerusalem, he had mercy and said, "Enough" (2 Samuel 24:16).

The place where this mercy was given is carefully noted ("by the threshing floor of Araunah the Jebusite," v. 16) for reasons that will soon become clear.

David's Confession (Again) (v. 17)

Verse 16 has given us the Lord's perspective on the destruction he had sent. Verse 17 gives us David's perspective.

Then David spoke to the LORD when he saw the angel who was striking the people, and said, "Behold, I have sinned, and I have done wickedly. But these sheep, what have they done? Please let your hand be against me and against my father's house." (v. 17)

The translation is more confusing than it needs to be. The Hebrew does not as clearly show as the English ("Then") that David's words to the Lord were subsequent to what happened in verse 16. This could be a flashback.[28] Furthermore the Hebrew is also less clear than the English implies about whether the angel/messenger was striking the people at the time David saw him or *had been* striking the people prior to David's seeing him.[29]

In other words, it is *possible* (but not necessary) that David's prayer in verse 17 was answered by the *subsequent* mercy shown by the Lord in verse 16. However, the narrator has presented the sequence of events in such a way that we cannot conclude that David's prayer *caused* the end of the destruction. The Lord's mercy did not *depend* on David's prayer, even if it may have been given in answer to that prayer. The plague ended at "the appointed time" (v. 15), that is, by the Lord's gracious but sovereign decision.

David's prayer repeated his confession of sin (without shedding any further light on the precise nature of his offense). He asked that the Lord's judgment be directed at him and his house, not at the people ("these sheep," v. 17), protesting their innocence. We do not know the answer to his question ("what have they done?" v. 17) any more than David did. We do know, however, that he was mistaken to think that they were innocent (v. 1).

Nonetheless we should certainly take careful note of King David's willingness to lay down his life for his sheep. Once again we find, even in the context of David's inadequacy, a wonderful anticipation of the Good Shepherd who has now done just that (John 10:11, 15).

The Word of the Lord (Again) (v. 18)

The word of the Lord came again to David by the prophet Gad.

> And Gad came that day to David and said to him, "Go up, raise an altar to the LORD on the threshing floor of Araunah the Jebusite." (v. 18)

This time the Lord required David to go to the place where the Lord's mercy had brought an end to the punishment. The threshing floor of Araunah the Jebusite[30] was an elevated location (hence, "Go up," v. 18). Subsequent events will indicate that it was on the high ground north of the city proper.

At that location David was to "raise an altar to the LORD" (v. 18), just as Noah, Abraham, Joshua, Samuel, and even Saul had done at significant moments in Israel's history (Genesis 8:20; 12:7, 8; Joshua 8:30; 1 Samuel 7:17; 14:35).

David's Faith (Again) (v. 19)

"So David went up at Gad's word, as the LORD commanded" (v. 19). As David had trusted himself to the Lord's mercy in verse 14, so his faith was now expressed in immediate obedience to the Lord's command.

The Wrath of God and Atonement (vv. 20–25)

The detail in which the story of David's acquisition of Araunah's threshing floor is told suggests that this—the last event recorded in the books of

Samuel—must be rather important. Curiously most space is given to the account of how the site was acquired.

The Place (vv. 20–24)

> And when Araunah looked down, he saw the king and his servants coming on toward him. And Araunah went out and paid homage to the king with his face to the ground. And Araunah said, "Why has my lord the king come to his servant?" David said, "To buy the threshing floor from you, in order to build an altar to the LORD, that the plague may be averted from the people." Then Araunah said to David, "Let my lord the king take and offer up what seems good to him. Here are the oxen for the burnt offering and the threshing sledges and the yokes of the oxen for the wood. All this, O king, Araunah gives to the king." And Araunah said to the king, "May the LORD your God accept you." But the king said to Araunah, "No, but I will buy it from you for a price. I will not offer burnt offerings to the LORD my God that cost me nothing." So David bought the threshing floor and the oxen for fifty shekels of silver. (vv. 20–24)

The interchange between King David and the Jebusite owner of the threshing floor is recounted with a touch of humor. It was typical of oriental bargaining, starting with a generous but unacceptable offer and ending in a deal.[31] We should note at least four important points.

First, the site came into Israelite ownership through a legitimate transaction. It was not seized by the king's power, nor was it taken in battle. Its ownership was beyond dispute. The importance of this has to do, no doubt, with the future use of this site.

Second, David (and Araunah for that matter) understood that an altar was for offering sacrifices. This was implicit in the Lord's command to raise up an altar.

Third, David's refusal to "offer burnt offerings to the LORD my God that cost me nothing" is striking (v. 24). "That cost me nothing" renders a Hebrew word that elsewhere is translated "without cause." It would be as inappropriate for David to offer sacrifices that had cost him nothing as it would be to shed innocent blood "without cause" (see 1 Samuel 19:5; 25:31).

Fourth, David knew there was a connection between the altar he had been told to build (and the sacrifices that would be offered) and the stopping of the plague ("that the plague may be averted from the people," 2 Samuel 24:21). This is puzzling because we have already been told of the Lord's decision to stop the destruction (v. 16). Of course, David may not have known about this since it would take some time for it to be clear that the pestilence had ceased. The subtle but important point is that while the altar and the sacrifices were no doubt very important (even necessary), the account is framed in such a way that excludes the idea that the sacrifices *caused* the plague to stop. The Lord did that (v. 16) at "the appointed time" (v. 15).

The Sacrifices (v. 25a)

"And David built there an altar to the LORD and offered burnt offerings and peace offerings" (v. 25a). The last act of David recorded in the books of Samuel was the offering of sacrifices. "Burnt offerings" (see Leviticus 1) were the most common of all Old Testament sacrifices. The main purpose was to atone for human sin by propitiating God's wrath.[32] "Peace offerings" (see Leviticus 3) were a celebration of peace with God and all that flows from that blessing.[33]

The Wrath of God Averted (v. 25b)

The book of 2 Samuel closes with these words: "So the LORD responded to the plea for the land, and the plague was averted from Israel" (v. 25b, echoing 21:14b).

That, of course, is good news. But we do not need to turn very many pages in the Bible to find that the people of this kingdom aroused the anger of the Lord again and again (see 1 Kings 14:9, 15; 15:30; 16:2, 7, 13, 26, 33; 21:22; 22:53[34]).

However, what David did at the threshing floor of Araunah was of historic importance. In due course David's son Solomon built the temple at this place, where burnt offerings would be offered for the ongoing sins of Israel for a long time to come (see 1 Chronicles 22:1).

The books of Samuel began with the visits of a country family to the "temple" at Shiloh (1 Samuel 1:9), where sacrifices were offered (1 Samuel 1:3) by corrupt priests (1 Samuel 2:12). The concluding chapter of this part of Israel's history presents King David (a much better man than Hophni and Phinehas, but also a deeply flawed man) offering sacrifices on the site of the future temple. First Samuel began with Israel's need for leadership that could save them from their enemies, themselves, and the wrath of God. Second Samuel concludes with the promised kingdom still unrealized.

David's inadequacy to save his people in any final sense from their enemies, themselves, and the wrath of God is clear. And yet in a number of wonderful ways in the final scenes of the books of Samuel David anticipates the Son of David who came 1,000 years later. David's great problem was that he was as guilty as his people. He knew that (vv. 10, 17). He was *willing* to die for his sheep (v. 17), but could not. Jesus did.

A short distance from the threshing floor of Araunah the perfect and complete sacrifice for the sins of the whole world was made when Jesus died on the cross. The New Testament proclaims the news that "There is therefore now no condemnation for those who are in Christ Jesus" because "God has done what the law, weakened by the flesh, could not do. By sending his own Son in the likeness of sinful flesh and for sin, he condemned sin in the flesh" (Romans 8:1, 3).

Those who are "in Christ Jesus" (that is, those who belong to him, who trust in him, who live under his Lordship) pray with confident and joyful longing, "Your kingdom come!"

Soli Deo gloria!

Notes

Introduction: Kingdom Matters

1. As I write this, I have before me a selection of no fewer than eight major studies of David published in recent years, each with its distinct point of view: Steven L. McKenzie, *King David: A Biography* (Oxford: Oxford University Press, 2000); John Goldingay, *Men Behaving Badly* (Carlisle, UK and Waynesboro, GA: Paternoster, 2000); Jonathan Kirsch, *King David: The Real Life of the Man Who Ruled Israel* (Crows Nest, NSW, Australia: Allen & Unwin, 2001); Baruch Halpern, *David's Secret Demons: Messiah, Murderer, Traitor, King*, The Bible in its World (Grand Rapids, MI and Cambridge, UK: Eerdmans, 2001); Gary Greenberg, *The Sins of King David: A New History* (Naperville, IL: Sourcebooks, Inc., 2002); Paul Borgman, *David, Saul, & God: Rediscovering an Ancient Story* (Oxford: Oxford University Press, 2008); John Van Seters, *The Biblical Saga of King David* (Winona Lake, IN: Eisenbrauns, 2009); Tod Linafelt, Claudia V. Camp, and Timothy Beal, eds., *The Fate of King David: The Past and Present of a Biblical Icon* (New York and London: T & T Clark, 2010).

2. This is a particular application of the general principle that has been helpfully explained in the writings of Graeme Goldsworthy: "It is important that we understand very clearly that this fact of the Old Testament's progression towards a fulfillment in the New is not merely an invitation to understand Jesus Christ as the end of the process. It is also a demand that the whole Bible be understood in the light of the gospel. It means that Jesus Christ is the key to the interpretation of the whole Bible, and the task before us is to discern *how* he interprets the Bible." Graeme Goldsworthy, *Gospel and Kingdom: A Christian Interpretation of the Old Testament* (Exeter, UK: Paternoster, 1981), p. 88.

3. My use of the word "story" here (and throughout this commentary) should not be misunderstood to imply a *mere* story. The Bible's message is that the story of David and of Jesus is true, both as history (these men actually lived and the "story" gives a true account of their lives) and in significance (David and Jesus *are* as important as the "story" indicates). I am using the word "story" simply to stress that we know both David and Jesus through the *narrative accounts* of their lives that the Bible presents.

4. The expression "the gospel of the kingdom" occurs only three times in the New Testament (Matthew 4:23; 9:35; 24:14; but see also Matthew 13:11, 19; 16:19; Mark 4:11; Luke 4:43; 8:1, 10; 9:11; 16:16; Acts 8:12). However, it is virtually synonymous with a range of expressions that suggest something of the wonder of "the kingdom." The gospel of the kingdom is also "the gospel of *the grace of God*" (Acts 20:24); "the gospel of *the glory of Christ*" (2 Corinthians 4:4); "the gospel of *your salvation*" (Ephesians 1:13); "the gospel of *peace*" (Ephesians 6:15); "the gospel of *the glory of the blessed God*" (1 Timothy 1:11).

5. The Greek word behind "gospel" (and the corresponding Hebrew term) means "news of a significant nature." See Graeme Goldsworthy, "Gospel," in T. Desmond Alexander and Brian S. Rosner, eds., *New Dictionary of Biblical Theology*

(Leicester, UK and Downers Grove, IL: Inter-Varsity Press and InterVarsity Press, 2000), pp. 521–524.

6. See John Bright's classic treatment *The Kingdom of God: The Biblical Concept and Its Meaning for the Church* (Nashville and New York: Abingdon Press, 1953), p. 17; also Goldsworthy, *Gospel and Kingdom*, pp. 90, 91.

7. The vocabulary of "king" and "kingdom" (though extensive as the selection of references in these paragraphs show) does not give a full indication of the prominence of this idea to the New Testament's message. In the course of our exposition of 2 Samuel we will have cause to note that the title "Christ" (or "Messiah"), applied to Jesus, is a *royal* title (see Mark 15:32; Luke 23:2; Acts 8:12; 28:31; 2 Timothy 4:1; 2 Peter 1:11; Revelation 11:15; 12:10). Furthermore to call Jesus Lord is virtually exactly the same as acknowledging him as king (see Matthew 7:21; Acts 28:31; 2 Timothy 4:18; 2 Peter 1:11). The theme of the kingdom is therefore present wherever the Lordship or Messiahship of Jesus is in view.

8. Thomas Jefferson's famous words in the United States Declaration of Independence, approved by the Congress on July 4, 1776 (two years into the American War of Independence), were a deliberate rejection of the dominant alternative political theory, the divine right of kings.

9. "It is at once apparent that the idea [of the kingdom of God] is broader than the term, and we must look for the idea where the term is not present." John Bright, *The Kingdom of God*, p. 18.

10. Note how God's kingship (reign) and creation are related themes in Psalm 93:1; 96:10; 97:1–5; 104:1, 2; 146:6, 10.

11. "I will . . . be your God, and you shall be my people" (Leviticus 26:12; cf. Genesis 17:8; Exodus 6:7).

12. The understanding of the book of 1 Samuel reflected in this paragraph is expounded in the previous volume in this series, John Woodhouse, *1 Samuel: Looking for a Leader*, Preaching the Word (Wheaton, IL: Crossway Books, 2008).

13. See 1 Samuel 26:23 and Woodhouse, *1 Samuel*, pp. 494, 495 and p. 621, note 16.

14. See the whole of Jeremiah 33:14–26; also Isaiah 9:6, 7; 11:1–5; 16:5; 55:3–5; Jeremiah 23:5, 6; 30:9; Ezekiel 34:23, 24; 37:24–28; Hosea 3:5; Amos 9:11, 12; Micah 5:2, 4; Zechariah 12:7—13:1.

Chapter One: A Dead King, a Victorious King, and a Time of Waiting

1. This is to ignore (as we should) a three-year illegitimate reign by Gideon's son Abimelech after his massacre of his seventy brothers (Judges 9:1–6, 22). See the thoroughly negative estimate of this kingship in the parable told by Abimelech's only surviving brother, Jotham, in Judges 9:7–21.

2. John Bright, *A History of Israel*, Third Edition (London: SCM, 1980), p. 469. The dates cannot be confidently determined with precision. Kenneth Kitchen proposes 1042–1010 BC in K. A. Kitchen, *On the Reliability of the Old Testament* (Grand Rapids, MI and Cambridge, UK: Eerdmans, 2003), p. 83.

3. Bright places David's reign approximately 1000–961 BC. Bright, *History*, p. 469. Kitchen's proposal is 1010–970 BC. Kitchen, *Reliability*, p. 83.

4. Compare the corresponding opening words (with exactly the same Hebrew construction) of the book of Joshua, "After the death of Moses . . ." (Joshua 1:1a)

and of the book of Judges, "After the death of Joshua . . ." (Judges 1:1a). Cf. Ronald F. Youngblood, *1 & 2 Samuel*, in Tremper Longman III and David E. Garland, eds., *The Expositor's Bible Commentary*, Revised Edition, vol. 3 (Grand Rapids, MI: Zondervan, 2009), p. 293. In each of these three cases the death of a leader marked the end of one era of Israel's history and raised serious questions about Israel's future in the light of this event. The book that follows these opening words, in each case, proceeds to provide answers to these questions. Also note "After the death of Ahab" in 2 Kings 1:1, but there the Hebrew wording is slightly different and does not give the very opening words of the book. The only other occurrence in the Old Testament of precisely the same Hebrew phrase as in 1 Samuel 1:1a (with a different personal name) is "After the death of Abraham" in Genesis 25:11. Contra P. Kyle McCarter Jr., *II Samuel: A New Translation with Introduction, Notes & Commentary*, The Anchor Bible, vol. 9 (Garden City, NY: Doubleday, 1984), p. 57 who suggests the expression is more common than this.

5. For the evidence see P. Kyle McCarter Jr., *I Samuel: A New Translation with Introduction, Notes & Commentary*, The Anchor Bible, vol. 8 (Garden City, NY: Doubleday, 1980), pp. 3, 4; Tony. W. Cartledge, *1 & 2 Samuel*, Smyth & Helwys Bible Commentary (Macon, GA: Smyth & Helwys, 2001), p. 349.

6. It may appear strange to refer to the second of the two books (as we now find them in the Bible) by the name of Samuel since Samuel's name does not appear anywhere in 2 Samuel. He died long *before* the death of Saul (1 Samuel 25:1). However the comment of Peter Ackroyd is apposite: "It was . . . with a quite proper instinct that the two books came to bear the name of Samuel, for thus it is made clear that to the author the story the books tell reveals the working out of a divine purpose, and Samuel fittingly represents the declaring of that purpose." Peter R. Ackroyd, *The Second Book of Samuel*, Cambridge Bible Commentary (Cambridge: Cambridge University Press, 1977), p. 1.

7. The division at the end of 1 Samuel 31, whenever it was made (usually supposed to be introduced by the translators responsible for the Septuagint; so A. A. Anderson, *2 Samuel*, Word Biblical Commentary 11 [Dallas: Word Books, 1989], p. xxv), makes obvious sense and recognizes the major break in the story that runs from 1 Samuel 1 to 2 Samuel 24 (and beyond, eventually to the end of 2 Kings).

8. For a long time scholars have debated the appropriate literary divisions of the narrative found in the books of Samuel (and extending into the books of Kings). The debate has been dominated by historical-critical questions (that is, questions about the earlier forms that the material may have had before being put together into the text we now have). McCarter, for example, maintains that the story of David's rise to power, in its earliest form, extended from 1 Samuel 16:14 to 2 Samuel 5:10. McCarter, *II Samuel*, p. 61. Likewise Brueggemann: "Critical scholarship . . . is nearly unanimous in its judgment that the first four chapters of II Samuel are a continuation of the literary unit beginning in I Samuel 16." Walter Brueggemann, *First and Second Samuel*, Interpretation: A Bible Commentary for Teaching and Preaching (Louisville: John Knox Press, 1990), p. 210. Without disputing that the present narrative may have drawn on earlier sources, our task as readers or expositors of the Bible is to understand the books in their present form. The identification of sources that may have been employed is of limited value for this task.

9. See John Woodhouse, *1 Samuel: Looking for a Leader*, Preaching the Word (Wheaton, IL: Crossway, 2008), pp. 35, 155.

10. The Hebrew has an unusual expression here: the definite article attached to "Amalek." This occurs nowhere else in the Old Testament and is assumed by most commentators (with some manuscript and version support) to be an error for either "the Amalek*ites*" or "Amalek" (without the definite article). So, for example, S. R. Driver, *Notes on the Hebrew Text and the Topography of the Book of Samuel with an Introduction on Hebrew Palaeography and Facsimiles of Inscriptions and Maps*, 2nd edition (Oxford: Clarendon, 1913), p. 232; McCarter, *II Samuel*, p. 56. However it is also possible that "Amalek" intentionally recalls earlier significant references to "Amalek" (1 Samuel 14:48; 15:2, 3, 5, 6, 7, 8, 18, 20, 32; 28:18; 30:18 [in several of these texts the ESV has translated the Hebrew "Amalek" as "the Amalek*ites*"]). "Amalek*ite(s)*" is a less frequently used term in the Hebrew (in 1 Samuel only at 15:6, 15; 27:8; 30:1, 13). Certainly "Amalek" in 1:1 is more likely to recall the injunctions against this people in Exodus 17:14; Numbers 24:20; Deuteronomy 25:17, 19. The addition of the definite article in 1:1 may be intended to restrict the reference to the particular representatives of Amalek in David's recent experience in 1 Samuel 30.

11. A quite literal translation of 1 Samuel 13:14; see Woodhouse, *1 Samuel*, pp. 235, 286, 287.

12. Cf. 7:21.

13. Interpreters of the books of Samuel often puzzle over the difference between Saul and David, seeking a reason why Saul was rejected, but David forgiven. They rightly notice that David's decisive sins (2 Samuel 11) were, on any normal measure, greater than Saul's (1 Samuel 15). Furthermore, Saul (like David in this respect) did try to repent (see 1 Samuel 15:24, 25). Some seek a difference in the men themselves to account for their different treatment by God. Vannoy provides a good example of this approach: "The question arises, 'Why did God treat these two sinful men so differently?' The answer lies in the general pattern of covenant consistency or inconsistency reflected in their lives, as well as in the character of their attitudes after they had sinned." J. Robert Vannoy, *1–2 Samuel*, Cornerstone Biblical Commentary, 4a (Wheaton, IL: Tyndale House, 2009), p. 27. Likewise Paul Borgman, *David, Saul, & God: Rediscovering an Ancient Story* (Oxford: Oxford University Press, 2008) is a book-length attempt to demonstrate that the critical purpose of the narrative of 1 and 2 Samuel is to reveal the difference between David and Saul that accounts for God rejecting one but not the other. In my judgement this is like arguing that the difference in God's treatment of Israel and, say, Egypt lay in the fact that Israel displayed (admittedly imperfectly) a degree of conformity to God's Law not seen in Egypt. The argument is nonsense (see Deuteronomy 7:6–8). Israel may well have displayed behavior "better" than that found in Egypt, but this was a *consequence* of God's grace shown to Israel, not the *basis* of it. There certainly were differences between the character and behavior of David and Saul. The question is whether these were the *basis* of their different treatment by God or, as I understand the narratives to be saying, the *consequence* of the grace that was shown to David but not to Saul.

14. See the summary in Woodhouse, *1 Samuel*, p. 545.

15. The emphasis on the two events as contemporaneous is accomplished in 1:1, 2 by reference to the fact that the man arrived with the news of Saul's death "on

the third day" after David's victory. Since we already know that it had taken David three days to travel from the region of Saul's battle with the Philistines (1 Samuel 30:1), it follows that both Saul's death and David's striking of the Amalekites occurred about three days before the messenger arrived in Ziklag. Similarly Young-blood, *1 & 2 Samuel*, p. 296; David G. Firth, *1 & 2 Samuel*, Apollos Old Testament Commentary 8 (Nottingham, UK and Downers Grove, IL: Apollos and InterVarsity Press, 2009), p. 321; J. P. Fokkelman, *Narrative Art and Poetry in the Books of Samuel: a full interpretation based on stylistic and structural analyses, Volume 2: The Crossing Fates (I Sam. 13—31 & II Sam. 1)* (Netherlands: Van Gorcum, Assen, 1986), p. 631.

16. On the Amalekites and their place in the Bible story more broadly, see Woodhouse, *1 Samuel*, pp. 260, 261.

17. Cf. Robert P. Gordon, *1 & 2 Samuel: A Commentary* (Exeter, UK: Paternoster, 1986), p. 208.

18. The words are taken from the second line of James Montgomery's hymn, "Hail to the Lord's Anointed."

19. For the location of Ziklag and the significance of Achish's land grant to David, see Woodhouse, *1 Samuel*, pp. 502, 503.

20. "The Scriptures" according to which Christ was raised "on the third day" in 1 Corinthians 15:4 have long puzzled commentators. There is no direct prediction in the Old Testament that the Messiah would rise "on the third day." We ought not to overlook the fact that "on the third day" or an equivalent phrase is quite common in the Old Testament, and a number of these texts may play no role in any pattern that anticipates the resurrection of Jesus on the third day (see, for example, 1 Samuel 20:5, 12, 19; 30:1). Gordon Fee offers a helpful summary of possibilities, favoring the rather imprecise view that "the OT as a whole bears witness to the resurrection on the third day." Gordon D. Fee, *The First Epistle to the Corinthians*, The New International Commentary on the New Testament (Grand Rapids, MI: Eerdmans, 1987), pp. 726–728.

Chapter Two: Who Says Crime Doesn't Pay?

1. For the relative locations of Ziklag and Mount Gilboa, see Maps 5-6, 5-7 in John D. Currid and David P. Barrett, *Crossway ESV Bible Atlas* (Wheaton, IL: Crossway, 2010), p. 124.

2. A basic rule for understanding a narrative text is that the narrator's voice is authoritative. While this is especially so in Biblical narrative texts, where the narrator is the voice through whom the Holy Spirit speaks, it is a broader principle that the narrator is the authoritative voice of any narrative. The various characters in a narrative may or may not be reliable, but the narrator himself is to be trusted in any reliable narrative. An instructive illustration of this principle applied to Scripture is found is Jesus' words in Matthew 19:5, 6, where the words of *the narrator* in Genesis 2:24 are quoted as spoken by *God*.

3. The Hebrew idiom (often untranslated in English versions; see, for example, the NIV) emphasizes "the immediate presence of an object or a fact." Thomas O. Lambdin, *Introduction to Biblical Hebrew* (London: Darton, Longman and Todd, 1973), p. 150; see also pp. 168–170. In this context the fact concerned (the man who had arrived in Ziklag) was immediately present *to David*.

4. The description of the man with torn clothes and dirt on his head is identical in 1 Samuel 4:12 and 2 Samuel 1:2, except that different words for "clothes" are used.

5. Reminiscent, that is, for the reader, not for any character in the narrative (none of whom were around for the Shiloh incident). The story needs to be heard at several levels. While we are invited to witness what happened *from David's point of view*, we are also expected to have our own point of view *as readers who have been informed by the preceding narrative*.

6. Davis sees here "all the signs of genuine grief," but sees the signs as deceptive. Dale Ralph Davis, *Expositions of the Book of 2 Samuel: Out of Every Adversity* (Geanies House, Fearn, UK: Christian Focus, 1999), p. 13. Polzin calls his appearance "his behavioural lie." Robert Polzin, *David and the Deuteronomist: A Literary Study of the Deuteronomic History. Part Three, 2 Samuel*, Indiana Studies in Biblical Literature (Bloomington and Indianapolis: Indiana University Press, 1993), p. 7.

7. Goldman anticipates the ambiguity that will emerge as the story unfolds: is he "recognizing David as Saul's successor; or grovelling in the hope of reward for his tidings"? S. Goldman, *Samuel: Hebrew Text & English Translation with an Introduction and Commentary*, Soncino Books of the Bible (London, Jerusalem, and New York: The Soncino Press, 1949), p. 186. "Perhaps the gesture of obeisance is already meant to be an act of homage to the future king. . . ." Hans Wilhelm Hertzberg, *I & II Samuel: A Commentary*, Old Testament Library (London: SCM Press, 1964), p. 236.

8. John Calvin, *Sermons on 2 Samuel Chapters 1—13*, trans. Douglas Kelly (Edinburgh: Banner of Truth, 1992), p. 12.

9. The only other occurrences of this verb in 1 Samuel are 1 Samuel 20:29 (Jonathan), 22:20 (Ahitub) (each is an involvement in David's experience of "escaping" from Saul), and 30:17 (Amalekites who "escaped" from David).

10. Cf. Polzin, *2 Samuel*, p. 4, who nonetheless, in my opinion, takes the identification of the man with David too far: "The narrator confronts David with his alter ego, and the reader with David's double." Polzin, *2 Samuel*, p. 5.

11. P. Kyle McCarter Jr., *II Samuel: A New Translation with Introduction, Notes & Commentary*, The Anchor Bible, vol. 9 (Garden City, NY: Doubleday, 1984), p. 56.

12. "The author of Samuel established a deliberate connection between the two stories in order to set up an analogy between the fates of Saul's house and of Eli's . . . just as Eli and his sons die on the same day . . . so do Saul and his." Ronald F. Youngblood, *1 & 2 Samuel*, in Tremper Longman III and David E. Garland, eds., *The Expositor's Bible Commentary*, Revised Edition, vol. 3 (Grand Rapids, MI: Zondervan, 2009), p. 296, quoting Moshe Garsiel. Likewise David G. Firth, *1 & 2 Samuel*, Apollos Old Testament Commentary 8 (Nottingham, UK and Downers Grove, IL: Apollos and InterVarsity Press, 2009), p. 321.

13. Some prefer to translate the word for "people" in this and similar contexts as "army." A. A. Anderson, *2 Samuel*, Word Biblical Commentary 11 (Dallas: Word, 1989), p. 7. While the context does indicate that the people referred to are the fighting men on the field of battle, it is probably better to retain the reference to them as "the people" rather than "the army" in order to maintain the connection with such expressions as "the people [same word] of the LORD" in 1:12.

14. Goldman, *Samuel*, p. 186.

15. The description of the man as a "young man" may remind us of the key role played by a number of young men so far in the story of 1 and 2 Samuel. The Hebrew word is variously rendered in the ESV as "child," "boy," "servant," "young man." Those who have been so designated previously are: Samuel (1 Samuel 1:22, 24, 25, 27; 2:18, 21, 26; 3:1, 8); the servant of Eli's corrupt sons (1 Samuel 2:13, 15); Eli's sons themselves (1 Samuel 2:17); the baby Ichabod (1 Samuel 4:21); Saul's companion on the donkey search (1 Samuel 9:3, 5, 7, 8, 10, 22, 27; 10:14); Jonathan's armor-bearer (1 Samuel 14:1, 6) or servant (1 Samuel 20:21, 35, 36, 37, 38, 39, 40, 41); Jesse's sons (1 Samuel 16:11); Saul's servant(s) (1 Samuel 16:18; 26:22); David (1 Samuel 17:33, 42, 55, 58); David's men (1 Samuel 21:2, 4, 5; 25:5, 8, 9, 25, 27); Nabal's and Abigail's servants (1 Samuel 25:8, 14, 19); the Egyptian David found near Ziklag (1 Samuel 30:13); the Amalekites who escaped from David (1 Samuel 30:17). See John Woodhouse, *1 Samuel: Looking for a Leader*, Preaching the Word (Wheaton, IL: Crossway, 2008), pp. 558, note 28; 602, note 6.

16. Fokkelman may overstate the matter slightly when he calls this phrase "a hint by the narrator who wants us to reflect sceptically on the true nature of this message." J. P. Fokkelman, *Narrative Art and Poetry in the Books of Samuel: a full interpretation based on stylistic and structural analyses, Volume 2: The Crossing Fates (I Sam. 13–31 & II Sam. 1)* (The Netherlands: Van Gorcum, Assen, 1986), p. 636. Cf. Robert Alter, *The David Story: A Translation with Commentary of 1 and 2 Samuel* (New York and London: W. W. Norton & Company, 1999), p. 195.

17. Twice he uses the idiom "behold" (cf. verse 2), although the ESV only reproduces it once. He actually says, "And behold, there was Saul . . . and behold, the chariots." The effect is to focus on the immediacy of the scene, this time from the point of view of the speaker as an eyewitness to what he describes.

18. "It was entirely by chance that I happened to be . . ." Anderson, *2 Samuel*, p. 4.

19. Alter, *David*, p. 196. Fokkelman comments, "We understand that the narrator gives us a knowing wink, for no one just happens to be on a battlefield coincidentally." J. P. Fokkelman, "A Lie, Born of Truth, Too Weak to Contain It: A Structural reading of 2 Sam. I 1–16," in *Prophets, Worship and Theodicy: Studies in Prophetism, Biblical Theology and Structural and Rhetorical Analysis and on the Place of Music in Worship: Papers Read at the Joint British-Dutch Old Testament Conference at Woudschoten 1982*, Oudtestamentische Studiën 23 (Leiden: E.J. Brill, 1984), p. 48.

20. See Woodhouse, *1 Samuel*, p. 547.

21. Earlier a spear had been one of Goliath's weapons of choice (1 Samuel 17:7, 45), but David knew that "the LORD saves not with sword and spear" (1 Samuel 17:47).

22. "Horsemen" represents an unparalleled expression in Hebrew that could be rendered rather literally "masters of the horsemen [or horses]." McCarter has "cavalry officers." McCarter, *II Samuel*, p. 57.

23. See McCarter, *II Samuel*, p. 59; cf. Firth, *1 & 2 Samuel*, p. 322.

24. There have been attempts to harmonize the narrator's account in 1 Samuel 31 with the messenger's report in 2 Samuel 1:6–10, but these are unconvincing. See Robert P. Gordon, *1 & 2 Samuel: A Commentary* (Exeter, UK: Paternoster, 1986), p. 208.

25. Although it should be noted that Saul was not a great one at remembering names. See 1 Samuel 17:55–58 in context.

26. Strangely Ackroyd appears to miss the fact that the identification of the young man as an Amalekite comes only in verse 8b: "the narrator underlines the point already made." Peter R. Ackroyd, *The Second Book of Samuel*, Cambridge Bible Commentary (Cambridge: Cambridge University Press, 1977), p. 21.

27. "As soon as the ancient audience learned the messenger's identity (v. 8), it would have begun to suspect him of treachery, for treachery was what it had come to expect of Amalekites . . . and its cynicism had just been reinforced by the story of the rape of Ziklag in I Sam 30:1–3." McCarter, *II Samuel*, p. 64.

28. For the background see Woodhouse, *1 Samuel*, pp. 260, 261.

29. One analysis of the whole section of 1:1–16 points out that the word "I" in the phrase "I am an Amalekite" in verse 8 "proves to be the 119th of the total of 237 words, and hence exactly the middle word!" Fokkelman, *Fates*, p. 637; also Fokkelman, "Lie," p. 41. While such a detail may be exaggerated in significance, Fokkelman is surely correct that "the issue of v. 8, the messenger's identity, is of a special nature." Fokkelman, "Lie," pp. 40, 41.

30. Ackroyd, *Second Samuel*, p. 20.

31. Interestingly "the Rabbinical commentators make him to have been Doeg, or his son, or the son of Agag." Henry Preserved Smith, *A Critical and Exegetical Commentary on the Books of Samuel*, The International Critical Commentary (Edinburgh: T. & T. Clark, 1899), p. 255. Also Gordon, *1& 2 Samuel*, p. 210.

32. "Kill" represents a Hebrew word that "refers to dispatching or 'finishing off' someone already wounded and near death. Cf. Judg 9:54; I Sam 14:13; 17:51." McCarter, *II Samuel*, p. 59. Cf. Youngblood, *1 & 2 Samuel*, p. 297.

33. The Hebrew word occurs nowhere else and is uncertain in meaning. Suggestions include "dizziness" (McCarter, *II Samuel*, pp. 59, 60); "terrible pain" (J. Robert Vannoy, *1–2 Samuel*, Cornerstone Biblical Commentary, 4a [Wheaton, IL: Tyndale House, 2009], p. 266); "throes of death" (NEB; Firth, *1 & 2 Samuel*, p. 319); "the hand of death" (Anderson, *2 Samuel*, p. 4).

34. The last phrase represents Hebrew that is difficult. The RV has "because my life is yet whole in me." Fokkelman puts it, "although all my life is still in me." Fokkelman, *Fates*, p. 637. Alter suggests that it is "most simply construed as a broken-off sentence that the failing Saul does not have the strength to complete . . . 'for while life is still within me . . .'" (Alter, *David*, p. 196).

35. Scholars, generally under the influence of the methods and assumptions of historical criticism, have made an inordinate effort arguing about the truthfulness or otherwise of the Amalekite's account of Saul's death. For example: "It is inappropriate to assume the Amalekite is a liar, since the text does not note this." Karl Budde, cited by Antony F. Campbell, S.J., *2 Samuel*, The Forms of the Old Testament Literature 8 (Grand Rapids, MI: Eerdmans, 2005), p. 18. "[N]owhere does the text stigmatize him as such [a liar]." "We, the audience, are aware of ch. 31 and we are free to regard the Amalekite as an opportunistic liar or to regard his story as a different tradition of Saul's end." Campbell, *2 Samuel*, pp. 18, 19. For an example of source criticism used to explain the contradictions between 1 Samuel 31 and the Amalekite's story, see Smith, *Samuel*, pp. 254, 255. Mauchline thinks the Amalekite story "rings true." John Mauchline, *1 and 2 Samuel*, New Century Bible (London:

Oliphants, 1971), p. 197. Brueggemann insists that "there is no way to adjudicate the question of the historicity of either narrative." Walter Brueggemann, *First and Second Samuel*, Interpretation: A Bible Commentary for Teaching and Preaching (Louisville: John Knox Press, 1990), p. 213. These arguments overlook the simple principle that the narrator is the authoritative voice in a narrative. Many recent commentators recognize this. See Alter, *David*, p. 197; Davis, *2 Samuel*, p. 14; McCarter, *II Samuel*, p. 63; Polzin, *2 Samuel*, p. 3; Gordon, *1 & 2 Samuel*, p. 208; Youngblood, *1 & 2 Samuel*, p. 299; Bill T. Arnold, "The Amalekite's Report of Saul's Death: Political Intrigue of Incompatible Sources?" *JETS* 32/3(1989), p. 209. For similar good sense in an older commentator see C. F. Keil and F. Delitzsch, *Biblical Commentary on the Books of Samuel* (Grand Rapids, MI: Eerdmans, 1950), p. 286. Fokkelman sums up the matter well: "A good lie cannot be recognized as such, and the narrator is too professional to take the punch out of his own story by giving away that the Amalekite is an adept liar." Fokkelman, "Lie," p. 40.

36. ". . . the very reason for the strength of his lie is that it contains so much truth!" Fokkelman, "Lie," p. 46.

37. This object was placed on the king at his installation (2 Kings 11:12). "Its precise nature is not known. Though often translated, somewhat misleadingly, as 'crown' (RSV), it is more likely to have been an emblem worn on the forehead. . . ." McCarter, *II Samuel*, p. 60.

38. Anderson, *2 Samuel*, p. 10.

39. "My lord" is by no means restricted to contexts referring to a king (1 Samuel 1:15, 26) but is fitting in such a setting. This is how Abigail had addressed David, with her remarkable understanding of his future role (fourteen times in 1 Samuel 25:24–31). It was how David addressed Saul (1 Samuel 24:6, 8, 10; 26:17, 18, 19; cf. 22:12) and Achish (1 Samuel 29:8). Soon it will be used by those who want to acknowledge David as the king (3:21; 4:8; 9:11).

40. "This leads to the conclusion that his account is a genuine eyewitness testimony, only embedded with lies at two points where this was necessary for the attainment of his clandestine goal." Fokkelman, "Lie," p. 47. "The man replaces Saul's arms-bearer by himself and replaces the companion-at-arms' refusal by his own consent." Fokkelman, *Fates*, p. 640.

41. So Mauchline, *1 and 2 Samuel*, p. 197; against Anderson, *2 Samuel*, p. 10, who thinks that the Amalekite did not realize that David was Israel's future king. If that were the case, why did he come to Ziklag?

Chapter Three: Crime *Doesn't* Pay

1. This is an important feature of much Biblical narrative, which is less committed to chronological order than we might expect. Flashbacks and what we might call flash-forwards are quite common on a small and larger scale. For examples and discussion of this narrative technique as it is found in 1 Samuel, see John Woodhouse, *1 Samuel: Looking for a Leader*, Preaching the Word (Wheaton, IL: Crossway, 2008), pp. 40, 64, 100, 219, 258, 296, 314, 334, 343, 545, 585 note 1, 605 note 15, 608 note 1.

2. For this connection see C. F. Keil and F. Delitzsch, *Biblical Commentary on the Books of Samuel* (Grand Rapids, MI: Eerdmans, 1950), pp. 286, 287.

3. See the discussion of this relationship in Woodhouse, *1 Samuel*, pp. 347–350.

4. So Keil and Delitzsch, *Samuel*, p. 286; against the view that the first expression refers to the army and the second to the nation (S. Goldman, *Samuel: Hebrew Text & English Translation with an Introduction and Commentary*, Soncino Books of the Bible [London, Jerusalem, and New York: The Soncino Press, 1949], p. 188).

5. Note Calvin's comment: "It is quite certain that the well-being of the Church was more precious to David than his own life." John Calvin, *Sermons on 2 Samuel Chapters 1–13*, trans. Douglas Kelly (Edinburgh: Banner of Truth, 1992), p. 1.

6. "Immediately after the Amalekite had finished speaking, not at the conclusion of the day's fast, verse 12 being parenthetical." Goldman, *Samuel*, p. 188. Similarly J. P. Fokkelman, *Narrative Art and Poetry in the Books of Samuel: a full interpretation based on stylistic and structural analyses, Volume 2: The Crossing Fates (I Sam. 13–31 & II Sam. 1)* (The Netherlands: Van Gorcum, Assen, 1986), p. 643. "The sequence of the text need not be taken to imply that the judgment of the Amalekite was delayed a day." Antony F. Campbell, S.J., *2 Samuel*, The Forms of the Old Testament Literature 8 (Grand Rapids, MI: Eerdmans, 2005), p. 20.

7. J. P. Fokkelman, "A Lie, Born of Truth, Too Weak to Contain It: A Structural reading of 2 Sam. I 1–16," in *Prophets, Worship and Theodicy: Studies in Prophetism, Biblical Theology and Structural and Rhetorical Analysis and on the Place of Music in Worship: Papers Read at the Joint British-Dutch Old Testament Conference at Woudschoten 1982*, Oudtestamentische Studiën 23 (Leiden: E.J. Brill, 1984), p. 49.

8. See Roland de Vaux, *Ancient Israel: Its Life and Institutions*, trans. John McHugh (London: Darton, Longman & Todd, 1973), pp. 74–76. The following comments are indebted to this summary of the place of the resident alien in Israel. See also Diether Kellermann, "*gur*," in G. Johannes Botterweck and Helmer Ringgren, eds., *Theological Dictionary of the Old Testament*, vol. 2 (Grand Rapids, MI: Eerdmans, 1975), pp. 439–449.

9. Again compare Doeg the Edomite who was a prominent servant of Saul (1 Samuel 21:7).

10. Cf. Fokkelman, "Lie," p. 49.

11. The exact expression "the LORD's anointed" occurs eleven times in the Old Testament, all but one of which are in the books of Samuel. A. A. Anderson, *2 Samuel*, Word Biblical Commentary 11 (Dallas: Word, 1989), p. 9.

12. As Fokkelman does! Fokkelman, "Lie," p. 50.

13. "Both [v. 1a and v. 16d] refer to Saul's end, but how differently! . . . The whole of the story concerns nothing other than the difference between v. 1a and v. 16d." Fokkelman, "Lie," pp. 42, 43.

14. Cf. 1 Kings 2:32; Ezekiel 22:4. So Fokkelman, *Fates*, p. 645. Campbell prefers to refer the phrase to the blood of the alleged killer, thus absolving David of bloodguilt. Campbell, *2 Samuel*, p. 20. For a general discussion of the use of the word "blood" in the Bible, see Alan Stibbs, *His Blood Works: The Meaning of the Word 'Blood' in Scripture* (Fearn, Ross-shire, UK: Christian Heritage, 2011), particularly pp. 21–24.

15. Fokkelman, *Fates*, p. 645.

16. Cf. J. Robert Vannoy, *1—2 Samuel*, Cornerstone Biblical Commentary, 4a (Wheaton, IL: Tyndale House, 2009), p. 267.

Chapter Four: What the Victorious King Said About the Dead King

1. Hans Wilhelm Hertzberg, *I & II Samuel: A Commentary*, Old Testament Library (London: SCM Press, 1964), p. 238.

2. Cf. David L. Zapf, "How are the mighty fallen! A study of 2 Samuel 1:17–27," *Grace Theological Journal* 5/1(1984), p. 116. "A lament is an expression of *thoughtful* grief." Dale Ralph Davis, *Expositions of the Book of 2 Samuel: Out of Every Adversity* (Geanies House, Fearn, UK: Christian Focus, 1999), p. 21.

3. It is therefore significantly more than "a vehicle by which Israel can continue her mourning." Davis, *2 Samuel*, p. 18.

4. Note that both 1 Samuel 1 and 2 Samuel 1 involve much weeping. See 1 Samuel 1:7, 8, 10; 2 Samuel 1:12, 24.

5. On the relationship between the beginnings of the two books see Robert Polzin, *David and the Deuteronomist: A Literary Study of the Deuteronomic History. Part Three, 2 Samuel*, Indiana Studies in Biblical Literature (Bloomington and Indianapolis, IN: Indiana University Press, 1993), p. 1; J. P. Fokkelman, *Narrative Art and Poetry in the Books of Samuel: a full interpretation based on stylistic and structural analyses, Volume 2: The Crossing Fates (I Sam. 13—31 & II Sam. 1)* (The Netherlands: Van Gorcum, Assen, 1986), p. 667, 668, 680. "Structurally, Samuel is built around three major poetic blocks: Hannah's Song (1 Sam. 2:1–10), David's lament (2 Sam. 1:17–27) and David's two reflective pieces (2 Sam. 22:1—23:7). Kingship is central in each poem. Hannah's song anticipates kingship. In David's lament, Saul's failure to provide the kingship required is considered, while the reflective pieces consider how kingship can make a positive contribution. Hannah's Song and the reflective pieces are the book's boundaries, and the lament is its turning point as we move from Saul to David." David G. Firth, *1 & 2 Samuel*, Apollos Old Testament Commentary 8 (Nottingham, UK and Downers Grove, IL: Apollos and InterVarsity Press, 2009), p. 321. ". . . both songs [Hannah's and David's] mention 'bows' and the 'mighty' and often in close connection (1 Samuel 2:4; 2 Samuel 1:17, 22, 25, 27) and both talk about death and life in close proximity (1 Samuel 2:6; 2 Samuel 2:23)." Andrew Reid, *1 and 2 Samuel: Hope for the Helpless*, Reading the Bible Today (Sydney South, NSW. Australia: Aquila Press, 2008), p. 155.

6. C. F. Keil and F. Delitzsch, *Biblical Commentary on the Books of Samuel* (Grand Rapids, MI: Eerdmans, 1950), p. 288.

7. "David faced a unique problem here: his lament is for two fallen heroes, with each of whom he had a very different relationship. Now it is never easy to compose a eulogy for two at the same time, and it is still harder to compose a eulogy for two men when the relationships are so very different as David's with Saul and Jonathan. . . . That he succeeded in a way which gives complete esthetic satisfaction is the measure of his skill." William L. Holladay, "Form and Word-play in David's Lament over Saul and Jonathan," *Vetus Testamentum* 20 (1970), p. 188.

8. Although the ESV conveys the essential point of verse 18a, it does omit one difficult word that appears at the end of the clause in Hebrew. It is the Hebrew word for "bow," which occurs again in verse 22 ("the bow of Jonathan"). Various options have been followed to account for this word in verse 18. (a) Some simply regard it as a mistake and omit the word, with some support from ancient versions. This is what the ESV, following the RSV, has done. Also P. Kyle McCarter Jr., *II Samuel: A New Translation with Introduction, Notes & Commentary*, The Anchor Bible, vol. 9

(Garden City, NY: Doubleday, 1984), p. 68. (b) Others have taken "bow" as the object of "teach," as the KJV: "Also he bade them teach the children of Judah *the use of* the bow." Calvin commented on the words, taken in this sense: "It was especially to encourage the children of Judah to practice shooting with the bow and to engage in military exercises so as not to lose courage after such a terrible defeat." John Calvin, *Sermons on 2 Samuel Chapters 1–13*, trans. Douglas Kelly (Edinburgh: Banner of Truth, 1992), p. 19. (c) Others have taken "Bow" to be the title of the following poem. So NRSV: "He ordered that The Song of the Bow be taught to the people of Judah"; similarly RV; NIV; HSCB; also Keil and Delitzsch, *Samuel*, pp. 288, 289; Hertzberg, *I & II Samuel*, p. 238; Zapf, "How are the mighty fallen!" pp. 116, 117; Davis, *2 Samuel*, p. 19, note 2. (d) Still others have suggested that the word concerned may be a musical term, now of unknown meaning, comparable to terms found in the superscriptions to some Psalms. See the ESV note. (e) Fokkelman proposes revocalizing the Hebrew word to give the sense "instructions to the Judeans concerning painful realities." Fokkelman, *Fates*, p. 651, followed by Robert Alter, *The David Story: A Translation with Commentary of 1 and 2 Samuel* (New York and London: W. W. Norton & Company, 1999), p. 198; Firth, *1 & 2 Samuel*, pp. 317, 318. The Hebrew text is probably best understood along the lines of (c), the "Bow" being a suggestive symbol of both the situation and the content of the following lament (see the occurrences of the word in verse 22 and 1 Samuel 31:3; also 1 Samuel 2:4). The "bow" has featured especially in David's experience with Jonathan in 1 Samuel 18:4 and implicitly in 1 Samuel 20 (with several references to "arrows").

9. However, see our later discussion of this phrase.

10. Cf. Ronald F. Youngblood, *1 & 2 Samuel*, in Tremper Longman III and David E. Garland, eds., *The Expositor's Bible Commentary*, Revised Edition, vol. 3 (Grand Rapids, MI: Zondervan, 2009), p. 303.

11. The force of "behold" here is to draw attention to something assumed to be well-known to the reader. Fokkelman, *Fates*, p. 649. As in the other three occurrences of this idiom in the present chapter (see vv. 2, 6) a certain sense of the immediacy of the thing described is emphasized—here the readers' familiarity with the Book of Jashar.

12. It is referred to also in Joshua 10:13, where we learn that another poem in the book was Joshua's words about the sun standing still (Joshua 10:12b, 13).

13. Examples of the various ways in which the poem's structure has been analyzed include:

I. vv. 19–24; II. vv. 25, 26; III. v. 27. Keil and Delitzsch, *Samuel*, p. 289.

I. (a) v. 19a; (b) v. 19b; II. (a) v. 20; (b) vv. 21, 22; III. (a) v. 23; (b) vv. 24–25a; (c) vv. 25b–27. Antony F. Campbell, S. J., *2 Samuel*, The Forms of the Old Testament Literature 8 (Grand Rapids, MI: Eerdmans, 2005), p. 22.

Theme and refrain: v. 19; I. vv. 20, 21; II. vv. 22, 23; III. vv. 24–27. Fokkelman, *Fates*, p. 676.

Different analyses of the structure are not necessarily contradictory. It can be simply a matter of emphasis given to different features of what is a wonderfully rich and complex text.

14. The ESV smooths over slightly awkward Hebrew by repeating the words "He said." The Hebrew only has these words at the beginning of the verse.

15. These are two different Hebrew words with exactly the same form. Which word is intended can only be deduced from the context. Here the context does not resolve the question, as we will see. See William L. Holladay, *A Concise Hebrew and Aramaic Lexicon of the Old Testament: based upon the lexical work of Ludwig Koehler and Walter Baumgartner* (Leiden: E.J. Brill, 1971), p. 302; also Francis Brown, S. R. Driver, and Charles Briggs, *A Hebrew and English Lexicon of the Old Testament* (Oxford: Clarendon Press, 1907), p. 840. (Note that the word translated "ornaments" in 1:24 is a different word.)

16. It is a case of deliberate ambiguity according to Zapf: "How are the mighty fallen!" p. 107. "[W]e must keep both possibilities open, for the benefit of the semantic spaces that the poem opens." Fokkelman, *Fates*, p. 652.

17. See this term later in the poem in verses 22, 25. See also 1 Samuel 17:52 (ESV, "wounded"); 31:1, 8; (ESV, "slain"); 2 Samuel 23:8, 18 (ESV, "killed"). In all these contexts the word refers to the violent ending of a life.

18. The word will be used unambiguously with the meaning "gazelle" in 2:18. This sense in 1:19 is rejected by Keil and Delitzsch, *Samuel*, p. 289, who prefer "The ornament." The NIV has "A gazelle," unfortunately omitting the definite article ("the").

19. Cf. Walter Brueggemann, *First and Second Samuel*, Interpretation: A Bible Commentary for Teaching and Preaching (Louisville: John Knox Press, 1990), p. 215.

20. "Tell" is a repeated word in the preceding narrative (1:4, 5, 6, 13), referring precisely to the news David here wants kept quiet.

21. The ESV "to carry the good news" in 1 Samuel 31:9 represents the same verb as "publish" in 2 Samuel 1:20. This is the word from which, via the Greek translation, we get the word "evangelize." It is possible that the "good news" of Saul's death was proclaimed by sending Saul's severed head on a journey around the land. See John Woodhouse, *1 Samuel: Looking for a Leader*, Preaching the Word (Wheaton, IL: Crossway, 2008), p. 551.

22. Similarly Fokkelman, *Fates*, p. 659.

23. For the relative locations of the places mentioned in the lament (Gath, Ashkelon, and Gilboa) see Maps 5-6 and 5-7 in John D. Currid and David P. Barrett, *Crossway ESV Bible Atlas* (Wheaton, IL: Crossway, 2010), p. 124.

24. Alter, *David*, p. 199.

25. This seems to be the view of Firth, *1 & 2 Samuel*, p. 325.

26. "[H]e knew that the Philistines would mock not only the people of Israel, but most especially the religion that God had given them." Calvin, *Sermons*, p. 29. Similarly Davis, *2 Samuel*, p. 22.

27. The phrase "fields of offerings" has occasioned considerable debate. On the one hand the sense may simply be fields fertile enough to yield "offerings" of first fruit. So Keil and Delitzsch, *Samuel*, p. 290. On the other hand it has been proposed that the word rendered "offerings" may mean "lofty" and refer to the elevated fields of the Gilboa region: "even you lofty fields." So D. N. Freedman, "The Refrain in David's Lament over Saul and Jonathan," in *Ex Orbe Religionum: Studia Geo Widen-*

gren, Studies in the History of Religions/Supplement to Numen 21 (Leiden: E.J. Brill, 1972), p. 141; J. P. Fokkelman, *"sdy trwmt* in II Sam 1:21a—A Non-existent Crux," *Zeitschrift für die alttestamentliche Wissenschaft* 91(1979), p. 290; Zapf, "How are the mighty fallen!" p. 108; Alter, *David*, p. 199. Various proposals for either emending or translating this line are helpfully outlined in Youngblood, *1 & 2 Samuel*, pp. 308, 309.

28. "God had willed to shame his people far more than if Saul had been killed in private. . . . Rather, it was as though Saul had been lifted up on a mountain, so that it would be widely known—'Saul is dead.'" Calvin, *Sermons*, p. 28.

29. "Even nature is to join the mourning." Keil and Delitzsch, *Samuel*, p. 290.

30. Similarly Fokkelman, *Fates*, p. 662.

31. Ibid., p. 663; Alter, *David*, p. 199.

32. Calvin takes it this way: "the shield of Saul, as though he had not been anointed by God." Calvin, *Sermons*, p. 32. Similarly Zapf, "How are the mighty fallen!" p. 119; Fokkelman, *Fates*, p. 663; Alter, *David*, p. 199.

33. Most Hebrew manuscripts have a form of the word "anointed" in 1:21 that is identical to the term used again and again in the books of Samuel for *"the Lord's anointed,"* who until now has been Saul (see 1 Samuel 2:10, 35; 12:3, 5; 24:6, 10; 26:9, 11, 16, 23; 2 Samuel 1:14, 16; 19:21; 22:51; 23:1). About twenty Hebrew manuscripts have a slightly different Hebrew form for "anointed," but there is no discernible difference in meaning. See Youngblood, *1 & 2 Samuel*, p. 309.

34. Keil and Delitzsch, *Samuel*, p. 291 who cite Deuteronomy 32:42; Isaiah 34:5, 6; Jeremiah 46:10.

35. In Hebrew the parallel between verses 19a and 25b is clear. The only differences between the two lines are the omission of the vocative "O Israel" in the later verse and the replacement of "the gazelle" with "Jonathan" as the first word of the respective lines. The ESV, following the RSV, has slightly obscured the parallel by varying the translation of exactly the same Hebrew verb from "is slain" to "lies slain."

36. Similarly Fokkelman, *Fates*, p. 670. Reid helpfully suggests that the identification of Jonathan as "the gazelle" may "contain an allusion to the defining moment in Jonathan's career. . . . In 1 Samuel 14:13 he scrambles upon all fours with his armour-bearer toward the Philistines." Reid, *1 & 2 Samuel*, p. 153.

37. "[T]he death of Jonathan has become the first and the last subject of the entire poem." Fokkelman, *Fates*, p. 671.

38. On the meaning of this "love" and the political dimensions implied, see Woodhouse, *1 Samuel*, p. 349 and the literature cited on p. 605, note 11.

39. On the significance of this verse, see ibid., p. 350.

40. "[T]here is no doubt about David's love for Jonathan, but he does not speak about that now. He only shows what radiance, warmth and love he received. The current flows only one direction and David puts it in this way in order to honour Jonathan and give his own gratitude dignified and beautiful form." Fokkelman, *Fates*, p. 672. I will suggest that the emphasis on Jonathan's love for David is more than this. It provides an example for Israel to follow.

41. A Hebrew verb translated "pleasant" in verse 26 is cognate with the adjective translated "lovely" in verse 23; likewise "love" in verse 26 (twice) echoes "beloved" in verse 23.

42. A recent example is Jonathan Kirsch, *King David: The Real Life of the Man Who Ruled Israel* (Crows Nest, NSW, Australia: Allen & Unwin, 2001), pp. 129–132.

43. See Woodhouse, *1 Samuel*, pp. 347, 348 and p. 604, notes 4, 6, 7.

44. As Alter emphasizes. Alter, *David*, p. 201.

45. So Keil and Delitzsch, *Samuel*, p. 292; also Zapf, "How are the mighty fallen!" p. 122.

46. Calvin's words are apt: "Let us learn to run to God, who controlled his servant David and bestowed on him the grace of being able to stamp on those violent passions which could have moved him to hatred and bitterness towards Saul." Calvin, *Sermons*, p. 18.

47. "[David] parades himself as the (new) leader who has the position and the power to arrange and interpret the meanings of the disaster, as a man of spiritual authority who can shape his vision on the high level of poetry and who, as the creator of *the* text of national mourning really has instruction to offer to his followers." Fokkelman, *Fates*, pp. 673, 674.

48. Commentators often see David's lament in terms of justifying David. "Despite appearances [David] stands fully on the side of Israel." Ibid., p. 648. More importantly the lament is a call to Israel to stand fully on the side of David. Even further from the mark is the view that David's lament reflects a troubled conscience: "for the deaths that he here bewails David may have felt at least in part responsible. . . . One may wonder . . . whether David is not 'overcompensating' in his lament for a guilty conscience." Gevirtz, cited by Zapf, "How are the mighty fallen!" pp. 99, 100. Calvin's words are again more helpful: "In order to help the people understand the situation better, he sent them a hymn of lamentation—for if he had not done something, they could have been seriously alienated from him. For who would ever have judged these to have been his feelings?" Calvin, *Sermons*, p. 20.

Chapter Five: Who Will Have This King?

1. For further discussion of this important but often misunderstood expression, see John Woodhouse, *1 Samuel: Looking for a Leader*, Preaching the Word (Wheaton, IL: Crossway, 2008), pp. 235, 236, 286, 287.

2. John Calvin, *Sermons on 2 Samuel Chapters 1—13*, trans. Douglas Kelly (Edinburgh: Banner of Truth, 1992), p. 61.

3. After the mention of the Philistines in David's lament (1:20), the only references to them before 5:17 are David's recollection of his dealings with them long ago (3:14) and Abner's belated acknowledgment of the Lord's promise that David would deliver Israel from the Philistines (3:18). Remarkably the Philistines themselves do not appear in the narrative as active participants from the time of Saul's death in 1 Samuel 31 to the establishment of David as king in Jerusalem at least seven and a half years later in 2 Samuel 5.

4. Cf. Walter Brueggemann, *First and Second Samuel*, Interpretation: A Bible Commentary for Teaching and Preaching (Louisville: John Knox Press, 1990), p. 219.

5. See 1 Samuel 8:10; 9:2 and Woodhouse, *1 Samuel*, p. 155.

6. Cornelius Van Dam argues, against the prevailing view, that these revelations involved prophecy. Cornelius Van Dam, *The Urim and Thummim: A Means of*

Revelation in Ancient Israel (Winona Lake, IN: Eisenbrauns, 1997), pp. 215–232. For the prevailing view see P. Kyle McCarter Jr., *I Samuel: A New Translation with Introduction, Notes & Commentary*, The Anchor Bible, vol. 8 (Garden City, NY: Doubleday, 1980), pp. 249, 250.

7. So Calvin, *Sermons*, pp. 50, 51; C. F. Keil and F. Delitzsch, *Biblical Commentary on the Books of Samuel* (Grand Rapids, MI: Eerdmans, 1950), p. 292; P. Kyle McCarter Jr., *II Samuel: A New Translation with Introduction, Notes & Commentary*, The Anchor Bible, vol. 9 (Garden City, NY: Doubleday, 1984), p. 83.

8. "Went up" (v. 2) and "brought up" (v. 3) translate forms of the Hebrew verb "to go up."

9. S. R. Driver, *Notes on the Hebrew Text and the Topography of the Book of Samuel with an Introduction on Hebrew Palaeography and Facsimiles of Inscriptions and Maps*, 2nd edition (Oxford: Clarendon, 1913), p. 239.

10. "[T]he ultimate motivating force is shown to have been Yahweh's will, not David's ambition." McCarter, *II Samuel*, p. 83.

11. Fokkelman regards David's question as "difficult to regard as open" because "he already knows where he is going." J. P. Fokkelman, *Narrative Art and Poetry in the Books of Samuel: a full interpretation based on stylistic and structural analyses, Volume 3: Throne and City (II Sam. 2–8 & 21–24)* (The Netherlands: Van Gorcum, Assen, 1990), p. 27. On the contrary, David's question was open to the answer "No" or "Not yet" as well as to the answer he actually received.

12. "The text is silent on the Philistines' view of David's move to kingship in Hebron, but one can assume they countenanced it as a reasonable act on the part of their vassal opposing the house of Saul." Robert Alter, *The David Story: A Translation with Commentary of 1 and 2 Samuel* (New York and London: W. W. Norton & Company, 1999), p. 202.

13. See Map 5-8 in John D. Currid and David P. Barrett, *Crossway ESV Bible Atlas* (Wheaton, IL: Crossway, 2010), p. 126. For more details about Hebron see Paul Wayne Ferris Jr., "Hebron," in David Noel Freedman, ed., *The Anchor Bible Dictionary*, vol. 3 (New York: Doubleday, 1992), pp. 107, 108; S. M. Ortiz, "Hebron," in Bill T. Arnold and H. G. M. Williamson, *Dictionary of the Old Testament: Historical Books* (Downers Grove, IL and Leicester, UK: InterVarsity Press and Inter-Varsity Press, 2005), pp. 390–392.

14. This is recognized in Ronald Clements, *Abraham and David: Genesis 15 and Its Meaning for Israelite Tradition*, Studies in Biblical Theology, Second Series, 5 (London: SCM, 1967), p. 47 (although I am unpersuaded by much in the historical-critical approach of this study).

15. The text meticulously describes David's obedience to both words he had received from the Lord: "Go up" (v. 1a), "David went up" (v. 2, same verb), "To Hebron" (v. 1b), "there" (v. 2).

16. While the Hebrew of Genesis 12:4 uses a different verb from 2 Samuel 2:2, in both cases the reported obedience echoes directly the Lord's word in Genesis 12:1 and 2 Samuel 2:1 respectively.

17. Curiously Ahinoam was also the name of Saul's (only) wife (1 Samuel 14:50). If, remarkably, David had taken *that* Ahinoam as his wife (as suggested by J. Levenson, "1 Samuel 25 as Literature and History," *Catholic Biblical Quarterly* 40 [1978], p. 27, and regarded as "plausible" by Ronald F. Youngblood, *1 & 2 Samuel*, in

Tremper Longman III and David E. Garland, eds., *The Expositor's Bible Commentary*, Revised Edition, vol. 3 (Grand Rapids, MI: Zondervan, 2009), p. 252, but "unlikely" by Diana V. Edelman, "Ahinoam," in David Noel Freedman, ed., *The Anchor Bible Dictionary*, vol. 3 (New York: Doubleday, 1992), p. 118), we would expect some comment to that effect from the Biblical writer. On the contrary, the historian's identification of David's wife as "Ahinoam *of Jezreel*" probably distinguishes her from Saul's wife whose hometown is not known. David's wife is therefore almost certainly another Ahinoam (so, for example, McCarter, *I Samuel*, p. 400), but there is at least a subtle irony in David's taking a wife with the same name as Saul's wife.

18. The Jezreel that was Ahinoam's hometown was not the northern Jezreel near Gilboa, but a town near Maon and Carmel (see Joshua 15:55, 56), the setting for the story in 1 Samuel 25. This Carmel is not the famous northern coastal mountain range, but a town about seven miles southeast of Hebron, where Saul once erected a monument to himself (1 Samuel 15:12).

19. McCarter, *II Samuel*, p. 84.

20. "Widow" is a correct inference from the context. The word means "woman" or "wife." There is, therefore, no explicit emphasis on Abigail's widowhood, just a repeated reminder of her earlier relationship to Nabal.

21. Note that Saul once recognized that David, for his part, refused to be Saul's enemy (1 Samuel 24:19).

22. David's "friends," even at this early stage, may anticipate the role that would later become known as "the king's friend" (see 2 Samuel 16:16; 1 Kings 4:5; 1 Chronicles 27:33; cf. Proverbs 22:11). Roland de Vaux, *Ancient Israel: Its Life and Institutions*, trans. John McHugh (London: Darton, Longman & Todd, 1973), pp. 122, 123; Diether Kellermann, *"rea'*," in G. Johannes Botterweck and Helmer Ringgren, eds., *Theological Dictionary of the Old Testament*, vol. 13 (Grand Rapids, MI and Cambridge. UK: Eerdmans, 2004), pp. 529, 530. The idea emerges in an interesting context in John 19:12.

23. "[I]t is as though they were replying 'Amen', and ratifying what had been done. We should understand, therefore, that David is not elected king here by the desire of men, but that he received approbation because God authorised it, and thus men agree with it." Calvin, *Sermons*, p. 56. Contrary to McCarter who claims to know too much when he says that here "the basis for his election is popular initiative rather than prophetically mediated divine designation, as also in 5:3." McCarter, *II Samuel*, p. 84.

24. Dale Ralph Davis, *Expositions of the Book of 2 Samuel: Out of Every Adversity* (Geanies House, Fearn, UK: Christian Focus, 1999), pp. 28, 29.

25. Jabesh-*gilead* means "Jabesh *in* Gilead." *Gilead* is the geographical term applied to all or part of the land east of the Jordan River. The narrower use of the term applies to that area approximately north of the Dead Sea and south of Lake Galilee. The term is also used more generally for the lands east of the Jordan beyond these limits. K. A. Kitchen, "Gilead," in J. D. Douglas, ed., *The Illustrated Bible Dictionary*, Part 1 (Leicester, UK and Wheaton, IL: Inter-Varsity Press and Tyndale House, 1980), pp. 561, 562.

26. Indeed there are reasons to suppose that Saul may have had a family connection with Jabesh-gilead. On this and for a brief outline of the history of this community prior to its involvements with Saul see Woodhouse, *I Samuel*, pp. 193, 194.

27. The ESV follows the RSV and omits "this," thereby obscuring the fact that the good David was promising to do was the very good he had prayed that the Lord would do (see the exposition of verse 6b). Several English versions recognize the importance of "this" (so KJV, NIV, HCSB).

28. Francis I. Andersen, "Yahweh, the Kind and Sensitive God," in Peter T. O'Brien and David G. Peterson, eds., *God Who Is Rich in Mercy: Essays Presented to Dr. D. B. Knox* (Homebush West, NSW, Australia: Lancer Books, 1986), p. 81. In this important study Francis Andersen has shown that *khesed* is associated with such qualities as love, grace, and compassion rather than obligation and duty (which "loyalty" implies). A feel for the word's meaning can be gained by reviewing its four occurrences in 1 Samuel (15:6, "kindness," 20:8, "kindly," and 20:14, 15, "steadfast love"). Some take a different view along the lines that *khesed* means "a responsible keeping of faith with another with whom one is in a relationship." Sakenfeld, cited by McCarter, *II Samuel*, p. 84.

29. Calvin, *Sermons*, p. 60.

30. Keil and Delitzsch, *Samuel*, p. 294.

31. Calvin, *Sermons*, p. 60.

32. Unfortunately this is the impression given by the ESV with its omission of "this." The REB makes matters worse by emphasizing the misunderstanding: "I for my part will show you favor *too*."

33. "The speaker has placed his activity on the same level as God's and in so doing has taken his place right next to God." Fokkelman, *Throne*, p. 32. We will see a particular instance of King David doing "the kindness [*khesed*] of God" to a member of Saul's household in 2 Samuel 9 (see v. 3).

34. "Be valiant" in 2:7 echoes "the valiant men" of Jabesh-gilead who dared to recover the bodies of Saul and his sons from under the noses of the Philistines (1 Samuel 31:12).

35. In the Hebrew text the emphatic "me" (literally "even me") in verse 7 quite strikingly corresponds to the emphatic "I" (literally "even I") in verse 6b.

36. "The promotion of Ish-bosheth as king was not only a continuation of the hostility of Saul towards David, but also an open act of rebellion against Jehovah, who had rejected Saul and chosen David prince over Israel, and who had given such distinct proofs of this election in the eyes of the whole nation, that even Saul had been convinced of the appointment of David to be his successor upon the throne." Keil and Delitzsch, *Samuel*, p. 292.

37. There has been the suggestion that this son of Saul is the one named Ishvi in 1 Samuel 14:49. So Driver, *Notes*, p. 120. However, Ishvi may rather have been another son of Saul who died in childhood. Diana V. Edelman, "Ish-bosheth," in David Noel Freedman, ed., *The Anchor Bible Dictionary*, vol. 1 (New York: Doubleday, 1992), p. 509.

38. See Francis Brown, S. R. Driver, and Charles Briggs, *A Hebrew and English Lexicon of the Old Testament* (Oxford: Clarendon Press, 1907), p. 127.

39. For the possibility of the Hebrew *baal* referring to God, see Hosea 2:16.

40. Other examples of names in which "baal" appears to have been replaced by "bosheth" are Saul's grandson Merib-baal (1 Chronicles 8:34) who is Mephibosheth in 4:4 and Jerubbaal (that is, Gideon, Judges 6:32; 1 Samuel 12:11) who is Jerub-besheth in 11:21.

41. Similarly McCarter, *II Samuel*, p. 87; Alter, *David*, p. 203.

42. See Map 5-8 in Currid, *Atlas*, p. 126.

43. "[T]he transfer of the Israelite seat of government to Transjordan is understandable in the light of the political situation that must have prevailed in Palestine after the Philistine victory at Gilboa. The heartland of Saul's kingdom in the Benjaminite hills was now too vulnerable to serve as the seat of the rump government that Abner set up in Ishbaal's name, and the more remote forests of Gilead offered refuge and security to Ishbaal, just as they would to David later on (cf. 17:21–29)." McCarter, *II Samuel*, p. 87.

44. Cf. Fokkelman, *Throne*, p. 39.

45. The situation is in fact more complicated than I have indicated. There are texts prior to 2:8–10 where "Israel" refers to the northern tribes, distinguished from the southern tribe of "Judah" (see 1 Samuel 11:8; 17:52; 18:16). This may suggest that the division that came to clear expression with the appointment of Ish-bosheth went back much further historically. However, it is also possible that these texts reflect the perspective of the writer who was writing at a time after 2 Samuel 2 or even 1 Kings 12. It remains valid to see the heart of the division between "Israel" and "Judah" to be based on the rejection and the acceptance of David as king.

46. The term in the Hebrew text usually refers to Assyria (Genesis 2:14; Numbers 24:22, 24; Psalm 83:8). Since this is hardly possible in this context, either there is an error in the text needing to be amended (so Keil and Delitzsch, *Samuel*, p. 295, especially note 1; McCarter, *II Samuel*, pp. 82, 83) or 'ashuri is an otherwise unknown place name (so Youngblood, *1 & 2 Samuel*, p. 315; David G. Firth, *1 & 2 Samuel*, Apollos Old Testament Commentary 8 [Nottingham, UK and Downers Grove, IL: Apollos and InterVarsity Press, 2009], p. 333). The simplest emendation may be to change the vowels so that it reads "the Asherites." So Alter, *David*, p. 203; cf. Robert P. Gordon, *1 & 2 Samuel: A Commentary* (Exeter, UK: Paternoster, 1986), p. 214.

47. So J. Robert Vannoy, *1—2 Samuel*, Cornerstone Biblical Commentary, 4a (Wheaton, IL: Tyndale House, 2009), p. 276, but contrary to several commentators who take "Israel" in the narrow sense of the northern tribes excluding Judah—for example Keil and Delitzsch, *Samuel*, p. 295; Gordon, *1& 2 Samuel*, p. 214. One interpretation of the extent of Ish-bosheth's and David's kingdoms is represented in Map 5-8 in Currid, *Atlas*, p. 126. (Note that the text under this map erroneously says that David and Ish-bosheth fought each other for seven years. Ish-bosheth was only king for two years, 2:10.)

48. For this understanding of 1 Samuel 13:1 see Woodhouse, *1 Samuel*, pp. 228, 229 where it is argued that the "two years" of Saul's reign began in 1 Samuel 11:15 and ended in 1 Samuel 15:28. It really lasted only two short years.

49. So Keil and Delitzsch, *Samuel*, p. 296; likewise McCarter, *II Samuel*, p. 89.

50. Fokkelman thinks that verse 8 is probably a flashback and that Ish-bosheth and David were installed "more or less at the same time." This requires reading the figures in verse 10 non-literally. This is not persuasive. Fokkelman, *Throne*, p. 37.

51. Once the question of chronology is raised (as it is by verse 11), it is clear that we do not know how much time elapsed between David's anointing in Hebron (v. 4a) and the news about the men of Jabesh-gilead reaching him. It happened some time in David's first five years as king in Hebron.

Chapter Six: Human Politics and the Kingdom

1. Arthur Delbridge, ed., *The Macquarie Dictionary*, Revised Edition (Dee Why, NSW, Australia: Macquarie Library Pty Ltd, 1985), p. 1318. It should be noted that this is an *Australian* dictionary!

2. For any readers fortunate enough to be puzzled by this reference, *West Wing* was a popular American television political drama with a president of the United States who was, sadly, too good to be true.

3. The only mention of Joab previously in the narrative was at 1 Samuel 26:6 where Abishai is referred to as "Joab's brother."

4. It is a little surprising that the family connection between David and the three brothers is not stated anywhere in the books of Samuel. It may be that the relationship was so well known that it was assumed knowledge for the audience of 1 and 2 Samuel.

5. For the locations of Mahanaim, Hebron, and Gibeon, see Map 5-8 in John D. Currid and David P. Barrett, *Crossway ESV Bible Atlas* (Wheaton, IL: Crossway, 2010), p. 126.

6. This pool is likely to be part of the impressive water system uncovered by archaeologists in the 1950s and discussed in Patrick M. Arnold, "Gibeon," in David Noel Freedman, ed., *The Anchor Bible Dictionary*, vol. 2 (New York: Doubleday, 1992), pp. 1010–1013 and the literature cited there. Also Robert P. Gordon, *1 & 2 Samuel: A Commentary* (Exeter, UK: Paternoster, 1986), pp. 214, 215. See the fine full-color photograph of a water chamber in Gibeon in Currid, *Atlas*, p. 144.

7. The Hebrew word means "together," "with each other," "all together," "equally." It may suggest "all at once," indicating that the two groups arrived at the pool simultaneously. Francis Brown, S. R. Driver, and Charles Briggs, *A Hebrew and English Lexicon of the Old Testament* (Oxford: Clarendon Press, 1907), p. 403. The term is rendered "together" in the KJV but is omitted in most modern translations. It will appear again in verse 16 with terrible significance, as we will see.

8. For a detailed analysis of the symmetry here see J. P. Fokkelman, *Narrative Art and Poetry in the Books of Samuel: a full interpretation based on stylistic and structural analyses, Volume 3: Throne and City (II Sam. 2—8 & 21—24)* (The Netherlands: Van Gorcum, Assen, 1990), pp. 41, 42.

9. The sense of the nation as a family is suggested by "the *house* of Israel," meaning the whole people of the Lord (1:12), and "the house of Judah," the part of the family that had made David king (2:7).

10. "[O]ne might perhaps better understand the passage as referring to a sudden change from a game to something more serious, or to a battle trick that both sides try to implement simultaneously but that then goes wrong." R. Bartelmus, "*sakhaq/tsakhaq*," in G. Johannes Botterweck, Helmer Ringgren, and Heinz-Josef Fabry, eds., *Theological Dictionary of the Old Testament*, vol. 14 (Grand Rapids, MI: Eerdmans, 2004), p. 69. This understanding is rejected by P. Kyle McCarter Jr., *II Samuel: A New Translation with Introduction, Notes & Commentary*, The Anchor Bible, vol. 9 (Garden City, NY: Doubleday, 1984), p. 95, but something along the same lines is advocated by Hans Wilhelm Hertzberg, *I & II Samuel: A Commentary*, Old Testament Library (London: SCM Press, 1964), p. 251 ("harmless military exercises") and John Mauchline, *1 and 2 Samuel*, New Century Bible (London: Oliphants, 1971), p. 205 ("a mock battle or acted drama"). Fokkelman thinks that the bloody outcome indicates what Abner meant by "making sport" and that his choice

of words was "probably the understatement of an old war-horse, part of military jargon from time immemorial, full of euphemisms which denote the most terrible things, but avoid adding more pain to the soft heart hidden behind the soldier's rough exterior." Fokkelman, *Throne*, p. 44.

11. Fokkelman, *Throne*, p. 46. Other proposals for rendering "Helkath-haz-zurim" include "field of the sharp edges," C. F. Keil and F. Delitzsch, *Biblical Commentary on the Books of Samuel* (Grand Rapids, MI: Eerdmans, 1950), p. 297; "The Field of Flints," Robert Alter, *The David Story: A Translation with Commentary of 1 and 2 Samuel* (New York and London: W. W. Norton & Company, 1999), p. 205; "Field of the Sword-edges," Everett Fox, *Give Us a King!: Samuel, Saul, and David: A New Translation of Samuel I and II with an Introduction and Notes* (New York: Shocken Books, 1999), p. 158.

12. Or "Are you Asahel?" Alter, *David*, p. 206.

13. Literally it was a one-word answer: "I."

14. Note how verses 24a and 19a are exactly parallel. Fokkelman, *Throne*, p. 56.

15. For details see Susan E. McGarry, "Ammah," in David Noel Freedman, ed., *The Anchor Bible Dictionary*, vol. 1 (New York: Doubleday, 1992), p. 189.

16. "The way of [not necessarily "to," as in ESV] the wilderness of Gibeon" may have referred to a west-east route from Gibeon to the Jordan River.

17. Since Abner and his people would have reached the hill first (they were the ones being pursued), verse 25 could be translated with a pluperfect, "And the people of Benjamin *had* gathered . . ."

18. Similarly Fokkelman, *Throne*, p. 58.

19. This rendering of the verse follows the sense of the KJV and RSV and is supported by Keil and Delitzsch, *Samuel*, p. 298; Fokkelman, *Throne*, p. 369. Fokkelman spells out the sense: "if you had not proposed a tournament this morning, then as far as I am concerned there would have been no need for a fight." Fokkelman, *Throne*, p. 60. Other proposals (involving emendations of the Hebrew text) include: "if you had not spoken, surely the men would not have given up the pursuit of their brothers until the morning" (ESV; likewise HCSB; NRSV); "had you but spoken, from this morning the troops would have given up pursuit of their brothers," Alter, *David*, p. 207.

20. The Hebrew is simply "And." "So" in the ESV depends on the translation of the previous verse.

21. "The whole morning" (ESV) represents difficult Hebrew. The RV has "and went through all Bithron . . ." suggesting an otherwise unknown place name. It may be a reference to the Jabbok valley. So Gordon, *1 & 2 Samuel*, p. 216.

22. "The Arabah" is a term that refers to all or part of the rift valley that runs south from Lake Galilee via the Dead Sea to the Gulf of Aqaba. Between Lake Galilee and the Dead Sea it provides the course of the Jordan River. McCarter, *II Samuel*, p. 97. In this context "through the Arabah" appears to refer to crossing the Jordan Valley. S. R. Driver, *Notes on the Hebrew Text and the Topography of the Book of Samuel with an Introduction on Hebrew Palaeography and Facsimiles of Inscriptions and Maps*, 2nd edition (Oxford: Clarendon, 1913), pp. 244, 245.

Chapter Seven: Ambitious Opportunism and the Kingdom

1. On the chronology, see 2:10, 11.

2. The Hebrew word behind "war" here is the same as the word translated "battle" in 2:17. The long "war" was the continuation of that daylong "battle."

3. Note, however, that "the house of David," in the sense of a dynasty, appears as early as 1 Samuel 20:16.

4. J. P. Fokkelman, *Narrative Art and Poetry in the Books of Samuel: a full interpretation based on stylistic and structural analyses, Volume 3: Throne and City (II Sam. 2–8 & 21–24)* (The Netherlands: Van Gorcum, Assen, 1990), p. 63.

5. So C. F. Keil and F. Delitzsch, *Biblical Commentary on the Books of Samuel* (Grand Rapids, MI: Eerdmans, 1950), p. 299.

6. Note "house of Israel" referring to the whole nation in 1 Samuel 7:2, 3.

7. Cf. J. Robert Vannoy, *1—2 Samuel*, Cornerstone Biblical Commentary, 4a (Wheaton, IL: Tyndale House, 2009), p. 280.

8. Apart from 1 Chronicles 3:1, where Chileab is called "Daniel."

9. During the turbulent days in the years to come Absalom will seek refuge in the land of his mother's family (13:37, 38; 14:23, 32; 15:8).

10. The reference to the last mother in the list as "David's wife" is probably stylistic, rounding off the list. "David's wife" applies to each woman mentioned, but placing the phrase only at the end avoids much repetition.

11. "In theory the children could have all been born in the same week." Fokkelman, *Throne*, p. 64, note 71.

12. Indeed the precise meaning of the Hebrew word is not certain. One suggestion is: "Slave women who belonged to wealthy households and bore children but did not share all the legal privileges of wives." P. Kyle McCarter Jr., *II Samuel: A New Translation with Introduction, Notes & Commentary*, The Anchor Bible, vol. 9 (Garden City, NY: Doubleday, 1984), p. 148. Anderson considers it likely "that in most cases she was a legitimate wife of second rank, perhaps mainly drawn from the lower or slave classes." A. A. Anderson, *2 Samuel*, Word Biblical Commentary 11 (Dallas: Word, 1989), p. 56.

13. This text calls Keturah Abraham's "concubine." According to Genesis 25:1, Keturah was Abraham's second "wife," whom he took after the death of Sarah. This raises questions about the range of meanings of the Hebrew word usually translated "concubine." See Richard M. Davidson, *Flame of Yahweh: Sexuality in the Old Testament* (Peabody, MA: Hendrickson Publishers, 2007), p. 186, who nonetheless fails, in my opinion, to adequately recognize that in Hebrew "wife/wives" and "woman/women" are represented by the same word. Also see Gordon P. Hugenberger, *Marriage as a Covenant: Biblical Law and Ethics as Developed from Malachi* (Grand Rapids, MI: Baker, 1994), p. 107, note 96.

14. These texts may apply to a concubine, although the word itself is not used anywhere in the Law. On some of the issues involved in Exodus 21:7–11, see Davidson, *Flame*, pp. 191–193, who rightly points out (among other things) that case laws do not legitimate the circumstances they presuppose, but rather prescribe what must happen if such circumstances arise.

15. For some details see J. A. Thompson, "Concubine," in J. D. Douglas, ed., *The Illustrated Bible Dictionary*, Part 1 (Leicester, UK and Wheaton, IL: Inter-Varsity Press and Tyndale House, 1980), p. 308.

16. Ezekiel 23:20 uses the word usually translated "concubines" in a clear moral judgment, but in this context the word refers to male lovers (KJV, "paramours"; ESV, "lovers").

17. The evidence for this proposition is set out well in Roland de Vaux, *Ancient Israel: Its Life and Institutions*, trans. John McHugh (London: Darton, Longman & Todd, 1973), pp. 24–29.

18. "The Edenic divine norm of heterosexual monogamy summarized in Gen 2:24 is assumed throughout the rest of OT Scripture." Davidson, *Flame*, p. 177.

19. "The texts in question deal with the concubines of patriarchs, kings, a Levite, one of the 'major judges,' and a tribal ancestor." K. Engelken, *"pilegesh,"* in G. Johannes Botterweck, Helmer Ringgren, and Heinz-Josef Fabry, eds., *Theological Dictionary of the Old Testament*, vol. 9 (Grand Rapids, MI: Eerdmans, 1998), p. 550.

20. Davidson argues that the narratives nonetheless signal disapproval. "Although these biblical narratives provide no explicit verbal condemnation of this practice [plural marriages, including concubines], the narrator presents each account in such a way as to underscore a theology of disapproval. The record of polygamous relationships bristles with discord, rivalry, heartache, and even rebellion, revealing the motivations and/or disastrous consequences that invariably accompanied such departures from the Edenic ideal. Here as elsewhere in the Hebrew Bible, a narrative theology of divine disapproval often speaks even louder, and more eloquently, than explicit condemnation." Davidson, *Flame*, p. 180.

21. It is worth noting that Deuteronomy 17:17 (forbidding the king in Israel from acquiring "many wives for himself") could be applied to concubines, since the Hebrew for "wives" also means "women."

22. The narrator continues to marginalize Ish-bosheth as much as possible. His name does not appear in the Hebrew here, which simply has, "And he said to Abner . . ." The context (*"my father's* concubine") clearly tells us that the speaker was Ish-bosheth.

23. See the insightful discussion of the significance of Abner's act in Walter Brueggemann, *First and Second Samuel*, Interpretation: A Bible Commentary for Teaching and Preaching (Louisville: John Knox Press, 1990), pp. 225, 226.

24. Compare David's self-deprecating expression "a dead dog" in 1 Samuel 24:14 and Goliath's "Am I a dog?" in 1 Samuel 17:43. For some attempts to interpret the sense of "a dog's head" more precisely see McCarter, *II Samuel*, p. 113.

25. "[H]ere, as always, *khesed* is the action of the powerful for the helpless, not the duty of an inferior to a superior." Francis I. Andersen, "Yahweh, the Kind and Sensitive God," in Peter T. O'Brien and David G. Peterson, eds., *God Who Is Rich in Mercy: Essays Presented to Dr. D. B. Knox* (Homebush West, NSW, Australia: Lancer Books, 1986), p. 62.

26. Firth thinks that Abner's claim of loyalty to Saul performs the function of a denial. David G. Firth, *1 & 2 Samuel*, Apollos Old Testament Commentary 8 (Nottingham, UK and Downers Grove, IL: Apollos and InterVarsity Press, 2009), p. 347. This puts the wrong weight on the word *khesed*, which does not mean "loyalty."

27. As implausibly suggested by Firth, *1 & 2 Samuel*, p. 347.

28. "From Dan [to the north of Lake Galilee] to Beersheba [to the south]" was a way of describing the full extent of Israel's land (see Judges 20:1; 1 Samuel 3:20; 2 Samuel 17:11; 24:2, 15; 1 Kings 4:25; 1 Chronicles 21:2; 2 Chronicles 30:5).

29. Again the narrator does not name Ish-bosheth. Literally, this simply reads, "And he could not answer . . ."

30. The Hebrew word translated "on his behalf" in verse 12 may mean "on the spot." That is, Abner sent the messengers to David while still face-to-face with Ish-bosheth. So Fokkelman, *Throne*, pp. 370, 371. Keil and Delitzsch, *Samuel*, p. 302 reject this understanding.

31. The Hebrew of this question is quite difficult. See McCarter, *II Samuel*, p. 107. There is no definite article on "land," and the word translated "saying" is repeated after the question. Fokkelman suggests, "Who has a country? That is to say, just make your covenant with me." Fokkelman, *Throne*, pp. 79, 80.

32. So Keil and Delitzsch, *Samuel*, p. 302.

33. Fokkelman, *Throne*, p. 80.

34. "Michal's coming represents and symbolizes the coming of Israel." Fokkelman, *Throne*, p. 82.

35. David referred to 100 Philistine foreskins. This is the price that Saul set (1 Samuel 18:25), although in the event David had doubled it (1 Samuel 18:27).

36. Paltiel is called Palti in the only other reference to him by name (1 Samuel 25:44).

37. This assumes that this Gallim is the same as the place mentioned in Isaiah 10:30. McCarter, *I Samuel*, p. 400. Bahurim was a town in Benjamin on the way from Jerusalem to the Jordan valley. See Map 5-12 in John D. Currid and David P. Barrett, *Crossway ESV Bible Atlas* (Wheaton, IL: Crossway, 2010), p. 129.

38. If our understanding of the chronology of events is correct, it would be better to omit "then" from the ESV, which is an interpretive addition by the translators.

39. Note the shift of the narrator's point of view from the north in verse 19 from which "Abner went" to Hebron in verse 20 to which "Abner came." This change of scene is marked by a paragraph break in the ESV.

40. Literally what Abner reported to David was "all that was good in the eyes of Israel and in the eyes of all the house of Benjamin." They saw *David* as "good."

41. "My lord the king" had been David's deferential form of address to Saul in 1 Samuel 24:8; 26:19 and to Achish in 1 Samuel 29:8. From this point in the narrative it will be frequently used by persons addressing David. The context usually suggests a strong note of deference, real or feigned (4:8; 9:11; 13:33; 14:9, 12, 15, 17, 18, 19, 22; 15:15, 21; 16:4, 9; 18:28, 31, 32; 19:19, 20, 27, 28, 30, 35, 37; 24:3, 21, 22).

42. Exactly the same expression is used in God's word to Jeroboam in 1 Kings 11:37.

Chapter Eight: Personal Vengeance and the Kingdom

1. See P. Kyle McCarter Jr., *II Samuel: A New Translation with Introduction, Notes & Commentary*, The Anchor Bible, vol. 9 (Garden City, NY: Doubleday, 1984), p. 117.

2. "Just then" captures well the effect here of a Hebrew idiom we noted in 1:2, 6, 18, where the ESV has "behold" (see also 3:12). The word here conveys a "notation of surprise." J. P. Fokkelman, *Narrative Art and Poetry in the Books of Samuel: a full interpretation based on stylistic and structural analyses, Volume 3: Throne and City (II Sam. 2–8 & 21–24)* (The Netherlands: Van Gorcum, Assen, 1990), p. 97.

3. The Hebrew says literally, "they told Joab," without identifying "they," perhaps suggesting general gossip as the source from which Joab heard.

4. The wording of verse 23b is closer to verse 22b and 21e than the English suggests. "Let him go" represents the same Hebrew verb as "sent him away."

5. Contrast the way in which Ish-bosheth is given little respect by either Abner or the narrator in the corresponding scene where Abner was angry with Saul's son (3:7–11).

6. "He is quite gone" (KJV); "you let him . . . get clean away" (REB). In Hebrew the end of verses 21, 22, 23, and 24 are almost identical. Literally:

"and David sent Abner and he went in peace" (v. 21).
"for he sent him and he went in peace" (v. 22).
"and he sent him and he went in peace" (v. 23).
"you sent him and he went completely" (v. 24).

Alter sees the substitution of "went completely" for "went in peace" as ominous "especially because 'to go' sometimes occurs in the Bible as a euphemism for dying." Robert Alter, *The David Story: A Translation with Commentary of 1 and 2 Samuel* (New York and London: W. W. Norton & Company, 1999), p. 212. This seems overly subtle.

7. David's "going out and coming in" (v. 25) "is an expression for leadership in battle." See 1 Samuel 18:16; 29:6; Numbers 27:17. Robert P. Gordon, *1 & 2 Samuel: A Commentary* (Exeter, UK: Paternoster, 1986), p. 160.

8. Driver suggests a possible location about a mile north of Hebron, on the road to Jerusalem. S. R. Driver, *Notes on the Hebrew Text and the Topography of the Book of Samuel with an Introduction on Hebrew Palaeography and Facsimiles of Inscriptions and Maps*, 2nd edition (Oxford: Clarendon, 1913), p. 250. Josephus says it was twenty stadia (about two miles) from Hebron. C. F. Keil and F. Delitzsch, *Biblical Commentary on the Books of Samuel* (Grand Rapids, MI: Eerdmans, 1950), p. 306.

9. Fokkelman sees "David did not know" as the beginning of a theme that will run through David's story—"whether or not, how and how far, David is losing his grip on developments and is even a prey to continuing, fresh deception." Fokkelman, *Throne*, p. 101.

10. There are three Hebrew words translated in verse 27 as "and he struck him," "the stomach," and "he died." Each of these words appears in exactly the same form in 2:23.

11. "This act of Joab . . . was a treacherous act of assassination, which could not even be defended as blood-revenge, since Abner had slain Asahel in battle after repeated warnings, and only for the purpose of saving his own life." Keil and Delitzsch, *Samuel*, p. 306.

12. Fokkelman sees an implicit criticism of David here: "how much David is overtaken by events and can do nothing more than react." Fokkelman, *Throne*, p. 105. I think this is too subtle.

13. It is a "technical term of exoneration; [it] declares that liability for a situation deemed to be an offense is denied." G. Warmuth, "*naqa*," in G. Johannes Botterweck, Helmer Ringgren, and Heinz-Josef Fabry, eds., *Theological Dictionary of the Old Testament*, vol. 9 (Grand Rapids, MI: Eerdmans, 1998), p. 557. The word was used once before of David when Jonathan said to Saul, "Why then will you sin against *in-*

nocent blood by killing David without cause?" (1 Samuel 19:5). See 2 Samuel 14:9 ("let the king and his throne be *guiltless*"); also Joshua 2:19. The legal sense of the term can be seen in Genesis 44:10 ("innocent"); Exodus 21:28 ("shall not be liable").

14. For "one who has a discharge," see Leviticus 15; "who is leprous" refers to various types of skin disease (not Hansen's disease); "who holds a spindle" is variously interpreted ("is an effeminate," Gordon, *1 & 2 Samuel*, p. 220; "a man being reduced to women's work," Alter, *David*, p. 214; "one who leans upon a stick, that is a lame person," Keil and Delitzsch, *Samuel*, p. 306; similarly "clings to a crutch," McCarter, *II Samuel*, p. 118; "an expression which indicates the oppression of forced labour," Fokkelman, *Throne*, p. 106, following S. W. Holloway, "Distaff, Crutch, or Chain Gang: the Curse on the House of Joab in 2 Samuel iii 29," *Vetus Testamentum* 37 [1987], pp. 370–375). The remaining items, "who falls by the sword" and "who lacks bread," are clear. The result is a wide-ranging list of suffering and troubles.

15. Gordon, *1 & 2 Samuel*, p. 220.

16. Keil and Delitzsch, *Samuel*, p. 306.

17. Grammatically the antecedent of "him" could be Joab or David. The context, however, suggests that "all the people" were all those who could hear the words that David spoke; "him" is David. We may assume that Joab's men were included in the addressees. Contra Fokkelman, *Throne*, p. 108, who takes "all the people who were with him [Joab]" to refer to the army.

18. "Before Abner" means "*preceding* the bier in the funeral procession." Driver, *Notes*, p. 251. Also Fokkelman, *Throne*, p. 108, note 56.

19. On the sense of the Hebrew word *nabal*, translated here "fool," see the discussion of Nabal's foolishness in John Woodhouse, *1 Samuel: Looking for a Leader*, Preaching the Word (Wheaton, IL: Crossway, 2008), pp. 473–476. Another illuminating use of the Hebrew word is 13:13 (the plural is rendered "outrageous fools" in the ESV). McCarter argues for a stronger and more precise meaning for *nabal* as "someone who has severed himself from society by socially destructive behaviour and has become an outcast, a moral pariah." McCarter, *II Samuel*, p. 323.

20. For this rendering see Fokkelman, *Throne*, p. 111.

21. Keil and Delitzsch, *Samuel*, p. 307.

22. "Wicked" is literally "sons of wickedness." Note the plural, referring to both Joab and Abishai.

23. The simplest sense is probably "all the people (who were present that day) and all Israel (the northern tribes whom Abner had previously persuaded of David's goodness," 3:19).

24. The range of meaning can be seen in such texts as 1 Samuel 8:12; 22:7; 29:3, 4, 9 ("commanders"); 12:9; 14:50; 17:18, 55; 18:13; 26:5; 2 Samuel 2:8 ("commander"); 1 Samuel 18:30 (KJV, "princes"); 22:2 (KJV, "captain").

25. Fokkelman sees a negative note in the term even in this context: "The dismay and bewilderment which Abner's assassination has stirred up in David bring him into contact with his own vulnerability." Fokkelman, *Throne*, p. 117.

26. See Alter, *David*, p. 216.

27. "Because he does not feel he can cope with them, he is forced to fall back on divine retribution for their behaviour." Fokkelman, *Throne*, p. 118. Also Keil and Delitzsch, *Samuel*, p. 308; David G. Firth, *1 & 2 Samuel*, Apollos Old Testament

Commentary 8 (Nottingham, UK and Downers Grove, IL: Apollos and InterVarsity Press, 2009), p. 352.

Chapter Nine: Wicked Violence and the Kingdom

1. See the perceptive discussion of "the idolization of success" written in the context of Hitler's Germany in Dietrich Bonhoeffer, *Ethics* (London: SCM, 1955), pp. 56–59.

2. See Map 5-8 in John D. Currid and David P. Barrett, *Crossway ESV Bible Atlas* (Wheaton, IL: Crossway, 2010), p. 126.

3. The Hebrew text lacks "Ish-bosheth" here, in keeping with the narrator's practice of often avoiding this name and thus marginalizing the person, as we saw in 3:7, 11. For another explanation that judges the omission here to be in need of correction, see P. Kyle McCarter Jr., *II Samuel: A New Translation with Introduction, Notes & Commentary*, The Anchor Bible, vol. 9 (Garden City, NY: Doubleday, 1984), p. 124; Ronald F. Youngblood, *1 & 2 Samuel*, in Tremper Longman III and David E. Garland, eds., *The Expositor's Bible Commentary*, Revised Edition, vol. 3 (Grand Rapids, MI: Zondervan, 2009), pp. 340, 341.

4. The Hebrew term often refers to a reaction to perceiving an impending disaster. The only other occurrence of this verb in the books of Samuel refers to Saul's terrified reaction to the message of doom he heard from the ghost of Samuel (1 Samuel 28:21, where the verb is intensified with the Hebrew for "very"). For other examples of the term see also Genesis 45:3; Exodus 15:15; Judges 20:41 (in these texts the ESV has "dismayed"); Psalm 2:5 ("terrify").

5. This raises a question about the earlier statement that "all Israel" understood David's innocence in the matter of Abner's death (3:37). In the light of 4:1b we should understand that 3:37 anticipates the response of "all Israel" *in due course* to the news about David's behavior at the funeral. They heard about Abner's death (4:1) *before* they heard about David at the funeral (3:37). Such chronological unevenness is a feature we find in many places in Biblical narratives.

6. Again we notice the narrator apparently avoiding Ish-bosheth's name.

7. Youngblood compares the same phrase in 1 Kings 11:24, where the ESV has "leader of a marauding band." Youngblood, *1 & 2 Samuel*, p. 337.

8. The same word is also used for the "raid" Joab had been on as David was making peace with Abner in 3:22.

9. The location of Beeroth is uncertain. A possible location just to the south of Gibeon is indicated on Map 4-10 in Currid, *Atlas*, p. 105.

10. McCarter, *II Samuel*, pp. 127, 128.

11. The location of Gittaim is uncertain. A possible location about fifteen miles northwest of the suggested location of Beeroth is indicated on Map 9-2 in Currid, *Atlas*, p. 180.

12. We will much later learn that the situation was not quite as simple as this. There were also other surviving sons and grandsons of Saul (21:8). We do not know why they are not mentioned at this point in the story.

13. Mephibosheth's name, like that of his uncle Ish-bosheth (as we saw in 2:8), appears to be an unfortunate nickname. The evidence is incomplete and open to a number of interpretations, but it is likely that the "bosheth" part of the name is a substitute for "baal" and means "shame." In 1 Chronicles 8:34; 9:40 this man is called Merib-baal. The variation in the first part of the names is more difficult to explain.

For one rather complicated proposal, see McCarter, *II Samuel*, pp. 124, 125. See also Youngblood, *1 & 2 Samuel*, p. 341.

14. Gibeah, Gibeon, and a possible location of Beeroth are all within a few miles of each other in the hills of Benjamin.

15. This estimate is based on the following observations: (a) David began his reign in Hebron shortly after Saul's death (2:1–4); (b) David reigned over Judah in Hebron for seven and a half years (2:11); and (c) the interval between Abner's death and David's becoming king over Israel (5:3) was probably at the most a matter of months, not years.

16. When the brothers were first introduced, the order was Baanah, then Rechab (v. 2). This may reflect their ages, Baanah being the older. In the narrative from verse 5 onward the order of the names is reversed, possibly suggesting that Rechab (the younger?) was the initiator of the action. Similarly Youngblood, *1 & 2 Samuel*, p. 338.

17. There is a major text critical issue with 4:6. The RSV follows the Septuagint: "And behold, the doorkeeper of the house had been cleaning wheat, but she grew drowsy and slept; so Rechab and Ba'anah his brother slipped in" (similarly REB). This is quite different from the Hebrew of the Masoretic text followed by KJV, ESV, HCSB, NIV, and NRSV. There are a number of difficulties with the Hebrew text of this verse, and these have led a number of commentators to prefer the Septuagint; so Peter R. Ackroyd, *The Second Book of Samuel*, Cambridge Bible Commentary (Cambridge: Cambridge University Press, 1977), p. 51; Robert Alter, *The David Story: A Translation with Commentary of 1 and 2 Samuel* (New York and London: W. W. Norton & Company, 1999), p. 218; Walter Brueggemann, *First and Second Samuel*, Interpretation: A Bible Commentary for Teaching and Preaching (Louisville: John Knox Press, 1990), p. 234; J. P. Fokkelman, *Narrative Art and Poetry in the Books of Samuel: a full interpretation based on stylistic and structural analyses, Volume 3: Throne and City (II Sam. 2–8 & 21–24)* (The Netherlands: Van Gorcum, Assen, 1990), pp. 125, 126; Robert P. Gordon, *1 & 2 Samuel: A Commentary* (Exeter, UK: Paternoster, 1986), p. 222; McCarter, *II Samuel*, pp. 125, 126; Smith, *Samuel*, p. 284. However the text-critical principle of favoring the more difficult reading could suggest that the Hebrew is to be preferred; so A. A. Anderson, *2 Samuel*, Word Biblical Commentary 11 (Dallas: Word, 1989), p. 70; Dale Ralph Davis, *Expositions of the Book of 2 Samuel: Out of Every Adversity* (Geanies House, Fearn, UK: Christian Focus, 1999), p. 43, note 3; David G. Firth, *1 & 2 Samuel*, Apollos Old Testament Commentary 8 (Nottingham, UK and Downers Grove, IL: Apollos and InterVarsity Press, 2009), p. 354; C. F. Keil and F. Delitzsch, *Biblical Commentary on the Books of Samuel* (Grand Rapids, MI: Eerdmans, 1950), p. 310, note 1; Youngblood, *1 & 2 Samuel*, p. 341. Hans Wilhelm Hertzberg, *I & II Samuel: A Commentary*, Old Testament Library (London: SCM Press, 1964), p. 264 and John Mauchline, *1 and 2 Samuel*, New Century Bible (London: Oliphants, 1971), p. 213 offer hypotheses that involve accepting parts of both the Septuagint and the Masoretic text. In the absence of convincing arguments either way, there is good sense in following the Hebrew text and grappling with its three (relatively minor) difficulties. The first is that the Hebrew text of the verse begins with a word often understood to be the *feminine* form of "they." However, the same word can also mean "here" or "to here" (as it does in 5:6). While a little unusual, the narrator may be vividly describing the scene from a point of view in Mahanaim: "And they came *here*, into the midst of

the house . . ." (so KJV, RV). The second difficulty with the Hebrew text is that the expression translated "*as if* to get wheat" actually means "getting wheat," the sense of which is not clear. As an objection to the Hebrew text this seems overly subtle. If the narrator is describing the scene *as it appeared*, then a reference to the men going into the house to fetch wheat (for their men from Ish-bosheth's granary?) is reasonable and the ESV wording unobjectionable. The third difficulty is that the information in verse 6 of the Hebrew text is almost all repeated in verse 7. However, this is a difficulty only when we overlook the common use of repetition in Biblical narrative (close at hand compare 3:22 and 3:23.) Fokkelman, in my opinion, overstates the difficulties with the Masoretic text. Fokkelman, *Throne*, p. 125.

18. "Stabbed him" in 4:6 represents precisely the same Hebrew word (in a plural form) as "struck him" in 2:23 and 3:27. The same word for "stomach" is also found in each of the three verses (preceded by the same preposition in the former two).

19. Fokkelman's objections to the Hebrew text of 4:6 includes that "escaped" is "incongruous" because there appears to have been no danger to the two killers. Fokkelman, *Throne*, p. 125. On the contrary, the use of the word implies that there *was* danger, as there undoubtedly would have been.

20. In verses 7, 8 there are four explicit references to this hideous object, ensuring that it is kept before our eyes: "they . . . beheaded him" (literally, "they removed *his head*"), "they took *his head*," "they . . . brought *the head of Ish-bosheth*," they showed it to the king, saying (literally), "Behold, *the head of Ish-bosheth*."

21. Gordon, *1 & 2 Samuel*, p. 223.

22. The Hebrew word translated "life" in verses 8, 9 is *nephesh*, traditionally "soul" (so KJV in v. 9).

23. David still knew and trusted God at the end of his life in precisely these terms (1 Kings 1:29).

24. The phrase repeated through the account in 2 Samuel 1, literally "the young man who was telling" (1:5, 6, 13), is echoed here in 4:10 where "one told me" is literally "the one who was telling me."

25. David mimics the speech of the sons of Rimmon who likewise began with "Behold" (ESV, "Here is," v. 8).

26. Similarly Fokkelman, *Throne*, p. 129.

Chapter Ten: Coming to the King

1. Fokkelman estimates that all the tribes of Israel would be one or two million people. J. P. Fokkelman, *Narrative Art and Poetry in the Books of Samuel: a full interpretation based on stylistic and structural analyses, Volume 3: Throne and City (II Sam. 2–8 & 21–24)* (The Netherlands: Van Gorcum, Assen, 1990), p. 137.

2. So C. F. Keil and F. Delitzsch, *Biblical Commentary on the Books of Samuel* (Grand Rapids, MI: Eerdmans, 1950), p. 313.

3. Alternatively it is possible that the Hebrew word for "tribes" here means "chiefs." So A. A. Anderson, *2 Samuel*, Word Biblical Commentary 11 (Dallas: Word, 1989), p. 75; cf. P. Kyle McCarter Jr., *II Samuel: A New Translation with Introduction, Notes & Commentary*, The Anchor Bible, vol. 9 (Garden City, NY: Doubleday, 1984), p. 130. Since Judah had already anointed David as their king (2:4), "Israel" here and in verse 3 refers to the northern tribes who had not yet done so.

4. "The speech of the tribes ... relays the general's arguments to the king: which proves just how far Abner's analysis has penetrated those involved; his arguments are even elaborated on and spruced up." Fokkelman, *Throne*, p. 138.

5. Adam said of the woman who was given to him that she was "bone of my bones and flesh of my flesh" (Genesis 2:23). Laban said to Jacob, "Surely you are my bone and my flesh" (Genesis 29:14). Abimelech, in his bid to rule over the leaders of Shechem, said, "I am your bone and your flesh" (Judges 9:2). David will in due course say to the elders of Judah (and Amasa), "you are my bone and my flesh" (19:12, 13). Contra Brueggemann: "The formula of 'flesh and bone' is probably not a statement about biological kinship, but it recognizes that the two parties have long stood together in strength (bone) and in weakness (flesh)." Walter Brueggemann, *First and Second Samuel*, Interpretation: A Bible Commentary for Teaching and Preaching (Louisville: John Knox Press, 1990), p. 237.

6. So Keil and Delitzsch, *Samuel*, p. 313. There is no need to invoke David's marriage to Michal to legitimate the claim, as suggested by Antony F. Campbell, S.J., *2 Samuel*, The Forms of the Old Testament Literature 8 (Grand Rapids, MI: Eerdmans, 2005), p. 55, which in any case only tied David to the tribe of Benjamin, not to "all the tribes of Israel."

7. *Incarnation* is the term theologians use to refer to what happened when Jesus was born, most concisely stated: "The Word [of God] became flesh and dwelt among us" (John 1:14). Less concisely the incarnation is "the act whereby the eternal Son of God, the Second Person of the Holy Trinity, without ceasing to be what he is, God the Son, took into union with himself what he before that act did not possess, a human nature." R. L. Reymond, "Incarnation," in Walter A. Elwell, ed., *Evangelical Dictionary of Theology*, Second Edition, (Grand Rapids, MI: Baker Academic, 2001), p. 601.

8. A more literal translation of the opening of their speech conveys the emphasis: "Look at us!—your bone and your flesh *we* [the pronoun is emphatic] are."

9. In support of this understanding notice that they say "*we* are *your* bone and flesh," not "*you* are *our* bone and flesh." They were saying that *they* belonged to *him* rather than that *he* belonged to *them*.

10. In English translations of the New Testament the word "church" translates the Greek *ekklesia*, which means "gathering," "assembly." The word often refers to the local gathering of Christian believers who are God's gathering ("the church of God") in that place (cf. 1 Corinthians 1:2). See John Woodhouse, *Colossians and Philemon: So Walk in Him*, Focus on the Bible (Fearn, Ross-shire, UK: Christian Focus, 2011), pp. 61–63, 82.

11. Just as the previous sentence emphasizes "we," so verse 2 has an emphatic "you" (three times): "it was *you* ... *You* shall be ... *you* shall be."

12. Robert P. Gordon, *1 & 2 Samuel: A Commentary* (Exeter, UK: Paternoster, 1986), p. 160. Similarly Anderson, *2 Samuel*, p. 75.

13. For a discussion of this text in this connection, see Woodhouse, *Colossians*, pp. 139–143.

14. Clearly "Israel" in God's promise refers to the whole nation, not just the northern tribes as in verses 1, 3.

15. The bracketed words have been added to the ESV, following the Hebrew quite literally.

16. After David's anointing in 1 Samuel 16 the only explicit words from God recorded in 1 Samuel are the message from the prophet Gad that David should go into Judah (1 Samuel 22:5), guidance (presumably using the priestly ephod) with regard to Keilah (1 Samuel 23:2, 4, 11, 12), and the word of the departed Samuel to Saul (1 Samuel 28:15–19). Perhaps Abigail's speech should be regarded as prophetic (1 Samuel 25:24–31). In the early chapters of 2 Samuel the only word from the Lord is the call to go up to Hebron (2:1).

17. See the discussion of where Abner had learned the Lord's promise in the terms he expressed in 3:18 in Keil and Delitzsch, *Samuel*, p. 304.

18. J. Robert Vannoy, *1–2 Samuel*, Cornerstone Biblical Commentary, 4a (Wheaton, IL: Tyndale House, 2009), p. 292.

19. So Brueggemann, *First and Second Samuel*, p. 239. For a brief discussion of the term and various views about its meaning, see John Woodhouse, *1 Samuel: Looking for a Leader*, Preaching the Word (Wheaton, IL: Crossway, 2008), p. 579, note 26.

20. "By a return to the metaphor of shepherd and sheep at the end of this long narrative, we are able to see how the initial act in I Samuel 16:1–13 with this shepherd boy has had its focus from the outset on the outcome of II Samuel 5:2. It is Yahweh's overriding intention in the narrative that the shepherd boy should become the shepherd of Israel." Brueggemann, *First and Second Samuel*, pp. 237, 238.

21. The powerful application of David's earlier occupation as a shepherd to his calling to be "shepherd" over God's people is strikingly like Jesus calling the fishermen, Simon Peter and Andrew, to become "fishers of men" (Matthew 4:18, 19).

22. Gordon, *1 & 2 Samuel*, p. 225.

23. The last line of Matthew 2:6 corresponds exactly with the wording of the Septuagint of the corresponding phrase in 2 Samuel 5:2.

24. The only other appearance of "all the elders of Israel" in the books of Samuel is 17:4 where they agree with Absalom on a plan to kill David! "The elders of Israel" (without the "all") appear in 1 Samuel 4:3; 2 Samuel 3:17; 17:15.

25. Ronald F. Youngblood, *1 & 2 Samuel*, in Tremper Longman III and David E. Garland, eds., *The Expositor's Bible Commentary*, Revised Edition, vol. 3 (Grand Rapids, MI: Zondervan, 2009), p. 344.

26. Actions "before the LORD" include praying (1 Samuel 1:12, 15; 2 Samuel 7:18), worship/serving (1 Samuel 1:19; 2:18; cf. 15:30, 31), surviving (1 Samuel 6:20), pouring out water (1 Samuel 7:6), assembling (1 Samuel 10:19), laying up a book (1 Samuel 10:25), offering sacrifices (1 Samuel 11:15; 2 Samuel 6:17), testifying and pleading (1 Samuel 12:3, 7), execution (1 Samuel 15:33; 2 Samuel 21:6, 9), placing bread (1 Samuel 21:6), detention (1 Samuel 21:7), making a covenant (1 Samuel 23:18; 2 Samuel 5:3), being cursed (1 Samuel 26:19), being guiltless (2 Samuel 3:28), dancing and making merry (2 Samuel 6:5, 14, 16, 21). While in some of these contexts "before the LORD" virtually means "before the ark of the covenant," the reference is to the reality of the Lord's presence whether or not this is associated with the ark.

27. See Woodhouse, *1 Samuel*, pp. 209, 212.

28. See Vannoy, *1—2 Samuel*, pp. 108–114, 292.

Chapter Eleven: "On Zion, My Holy Hill"

1. For an insightful study, see William J. Dumbrell, *The End of the Beginning: Revelation 21—22 and the Old Testament* (Eugene, OR: Wipf and Stock, 2001).

2. Various helpful essays exploring contemporary perspectives on Jerusalem are to be found in P. W. L. Walker, ed., *Jerusalem Past and Present in the Purposes of God* (Cambridge: Tyndale House, 1992), pp. 99–204.

3. See Colin Chapman, *Whose Promised Land?* (Tring, UK, Belleville, MI, and Sydney, Australia: Lion Publishing, 1983), pp. 9–12.

4. Two helpful essays in this regard are Chris Wright, "A Christian Approach to Old Testament Prophecy concerning Israel" and Gordon McConville, "Jerusalem in the Old Testament," both in Walker, *Jerusalem*, pp. 1–19 and 21–51 respectively. See also P. W. L. Walker, "Jerusalem," in T. Desmond Alexander and Brian S. Rosner, eds., *New Dictionary of Biblical Theology* (Leicester, UK and Downers Grove, IL: Inter-Varsity Press and InterVarsity Press, 2000), pp. 589–592.

5. Contra A. A. Anderson, *2 Samuel*, Word Biblical Commentary 11 (Dallas: Word, 1989), pp. 77, 78 who favors something more like the latter.

6. See John Woodhouse, *1 Samuel: Looking for a Leader*, Preaching the Word (Wheaton, IL: Crossway, 2008), pp. 342, 343.

7. The two earlier mentions of Jerusalem in the books of Samuel (1 Samuel 17:54; 2 Samuel 5:5) anticipate the events of 2 Samuel 5:6–16.

8. These were David's own followers (numbering about 600) who had been with him through his years on the run, in exile, and for the last seven and a half years in Hebron. See 1 Samuel 22:2, 3; 23:5, 8, 13, 24, 26; 24:2, 3, 6, 7, 22; 25:13, 20; 27:3, 8; 29:2, 11; 30:1, 3, 31; 2 Samuel 2:3.

9. Historical knowledge of Jerusalem dates as early as about 2500 BC. Anderson, *2 Samuel*, pp. 81, 82.

10. The Hebrew in this clause has singular nouns: "the Jebusite, the inhabitant of the land." "The Jebusite" is probably to be understood as a collective rather than as a reference to the Jebusite ruler of the city. Anderson, *2 Samuel*, p. 79.

11. S. R. Driver, *Notes on the Hebrew Text and the Topography of the Book of Samuel with an Introduction on Hebrew Palaeography and Facsimiles of Inscriptions and Maps*, 2nd edition (Oxford: Clarendon, 1913), p. 258.

12. The interpretation of the words attributed to the Jebusites in verse 6 has occasioned considerable debate. See P. Kyle McCarter Jr., *II Samuel: A New Translation with Introduction, Notes & Commentary*, The Anchor Bible, vol. 9 (Garden City, NY: Doubleday, 1984), pp. 134–138.

13. McCarter, *II Samuel*, p. 139.

14. The part of Jerusalem called Zion today (in the south*west*) is not the Biblical Zion. Driver, *Notes*, p. 258.

15. In the historical books of Samuel, Kings, and Chronicles "Zion" occurs just six times, whereas in the Psalms and the Prophets it occurs 39 and 108 times respectively.

16. See Jon D. Levenson, "Zion Traditions," in *Anchor Bible Dictionary*, vol. 6 (New York: Doubleday, 1992), pp. 1098–1102.

17. See the excellent representation in John D. Currid and David P. Barrett, *Crossway ESV Bible Atlas* (Wheaton, IL: Crossway, 2010), p. 127; also pp. 296, 297.

18. In the Old Testament this Hebrew word occurs only here ("gutter," KJV; "water shaft," ESV, HCSB, NIV, NRSV) and in Psalm 42:7 (where it is translated "water-spouts," KJV; "waterfalls," ESV, HCSB, NIV; "cataracts," NRSV).

19. This shaft, made by the Jebusites in the Late Bronze Age to give access from within the city to the water supply of the Gihon Spring, was discovered by Charles Warren in 1867. McCarter, *II Samuel*, p. 139.

20. Robert Alter, *The David Story: A Translation with Commentary of 1 and 2 Samuel* (New York and London: W. W. Norton & Company, 1999), p. 222. See Map 5-9 in Currid, *Atlas*, p. 126. For a survey of archaeological work supporting the plausibility of this interpretation see Ronald F. Youngblood, *1 & 2 Samuel*, in Tremper Longman III and David E. Garland, eds., *The Expositor's Bible Commentary*, Revised Edition, vol. 3 (Grand Rapids, MI: Zondervan, 2009), pp. 349–351.

21. One problem is that the word translated "get up" usually means "touch," "strike," or "reach." Furthermore the Hebrew does not have "to attack."

22. So Anderson, *2 Samuel*, p. 84. See Robert P. Gordon, *1 & 2 Samuel: A Commentary* (Exeter, UK: Paternoster, 1986), p. 227. Similarly J. P. Fokkelman, *Narrative Art and Poetry in the Books of Samuel: a full interpretation based on stylistic and structural analyses, Volume 3: Throne and City (II Sam. 2—8 & 21—24)* (The Netherlands: Van Gorcum, Assen, 1990), p. 161.

23. Other suggestions for the critical Hebrew term include "dagger," "pitchfork," and "grappling-iron." Different again is the rendering of David's words proposed by Keil and Delitzsch: "Everyone who smites the Jebusites, let him hurl into the waterfall (*i.e.* down the precipice) both the lame and blind, who are hateful to David's soul." C. F. Keil and F. Delitzsch, *Biblical Commentary on the Books of Samuel* (Grand Rapids, MI: Eerdmans, 1950), p. 315. For an outline of a wide range of interpretations see McCarter, *II Samuel*, pp. 139, 140. McCarter translates David's words, "Whoever smites a Jebusite, let him strike at the windpipe, for David hates the lame and the blind" (p. 135).

24. I therefore think it unlikely that the exclusion of the blind and the lame from "the house" in verse 8b is a reference to Mephibosheth (who was not blind). Contra R. A. Carlson, *David the Chosen King: A Traditio-historical Approach to the Second Book of Samuel* (Stockholm: Almqvist & Wiksell, 1964), p. 24 (who relates "the blind" to Zedekiah in 2 Kings 25:7).

25. Driver, *Notes*, p. 260.

26. So Youngblood, *1 & 2 Samuel*, p. 351. Cf. Alter, *David*, p. 222.

27. "The revulsion of David for the Jebusites barred them from associating with him from that day onward." Youngblood, *1 & 2 Samuel*, p. 351.

28. This exclusion is not related to the requirements that priests or sacrificial animals should not be blind or lame (Leviticus 21:18; Deuteronomy 15:21). Contra McCarter, *II Samuel*, p. 140.

29. W. D. Davies and Dale C. Allison, *The Gospel According to Saint Matthew*, vol. 3, International Critical Commentary on the Holy Scriptures of the Old and New Testaments (London and New York: T&T Clark, 1997), p. 140. Similarly Gordon, *1 & 2 Samuel*, p. 227; Walter Brueggemann, *First and Second Samuel*, Interpretation: A Bible Commentary for Teaching and Preaching (Louisville: John Knox Press, 1990), p. 241; Youngblood, *1 & 2 Samuel*, p. 352.

30. The narrative has followed David from Bethlehem (1 Samuel 16:1, 13) to Gibeah (1 Samuel 16:21) (via the Valley of Elah, 1 Samuel 17:19, 20), then to Ra-

mah (1 Samuel 19:18), Nob (1 Samuel 21:1), Gath (1 Samuel 21:10), the cave of Adullam (1 Samuel 22:1), Mizpeh in Moab (1 Samuel 22:3), back to the forest of Hereth in Judah (1 Samuel 22:5), then Keilah (1 Samuel 23:5), Horesh in the wilderness of Ziph (1 Samuel 23:14, 15), the wilderness of Moan (1 Samuel 23:24), Engedi (1 Samuel 23:29), the wilderness of Paran near Carmel (1 Samuel 25:1, 5), the hill of Hachilah (1 Samuel 26:1), Gath (again, 1 Samuel 27:3), Ziklag (1 Samuel 27:6), Aphek (1 Samuel 29:1, 2), back to Ziklag (1 Samuel 30:1; 2 Samuel 1:1), Hebron (2 Samuel 2:1, 2), Jerusalem (2 Samuel 5:6). These movements can be helpfully traced on Maps 5-4, 5-5, 5-6 in Currid, *Atlas*, pp. 122–124.

31. See further references to the Millo in 1 Kings 9:15, 24; 11:27; 2 Kings 12:20. "Millo" means "filling" and, according to Driver, *Notes*, p. 262, probably denotes a mound or rampart of earth.

32. Anderson, *2 Samuel*, p. 85; Youngblood, *1 & 2 Samuel*, p. 352. See Photo 5-2 in Currid, *Atlas*, p. 129.

33. The description of David in verse 10 is reminiscent of the description of Samuel in 1 Samuel 2:26. Fokkelman, *Throne*, p. 165.

34. Further see Anderson, *2 Samuel*, p. 86; Woodhouse, *1 Samuel*, p. 556, note 3.

35. Indeed, although the writer records David's taking of Jerusalem at the beginning of his account of David's reign over all Israel, this does not mean that the event necessarily took place immediately after the anointing of 5:3. The events in 5:6–25 are arranged thematically, not chronologically. So Alter, *David*, p. 221. However 5:5 indicates that the whole of David's reign over all Israel was from Jerusalem. Keil and Delitzsch, *Samuel*, pp. 314, 315.

36. Hiram became king of Tyre more than twenty years after David was anointed king over all Israel, and so the events of verse 11 may be understood to have occurred much later than the conquest of Jerusalem described in verses 6–9. Youngblood, *1 & 2 Samuel*, p. 353. Difficulties in assessing the evidence for the dating of these events is carefully weighed in Keil and Delitzsch, *Samuel*, pp. 319–321, note 1.

37. See Map 5-8 in Currid, *Atlas*, p. 126.

38. Some of the Sidonian women Solomon loved (1 Kings 11:1) may have come from Tyre, since Tyre (the capital of Phoenicia) and nearby Sidon are often closely associated (see Jeremiah 25:22; 27:3; 47:4; Ezekiel 27:8; Joel 3:4; Zechariah 9:2), and Phoenicians were called Sidonians. McCarter, *II Samuel*, p. 145.

39. Similarly Brueggemann, *First and Second Samuel*, p. 246: "Hiram embodies what is most successful in the world, commercialism. He also represents what is most dangerous to Israel, cedars and self-sufficiency. David has joined the nations. . . . Verse 11 sounds like a historical report, but it is in fact an ominous act of warning."

40. Clearly "Israel" here refers to the whole nation, as in 5:2, not just the northern tribes as in 5:1, 3.

41. "Taking many wives was indeed prohibited in the law of the king in Deut. xvii. 17; but as a large harem was considered from time immemorial as part of the court of an oriental monarch, David suffered himself to be seduced by that custom to disregard this prohibition, and suffered many a heartburn afterwards in consequence. . . ." Keil and Delitzsch, *Samuel*, p. 322.

42. Everywhere else in the Old Testament where "wives and concubines" are mentioned, "wives" comes first (2 Samuel 19:5; 1 Kings 11:3; 2 Chronicles 11:21; Daniel 5:2, 3, 23). K. Engelken, *"pilegesh,"* in G. Johannes Botterweck, Helmer Ring-

gren, and Heinz-Josef Fabry, eds., *Theological Dictionary of the Old Testament*, vol. 9 (Grand Rapids, MI: Eerdmans, 1998), p. 550.

43. Youngblood, *1 & 2 Samuel*, p. 355.

44. We considered the Biblical references to "concubines" when we considered Saul's concubine, Rizpah, in 3:7.

45. "*From* Jerusalem" is ambiguous and may simply mean "*in* Jerusalem," as 1 Chronicles 14:3 has it. So Youngblood, *1 & 2 Samuel*, p. 357.

46. This is not the famous prophet by the same name. In the genealogy of Jesus according to Luke, Jesus' ancestry is traced back to David via this Nathan (Luke 3:31).

Chapter Twelve: "The Nations Rage and the Peoples Plot in Vain"

1. It should be noted that the troubles associated with the earthly city of Jerusalem today are not directly relevant to this discussion. The New Testament, through the life and work of Jesus Christ, shifts the focus of attention from the earthly Jerusalem to the heavenly Jerusalem. See P. W. L. Walker, "Jerusalem," in T. Desmond Alexander and Brian S. Rosner, eds., *New Dictionary of Biblical Theology* (Leicester, UK and Downers Grove, IL: Inter-Varsity Press and InterVarsity Press, 2000), pp. 590–592.

2. For an argument that Saul ought to have attacked the Philistines here, see John Woodhouse, *1 Samuel: Looking for a Leader*, Preaching the Word (Wheaton, IL: Crossway, 2008), pp. 172–176; also V. Philips Long, *The Reign and Rejection of King Saul*, SBL Dissertation Series, 118 (Atlanta: Scholars Press, 1989), pp. 51–55.

3. There have been three references to the Philistines (1:20; 3:14, 18), only the last of which may allude to the contemporary situation. Nothing, however, is said in 1:1—5:16 about the activity of the Philistines after their crushing defeat of the Israelites at Mount Gilboa.

4. Similarly J. P. Fokkelman, *Narrative Art and Poetry in the Books of Samuel: a full interpretation based on stylistic and structural analyses, Volume 3: Throne and City (II Sam. 2—8 & 21—24)* (The Netherlands: Van Gorcum, Assen, 1990), p. 170.

5. David was also the man whom the Lord had "sought" (1 Samuel 13:14). All of these verses use the same Hebrew verb "to seek."

6. This is close to the view of Fokkelman, *Throne*, p. 171, who translates the phrase, "'withdrew himself into the fortress,' meaning Jerusalem itself." He argues that in context "the stronghold" in verse 17 must be read in the light of the same word occurring twice in the preceding lines (vv. 7, 9). The main problem with this is the verb "went down." If David was in Jerusalem, he would not go "down" to the elevated fortress of Zion. Likewise if he was outside the city, he would go "up" into it. There is evidence that the verb concerned can occasionally mean "go up." William L. Holladay, *A Concise Hebrew and Aramaic Lexicon of the Old Testament: based upon the lexical work of Ludwig Koehler and Walter Baumgartner* (Leiden: E.J. Brill, 1971), p. 143. Fokkelman argues that the Hebrew verb does not necessarily mean "went *down*" and argues for the sense here "withdrew" (this had been rejected by C. F. Keil and F. Delitzsch, *Biblical Commentary on the Books of Samuel* [Grand Rapids, MI: Eerdmans, 1950], pp. 323, 324) or "entered into battle." Fokkelman suggests that the verbs rendered "went up" and "went down" in 5:17 refer to opposite military moves rather than "the high/low distinction." Fokkelman, *Throne*, p. 171,

note 43. Alternatively Alter argues simply that David may have gone "down" to the stronghold in the city "because his residence in Jerusalem could be topographically above the stronghold." Robert Alter, *The David Story: A Translation with Commentary of 1 and 2 Samuel* (New York and London: W. W. Norton & Company, 1999), p. 223. Several commentators take the contrary view that "the stronghold" of 5:17 cannot be the stronghold of Zion, usually supported by reference to the verb "went down." So S. R. Driver, *Notes on the Hebrew Text and the Topography of the Book of Samuel with an Introduction on Hebrew Palaeography and Facsimiles of Inscriptions and Maps*, 2nd edition (Oxford: Clarendon, 1913), p. 263; Keil and Delitzsch, *Samuel*, p. 323; Dale Ralph Davis, *Expositions of the Book of 2 Samuel: Out of Every Adversity* (Geanies House, Fearn, UK: Christian Focus, 1999), p. 58, note 18. There is a slight difference in the Hebrew word for "stronghold" in verse 17 compared to the preceding two occurrences, which Youngblood argues suggests a distinction. Ronald F. Youngblood, *1 & 2 Samuel*, in Tremper Longman III and David E. Garland, eds., *The Expositor's Bible Commentary*, Revised Edition, vol. 3 (Grand Rapids, MI: Zondervan, 2009), p. 359. Some therefore think that "the stronghold" was the cave of Adullam or nearby (see 1 Samuel 22:1, 4; 24:22). So Keil and Delitzsch, *Samuel*, p. 324; A. A. Anderson, *2 Samuel*, Word Biblical Commentary 11 (Dallas: Word, 1989), p. 92; P. Kyle McCarter Jr., *II Samuel: A New Translation with Introduction, Notes & Commentary*, The Anchor Bible, vol. 9 (Garden City, NY: Doubleday, 1984), pp. 153, 158; Robert P. Gordon, *1 & 2 Samuel: A Commentary* (Exeter, UK: Paternoster, 1986), p. 229. Corroborative evidence for "the stronghold" being Adullam may be found in 23:13, 14 if the event recounted there took place in the context of this conflict with the Philistines, which is possible but not certain. Adullam was roughly seventeen miles southwest of Jerusalem and ten miles northwest of Hebron. In my opinion none of the arguments advanced is weighty enough to undermine the straightforward assumption that "the stronghold" in verse 17 would be the one that has just been mentioned (twice) in the immediate context.

7. See Map 5-10 in John D. Currid and David P. Barrett, *Crossway ESV Bible Atlas* (Wheaton, IL: Crossway, 2010), p. 128. Although the location is not certain, this must be about right if our understanding of this episode is correct.

8. So Gershon Edelstein, "Rephaim, Valley of," in David Noel Freedman, ed., *The Anchor Bible Dictionary*, vol. 5 (New York: Doubleday, 1992), pp. 676, 677. Against this Anderson probably reads too much into the verb "spread out," suggesting that it means "to plunder, gather spoils." Anderson, *2 Samuel*, p. 92; likewise McCarter, *II Samuel*, p. 157.

9. See T. C. Mitchell, "Rephaim," in J. D. Douglas, ed., *The Illustrated Bible Dictionary*, Part 3 (Leicester, UK and Wheaton, IL: Inter-Varsity Press and Tyndale House, 1980), p. 1328. The Septuagint has "the Valley of the Titans."

10. Here "go up" should not be pressed to mean that he would move to a higher place, but is probably to be understood in such a context as virtually meaning "attack." So McCarter, *II Samuel*, p. 154.

11. Literally the last sentence of verse 20 is, "Therefore he called the name of that place Baal-perazim." This suggests that David named the place. Contra Fokkelman who translates this, "that is why one calls this place Baal of Breaches." Fokkelman, *Throne*, p. 173.

12. This is an interesting example of the Hebrew "Baal" (which means lord or master) referring to God, despite the fact that it was also the name of a pagan deity of Canaan.

13. For this understanding of what happened, see Woodhouse, *1 Samuel*, p. 551.

14. Similarly Keil and Delitzsch, *Samuel*, p. 325; Anderson, *2 Samuel*, p. 93; McCarter, *II Samuel*, p. 154.

15. Gordon, *1& 2 Samuel*, p. 229.

16. The type of tree is uncertain. Other possibilities include "mulberry trees" (KJV; RV), "poplar trees" (NIV), "aspens" (REB), "willows" (Alter, *David*, p. 224). Perhaps we should admit ignorance and simply transliterate this "baka-shrubs" (so Holladay, *Lexicon*, p. 39). It is even possible that the Hebrew word is not the name of a tree or shrub at all but a place name. So McCarter, *II Samuel*, p. 156.

17. "Look sharp." Driver, *Notes*, p. 264.

18. Similarly McCarter, *II Samuel*, p. 155.

19. As often suggested. For example, Anderson, *2 Samuel*, p. 94; Alter, *David*, p. 224.

20. Because the corresponding passage in 1 Chronicles 14:16 has "from Gibeon to Gezer," most commentators want to change "Geba" in 5:25 to "Gibeon." So Keil and Delitzsch, *Samuel*, p. 326; Anderson, *2 Samuel*, p. 90; McCarter, *II Samuel*, pp. 152, 153; Youngblood, *1 & 2 Samuel*, p. 362. This is possible (and supported by the Septuagint) but unnecessary. The extent of the Philistines expulsion from Israelite territory could be described in either way. See Map 5-10 in Currid, *Atlas*, p. 128 (where the reference should be to 1 Chronicles 14 [not 11]:8–16). The version in 5:25 indicates more fully the scope of David's victory. Similarly Alter, *David*, p. 224.

Chapter Thirteen: "Rejoice with Trembling"

1. The preposition "from" sounds strange here, where we expect "to." Some emend the Hebrew to obtain a smoother sense. So NIV; REB; A. A. Anderson, *2 Samuel*, Word Biblical Commentary 11 (Dallas: Word, 1989), p. 97; Robert Alter, *The David Story: A Translation with Commentary of 1 and 2 Samuel* (New York and London: W. W. Norton & Company, 1999), p. 225; P. Kyle McCarter Jr., *II Samuel: A New Translation with Introduction, Notes & Commentary*, The Anchor Bible, vol. 9 (Garden City, NY: Doubleday, 1984), p. 162. However, it seems that in this condensed narrative the writer wastes no words telling us about David's movement *to* the town. All interest is in what he planned to bring *from* the town. See C. F. Keil and F. Delitzsch, *Biblical Commentary on the Books of Samuel* (Grand Rapids, MI: Eerdmans, 1950), p. 329.

2. The figure seventy is the sum of the twenty years of 1 Samuel 7:2 (on which see John Woodhouse, *1 Samuel: Looking for a Leader*, Preaching the Word [Wheaton, IL: Crossway, 2008], pp. 125, 126), the forty years of Saul's reign (Acts 13:21), and, say, ten years since David had first become king in Hebron (5:5). Brueggemann is surely mistaken to think that the twenty years of 1 Samuel 7:2 is the entire period from when the ark was left at Kiriath-jearim to the time when David brought it up from there. Walter Brueggemann, *First and Second Samuel*, Interpretation: A Bible Commentary for Teaching and Preaching (Louisville: John Knox Press, 1990), p. 247.

3. Anderson, *2 Samuel*, p. 100.

4. Much more detail about David's preparations here is given in 1 Chronicles 13:1–5, but we will focus on the report before us.

5. The verb translated "gathered" is often (but by no means exclusively) used for mustering troops for battle (1 Samuel 13:5, 11; 17:1, 2; 2 Samuel 10:15, 17; 12:28, 29; 17:11; 23:11).

6. We should remember that the Hebrew word for "thousand" may refer to a military unit of unspecified size. John W. Wenham, "Large Numbers in the Old Testament," *Tyndale Bulletin* 18 (1967), pp. 19–53. Likewise McCarter, *II Samuel*, p. 168; but contra Alter, *David*, p. 225. We may also recall that in the earlier conflict with the Philistines, when the ark was captured, the Israelite fatalities numbered "thirty thousand" (1 Samuel 4:10). Robert Polzin, *David and the Deuteronomist: A Literary Study of the Deuteronomic History. Part Three, 2 Samuel*, Indiana Studies in Biblical Literature (Bloomington and Indianapolis, IN: Indiana University Press, 1993), pp. 60, 61.

7. Some think that "again" points back to these incidents. So Anderson, *2 Samuel*, p. 101; Ronald F. Youngblood, *1 & 2 Samuel*, in Tremper Longman III and David E. Garland, eds., *The Expositor's Bible Commentary*, Revised Edition, vol. 3 (Grand Rapids, MI: Zondervan, 2009), p. 366; J. P. Fokkelman, *Narrative Art and Poetry in the Books of Samuel: a full interpretation based on stylistic and structural analyses, Volume 3: Throne and City (II Sam. 2–8 & 21–24)* (The Netherlands: Van Gorcum, Assen, 1990), p. 184.

8. So Keil and Delitzsch, *Samuel*, p. 328.

9. The Hebrew transliterated here "Baale" is a plural construct form of *baal*, which is either the name of a Canaanite deity or means "lord, master." This has led to a misunderstanding of the phrase, reflected in some of the ancient versions: "all the people who were with him from *the lords* (or, *citizens*) *of Judah*." However "from there" indicates that Baale-judah is a place name. See Keil and Delitzsch, *Samuel*, pp. 328, 329.

10. This is made explicit in 1 Chronicles 13:6, which says that David went "to Baalah, that is, to Kiriath-jearim that belongs to Judah." See Joshua 15:9, 60; 18:14 for other variations of the name of this place.

11. Francis Brown, S. R. Driver and Charles Briggs, *A Hebrew and English Lexicon of the Old Testament* (Oxford: Clarendon Press, 1907), p. 900.

12. For a discussion of other possibilities see S. R. Driver, *Notes on the Hebrew Text and the Topography of the Book of Samuel with an Introduction on Hebrew Palaeography and Facsimiles of Inscriptions and Maps*, 2nd edition (Oxford: Clarendon, 1913), pp. 265, 266; Anderson, *2 Samuel*, p. 101.

13. The places relevant to this episode can be located on Map 5-10 in John D. Currid and David P. Barrett, *Crossway ESV Bible Atlas* (Wheaton, IL: Crossway, 2010), p. 128.

14. There is some uncertainty about the Hebrew text here. Following the Septuagint, many argue (unpersuasively in my opinion) that "ark" in 1 Samuel 14:18 should be "ephod."

15. See Woodhouse, *1 Samuel*, pp. 569, 570, note 2.

16. The Hebrew has an unusual double use of the word "name," which we may represent literally: "which is called by the name, the name of the Lord of hosts . . ." (cf. rv). See Keil and Delitzsch, *Samuel*, pp. 329, 330; followed by Youngblood, *1 &*

2 Samuel, p. 367. It is common to emend the text, deleting one "name." So Fokkelman, *Throne*, p. 377; McCarter, *II Samuel*, p. 163.

17. See G. T. Manley and F. F. Bruce, "God, names of," in J. D. Douglas, ed., *The Illustrated Bible Dictionary*, Part 1 (Leicester, UK and Wheaton, IL: Inter-Varsity Press and Tyndale House, 1980), pp. 571–573.

18. It should be acknowledged that the instructions were originally given when the ark was part of the furnishings of the tabernacle and, particularly in Numbers 4, referred specifically to the Israelites setting out on their journey from Mount Sinai to the promised land (Numbers 4:5). The history of the tabernacle (or tent of meeting) in the period covered by 1 and 2 Samuel is unclear. Since the Philistine victory over Israel in 1 Samuel 4, we presume that Shiloh (where the tabernacle had stood since Joshua 18:1; see 1 Samuel 1:3, 9; 2:22) was destroyed (see Psalm 78:60–64; Jeremiah 7:12, 14; 26:6, 9). Was the tabernacle also destroyed at that time? It may have been moved to Nob (see 1 Samuel 21:1–9), or perhaps a new tabernacle was reconstructed there. Later the tabernacle stood at Gibeon (1 Chronicles 16:39; 21:29; 2 Chronicles 1:3, 5; cf. 1 Kings 3:4). Whether this was actually the tabernacle made by Moses (one understanding of 1 Chronicles 21:29) or another tabernacle built according to the same plan is not certain. The ark at Kiriath-jearim (as far as we know) was not in the tabernacle. However, it is reasonable to expect that even in these unusual circumstances God's instructions about the ark should be followed as fully as the circumstances allowed.

19. The Hebrew text repeats the words "and brought it out of the house of Abinadab, which was on the hill" from verse 3 at the beginning of verse 4. See ESV note; also RV. This is reasonably regarded by almost all commentators as a scribal error. See Keil and Delitzsch, *Samuel*, p. 331.

20. Since, as we have noted, some seventy years had passed since the ark was left in the house of Abinadab, it is likely (although not necessary) that the "sons" of Abinadab here means "grandsons." Keil and Delitzsch, *Samuel*, pp. 330, 331. Some have argued, on the contrary, that "Uzzah" is a variation of the "Eleazar" of 1 Samuel 7:1 (McCarter, *II Samuel*, p. 169), and/or that "Ahio" should be translated "his brother" (Antony F. Campbell, S.J., *2 Samuel*, The Forms of the Old Testament Literature 8 [Grand Rapids, MI: Eerdmans, 2005], p. 66).

21. For reasons to think that Abinadab was a Levite, see Woodhouse, *1 Samuel*, p. 125.

22. This is the same Hebrew verb that we saw in 2:14, where it was (unusually) rendered "compete." The basic meaning has been defined as a "cheerful activity consisting of different, varying, and sequential individual actions." E. Jenni, cited by R. Bartelmus, "*sakhaq/tsakhaq*," in G. Johannes Botterweck, Helmer Ringgren, and Heinz-Josef Fabry, eds., *Theological Dictionary of the Old Testament*, vol. 14 (Grand Rapids, MI: Eerdmans, 2004), pp. 62.

23. There is some uncertainty about the exact meaning of some of the terms here, as well as a textual problem (see ESV note), but the picture is clear enough. The main issues are clearly presented by Youngblood, *1 & 2 Samuel*, pp. 367, 376.

24. It is even uncertain that Nacon is a name. It could be "the threshing-floor of the stroke," for reasons that will soon be obvious. Keil and Delitzsch, *Samuel*, p. 332. Other suggested interpretations of the phrase "threshing floor of Nacon" are listed by McCarter, *II Samuel*, p. 164.

25. "Stumbled" should probably be "let [the ark] drop." Similarly Driver, *Notes*, p. 267; Robert P. Gordon, *1 & 2 Samuel: A Commentary* (Exeter, UK: Paternoster, 1986), p. 232.

26. The triple reference to the location of Uzzah's death ("there" twice; "*with* the ark of God") contributes to the problems raised by this scene. Uzzah was *there* (to all appearances at least) conscientiously performing his duty *with* the ark when he died.

27. The actual number who died is unclear because of some uncertainty about the text. See Woodhouse, *1 Samuel*, p. 572, note 33.

28. We are not helped by the fact that the Hebrew word translated "error" occurs only here in the whole Old Testament. It is difficult to be sure of its meaning. Renderings include "irreverence" (HSCB), "irreverent act" (NIV), "imprudent action" (REB), "crime" (JB). These are all guesses based largely on an interpretation of the context. For an etymological argument for the sense of irreverence see R. A. Carlson, *David the Chosen King: A Traditio-historical Approach to the Second Book of Samuel* (Stockholm: Almqvist & Wiksell, 1964), p. 79. In my opinion the vague "error" is best because it preserves the vagueness of the Hebrew, which I think does not provide an *explanation* of God's action. I do not believe it is helpful to try to resolve this by reference to 1 Chronicles 13:10 which has, in place of "because of his error," "because he put out his hand to the ark." On the one hand, the question as to why this was an offense deserving death remains unanswered. On the other hand, our task here is to listen to the text before us with its nuances and difficulties.

29. Similarly Keil and Delitzsch, *Samuel*, p. 333.

30. An overly literal translation shows this: "the LORD had burst through a breach against Uzzah" (6:8); "*the LORD has burst through* my enemies before me like *a breach* of water" (5:20).

31. "That place is called . . ." is more literally, "he called that place . . ."

32. "To this day" refers to the time of the writer, indicating that the events recounted have effects observable in the later world in which the narrative was being told. See also 1 Samuel 5:5; 6:18; 27:6; 30:25; 2 Samuel 4:3; 18:18.

33. Derek Kidner, *Psalms 1—72*, Tyndale Old Testament Commentaries (London: Inter-Varsity Press, 1973), p. 113.

34. You might like to follow this theme through the following selection of some of the relevant texts: Deuteronomy 6:2, 13, 24; 10:12, 20; 13:4; 14:23; 17:19; 31:12, 13; Joshua 4:24; 24:14; Job 28:28; 1 Samuel 12:14, 24; 2 Kings 17:28, 36, 39; Psalm 15:4; 19:9; 22:23; 25:14; 33:8, 18; 34:7, 9, 11; 67:7; 76:7; 85:9; 103:11, 17; 111:10; 115:11, 13; 118:4; 135:20; 145:19; 147:11; Proverbs 1:7, 29; 2:5; 3:7; 8:13; 9:10; 10:27; 14:26, 27; 15:16, 33; 24:21; 16:6; 19:23; 22:4; 23:17; Isaiah 11:2, 3; Matthew 10:28; Luke 1:50; Acts 9:31; 2 Corinthians 5:11; Revelation 19:5.

35. For a less positive estimate of David's fear see David G. Firth, *1 & 2 Samuel*, Apollos Old Testament Commentary 8 (Nottingham, UK and Downers Grove, IL: Apollos and InterVarsity Press, 2009), p. 376.

36. "Obed-edom" means "servant of Edom," Edom being either a god or a tribe. Youngblood, *1 & 2 Samuel*, p. 369. "Gittite" is very surprising. It normally means someone from the Philistine town of Gath (as in 15:18; 21:19). Was Obed-edom, therefore, a Philistine who had come over to David (like Ittai the Gittite later, 15:19, 22; 18:2), perhaps during David's time of serving in the army of the king of

Gath (1 Samuel 27)? So Driver, *Notes*, p. 269; McCarter, *II Samuel*, p. 170; Fokkelman, *Throne*, p. 192; contra Dale Ralph Davis, *Expositions of the Book of 2 Samuel: Out of Every Adversity* (Geanies House, Fearn, UK: Christian Focus, 1999), p. 66, note 8. This seems likely, despite the fact that soon after this time there was a Levite named Obed-edom (1 Chronicles 15:18, 24; 16:38). This is usually (and I think rightly) assumed to be the same person, although Thompson distinguishes these as different individuals. David L. Thompson, "Obed-edom," in David Noel Freedman, ed., *The Anchor Bible Dictionary*, vol. 5 (New York: Doubleday, 1992), pp. 5, 6. Thompson finds four different individuals in the Old Testament with the name Obed-edom. Some argue, on the basis of Obed-edom the Levite in 1 Chronicles, that Obed-edom in 2 Samuel 6 was an Israelite, and "Gittite" is a reference to the Levitical city of Gath-rimmon in the tribe of Dan (Joshua 19:45; 21:24). So Keil and Delitzsch, *Samuel*, p. 334. On balance it seems more likely that as a result of the responsibility given here to the foreigner Obed-edom and the evident blessing of the Lord, he was later included (irregularly) in the company of the Levites with responsibility for the ark. So Gordon, *1 & 2 Samuel*, p. 233.

Chapter Fourteen: The Joy of Humility and the Misery of Pride

1. We may check what we imagine against the much more detailed account in 1 Chronicles 15:1—16:3.

2. The only other occurrence in the books of Samuel of the Hebrew word translated here "rejoicing" is in 1 Samuel 18:6 (ESV, "songs of joy"); the women were rejoicing with singing, dancing, and music over David's defeat of Goliath.

3. "Those who bore" translates a plural participle of the verb "to carry," the verb used for the lawful "carrying" of the ark by Levites in Exodus 25:14; Numbers 4:15; 7:9; Deuteronomy 10:8.

4. Youngblood argues that a sacrifice was made *every* six steps. Ronald F. Youngblood, *1 & 2 Samuel*, in Tremper Longman III and David E. Garland, eds., *The Expositor's Bible Commentary*, Revised Edition, vol. 3 (Grand Rapids, MI: Zondervan, 2009), p. 370. Similarly R. A. Carlson, *David the Chosen King: A Traditio-historical Approach to the Second Book of Samuel* (Stockholm: Almqvist & Wiksell, 1964), p. 87; P. Kyle McCarter Jr., *II Samuel: A New Translation with Introduction, Notes & Commentary*, The Anchor Bible, vol. 9 (Garden City, NY: Doubleday, 1984), p. 171 (McCarter recognizes that the text must be emended to give this sense). While this is possible (especially if Obed-edom's house was very close to Jerusalem), the text only says that this happened after the first six steps. So C. F. Keil and F. Delitzsch, *Biblical Commentary on the Books of Samuel* (Grand Rapids, MI: Eerdmans, 1950), p. 335; S. R. Driver, *Notes on the Hebrew Text and the Topography of the Book of Samuel with an Introduction on Hebrew Palaeography and Facsimiles of Inscriptions and Maps*, 2nd edition (Oxford: Clarendon, 1913), p. 269; Hans Wilhelm Hertzberg, *I & II Samuel: A Commentary*, Old Testament Library (London: SCM Press, 1964), p. 279; A. A. Anderson, *2 Samuel*, Word Biblical Commentary 11 (Dallas: Word, 1989), p. 105; Robert P. Gordon, *1 & 2 Samuel: A Commentary* (Exeter, UK: Paternoster, 1986), p. 233; Robert Alter, *The David Story: A Translation with Commentary of 1 and 2 Samuel* (New York and London: W. W. Norton & Company, 1999), p. 227.

5. Contra McCarter: "after the first six paces of the journey, which showed David that Yahweh would now allow the ark to be brought into the City of David, sacrifices were made in gratitude." McCarter, *II Samuel*, p. 171.

6. The Hebrew of "danced . . . with all his might" is difficult, as the verb occurs nowhere else on the Old Testament. McCarter proposes "strumming on a sonorous instrument." Ibid.

7. It may be significant that at this new beginning in Israel's leadership, David was dressed like the young Samuel when the Lord had earlier provided new leadership for Israel.

8. Although against this see McCarter, *II Samuel*, p. 171.

9. Could we go so far as to say that the linen ephod indicates that David saw himself "as the head of the priestly nation of Israel"? So Keil and Delitzsch, *Samuel*, p. 336.

10. The "shouting" may remind us of the "shout" (same word) in 1 Samuel 4:5 when the ark was brought into the Israelite camp at Ebenezer. Gordon, *1 & 2 Samuel*, p. 234.

11. The beginning and the end of the story of Michal and David involve two very different "through the window" episodes. Alter, *David*, p. 228.

12. These three texts use the verb translated here "despised," which refers to a contemptuous attitude, seen in those who think nothing of the Lord (see 2 Samuel 12:9, 10; also Proverbs 14:2; 19:16). See M. Görg, "*bazah*," in G. Johannes Botterweck and Helmer Ringgren, eds., *Theological Dictionary of the Old Testament*, vol. 2 (Grand Rapids, MI: Eerdmans, 1975), pp. 60–65.

13. Anderson, *2 Samuel*, p. 106.

14. Keil and Delitzsch are certain that David's tent would have been constructed "according to the type of the Mosaic tabernacle." Keil and Delitzsch, *Samuel*, p. 337. On the tabernacle's locations through this period see note 18 to Chapter 13 above. The tabernacle only came to Jerusalem when the temple had been built (1 Kings 8:4; 2 Chronicles 5:5).

15. Gordon J. Wenham, *The Book of Leviticus*, The New International Commentary on the Old Testament (Grand Rapids, MI: Eerdmans, 1979), pp. 63, 58.

16. Wenham, *Leviticus*, pp. 75, 77.

17. Here we may see an anticipation of the King who will ascend on high and give gifts to men (Ephesians 4:8, a version of Psalm 68:18). Similarly Gordon, *1 & 2 Samuel*, p. 234.

18. Compare the superficially similar but very different welcome Saul and David received in 1 Samuel 18:6, 7.

19. "Honored" translates a verbal form of the Hebrew for "glory." In this way Michal's words inadvertently signal that the "glory" that had departed from Israel when the ark was captured by the Philistines seventy years earlier (see 1 Samuel 4:22) had now returned. The problem for Michal was that this was not the kind of glory she wanted. Similarly Alter, *David*, p. 229.

20. Similarly Keil and Delitzsch, *Samuel*, p. 338; Anderson, *2 Samuel*, p. 107; contra Hertzberg who says that it should "certainly not be described as 'Michal's pride.'" Hertzberg, *I & II Samuel*, p. 281.

21. See comments on these passages in this connection in John Woodhouse, *1 Samuel: Looking for a Leader*, Preaching the Word (Wheaton, IL: Crossway, 2008), pp. 332, 350, 381, 382, 513.

22. Following the Septuagint, the ESV has "in your eyes." Also Anderson, *2 Samuel*, p. 99. I favor the Hebrew ("in my eyes"), which emphasizes David's humility. Similarly Keil and Delitzsch, *Samuel*, p. 338, 339; Alter, *David*, p. 229.

23. David used the term that we noted in 5:2 (ESV, "prince"). It seems to be a deliberate alternative to "king," avoiding the connotations of worldly power and pomp associated with that term.

24. The Hebrew word translated "celebrate" is also the word used in 6:5.

25. William L. Holladay, *A Concise Hebrew and Aramaic Lexicon of the Old Testament: based upon the lexical work of Ludwig Koehler and Walter Baumgartner* (Leiden: E. J. Brill, 1971), p. 319.

26. The word means "low." See Job 5:11; Psalm 138:6; Proverbs 29:23; Isaiah 57:15; Ezekiel 17:14, 24; 21:26; 29:14, where the ESV has "low," "lowly," or "humble."

27. Contra McCarter, *II Samuel*, p. 187.

28. Similarly Hertzberg, *I & II Samuel*, p. 281.

29. In 21:8 "Michal" appears in most Hebrew manuscripts, but this is widely recognized as a scribal error.

30. The ark was "a vehicle for royal legitimation" according to Walter Brueggemann, *First and Second Samuel*, Interpretation: A Bible Commentary for Teaching and Preaching (Louisville: John Knox Press, 1990), p. 247.

31. Brueggemann is correct to observe: "Popular use of this text to justify liturgic dance is quite beside the point." Brueggemann, *First and Second Samuel*, p. 253.

Chapter Fifteen: The Most Important Words in the World

1. The crucial piece of historical data is that Hiram's reign as king of Tyre overlapped with David's as king of Israel only by the last few years of the latter. John Bright, *A History of Israel*, Third Edition (London: SCM, 1980), p. 204, note 46. Since Hiram was involved in the building of David's "house" (5:11) and this house is crucial to the situation in 7:1, it seems that 2 Samuel 7 belongs somewhere in the last few (eight or nine on Bright's reckoning) years of David's reign. Similarly Paul R. Williamson, *Sealed with an Oath: Covenant in God's Unfolding Purpose*, New Studies in Biblical Theology 23 (Downers Grove, IL: InterVarsity Press, 2007), p. 123; contra C. F. Keil and F. Delitzsch, *Biblical Commentary on the Books of Samuel* (Grand Rapids, MI: Eerdmans, 1950), p. 346.

2. Similarly Keil and Delitzsch, *Samuel*, p. 341.

3. The text of 2 Samuel 6 is also vague about the time at which the events recorded there occurred. Since it is possible that these, too, occurred quite late in David's reign, the time that elapsed between 2 Samuel 6 and 2 Samuel 7 may not have been great.

4. "House" will soon become the key word of this entire chapter (it occurs fifteen times in the twenty-nine verses).

5. Similarly A. A. Anderson, *2 Samuel*, Word Biblical Commentary 11 (Dallas: Word, 1989), p. 116. Alternatively Alter sees the "rest" of 7:1 as "partial, and temporary, because the subsequent chapters report further military campaigns." Robert Alter, *The David Story: A Translation with Commentary of 1 and 2 Samuel* (New York and London: W. W. Norton & Company, 1999), p. 231. This assumes a lot about the arrangement of the text reflecting the chronology of events. McCarter makes the

same assumption and also disregards the point made here that the narrator seems to be describing David's point of view, which will indeed be corrected in due course by the word of the Lord. McCarter solves the problem he sees by deleting the whole phrase about rest from the enemies, without textual evidence. P. Kyle McCarter Jr., *II Samuel: A New Translation with Introduction, Notes & Commentary*, The Anchor Bible, vol. 9 (Garden City, NY: Doubleday, 1984), p. 191.

6. The words in italics are emphasized by the Hebrew word order.

7. Hebrew has a number of words for "rest." The one used in 7:1 is not the word from which we get "Sabbath," but, as the following references illustrate, was used in connection with the Sabbath and with God's promise of "rest."

8. The phrases in Deuteronomy 12:10; 25:19; 2 Samuel 7:1 are almost identical in the Hebrew.

9. Literally, "in the midst of the curtain."

10. The abrupt introduction of Nathan into the story at this point may reflect the fact that this was late in David's reign, when Nathan (in circumstances that have not been recorded) had become established as a prophet in David's circle.

11. The house envisaged in this chapter will first be called a "temple" in 1 Kings 7:21, only after David's death.

12. Here I am disagreeing with Gordon who regards David as "a fairly typical near eastern king in this regard." Robert P. Gordon, *1 & 2 Samuel: A Commentary* (Exeter, UK: Paternoster, 1986), p. 236.

13. See, for example, 1 Samuel 9:16 and the discussion in John Woodhouse, *1 Samuel: Looking for a Leader*, Preaching the Word (Wheaton, IL: Crossway, 2008), p. 162.

14. I therefore take issue with commentators like McCarter: "David's words in v. 2 must be understood as the expression of a wish to build a temple." McCarter, *II Samuel*, p. 196; or Fokkelman: "the issue is David's desire to build a temple for God." J. P. Fokkelman, *Narrative Art and Poetry in the Books of Samuel: a full interpretation based on stylistic and structural analyses, Volume 3: Throne and City (II Sam. 2—8 & 21—24)* (The Netherlands: Van Gorcum, Assen, 1990), p. 208. I do not believe it was as clear as that, and these interpreters have perhaps missed a subtle significance in the absence of the word "temple" in 2 Samuel 7.

15. Similarly McCarter, *II Samuel*, p. 197.

16. The last time this phrase appeared in the narrative was when the Lord rejected Saul (1 Samuel 15:10, 11). The only other occurrence of the phrase in the books of Samuel is 24:11. There had been a time when "the word of the LORD was rare" (1 Samuel 3:1, 7), a situation that changed with the calling of Samuel to be a prophet (1 Samuel 3:21; 4:1; see 9:27; 15:10, 23, 26).

17. In the Old Testament the following persons are called by God "my servant": Abraham (Genesis 26:24), Moses (Numbers 12:7, 8; Joshua 1:2, 7; 2 Kings 21:8; Malachi 4:4), Caleb (Numbers 14:24), David (2 Samuel 3:18; 7:5, 8; 1 Kings 11:13, 32, 34, 36, 38; 14:8; 2 Kings 19:34; 20:6; Psalm 89:3, 20; Isaiah 37:35; Jeremiah 33:21, 22, 26; Ezekiel 34:23, 24; 37:24, 25), Job (Job 1:8; 2:3; 42:7, 8), Isaiah (Isaiah 20:3;), Eliakim (Isaiah 22:20), the servant of the Lord (sometimes identified as Israel) in Isaiah 41:8, 9; 42:1, 19; 43:10; 44:2, 21; 45:4; 49:3, 6; 52:13; 53:11 (see Matthew 12:18), Israel (Jeremiah 30:10; 46:27, 28; Ezekiel 28:25), the king of Babylon (Jeremiah 25:9; 27:6; 43:10), Zerubbabel (Haggai 2:23), and a promised unnamed

king (Zechariah 3:8). The boy Samuel had understood himself to be the Lord's "servant" (1 Samuel 3:10). David had called himself Saul's "servant" (1 Samuel 17:32, 34, 36; 26:18, 19; cf. 19:4; 22:8; 29:3) and in that context also Jonathan's "servant" (1 Samuel 20:7, 8). This was a common enough way of referring to the king's subjects (see 1 Samuel 22:17), and could be a form of courteous speech (as in 1 Samuel 25:8). David even called himself Achish's "servant" (1 Samuel 27:5; 28:2; 29:8), but this was part of an elaborate deception (1 Samuel 27:12). On two occasions we have heard David refer to himself as the Lord's "servant" (1 Samuel 23:10, 11; 25:39). Only once (before 2 Samuel 7) have we indirectly heard the Lord refer to David as "my servant" (2 Samuel 3:18). This will not be the last time this important phrase is applied to him (see 1 Kings 3:6; 8:24, 25, 26, 66; 2 Kings 8:19; the titles of Psalms 18, 36; Psalm 78:70; 89:39; 132:10; 144:10; Luke 1:69; Acts 4:25), and it will become important in David's self-understanding (ten times in 2 Samuel 7:19–29; see also 24:10; Psalm 19:11, 13; 27:9; 31:16; 69:17; 86:2, 4, 16; 109:28; 143:2, 12).

18. See 1 Samuel 2:27; 10:18; 15:2; 2 Samuel 7:5, 8. The next time David will hear these words will be the devastating message delivered by Nathan in 12:7, 11. See also 24:12.

19. On this phrase, see Woodhouse, *1 Samuel*, pp. 64, 562, note 2.

20. Those who see 7:5 as in principle an absolute rejection of a temple can only do so on the basis of some view of the text as a composition of contradictory sources. See, for example, Anderson, *2 Samuel*, pp. 118, 119. Any reading of the text as it stands must understand the question in the context that includes 7:13.

21. This is clear in the Hebrew, which gives this emphasis by the pronoun used and by its position in the sentence. Similarly Fokkelman, *Throne*, p. 216.

22. It is possible (but less obvious) that the question also presents a contrast between David and the Lord: "Are *you* going to build *me* a house?"—the implied answer being, "No, David *I* am going to build *you* a house" (see 7:11c). So McCarter, *II Samuel*, p. 198.

23. In Hebrew 7:6 begins with a conjunction, usually translated "for" or "because." What follows therefore provides reasons for the implied answer to the rhetorical question of the previous verse. "No, David, you are not the one to build me a house to dwell in *because* . . ."

24. The date of the exodus is debated. Here I follow the dates proposed by Bright, *History*, pp. 468, 469.

25. The Hebrew word for "dwelling" here is the word often translated "tabernacle." The phrase could be rendered "in a tent (that is, a tabernacle)." So Anderson, *2 Samuel*, p. 110.

26. In this snapshot of the history from Egypt to Jerusalem, the period when the ark was housed in something called a "temple" in Shiloh (1 Samuel 1:9; 3:3) is not mentioned. Since this was certainly not "a house of cedar" and was probably not a great deal more than some minor additions to the tabernacle, the argument is hardly affected. Nor is it relevant here that the ark was placed in the "house" of Abinadab (1 Samuel 7:1) for many years and in the "house" of Obed-edom for three months (6:10, 11). In the unusual circumstances involved, it is unlikely that the Lord would refer to these houses as "my dwelling."

27. The Hebrew word here usually means "tribes" (as in 1 Samuel 2:28; 9:21; 10:19, 20, 21; 15:17; 2 Samuel 5:1; 15:2, 10; 19:9; 20:14; 24:2). It can also mean

"rod" (7:14), "javelin" (18:14), or "staff" (23:21). Since these meanings do not seem to fit the context here (how would "tribes" "shepherd" people?), many commentators amend the text in some way, sometimes (as ESV) under the influence of 1 Chronicles 17:6. See Ronald F. Youngblood, *1 & 2 Samuel*, in Tremper Longman III and David E. Garland, eds., *The Expositor's Bible Commentary*, Revised Edition, vol. 3 (Grand Rapids, MI: Zondervan, 2009), p. 384. For a defense of the unamended Hebrew text see Keil and Delitzsch, *Samuel*, p. 342, disputed by S. R. Driver, *Notes on the Hebrew Text and the Topography of the Book of Samuel with an Introduction on Hebrew Palaeography and Facsimiles of Inscriptions and Maps*, 2nd edition (Oxford: Clarendon, 1913), pp. 274, 275, but defended again by Fokkelman, *Throne*, p. 218.

Chapter Sixteen: The Promise

1. In this brief paragraph I have left out much. For an excellent brief outline of how the whole Bible works together to inform and build faith in God's promise, see Graeme Goldsworthy, *Gospel and Kingdom: A Christian Interpretation of the Old Testament* (Exeter, UK: Paternoster, 1981).

2. It is highly significant that the first verse of the New Testament introduces Jesus as "the son of David, the son of Abraham" (Matthew 1:1). To understand Jesus it is fundamentally important to understand his connection to Abraham and to David. Matthew 1:2–16 then shows the connection in the form of a genealogy that begins with Abraham and moves, via David, to Jesus.

3. Literally "And now," a Hebrew idiom often used in drawing a conclusion from what has just been said. Francis Brown, S. R. Driver and Charles Briggs, *A Hebrew and English Lexicon of the Old Testament* (Oxford: Clarendon Press, 1907), p. 774.

4. On the meaning of the title "the LORD of hosts," see John Woodhouse, *1 Samuel: Looking for a Leader*, Preaching the Word (Wheaton, IL: Crossway, 2008), p. 556, 557, note 3.

5. "You" and "your" in 7:8b–16 are all singular and refer to David.

6. I have previously argued that the word misleadingly translated here "prince" does not have royal connotations and in some contexts represents a deliberate avoidance of "king." See 1 Samuel 9:16; 10:1; 13:14; 25:30; 2 Samuel 5:2; 6:21. Woodhouse, *1 Samuel*, pp. 162, 579, note 26.

7. The most natural reading of the tenses of the Hebrew verbs in this passage supports the understanding given here. This is convincingly argued by J. P. Fokkelman, *Narrative Art and Poetry in the Books of Samuel: a full interpretation based on stylistic and structural analyses, Volume 3: Throne and City (II Sam. 2–8 & 21–24)* (The Netherlands: Van Gorcum, Assen, 1990), pp. 223–226. However, several commentators regard a reference to the future here as impossible because the matters referred to had already happened. For example, Hans Wilhelm Hertzberg, *1 & II Samuel: A Commentary*, Old Testament Library (London: SCM Press, 1964), p. 285; A. A. Anderson, *2 Samuel*, Word Biblical Commentary 11 (Dallas: Word, 1989), p. 120. This, in my opinion, is to miss the subtlety of the Lord's words: things that seemed to have been accomplished had yet to reach their intended end.

8. Note again that "you" in 7:9b is singular, referring to David.

9. The Hebrew verb for "plant" is the same as in 7:10.

10. The Hebrew word for "place" here is a very slight variant on the word in 7:10. The land is referred to with the word "place" in Deuteronomy 11:24; Joshua 1:3; 1 Samuel 12:8.

11. On this understanding "your own mountain," "the place," and "the sanctuary" in Exodus 15 are metaphorical references to the land itself, since that is where the Lord would "plant" the people. Some consider the "mountain" to be Mount Zion and "the sanctuary" to be the temple. While possible, I think the leading idea of the people being "planted" in the land suggests the understanding adopted here. For a brief survey of views see J. P Hyatt, *Exodus*, New Century Bible (London: Oliphants, 1971), pp. 167, 168.

12. For the view that the "place" in 7:10 is the temple that Solomon will build, see P. Kyle McCarter Jr., *II Samuel: A New Translation with Introduction, Notes & Commentary*, The Anchor Bible, vol. 9 (Garden City, NY: Doubleday, 1984), pp. 202, 203.

13. "You" in 7:11b is again singular and refers to David.

14. Notice how two promises concerning David (vv. 9b, 11b) bracket the promises concerning Israel (vv. 10, 11a). Similarly Fokkelman, *Throne*, p. 227.

15. Similarly Paul R. Williamson, *Sealed with an Oath: Covenant in God's Unfolding Purpose*, New Studies in Biblical Theology 23 (Downers Grove, IL: InterVarsity Press, 2007), p. 124.

16. The brief change to the third person references to the Lord in verse 11c, d adds rhetorical weight to these words, which thus stand out from the words spoken in the first person before and after. Similarly Fokkelman, *Throne*, p. 228.

17. The italicized words are emphasized in the Hebrew. The emphasis on both words has been highlighted by McCarter, *II Samuel*, p. 198.

18. "The LORD" and "you" are emphasized in this sentence by their repetition. The word order in Hebrew gives prominence to the word "house," signaling the return to that topic. "As for a house, *he* will build one for *you*." See McCarter, *II Samuel*, p. 190; also Fokkelman, *Throne*, p. 228.

19. The different kind of house is hinted at in the avoidance of the word "build" in 7:11d, compared to 7:5b. The word used (ESV, "make") is the one used in Nathan's reply to David in 7:3 (ESV, "do"). The word "build" will return in 7:13 when a literal, physical "house" is again on view.

20. The Hebrew phrase translated "who shall come from your body" repeats exactly the same phrase in Genesis 15:4 (ESV: "your very own son"). This is a further indication that the fabric of this message to David is woven from the cords of the promise to Abraham. The only other occurrence of this precise phrase in the Old Testament is in 16:11 (ESV: "my own son"), where David seems to have thought that Absalom may have been the one the Lord was raising up to succeed him. Similarly Fokkelman, *Throne*, p. 230.

21. Hebrew has several words rendered "kingdom" in English translations. According to the standard lexicons *melukah* means position or rank of king, royalty, kingship (1 Samuel 10:16, 25; 11:14; 14:47; 18:8; 2 Samuel 12:26; 16:8); *mamlakuth* means royal power, dominion, kingdom (1 Samuel 15:28; 2 Samuel 16:3); *malkuth* means royalty, royal power, reign, dominion, royal dignity, kingship, kingdom, realm (1 Samuel 20:31); *mamlakah* means kingdom, sovereignty, dominion, reign, royal power, or dignity (1 Samuel 10:18; 13:13, 14; 24:20; 27:5; 28:17;

2 Samuel 3:10, 28; 5:12, 13, 16). See the relevant entries in Brown, Driver, and Briggs, *Lexicon* and William L. Holladay, *A Concise Hebrew and Aramaic Lexicon of the Old Testament: based upon the lexical work of Ludwig Koehler and Walter Baumgartner* (Leiden: E. J. Brill, 1971). Precise distinctions between these terms are difficult to discern. They may be regarded as essentially synonymous. Contextual considerations will shape the more exact meaning in each case.

22. Similarly S. R. Driver, *Notes on the Hebrew Text and the Topography of the Book of Samuel with an Introduction on Hebrew Palaeography and Facsimiles of Inscriptions and Maps*, 2nd edition (Oxford: Clarendon, 1913), p. 276, note 1; Fokkelman, *Throne*, p. 231.

23. In 7:13a "He" is emphatic in the same way as "you" in 7:5b and "I" in 7:8b.

24. Including the last word of the chapter, which is a slight variant on the phrase.

25. For example, the same expression (translated "forever") in 1 Samuel 1:22 refers to the time that Hannah promised Samuel would dwell in Shiloh (which was not all eternity). Consider also the sense of "forever" in 1 Samuel 2:30, 35; 20:23; 2 Samuel 3:28. However, "forever" can mean for all time without end (see 1 Samuel 2:32; 3:14). The context must be considered in each case.

26. See further Oscar Cullmann, *The Christology of the New Testament* (London: SCM, 1963), pp. 272–275.

27. See the similar argument that 7:14 is "adoption language" in McCarter, *II Samuel*, p. 207.

28. Similarly Driver, *Notes*, p. 276.

29. For example, the record of the wicked king Manasseh in 2 Kings 21 does not suggest that this promise kept him in the Lord's steadfast love. Nonetheless the Lord raised up his righteous son Josiah (2 Kings 22:1, 2).

30. It is interesting to notice how these words from Heaven at Jesus' baptism not only echo Isaiah 42:1, but also identify Jesus in terms of 7:14a, while indicating that he is the *first* such person to whom 7:14b does *not* apply.

31. The Hebrew has "before you (singular)." The ESV and others have followed the Septuagint here, but probably wrongly. Similarly Fokkelman, *Throne*, p. 235, note 55.

32. The italicized words in this paragraph represent forms of the same Hebrew word.

33. Similarly Fokkelman, *Throne*, pp. 233, 234.

34. Jesse was David's father (1 Samuel 16:1).

35. For a study of Matthew 16:16–19 that recognizes this passage's links with 2 Samuel 7, see Ben F. Meyer, *The Aims of Jesus* (London: SCM, 1979), pp. 185–197.

Chapter Seventeen: The King's Prayer

1. For a helpful discussion of the priority of *hearing* over *seeing* in a Biblical understanding of our knowledge of God, see Michael Horton, *The Christian Faith: A Systematic Theology for Pilgrims on the Way* (Grand Rapids, MI: Zondervan, 2011), pp. 80–94.

2. Sitting for prayer is unusual in the Bible. Keil and Delitzsch insist that the verb should be translated "remained, tarried," not "sat," because sitting was not the posture assumed for prayer before the Lord. C. F. Keil and F. Delitzsch, *Biblical Commentary on the Books of Samuel* (Grand Rapids, MI: Eerdmans, 1950), pp. 349, 350. Similarly P. Kyle McCarter Jr., *II Samuel: A New Translation with*

Introduction, Notes & Commentary, The Anchor Bible, vol. 9 (Garden City, NY: Doubleday, 1984), p. 236. However, Gordon notes the suggestion that David's sitting here has to do with "the special prerogative of the Davidic kings" and refers to Psalm 110:1. Robert P. Gordon, *1 & 2 Samuel: A Commentary* (Exeter, UK: Paternoster, 1986), p. 241.

3. For an important study of what it means in the Psalms to praise God, see Claus Westermann, *Praise and Lament in the Psalms* (Edinburgh: T. & T. Clark, 1965), pp. 15–35.

4. "Thus far" may also be understood to refer to the situation described in 7:1. However, David now understood that situation differently in the light of the word of the Lord.

5. Of the fifteen occurrences of the word "house" in this chapter, seven are in David's prayer.

6. The Hebrew name for God, YHWH (see Exodus 3:13–15; 6:2, 3), was not uttered in the public reading of the Hebrew Scriptures. Instead the reader substituted the Hebrew for "my lord." This was almost certainly motivated by the view that God's name was too holy to be spoken. When vowel marks were added to the consonantal Hebrew text, this convention of reading was represented by the vowels of "my lord" being added to the consonants YHWH. The resulting hybrid word (which we may represent as YeHoWaH) preserved the written consonants of the inspired Scriptures, but the vowels reminded the reader to say "my lord" at this point. In time the original pronunciation of YHWH was forgotten ("Yahweh" is an informed guess that has caught on). When the Old Testament was translated into Greek, YHWH was represented by *kurios*, the Greek for "Lord." Most English translations of the Old Testament followed this convention but put "Lord" in small capital letters to distinguish YHWH from the ordinary Hebrew word for "Lord." When the Hebrew has both the ordinary word for "Lord" and the name YHWH, some English translations adapted the convention and printed "Lord God" (to avoid "Lord Lord," which would sound odd). For further details, see G. T. Manley and F. F. Bruce, "God, names of," in J. D. Douglas, ed., *The Illustrated Bible Dictionary*, Part 1 (Leicester, UK and Wheaton, IL: Inter-Varsity Press and Tyndale House, 1980), pp. 571, 572.

7. The precise Hebrew expression ("my lord Yahweh") occurs in 7:18, 19 (twice), 20, 22(?), 28, 29. In verse 25 "O Lord God" represents a different phrase, literally "Yahweh God." In verse 22 many Hebrew manuscripts have "Yahweh God" (as in verse 25, represented in ESV as "O Lord God" [similarly KJV, RSV, NRSV]), but others have "my lord Yahweh" (followed by HCSB, NIV). In verse 22 (and perhaps verse 25) "my Lord Yahweh" is probably original. So S. R. Driver, *Notes on the Hebrew Text and the Topography of the Book of Samuel with an Introduction on Hebrew Palaeography and Facsimiles of Inscriptions and Maps*, 2nd edition (Oxford: Clarendon, 1913), p. 277; McCarter, *II Samuel*, p. 234; A. A. Anderson, *2 Samuel*, Word Biblical Commentary 11 (Dallas: Word, 1989), p. 125.

8. The expression "my Lord Yahweh" was also used by Moses as he wondered at the Lord's mighty acts for his people (Deuteronomy 3:24; 9:26; but nowhere else in the books of Exodus to Deuteronomy), Joshua as he questioned the Lord's purpose in these great acts (Joshua 7:7; but nowhere else in the book of Joshua), Gideon and Samson in similarly awesome contexts (Judges 6:22; 16:28; but nowhere else in the book of Judges). See W. C. Kaiser, "The Blessing of David, the Charter for

Humanity," in J. H. Skilton, ed., *The Law and the Prophets: Old Testament Studies Prepared in Honor of Oswald Thompson Allis* (Philadelphia: Presbyterian and Reformed, 1974), p. 311. Similarly R. A. Carlson, *David the Chosen King: A Traditio-historical Approach to the Second Book of Samuel* (Stockholm: Almqvist & Wiksell, 1964), p. 127; Ronald F. Youngblood, *1 & 2 Samuel*, in Tremper Longman III and David E. Garland, eds., *The Expositor's Bible Commentary*, Revised Edition, vol. 3 (Grand Rapids, MI: Zondervan, 2009), p. 395. See also 1 Kings 2:26; 8:53. The expression is common in the book of Ezekiel.

9. This is further subtle confirmation of the significance of David's reign beginning in Abraham's town of Hebron (2:1–4).

10. Strictly speaking "my servant David" were words spoken to Nathan, but were not included in the words he was instructed to speak to David (7:5a, 8a). However, we can deduce from David's repetitions of "your servant" that Nathan really did speak "all these words" to David, including the instructions that had been addressed to the prophet. Contra J. P. Fokkelman, *Narrative Art and Poetry in the Books of Samuel: a full interpretation based on stylistic and structural analyses, Volume 3: Throne and City (II Sam. 2—8 & 21—24)* (The Netherlands: Van Gorcum, Assen, 1990), p. 237.

11. Literally David's words here are, "and this is the law [*torah*] of man [or mankind], O Lord GOD!" Interpretations vary widely, depending largely on the meaning attributed to the Hebrew *torah* and the sense of the genitive ("of"). The following are representative of the range of understandings. (1) "This is the manner of man [not of God]." Francis Brown, S. R. Driver, and Charles Briggs, *A Hebrew and English Lexicon of the Old Testament* (Oxford: Clarendon Press, 1907), p. 436; so KJV. But *torah* does not mean "manner" anywhere else. (2) Keil and Delitzsch propose that "this is the law of man" means that God has behaved toward David in the way in which he requires (in the Law) humans to act toward one another, namely to love their neighbor. C. F. Keil and F. Delitzsch, *Biblical Commentary on the Books of Samuel* (Grand Rapids, MI: Eerdmans, 1950), pp. 350, 351. But the antecedent of "this" is better understood as the promise itself rather than the divine kindness involved. (3) "Is this your usual way of dealing with man?" (NIV; supported by Joyce Baldwin, *1 and 2 Samuel*, Tyndale Old Testament Commentaries [Leicester, UK: Inter-Varsity Press, 1988], p. 217). The previous two objections apply again, and the phrase is probably an exclamation rather than a question. (4) "This decree . . . is for a mere human!" But there is a definite article that is ignored in "*a* mere human." (5) "May this be instruction for the people" (NRSV). This is close to Firth's proposal "that the evidence of grace in such actions by Yahweh acts as instruction (*torah*) for all people." David G. Firth, *1 & 2 Samuel*, Apollos Old Testament Commentary 8 (Nottingham, UK and Downers Grove, IL: Apollos and InterVarsity Press, 2009), p. 390. See my objection to (2). (6) "This is a revelation for mankind" (HCSB; similarly ESV). Other scholars despair and amend the text rather arbitrarily (so RSV; Hans Wilhelm Hertzberg, *I & II Samuel: A Commentary*, Old Testament Library [London: SCM Press, 1964], p. 282; John Mauchline, *1 and 2 Samuel*, New Century Bible [London: Oliphants, 1971], p. 231; McCarter, *II Samuel*, p. 233) or admit defeat (so Driver, *Notes*, p. 276). Still others omit the phrase (JB, REB). The exposition here is similar to Kaiser, "Blessing," pp. 298–318, who paraphrases: "This is the charter by which humanity will be directed." This is similar to (6) above.

12. See the similar use of the word "know" in Genesis 18:19 (ESV, "chosen"); Hosea 5:3; 13:5; Amos 3:2.

13. I prefer to omit the ESV's "it" from the end of verse 21, following the Hebrew quite literally.

14. Similarly McCarter, *II Samuel*, p. 236.

15. Therefore 7:21 confirms the understanding argued elsewhere that "a man after [God's] own heart" (1 Samuel 13:14) does not mean a man with a godly heart but a man of God's choice. It speaks of the place the man has in God's heart, not the place God has in the man's heart. See further John Woodhouse, *1 Samuel: Looking for a Leader*, Preaching the Word (Wheaton, IL: Crossway, 2008), pp. 235, 286, 287. Also P. Kyle McCarter Jr., *I Samuel: A New Translation with Introduction, Notes & Commentary*, The Anchor Bible, vol. 8 (Garden City, NY: Doubleday, 1980), p. 229; McCarter, *II Samuel*, p. 236.

16. "If there was nothing meritorious in David (vv. 18, 20), then the explanation of Yahweh's kindness must lie in his own will and purpose." Gordon, *1 & 2 Samuel*, p. 241. Contra Fokkelman, *Throne*, p. 241.

17. "Because of" at the beginning of 7:21 indicates that the Lord's word is the effective cause or reason for God's action. In a similar way the ark of God was the cause or reason for the blessing of the household of Obed-edom ("because of" in 6:12 represents the same Hebrew expression). Elsewhere this preposition is translated "for the sake of" or "on account of." See 1 Samuel 12:22; 23:10; 2 Samuel 5:12; 9:1, 7. In these different cases it points to the effective cause or reason for an action. For further details, see Brown, Driver and Briggs, *Lexicon*, p. 271.

18. The Hebrew has an additional expression here that means "for your [singular] land." Most commentators (for example Anderson, *2 Samuel*, p. 125) regard this as an error, although the ideas of the promised land belonging to the Lord (Psalm 85:1) and of the exodus having as its goal the blessing of that land and life in it are well documented (Deuteronomy 7:13; 8:10; 11:29; 15:4; 26:15; 28:12; 33:13). For an argument that the phrase means "to your land," extending the "great and awesome things" to the conquest, see Keil and Delitzsch, *Samuel*, p. 353.

19. The Hebrew, unusually, has a plural verb here. "The construing of *Elohim* [God] with a plural arises from the fact, that in this clause it not only refers to the true God, but also includes the idea of the gods of other nations. The idea, therefore, is not, 'Is there any nation upon earth to which the only true God went?' but, 'Is there any nation to which the deity worshipped by it went, as the true God went to Israel to redeem it for His own people?'" Keil and Delitzsch, *Samuel*, p. 352.

20. Strictly speaking a more literal translation indicates a threefold purpose: ". . . God went *to redeem* for himself a people and *to make* himself a name and *to do* . . ."

21. The Hebrew text has "nations," which supports the view that David was speaking not only of the exodus but also of the conquest. So Keil and Delitzsch, *Samuel*, p. 353.

22. The movement from address to God ("you" singular) to address to the people ("you" plural) is accompanied by a movement to third person reference to God ("*his* people," "*him*self") and back to second person again ("*your* people," "*you* redeemed," "*your*self") within this verse. See Keil and Delitzsch, *Samuel*, pp. 352, 353.

23. Such movements from words addressed to God to words spoken about God and words spoken to other people are quite common in the Psalms. See, for example, Psalm 3: verses 1–3 (to the Lord), 4–6 (about the Lord), 7 (to the Lord), 8 (about *and* to the Lord); Psalm 4: verse 1 (to the Lord), 2–6 (to men), 7, 8 (to the Lord).

24. Similarly Youngblood, *1 & 2 Samuel*, pp. 396, 397.

25. Brown, Driver, and Briggs, *Lexicon*, p. 774. The same Hebrew phrase is repeated at the beginning of verses 28 (ESV, "And now") and 29 (ESV, "Now therefore").

26. Interestingly the divine name here ("the LORD of Hosts") is the "name" by which the ark was called according to 6:2.

Chapter Eighteen: "I Will Make the Nations Your Heritage"

1. The Hebrew phrase translated "After this" (NIV, "In the course of time") is used as a general expression of transition in the narrative and should not necessarily be pressed in a chronological sense, although in many contexts it does convey this. The phrase occurs in a general sense in 10:1; 13:1 (ESV, "now"). Similarly C. F. Keil and F. Delitzsch, *Biblical Commentary on the Books of Samuel* (Grand Rapids, MI: Eerdmans, 1950), p. 355; P. Kyle McCarter Jr., *II Samuel: A New Translation with Introduction, Notes & Commentary*, The Anchor Bible, vol. 9 (Garden City, NY: Doubleday, 1984), p. 251. However, according to Youngblood the phrase "always inaugurates a new section" in the narrative. Ronald F. Youngblood, *1 & 2 Samuel*, in Tremper Longman III and David E. Garland, eds., *The Expositor's Bible Commentary*, Revised Edition, vol. 3 (Grand Rapids, MI: Zondervan, 2009), p. 419.

2. The Hebrew verb translated "defeated" in the ESV of 8:1, 2, 3, 9, 10 and "struck/striking down" in 8:5, 13 is used of David "striking down" the Amalekites in 1:1 (and the striking down of one particular Amalekite in 1:15), the Jebusites in 5:8, the Philistines in 5:20 ("defeated"), 24, 25. It is also used of other killings that have taken place in this story (2:22, 23, 31; 3:27; 4:6, 7; 6:7). In all these occurrences it indicates violent killing.

3. See Map 5-1 in John D. Currid and David P. Barrett, *Crossway ESV Bible Atlas* (Wheaton, IL: Crossway, 2010), p. 120.

4. See also Judges 10:6, 7.

5. Although he had more success than has been recorded in detail. See 1 Samuel 14:47.

6. It "denotes . . . the shame, dishonor, and loss of prestige brought about by defeat, the humiliation associated with the entire complex of events." S. Wagner, "*kn'*," in G. Johannes Botterweck, Helmer Ringgren, and Heinz-Josef Fabry, eds., *Theological Dictionary of the Old Testament*, vol. 7 (Grand Rapids, MI: Eerdmans, 1995), p. 206.

7. So Keil and Delitzsch, *Samuel*, p. 356; S. R. Driver, *Notes on the Hebrew Text and the Topography of the Book of Samuel with an Introduction on Hebrew Palaeography and Facsimiles of Inscriptions and Maps*, 2nd edition (Oxford: Clarendon, 1913), p. 279; J. P. Fokkelman, *Narrative Art and Poetry in the Books of Samuel: a full interpretation based on stylistic and structural analyses, Volume 3: Throne and City (II Sam. 2–8 & 21–24)* (The Netherlands: Van Gorcum, Assen, 1990), p. 257; Youngblood, *1 & 2 Samuel*, p. 401. McCarter interprets the expression "the bridle of the water channel." McCarter, *II Samuel*, p. 243.

8. David's triumph over the Philistines was remembered (see 19:9). Although hostility from the Philistines would emerge again much later in his reign (21:15—22, which, as we will see, seems to recount events in David's older age), they were never again the threat to the nation that they had been. After David's reign the only serious conflict with the Philistines recorded in 1 and 2 Kings is in the days of Hezekiah (2 Kings 18:8).

9. See Map 5-1 in Currid, *Atlas*, p. 120.

10. See Deuteronomy 2:9.

11. See John Woodhouse, *1 Samuel: Looking for a Leader*, Preaching the Word (Wheaton, IL: Crossway, 2008), p. 429.

12. For example, Youngblood, describes the event as "David's atrocity" (Youngblood, *1 & 2 Samuel*, p. 402), and Gordon calls it "savage and arbitrary treatment" (Robert P. Gordon, *1 & 2 Samuel: A Commentary* [Exeter, UK: Paternoster, 1986], p. 242).

13. John Calvin, *Sermons on 2 Samuel Chapters 1—13*, trans. Douglas Kelly (Edinburgh: Banner of Truth, 1992), p. 406.

14. Moab continued to be a source of difficulty for the Israelites, including the introduction of pagan worship in the days of Solomon (1 Kings 11:1, 7, 33; also 2 Kings 1:1; 3:5, 7; 13:20; 24:2). At a later time Moab was a nation known for its wickedness (Amos 2:1–3; Zephaniah 2:8–11).

15. Elsewhere called "Aram-Zobah" (Psalm 60 title) and "the Syrians of Zobah" (10:6, 8). According to Genesis 10:22, 23 Arameans (usually translated in English versions as "Syrians") were descendants of Shem. (Genesis 22:21 indicates that a different Aram was descended from Abraham's brother, Nahor.) "Aram" seems to be a term applied to a broad geographical area north and northeast of Israel covering Syria, Lebanon, and upper Mesopotamia. Hence Jacob (or Abraham) was remembered as "a wandering Aramean" (Deuteronomy 26:5).

16. Zobah seems to have occupied territory between Hamath to its north and Damascus to its south. See Map 5-1 in Currid, *Atlas*, p. 120. Precise details of the location are not known. It was at the time apparently the most powerful nation north and east of Israel. So Gordon, *1& 2 Samuel*, p. 243; Robert Alter, *The David Story: A Translation with Commentary of 1 and 2 Samuel* (New York and London: W. W. Norton & Company, 1999), p. 237.

17. The first mention of Zobah is 1 Samuel 14:47, which indicates that "the kings of Zobah" were enemies of Saul.

18. See John Bright, *A History of Israel*, Third Edition (London: SCM, 1980), p. 202, note 38. Contra Keil and Delitzsch, *Samuel*, p. 359.

19. The probable history of conflict between Aram-Zobah and King David is conveniently outlined in J. A. Lund, "Aram, Damascus and Syria," in Bill T. Arnold and H. G. M. Williamson, *Dictionary of the Old Testament: Historical Books* (Downers Grove, IL and Leicester, UK: InterVarsity Press and Inter-Varsity Press, 2005), pp. 41, 42.

20. Literally "his hand." The Hebrew may refer to a monument, as it does in 1 Samuel 15:12; 2 Samuel 18:18. So McCarter, *II Samuel*, pp. 247, 248; Alter, *David*, p. 237; also NRSV, REB, and NIV.

21. "Euphrates" is an interpretive addition. The Hebrew has simply "the river" (also in 10:16). While some have argued that another river is intended, most agree

that it is the Euphrates. For a discussion of the evidence see Driver, *Notes*, p. 281; McCarter, *II Samuel*, pp. 272, 273.

22. So McCarter, *II Samuel*, p. 247, although with a different understanding of the events themselves (see next note).

23. The text is not clear whether it was Hadadezer or David who was going to "restore his power at the river Euphrates." It is possible that it was David: "Surely it was David, in the flush of recent victories, who was marching to the Euphrates to leave a monument to himself." McCarter, *II Samuel*, p. 247. However, "restore" is then a strange word to use. Most commentators regard the subject here as Hadadezer. So Keil and Delitzsch, *Samuel*, p. 358; Driver, *Notes*, p. 281; Alter, *David*, p. 237; Gordon, *1 & 2 Samuel*, p. 243; also HSCB and REB.

24. Note that the Hebrew word for "thousand" can also refer to a military unit of unspecified size. McCarter maintains it could be as small as a dozen. McCarter, *II Samuel*, p. 249.

25. There is a later reference to Hadadezer in 1 Kings 11:23–25, from which we learn that David's victory here ("the killing by David" in 1 Kings 11:24 [literally, "David's killing them," which seems to be a reference to David's defeat of Hadadezer in 8:3–8]) led to someone named Rezon deserting from Hadadezer's army. Rezon gathered a band of followers who made him (or themselves [in the Hebrew the end of 1 Kings 11:24 is literally "they reigned in Damascus"]) king(s) in Damascus. From there "he was an adversary of Israel all the days of Solomon" (1 Kings 11:25).

26. Cf. J. Robert Vannoy, *1—2 Samuel*, Cornerstone Biblical Commentary, 4a (Wheaton, IL: Tyndale House, 2009), p. 313, who suggests that this "might represent the first step in a process that culminated in David's sin of counting the fighting men of Israel (ch 24) and led to even more serious trouble among succeeding kings."

27. An alternative translation to "garrisons" is "governors." There is a similar ambiguity in 1 Samuel 10:5; 13:4, 5. The point is the same: David was in control of Damascus.

Chapter Nineteen: A Kingdom of Justice and Righteousness

1. While our interest is in the text of Scripture in the form in which it has come to us, Robert Good has argued that 2 Samuel 8 may have been based on an inscription contemporary with the reign of David. Robert M. Good, "2 Samuel 8," *Tyndale Bulletin* 51/1 (2001): 129–138.

2. The Hebrew phrase translated in the ESV here as "justice and equity" is usually rendered "justice and righteousness" (see Genesis 18:19; 1 Kings 10:9; 2 Chronicles 9:8; Job 37:23; Psalm 33:5; 72:1; 99:4; 103:6; 106:3; Proverbs 8:20; 21:3; Isaiah 1:27; 5:7, 16; 9:7; 28:17; 32:16; 33:5; 56:1; 59:9, 14; Jeremiah 4:2; 9:24; 22:3, 15; 23:5; 33:15; Ezekiel 45:9; Amos 5:7, 24; 6:12).

3. The corresponding text in 1 Chronicles 18:8 suggests that "Betah" may be a variation of "Tibhath" (precise location unknown). Some think the location of Berothai may be modern Bereitan, about thirty miles north-northwest of Damascus (Robert P. Gordon, *1 & 2 Samuel: A Commentary* [Exeter, UK: Paternoster, 1986], p. 244; P. Kyle McCarter Jr., *II Samuel: A New Translation with Introduction, Notes & Commentary*, The Anchor Bible, vol. 9 [Garden City, NY: Doubleday, 1984], p. 250). Other possible locations for Betah and Berothai are indicated on Map 5-1

in John D. Currid and David P. Barrett, *Crossway ESV Bible Atlas* (Wheaton, IL: Crossway, 2010), p. 120.

4. Thus Brueggemann (mistakenly in my view) calls this "David's rapacious way" and compares it with his "taking" in 11:4. Walter Brueggemann, *David's Truth: In Israel's Imagination & Memory* (Philadelphia: Fortress, 1985), p. 81.

5. Located on the east bank of the Orontes River. See Map 5-1 in Currid, *Atlas*, p. 120.

6. Frequently Hamath is mentioned in a somewhat obscure phrase, "Lebo-hamath" (ESV; NRSV). The phrase may mean "[to] the entrance of Hamath" (HCSB), and various proposals have been made as to what that "entrance" might be.

7. There seems to be a story behind the name of Toi's son. Here he is called Joram, which is a Hebrew name meaning "The LORD is exalted." His original name is given in 1 Chronicles 18:10 as Hadoram ("Hadad is exalted"). We may reasonably presume that the change of name was made by David and, if accepted, would constitute an acknowledgment of the Lord by Toi and his son. Cf. Gordon, *1& 2 Samuel*, pp. 244, 245; Ronald F. Youngblood, *1 & 2 Samuel*, in Tremper Longman III and David E. Garland, eds., *The Expositor's Bible Commentary*, Revised Edition, vol. 3 (Grand Rapids, MI: Zondervan, 2009), p. 405.

8. The phrase translated "to ask about his health" may refer to a conventional greeting, signifying goodwill, but it may imply more. The Hebrew could be rendered quite literally, "to ask for [terms of] peace." So Dale Ralph Davis, *Expositions of the Book of 2 Samuel: Out of Every Adversity* (Geanies House, Fearn, UK: Christian Focus, 1999), p. 93.

9. The Hebrew has "Aram" and, given the prominence of "Aram" in the preceding narrative, emendation to (the very similar word in Hebrew) "Edom" is unnecessary. So J. P. Fokkelman, *Narrative Art and Poetry in the Books of Samuel: a full interpretation based on stylistic and structural analyses, Volume 3: Throne and City (II Sam. 2–8 & 21–24)* (The Netherlands: Van Gorcum, Assen, 1990), pp. 255, note 96, 385. Contra McCarter, *II Samuel*, p. 245; Gordon, *1& 2 Samuel*, p. 245; Robert Alter, *The David Story: A Translation with Commentary of 1 and 2 Samuel* (New York and London: W. W. Norton & Company, 1999), p. 238.

10. The list of defeated enemies who contributed to the wealth "dedicated to the LORD" goes beyond the victories already mentioned. In particular the Ammonites are noted. The account of their defeat will be given in 2 Samuel 10—12. David's defeat of the Amalekites (at least some of them) was recounted in 1 Samuel 30 and referred to in 2 Samuel 1:1.

11. So Walter Brueggemann, *First and Second Samuel*, Interpretation: A Bible Commentary for Teaching and Preaching (Louisville: John Knox Press, 1990), p. 262.

12. It is even less likely in the Hebrew, which reads simply, "And David made a name," without the additional words "for himself."

13. A few Hebrew manuscripts have "Edom," and this is accepted by C. F. Keil and F. Delitzsch, *Biblical Commentary on the Books of Samuel* (Grand Rapids, MI: Eerdmans, 1950), p. 363; A. A. Anderson, *2 Samuel*, Word Biblical Commentary 11 (Dallas: Word, 1989), p. 130; Gordon, *1& 2 Samuel*, p. 245; Fokkelman, *Throne*, p. 384; Alter, *David*, p. 238; Davis, *2 Samuel*, p. 91, note 1. The superscription to Psalm 60 provides some support for the idea that the Valley of Salt was in Edom. Further support for the emendation may be found in 1 Chronicles 18:12.

14. See Map 5-1 in Currid, *Atlas*, p. 120.

15. For a brief outline of Edom's hostilities, see John Woodhouse, *1 Samuel: Looking for a Leader*, Preaching the Word (Wheaton, IL: Crossway, 2008), p. 412.

16. The Hebrew word for "all" appears nine times: verses 4 ("*all* the chariot horses"), 6 ("*wherever* he went"), 9 ("the *whole* army of Hadadezer"), 11 ("*all* the nations"), 14 ("*all* Edom," "*all* the Edomites," and "*wherever* he went"), and 15 ("*all* Israel" and "*all* his people").

17. The ESV's "equity" unnecessarily narrows the sense of the phrase.

18. The only other place where the two words in question appear in the same verse prior to 8:15 is Deuteronomy 33:21. (By "prior to" I am referring to the canonical order of the text, not to any supposed time of writing.)

19. In this paragraph I have surveyed the occurrences of the precise Hebrew phrase usually rendered "justice and righteousness" (or close variations of it). A further group of texts that reflect the same idea are poetic texts where the two words are used in parallel (Psalm 36:6; 72:1; 106:3; Proverbs 8:20; 16:8; Isaiah 1:27; 5:7, 16; 28:17).

20. The use of the Hebrew term *mishpat* in these contexts is discussed in Woodhouse, *1 Samuel*, pp. 55, 148, 149, 187, 188, 505, 560, note 10.

21. There are many studies of the concept of "righteousness" in the Bible, and the subject is controversial in several respects. For our purposes here I have found two studies useful: E. R. Achtemeier, "Righteousness in the OT," in George Arthur Buttrick, ed., *The Interpreter's Dictionary of the Bible*, vol. 4 (Nashville and New York: Abingdon Press, 1962), pp. 80–85 (emphasizing that "righteousness" is a relational concept); and H. Ringgren and B. Johnson, "*tsadaq*," in G. Johannes Botterweck, Helmer Ringgren, and Heinz-Josef Fabry, eds., *Theological Dictionary of the Old Testament*, vol. 12 (Grand Rapids, MI: Eerdmans, 2003), pp. 239–264 (a comprehensive survey of the uses of the relevant vocabulary in the Old Testament).

22. David's refusal to harm Saul was "righteous" (1 Samuel 24:18; 26:23).

23. This ordered state of affairs was undone when God's judgment fell on this people (Isaiah 3:1—5).

24. The Hebrew word suggests "causing remembrance."

25. So McCarter, *II Samuel*, p. 255.

26. So S. R. Driver, *Notes on the Hebrew Text and the Topography of the Book of Samuel with an Introduction on Hebrew Palaeography and Facsimiles of Inscriptions and Maps*, 2nd edition (Oxford: Clarendon, 1913), p. 283; Keil and Delitzsch, *Samuel*, p. 365.

27. This means that Zadok's father, Ahitub, was a different person from the grandson of Eli mentioned in 1 Samuel 14:3; 22:9, 11, 12, 20. A careful reader would assume this even without the information provided by 1 Chronicles. After Saul's slaughter of the priests at Nob, only Abiathar survived from the family of Eli (1 Samuel 22:20). If Zadok had been a son of Eli's grandson, Ahitub, then he would have been a brother of the Ahimelech who died at Nob and would have died there also.

28. Despite the exact replication of the information in 8:17 in 1 Chronicles 18:16, many scholars consider the text of the former to be mistaken (the mistake being reproduced in the later text). So Alter, *David*, p. 239. The Biblical material is quite straightforward and consistent once allowance is made for the obvious phenom-

enon of personal names applying to more than one person. So Keil and Delitzsch, *Samuel*, pp. 366, 367; Youngblood, *1 & 2 Samuel*, pp. 410, 411. Some who discount this explanation have argued that since Abiathar's father's name was Ahimelech and his grandfather was Ahitub (1 Samuel 22:20), 8:17 should read, "Zadok and Abiathar, son of Ahimelech, son of Ahitub, were priests." See, for example, Driver, *Notes*, p. 283; McCarter, *II Samuel*, p. 251; J. Robert Vannoy, *1–2 Samuel*, Cornerstone Biblical Commentary, 4a (Wheaton, IL: Tyndale House, 2009), p. 314. This emendation (leaving Zadok without any genealogy here) has been part of various speculations about Zadok's origins. Views are conveniently surveyed by D. W. Rooke, "Zadok, Zadokites," in Bill T. Arnold and H. G. M. Williamson, *Dictionary of the Old Testament: Historical Books* (Downers Grove, IL and Leicester, UK: InterVarsity Press and Inter-Varsity Press, 2005), pp. 1012–1016. Rooke's own conclusions, however, are unnecessarily skeptical.

29. On this promise and the ways in which it has been fulfilled, see Woodhouse, *1 Samuel*, pp. 71, 72.

30. See Roland de Vaux, *Ancient Israel: Its Life and Institutions*, trans. John McHugh (London: Darton, Longman & Todd, 1973), p. 131.

31. Strangely, in the books of Samuel the only leader to have an acceptable son was Saul! Jonathan was outstanding and perhaps the least flawed character in the whole narrative.

32. The Hebrew syntax of the clause is a little unusual. Fokkelman suggests that it may mean that the sons had *become* priests. Fokkelman, *Throne*, p. 263, note 107. Cf. McCarter, *II Samuel*, p. 254.

33. The troubling tone will be stronger if we understand that only a member of the tribe of Levi, more particularly the line of Aaron, may be a "priest" (see Numbers 3:3, 10; 10:8). On this understanding some think that David's sons could not have been priests. They propose either: (a) an emendation of the text at this point (Gordon J. Wenham, "Were David's Sons Priests?," *Zeitschrift für die alttestamentliche Wissenschaft* 87[1975]: 79–82 has argued that "priests" was originally a word meaning "administrators (of royal estates)"); or (b) another meaning for the Hebrew word (Calvin thought that the expression means that "David took pains to have [his sons] instructed and taught the requirements of the Law"; John Calvin, *Sermons on 2 Samuel Chapters 1–13*, trans. Douglas Kelly [Edinburgh: Banner of Truth, 1992], p. 246. Keil and Delitzsch suggest that the word means "the king's confidential advisers." Keil and Delitzsch, *Samuel*, p. 369).

These suggestions have their own problems: (a) McCarter argues reasonably that the controversial reading is unlikely to have arisen mistakenly from a less controversial one. McCarter, *II Samuel*, p. 255. (b) Driver just as persuasively insists that the well-known Hebrew word must mean "priests" here as it does everywhere else. Driver, *Notes*, p. 284, 285.

However, the restriction of the priesthood to the descendants of Aaron (from which the difficulties of this text arise) may have applied only to the particular priestly functions associated with the tabernacle. In David's kingdom Zadok and Ahimelech served as priests in this sense (v. 17). But there may have been other people called "priests" who were not priests in the strictest sense (that is, with the prescribed duties in the tabernacle). Similarly Youngblood, *1 & 2 Samuel*, p. 412. In particular there may have been people who served the king in some "priest" capacity but who were not "priests" in the stricter sense (consider Ira the Jairite [therefore not a Levite] who was "David's priest" in 20:26 and Zabud son of Nathan [probably not a Levite] who was "priest and king's friend" in 1 Kings 4:5). Similarly Driver, *Notes*, p. 285; McCarter, *I Samuel*, pp. 256, 257; cf. Alter, *David*, p. 239. The fact that the designation of David's sons as "priests" in verse 18b is separated in the list from Zadok and Ahimelech in verse 17 is consistent with this suggestion. So Fokkelman, *Throne*, p. 263. Carl Armerding has argued that there was a royal priesthood in Israel, ultimately based on the king-priest Melchizedek (Genesis 14:18). In his view David's sons participated in this but not in the Aaronic priesthood. C. E. Armerding, "Were David's Sons Really Priests?" in G. Hawthorne, ed., *Current Issues in Biblical and Patristic Interpretation: Studies in Honor of Merrill C. Tenney Presented by his Former Students* (Grand Rapids: Eerdmans, 1975), pp. 75–86. Armerding's case is attractive but in my opinion not persuasive (so also Vannoy, *1—2 Samuel*, p. 317, note 4).

34. Perhaps this is "a stick of dynamite placed by the narrator under the perfection. It is conceivable that we ought to assimilate v. 18b as the first hint of David's approaching *hubris*." Fokkelman, *Throne*, p. 262. (In my view it would be the *second* hint!)

Chapter Twenty: The Kindness of the King

1. Many scholarly discussions regard 2 Samuel 9 as the beginning of a new section of the narrative. So, for example, P. Kyle McCarter Jr., *II Samuel: A New Translation with Introduction, Notes & Commentary*, The Anchor Bible, vol. 9 (Garden City, NY: Doubleday, 1984), pp. 263–265; Ronald F. Youngblood, *1 & 2 Samuel*, in Tremper Longman III and David E. Garland, eds., *The Expositor's Bible Commentary*, Revised Edition, vol. 3 (Grand Rapids, MI: Zondervan, 2009), p. 415. This view is influenced by a number of factors, particularly the theory of Leonard Rost (originally published in 1926; English translation: Leonhard Rost, *The Succession to the Throne of David*, Historical Texts and Interpreters in Biblical Scholarship [Sheffield, UK: The Almond Press, 1982]) that 2 Samuel 9—20 plus 1 Kings 1, 2 originally constituted a "Succession Narrative." Subsequent discussion developing, modifying, or challenging Rost's proposal is voluminous. Among the many works, note R. N. Whybray, *The Succession Narrative: A Study of II Sam. 9—20 and I Kings 1 and 2*, Studies in Biblical Theology, Second Series 9 (London: SCM, 1968), accepting the basic literary proposal, but arguing for "wisdom" influence on the so-called "Succession Narrative"; James W. Flanagan, "Court History or Succession Document? A Study of 2 Samuel 9–20 and 1 Kings 1–2," *Journal of Biblical Literature* 91(1972): 172–191, arguing that the "History of David's Court" (as he called it) was not originally a "succession" document; Gillian Keys, *The Wages of Sin: A Reappraisal of the 'Succession Narrative,'* Journal for the Study of the Old Testament Supplement Series 221 (Sheffield, UK: Sheffield Academic Press, 1996), challenging the idea of "succession" as the main theme of the so-called "Succession Narrative"; Serge Frolov, "Succession Narrative: A 'Document' or a Phantom?" *Journal of Biblical Literature* 121/1 (2002): 81–104, arguing against the idea of a distinct document within the present text.

For the purposes of this exposition I have given precedence to the relationship of 2 Samuel 9 to what *precedes* it in the text before us for the following reasons (similarly C. F. Keil and F. Delitzsch, *Biblical Commentary on the Books of Samuel* [Grand Rapids, MI: Eerdmans, 1950], p. 370; Robert Alter, *The David Story: A Translation with Commentary of 1 and 2 Samuel* [New York and London: W. W. Norton & Company, 1999], p. 240):

(1) The opening words ("And David said") do not suggest that a new section begins here. It is naturally understood as a continuation of the story from 7:29, which has been briefly interrupted by the summary description of David's reign in chapter 8.

(2) Second Samuel 9 provides a wonderful particular example of David doing "justice and righteousness for all the people," and thus makes a fine sequel to 2 Samuel 8.

(3) The connections between 2 Samuel 9 and what has gone before (particularly 1 Samuel 20; 2 Samuel 2:6; 4:1–12) are at least as important as links with what follows (particularly 16:1–4; 19:25–31).

(4) The generally positive estimation of David's conduct that we have seen since 2 Samuel 1 (or rather since 1 Samuel 16) continues in 2 Samuel 9 and, as we will see, into chapter 10. Only in 2 Samuel 11 is there a major change to this perspective.

2. Chronological precision is not possible or needed. We know that Mephibosheth was five years old when Saul and Jonathan died at the battle of Gilboa (4:4). David became king over Judah shortly after that (for the sake of argument, let us suppose six months later, 2:1–4). Then after another seven and a half years he became king over all Israel (5:5). At that time (on this reasoning) Mephibosheth was thirteen years old. We will shortly learn that at the time of the events recounted in 2 Samuel 9 Mephibosheth had a young son (9:12 seems to report this as a contemporary state of affairs). If Mephibosheth was about twenty years old at this time, then David had been king of Israel for about seven years. It could easily have been longer, but not a great deal shorter. Some reasonably suggest that 2 Samuel 9 is set in about the middle of David's reign. So Keil and Delitzsch, *Samuel*, p. 370; J. Robert Vannoy, *1—2 Samuel*, Cornerstone Biblical Commentary, 4a (Wheaton, IL: Tyndale House, 2009), p. 319.

3. Calvin makes much of the delay in David's acting on his promise to Jonathan. "But the fact that he waited so long and did not carry out the oath made with Jonathan shows that he forgot it, as though prosperity had intoxicated him." John Calvin, *Sermons on 2 Samuel Chapters 1—13*, trans. Douglas Kelly (Edinburgh: Banner of Truth, 1992), p. 430; similarly Vannoy, *1—2 Samuel*, p. 319. In my opinion it is preferable to recognize that we simply do not know whether or not there were justifiable reasons for the delay before the question of 9:1 was asked. Certainly the Bible writer does not think that the matter is worth explicit comment. He does not even give us enough information to know for sure how long the delay was.

4. Some argue that the question makes more sense after the events of 21:1–14 and therefore conclude that these events occurred chronologically before those of 2 Samuel 9. So McCarter, *II Samuel*, pp. 260, 263. In the text as we have it this is not

possible because 21:7 indicates that Mephibosheth was known to David at that time. So Vannoy, *1—2 Samuel*, p. 319.

5. Francis I. Andersen, "Yahweh, the Kind and Sensitive God," in Peter T. O'Brien and David G. Peterson, eds., *God Who Is Rich in Mercy: Essays presented to Dr. D. B. Knox* (Homebush West, NSW, Australia: Lancer Books, 1986), p. 81. I am persuaded by the argument of Andersen that the Hebrew *khesed* does not mean (as is often suggested) "loyalty," the outworking of the obligations involved in a preexisting relationship. So, for example, Walter Brueggemann, *First and Second Samuel*, Interpretation: A Bible Commentary for Teaching and Preaching (Louisville: John Knox Press, 1990), p. 267; Alter, *David*, p. 240; Dale Ralph Davis, *Expositions of the Book of 2 Samuel: Out of Every Adversity* (Geanies House, Fearn, UK: Christian Focus, 1999), p. 100. Rather *khesed* is mercy, kindness shown toward one in need by one with the power to help, but not necessarily with any obligation to help. See John Woodhouse, *1 Samuel: Looking for a Leader*, Preaching the Word (Wheaton, IL: Crossway, 2008), p. 611, note 14.

6. According to Saul, the Kenites showed this surprising "kindness" to the people of Israel when they came out of Egypt (1 Samuel 15:6). This was also the word Abner used to describe his dealings with Ish-bosheth prior to their falling out (esv, "steadfast love," 3:8).

7. In Hebrew it is a one-word reply—"Your-servant," possibly reflecting the formality of the conversation.

8. I have given more weight to the expression "the kindness of God" than is generally recognized by understanding these words in the light of 2:6 (which also seems to me to be more significant than often noticed). For example, Fokkelman interprets the expression as meaning simply kindness "which is pleasing to God and for which he sets the standard." J. P. Fokkelman, *Narrative Art and Poetry in the Books of Samuel: a full interpretation based on stylistic and structural analyses, Volume 1: King David (II Sam. 9—20 & I Kings 1—2)* (The Netherlands: Van Gorcum, Assen, 1981), p. 26. Cf. "love and kindness shown in God, and for God's sake (Luke vi. 36)" (Keil and Delitzsch, *Samuel*, p. 370); "kindness like that of God" (Youngblood, *1 & 2 Samuel*, p. 417). Alter regards "of God" merely as an intensifier. Alter, *David*, p. 240.

9. Precisely the same phrase is used in 4:4 and 9:3.

10. So Brueggemann, *First and Second Samuel*, p. 267; Alter, *David*, p. 241. The word translated "crippled" is related to a verb frequently (especially in the preceding chapter) used in this narrative for striking down (that is, killing) enemies (see, for example, 1:1, 15; 2:23, 31; 3:27; 4:6; 5:8, 25; 8:1, 2, 3, 5, 9, 10, 13). The son of Jonathan was already "struck down" (metaphorically) in his feet.

11. So S. R. Driver, *Notes on the Hebrew Text and the Topography of the Book of Samuel with an Introduction on Hebrew Palaeography and Facsimiles of Inscriptions and Maps*, 2nd edition (Oxford: Clarendon, 1913), p. 286. A location further north, beyond Jabesh-Gilead, is suggested on Map R-15 in John D. Currid and David P. Barrett, *Crossway ESV Bible Atlas* (Wheaton, IL: Crossway, 2010), p. 290.

12. Literally, "Behold, your-servant." This two-word response was a slight expansion on Ziba's one-word reply in verse 2. "Behold" draws attention to and adds emphasis to Mephibosheth's submission to David expressed in the one word (in Hebrew), "your-servant."

13. Various ways of describing the structure of 2 Samuel 9 (including mine) have verse 7 at the center or turning point of the chapter. See Davis, *2 Samuel*, p. 103; Youngblood, *1 & 2 Samuel*, p. 415.

14. The expression is all the more wonderful in its New Testament setting. See it, for example, in Matthew 28:5, 10; Luke 1:13, 30; 2:10; Revelation 1:17.

15. First Samuel 20, which, as we have seen, provides important background for 2 Samuel 9, is the only other place in the books of Samuel where a "table" is mentioned. Furthermore it is the king's table (Saul's this time), and the matter of eating at the king's table is important to that story. David's failure to eat at Saul's table signified and inflamed the hostility between them. Jonathan's kindness saved David. Now the "kindness" David had then promised to show to Jonathan's house results in Mephibosheth's eating at David's table, a sign and expression of the favor of the king. For further discussion of the links between 1 Samuel 20 and 2 Samuel 9 see Fokkelman, *David*, pp. 29, 30. The supposition that David brought Mephibosheth into his household in order to keep an eye on this potential rival for the throne (so Hans Wilhelm Hertzberg, *I & II Samuel: A Commentary*, Old Testament Library [London: SCM Press, 1964], pp. 300, 301; McCarter, *II Samuel*, p. 265; John Mauchline, *1 and 2 Samuel*, New Century Bible [London: Oliphants, 1971], p. 241) is not suggested by the text and is contrary to its tone.

16. "Grandson" is a correct interpretation (here and twice in the next verse), although the Hebrew has simply "son." The Hebrew thus links Mephibosheth directly to Saul, adding to the astonishing quality of David's kindness.

17. Contra Youngblood, *1 & 2 Samuel*, p. 418.

18. Similarly, though for different reasons, Fokkelman, *David*, p. 28.

19. There is a textual difficulty with "David's table." The ESV follows the Septuagint, as do many commentators including Keil and Delitzsch, *Samuel*, p. 371; McCarter, *II Samuel*, p. 259; Alter, *David*, p. 242. The Hebrew text has "my table," suggesting rather awkwardly that the words were spoken by David. Hence RV: "As for Mephibosheth, *said the king*, he shall eat at my table, as one of the king's sons." For alternative (but in my opinion less probable) interpretations of the Hebrew text, see A. Graeme Auld, *I & II Samuel: A Commentary*, Old Testament Library (Louisville: Westminster John Knox Press, 2011), p. 237. Fokkelman "solves" the problem by deleting the line on the grounds of the symmetry he is then able to find in the text. Fokkelman, *David*, p. 27.

20. See 1 Chronicles 8:34–40 and 9:40–44 for the many descendants of Saul from Mephibosheth's (there called Merib-baal) son Mica (Micah).

Chapter Twenty-One: Those Who Despise the Kindness of the King

1. So REB, HCSB, NIV has "show contempt for."

2. Note the phrase "After this" (or "In the course of time," NIV) that opens 2 Samuel 10 (cf. 2:1; 8:1; 13:1 [ESV "Now"]; 15:1; 21:18), "a phrase that always inaugurates a new section." Ronald F. Youngblood, *1 & 2 Samuel*, in Tremper Longman III and David E. Garland, eds., *The Expositor's Bible Commentary*, Revised Edition, vol. 3 (Grand Rapids, MI: Zondervan, 2009), p. 419, where other sound reasons for regarding 2 Samuel 10—12 as a distinct literary unit are noted. However, readers may notice that in this exposition I have chosen to make a major division at the end of 2 Samuel 10 rather than the more obvious place from a literary point of

view, at the beginning of chapter 10. This is because I have given more weight to the continuity of subject matter (the kindness of King David) than to literary patterns (or even, on this occasion, plot). I have no objection to the alternative way of dividing the material, but I want to make the point that this complex text has more than one line running through it. Literary structural features do not control everything.

3. This is generally agreed among the commentaries. Keil and Delitzsch add that the subjugation of Moab (8:2) "had certainly taken place a short time before," which probably had increased the national hatred and enmity of the chiefs of the Ammonites toward David and Israel. C. F. Keil and F. Delitzsch, *Biblical Commentary on the Books of Samuel* (Grand Rapids, MI: Eerdmans, 1950), p. 374. McCarter's argument that this episode (2 Samuel 10) occurred after Absalom's rebellion (2 Samuel 15—18) is not convincing and raises more problems than it solves. P. Kyle McCarter Jr., *II Samuel: A New Translation with Introduction, Notes & Commentary*, The Anchor Bible, vol. 9 (Garden City, NY: Doubleday, 1984), p. 270.

4. For a brief summary of the role of the Ammonites in the Old Testament see John Woodhouse, *1 Samuel: Looking for a Leader*, Preaching the Word (Wheaton, IL: Crossway, 2008), p. 194.

5. "Deal loyally" in the ESV represents the same Hebrew expression that we have seen repeatedly in 2 Samuel 9, translated there as "show kindness" (9:1, 3, 7). It is therefore clear in the Hebrew text that 2 Samuel 10 continues this theme of the *kindness* of King David, now applied in an even more surprising way than in chapter 9.

6. The Hebrew preposition rendered here "as" could mean "because" (providing the *reason* for David's proposed treatment of Hanun) or "just as" (indicating that David's treatment of Hanun would be *of the same kind* as Nahash's treatment of him). See William L. Holladay, *A Concise Hebrew and Aramaic Lexicon of the Old Testament: based upon the lexical work of Ludwig Koehler and Walter Baumgartner* (Leiden: E. J. Brill, 1971), pp. 149, 150.

7. It does not follow, as some suppose, that Nahash had become a friendly power toward Israel or subservient to them, any more than the Philistines had. Contra J. P. Fokkelman, *Narrative Art and Poetry in the Books of Samuel: a full interpretation based on stylistic and structural analyses, Volume 1: King David (II Sam. 9—20 & I Kings 1—2)* (The Netherlands: Van Gorcum, Assen, 1981), p. 43; Walter Brueggemann, *First and Second Samuel*, Interpretation: A Bible Commentary for Teaching and Preaching (Louisville: John Knox Press, 1990), p. 269. Nor need we suppose that there had been any formal treaty arrangement between David and Nahash, contra Youngblood, *1 & 2 Samuel*, 422.

8. ". . . our own good intentions will often be frustrated, and yet God will not fail to approve what we tried to do . . . when we have done our duty, let us not be too clever in figuring out what shall come of it. Let us take refuge in God, who knows exactly how to work it all out." John Calvin, *Sermons on 2 Samuel Chapters 1—13*, trans. Douglas Kelly (Edinburgh: Banner of Truth, 1992), pp. 448, 449.

9. See Map 5-11 in John D. Currid and David P. Barrett, *Crossway ESV Bible Atlas* (Wheaton, IL: Crossway, 2010), p. 128.

10. The same Hebrew word is variously rendered in the ESV: "commander(s)" in 2:8; 10:16, 18; 18:1, 5; 19:6, 13; 23:19; 24:2; 24:4; "prince" in 3:38; "captains" in 4:2. See also Woodhouse, *1 Samuel*, p. 626, note 15.

11. Note Calvin's wise words: "Now here we see, above all, what distrust is. That is why it is not good for us to be consumed by a distrustful spirit—like many people who, thinking they are wise, consider everything doubtful and accept nothing without suspicion. We see some who are so wicked that they actually cultivate this distrustful attitude out of ambition and vanity: 'I must distrust everything and know how to disguise my feelings'. What is the outcome? Their attitude causes wars and quarrels. Well, when we are consumed by this sort of distrust, it is certain that we will start fires to which there will be neither end nor measure, and we will not be able to put them out once they have been started. . . . Hence, let us learn not to be influenced by our own malice to put a bad interpretation on what could be taken as good, and if something is done which we could doubt, still let us not do so." Calvin, *Sermons*, pp. 451, 452.

12. See Map 5-11 in Currid, *Atlas*, p. 128.

13. See Map 4-13 in Currid, *Atlas*, p. 107. In Joshua 13:25 "Aroer, which is east of Rabbah" should be translated "Aroer, near Rabbah" (NIV). The precise location of this Aroer is unknown, but it was probably west of Rabbah, marking the eastern border of Gad's territory, thus excluding Rabbah.

14. Interestingly the Hebrew word for "beard" is a cognate of the word for "old" or "elder," perhaps suggesting that the beard was associated with the dignity of age and maturity in the community.

15. Keil and Delitzsch, *Samuel*, p. 375, note 1.

16. So S. R. Driver, *Notes on the Hebrew Text and the Topography of the Book of Samuel with an Introduction on Hebrew Palaeography and Facsimiles of Inscriptions and Maps*, 2nd edition (Oxford: Clarendon, 1913), p. 287; Alter, *David*, p. 245.

17. So Keil and Delitzsch, *Samuel*, p. 374.

18. Although McCarter perhaps sees too much: "Removal of the beard symbolically deprives a man of his masculinity. Cutting off the skirt may be palliative for castration, and, in any case, it bares the testicles, and thus—by the same kind of transference that led Oedipus to gouge out his eyes after discovering that he had been sleeping with his mother—it exposes the 'eyes' of the secret spies." McCarter, *II Samuel*, pp. 270, 271.

19. So, explicitly, NIV.

20. The Hebrew words for "honoring" and "ashamed" in 10:3, 5 are opposites of each other as illustrated by Psalm 4:2. What being put to shame could mean is elaborated in a number of the Psalms (see Psalm 35:4–8, 26; 40:14; 70:2; 71:13; 109:28, 29).

21. This is the only reference to Jericho in the books of Samuel. The city is famous for being the starting point for the conquest of the land under Joshua (Joshua 2; 6).

22. Also Genesis 34:30; Exodus 5:21.

23. ". . . they certainly thought that they would never be able to obtain pardon from David. So it is with all the wicked whom God clearly forces . . . to feel their evil. Yet he does not give them the grace of arriving at the remedy." Calvin, *Sermons*, p. 455.

24. Throughout this chapter (as in 2 Samuel 8) "Syrians" in the ESV represents "Aram" in the Hebrew, a term that seems to apply to a broad geographical area north and northeast of Israel covering Syria, Lebanon, and upper Mesopotamia. The reference here is made more specific with a qualifying term "Aram *of Beth-rehob*," "Aram *of Zobah*." Cf. 8:6.

25. The precise location of Rehob is unknown. See Map 5-11 in Currid, *Atlas*, p. 128. Since Hadadezer, king of Zobar, was called "the son of Rehob" (8:3, 12), he may have come from this city.

26. See Map 5-11 in Currid, *Atlas*, p. 128.

27. As we have noted before, the Hebrew word for "thousand" is ambiguous because it may also mean a military unit of unspecified size. See, for example, 6:1. Contra Youngblood who asserts that it is "virtually certain that the word [*'elep*] is intended in its ordinary sense of 'thousand' throughout this chapter." Youngblood, *1 & 2 Samuel*, p. 424.

28. See Deuteronomy 3:14; Joshua 13:11, 13; also Map 5-11 in Currid, *Atlas*, p. 128.

29. See Judges 11:3, 5; also Map 5-11 in Currid, *Atlas*, p. 128.

30. The term is sometimes translated "heroes" (as in Jeremiah 48:14). For a full survey of the term and its use, see H. Kosmala, "*gabhar*," in G. Johannes Botterweck and Helmer Ringgren, eds., *Theological Dictionary of the Old Testament*, vol. 2 (Grand Rapids, MI: Eerdmans, 1975), pp. 367–382, particularly pp. 373–377.

31. Contra Robert Alter, *The David Story: A Translation with Commentary of 1 and 2 Samuel* (New York and London: W. W. Norton & Company, 1999), p. 246.

32. In Hebrew the expression "came out and drew up in battle array" is an exact echo of "come out to draw up for battle" in 1 Samuel 17:8.

33. See 1 Chronicles 19:7 and Map 5-11 in Currid, *Atlas*, p. 128.

34. The last time we heard of Abishai was in connection with the revenge killing of Abner by the two brothers Joab and Abishai (3:30). Those two were quite a team!

35. In Hebrew "you" in verses 11, 12 is singular, referring directly to Abishai. By implication the words apply to all those engaged in this action under Abishai's leadership.

36. The Hebrew words translated "help" in 10:11 usually mean more than that. See, for example, 1 Samuel 2:1 ("I rejoice in your *salvation*"); 1 Samuel 14:45 ("this great *salvation* in Israel"); 2 Samuel 3:18 ("I will *save* my people Israel"); 8:6, 14 ("the LORD *gave victory* to David").

37. Precisely the same Hebrew word is translated "save" in 10:19.

38. The Hebrew verb meaning "to be strong" appears twice in verse 11 with respect to the Ammonites and twice in verse 12 with respect to Abishai and Joab.

39. I prefer "the LORD will do." In this context Joab's words sound more like a statement of confident faith ("the LORD will do") than a hopeful wish ("may the LORD do").

40. Compare the words of Eli in 1 Samuel 3:18: "Let [the LORD] do what seems good to him," which similarly could be translated, quite literally, "He [the LORD] will do the good in his eyes." Also see 2 Samuel 15:26; Job 1:21; 2:10.

41. Indeed the next reference to God in the narrative will be at the end of chapter 11, where we will hear that something "was *evil* in the eyes of the LORD" (11:27b AT).

42. "We see, therefore, that Joab's uncertainty was not lack of faith, for we can certainly doubt, although we embrace the promises of God and hold them as absolutely certain and infallible. What we doubt are the things which are not clear to us. That is how he wants us to remain in suspense about many things and to leave it all to his secret counsel and his providence." Calvin, *Sermons*, p. 465.

43. So Keil and Delitzsch, *Samuel*, p. 379, with reference to the common understanding of 11:1 as a reference to "the spring of the year."

44. As in 8:3, the Hebrew is simply "the river," but this certainly refers to the Euphrates.

45. See Map 5-11 in Currid, *Atlas*, p. 128. The evidence is outlined in Henry O. Thompson, "Helam," in David Noel Freedman, ed., *The Anchor Bible Dictionary*, vol. 3 (New York: Doubleday, 1992), pp. 116, 117.

46. In 1 Chronicles 19:16, 18 he is called Shophach. His appearance in Biblical history is limited to the present episode.

47. It is improbable that the 700 charioteers and 40,000 horsemen "David killed" were all struck down by the king himself!

48. The opening words of verse 19 exactly echo verse 15: "And/But when . . . saw that they had been defeated by Israel . . . ," thus drawing attention to the different responses to similar circumstances.

Chapter Twenty-Two: The Disaster

1. I warmly commend the exposition of the story of David and Bathsheba by John Bright who argues profoundly against a merely moralistic application of this (or any other) Old Testament text. John Bright, *The Authority of the Old Testament* (London: SCM Press, 1967), pp. 226–233.

2. This background is "indispensable" according to J. P. Fokkelman, *Narrative Art and Poetry in the Books of Samuel: a full interpretation based on stylistic and structural analyses, Volume 1: King David (II Sam. 9—20 & I Kings 1—2)* (The Netherlands: Van Gorcum, Assen, 1981), p. 41. Contra Ackroyd, who rather surprisingly sees "no link" between the campaigns of 11:1 and 10:1–14. Peter R. Ackroyd, *The Second Book of Samuel*, Cambridge Bible Commentary (Cambridge: Cambridge University Press, 1977), p. 100.

3. So P. Kyle McCarter Jr., *II Samuel: A New Translation with Introduction, Notes & Commentary*, The Anchor Bible, vol. 9 (Garden City, NY: Doubleday, 1984), p. 285, who points out that the interpretation of "the return of the year" (1 Kings 20:22, 26; 2 Chronicles 36:10) as a reference to springtime (see Robert P. Gordon, *1 & 2 Samuel: A Commentary* [Exeter, UK: Paternoster, 1986], p. 252) is dubiously based on the present passage. See also Moshe Garsiel, "The Story of David and Bathsheba: A Different Approach," *The Catholic Biblical Quarterly* 55 (1993), pp. 249, 251.

4. The two words are very similar in the consonants of Hebrew: "messengers" has one additional silent consonant. The consonants of the standard Hebrew text suggest "messengers," but consistent with 1 Chronicles 20:1, a number of other Hebrew manuscripts, and most ancient translations, the vocalization suggests "kings." Most commentators regard "kings" as the correct reading. So, for example, S. R. Driver, *Notes on the Hebrew Text and the Topography of the Book of Samuel with an Introduction on Hebrew Palaeography and Facsimiles of Inscriptions and Maps*, 2nd edition (Oxford: Clarendon, 1913), p. 289; C. F. Keil and F. Delitzsch, *Biblical Commentary on the Books of Samuel* (Grand Rapids, MI: Eerdmans, 1950), p. 381; Gordon, *1 & 2 Samuel*, p. 252; Robert Alter, *The David Story: A Translation with Commentary of 1 and 2 Samuel* (New York and London: W. W. Norton & Company, 1999), p. 249; Ronald F. Youngblood, *1 & 2 Samuel*, in Tremper Longman III

and David E. Garland, eds., *The Expositor's Bible Commentary*, Revised Edition, vol. 3 (Grand Rapids, MI: Zondervan, 2009), p. 431; McCarter, *II Samuel*, p. 279. "Messengers" is regarded as "the true reading" by A. E. Cowley, *Gesenius' Hebrew Grammar as edited and enlarged by the late E. Kautzsch*, Second English Edition (Oxford: Clarendon Press, 1910), p. 81; likewise Fokkelman, *David*, pp. 50, 51. The textual uncertainty makes little difference to the assertion that the events of 2 Samuel 11 began about a year after the events of 2 Samuel 10, whether that was the time the *messengers* were sent out by David (10:2) or the Syrian *kings* went out (a month or so later?, 10:8). Polzin's description of this textual issue as "deliciously ambiguous" is more ingenious than persuasive. Robert Polzin, *David and the Deuteronomist: A Literary Study of the Deuteronomic History. Part Three, 2 Samuel*, Indiana Studies in Biblical Literature (Bloomington and Indianapolis: Indiana University Press, 1993), p. 109; cf. Alter, *David*, p. 249.

5. Admittedly the use of the definite article in the Hebrew here is not decisive. However, following a story of kings (and also messengers, although they are not designated by that word) going out (10:2, 8), it is natural to understand "*the* kings/ messengers" in 11:1 as a reference to the events just narrated. Indeed "the kings" had been mentioned in the previous verse (10:19; cf. "king" in 10:5, 6). I suspect that the chapter division has been a factor in obscuring this link between the episodes. For a discussion of the origin and significance of the chapter divisions in the Old Testament, see John Woodhouse, *1 Samuel: Looking for a Leader*, Preaching the Word (Wheaton, IL: Crossway, 2008), p. 572, note 3.

6. So McCarter translates: "When the time of year at which the kings had marched out came around again . . ." McCarter, *II Samuel*, p. 277. Similarly Fokkelman, *David*, p. 51. If this understanding is correct, it downplays the negative force often seen in the words, "But David remained at Jerusalem." The text is not referring to what kings in general were expected to be doing at this time of the year. Contra, for example, Gordon, *1 & 2 Samuel*, p. 252.

7. There is no obvious difference in the forces sent in 11:1 and 10:7 ("all the host of the mighty men"). The added emphasis now is that "all Israel" was represented by the army.

8. The verb "to send" occurs twelve times in 2 Samuel 11 (and eight times in 2 Samuel 10).

9. The Hebrew verb suggests much damage was done to the Ammonites. They "destroyed" them (NIV). Cf. 1 Samuel 6:5; 23:10; 26:9, 15; 2 Samuel 1:14; 20:20; 24:16.

10. There was not necessarily anything reprehensible in the fact that "David sent Joab" while remaining in Jerusalem himself. Cf. J. Robert Vannoy, *1—2 Samuel*, Cornerstone Biblical Commentary, 4a (Wheaton, IL: Tyndale House, 2009), pp. 331, 332; McCarter, *II Samuel*, p. 285. Those who see an implied criticism of David's remaining in Jerusalem while his troops were away fighting (as, for example, Alter, *David*, pp. 249, 250) have, in my opinion, misunderstood the beginning of verse 1 to be saying that kings were expected to go out to battle at this time of year and overlook the fact that David's remaining in Jerusalem during a campaign was not unusual. It was "a normal procedure" (Ackroyd, *Second Samuel*, p. 100). So Antony F. Campbell, S.J., *2 Samuel*, The Forms of the Old Testament Literature 8 (Grand Rapids, MI: Eerdmans, 2005), p. 114. Garsiel has supported this conclusion with historical arguments that (1) it is improbable that all local kings made a practice

of fighting in the springtime, and (2) it was probably not in fact standard practice for kings to participate personally in every battle (see already 10:7; also 21:17). Garsiel, "David and Bathsheba," pp. 250, 251.

11. "Late one afternoon" is literally "at the time of the evening." The phrase echoes "at the time of . . ." in verse 1b.

12. The same expression is used of Rebekah in Genesis 24:16, Queen Vashti in Esther 1:11, and Esther in Esther 2:7.

13. Not all agree. "Bathsheba is not to be regarded as free from blame. The very act of bathing in the uncovered court of a house in the heart of the city, into which it was possible for any one to look down from the roofs of the houses on higher ground, does not say much for her feminine modesty, even if this was not done with an ulterior purpose, as some commentators suppose." Keil and Delitzsch, *Samuel*, p. 383. "But she should have exercised discretion, so as not to be seen. For a chaste and upright woman will not show herself in such a way as to allure men, nor be like a net of the devil to 'start a fire'. Bathsheba, therefore, was immodest in that regard." John Calvin, *Sermons on 2 Samuel Chapters 1—13*, trans. Douglas Kelly (Edinburgh: Banner of Truth, 1992), p. 481. Similarly Hans Wilhelm Hertzberg, *I & II Samuel: A Commentary*, Old Testament Library (London: SCM Press, 1964), p. 309.

14. The word rendered "inquired" can mean "to seek," "to care about."

15. The negative question ("Is not this . . . ?") "is used, as it frequently is, in the sense of an affirmation, 'it is indeed so.'" Keil and Delitzsch, *Samuel*, p. 383. See Cowley, *Grammar*, p. 474.

16. So Youngblood, *1 & 2 Samuel*, p. 430. However, Gordon doubts that this was the case. Gordon, *1 & 2 Samuel*, p. 253. Likewise Ackroyd, *Second Samuel*, p. 101.

17. Although references to Ahithophel as David's counselor come later in the story (beginning at 15:12), it is reasonable to assume that his involvement with David had begun by the time of 2 Samuel 11.

18. Cf. Vannoy, *1—2 Samuel*, p. 338, note 6.

19. The Hittites were among the occupants of the land that was promised to Abraham (Genesis 15:20; see also Numbers 13:29; Joshua 1:4; 11:3). They were among those whom the Israelites were required to "devote . . . to complete destruction" (Deuteronomy 20:16–18). They fought against Israel in the days of Joshua (Joshua 9:1, 2). Israel failed to completely destroy the Hittites, and intermarriage with them contributed to Israel's unfaithfulness to the Lord (Judges 3:5, 6). By the time of David, Ahimelech (1 Samuel 26:6) and Uriah are examples of Hittites who had been fully integrated into Israel's life and faith, as is evidenced by their Hebrew names and their recorded behavior.

20. Ackroyd, *Second Samuel*, p. 101.

21. Samuel had protested at the appointment of Saul that his own leadership of Israel had not consisted of "taking" (1 Samuel 12:3–5).

22. Contra Gordon: "a degree of complicity might reasonably be inferred." Gordon, *1 & 2 Samuel*, p. 253.

23. Early Jewish commentaries on this incident went to extraordinary lengths to vindicate David, suggesting, among other things, that Uriah had divorced his wife before going to war (it was not therefore technically adultery). For details see McCarter, *II Samuel*, p. 288. More credible is the following comment: "The success of all [David's] undertakings, and the strength of his government, which increased

year by year, had made him feel so secure, that in the excitement of undisturbed prosperity, he allowed himself to be carried away by evil lusts, so as to stain his soul not only with adultery, but also with murder, and fell all the deeper because of the height to which his God had exalted him." Keil and Delitzsch, *Samuel*, p. 372. The fact remains that such explanations appear to be of no interest to the Bible writer at this point.

24. The Hebrew participle here provides a circumstantial clause rather than something that Bathsheba did subsequent to the act of adultery. Driver, *Notes*, p. 289; McCarter, *II Samuel*, p. 286; Hertzberg, *I & II Samuel*, p. 306, note a. Calvin seems to have missed this, misunderstanding verse 4e as an attempt by her to deal with the guilt of her adultery after the event: "Bathsheba was convicted of her evil after she had committed adultery with David." Calvin then criticizes her for resorting merely to a ritual cleansing without going on to true repentance. Calvin, *Sermons*, pp. 487–489.

25. For an excellent introduction to the meaning of the system, see Gordon J. Wenham, *The Book of Leviticus*, The New International Commentary on the Old Testament (Grand Rapids, MI: Eerdmans, 1979), pp. 15–32.

26. Cf. Walter Brueggemann, *First and Second Samuel*, Interpretation: A Bible Commentary for Teaching and Preaching (Louisville: John Knox Press, 1990), p. 274.

Chapter Twenty-Three: The Deceitful Heart

1. There is reason to think that this may have been the maximum penalty imposed and that the adulterer's fate depended on the wronged husband's decision (see Proverbs 6:32–35). Elaine Adler Goodfriend, "Adultery," in David Noel Freedman, ed., *The Anchor Bible Dictionary*, vol. 1 (New York: Doubleday, 1992), p. 83.

2. Note that Bathsheba was not consulted. Fokkelman suggests that "Evidently, Bathsheba is simply expected to consent to all of this if it succeeds." J. P. Fokkelman, *Narrative Art and Poetry in the Books of Samuel: a full interpretation based on stylistic and structural analyses, Volume 1: King David (II Sam. 9—20 & I Kings 1—2)* (The Netherlands: Van Gorcum, Assen, 1981), p. 53. We do not know, however, whether Bathsheba knew anything of David's cover-up scheme. Indeed did she ever learn what he had done?

3. In an important study of this story Meir Sternberg has argued that it is told in such a way that readers are forced to fill in various gaps deliberately left unfilled by the narrator. Meir Sternberg, *The Poetics of Biblical Narrative: Ideological Reading and the Drama of Reading*, Indiana Studies in Biblical Literature (Bloomington, IN: Indiana University Press, 1987), pp. 190–222. This is not so much a matter of a reader imaginatively and arbitrarily creating details to add to the story as it is told. It is, rather, that the story is told in such a way as to provoke questions that a thoughtful reader is forced to ponder, and perhaps answer. What is meant will become clearer as we work through the story.

4. William L. Holladay, *A Concise Hebrew and Aramaic Lexicon of the Old Testament: based upon the lexical work of Ludwig Koehler and Walter Baumgartner* (Leiden: E. J. Brill, 1971), p. 371.

5. Compare the three occurrences of *shalom* ("peace") in 3:21–23.

6. Cf. Fokkelman, *David*, p. 53.

7. So Ronald F. Youngblood, *1 & 2 Samuel*, in Tremper Longman III and David E. Garland, eds., *The Expositor's Bible Commentary*, Revised Edition, vol. 3 (Grand Rapids, MI: Zondervan, 2009), p. 434; P. Kyle McCarter Jr., *II Samuel: A New Translation with Introduction, Notes & Commentary*, The Anchor Bible, vol. 9 (Garden City, NY: Doubleday, 1984), p. 286; Walter Brueggemann, *First and Second Samuel*, Interpretation: A Bible Commentary for Teaching and Preaching (Louisville: John Knox Press, 1990), p. 274.

8. Cf. Robert Alter, *The David Story: A Translation with Commentary of 1 and 2 Samuel* (New York and London: W. W. Norton & Company, 1999), p. 251.

9. The Hebrew word for "present" here is associated with food in Genesis 43:34; Amos 5:11; Jeremiah 40:5; and possibly Esther 2:18.

10. Thus Keil and Delitzsch: "Uriah had his suspicions aroused. The connection between his wife and David may not have remained altogether a secret, so that it may have reached his ears as soon as he arrived in Jerusalem." C. F. Keil and F. Delitzsch, *Biblical Commentary on the Books of Samuel* (Grand Rapids, MI: Eerdmans, 1950), p. 384.

11. Notice how "he did not go down to his house" becomes a refrain-like line echoing and inverting "Go down to your house" in verse 8a. See verses 9, 10 (twice), 11. Our passage closes with the words "to his house he did not go down" (v. 13 AT).

12. The suggestion of Youngblood that the word for "journey" here may mean a military campaign and that the celibacy of those going into battle (1 Samuel 21:4, 5) may be implied is, in my opinion, a little far-fetched. Youngblood, *1 & 2 Samuel*, p. 434.

13. "In booths" could be a place name, "in Succoth." So Fokkelman, *David*, p. 55, note 9; Youngblood, *1 & 2 Samuel*, p. 435; McCarter, *II Samuel*, p. 287; contra Alter: "Uriah's point is that neither the Ark nor the troops enjoy proper shelter (while David is 'sitting in Jerusalem')." Alter, *David*, p. 252; also Robert P. Gordon, *1 & 2 Samuel: A Commentary* (Exeter, UK: Paternoster, 1986), p. 254. On this matter see Y. Yadin, "Some Aspects of the Strategy of Ahab and David," *Biblica* 36 (1955), pp. 332–351; Michael M. Homan, "Booths or Succoth? A Response to Yigael Yadin," *Journal of Biblical Literature* 118 (1999), pp. 691–697. The main objection to understanding the expression as meaning "in booths" is that this is not the usual word for the "tent" in which the ark was housed (7:2), nor for the shelter of soldiers in the field. It may be replied that Uriah's words have a rhetorical force, and "booths" may have served his purpose well, with the associations this term had in Israel (see Leviticus 23:42, 43). The main (but not conclusive) objection to the sense "in Succoth" is that Succoth was probably not close enough to Rabbah to be the location of the army that was besieging Rabbah (11:1). See Map 4-19 in John D. Currid and David P. Barrett, *Crossway ESV Bible Atlas* (Wheaton, IL: Crossway, 2010), p. 111.

14. See 1 Samuel 3:3; 4:3–22; 5:1—7:2; 14:18; 2 Samuel 6:1—7:3. For a fuller discussion of the ark and its history and significance, see the exposition of 6:1–11 in this book.

15. T. Kronholm, "*sakak*," in G. Johannes Botterweck, Helmer Ringgren, and Hienz-Josef Fabry, eds., *Theological Dictionary of the Old Testament*, vol. 10 (Grand Rapids, MI: Eerdmans, 1999), pp. 236–254, especially pp. 244–246.

16. There is little evidence to support the assertion of Halpern: "The point is not that Uriah is declining special privileges. Rather, intercourse would render him ritu-

ally unclean for combat." Baruch Halpern, *David's Secret Demons: Messiah, Murderer, Traitor, King*, The Bible in Its World (Grand Rapids, MI and Cambridge, UK: Eerdmans, 2001), pp. 35, 36. Even a strict understanding of Deuteronomy 23:9–11 would not forbid Uriah from sleeping with his wife, since he was not in the camp, and in any case he would have ample opportunity to bathe before returning to camp.

17. So Fokkelman, *David*, p. 56. If "my lord" in both of its occurrences refers to Joab, then Uriah could have been suggesting that Joab, but no longer David, had his allegiance. However, in this case I suspect that the ambiguity is too subtle to be deliberate.

18. In the Hebrew "I" is emphatic. "*I* am not one to do such a thing." Others, of course, might.

19. "Uriah . . . responds with such a reasonable and respectable answer that David thereafter has no opportunity to insist again without arousing amazement." Fokkelman, *David*, p. 54.

20. "David, therefore, should have been touched, and have been instructed by these words which God put in the mouth of Uriah." John Calvin, *Sermons on 2 Samuel Chapters 1—13*, trans. Douglas Kelly (Edinburgh: Banner of Truth, 1992), p. 500.

21. On Day 1 he arrived (v. 7). On Night 1 he slept at the door of the king's house (v. 9). On Day 2 he had the interview with David (vv. 10–12a). On the same day he ate and drank with David (v. 13a). On Night 2 he again slept with the servants (v. 13b). On Day 3 he returned to the battlefront (v. 14). Contra Fokkelman, *David*, p. 57 who understands the end of verse 12 differently and has Uriah departing on a fourth day.

22. For the sense of the Hebrew verb, see Jeremiah 51:7; Habakkuk 2:15. The Hebrew may be understood to mean that David *attempted* to make Uriah drunk.

23. The Hebrew of verse 13d adds a rhetorical flourish by an unusual word order: "but *to his house* he did not go down." These words aptly conclude the episode.

24. Cf. Peter R. Ackroyd, *The Second Book of Samuel*, Cambridge Bible Commentary (Cambridge: Cambridge University Press, 1977), p. 102.

Chapter Twenty-Four: The Murderer

1. For this understanding of the often-misunderstood expression "a man after [God's] own heart," see John Woodhouse, *1 Samuel: Looking for a Leader*, Preaching the Word (Wheaton, IL: Crossway, 2008), pp. 235, 236 and 286, 287.

2. Strictly, since this is a minor flashback following verse 14, "had written" would be a better translation.

3. The imperative "Set" (addressed to Joab) is, curiously, plural. This has led some to suspect a textual error and to emend the text, following the Septuagint, to a verb meaning "Send." The meaning is not substantially affected. See S. R. Driver, *Notes on the Hebrew Text and the Topography of the Book of Samuel with an Introduction on Hebrew Palaeography and Facsimiles of Inscriptions and Maps*, 2nd edition (Oxford: Clarendon, 1913), p. 290; P. Kyle McCarter Jr., *II Samuel: A New Translation with Introduction, Notes & Commentary*, The Anchor Bible, vol. 9 (Garden City, NY: Doubleday, 1984), p. 281. Nonetheless the plural may be because David was issuing an order that applied to the whole army ("draw back" is also plural).

4. "Besieged" in 11:1 and "besieging" in verse 16 are different Hebrew words. The former is the technical term for a siege (1 Samuel 23:8; 2 Samuel 20:15; 1 Kings 15:27; 16:17; 2 Kings 16:5). The latter is a more general word meaning "watch, guard, observe." Joab was *watching* the besieged city as he responded to the letter that Uriah brought him from David.

5. Because, of course, he had been "watching"! See previous note.

6. Literally "from the people, from the servants of David."

7. This is another minor flashback like verse 15. Strictly, therefore, "had instructed" would be better. Cf. J. P. Fokkelman, *Narrative Art and Poetry in the Books of Samuel: a full interpretation based on stylistic and structural analyses, Volume 1: King David (II Sam. 9—20 & I Kings 1—2)* (The Netherlands: Van Gorcum, Assen, 1981), p. 64.

8. Contra McCarter, who adjusts the text to make it David who actually makes this response, because he considers that "it is unreasonable to suppose that Joab would anticipate David's remonstrance in every detail." McCarter, *II Samuel*, p. 282; likewise Hans Wilhelm Hertzberg, *I & II Samuel: A Commentary*, Old Testament Library (London: SCM Press, 1964), p. 307, note a.

9. See Map 5-11 in John D. Currid and David P. Barrett, *Crossway ESV Bible Atlas* (Wheaton, IL: Crossway, 2010), p. 128.

10. The stone in question would have been "the smaller, upper stone of a hand-operated grain grinder." Barry G. Webb, *The Book of Judges*, The New International Commentary on the Old Testament (Grand Rapids, MI: Eerdmans, 2012), p. 293.

11. Jerubbesheth is a variation on the name Jerubbaal that was given to Gideon (Judges 6:32; 7:1), with "baal" replaced by "besheth," in the same way as Ish-baal became Ish-bosheth (see 2:8) and Meri-baal became Mephibosheth (see 4:4).

12. Contra Alter: "Thus the narrative makes palpable the inexorable public knowledge of David's crime." Robert Alter, *The David Story: A Translation with Commentary of 1 and 2 Samuel* (New York and London: W. W. Norton & Company, 1999), p. 255.

13. There is an indirect allusion to the Lord in the mention of the ark in 11:11, but even that was on the lips of Uriah, not David.

Chapter Twenty-Five: Shattered by the Word of God

1. God has been mentioned in the speech of characters in the story (9:3; 10:12), but God has not appeared explicitly as a participant in the narrative since 8:14b. After 2 Samuel 12 the Lord does not appear again as a character in the narrative until 21:1. J. P. Fokkelman, *Narrative Art and Poetry in the Books of Samuel: a full interpretation based on stylistic and structural analyses, Volume 1: King David (II Sam. 9—20 & I Kings 1—2)* (The Netherlands: Van Gorcum, Assen, 1981), p. 71 makes similar observations.

2. The child conceived in the act of adultery had been born before Nathan came to David (11:27; 12:14). Cf. C. F. Keil and F. Delitzsch, *Biblical Commentary on the Books of Samuel* (Grand Rapids, MI: Eerdmans, 1950), p. 388.

3. It is not certain that the events of 2 Samuel 11 are behind Psalm 32, but it seems very likely.

4. David "sent" in 11:1, 3, 4, 6, 12, 14, 27. Bathsheba "sent" in 11:5. Joab "sent" in 11:6, 18, 22.

5. "[W]e should, in the first place, listen to his account just as David does, as a historical event." Fokkelman, *David*, p. 72. "Perhaps David took this as an actual case." Dale Ralph Davis, *Expositions of the Book of 2 Samuel: Out of Every Adversity* (Geanies House, Fearn, UK: Christian Focus, 1999), p. 122. Alter thinks that David should have been more sensitive to literary form. "Given the patently literary character of Nathan's tale, which would have been transparent to anyone native to ancient Hebrew culture, it is a little puzzling that David should so precipitously take the tale as a report of fact requiring judicial action. . . . David's compensatory zeal to be a champion of justice overrides any awareness he might have of the evident artifice of the story." Robert Alter, *The David Story: A Translation with Commentary of 1 and 2 Samuel* (New York and London: W. W. Norton & Company, 1999), p. 257.

6. The Hebrew emphasizes the "togetherness" of this scene with a word meaning "together" at this point. Cf. Fokkelman, *David*, p. 74. See REB.

7. "Arms" can be rendered "lap" or "bosom."

8. Importantly (in due course) the same verb "to lie" was used in this sense in 11:4, 11 (but ironically not in 11:9, 13).

9. Cf. Robert P. Gordon, *1 & 2 Samuel: A Commentary* (Exeter, UK: Paternoster, 1986), p. 257.

10. The messenger also "came" to David (11:22), as did Nathan (12:1).

11. "Unwilling" translates the same verb rendered "pity" in verse 6.

12. Walter Brueggemann, *First and Second Samuel*, Interpretation: A Bible Commentary for Teaching and Preaching (Louisville: John Knox Press, 1990), p. 280.

13. Fokkelman, *David*, p. 75.

14. In particular the eighth-century prophets Amos and Hosea confronted injustices in which the rich took advantage of the poor. See Hosea 4:2; Amos 2:6, 7.

15. David had used almost exactly the same words (with the same oath) about Abner in 1 Samuel 26:16. Saul had used the phrase "son of death" concerning David in 1 Samuel 20:31. On the significance of the expression in 1 Samuel, see John Woodhouse, *1 Samuel: Looking for a Leader*, Preaching the Word (Wheaton, IL: Crossway, 2008), p. 492.

16. For these reasons I am not persuaded by Fokkelman's view that David's reaction to Nathan's story shows his "good side." Fokkelman, *David*, p. 79. On the contrary, he seems to care only about evil in others (and magnifies it).

17. There is also an echo of the word "pity" in verse 4, noted above.

18. The brevity of the Hebrew of these two messages is starker than the English translations: "Pregnant I." "You the-man."

19. Fokkelman, *David*, p. 78.

20. Of course, the story should not be pressed in all its details. David did not kill Bathsheba (the lamb in the story); he killed Uriah ("the poor man"). The traveler who came to the rich man should not be identified, for example, with the lust that overcame David.

21. I find Fokkelman's slightly unconventional formal analysis of verses 7b–12 convincing and follow it here. Fokkelman, *David*, pp. 83–87. The critical point is that verse 10a concludes the first part of the speech, and verse 10b begins the second part. The two parts then deal neatly with David's two crimes. This requires the following small changes to the punctuation found in almost all English versions of verses 10, 11: "Now therefore the sword shall never depart from your house.

Because you have despised me and have taken the wife of Uriah the Hittite to be your wife, thus says the Lord, 'Behold . . .'"

22. The reference to the Lord giving "your master's [Saul's] wives into your arms" is puzzling. On the one hand, as far as we know, Saul had only one wife (1 Samuel 14:50) and one concubine (3:7). On the other hand, although David did have a wife of the same name as Saul's (Ahinoam, 1 Samuel 25:43), as we saw in the exposition of 2:2, this was almost certainly not the same woman. David's wife was Ahinoam *of Jezreel*. Furthermore Saul's concubine was taken by Abner, not by David (3:7). While the Lord therefore made it possible, in principle, for David to take over Saul's harem (if he had had one), it seems that this did not happen. "I gave you . . . your master's wives" should probably not, therefore, be taken literally, but as a way of referring to Saul's household. Similarly Keil and Delitzsch, *Samuel*, pp. 389, 390; Gordon, *1 & 2 Samuel*, pp. 257, 258; Davis, *2 Samuel*, p. 125, note 4. The sentence ("I gave you . . . your master's wives into your arms") also serves the purposes of (a) introducing the idea of sexual relations and (b) creating the first of several verbal links between this word of the Lord and the story ("into your arms," v. 8 echoes "in his arms," v. 3).

23. Fokkelman, *David*, p. 84.

24. This promise is called "the word of the Lord" in 7:4 and is referred to by David as "your word" (7:21 AT), "the word that you have spoken" (7:25), and "your words" (7:28).

25. The Hebrew focuses on the objects of the verbs: "*Uriah the Hittite* you have struck down . . . *his wife* you have taken . . . *him* you have killed."

26. The reference to Uriah's wife in verse 9 does not focus on the adultery as such, but on the theft involved. "David is a robber and Uriah is his victim" as in the story of the rich man and the poor man. Fokkelman, *David*, p. 86.

27. Contrary to ESV and others, there should, in my opinion, be a full stop after "house." See note 21.

28. It is of no consequence that, strictly speaking, Uriah was killed by arrows (11:24). "Sword" was David's word for the instrument of the murder (11:25).

29. The Hebrew has a rather unusual and strong word here for "Because." It appeared in David's furious words "*because* he did this thing" (v. 6). The word in question occurs only in these two places in the books of Samuel. It connects the Lord's pronouncement concerning David with David's judgment on the rich man. "Thus the judge meets his own judgement from the highest judge." Fokkelman, *David*, p. 86.

30. On the punctuation, see note 21.

31. The wording of verse 10c is similar to the clause in verse 9. However, now the focus is on Uriah's wife becoming David's wife—in other words, the adultery. Fokkelman, *David*, p. 86.

32. Those who account for David's different treatment by God, when compared to Saul, by reference to qualities in David tend to emphasize the authenticity of David's repentance and the lack of excuses or prevarication. This is seriously misleading. See note 1 to Chapter 26 below.

33. "Also" in the ESV is misleading here. The Hebrew word in this context does not mean that the Lord was *another* person who put away David's sin, nor that putting away David's sin was *another* thing that the Lord did. The Hebrew word simply adds emphasis to "the Lord." "The Lord *himself* has put away your sin." Cf. Fokkelman, *David*, p. 87.

34. Some see a textual problem here. As the ESV note indicates, the Hebrew has "the enemies of the Lord," but the words "the enemies of" are omitted in the ESV text (likewise NIV, REB, HCSB). The RV offers a sensible rendering of the Hebrew as it stands: "Howbeit, because by this deed thou hast given great occasion to the enemies of the Lord to blaspheme . . ." Likewise Francis Brown, S. R. Driver, and Charles Briggs, *A Hebrew and English Lexicon of the Old Testament* (Oxford: Clarendon Press, 1907), p. 611; Fokkelman, *David*, p. 451. However, some consider that "the enemies of" has been added to the text to avoid the impression that David had scorned the Lord. So Gordon, *1 & 2 Samuel*, p. 259. The argument for emending the text is unconvincing in the light of verses 9, 10 of this chapter, which plainly state that David *had* despised the Lord.

35. I recommend the extended reflection on these matters in John Calvin, *Sermons on 2 Samuel Chapters 1—13*, trans. Douglas Kelly (Edinburgh: Banner of Truth, 1992), pp. 575–581. One pertinent point: we should not be deceived into thinking that this life is all there is when we consider the tragedy of anyone's death.

Chapter Twenty-Six: Restoration

1. When, in similar circumstances, Saul had said, "I have sinned" (1 Samuel 15:24, 30), he did not receive the same grace. It is often pointed out that the simple straightforward repentance of David was better than Saul's. "He bowed to the prophetic word without any of the casuistry or self-justification that marks the confrontations between Samuel and Saul in similar circumstances (*e.g.* 1 Sa. 15:13ff.)." Robert P. Gordon, *1 & 2 Samuel: A Commentary* (Exeter, UK: Paternoster, 1986), p. 256. "There is no excuse, no cloaking, no palliative of sin. There is no searching for a loophole . . . no pretext put forward, no human weakness pleaded. He acknowledges his guilt openly, candidly, and without prevarication." C. F. Keil and F. Delitzsch, *Biblical Commentary on the Books of Samuel* (Grand Rapids, MI: Eerdmans, 1950), p. 391, citing the Berleburg Bible. These observations are true but misconstrued. Davis identifies the problem: "we still assume that intensity of repentance contributes to atonement." Dale Ralph Davis, *Expositions of the Book of 2 Samuel: Out of Every Adversity* (Geanies House, Fearn, UK: Christian Focus, 1999), p. 127. David's repentance took place in the context of grace (expressed in the promises of 2 Samuel 7). That is why David's repentance met with grace. Saul's repentance took place in the context of the warning of 1 Samuel 12:15. David's behavior was different from Saul's because of the grace of God toward him. It is not the case that God was gracious toward him *because* he was the better man.

2. The ESV inserts "therefore" here, although the Hebrew presents a simple sequence of events without the inference conveyed by "therefore." Indeed, in the context what David did was not obviously the logical thing to do at this point.

3. Cf. John Calvin, *Sermons on 2 Samuel Chapters 1—13*, trans. Douglas Kelly (Edinburgh: Banner of Truth, 1992), p. 590.

4. This observation is based on the tenses of the Hebrew verbs. Gordon, *1 & 2 Samuel*, p. 259.

5. "The elders of his house" were, no doubt, "the oldest and most confidential servants." Keil and Delitzsch, *Samuel*, p. 392.

6. Cf. Robert Alter, *The David Story: A Translation with Commentary of 1 and 2 Samuel* (New York and London: W. W. Norton & Company, 1999), p. 261.

7. So Alter, *David*, p. 261. The Hebrew word for "evil" does not always mean moral evil. In some contexts it means "harmful." See, for example, 1 Samuel 16:14 and the discussion of this point in John Woodhouse, *1 Samuel: Looking for a Leader*, Preaching the Word (Wheaton, IL: Crossway, 2008), p. 295.

8. So Gordon, *1 & 2 Samuel*, p. 259.

9. The word "washed" reminds us again of what Uriah has refused to do (11:8), and indeed of what Bathsheba was doing when David first spied her from his rooftop (11:2; ESV, "bathing"). The same Hebrew word occurs in these three places. Fokkelman points out that the "washing" of Bathsheba had to do with her purity (11:4), and the refusal of Uriah to "wash" represented his immaculate behavior. At last David had come to participate in the kind of proper conduct displayed by Bathsheba and Uriah. J. P. Fokkelman, *Narrative Art and Poetry in the Books of Samuel: a full interpretation based on stylistic and structural analyses, Volume 1: King David (II Sam. 9—20 & I Kings 1—2)* (The Netherlands: Van Gorcum, Assen, 1981), p. 93.

10. See a fuller discussion of this important matter in Calvin, *Sermons*, pp. 584–589.

11. Too much should not be read into "I shall go to him," as Calvin perhaps does: "he was showing here the hope that he had of life after death." Calvin, *Sermons*, p. 592. David's words do not necessarily imply an understanding of life beyond death, just that the time would come when he, too, would die. Similarly Davis, *2 Samuel*, p. 130, note 12. However, some commentators are a little too emphatic that Old Testament believers knew nothing about life beyond death (see, for example, Hannah in 1 Samuel 2:6 or David in Psalm 16:10).

12. Indeed this is the first time since 11:3 that Bathsheba has been referred to by her own name.

13. The Hebrew text is uncertain here. The ESV has "he," following the consonantal Hebrew text. However, the vowels suggest "she," and this is supported by a number of ancient versions and followed by REB and HCSB. The NIV avoids the problem with "they." It is likely that the more surprising reading (that Bathsheba was the one who named Solomon) is the original. Similarly P. Kyle McCarter Jr., *II Samuel: A New Translation with Introduction, Notes & Commentary*, The Anchor Bible, vol. 9 (Garden City, NY: Doubleday, 1984), pp. 298, 303; Alter, *David*, p. 262.

14. A rather different account of the origin of Solomon's name is given by David in 1 Chronicles 22:9. This suggests that there was more to the naming than the writer of 2 Samuel tells us.

15. Slightly more literal is "And the LORD loved him and sent a message by Nathan the prophet and called his name Jedidiah." The ESV might suggest that David did the naming this time, whereas the Hebrew syntax suggests that either the Lord or Nathan "called his name Jedidiah."

16. Fokkelman, *David*, p. 94.

17. Alter, *David*, p. 263.

18. Cf. Gordon, *1 & 2 Samuel*, p. 260.

19. Keil and Delitzsch, *Samuel*, p. 396.

20. Gordon, *1 & 2 Samuel*, p. 260.

21. Cf. Keil and Delitzsch, *Samuel*, p. 395.

22. Supported by Alter, *David*, p. 264.

23. This is supported by 1 Chronicles 20:3, which in the Hebrew is not ambiguous (see ESV margin). So Keil and Delitzsch, *Samuel*, p. 396.

Chapter Twenty-Seven: Like Father, Like Son

1. Matthew Henry on 2 Samuel 13, in *Commentary on the Whole Bible*; http://www.sacred-texts.com/bib/cmt/henry/sa2013.htm.

2. The narrative in 13:1–22 has received much attention from scholars interested in the narrative art of the Bible. The structure of the story, as outlined here, follows fairly closely a proposal by George Ridout, "The Rape of Tamar: A Rhetorical Analysis of 2 Sam 13:1–22," in Jared J. Jackson and Martin Kessler, eds., *Rhetorical Criticism: Essays in Honor of James Muilenburg*, Pittsburgh Theological Monograph Series, Number 1 (Pittsburgh: The Pickwick Press, 1974), pp. 75–84. Other valuable studies include J. P. Fokkelman, *Narrative Art and Poetry in the Books of Samuel: a full interpretation based on stylistic and structural analyses, Volume 1: King David (II Sam. 9—20 & I Kings 1—2)* (The Netherlands: Van Gorcum, Assen, 1981), pp. 99–114 (who follows Ridout quite closely); C. Conroy, *Absolom, Absolom! Narrative and Language in 2 Sam 13—20*, Analecta Biblica 81 (Rome: Biblical Institute, 1978), pp. 17–39.

3. This is similar to Ridout, "The Rape of Tamar," p. 81 and Fokkelman, *David*, p. 100.

4. The episode begins, more literally, "And it came to pass after this . . ." This marks the beginning of a new section of the narrative, namely the story of Absalom (2 Samuel 13—20). A subdivision within this will be similarly marked at 15:1.

5. The Hebrew word translated "anything" is often used for something bad, sometimes euphemistically. For example (with various English renderings), see Genesis 22:12; 40:15; 1 Samuel 12:4, 5; 20:26; 25:21; 29:3. Francis Brown, S. R. Driver, and Charles Briggs, *A Hebrew and English Lexicon of the Old Testament* (Oxford: Clarendon Press, 1907), pp. 548, 549.

6. Dale Ralph Davis, *Expositions of the Book of 2 Samuel: Out of Every Adversity* (Geanies House, Fearn, UK: Christian Focus, 1999), p. 136; M. Tsevat, "*bethulah*," in G. Johannes Botterweck and Helmer Ringgren, eds., *Theological Dictionary of the Old Testament*, vol. 2 (Grand Rapids, MI: Eerdmans, 1975), pp. 338–343.

7. "The maidenly modesty of Tamar evidently raised an insuperable barrier to the gratification of his lusts." C. F. Keil and F. Delitzsch, *Biblical Commentary on the Books of Samuel* (Grand Rapids, MI: Eerdmans, 1950), p. 397.

8. Fokkelman argues that "the horror of incest" was not the concern of this narrative. Fokkelman, *David*, p. 103. The fact that Abraham was married to his half-sister (Genesis 20:12) is not decisive, since that was before the giving of the Law. After the Law was given, anyone who took God's Law seriously would know that sex between a brother and his half-sister was forbidden. Similarly Davis, *2 Samuel*, p. 134, note 2.

9. It is possible that "friend" refers to an official position of companion and counselor to the prince. Cf. 2 Samuel 15:37; 1 Kings 4:5. So Robert Alter, *The David Story: A Translation with Commentary of 1 and 2 Samuel* (New York and London: W. W. Norton & Company, 1999), p. 265; Andrew E. Hill, "A Jonadab Connection in the Absalom Conspiracy?" *Journal of the Evangelical Theological Society* 30/4(1987), p. 387. However, 16:16, 17 suggests that "friend" in this royal context was a mutual relationship (Hushai was David's friend, and David was Hushai's friend).

10. In my opinion this reply counts against Fokkelman's argument that incest is not part of the issue in this story. I agree that the act of Amnon a little later in the story is rape, but I disagree that it is "not incest." Fokkelman, *David*, p. 103.

11. The word order of the Hebrew sentence supports this understanding. "Tamar, my brother Absalom's sister" is emphasized at the beginning of the sentence. This is followed by an emphatic form of the pronoun "I."

12. Without explanation Alter has "your brother" here, meaning Absalom. There is no obvious justification for this reading. Alter, *David*, p. 266.

13. As I think Fokkelman does: "I consider it improbable that the Jonadab of 13:4–6 had already cynically premeditated rape [see 13:32]. It seems preferable to me to place no more responsibility on Jonadab than for that which he himself proposes in v. 5: a deception, admittedly not very morally elevated, in order that Amnon secure a private meeting with Tamar." Fokkelman, *David*, p. 109. Alter is less definite, but recognizes the ambiguity of Jonadab's intentions. Alter, *David*, p. 266. Contra Keil and Delitzsch, *Samuel*, p. 397. For a thoroughly damning estimate of Jonadab's character, see Davis, *2 Samuel*, pp. 137–139.

14. It has been argued that Jonadab's advice to Amnon was part of a wider conspiracy in which he was working with Absalom to achieve Absalom's designs to usurp his father's throne. This was, then, the first step in removing Amnon as an obstacle to that goal. Hill, "Jonadab Connection," pp. 387–390. In my opinion this hypothesis is a plausible explanation of the perplexing role of Jonadab but remains uncertain and is a lot to infer from a text that refrains from any explicit reference to Jonadab's role in the supposed conspiracy.

15. Similarly Fokkelman, *David*, p. 105. Alter points out that the verb here is associated with the idea of sexual arousal in the Song of Solomon (4:9, ESV, "captivated"). Alter, *David*, p. 267.

16. ". . . the spoiled prince who is constantly served at every whim." Fokkelman, *David*, p. 106.

17. Significantly, David's adultery was described with the words "he *lay* with her" (11:4). Of course, it is the context that makes the word sinister. The same word is used of proper sexual relations in marriage (11:11; 12:24).

18. Fokkelman, *David*, p. 104. Cf. Song of Solomon 4:9, 10, 12; 5:1, 2.

19. The word for "fool" is *nabal*, reminding us of the fool Nabal who refused to listen to sound advice and suffered the consequences (1 Samuel 25).

20. Similarly Keil and Delitzsch, *Samuel*, p. 399; Alter, *David*, p. 268. Fokkelman argues that Tamar's suggestion offered a "genuine alternative" and that Amnon's crime was rape, not incest, citing the example of Abraham in Genesis 20:12. Amnon's crime was certainly rape, but it was *also* incest.

21. "The king understands about lust and desire. He would permit the relationship." Walter Brueggemann, *First and Second Samuel*, Interpretation: A Bible Commentary for Teaching and Preaching (Louisville: John Knox Press, 1990), p. 287.

22. Similarly Brueggemann, *First and Second Samuel*, p. 287.

23. The word is used in connection with rape in Genesis 34:2. Other contexts include Genesis 15:13 ("afflicted"); Leviticus 16:29 ("afflict"); Numbers 24:24 ("afflict"); Deuteronomy 21:14 ("humiliated"); Judges 16:5 ("overpower"), 6 ("subdue"); 1 Kings 11:39 ("afflict"); Job 37:23 ("violate").

24. The Hebrew has "with" in verse 11 ("lie *with* me"). Even 11:4 has "he lay *with* her." In 13:14b "with her" is replaced by "her" as the direct object of "lay." Fokkelman, *David*, p. 105.

25. Similarly Alter, *David*, p. 269.

26. "[P]sychologically so accurate and so brilliantly formulated." Fokkelman, *David*, p. 107.

27. So Alter, *David*, p. 269.

28. Brueggemann, *First and Second Samuel*, p. 287.

29. Alter, *David*, p. 269.

30. "He who seeks intercourse pretends to be able to reciprocate tenderness, to make deep contact, and to taste the union of true love. Amnon's act of violence reveals him as someone incapable of contact and as an uncouth egoist. The worst for him is that there is a witness present, and Tamar is this very witness. From then on he will no longer be able to see her, for such a meeting would be a repeated, extremely shameful unmasking and intolerable confrontation with his own shortcomings as a person. Therefore, Amnon pushes his half-sister as far away as he can with his hate." Fokkelman, *David*, pp. 107, 108.

31. The ESV adds "my brother," following the Septuagint. So also Fokkelman, *David*, p. 452; but see contrary argument in Alter, *David*, p. 269. The Hebrew does not have this expression. If we follow the Hebrew, it suggests that prior to the violation Tamar could call Amnon "my brother" (v. 12), but not afterward. So NIV, REB, HCSB. There are other difficulties in the Hebrew of this verse. See the helpful discussions of the unamended text in Keil and Delitzsch, *Samuel*, p. 399; Ronald F. Youngblood, *1 & 2 Samuel*, in Tremper Longman III and David E. Garland, eds., *The Expositor's Bible Commentary*, Revised Edition, vol. 3 (Grand Rapids, MI: Zondervan, 2009), p. 468.

32. See Alter, *David*, pp. 269, 270.

33. Keil and Delitzsch, *Samuel*, p. 399.

34. Exactly the same description as Joseph's famous "coat of many colors" (Genesis 37:3, which can be translated "a robe with long sleeves"). See the discussion of the two garments in Alter, *David*, p. 270.

35. The correspondence between the intervention of Jonadab in verses 3–5 and the intervention of Absalom here is one of the less convincing aspects to the outline of the story that we have followed here. Fokkelman includes this element, although Ridout does not. Fokkelman, *David*, p. 100; Ridout, "The Rape of Tamar," p. 81. However, this uncertainty does not undermine the more obvious correspondences that shape the narrative.

36. Readers will notice that "with me" was Amnon's language for what he wanted to do to her (v. 11). Alter calls this an "oblique euphemism for rape." Alter, *David*, p. 270. Similarly Keil and Delitzsch, *Samuel*, p. 400.

37. The word can have the sense "keep inactive" about something, as in 19:10 (ESV, "say nothing").

38. Similarly Fokkelman, *David*, p. 111. Cf. Alter, *David*, p. 271.

39. Literally "this thing," just as in 11:25 (ESV, "this matter"); 12:6, 14 ("this deed").

40. The Hebrew has "your heart."

41. Similarly Brueggemann, *First and Second Samuel*, p. 289.

42. That is, "as one laid waste, with the joy of her life hopelessly destroyed." Keil and Delitzsch, *Samuel*, p. 400.

43. There are references back to her in verse 22 and 13:32; 1 Chronicles 3:9. In due course Absalom will name a beautiful daughter after Tamar (14:27).

44. The version is the Septuagint, supported by the Qumran Samuel scroll. The REB includes the words in question, and McCarter argues for their originality. P. Kyle McCarter Jr., *II Samuel: A New Translation with Introduction, Notes & Commentary*, The Anchor Bible, vol. 9 (Garden City, NY: Doubleday, 1984), pp. 319, 320. Alter thinks they are an "explanatory gloss, an effort to make sense of David's silence." Alter, *David*, p. 271. Likewise Keil and Delitzsch, *Samuel*, p. 400.

45. "In this case [David's] powerlessness can be explained on the basis of awkwardness and embarrassment aroused in David by the discovery that he had been misled when he did Amnon a favour in sending Tamar to visit him. But below this lies an even more fundamental embarrassment and powerlessness, that of a father who cannot be a match for his spoiled and/or ambitious sons. We may not neglect the unambiguous evidence for this in Chs. 15 and 18 and 1 Kings 1 in our explanation of 13:21." Fokkelman, *David*, p. 112.

Chapter Twenty-Eight: Vengeance and the Kingdom

1. Literally "two years, days," that is, two years of days. The expression conveys the period of time ("two years"), with the content of the period ("days") in apposition. There were many painful "days" in those "two years." See A. E. Cowley, *Gesenius' Hebrew Grammar as edited and enlarged by the late E. Kautzsch*, Second English Edition (Oxford: Clarendon Press, 1910), p. 424.

2. The locations of both Baal-hazor and Ephraim are not certain. See Map 5-12 in John D. Currid and David P. Barrett, *Crossway ESV Bible Atlas* (Wheaton, IL: Crossway, 2010), p. 129. See Henry O. Thompson, "Ephraim (Place)," in David Noel Freedman, ed., *The Anchor Bible Dictionary*, vol. 2 (New York: Doubleday, 1992), p. 556.

3. So Robert Alter, *The David Story: A Translation with Commentary of 1 and 2 Samuel* (New York and London: W. W. Norton & Company, 1999), p. 271. Compare 1 Samuel 25:2, 8.

4. I find Fokkelman's understanding of Absalom's machinations convincing, and the following exposition is indebted to his insights. "Absalom leaves nothing to chance. . . . Absalom has foreseen every step with subtle precision and attains exactly what he wishes." J. P. Fokkelman, *Narrative Art and Poetry in the Books of Samuel: a full interpretation based on stylistic and structural analyses, Volume 1: King David (II Sam. 9—20 & I Kings 1—2)* (The Netherlands: Van Gorcum, Assen, 1981), p. 115. Contra: "It could be that the opportunity against Amnon only emerges late in the process." Walter Brueggemann, *First and Second Samuel*, Interpretation: A Bible Commentary for Teaching and Preaching (Louisville: John Knox Press, 1990), p. 289.

5. Since this is now in effect a flashback explaining how the situation summarized in verse 23 came about, "had come" would be more strictly accurate.

6. Literally, "be heavy upon you." See the expression in Nehemiah 5:18.

7. A small Hebrew word, rendered "please" in the previous verse, appears again in David's reply. While it is difficult to translate, it does contribute to the sense of a respectful, polite conversation.

8. The expression "pressed him" is exactly the same as in verse 25b.

9. The ESV ("he let Amnon and all the king's sons go with him") fails to render the important word "sent." The king's authority was behind this, not just his permission. David's and others' "sending" has been a feature of the narrative through 2 Samuel 11—13. In this chapter David "sent" a message to Tamar (v. 7), and Amnon "sent" Tamar away (vv. 16, 17 [ESV "put out"]).

10. So Alter, *David*, p. 272. "Servants" in verse 28 is a different Hebrew word from the one for David's "servants" in verse 24 and may have a less formal connotation. These were Absalom's "boys."

11. Similarly Fokkelman, *David*, p. 117.

12. The "I" in "Have I not commanded you?" is strikingly emphatic: "Am I not the one who commanded you?"

13. Fokkelman, *David*, p. 125.

14. The mule was "the customary mount for royal personages." Alter, *David*, p. 272. See 2 Samuel 18:9; 1 Kings 1:33, 38, 44.

15. The word means "something heard." See its use in 1 Samuel 2:24; 4:19; 2 Samuel 4:4.

16. Fokkelman, *David*, p. 118.

17. Not exclusively so, but there are many examples of the use of this word (variously translated) in military contexts. For example 1 Samuel 4:2; 7:11; 11:11; 13:3, 4; 14:14; 2 Samuel 1:1; 2:31; 5:8.

18. The identical phrase is used of God's conquest of the Egyptians in Psalm 106:11. See the almost identical expression in Numbers 26:65; cf. 2 Samuel 17:12.

19. Fokkelman has another suggestion, namely that the rumor may have been planted earlier by Absalom himself: "yet another product of Absalom's perfect organization?" Fokkelman, *David*, p. 118.

20. Contra Brueggemann, *First and Second Samuel*, p. 290.

21. Similarly Andrew E. Hill, "A Jonadab Connection in the Absalom Conspiracy?" *Journal of the Evangelical Theological Society* 30/4(1987), p. 390; also Ronald F. Youngblood, *1 & 2 Samuel*, in Tremper Longman III and David E. Garland, eds., *The Expositor's Bible Commentary*, Revised Edition, vol. 3 (Grand Rapids, MI: Zondervan, 2009), p. 472. These authors go further and claim that Jonadab had been a coconspirator with Absalom to remove Amnon, clearing the way for Absalom's attempt to take the throne.

22. Jonadab's speech has a clear rhetorical structure (Fokkelman, *David*, pp. 118, 119):

A. Let not my lord suppose
B. that they have killed all the young men, the king's sons,
C. for Amnon alone is dead.
X. For by the command of Absalom this has been determined from the day he violated his sister Tamar.
A¹. Now therefore let not my lord the king so take it to heart as to suppose
B¹. that all the king's sons are dead,
C¹. for Amnon alone is dead.

23. Similarly Fokkelman, *David*, p. 119.

24. The Hebrew could mean, "it was placed upon the mouth of Absalom" (Absalom had an obligation to do something about this, which he has done by his orders), or "by the mouth of Absalom it was set" (Absalom has said that this must be done).

25. "Fled" in verses 34, 37, and 38 is a different Hebrew word from that used in verse 29. In verse 34 it is the word used repeatedly of David's fleeing from Saul (1 Samuel 19:12, 18; 20:1; 21:10; 22:17; 27:4; cf. 22:20; 23:6). In due course this word will refer to David's fleeing from Absalom (15:14; 19:9). It refers to "evasion of and escape from continuing, unpleasant, dangerous situations." J. Gamberoni, "*barach*," in G. Johannes Botterweck and Helmer Ringgren, eds., *Theological Dictionary of the Old Testament*, vol. 2 (Grand Rapids, MI: Eerdmans, 1975), p. 250. The word for the fleeing of the princes in verse 29 is often used of armies defeated in battle and suggests defeat and shame (1 Samuel 4:10, 17; 17:24, 51; 19:8; 30:17; 31:1, 7; 2 Samuel 1:4; 10:13, 14, 18; 17:2; 18:3, 17; 19:3, 8; 23:11; 24:13). J. Reindl, "*nua*," in G. Johannes Botterweck, Helmer Ringgren, and Heinz-Josef Fabry, eds., *Theological Dictionary of the Old Testament*, vol. 9 (Grand Rapids, MI: Eerdmans, 1998), p. 291.

26. "Behind him" may mean "west of him." So NIV; HCSB; C. F. Keil and F. Delitzsch, *Biblical Commentary on the Books of Samuel* (Grand Rapids, MI: Eerdmans, 1950), p. 403. Alter translates this, "going round the side of the mountain from the road behind it." Alter, *David*, p. 273.

27. Not now "*all* the king's sons" as in verses 23, 27, 29, 30, 32, 33. Two were now missing.

28. The suggestion of Brueggemann that the princes may have brought back Amnon's body is unlikely, given the circumstances of their departure from Baal-hazor. Brueggemann, *First and Second Samuel*, p. 290.

29. See Map 5-12 in Currid, *Atlas*, p. 129.

30. "Most likely David does not know. The denseness of the king's loss is so thick he cannot sort it out." Brueggemann, *First and Second Samuel*, p. 291.

31. The difficulties of the verse as it stands in the Hebrew text are as follows. (a) The first verb (ESV, "longed") is feminine in form, but the text lacks a feminine subject. The ESV has supplied a grammatically feminine subject ("spirit"), with some support from the ancient versions, but this may be just an ancient attempt to solve the problem of the Hebrew text rather than evidence of a superior Hebrew text. It is possible that the implied subject is the circumstances described in verse 38. So Keil and Delitzsch, *Samuel*, p. 405; cf. Fokkelman, *David*, p. 452. (b) The verb translated "longed" usually means "complete," "finish," "end with," or "destroy," as it does in verse 36 (ESV, "finished"), but may mean "hold back" (Keil and Delitzsch, *Samuel*, pp. 404, 405). (c) The infinitive verb "to go out" followed by the preposition "to" can refer to a military action against an enemy ("to march out against") as, for example, in 11:23 (cf. 1 Samuel 17:20, 55; 28:1; 29:6). (d) The conjunction translated "because" can mean "but." (e) The verb translated "was comforted" may refer to the period of mourning (as perhaps in Genesis 38:12) or can mean "to be sorry for." Fokkelman, *David*, p. 453.

32. The discussions in Keil and Delitzsch, *Samuel*, pp. 404, 405 and Fokkelman, *David*, p. 452, 453 have informed this rendering.

Chapter Twenty-Nine: Foolish Schemes

1. There is nothing in the Hebrew corresponding to "went out" in the ESV, and the preposition in question can certainly mean "against," as its use in 14:7, 13 shows (although it can have a range of meanings). This understanding of verse is supported by C. F. Keil and F. Delitzsch, *Biblical Commentary on the Books of Samuel* (Grand Rapids, MI: Eerdmans, 1950), p. 406, citing Daniel 11:28 as the only close parallel; also J. P. Fokkelman, *Narrative Art and Poetry in the Books of Samuel: a full interpretation based on stylistic and structural analyses, Volume 1: King David (II Sam. 9—20 & I Kings 1—2)* (The Netherlands: Van Gorcum, Assen, 1981), p. 126, 127; A. A. Anderson, *2 Samuel*, Word Biblical Commentary 11 (Dallas: Word, 1989), p. 187; Dale Ralph Davis, *Expositions of the Book of 2 Samuel: Out of Every Adversity* (Geanies House, Fearn, UK: Christian Focus, 1999), p. 143. Others prefer a translation that does not indicate whether David's attitude to Absalom was positive or negative. For example, "And Joab son of Zeruiah knew that the king's mind was *on* Absalom." Robert Alter, *The David Story: A Translation with Commentary of 1 and 2 Samuel* (New York and London: W. W. Norton & Company, 1999), p. 275; similarly HCSB; P. Kyle McCarter Jr., *II Samuel: A New Translation with Introduction, Notes & Commentary*, The Anchor Bible, vol. 9 (Garden City, NY: Doubleday, 1984), p. 344.

2. As supposed, for example, by Keil and Delitzsch: ". . . the principal reason no doubt was that Absalom had the best prospect of succeeding to the throne, and Joab thought this the best way to secure himself from punishment for the murder which he had committed. But the issue of events frustrated all such hopes. Absalom did not succeed to the throne, Joab did not escape punishment, and David was severely chastised for his weakness and injustice." Keil and Delitzsch, *Samuel*, p. 406.

3. This is the first mention of Tekoa in the Bible. The town appears a number of times subsequent to 2 Samuel 14. Many years later the prophet Amos would come from Tekoa (Amos 1:1). See also 2 Chronicles 11:6; 20:20; Jeremiah 6:1; Nehemiah 3:5, 27. For the location see Map 5-12 in John D. Currid and David P. Barrett, *Crossway ESV Bible Atlas* (Wheaton, IL: Crossway, 2010), p. 129.

4. The woman almost certainly used her considerable skill in leading the conversation with the king to its desired conclusion. Joab did not, therefore, give her a script to follow. What she said, however, had originated with Joab.

5. Fokkelman, *David*, p. 127.

6. The Hebrew of the Masoretic Text has "said" rather than "came," providing a slightly awkward repetition with "and said" later in the sentence. The Masoretic Text is well defended by Keil and Delitzsch, *Samuel*, pp. 406, 407 and followed by Alter, *David*, p. 276.

7. See Psalm 72:1–4, 12–14; Isaiah 11:3–5. Prior to the introduction of the monarchy in Israel this was a task of a "judge." See 1 Samuel 7:15–17.

8. The ESV ("*they* would destroy") reflects an emendation with little support from the ancient versions. See McCarter, *II Samuel*, p. 338. I prefer to follow the Hebrew ("and so *we* will destroy . . .") and consequently would include this sentence in the woman's quotation of the family's words. Similarly NIV, REB, HCSB; also Keil and Delitzsch, *Samuel*, p. 407, 408; Robert P. Gordon, *1 & 2 Samuel: A Commentary* (Exeter, UK: Paternoster, 1986), p. 267; Alter, *David*, p. 276.

9. "I" is emphatic in the Hebrew, as though the king had said, "Leave it to me. I will deal with it."

10. Keil and Delitzsch, *Samuel*, p. 408.

11. See Roland de Vaux, *Ancient Israel: Its Life and Institutions*, trans. John McHugh (London: Darton, Longman & Todd, 1973), pp. 21, 22, 160, 161.

12. Note the identical oath in both cases, "As the LORD lives."

13. Fokkelman, *David*, p. 131, note 6.

14. The Hebrew of this half-sentence is difficult, probably expressing the woman's awkwardness in virtually indicting the king (so Alter, *David*, p. 278). She was, after all, not a prophet of the Lord like Nathan.

15. This sounds to me almost like a proverbial saying (fitting for a "wise" woman, 13:2) and therefore general in its meaning. Fokkelman rejects this and argues that the woman was speaking in the name of the people ("we") and indicating the terrible consequences of David's failure with regard to Absalom: "We will all die!" Fokkelman, *David*, p. 136, note 16.

16. Cf. 1 Samuel 26:19, where "the heritage of the LORD" seems to mean Israel as God's people, as in Deuteronomy 32:9.

17. As it clearly does, for example, in 1 Samuel 6:21; 11:3, 4, 7, 9; 16:19; 19:11, 14, 15, 16, 20, 21; 23:27; 25:14, 42; 2 Samuel 2:5; 3:12, 14, 26; 5:11; 11:4, 19, 22, 25; 12:27. Indeed the only other places in the books of Samuel where this word seems to refer to a heavenly messenger ("angel") are 1 Samuel 29:9; 2 Samuel 19:27; 24:16, 17.

18. Literally, "hear."

19. "On the earth" could be better rendered "in the land." Alter regards the statement that David knew what was going on in the land of Israel as ironic. David's actions from here on show his lack of wisdom and that there was much in the land about which he knew nothing. Alter, *David*, p. 279.

20. "The woman's eventual admission that she has been sent by Joab (vv. 19–20) may itself be part of Joab's indirect message to David—something like, 'Bring Absalom back or I may side with him against you.'" Polzin, cited by Alter, *David*, p. 279.

21. Alter, *David*, p. 280. Fokkelman points out that the repeated use of the expression in the following chapters suggests that "David continues to see him as a child to the very end." Fokkelman, *David*, p. 145.

22. Both verses 20 and 24 have the same Hebrew verb that means "turn around" (ESV, "change" and "dwell apart in" respectively).

23. "Handsome" represents the same Hebrew word as "beautiful" in 1 Samuel 16:12; 25:3; 2 Samuel 13:1; 14:27. Cf. 1 Samuel 17:42.

24. Note that the Hebrew word rendered "handsome" here is the usual word for "good." For the sense of this verse and its emphasis on Saul's "good" appearance, see John Woodhouse, *1 Samuel: Looking for a Leader*, Preaching the Word (Wheaton, IL: Crossway, 2008), pp. 155, 156.

25. See also the Lord's rebuke of those who make their judgments of people by their appearance in 1 Samuel 16:7. See ibid., pp. 286, 287.

26. Gordon estimates between five and six pounds! Gordon, *1 & 2 Samuel*, p. 269.

27. So Keil and Delitzsch, *Samuel*, p. 412. It is possible that the sons were born after 18:18 (so Matthew Henry, cited by Davis, *2 Samuel*, p. 150, note 11). Fokkelman is hardly convincing in calling the former explanation "an attempt at harmo-

nization, in itself somewhat cheap . . ." Fokkelman, *David*, p. 150. Likewise Alter, *David*, p. 281, who thinks it strained.

28. It seems to me likely that this Tamar was born after the rape of Absalom's sister and that the naming of her therefore had added poignancy. While Alter is right to note that she is represented here as a woman, he is mistaken to conclude that she must have been a woman at the time of Absalom's confinement in Jerusalem. Alter, *David*, p. 281. The portrait of Absalom and his family in verses 25–27 is general and should not be forced into the chronological sequence of the narrative.

29. Similarly Alter, *David*, p. 281.

30. Walter Brueggemann, *First and Second Samuel*, Interpretation: A Bible Commentary for Teaching and Preaching (Louisville: John Knox Press, 1990), p. 298, who compares this with Luke 15:21, 22.

31. Fokkelman, *David*, p. 154.

32. Alter, *David*, p. 282.

Chapter Thirty: Politics and Power

1. It is highly likely that some of these psalms were composed by David during the period covered by 2 Samuel 15—19, but the circumstances behind any particular psalm are notoriously difficult to discern unless, of course, there is an explicit indication in the psalm's superscription (as, for example, Psalm 3).

2. The story of Absalom began in 13:1 (literally, "And it came to pass after this Absalom . . ."). Chapters 13, 14 will soon be seen as the prelude to chapters 15—19.

3. We have assumed that David's second-born son, Chileab, had died earlier than the events before us, since he is not mentioned after 3:3.

4. The Hebrew phrase at the beginning of 15:1 (literally, "And it came to pass from after this Absalom . . .") is very similar to the beginning of 13:1, where the story of Absalom really began (literally, "And it came to pass after this Absalom . . .").

5. I am not persuaded by Anderson's argument that Adonijah is more likely to have been the heir apparent at this time. A. A. Anderson, *2 Samuel*, Word Biblical Commentary 11 (Dallas: Word, 1989), p. 194. In the absence of any intervening factor the principal of primogeniture would be assumed, as it had been with Saul's son Jonathan (see 1 Samuel 14:49; 20:31). Only with Absalom's death did Adonijah develop aspirations to succeed David (on Adonijah, see 3:4; 1 Kings 1:5).

6. Similarly J. P. Fokkelman, *Narrative Art and Poetry in the Books of Samuel: a full interpretation based on stylistic and structural analyses, Volume 1: King David (II Sam. 9—20 & I Kings 1—2)* (The Netherlands: Van Gorcum, Assen, 1981), p. 166.

7. Although Absalom did not yet say, "I will be king," he acted in precisely the same way that Adonijah did some time later when he explicitly claimed the throne (1 Kings 1:5).

8. Similarly Robert Alter, *The David Story: A Translation with Commentary of 1 and 2 Samuel* (New York and London: W. W. Norton & Company, 1999), p. 283.

9. The Hebrew expression is a little unusual and literally reads, "by the hand of the way [or road] of the gate."

10. For a discussion of what we know about "the gate" as a court of justice, see Roland de Vaux, *Ancient Israel: Its Life and Institutions*, trans. John McHugh (London: Darton, Longman & Todd, 1973), pp. 152–155.

11. The Hebrew word is often used for a lawsuit.

12. The importance of the Hebrew word rendered "justice" in the books of Samuel was briefly reviewed in our discussion of 8:15.

13. Cf. REB: "you will get no hearing from the king." Also P. Kyle McCarter Jr., *II Samuel: A New Translation with Introduction, Notes & Commentary*, The Anchor Bible, vol. 9 (Garden City, NY: Doubleday, 1984), p. 353.

14. We do not know that there was widespread discontent with David's rule apart from Absalom's stirring it up. Too much credence should not be given to this man's portrait of how bad things had become. Alter has an alternative view: "The heart of Absalom's demagogic pitch is his exploiting what must have been widespread dissatisfaction over the new centralized monarchic bureaucracy with its imposition of taxes and corvées and military conscription: there is no one in this impersonal place to listen to you with a sympathetic ear, as I do." Alter, *David*, p. 283. Similarly Walter Brueggemann, *First and Second Samuel*, Interpretation: A Bible Commentary for Teaching and Preaching (Louisville: John Knox Press, 1990), p. 301. These views are more informed by the authors' own political viewpoints than by the text of 2 Samuel.

15. The Hebrew emphasizes "to me." C. F. Keil and F. Delitzsch, *Biblical Commentary on the Books of Samuel* (Grand Rapids, MI: Eerdmans, 1950), p. 415.

16. It is overreading the term "judge" to suggest that Absalom was hoping to fulfill the ideal initial expectations of the monarchy. Cf. Anderson, *2 Samuel*, p. 195.

17. For a brief discussion of the role of a "judge," see John Woodhouse, *1 Samuel: Looking for a Leader*, Preaching the Word (Wheaton, IL: Crossway, 2008), p. 130.

18. So Alter, *David*, p. 284.

19. Cf. Fokkelman, *David*, p. 166.

20. This possibly overly subtle observation is made by Alter, *David*, p. 284. The Hebrew word in question ("take hold of") occurs eighteen times in 2 Samuel.

21. Alter, *David*, p. 284.

22. The phrase "stole the hearts of" (with a different form of the same verb root) is translated "tricked" in the ESV of Genesis 31:20, 26, 27. Driver proposes the sense "duped." S. R. Driver, *Notes on the Hebrew Text and the Topography of the Book of Samuel with an Introduction on Hebrew Palaeography and Facsimiles of Inscriptions and Maps*, 2nd edition (Oxford: Clarendon, 1913), p. 311. Likewise Fokkelman, *David*, p. 168. Contra Keil and Delitzsch, *Samuel*, p. 415.

23. The Hebrew text has "forty years" in verse 7a, but this is generally agreed to be a textual error. Various interpretations that accept the reading "forty years" are outlined and rejected by Keil and Delitzsch, *Samuel*, pp. 415, 416. Several ancient versions support the emendation to "four years," which seems to be correct. The Hebrew for "forty" merely involves the addition of a plural ending to the word for "four." Two Hebrew manuscripts have "forty days." For a clear statement of the issues see C. Conroy, *Absolom, Absolom! Narrative and Language in 2 Sam 13—20*, Analecta Biblica 81 (Rome: Biblical Institute, 1978), p. 106, note 40.

24. I do not therefore think that the critical question is "why Absalom does not consider 'serving Yahweh in Jerusalem.'" Fokkelman, *David*, p. 170.

25. See our earlier discussion of 2:1.

26. It is possible that there were in Hebron people who were displeased with David's movement of his royal residence from Hebron to Jerusalem. This would add strategic value to Hebron for Absalom's real plans. So Keil and Delitzsch, *Samuel*, p. 416.

27. Keil and Delitzsch, *Samuel*, p. 416.

28. Similarly Fokkelman, *David*, p. 171.

29. While this is not the original meaning of the ancient name Jerusalem, this is what it sounds like in Hebrew. Cf. Hebrews 7:2.

30. We might add that Absalom himself introduced *shalom* to the conversation. When he said "Let me . . . *pay* my vow . . ." (v. 7), he used a word that means "make peace."

31. Keil and Delitzsch, *Samuel*, p. 416.

32. The translation is probably correct, but the Hebrew is ambiguous as to whether it was Absalom in Hebron or Ahithophel in Giloh who was offering sacrifices.

33. The Hebrew lacks "for." The expression is a little unusual in the context ("he sent Ahithophel"), but gives the impression that Ahithophel was already under Absalom's authority. Cf. Keil and Delitzsch, *Samuel*, p. 417.

34. Ahithophel's name, meaning "my brother is foolishness," is probably "a deliberate distortion satirizing the man's ill-used wisdom." So McCarter, *II Samuel*, p. 357, who suggests that the actual name was something like Ahiphelet. See 15:31. Cf. Ish-bosheth and Mephibosheth in our discussions of 2:8 and 4:4.

35. This conclusion is endorsed by a number of commentators such as Driver, *Notes*, p. 312; Hans Wilhelm Hertzberg, *I & II Samuel: A Commentary*, Old Testament Library (London: SCM Press, 1964), p. 337; Ronald F. Youngblood, *1 & 2 Samuel*, in Tremper Longman III and David E. Garland, eds., *The Expositor's Bible Commentary*, Revised Edition, vol. 3 (Grand Rapids, MI: Zondervan, 2009), p. 494, despite the skepticism of others such as Anderson, *2 Samuel*, pp. 153, 196; Dale Ralph Davis, *Expositions of the Book of 2 Samuel: Out of Every Adversity* (Geanies House, Fearn, UK: Christian Focus, 1999), p. 171, note 16. The facts are (a) Ahithophel had a son named Eliam (23:34); and (b) Bathsheba's father was named Eliam (11:3). It is reasonable (but not certain) to assume that it was the same man.

36. Gary A. Herion, "Giloh," in David Noel Freedman, ed., *The Anchor Bible Dictionary*, vol. 2 (New York: Doubleday, 1992), p. 1027.

37. Similarly Keil and Delitzsch, *Samuel*, p. 417.

38. See 1 Kings 15:27; 16:9, 16, 20; 2 Kings 9:14; 10:9; 11:14 (ESV, "treason"); 12:20; 14:19; 15:10, 15, 25, 30; 17:4 (ESV, "treachery"); 21:23, 24.

Chapter Thirty-One: The Darkest Day

1. See Map 12-10 in John D. Currid and David P. Barrett, *Crossway ESV Bible Atlas* (Wheaton, IL: Crossway, 2010), p. 233.

2. "One must think that the Gospel writers were acutely aware of this when they depicted Jesus' Maundy Thursday walk to the Mount of Olives in ways so graphically reminiscent of the 'passion' of the first *Meshiach* in 2 Samuel 15:13–37. Even the details of Judas' betrayal of Jesus, and his subsequent suicide, have no remote parallel anywhere in Scripture, with the remarkable exception of Ahithophel, who betrayed the Lord's anointed and thus opened the door to suicidal despair (2 Samuel

17:23)." Cited by Ronald F. Youngblood, *1 & 2 Samuel*, in Tremper Longman III and David E. Garland, eds., *The Expositor's Bible Commentary*, Revised Edition, vol. 3 (Grand Rapids, MI: Zondervan, 2009), p. 495, from James A. Wharton, "A Plausible Tale: Story and Theology in 2 Samuel 9—20, 1 Kings 1—2," *Interpretation* 35/4 (1981), pp. 341–354 (p. 353).

3. Unsurprisingly, opinions differ about the most appropriate divisions in this complex and sophisticated narrative. The chapter division suggests that the arrival of Hushai and David's conversation with him (15:32–37) belong with the passage before us. There are good reasons for this; most importantly, Hushai turns out to be the answer to David's prayer in verse 31. So, for example, Youngblood, *1 & 2 Samuel*, p. 495. On the significance of chapter divisions in the Old Testament, see John Woodhouse, *1 Samuel: Looking for a Leader*, Preaching the Word (Wheaton, IL: Crossway, 2008), p. 572, note 3. The division and structure of the passage presented here has benefited from J. P. Fokkelman, *Narrative Art and Poetry in the Books of Samuel: a full interpretation based on stylistic and structural analyses, Volume 1: King David (II Sam. 9—20 & I Kings 1—2)* (The Netherlands: Van Gorcum, Assen, 1981), pp. 175, 176.

4. Or "the informant." So Robert Alter, *The David Story: A Translation with Commentary of 1 and 2 Samuel* (New York and London: W. W. Norton & Company, 1999), p. 285. The Hebrew word here has the definite article and is different from the usual word for "messenger" (found, for example, in 11:4, 19, 22, 23, 25; a different word again is used in 15:10), which typically refers to someone "sent" with a message. Here the word is a participle of the verb translated "to inform" in verse 28 and "told" in verse 31. This person had not been sent by anyone. He was simply "the one who informed" David.

5. The Hebrew is grammatically singular, not, of course, suggesting one man, but all Israel *as one man*.

6. David's immediate response to the news makes me want to qualify Fokkelman's assertion that it was "almost a complete surprise to David . . . the king has for many years evidently closed his eyes to reality and deluded himself." Fokkelman, *David*, pp. 176, 177.

7. The verb "flee" is used repeatedly as David was on the run from Saul's hostility (1 Samuel 19:12, 18; 20:1; 21:10; 22:17, 20; 23:6; 27:4).

8. The superscription of Psalm 3 says, "A Psalm of David, when he fled from Absalom his son."

9. John records these words of Jesus before the departure from Jerusalem, and therefore they are closely reminiscent of the words of David. The other Gospels include similar words spoken in the Garden of Gethsemane (Matthew 26:46; Mark 14:42; cf. Luke 22:46).

10. Cf. Fokkelman, *David*, p. 178. The expression is translated "at his heels" in Judges 4:10.

11. There is a fuller consideration of concubines in the Old Testament in our discussion of 3:7.

12. Similarly Alter, *David*, p. 285.

13. Literally "the house of the distance." This may have been the actual name of a house, "the last house in the settled area beyond the walls of the city." Alter, *David*, p. 286. Similarly C. F. Keil and F. Delitzsch, *Biblical Commentary on the Books of Samuel* (Grand Rapids, MI: Eerdmans, 1950), p. 417.

14. Fokkelman, *David*, p. 179.

15. The Hebrew at this point begins to employ participles that impart "a sense of something like a present tense to the report of the action." Alter, *David*, p. 286. The servants, etc. "are passing by."

16. The expression "in his feet" (vv. 16a, 17a) is repeated here, such was the close loyalty of the Gittites to David.

17. So, for example, Alter, *David*, p. 286; Robert P. Gordon, *1 & 2 Samuel: A Commentary* (Exeter, UK: Paternoster, 1986), p. 273. Contra Keil and Delitzsch, *Samuel*, p. 418 who argue that 600 actual Philistines in David's service is not thinkable, but that the "six hundred Gittites" were the 600 old companions in arms that went with David to Gath (1 Samuel 27:2) and who afterward lived with him in Ziklag (1 Samuel 30:9). These were "[David's] men" who eventually followed him to Hebron (2:3) and Jerusalem (5:6). They were, on this argument, given the name "Gittites" because of their time in Gath, not because they were actually Philistines. The plausibility of this rather ingenious suggestion rests on the number 600 (more plausibly a coincidence, in my opinion; see 1 Samuel 13:15; 14:2) and the impossibility of Philistines being in David's service (which I do not accept). The suggestion becomes implausible (in my opinion) when we hear what David said to Ittai the Gittite in verses 19, 20.

18. Brueggemann seems to invert the perspective of the historian here by making the situation an implicit criticism of David: "David's military strength is not in a popular militia but in a paid guard." Walter Brueggemann, *First and Second Samuel*, Interpretation: A Bible Commentary for Teaching and Preaching (Louisville: John Knox Press, 1990), p. 303.

19. I deduce that Ittai was their leader from the following: (a) he was the one Gittite of the 600 that the king chose to address; (b) David invites him to take his "brothers" with him (v. 20); and (c) he appears a little later in the story as the commander of one third of David's army (18:2). It is possible that Ittai was a Philistine general who had entered David's service. Keil and Delitzsch, *Samuel*, p. 418. It is possible that Ittai was a leader of the Cherethites and Pelethites as well.

20. "You" and "your" in verses 19, 20 are singular.

21. See Joshua 3:14–17, where the verb rendered "passed by" and "passed on" in 15:23 occurs four times.

22. There may be further symbolism in the name. "Kidron" means "dark," and the threatening sense can be seen in Job 6:15, 16. Fokkelman comments on ". . . the rich symbolism of the Kidron here. David's crossing is fraught with disaster. As far as Absalom is concerned, David is going to his death, his flight acquires the emotional colour of mourning and shame. His son has consigned him to the dustbin of history and all are witnesses to his humiliation." Fokkelman, *David*, p. 185.

23. The allusion in John 18:1 to David's crossing of the Kidron is recognized by B. F. Westcott, *The Gospel According to St John: The Authorised Version with Introduction and Notes* (London: John Murray, 1896), p. 250; William Hendriksen, *A Commentary on the Gospel of John* (London: Banner of Truth, 1959), p. 376. The proposed allusion is noted without further comment by Raymond E. Brown, *The Gospel According to John (xiii-xxi)*, The Anchor Bible (London: Geoffrey Chapman, 1966), p. 806. The allusion is rejected by Rudolf Bultmann, *The Gospel of John: A Commentary* (Oxford: Basil Blackwell), p. 638, note 6.

24. Keil and Delitzsch, *Samuel*, p. 421.

25. Of course, David had been in "the wilderness" before, in his days as a fugitive from Saul (1 Samuel 23:14, 15, 24, 25; 24:1; 25:1, 4, 14, 21; 26:2, 3).

26. I suggest: "And behold, Zadok came also with all the Levites, bearing the ark of the covenant of God. And they set down the ark of God, and Abiathar offered sacrifices until the people had all passed out of the city." In this wording, the clause about Abiathar has been moved to more closely reflect the Hebrew and has been understood to mean that Abiathar "offered sacrifices" rather than "came up." Fokkelman describes how he imagines this happened in Fokkelman, *David*, p. 185, note 35. The Hebrew verb in question occurs in exactly the same form in 6:17 with the meaning "offer sacrifices." Cf. 1 Samuel 2:28; 2 Samuel 6:18; 24:22, 24, 25. Similarly NIV, HCSB; also Youngblood, *1 & 2 Samuel*, p. 501. Contra Keil and Delitzsch, *Samuel*, p. 421.

27. On Levites and the ark, see 1 Samuel 6:15, the only other reference to Levites in the books of Samuel.

28. For more information about the priests Zadok and Abiathar, see our discussion of 8:17.

29. I do not agree that sending the ark back to Jerusalem was "a surprising gesture of renunciation." Fokkelman, *David*, p. 186.

30. Or "Do you see?" Similarly NIV: "Do you understand?" Also Youngblood, *1 & 2 Samuel*, p. 499. There are difficulties with the ESV, "Are you a seer?"

31. "Thus David is indeed thinking, planning, and scheming. That does not cancel out his enormous faith, however. He does entrust himself to God, but such trust does not entail mindlessness or resignation." Brueggemann, *First and Second Samuel*, p. 304.

32. Keil and Delitzsch, *Samuel*, p. 422. So also Gordon, *1 & 2 Samuel*, p. 275.

33. This is the first of only two references to the Mount of Olives (here literally, "the ascent of the olives") in the Old Testament. Only in Zechariah 14:4 it is called "the Mount of Olives."

34. His head (and the people's heads) may have been "uncovered" (REB). Fokkelman, *David*, p. 188, note 37; Gordon, *1 & 2 Samuel*, p. 275. Whatever the translation, it refers to an expression of abject sorrow.

35. Gordon, *1 & 2 Samuel*, p. 275.

Chapter Thirty-Two: People Who Met David

1. In order to bring together these "people who met David," there is an overlap with the passage that we covered in our previous chapter.

2. The words "and may the LORD show . . . to you" in the ESV of verse 20 are not in the Hebrew text, but are found in the Septuagint and are included, for example, by J. P. Fokkelman, *Narrative Art and Poetry in the Books of Samuel: a full interpretation based on stylistic and structural analyses, Volume 1: King David (II Sam. 9—20 & I Kings 1—2)* (The Netherlands: Van Gorcum, Assen, 1981), p. 180; P. Kyle McCarter Jr., *II Samuel: A New Translation with Introduction, Notes & Commentary*, The Anchor Bible, vol. 9 (Garden City, NY: Doubleday, 1984), p. 365. However, the Septuagint may represent a reasonable interpretation of the Hebrew text as it stands rather than being evidence for a better text. On the other hand, another interpretation of the Hebrew could be "take your brothers back with you in grace and truth," that is, with

integrity. See the discussion in C. F. Keil and F. Delitzsch, *Biblical Commentary on the Books of Samuel* (Grand Rapids, MI: Eerdmans, 1950), p. 420. My understanding is that "Steadfast love and faithfulness!" expressed David's own goodwill toward Ittai and the Gittites. Cf. Robert Alter, *The David Story: A Translation with Commentary of 1 and 2 Samuel* (New York and London: W. W. Norton & Company, 1999), p. 287.

3. In the Hebrew of these two verses there are five emphatic pronouns, "you" three times in verse 19 and "I" twice in verse 20.

4. Hebrew has two words for "with." The other (and more common) one is used for "with the king" (v. 19) and for "with us" and "with you" (v. 20).

5. Keil and Delitzsch argue that David did not actually call Absalom "the king": "The words contain nothing more than the simple thought: Do you remain with whoever is or shall be king, since there is no necessity for you as a stranger to take sides at all." Keil and Delitzsch, *Samuel*, p. 419. This, I think, is not a natural understanding of David's words.

6. Fokkelman, *David*, p. 182.

7. "Little ones" can designate a man's whole family as in Exodus 12:37, where the same Hebrew word is rendered "women and children" in the ESV. Keil and Delitzsch, *Samuel*, p. 420.

8. "It is the migration of a small nation." Fokkelman, *David*, p. 183.

9. "[T]he Mount of Olives is about twenty-seven hundred feet high and rises about two hundred feet above the city itself." Ronald F. Youngblood, *1 & 2 Samuel*, in Tremper Longman III and David E. Garland, eds., *The Expositor's Bible Commentary*, Revised Edition, vol. 3 (Grand Rapids, MI: Zondervan, 2009), p. 500.

10. Fokkelman, *David*, p. 456. The Hebrew is literally, "where one [or he] would worship God."

11. The Hebrew word rendered "behold" occurs ten times in 2 Samuel 15, 16 (untranslated in 16:1, 5). In Hebrew it has the effect of emphasizing the immediacy of what is described. Here it suggests the presence of Hushai as unexpected and surprising. Cf. 1:2.

12. A. A. Anderson, *2 Samuel*, Word Biblical Commentary 11 (Dallas: Word, 1989), p. 205. Joshua 16:2 is generally understood to indicate that the Archites' territory lay to the south of the southern border of the land allotted to the people of Joseph, that is, in Benjamin. See Map 4-13 in John D. Currid and David P. Barrett, *Crossway ESV Bible Atlas* (Wheaton, IL: Crossway, 2010), p. 107.

13. The Hebrew can be read: "Hushai came . . . and Absalom was coming . . ." So Fokkelman, *David*, p. 192; contra Keil and Delitzsch, *Samuel*, p. 423 who see the two arrivals as "contemporaneous."

14. As Absalom approached the city from the south (from Hebron), the top of the Mount of Olives would have been in his line of sight. Similarly Fokkelman, *David*, p. 192.

15. For example, "one of his privy councillors." Keil and Delitzsch, *Samuel*, p. 423.

16. Similarly Fokkelman, *David*, pp. 191, 192, note 40.

17. See also 16:16, 17, where Absalom describes David as Hushai's "friend." This does not fit well with the idea that "friend" was a title.

18. Youngblood, *1 & 2 Samuel*, p. 503.

19. Ibid.

20. Contra Alter, *David*, p. 291, who regards Jonathan as Ziba's master.

21. Precisely the same Hebrew phrase is translated "your master's grandson" in the ESV of 9:9, 10.

22. Contra Alter, *David*, p. 291: "But David, overwhelmed by betrayals from within his own court, is suspicious of Mephibosheth's absence." Likewise "David's question to Ziba about Mephibosheth is not about the physical location of Saul's grandson. More likely it is about Mephibosheth's political sympathies. Whose side is he on?" Walter Brueggemann, *First and Second Samuel*, Interpretation: A Bible Commentary for Teaching and Preaching (Louisville: John Knox Press, 1990), p. 306.

23. In 9:13 "lived in Jerusalem" represents exactly the same Hebrew phrase.

24. The precise location is not certain. See Map 5-12 in Currid, *Atlas*, p. 129.

25. There is a similarity between "Bahurim" and the Hebrew word for weeping.

26. Norman H. Snaith, *Notes on the Hebrew Text of 2 Samuel xvi-xix* (London: The Epworth Press, 1945), p. 12.

27. Alter's rendering is an attractive alternative: "and here you are because of your evil . . ." Alter, *David*, p. 292. We are reminded that what David had done in 2 Samuel 11 was summed up as "evil in the eyes of the LORD" (11:27 AT). Shimei, of course, meant something else.

28. In Hebrew the plural of "blood" (as here) refers to shed blood.

29. On the harsh horror of the expression, see John Woodhouse, *1 Samuel: Looking for a Leader*, Preaching the Word (Wheaton, IL: Crossway, 2008), pp. 53, 54. Also 23:6.

30. There is a difference between describing oneself as a "dead dog" (as both David and Mephibosheth had done on different occasions, 1 Samuel 24:14; 2 Samuel 9:8) and calling someone else a "dead dog." The former expresses abject humility; the latter is a harsh insult.

31. The ESV wording, "the wrong done to me" is (in my opinion) an unnatural interpretation of "my iniquity," supported, however, by S. R. Driver, *Notes on the Hebrew Text and the Topography of the Book of Samuel with an Introduction on Hebrew Palaeography and Facsimiles of Inscriptions and Maps*, 2nd edition (Oxford: Clarendon, 1913), p. 318.

32. Literally David said, "What to me and to you . . . ?" The same idiom was used by Jesus in John 2:4.

33. Brueggemann, *First and Second Samuel*, p. 308.

34. Followed by the NIV ("my misery"), HCSB ("my affliction"), and REB ("my suffering").

35. See the fine discussion of this matter in Dale Ralph Davis, *Expositions of the Book of 2 Samuel: Out of Every Adversity* (Geanies House, Fearn, UK: Christian Focus, 1999), pp. 166–168. Also Keil and Delitzsch, *Samuel*, p. 426.

36. The words "at the Jordan" are lacking in the Hebrew but are found in the Septuagint. They accurately identify the location David had reached (see 17:22), but may have been added by a translator keen to clarify the vagueness of the Hebrew.

Chapter Thirty-Three: The Friend and the Traitor

1. It is unfortunately unfashionable in some academic circles today to read the psalms of David against the background of David's life recounted in 1 and 2 Samuel. It is therefore difficult to find modern commentaries on the Psalms that note the

probability of Ahithophel being the one spoken of in Psalm 41:9. However, the older commentaries were more comfortable with the obvious. Spurgeon, insightful as always, wrote about this verse, "This was Ahithophel to David, and Iscariot with our Lord." C. H. Spurgeon, *The Treasury of David* (Byron Center, MI: Associated Publishers and Authors, 1970), p. 287.

2. The narrator is picking up the story from 15:37, which noted Absalom's arrival in Jerusalem at about the time Hushai got there, after his climb down the west side of the Mount of Olives. In 16:1 the narrative went back to tell us that as Hushai had been making his way down that side of the mountain, David began the descent on the east side. Hushai's arrival at Jerusalem occurred at some time during David's eastward journey (16:1–14). Therefore "had come" is better than "came" (ESV) in 16:15. So REB; also Robert Alter, *The David Story: A Translation with Commentary of 1 and 2 Samuel* (New York and London: W. W. Norton & Company, 1999), p. 294.

3. Unknown to Absalom, even David had referred to him as "the king" (15:19).

4. The English idiom "Long live the king" emphasizes length of life. The Hebrew here is simply "Let the king *live*." The fact is that only one of the claimants to be king will live. Hushai's "Let the king live" is "an exercise in studied ambiguity." Ronald F. Youngblood, *1 & 2 Samuel*, in Tremper Longman III and David E. Garland, eds., *The Expositor's Bible Commentary*, Revised Edition, vol. 3 (Grand Rapids, MI: Zondervan, 2009), p. 511.

5. In comparable circumstances of uncertainty as to who was king, names were used: "Long live King Adonijah!" (1 Kings 1:25); "May my lord King David live forever!" (1 Kings 1:31); "Long live King Solomon!" (1 Kings 1:34, 39).

6. J. P. Fokkelman, *Narrative Art and Poetry in the Books of Samuel: a full interpretation based on stylistic and structural analyses, Volume 1: King David (II Sam. 9—20 & I Kings 1—2)* (The Netherlands: Van Gorcum, Assen, 1981), p. 206.

7. "His son" and "your father" are not the direct objects of "serve" in these two sentences (as in ESV, NIV, and other English versions). More literally, the Hebrew says, "Should it not be to the face of [that is, before] his son? As I have served to the face of [that is, before] your father . . ."

8. The last clause drops the verb "serve" (contra ESV, NIV, and other English versions). In his deliberate double-talk Hushai did not actually say that he would "serve Absalom."

9. In the Hebrew "have chosen" is singular, putting emphasis on the Lord's choice. The words "and this people and all the men of Israel" represent a subordinate idea. Similarly Fokkelman, *David*, p. 207, note 5.

10. As far as the books of Samuel are concerned, Saul had once been "him whom the LORD has chosen" (1 Samuel 10:24). David knew that the Lord had "chosen" him over Saul (6:21).

11. "And again" is literally, "And the second." This was presented clearly as a two-point speech.

12. Similarly Fokkelman, *David*, p. 208.

13. So Alter, *David*, p. 294.

14. Fokkelman is not certain that it was usual for a usurper to take over a harem, but "perhaps" it was so. Our consideration of 3:7 suggested that such an act would be understood as a grab at the throne. Fokkelman, *David*, p. 209, note 8.

15. Ibid., p. 209.

Chapter Thirty-Four: The Plan That Really Matters

1. The ESV offers a marginal reading for verse 3, following the Hebrew: "and I will bring all the people back to you. Like the return of the whole is the man whom you seek. And all the people will be at peace." This sentence is difficult in Hebrew (as it is in English), and that is probably why the Septuagint attempted an improvement, which is followed in the main text of the ESV. The Hebrew is, however, supported by other ancient versions and makes good, if slightly awkward, sense: the return of the whole nation to Absalom depends on the striking down of only one man, David, the man whom Absalom seeks. So C. F. Keil and F. Delitzsch, *Biblical Commentary on the Books of Samuel* (Grand Rapids, MI: Eerdmans, 1950), p. 429, note 1; J. P. Fokkelman, *Narrative Art and Poetry in the Books of Samuel: a full interpretation based on stylistic and structural analyses, Volume 1: King David (II Sam. 9—20 & I Kings 1—2)* (The Netherlands: Van Gorcum, Assen, 1981), pp. 213, 214, note 10; Ronald F. Youngblood, *1 & 2 Samuel*, in Tremper Longman III and David E. Garland, eds., *The Expositor's Bible Commentary*, Revised Edition, vol. 3 (Grand Rapids, MI: Zondervan, 2009), p. 519. Attempts at smoother English for verse 3b, paraphrasing the Hebrew, include: "The death of the man you seek will mean the return of all; all the people will be unharmed" (NIV); "When everyone returns except the man you're seeking, all the people will be at peace" (HCSB).

2. Similarly Youngblood, *1 & 2 Samuel*, p. 513.

3. Given the chronological unevenness that we often find in Biblical narrative, we should perhaps allow for the possibility that Ahithophel gave his advice in two parts (16:21 and 17:1–3). The fulfillment of the first part of that advice is then reported at a convenient point in the narrative, although it may have occurred at some later unspecified time. The difficulty of suggesting a plausible time when it may have happened does not necessarily disprove this possibility.

4. Similarly Fokkelman, *David*, p. 212.

5. The Hebrew behind "discouraged" is literally "weak of hands." It is not a direct statement about their state of mind, but a reference to the bodily weakness resulting from their physical, emotional, and mental exhaustion. Notice the contrast to what Ahithophel had said to Absalom a little earlier: "the *hands* of all who are with you will be *strengthened*" (16:21).

6. Fokkelman contrasts Ahithophel's political motive with Absalom's personal one, not acknowledging Ahithophel's very probable personal motive. Fokkelman, *David*, p. 213.

7. "Here speaks a sober politician, nay a wise statesman." Ibid., p. 213.

8. Similarly Fokkelman, *David*, p. 214.

9. The rhetorical skill of Hushai's speech is reflected in a simple but brilliant structure that has been discerned by S. Bar-Efrat, "Some Observations on the Analysis of Structure in Biblical Narrative," *Vetus Testamentum* 30/2 (1980), pp. 170, 171; see also Youngblood, *1 & 2 Samuel*, p. 514.

10. The use of vivid figures of speech in Hushai's speech ("like a bear robbed of her cubs in the field" and "like the heart of a lion") contrasts with the plain, honest language of Ahithophel's speech in the Hebrew text. This corroborates the view that the Septuagint of verse 3 (followed by ESV, REB), with its simile ("as a bride comes home to her husband") is not to be relied on.

11. The idea of being "gathered" is intensified in the Hebrew in a way difficult to convey in translation. Although he cannot have meant that "all Israel" (literally) be gathered to Absalom, he did intend a massive gathering that would be understood to fully represent "all Israel."

12. See Map 5-13 in John D. Currid and David P. Barrett, *Crossway ESV Bible Atlas* (Wheaton, IL: Crossway, 2010), p. 130.

13. "We" is emphasized in the Hebrew phrase in verse 12—literally, "and *we* upon him."

14. "Dew falls at night and is encountered plentifully in the morning by the peasant in Palestine. Dew is heavy and yet light. It falls silently, gradually and inimitably and is a blessing to the plants of the field. . . . The picture is also ironic, because the blessing of the gentle descent is fatal to David." Fokkelman, *David*, p. 218.

15. This is suggested by the order of words in the Hebrew sentence and the singular verb, "said."

16. It has been argued that verse 14 stands at the structural center of 2 Samuel 15—20. Youngblood, *1 & 2 Samuel*, p. 515.

17. "For" is a reasonable interpretation of the logical connection here. The Hebrew simply has "And."

18. There is a moral question here. Hushai's speech was intentionally deceptive. It contained deliberate untruths. See the reflections on telling lies in John Woodhouse, *1 Samuel: Looking for a Leader*, Preaching the Word (Wheaton, IL: Crossway, 2008), pp. 377, 378.

19. There is a reasonable argument for relocating this quotation mark: ". . . tell David, 'Do not stay tonight at the fords of the wilderness, but by all means pass over,' lest the king and all the people who are with him be swallowed up." The last clause would then be Hushai's explanation to Zadok and Abiathar of the urgency of the situation rather than part of the message to be taken to David. Fokkelman, *David*, p. 226.

20. Similarly Fokkelman, *David*, p. 225.

21. Or possibly "Well of the Runner." Fokkelman, *David*, p. 229.

22. See Joshua 15:7; 18:16; also Map 5-15 in Currid, *Atlas*, p. 133.

23. Similarly Fokkelman, *David*, p. 225.

24. So Fokkelman, *David*, p. 225. At this point the sequence of the narrative seems to correspond to the sequence of events.

25. See Map 5-12 in Currid, *Atlas*, p. 129.

26. Literally, "he and every man of Israel with him." The ESV ("with all the men of Israel," also NIV, HCSB) is not quite what the Hebrew actually says and introduces a problem unnecessarily. Absalom crossed the Jordan accompanied by every man of Israel who was "with him" (on his side), which was not "all the men of Israel."

27. The Hebrew has "Israelite" here, which has been changed by most English versions to "Ishmaelite," under the influence of 1 Chronicles 2:17 and some Septuagint manuscripts. It is generally argued that it would hardly be necessary in this context to identify a man as an "Israelite." However, the Hebrew may be a statement of political alliance rather than birth—an Israelite rather than a Judean (although born an Ishmaelite, 1 Chronicles 2:17). Cf. Robert P. Gordon, *1 & 2 Samuel: A Commentary* (Exeter, UK: Paternoster, 1986), p. 361, note 184.

28. The Hebrew is, literally, "had gone in to Abigal." Since the language refers to sexual relations rather than marriage as such, it has been suggested that Ithra had "seduced" Abigal. Keil and Delitzsch, *Samuel*, p. 433.

29. This is preferable to an understanding that restricts "Israel" here to the northern tribes. While Absalom had support from Israel in that more restricted sense, there is no reason to think that his base was limited.

30. See Map 5-12 in Currid, *Atlas*, p. 129.

31. The Hebrew here repeats the words "and parched grain" from earlier in the list. The repetition is defended by Keil and Delitzsch, *Samuel*, pp. 434, 435.

32. There is much more to the wilderness theme in the Bible. For a brief summary see R. E. Watts, "Wilderness," in T. Desmond Alexander and Brian S. Rosner, *New Dictionary of Biblical Theology* (Downers Grove, IL: InterVarsity Press, 2000), pp. 841–843.

Chapter Thirty-Five: When Love and Justice Do Not Meet

1. The expression "the men who were with him" in verse 1 (ESV) is identical in Hebrew to "the people with him" in the previous verse (17:29). Throughout 2 Samuel 18 the Hebrew for "the people" is variously rendered in the ESV: "the men" (vv. 1, 2b, 3, 7), "the army" (vv. 2a, 4, 6), "the people" (vv. 5, 8), "the troops" (v. 16a), "them" (v. 16b). This may be a fair representation of the referent of the Hebrew word in each context, but the Hebrew does not so clearly differentiate "the army" from "the people." The army represented the people so that, in principle, "the army" was "the people."

2. The terminology companies, regiments, and divisions is suggested by J. P. Fokkelman, *Narrative Art and Poetry in the Books of Samuel: a full interpretation based on stylistic and structural analyses, Volume 1: King David (II Sam. 9—20 & I Kings 1—2)* (The Netherlands: Van Gorcum, Assen, 1981), p. 237.

3. This confirms our earlier inference from 16:10 that both Joab and Abishai were with David as he fled from Jerusalem.

4. The Hebrew behind "I myself will also go out with you" is very forceful. "I myself" is emphatic. This is underlined by "also." "Will go out" is categorical: "will *indeed* go out."

5. The translation here depends on a slight emendation to the Hebrew (supported by some Hebrew manuscripts and ancient versions), which has "now" instead of "you." C. F. Keil and F. Delitzsch, *Biblical Commentary on the Books of Samuel* (Grand Rapids, MI: Eerdmans, 1950), p. 435.

6. So Fokkelman, *David*, p. 238.

7. So Keil and Delitzsch, *Samuel*, pp. 436, 437.

8. Hebrew: "land."

9. This is strongly argued by Keil and Delitzsch, *Samuel*, pp. 436, 437, but just as emphatically rejected by most more recent commentaries, such as P. Kyle McCarter Jr., *II Samuel: A New Translation with Introduction, Notes & Commentary*, The Anchor Bible, vol. 9 (Garden City, NY: Doubleday, 1984), p. 405; Robert P. Gordon, *1 & 2 Samuel: A Commentary* (Exeter, UK: Paternoster, 1986), p. 284; A. A. Anderson, *2 Samuel*, Word Biblical Commentary 11 (Dallas: Word, 1989), p. 224; Dale Ralph Davis, *Expositions of the Book of 2 Samuel: Out of Every Adversity* (Geanies House, Fearn, UK: Christian Focus, 1999), p. 183, note 3.

10. Keil and Delitzsch, *Samuel*, pp. 437, 438.

11. This is a small selection from hundreds of references to the land as the Lord's gift to Israel.

12. In Hebrew, "the great oak." When this account was written, the oak tree may have become well-known because of this incident.

13. Gordon, *1 & 2 Samuel*, p. 284, citing G. R. Driver who suggests that the two boughs "had been kept low down and held together by the surrounding branches; jolted by the impact of Absalom's weight, the fork became dislodged and its two arms closed round Absalom's neck as they sprang upwards, freed from entangling branches and carrying him with them."

14. For the belt as a symbol of a warrior's status, see also 1 Samuel 18:4; 2 Samuel 20:8; 1 Kings 2:5; 2 Kings 3:21 (ESV, "armor"); Isaiah 3:24; Ezekiel 23:15.

15. The Hebrew sentence, more literally translated, is, "I am not going to wait like this *before you*," suggesting that Joab was impatient with being treated as the man's inferior ("before you"). He was not going to be lectured at like this.

16. Keil and Delitzsch, *Samuel*, p. 412.

17. Genesis 14:17 is evidence that the location was known as the King's Valley at the time the book of Genesis was written or edited, which could have been after King David's time. In Abraham's day it was known as the Valley of Shaveh (meaning "level" or "smooth").

18. McCarter, *II Samuel*, p. 408.

19. "To this day" is an expression that occurs with varying frequency in Biblical history, often relating the events of the past to some witness to these events present in the writer's (and the early readers') day. See 1 Samuel 5:5; 6:18; 27:6; 30:25; 2 Samuel 4:3; 6:8.

20. It is possible that the news Ahimaaz wanted to carry concerned only the victory (v. 7). He may not yet have known about the death of Absalom. That will be his claim in verse 29.

21. The Hebrew word rendered "carry news" is typically translated into Greek with the vocabulary the New Testament uses for "preach the gospel." This and cognate words are variously rendered in the ESV of 2 Samuel 18:19–31: "carry news" (vv. 19, 20), "reward for the news" (v. 22), "news" (vv. 25, 27), "brings news" (v. 26), and "good news" (v. 31).

22. There is a debate as to whether the Hebrew words on view here mean "good" news. In my opinion the sense in which the news may be "good" depends on the context, the Hebrew vocabulary referring to important but not necessarily "good" news. Contra O. Schilling, "*bsr*," in G. Johannes Botterweck and Helmer Ringgren, eds., *Theological Dictionary of the Old Testament*, vol. 2 (Grand Rapids, MI: Eerdmans, 1975), pp. 313–316. A review of the use of this vocabulary in the books of Samuel illustrates the point. In 1 Samuel 4:17, "He who brought the news" represents a form of the verb we are discussing. In this case the news was disastrous for those to whom it was spoken, not "good" news at all. In 1 Samuel 31:9 the "good news" was "good" only from the point of view of the Philistines (similarly "publish" in 1:20; "bringing good news" in 4:10). See John Woodhouse, *1 Samuel: Looking for a Leader*, Preaching the Word (Wheaton, IL: Crossway, 2008), p. 551.

23. This word is translated "judge" in 1 Samuel 4:18; 7:6, 15, 16, 17; 8:1, 5, 6, 20; 2 Samuel 15:4, and its meaning is discussed in Woodhouse, *1 Samuel*, pp. 100,

130, 135. There is no doubt irony in the fact that Absalom's ambition had been to be "judge in the land" (15:4). The Lord had judged the would-be judge.

24. I take the last clause as the narrator's comment rather than Joab's words to Ahimaaz (as in the ESV). If Ahimaaz knew only of the victory, but not of Absalom's death (as he will claim in verse 29), then the reason for Joab's caution was explained to the reader, but not to Ahimaaz. So McCarter, *II Samuel*, p. 408; contra Davis, *2 Samuel*, p. 191, note 18.

25. The Hebrew has a definite article here and could suggest "the Cushite well-known to readers since this episode." However, the definite article in Hebrew does not have exactly the same force as in English and often should be translated with an indefinite article, "a Cushite." So REB, NIV. See A. E. Cowley, *Gesenius' Hebrew Grammar as edited and enlarged by the late E. Kautzsch*, Second English Edition (Oxford: Clarendon Press, 1910), p. 407.

26. "The Cushite" has sometimes been understood as a proper name, "Cushi." So KJV; a possibility noted, but not preferred, by Keil and Delitzsch, *Samuel*, p. 440; rejected as "wrong" by Gordon, *1& 2 Samuel*, p. 286.

27. See Map 1-2 in John D. Currid and David P. Barrett, *Crossway ESV Bible Atlas* (Wheaton, IL: Crossway, 2010), p. 55.

28. "He said" is not expressed in the Hebrew, but is clearly implied.

29. So Keil and Delitzsch, *Samuel*, p. 441, who regard this as "decisive proof" that the forest of Ephraim was on the west side of the Jordan.

30. So S. R. Driver, *Notes on the Hebrew Text and the Topography of the Book of Samuel with an Introduction on Hebrew Palaeography and Facsimiles of Inscriptions and Maps*, 2nd edition (Oxford: Clarendon, 1913), pp. 331, 332; Gordon, *1& 2 Samuel*, p. 286. Contra Keil and Delitzsch, *Samuel*, p. 441, who regard it as "utterly impossible" for the supposed circuitous route to be traversed more quickly than the direct route.

31. The NIV, JB, and HCSB wrongly have "good news" here. David did not deduce that a man running alone must be bringing *good* news, just that he must be bringing *news*. There are plenty of examples of lone messengers bringing bad news (see 1 Samuel 4:12; 2 Samuel 1:2). Fokkelman's interpretation of this scene as "David . . . feverishly engaged in self-deception" (Fokkelman, *David*, p. 255) is also dependent on the view that the vocabulary means *good* news, rather than news that may or may not be good. This understanding is reflected in a number of commentaries including Keil and Delitzsch, *Samuel*, p. 441; Ronald F. Youngblood, *1 & 2 Samuel*, in Tremper Longman III and David E. Garland, eds., *The Expositor's Bible Commentary*, Revised Edition, vol. 3 (Grand Rapids, MI: Zondervan, 2009), p. 531. The more neutral (and reasonable) view that a lone runner must be bringing *news* is suggested in Gordon, *1& 2 Samuel*, p. 286; Robert Alter, *The David Story: A Translation with Commentary of 1 and 2 Samuel* (New York and London: W. W. Norton & Company, 1999), p. 308.

32. The Hebrew explicitly uses the adjective "good" here. This supports the view that the word rendered "news" only means "*good* news" when the context makes that clear.

33. Cf. McCarter, *II Samuel*, p. 409; P. Kyle McCarter Jr., *I Samuel: A New Translation with Introduction, Notes & Commentary*, The Anchor Bible, vol. 8 (Garden City, NY: Doubleday, 1980), p. 322.

34. Among those who do not accord Ahimaaz the benefit of the doubt are Alter, *David*, p. 309; J. Robert Vannoy, *1—2 Samuel*, Cornerstone Biblical Commentary, 4a (Wheaton, IL: Tyndale House, 2009), p. 381; Davis, *2 Samuel*, p. 191.

35. Curiously it is the Cushite who used the "justice" vocabulary, as Ahimaaz had in verse 19. In verse 28 Ahimaaz did not use this language.

36. See the sensitive discussion of the issues in Vannoy, *1—2 Samuel*, pp. 380–382.

Chapter Thirty-Six: The Return of the King

1. "This gross exaggeration is a sarcastic variation of the loyalty of 18:3." J. P. Fokkelman, *Narrative Art and Poetry in the Books of Samuel: a full interpretation based on stylistic and structural analyses, Volume 1: King David (II Sam. 9—20 & 1 Kings 1—2)* (The Netherlands: Van Gorcum, Assen, 1981), p. 272.

2. "Speak kindly to your servants" is literally "speak to the heart of your servants." This is the language of love in, for example, Genesis 34:3.

3. So Fokkelman, *David*, p. 273, note 7; contra Robert P. Gordon, *1 & 2 Samuel: A Commentary* (Exeter, UK: Paternoster, 1986), p. 288.

4. Contra Keil and Delitzsch who deduce from the context that David "manifested his good-will in both looks and words." C. F. Keil and F. Delitzsch, *Biblical Commentary on the Books of Samuel* (Grand Rapids, MI: Eerdmans, 1950), p. 444.

5. In both verse 8b and 18:17 the word translated "home" is more literally "tent."

6. The words "when [or and] the word of all Israel has [or had] come to the king" may be the narrator's comment, explaining the circumstances that led to David's question. So Keil and Delitzsch, *Samuel*, p. 444. Fokkelman, with some support from the Septuagint, puts these words before verse 11. Similarly Gordon, *1 & 2 Samuel*, pp. 288, 289. The various possibilities make no substantial difference.

7. "David thus creates a distinction between Judah and Israel on his return, and this has very unfavourable consequences for the unity of his kingdom." Fokkelman, *David*, p. 292.

8. "My brothers" likewise does not elevate the tribe of Judah above the northern tribes. Rather the words probably allude to Deuteronomy 17:15: "One from among your brothers you shall set as king over you."

9. We do not know whether David had yet learned of Joab's role in Absalom's death. That is beside the point, however. Joab had been charged with Absalom's protection (18:5, 12) and had (at least) failed to do that.

10. "The replacement of the army commander is primarily the vengeance of a masochist detected." Fokkelman, *David*, p. 277. Similarly Gordon, *1 & 2 Samuel*, p. 289.

11. Similarly Dale Ralph Davis, *Expositions of the Book of 2 Samuel: Out of Every Adversity* (Geanies House, Fearn, UK: Christian Focus, 1999), p. 195.

12. The frequency of this verb is hidden in the English translation, which renders it variously in 19:15–41: "bring over," "cross," "go," "come over," "go over," and "bring on his way."

13. For a possible route see Map 5-12 in John D. Currid and David P. Barrett, *Crossway ESV Bible Atlas* (Wheaton, IL: Crossway, 2010), p. 129.

14. See Map 4-7 in Currid, *Atlas*, p. 101.

15. See John Woodhouse, *1 Samuel: Looking for a Leader*, Preaching the Word (Wheaton, IL: Crossway, 2008), p. 174.

16. Fokkelman, *David*, p. 299, note 1.

17. Gordon, *1& 2 Samuel*, p. 289.

18. We may support our cynicism about Shimei's sincerity by noting that in due course David himself still held Shimei's crimes against him (1 Kings 2:8, 9). This begs the question whether what David said on his deathbed was right or wrong, as well as the question whether Shimei acted in ways that spurned the mercy that he received here.

19. Strictly speaking the house of Joseph was the two large tribes of Ephraim and Manasseh, but "Joseph" here represents all of the northern tribes, "Israel" in the narrower sense. Cf. Joshua 16:1, 4; 17:17; 18:5; 1 Kings 11:28.

20. Gordon, *1& 2 Samuel*, p. 290. Cf. Mark 8:33.

21. This is based on the phrase "when he came to Jerusalem" in verse 25. The NIV has "from Jerusalem" because Mephibosheth lived in Jerusalem (9:13; 16:3), and in the context the king had not yet reached Jerusalem (he only reaches Gilgal by verse 40 and does not get to Jerusalem until 20:2). The Hebrew lacks a preposition at this point, but the most natural way to take the Hebrew phrase is, as in the ESV, "he came to Jerusalem." It seems most straightforward to understand that the following conversation took place later than the setting in the text, when the king had reached Jerusalem. P. Kyle McCarter Jr., *II Samuel: A New Translation with Introduction, Notes & Commentary*, The Anchor Bible, vol. 9 (Garden City, NY: Doubleday, 1984), p. 421. Such chronological unevenness is not unusual in Biblical narratives. An alternative but somewhat awkward rendering would be, "And when Jerusalem came to meet the king." Keil and Delitzsch, *Samuel*, p. 447, note 1.

22. In verses 41–43 a number of singular nouns and verbs are used in the Hebrew, making the speeches sound particularly personal. Literally, "my close relative. Why then are you [singular] angry . . . ?" (v. 42); "I have ten shares . . . I have more than you [singular] . . . Why then did you [singular] despise me? . . . Was I not the first to speak . . . my king?" This does not work well in English, and most translations use plurals throughout.

23. This is the third time that the verb "to steal" has been used in recent chapters, each time signaling a negative evaluation of an action. Absalom "stole the hearts of the men of Israel" (15:6). The people who had fought for David "stole" into Mahanaim because of David's grief (19:3). The people of Judah are here accused of "stealing" the king.

24. Rather than David's as suggested by Fokkelman, *David*, p. 316.

25. Fokkelman argues that David was directly responsible for the division among the people. "The schism between Israel and Judah is not a natural disaster but is the direct and expected result of the schismatic David." Fokkelman, *David*, p. 316. I am not convinced that this is fair. The tensions between "Israel and Judah" go back much further. They were evident at the beginning of David's reign (2 Samuel 2).

Chapter Thirty-Seven: An Unstable Kingdom

1. See John Woodhouse, *1 Samuel: Looking for a Leader*, Preaching the Word (Wheaton, IL: Crossway, 2008), pp. 53, 54.

2. In verse 14 the Hebrew does not have the name Sheba. The ESV has added it to clarify who "passed through."

3. The proposal that "son of Bichri" also suggests being stubborn, rebellious, and self-willed on the basis of a similar word *beker* meaning "camel" (cf. Isaiah 60:6; Jeremiah 2:23) is in my opinion unlikely. Ronald F. Youngblood, *1 & 2 Samuel*, in Tremper Longman III and David E. Garland, eds., *The Expositor's Bible Commentary*, Revised Edition, vol. 3 (Grand Rapids, MI: Zondervan, 2009), p. 549. More plausible is the suggestion that there may be a link between Bichri here and Becorath in 1 Samuel 9:1, 2, indicating that Sheba might have been of Saul's family. Robert P. Gordon, *1 & 2 Samuel: A Commentary* (Exeter, UK: Paternoster, 1986), p. 293.

4. For the sense of the word translated "portion," see 1 Samuel 30:24 (ESV, "share").

5. Although Sheba's call was not successful in his time, the secession of Israel from Judah, when it eventually came, was declared in words almost identical to Sheba's (1 Kings 12:16). "Sheba ben Bichri was before his time." Youngblood, *1 & 2 Samuel*, p. 550.

6. Literally, "went up," that is, from the Jordan Valley to the mountains. C. F. Keil and F. Delitzsch, *Biblical Commentary on the Books of Samuel* (Grand Rapids, MI: Eerdmans, 1950), p. 452.

7. The Hebrew word used here denotes strong allegiance. It is the word rendered "hold fast" in Genesis 2:24.

8. Similarly Keil and Delitzsch, *Samuel*, p. 452. Contra J. P. Fokkelman, *Narrative Art and Poetry in the Books of Samuel: a full interpretation based on stylistic and structural analyses, Volume 1: King David (II Sam. 9—20 & I Kings 1—2)* (The Netherlands: Van Gorcum, Assen, 1981), p. 320; Youngblood, *1 & 2 Samuel*, p. 550.

9. For the positive sense of this language, see 19:33.

10. So Walter Brueggemann, *First and Second Samuel*, Interpretation: A Bible Commentary for Teaching and Preaching (Louisville: John Knox Press, 1990), p. 330.

11. A quite literal rendering of the last clause of verse 3. Cf. Fokkelman, *David*, pp. 320, 459.

12. Keil and Delitzsch, *Samuel*, p. 453.

13. Fokkelman, *David*, p. 324.

14. The phrase "and escape from us" is difficult in Hebrew and has been variously rendered and interpreted: "'*tear out our eye*,' i.e. do us a serious injury," Keil and Delitzsch, *Samuel*, p. 453; "pluck out our eyes," Fokkelman, *David*, p. 325; "cause to remove our eye (from him)," that is, he will escape us, Dale Ralph Davis, *Expositions of the Book of 2 Samuel: Out of Every Adversity* (Geanies House, Fearn, UK: Christian Focus, 1999), p. 206, note 8.

15. On historical associations of Gibeon, see our discussion of 2:12.

16. Similarly Fokkelman, *David*, p. 328, note 14.

17. The Hebrew sentence signals Joab's leadership over Abishai not only by Joab being mentioned first, but also by the singular form of the verb "pursued." Joab is the grammatical subject of the verb. Abishai accompanied Joab in his pursuit.

18. Verse 10b is a summary statement of what "Joab and Abishai" did next. The more detailed account of what that involved is then given in verses 11–13, which explain how it was that "all the people" joined Joab and Abishai in the pursuit of Sheba.

19. The Hebrew lacks the name, but it is reasonable to infer that "he passed through" refers to "Sheba son of Bichri" at the end of the previous verse, especially as the person concerned went into the city of Abel. "It must be Sheba" according to Fokkelman, *David*, p. 460. Contra Keil and Delitzsch, *Samuel*, p. 455, who take Joab as the subject of "passed through."

20. The Hebrew text has "Berites," a reading defended by Keil and Delitzsch, *Samuel*, p. 455 and followed by HCSB. Some ancient versions, however, have "Bichrites," which seems more likely. See S. R. Driver, *Notes on the Hebrew Text and the Topography of the Book of Samuel with an Introduction on Hebrew Palaeography and Facsimiles of Inscriptions and Maps*, 2nd edition (Oxford: Clarendon, 1913), pp. 344, 345.

21. See Map 5-11 in John D. Currid and David P. Barrett, *Crossway ESV Bible Atlas* (Wheaton, IL: Crossway, 2010), p. 128.

22. For "all the men who were with Joab came" the Hebrew has "they came," but the ESV is certainly correct since the words "all the men who were with Joab" occur later in the verse (in Hebrew), confirming the obvious identity of "they." Cf. Fokkelman, *David*, p. 460.

23. We have learned from this story that "wise" is morally ambiguous. It can be the evil cleverness of Jonadab (13:3, ESV, "crafty"), or the treacherous ingenuity of Ahithophel (15:31), or the sound, though deceptive, advice of the woman from Tekoa (14:2–17).

24. Fokkelman, *David*, p. 332.

25. Keil and Delitzsch, *Samuel*, p. 455.

26. This vivid metaphor for a military attack was used in 17:16 with reference to what might have happened to David and the people with him.

27. See Woodhouse, *1 Samuel*, p. 169.

28. "The hill country of Ephraim" extended into the tribal territory of Benjamin, Sheba's tribe. See Map 4-13 in Currid, *Atlas*, p. 107.

29. I have reordered some of the items in the list in 8:15–18 so that they line up with corresponding items in 20:23–26.

30. The addition of the words "in command of" in 20:23, compared with "over" in 8:16, does not reflect the Hebrew, but has been introduced by the translator.

31. Alter, *David*, p. 328.

Chapter Thirty-Eight: A Problem in David's Kingdom: God's Wrath I

1. *Epilogue* is a better term than *appendix* or *appendices* to describe these chapters, bearing in mind the close connections this material has with the preceding history. See Robert Alter, *The David Story: A Translation with Commentary of 1 and 2 Samuel* (New York and London: W. W. Norton & Company, 1999), p. 329; Ronald F. Youngblood, *1 & 2 Samuel*, in Tremper Longman III and David E. Garland, eds., *The Expositor's Bible Commentary*, Revised Edition, vol. 3 (Grand Rapids, MI: Zondervan, 2009), p. 557; J. Robert Vannoy, *1—2 Samuel*, Cornerstone Biblical Commentary, 4a (Wheaton, IL: Tyndale House, 2009), pp. 393–396.

2. An arrangement along these lines has been widely recognized for a long time (well before it became trendy in scholarly circles to find such arrangements, imagined or otherwise, almost everywhere). See C. F. Keil and F. Delitzsch, *Biblical Commentary on the Books of Samuel* (Grand Rapids, MI: Eerdmans, 1950),

p. 458; Henry Preserved Smith, *A Critical and Exegetical Commentary on the Books of Samuel*, The International Critical Commentary (Edinburgh: T. & T. Clark, 1899), p. 373. Also Robert P. Gordon, *1 & 2 Samuel: A Commentary* (Exeter: Paternoster, 1986), p. 45; Alter, *David*, p. 329; Youngblood, *1 & 2 Samuel*, p. 558; and most modern commentaries.

3. It has been suggested that the famine may have occurred between the end of 2 Samuel 9 and the beginning of 2 Samuel 10. The plausibility of this suggestion rests on the difficulty (but not impossibility) of envisaging the three-year famine and the events of 2 Samuel 21 occurring anywhere in the unbroken sequence of events from 2 Samuel 10 to 2 Samuel 20. See the nuanced but finally unsatisfying discussion in J. P. Fokkelman, *Narrative Art and Poetry in the Books of Samuel: a full interpretation based on stylistic and structural analyses, Volume 3: Throne and City (II Sam. 2—8 & 21—24)* (The Netherlands: Van Gorcum, Assen, 1990), pp. 283, 284.

4. Alter, *David*, p. 329. Cf. 1 Kings 10:24.

5. We are not told how the Lord spoke to David. It may have been through a prophet (as in 2 Samuel 7, 12). It may have been by some other means. As usual the focus is on what the Lord said rather than how he said it. The direct quotation of the Lord's words indicates that this communication was clear and specific. It was not a hunch on David's part. See our discussion of 2:1.

6. "Bloodguilt" here represents the plural of the Hebrew word for "blood," which can refer to shed blood or to the guilt associated with the shedding of blood. Shimei used this plural when he called David a "man of blood," that is, a murderer (16:7, 8). See this idiom also in 1 Samuel 25:26, 33; cf. 2 Samuel 1:16; 3:28.

7. The Gibeonites had originally also inhabited the cities of Chephirah, Beeroth, and Kiriath-jearim (Joshua 9:17). See Map 4-10 in John D. Currid and David P. Barrett, *Crossway ESV Bible Atlas* (Wheaton, IL: Crossway, 2010), p. 105.

8. "Amorites" is a term that can refer to a particular ethnic group among the early inhabitants of Canaan (along with Hittites, Perizzites, Jebusites, and Hivites, Exodus 3:8, 17; 23:23; Joshua 9:1; etc.). It is also used as a general term for the pre-Israelite population in Canaan (as in Genesis 15:16; Joshua 24:15; 1 Samuel 7:14). The latter is the sense here because the Gibeonites were, more strictly speaking, Hivites (Joshua 9:7; 11:19).

9. "[T]he fact that they were settled in Benjaminite territory cannot have helped." Gordon, *1& 2 Samuel*, p. 299.

10. Similarly Youngblood, *1 & 2 Samuel*, p. 560.

11. Literally "Whatever you say I will do for you." Fokkelman, *Throne*, pp. 278, 386.

12. For symbolic use of "seven" as a number representing completion, see 1 Samuel 2:5. For a helpful survey of significant uses of "seven" in the Bible, see R. A. H. Gunner, "Number," in J. D. Douglas, ed., *The Illustrated Bible Dictionary*, Part 2 (Leicester, UK and Wheaton, IL: Inter-Varsity Press and Tyndale House, 1980), p. 1098.

13. So JB.

14. So Keil and Delitzsch, *Samuel*, p. 461. The only use of this Hebrew verb outside this chapter is Numbers 25:4.

15. See A. A. Anderson, *2 Samuel*, Word Biblical Commentary 11 (Dallas: Word, 1989), pp. 251, 252; Gordon, *1& 2 Samuel*, pp. 300, 301.

16. This is certainly the correct reading, despite "Michal" in a number of Hebrew manuscripts. So Keil and Delitzsch, *Samuel*, p. 461; Fokkelman, *Throne*, p. 387. See 1 Samuel 18:19.

17. "The Meholathite" distinguishes this Barzillai from "Barzillai the Gileadite" from Rogelim (2 Samuel 17:27; 19:31; 1 Kings 2:7). The designation probably indicates that this Barzillai's hometown was Abel-meholah (Judges 7:22; 1 Kings 4:12; 19:16). See Map 4-19 in Currid, *Atlas*, p. 111.

18. There had been another falling "together" (which occurred in Gibeon). See our discussion of 2:16.

19. Gordon, *1 & 2 Samuel*, p. 301.

20. This paragraph is indebted to the moving reflection on this scene in Fokkelman, *Throne*, pp. 285, 286.

21. Gordon, *1 & 2 Samuel*, p. 301.

22. Alter, *David*, p. 332.

23. See Map 5-8 in Currid, *Atlas*, p. 126.

24. The specific location of Zela is unknown. It is mentioned in Joshua 18:28.

Chapter Thirty-Nine: The Strength of David's Kingdom: His Mighty Men, Part 1

1. How this narrative shows Saul's failure to deal with the Philistines is discussed in John Woodhouse, *1 Samuel: Looking for a Leader*, Preaching the Word (Wheaton, IL: Crossway, 2008), pp. 172–177.

2. Alter suggests that the phrase may indicate an aging David, "but not yet the vulnerable sedentary monarch of the conflict with Absalom." Robert Alter, *The David Story: A Translation with Commentary of 1 and 2 Samuel* (New York and London: W. W. Norton & Company, 1999), p. 333.

3. Perhaps he lived in an inaccessible castle. C. F. Keil and F. Delitzsch, *Biblical Commentary on the Books of Samuel* (Grand Rapids, MI: Eerdmans, 1950), p. 464.

4. There are various views about the meaning of the two key terms, rendered in the ESV as "descendants" and "giants." For a useful survey of arguments, see Ronald F. Youngblood, *1 & 2 Samuel*, in Tremper Longman III and David E. Garland, eds., *The Expositor's Bible Commentary*, Revised Edition, vol. 3 (Grand Rapids, MI: Zondervan, 2009), pp. 566, 567.

5. See T. C. Mitchell, "Rephaim," in J. D. Douglas, ed., *The Illustrated Bible Dictionary*, Part 3 (Leicester, UK and Wheaton, IL: Inter-Varsity Press and Tyndale House, 1980), p. 1328.

6. The Hebrew word here is of uncertain meaning. It occurs nowhere else in the Old Testament.

7. The Hebrew lacks a word for "sword." Cf. "who wore new armor" (HCSB).

8. J. P. Fokkelman, *Narrative Art and Poetry in the Books of Samuel: A Full Interpretation Based on Stylistic and Structural Analyses, Volume 3: Throne and City (II Sam. 2—8 & 21—24* (The Netherlands: Van Gorcum, Assen, 1990), p. 295; contra Keil and Delitzsch, *Samuel*, p. 464.

9. The Hebrew behind "attacked the Philistine and killed him" in 21:17 is identical to "struck the Philistine and killed him" in 1 Samuel 17:50.

10. This probably means "administered an oath to him, *i.e.* fixed him by a promise on oath." Keil and Delitzsch, *Samuel*, p. 464.

11. "After this" should probably not be taken as a clear chronological indicator. It functions as a transitional phrase. Cf. "In the course of time . . ." (NIV). Young-blood, *1 & 2 Samuel*, p. 312.

12. See Map 5-10 in John D. Currid and David P. Barrett, *Crossway ESV Bible Atlas* (Wheaton, IL: Crossway, 2010), p. 128.

13. Dale C. Liid, "Hushah," in David Noel Freedman, ed., *The Anchor Bible Dictionary*, vol. 3 (New York: Doubleday, 1992), p. 338.

14. The wording at the end of verse 19 is identical to 1 Samuel 17:7a. On what a spear with a shaft like a weaver's beam would be like, see Woodhouse, *1 Samuel*, pp. 306, 307.

15. So Keil and Delitzsch, *Samuel*, p. 466. There are certainly good reasons, very widely accepted, to think that "Jaare-oregim" in 21:19 should be "Jair," as in 1 Chronicles 20:5. The word "oregim" appears at the end of both verses (translated "weaver's"), and its occurrence twice in 21:19 "is almost universally regarded" as a copying error. Robert P. Gordon, *1 & 2 Samuel: A Commentary* (Exeter, UK: Paternoster, 1986), p. 303. Since there is only a small difference between Jair and Jaare in Hebrew, there was probably another minor copying error (by the same sleepy scribe?). Furthermore, the Hebrew behind "Bethlehemite" (*beth-hallahmi*) is quite close to *eth-lahmi* ("Lahmi"). It is possible that our weary scribe made yet a third error.

16. There are other possibilities, including (1) the suggestion that Goliath was more a title than a personal name (so that two Philistine brothers were both "Goliath"); cf. Hans Wilhelm Hertzberg, *I & II Samuel: A Commentary*, Old Testament Library (London: SCM Press, 1964), p. 387; (2) the possibility that Elhanan was another name for David (just as Solomon had the name Jedidiah), see Gordon, *1 & 2 Samuel*, p. 303; and (3) that there were other textual transmission errors. For a brief outline and judicious evaluation of the possibilities, see D. F. Payne, in D. Guthrie and J. A. Motyer, *The New Bible Commentary Revised* (London: Inter-Varsity Press, 1970), pp. 318, 319.

17. Another man with the same name is mentioned in 2 Samuel 23:24; 1 Chronicles 11:26.

18. See note 15 above.

19. The same phrase in Jeremiah 15:10 is translated "a man of . . . contention." The reference seems to be to his taunting of Israel (v. 21). He was an "expert in derision, an agitator." Fokkelman, *Throne*, p. 298. See the term also in Proverbs 6:19 ("discord"); 10:12 ("strife").

20. Gath is so well-known to readers of this record by now as a Philistine city that the narrator does not need to tell us this time that the conflict was with the Philistines.

21. The same verb is used in 1 Samuel 17:10, 25, 26, 36, 45 (ESV, "defy" throughout).

Chapter Forty: The Hope of David's Kingdom: The Lord's Promise, Part 1

1. Precisely when David composed the words of this song is unclear. "On the day when the LORD delivered him from the hand of all his enemies, and from the hand of Saul" indicates that the background to the song was the Lord's deliverance of David from "all his enemies" (see 7:1) and "from . . . Saul." It was certainly after

he had received the promise in 2 Samuel 7, as we will soon see. Because of the confidence of the song (especially in vv. 21–25) some have argued that it must have been before the Bathsheba and Uriah affair (2 Samuel 11). This, as again we will see, is largely beside the point. The Bible historian has chosen to record the song near the end of the story of David's life, in the epilogue to his narrative. We hear the song in the light of all that precedes it in the books of Samuel, and all that precedes it is illuminated by the song. Cf. Hans Wilhelm Hertzberg, *I & II Samuel: A Commentary*, Old Testament Library (London: SCM Press, 1964), p. 393.

2. There are a number of small differences in the text of Psalm 18 compared with 2 Samuel 22. These will not concern us here. It is likely that the song David actually composed was adapted (by him?) for inclusion in the book of Psalms and possibly by the writer of the books of Samuel for inclusion there. Cf. C. F. Keil and F. Delitzsch, *Biblical Commentary on the Books of Samuel* (Grand Rapids, MI: Eerdmans, 1950), p. 469.

3. Hannah's son, Samuel, was an old man well before he anointed David as a lad in Bethlehem (see 1 Samuel 8:1; 16:13).

4. "The poem functions (together with 23:1–7) as a counterpart to the song of Hannah (I Sam. 2:1–10)." Walter Brueggemann, *First and Second Samuel*, Interpretation: A Bible Commentary for Teaching and Preaching (Louisville: John Knox Press, 1990), p. 339.

5. I am indebted to Fokkelman's masterful technical analysis of 2 Samuel 22 for the main lines of my understanding of the song's structure. However, I have modified and interpreted the structure in ways that do not always follow Fokkelman. J. P. Fokkelman, *Narrative Art and Poetry in the Books of Samuel: a full interpretation based on stylistic and structural analyses, Volume 3: Throne and City (II Sam. 2—8 & 21—24)* (The Netherlands: Van Gorcum, Assen, 1990), pp. 333–355.

6. Apart from the tone, which resonates with the opening lines of Hannah's prayer, David uses some of the very same words as Hannah: "rock," "horn," "salvation," "my enemies."

7. "Horn" is a striking and violent image. "The horn of my salvation" means "the horn that saved me." "The idea seems to be that the animal's horn is its glory and power, held high, perhaps in triumph after goring an enemy into submission." Robert Alter, *The David Story: A Translation with Commentary of 1 and 2 Samuel* (New York and London: W. W. Norton & Company, 1999), p. 9.

8. "Sheol" occurs only here and in Hannah's prayer (1 Samuel 2:6) in the books of Samuel.

9. Fokkelman, *Throne*, p. 341

10. Strictly the suffix meaning "them" appears only once in Hebrew, but it is implied in the second place.

11. Since this antecedent is far removed, some have interpreted "them" as referring to the arrows. So REB. See Robert P. Gordon, *1 & 2 Samuel: A Commentary* (Exeter, UK: Paternoster, 1986), p. 363, note 21.

12. "Took" may be a reference to God choosing David in the first place for his purposes (1 Samuel 16:1).

13. The word in question also occurs, of course, in Psalm 18:16, but since that is a repetition of 2 Samuel 22 it does not really count as a third use of the word.

14. "Come down" is the same Hebrew word as "came" in 22:10.

15. The Hebrew here uses a word cognate with "broad place" in 22:20.

16. The sense of the cognate Hebrew words (although English translations vary), particularly applied to the land God promised to his people, can be seen in Genesis 13:17; 26:22; 34:21; Exodus 34:24; Deuteronomy 12:20; 19:8; Judges 18:10; Isaiah 30:23; 33:21; 54:2; Hosea 4:16; Psalm 119:45; Job 36:16; Nehemiah 9:35; 1 Chronicles 4:40.

17. It is noteworthy that the Lord brought the people of Israel into the promised land because he "delight[ed]" in them (Numbers 14:8), just as David now says he brought David into "a broad place . . . because he delighted in me."

18. The verb translated "dealt with" in verse 21a is "repaid" in 1 Samuel 24:17 (twice), where it refers to actions that were definitely not deserved (the very opposite in fact). The expression translated "rewarded" in verse 21b and 25a is literally "caused to return to me."

19. Because of this problem some have argued that David composed this song *before* the Bathsheba and Uriah affair. Even if this is so (which I doubt), it does not remove the problem. Was David sinless before 2 Samuel 11? We have seen various indications that even then the great and good man had his flaws (see our discussions of 5:13, 14; 8:4), which of course he did. Furthermore, we must take seriously the fact that the writer of David's history chose to place the song asserting his "righteousness" here, near the end of his story, making sure that we would read it *after* we had heard of David's disastrous failings.

20. "Though he had sometimes *weakly* departed from his duty, he had never *wickedly* departed from his God." Matthew Henry, cited with approval in Dale Ralph Davis, *Expositions of the Book of 2 Samuel: Out of Every Adversity* (Geanies House, Fearn, UK: Christian Focus, 1999), p. 239, note 10. "David does not claim perfection in life's particulars but wholeheartedness in life's commitment." Ibid., p. 239. "David was not claiming anything approaching sinless perfection, nor was he making prideful self-righteous pronouncements; rather he was humbly saying that, unlike Saul, the general pattern of his life demonstrated that his heart's desire was to walk in the way of covenant faithfulness." J. Robert Vannoy, *1—2 Samuel*, Cornerstone Biblical Commentary, 4a (Wheaton, IL: Tyndale House, 2009), p. 408. The obvious problem with these views is that David sounds as though he was saying more than is claimed for him. Furthermore, if he was claiming that his heart was in the right place, even if his conduct left much to be desired, isn't that still a self-righteous pronouncement?

21. Therefore I consider that Alter has completely missed the point: "The profession of blamelessness scarcely accords with David's behavior in the body of the story." Alter, *David*, p. 340.

22. The Hebrew word is cognate with the word translated "kindness" in 9:1. That chapter is a good example of David being "merciful."

23. The Hebrew word suggests more than "man." Elsewhere it is rendered "mighty [man]" (1 Samuel 2:4; 2 Samuel 1:19, 21, 22, 25, 27; 10:7; 16:6; 17:8, 10; 20:7; 23:8, 9, 16, 22), "strong [man]" (1 Samuel 14:52), "champion" (1 Samuel 17:51).

24. Or "you show yourself shrewd" (NIV).

25. Fokkelman, *Throne*, p. 346.

26. The form of this Hebrew participle often conveys a passive meaning. Thus "purified" (ESV) is correct, but the NIV "pure" misses this subtlety (also REB, HCSB).

27. "Humble" does not refer to a virtue but to a condition. The HCSB has "afflicted."

28. The Hebrew here means "your answering." In context this makes sense. David's greatness has come from all that God has done in answer to his cries. The NIV has "help." The ESV seems to have followed the slightly different wording found in Psalm 18:35.

29. "Wide place" is the same idea (and a similar Hebrew word) as "broad place" in verse 20.

30. This seems to refer to the days of Saul, and probably also the rebellion of Absalom.

Chapter Forty-One: The Hope of David's Kingdom: The Lord's Promise, Part 2

1. J. P. Fokkelman, *Narrative Art and Poetry in the Books of Samuel: a full interpretation based on stylistic and structural analyses, Volume 3: Throne and City (II Sam. 2—8 & 21—24)* (The Netherlands: Van Gorcum, Assen, 1990), p. 355, note 59, who understands verse 1a to mean that the following poem is "the last to be included in the books of Samuel."

2. "[T]he prophetic will and testament of the great king, unfolding the importance of his rule in relation to the sacred history of the future." C. F. Keil and F. Delitzsch, *Biblical Commentary on the Books of Samuel* (Grand Rapids, MI: Eerdmans, 1950), pp. 484, 485. Cf. Ronald F. Youngblood, *1 & 2 Samuel*, in Tremper Longman III and David E. Garland, eds., *The Expositor's Bible Commentary*, Revised Edition, vol. 3 (Grand Rapids, MI: Zondervan, 2009), p. 590.

3. The general shape of this poem is widely recognized in various commentaries with minor variations. The divisions here follow the analysis of Fokkelman, *Throne*, pp. 355–362.

4. The ESV has verse 1 as the words of the narrator (the quotation marks begin at verse 2). In my judgment the quotation marks should begin at verse 1b: "The oracle of . . . " (so NIV).

5. The Hebrew word occurs 376 times in the Old Testament, 365 of which refer to an utterance of God. See H. Eising, *"neum,"* in G. Johannes Botterweck, Helmer Ringgren, and Heinz-Josef Fabry, eds., *Theological Dictionary of the Old Testament*, vol. 11 (Grand Rapids, MI: Eerdmans, 2001), pp. 109–113. The only other occurrence of the Hebrew word in the books of Samuel is 1 Samuel 2:30, where it again occurs twice (ESV, "declares"). It is possible that David's introductory words here deliberately echo the words of Balaam: *"The oracle of* Balaam *the son of* Beor, *the oracle of the man* whose eye is opened" (Numbers 24:3, 15; the italics indicate the words that the two texts have in common). I am not convinced, however, that this "indicates . . . that [David's] own prophetic utterance was intended to be a further expansion of Balaam's prophecy concerning the Star out of Jacob and the Sceptre out of Israel." Keil and Delitzsch, *Samuel*, p. 485.

6. Contra Fokkelman, *Throne*, p. 357, note 62. I would argue that "the son of Jesse" fittingly prepares for "was *raised*" in the next line.

7. See H. Kosmala, *"geber,"* in G. Johannes Botterweck and Helmer Ringgren, eds., *Theological Dictionary of the Old Testament*, vol. 2 (Grand Rapids, MI: Eerdmans, 1975), pp. 377–381.

8. Similarly REB. This alternative rendering depends on a quite rare Hebrew word being taken as a divine title (as perhaps in Hosea 7:16, ESV margin; 11:7). The other occurrences of the word in question are Genesis 27:39 (ESV, "on high"); 49:25 (ESV, "above"); Psalm 50:4 (ESV, "above").

9. The ambiguity of the Hebrew can be sensed in a literal translation: "the pleasant one of the songs of Israel." The Hebrew grammar allows this to be understood as "the pleasant one of songs (that is, the pleasant singer) of Israel" or "the pleasant object (the 'darling') of Israel's songs." See S. R. Driver, *Notes on the Hebrew Text and the Topography of the Book of Samuel with an Introduction on Hebrew Palaeography and Facsimiles of Inscriptions and Maps*, 2nd edition (Oxford: Clarendon, 1913), p. 357.

10. The "I" of the Psalms may often be understood not as David himself but as a later Davidic king. The distinction is slight because the king is still understood in terms of the promises made to David that, after all, focused on a "son" of David. On this matter, see John Woodhouse, "Reading the Psalms as Christian Scripture," in Andrew G. Shead, ed., *Stirred by a Noble Theme: The Book of Psalms in the Life of the Church* (Nottingham, UK: Apollos, 2013), pp. 46–73.

11. This opens an important subject that cannot be fully explored here. I have discussed some aspects in John Woodhouse, "The preacher and the living Word: Preaching and the Holy Spirit," in *When God's voice is heard: Essays on preaching presented to Dick Lucas*, eds. D. Jackman and C. Green (Leicester, UK: Inter-Varsity Press, 1995), pp. 43–61.

12. The English translations tend to turn this stark announcement into a general proverbial saying: "When one rules justly over men, ruling in the fear of God . . ." (v. 3c, d, ESV). The meaning is rather, "A ruler over the human race will arise, a just ruler, and will exercise his dominion in the spirit of the fear of God." Keil and Delitzsch, *Samuel*, p. 487.

13. W. Gross, *"masal,"* in G. Johannes Botterweck, Helmer Ringgren, and Heinz-Josef Fabry, eds., *Theological Dictionary of the Old Testament*, vol. 9 (Grand Rapids, MI: Eerdmans, 1998), p. 69.

14. Where, incidentally, the sun is said to "rule" (same word as "ruler" here, Genesis 1:16).

15. Some skeptics have denied the objective historicity of David's kingdom as the books of Samuel have presented it to us. Our knowledge and certainty of these things depends on the reliability of the witnesses. In this respect it is the same as all historical knowledge. Two valuable discussions of the questions surrounding the historical reliability of the Old Testament in general, including the kingdom of David, are K. A. Kitchen, *On the Reliability of the Old Testament* (Grand Rapids, MI and Cambridge, UK: Eerdmans, 2003) and Iain Provan, V. Philips Long, and Tremper Longman III, *A Biblical History of Israel* (Louisville: Westminster John Knox Press, 2003).

16. Similarly Driver, *Notes*, p. 360. Cf. "drawn up in full and guaranteed." Alter, *David*, p. 347.

17. "My salvation" (ESV, "my help") probably means both David's being saved and David's saving activity. Contra Fokkelman, *Throne*, p. 361. The whole line sug-

gests, "all the salvation promised to me and my house." Keil and Delitzsch, *Samuel*, p. 489.

Chapter Forty-Two: The Strength of David's Kingdom: His Mighty Men, Part 2

1. The ESV margin draws attention to textual or translation difficulties in verses 8 (twice), 18 (twice), 19, 20 (twice), 35. These are only some of the problems this passage presents. By and large the textual and translation uncertainties are not particularly important. I will generally follow the ESV and only draw attention to problems that impact the exposition. For a more detailed discussion (with differing assumptions) of these issues I recommend A. A. Anderson, *2 Samuel*, Word Biblical Commentary 11 (Dallas: Word, 1989), pp. 272–274; P. Kyle McCarter Jr., *II Samuel: A New Translation with Introduction, Notes & Commentary*, The Anchor Bible, vol. 9 (Garden City, NY: Doubleday, 1984), pp. 489–494; Ronald F. Youngblood, *1 & 2 Samuel*, in Tremper Longman III and David E. Garland, eds., *The Expositor's Bible Commentary*, Revised Edition, vol. 3 (Grand Rapids, MI: Zondervan, 2009), pp. 596–603. A useful interpretation of the available information relevant to the content of our passage is found in D. G. Schley, "David's Champions," in David Noel Freedman, ed., *The Anchor Bible Dictionary*, vol. 2 (New York: Doubleday, 1992), pp. 49–52.

2. The Hebrew word "means a particularly strong or mighty person who carries out, can carry out, or has carried out great deeds, and surpasses others in doing so." H. Kosmala, "*gabhar*," in G. Johannes Botterweck and Helmer Ringgren, eds., *Theological Dictionary of the Old Testament*, vol. 2 (Grand Rapids, MI: Eerdmans, 1975), p. 373.

3. Some confusion is possible because 23:8–12 describes "the three mighty men" and then verses 13–17 recount the exploits of a *different* three men, but also calls them "the three mighty men." Then there is a reference to "the three" and "the three mighty men" in verses 18 and 22 who appear to be the three of verses 8–12.

4. This Eleazar is not to be confused, of course, with Eleazar the son of Abinadab (1 Samuel 7:1).

5. This may have been the man named Dodai, one of David's officials mentioned in 1 Chronicles 27:4.

6. Possibly "son of an Ahohite," meaning a member of the clan of Ahoah, belonging to the tribe of Benjamin (1 Chronicles 8:4).

7. We know no more about Agee. He is mentioned only here in the Bible.

8. "Hararite" probably indicates a town, although it has not been identified with certainty. It is possible that Hararite means "mountain dweller" (the Hebrew for mountain is *har*). So Francis Brown, S. R. Driver, and Charles Briggs, *A Hebrew and English Lexicon of the Old Testament* (Oxford: Clarendon Press, 1907), p. 251.

9. A suggested location about fifteen miles west of Jerusalem is indicated on Map 4-22 in John D. Currid and David P. Barrett, *Crossway ESV Bible Atlas* (Wheaton, IL: Crossway, 2010), p. 114.

10. The wording of the Hebrew clause is identical in verses 10 and 12 despite a slight variation in the ESV.

11. The Hebrew for "victory" also means "salvation."

12. So C. F. Keil and F. Delitzsch, *Biblical Commentary on the Books of Samuel* (Grand Rapids, MI: Eerdmans, 1950), p. 496. Our exposition of 5:17 concluded

that David was probably in Jerusalem at the time of this Philistine advance. This probability is overturned if the present passage concerns the same events. In that case "the stronghold" of 5:17 was the cave of Adullam, not "the stronghold of Zion" (5:7). However the correspondence of the incident in 23:13–17 with the events in 5:17–25 is not certain.

13. See Map 5-6 in Currid, *Atlas*, p. 124.

14. Or, "a garrison of Philistines." Neither the context nor the Hebrew requires the definite articles. My understanding is that there was a Philistine garrison in Bethlehem as well as a band of the enemy camped in the Valley of Rephaim.

15. Cf. J. P. Fokkelman, *Narrative Art and Poetry in the Books of Samuel: a full interpretation based on stylistic and structural analyses, Volume 3: Throne and City (II Sam. 2—8 & 21—24)* (The Netherlands: Van Gorcum, Assen, 1990), p. 304, note 43.

16. See the same vocabulary in 2 Kings 3:26; 2 Chronicles 21:17; Isaiah 7:6; Jeremiah 39:2; Ezekiel 26:10; 30:16. Fokkelman, *Throne*, p. 305, note 44.

17. Robert P. Gordon, *1 & 2 Samuel: A Commentary* (Exeter, UK: Paternoster, 1986), p. 313.

18. It is unclear whether Abishai was in charge of "the thirty" (that is, the thirty mentioned in verse 13 and enumerated in verses 24–39; so ESV) or of "the three" (that is, the three heroes named in verses 8–12; so NIV). Most Hebrew manuscripts have "the three," and this accords with the Hebrew of 1 Chronicles 11:20. It is sufficient for us to understand that Abishai was a leader among leaders, who nonetheless was not included in the top rank of three heroes (even if he possibly commanded them).

19. For further details about Benaiah's role and who the Cherethites and the Pelethites were, see the exposition of 8:18.

20. The ESV has adopted the curious solution of transliterating the word rather than attempting a translation, an expedient already employed by the Septuagint. One proposed meaning is "warrior." So William L. Holladay, *A Concise Hebrew and Aramaic Lexicon of the Old Testament: based upon the lexical work of Ludwig Koehler and Walter Baumgartner* (Leiden: E. J. Brill, 1971), p. 26. The NIV has "Moab's two mightiest warriors." The REB and JB have "the two champions of Moab." The HCSB treats Ariel as a proper name and has "two sons of Ariel of Moab" (similarly RV).

21. Since the Hebrew for lion is very similar to "ariel," the wordplay produced may account for the use of the unusual word "ariel" in the first part of the verse.

22. The ESV "handsome" is more specific than the Hebrew, which suggests "a man of striking appearance." Fokkelman, *Throne*, p. 397. It is likely that his appearance was fearsome rather than handsome.

23. Probably the Cherethites and the Pelethites of 8:18; 20:23.

24. For alternative understandings of the numbers, see Youngblood, *1 & 2 Samuel*, p. 600.

25. For a more detailed discussion of the names and issues they raise, see ibid., pp. 601, 602.

26. See ibid., p. 600.

Chapter Forty-Three: A Problem in David's Kingdom: God's Wrath, Part 2

1. It is not entirely clear why "Israel and Judah" appears here. In verse 4 "the people of Israel" refers to the whole nation. However, when Joab reported the results

of the census in verse 9 Israel and Judah are distinguished. "It would seem that, even when the kingdom was united under David, Israel and Judah were, for some purposes, separate administrative entities." Robert P. Gordon, *1 & 2 Samuel: A Commentary* (Exeter, UK: Paternoster, 1986), p. 319.

2. It "belongs undoubtedly to the closing years of David's reign," according to C. F. Keil and F. Delitzsch, *Biblical Commentary on the Books of Samuel* (Grand Rapids, MI: Eerdmans, 1950), p. 501.

3. The fact that there is no explicit reference to the anger of the Lord in 21:1–14 is not important. The famine was certainly a consequence of the Lord's anger concerning the "bloodguilt" of Saul (21:1).

4. It is possible to translate the beginning of the verse, "The anger of the LORD continued to burn against Israel. . . ." See Dale Ralph Davis, *Expositions of the Book of 2 Samuel: Out of Every Adversity* (Geanies House, Fearn, UK: Christian Focus, 1999), p. 259, note 7.

5. One suggested reason for the Lord's anger was "the rebellions of Absalom and Sheba against the divinely established government of David." Keil and Delitzsch, *Samuel*, p. 503. That is possible, but not certain.

6. Compare the similar use of the same verb when David said to his persecutor Saul, "If it is the LORD who has *stirred you up* [or incited you] against me . . ." (1 Samuel 26:19).

7. Generally I have avoided using the parallel accounts in the books of Chronicles to interpret the books of Samuel because it has been my concern to understand specifically the text before us. It is probable that the writer(s) of the much later books of Chronicles presupposed that readers would be familiar with the books of Samuel. It is therefore more appropriate to draw on Samuel as we read Chronicles than vice versa. There is, of course, a place for doing both.

8. See Job 1:6–22, where Satan was responsible for various disasters that fell on Job, and yet Job was right to say, "The LORD gave, and the LORD has taken away . . ." (Job 1:21).

9. See Gordon, *1 & 2 Samuel*, p. 316.

10. The imperative "number" is plural in Hebrew, indicating that others were expected to assist Joab in the task (see v. 4).

11. See Map 5-13 in John D. Currid and David P. Barrett, *Crossway ESV Bible Atlas* (Wheaton, IL: Crossway, 2010), p. 130.

12. Youngblood takes "this thing" to mean David's seeing the Lord multiply the number of the people (which he understands to mean "troops"). Ronald F. Youngblood, *1 & 2 Samuel*, in Tremper Longman III and David E. Garland, eds., *The Expositor's Bible Commentary*, Revised Edition, vol. 3 (Grand Rapids, MI: Zondervan, 2009), p. 607. On the contrary, in my judgment, "this thing" is David's proposal to number the people.

13. Similarly Keil and Delitzsch, *Samuel*, p. 504.

14. The Hebrew has "and camped in Aroer," which may suggest that Aroer was the first of a number of bases from which the administrative work was done around the country.

15. As the ESV margin note indicates, the translation follows the Septuagint rather than the Hebrew, simply because the latter is unintelligible. There are problems with the Septuagint as well, but since the general route of the census collectors

is clear enough for the purposes of the passage, we will not concern ourselves with these issues. See Gordon, *1& 2 Samuel*, p. 318.

16. For a reconstruction of the route taken, see Map 5-13 in Currid, *Atlas*, p. 130.

17. Youngblood, *1 & 2 Samuel*, p. 609. This is generally regarded as excessively high.

18. P. Kyle McCarter Jr., *II Samuel: A New Translation with Introduction, Notes & Commentary*, The Anchor Bible, vol. 9 (Garden City, NY: Doubleday, 1984), p. 510.

19. Similarly Gordon, *1& 2 Samuel*, p. 319.

20. On three occasions the Lord had commanded Moses to number the people, and there is no suggestion that such actions were in any way inappropriate (see Exodus 30:11–16; Numbers 1:2; 26:2).

21. Compare the very similar experience of David in 1 Samuel 24:5. We might say that cutting a piece of cloth was not *in itself* a sin. But the circumstances (and perhaps the motive) in the cave that day meant that the action resulted in a severe attack of conscience for David.

22. This is argued by Raymond B. Dillard, "David's Census: Perspectives on II Samuel 24 and I Chronicles 21," in W. R. Godfrey and J. L. Boyd III, eds., *Through Christ's Word* (Philipsburg, NJ: P&R, 1985), pp. 94–107.

23. In the Hebrew "take away" in 24:10 is the same word that is translated "put away" in 12:13. I doubt that this is coincidental.

24. The same word was used by Samuel when telling Saul, "You have done foolishly" (1 Samuel 13:13).

25. The Hebrew has "seven" here, but the Septuagint has "three" (cf. 1 Chronicles 21:12). Arguments can be advanced in support of each reading, but the difference is not substantial in context.

26. "The morning" of verse 15 was presumably "the morning" of verse 11.

27. For a discussion of the Lord "regretting" in this context see John Woodhouse, *1 Samuel: Looking for a Leader*, Preaching the Word (Wheaton, IL: Crossway, 2008), pp. 263, 264, 276.

28. Davis, *2 Samuel*, p. 265, note 17.

29. J. P. Fokkelman, *Narrative Art and Poetry in the Books of Samuel: a full interpretation based on stylistic and structural analyses, Volume 3: Throne and City (II Sam. 2—8 & 21—24)* (The Netherlands: Van Gorcum, Assen, 1990), p. 324, note 77.

30. On Jebusites see our discussion of 5:6.

31. Compare the interchange between Abraham and Ephron the Hittite over the purchase of Sarah's burial plot (Genesis 23:10–16).

32. Gordon J. Wenham, *The Book of Leviticus*, The New International Commentary on the Old Testament (Grand Rapids, MI: Eerdmans, 1979), p. 63.

33. See the full discussion in ibid., pp. 76–84.

34. These references follow a refrain that runs through the history of the northern kingdom of Israel after the division of the kingdom of David and Solomon. It is clear, however, that the southern kingdom of Judah also continued to provoke the Lord to anger (2 Kings 21:6, 15; 22:17; 23:26; 24:20).

Scripture Index

General Index

Index of Sermon Illustrations

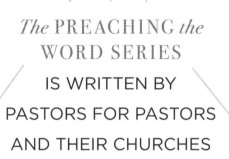

The PREACHING *the*
WORD SERIES

IS WRITTEN BY

PASTORS FOR PASTORS

AND THEIR CHURCHES